ONE OF THE NOTABLE BOOKS OF THE YEAR—*The New York Times*

"Who Spoke Up? *is far and away the best single history of the protest movement which helped get America out of Vietnam. It restores a much-needed sense of balance to our understanding of those awful years, and it does honor to the ordinary citizens who spoke up when officials in Washington were silent.*"
—Thomas Powers, author of
The Man Who Kept the Secrets

"*A passionate, partisan history of the movement against the war in Vietnam. . . . This well-written work painstakingly traces the development of the opposition to the war from its earliest stirring . . . to its mobilization of large segments of American society.*" —*Best Sellers*

"*This account of the antiwar movement of the Vietnam years provides many insights into the people and forces that came into play. . . . This narrative is most useful when it delves beneath events . . . to explore the complex tactical and other problems facing activists working outside conventional politics . . . to end a war.*" —*Publishers Weekly*

"*Zaroulis and Sullivan describe the guts and fervor of Americans who spoke up early and risked much to organize the grass-roots movement that hauled us out of Vietnam.*" —*Los Angeles Times Book Review*

Who Spoke Up?

Also by Nancy Zaroulis

THE LAST WALTZ
CALL THE DARKNESS LIGHT
THE POE PAPERS

Who Spoke Up?

AMERICAN PROTEST AGAINST
THE WAR IN VIETNAM
1963 - 1975

Nancy Zaroulis
and
Gerald Sullivan

An Owl Book

HOLT, RINEHART AND WINSTON
NEW YORK

Grateful acknowledgment is made to the following for permission to reprint their copyrighted material.

Excerpt from *The New Soldier* by John Kerry and Vietnam Veterans Against the War. Copyright © 1971 by Vietnam Veterans Against the War, Inc. Reprinted with permission of Macmillan Publishing Company.

Excerpt from *Out Now!* by Fred Halstead. Copyright © 1978 by the Anchor Foundation Inc. Reprinted by permission of the Anchor Foundation Inc. and Monad/Pathfinder Press.

Excerpt from *SDS* by Kirkpatrick Sale. Reprinted by permission of Random House, Inc.

Excerpt from *RN: The Memoirs of Richard Nixon*. Copyright © 1978 by Richard Nixon. Reprinted by permission of Warner Books, New York.

Excerpt from *Born on the Fourth of July* by Ron Kovic. Copyright © 1976 by Ron Kovic. Reprinted by permission of McGraw Hill Book Company.

Excerpts from "Trapped in a System," "An Open Letter to McCarthy Supporters," "Notes on a Generation Ready for the Dustbin" *(Liberation,* 1969) by Carl Oglesby. Reprinted by permission of the author.

Excerpts reprinted from the following articles appearing in *Liberation* magazine by permission of David Dellinger:
   "Coalition Politics . . ." by Staughton Lynd (June–July 1965)
   "A Call to Burn Draft Cards" (February 1967)
   "My name is Gary Rader" (November 1967)
   "Testimony I Would Have Given" by Staughton Lynd (March 1970)
   "In 1966 the Progressive Labor Party Dissolved Its Front Group" by
      Staughton Lynd (January 1971)
   "The Antiwar Movement Is Paying A Price" by David Dellinger (January 1971)

Published by Holt, Rinehart and Winston,
383 Madison Avenue, New York, New York 10017.
Published simultaneously in Canada by Holt,
Rinehart and Winston of Canada, Limited.

Library of Congress Cataloging in Publication Data
Zaroulis, N. L.
Who spoke up?
"An Owl book."
Bibliography: p.
Includes index.
1. Vietnamese Conflict, 1961–1975—Protest movements
—United States.   2. United States—Politics and
government—1963–1969.   3. United States—Politics and
government—1969–1974.   I. Sullivan, Gerald.   II. Title.
[DS559.62.U6Z37   1985]   959.704'38   85-8474
ISBN 0-03-005603-9 (pbk.)

First published in hardcover by Doubleday & Company, Inc.,
in 1984.
First Owl Book Edition—1985
Printed in the United States of America
10 9 8 7 6 5 4 3 2 1

ISBN 0-03-005603-9

Alter alterī

Acknowledgments

The staffs of the Boston Public Library, the Lamont Library (Harvard University), and the Library of the University of Massachusetts at Boston have been consistently helpful. C. R. Wolf Roberts and Frances Schlesinger at the University of Massachusetts at Boston gave crucial assistance.

For contributions of material and advice, we thank the Reverend Dr. William E. Alberts, James Brough, Ann Froines, Elissa L. A. Hamilton, Tommy Lott, Mark Pawlak, Myles Striar, Peter Sullivan, Amy Swerdlow, and Gordon Zahn. Katherine Zaroulis performed valuable emergency assignments. Timothy Sullivan's research was intelligent and thorough.

Thomas N. Brown, R. Joseph Shork, and Florian Weissenborn read the manuscript and made many worthwhile criticisms.

Kathleen Carspecken and Zoe Sleeth typed with great efficiency.

Our family endured with patience and good humor.

Finally, we are deeply grateful for the patience and generosity shown to us by those whom we interviewed; without their help this book would not have been possible.

Contents

CONTENTS

Our country, right or wrong.

When right, to be kept right;

When wrong, to be put right.

Carl Schurz
address to the
Anti-Imperialistic Conference
Chicago, October 17, 1899

This [the destruction of Vietnam]

is the crime our country is committing.

And this is what we must condemn,

lest a later generation ask of us,

as they ask of the Germans,

who spoke up?

I. F. Stone
I. F. Stone's Weekly
October 17, 1966

Foreword

AMERICAN PROTEST AGAINST the war in Vietnam was begun and sustained by American citizens who believed that in a representative democracy, individuals can make themselves heard and, more, can affect public policy.

To us, the antiwar movement during the Vietnam era is important not because it stopped the war, which it may or may not have done; rather, it is important because it existed. It is a reminder to Americans that times come when citizens can and, indeed, must challenge their government's authority.

Because it grew to include so many people, and because like the war it opposed it lasted for so many years, the antiwar movement was a protest unique in human history. Never before in time of war (declared or not) had so many citizens freely stood up to say to their government, "No. Stop!"

Every war has had its opponents. There was a sizable antiwar sentiment in Great Britain during the South African War (1899–1902), and in America there has always been during every war a small protest movement—most notably, until Vietnam, during the Mexican War in 1846–48 and the Philippine Insurrection in 1899–1901. But the Vietnam War was different: increasingly unpopular, undeclared and therefore in the opinion of many citizens illegal and unconstitutional as well, it was the most frustrating war in American history, and the ugliest, and the longest. The movement opposing it had years in which to grow.

Opposition to the war took many forms: letters to congressmen and presidents; advertisements in newspapers; signatures on petitions; vigils in town centers, at government buildings, installations, and other public places; lobbying congressmen; working to elect candidates sympathetic to the cause; tax refusal; draft refusal; desertion from the armed forces; nonviolent civil disobedience resulting in arrest, jailing, and court trials; nonviolent civil disobedience met by tear-gassing and/or violence from police and troops; legal mass marches and rallies of tens and hundreds of thousands of people; strikes on campus or at workplace; draft board raids to destroy records—burning them or pouring blood on them; illegal, violent acts such as trashing, burning buildings or setting off bombs; suicide.

The effectiveness of these tactics is still a matter for debate; probably it always will be.

The antiwar movement is widely perceived to have been a coming together of treasonous, violent, bomb-throwing youths, cowards who would not fight for their country, licentious hedonists who scorned the middle-class lifestyle, Communist dupes who took orders from Moscow, Peking, and Hanoi.

None of these perceptions accurately measures a movement so representative of America's diversity.

The antiwar movement was not a movement inspired or led by foreign powers. It was a homegrown movement of the Left which eventually encompassed the entire political spectrum; it was American-born and -bred. It was led for the most part by people who believed profoundly in their American heritage and who relied upon their Constitution, their Bill of Rights, and the tradition of their American Revolution as fundamental to their opposition to the war. The U.S. Government made repeated efforts to link the antiwar movement to an "international Communist conspiracy." No such link was ever found, despite intensive investigations by the Central Intelligence Agency (investigations illegal under its charter), the Federal Bureau of Investigation, and other government agencies. Because the antiwar movement was of the Left, it included some who clung to the belief that a workers' revolution would one day take place in the United States and that a socialist (or even Communist) government would be installed. But even they saw such an eventuality to be far in the future, and they were the "conservatives" in the Movement.

The antiwar movement was not a violent movement. It was begun and led by lifelong pacifists, many of them devoutly religious men and women who practiced nonviolence as part of their faith. Its membership was overwhelmingly peaceful.

The antiwar movement was not a movement of the young, although young people gave it needed energy, served by the hundreds of thousands as its "troops," and provided some of its leaders. It was conceived, nurtured, and largely directed by adults; people over thirty made up a large part of its membership. Its original inspiration came from two old men.

The antiwar movement was not a movement of cowards afraid to fight for their country. Its leaders and members endured years of harassment, surveillance, court trials, jailings, and, in the case of armed forces deserters or draft refusers, long separation from home, family, and friends. Their refusal to endorse what they perceived to be the wrong war in the wrong place at the wrong time caused them untold anguish.

The antiwar movement was not a movement of licentious counterculturals living a sexually promiscuous lifestyle. Its membership was ordinary citizens; its leadership was, for the most part, straight-living under the constant threat of government spying and the public spotlight in which they existed.

The antiwar movement was not a monolithic organization following the dictates of a "party line." It was a loose, shifting, often uneasy coalition of groups and individuals who often disagreed on every issue except their hatred of the war. Many times the antiwar movement fell apart only to come together again under the overwhelming need to oppose its government's policy in Vietnam, but it was never an untroubled alignment. At all times the social concern of its individual members guaranteed that they would have strong opinions on whatever question was being considered, whether it was what slogan to put on a placard, what protest tactic to use, or whether to include nonantiwar groups and their demands. From first to last, therefore, the antiwar movement was torn by bitter disagreements over tactics, policy, programs for action, and basic philosophical tenets. It was a movement comprised of as many as several hundred groups at the best of times; in lean years it kept going with the support of only a few.

Finally, the antiwar movement was not "anti-American." Rather, it was a movement arising from profound patriotism. Its members cared deeply about their country. In the bleak and bitter years when some of them, including some of the nation's best and brightest young people, turned their backs on America and spewed out a hatred of her born of massive ignorance and frustration, they were no longer of the antiwar movement even as they were no longer of America; they had left both far behind. The angriest among them were unwilling to acknowledge that in few countries of the world would they have found the freedom to protest that existed in the United States. In most countries they would have been silenced simply for voicing opposition; in many they would have been jailed or executed. Despite considerable effort by the government to discredit the antiwar protesters, to foster violence, to divide them by using provocateurs to sabotage their efforts, to force them to endure long and expensive trials, to frustrate them at every turn, the Movement survived nevertheless because, in the end, it spoke for America. It had traveled from the fringes of American politics into its very heart. The antiwar movement saved the nation's honor, and saved it not easily but by speaking truth to those who did not want to hear, by continuing to speak in the face of public indifference and hostility.

Until the very end—until beyond the end, in fact—the "system," the institutions of government intended not only to represent the people but to lead them, refused to listen. The system, in short, did not work. Presidents lied; Congress, ostrichlike, buried its head; federal and state courts allowed themselves to be prostituted in the government's service; and the highest Court consistently refused to entertain what the late Justice William O. Douglas called the single "most important issue of the sixties to reach the Court."

Only the press—most notably that portion of it that published the secret government history of the war known as the Pentagon Papers—acted minimally as it was intended to do; the Fourth Estate, by and large, performed its function somewhat better than the three constitutional branches of the government performed theirs, but even to say that is to say very little. The press tended to reflect the government's view of the antiwar movement as irrelevant, insignificant, violent, unrepresentative, and wrong. One prominent member of the antiwar movement, commenting on the 1971 publication of the Pentagon Papers, asks darkly, "What if it [Daniel Ellsberg's "leak" to the New York *Times]* had happened in 1968?" In other words, the courage of the press to question authority came slowly if at all.

Television, of course, actively helped the antiwar movement simply by doing its job, by reporting the fighting half a world away: the Vietnam War was the "living room war," and its horrors came home every night from coast to coast on the evening news. On the other hand, television performed far more poorly than the print media in presenting the antiwar movement itself: it wanted only the most eye-catching images, and almost invariably those were images of random violence like the sustained violence of the war.

The antiwar movement, like the war it opposed, consumed the passions of a generation—a "lost generation," it has been called, far more accurately, we believe, than the generation "lost" after the war fought "to make the world safe for democracy." And yet, in the end, perhaps they were not lost but only detoured. A few died; a few more disappeared; a few turned outlaw with tragic results for themselves and others. Most are alive and well and performing useful work—teaching, community organizing, politics, business, religious work, writing. Their political power is only now, in 1984, beginning to be felt.

When they had done with their task—when the war was over, at least for America, and the flag-draped caskets stopped coming home—they picked up their lives and went on. Like the boys who fought the war, they had no parades. They will probably never have a monument. Like the Abolitionists over a century ago, they gave voice to their consciences; but America (like all nations) is not grateful to those who would tell her she is wrong. And so, like the movement to abolish slavery, the antiwar movement has become quasi-mythical, half-buried in time, an increasingly dim and distorted historical presence remembered kindly by some, belittled and reviled by others, recalled inaccurately even by many who helped to make it happen.

We think that at least it should be remembered for what it was.

January 1984

NANCY ZAROULIS

GERALD SULLIVAN

Who Spoke Up?

Death by Fire

IN THE LATE afternoon of November 2, 1965, Norman R. Morrison, a thirty-two-year-old Quaker, walked to the river entrance to the Pentagon across the Potomac from the nation's capital, doused himself with kerosene from a can that he carried, and set himself on fire. He was about one hundred yards from Secretary of Defense Robert S. McNamara's office and within full view of its windows.

One of the witnesses to Morrison's immolation was his fifteen-month-old daughter, Emily. He had carried her to the site and then put her down about fifteen feet away before striking the match that was to bring his death. Hundreds of office workers saw the flames shooting six or seven feet high from his body; an army major jumped over a low parapet in an attempt to reach Morrison and beat out the fire, but he was too late to save the young Quaker's life. Within moments Morrison was burned beyond recognition, his face charred black, his body melted flesh like the victims of napalm or the bodies of the Buddhist monks in South Vietnam who had immolated themselves to protest the regime of the hated President Ngo Dinh Diem. Only the previous day in Saigon, a Buddhist monk had burned himself to death on the second anniversary of Diem's overthrow and assassination.

We do not know if Morrison learned of that most recent suicide in Vietnam before he killed himself, but we do know that he had been deeply troubled by the war in Southeast Asia. His associates at the Stony Run Friends Meeting in Baltimore, where he had been the executive secretary, said that he had been "grieving" for months over the United States' increasing military involvement in Vietnam; one of them recalled that "we had to talk him out of burning himself up last year. He wanted to do it when the monks in Saigon were killing themselves that way."

Three months before his death, Morrison had written a letter that was published in the Baltimore *Sun;* he said, in part:

> American youth cannot long be expected to respond to an anti-revolutionary call that is dressed up as patriotism. . . . President Johnson claims that Asian communism has provided an inspiration to our enemy, but why

1

should Americans be expected to die trying to chase down this inspiration? . . .

It is difficult to imagine that this will be a long war, but if it is it may give Americans enough time to decide that at least this type of war should be the last of its kind. . . .

Morrison's associates called his tactic of self-immolation "unprecedented" as a means of protest used by Quakers, however. "He must have been motivated by a desperate search to be heard by the American people and their leaders," said one. "Religion was the dominant force in his life," said another. He was haunted, they said, by the questions "What can a man do with his life? How can he best show his beliefs? When must thoughts give way to deeds?"

Morrison had testified to the pacifism that he shared with other Friends by withholding five dollars from his income tax in 1962, and again in 1963, as a "token protest" against federal military expenditures. More recently, he had protested the Administration's Vietnam policy by demonstrating against Secretary of State Dean Rusk when Rusk spoke at Johns Hopkins University in late October.

During the weekend before his suicide, Morrison had traveled to Philadelphia to attend a meeting of the American Friends Service Committee. There he heard speeches by Stephen G. Cary, an AFSC official recently returned from South Vietnam, and by William C. Davidon, chairman of the physics department at Haverford College. Both men were critical of American policy in South Vietnam.

On the day that he died, as he was having lunch with his wife, Anne, Morrison read a report from *Paris Match,* reprinted in *I. F. Stone's Weekly,* about a French priest in Vietnam whose church had been bombed by U.S. planes. The priest buried at least seven of his parishioners, all of whom had been "blown to bits."

The day after Morrison's death his body was cremated. His widow said of him:

> Norman Morrison has given his life to express his concern over the great loss of life and human suffering caused by the war in Vietnam.
>
> He was protesting the Government's deep military involvement in this war. He felt that all citizens must speak their true convictions about our country's actions.

"Who of us can comprehend what it is to live in 1965 and contain such concern . . . which extends to Vietnamese being killed, those killing them and people outside who are insensitive to this tragedy?" said a Friend. Added another, Morrison acted according to Quaker beliefs which state that one "must follow the light as he understands it . . . he was a mystic who believed that his self-sacrifice was a giving, not a taking of life."

"The Buddhist monk who burns himself alive does not think that he is destroying himself," explained a Vietnamese official in New York, responding to the Buddhist immolations two years before; "he believes in the good fruition of his act of self-sacrifice for the sake of others."

Carl Oglesby, president of Students for a Democratic Society at the time of

Morrison's death, thought that Morrison knew that the statement he was making would be incomprehensible to Americans: "He's not immolating himself for the Americans but for the Vietnamese. That ability to transfer your allegiance so profoundly to another culture . . ."

And, indeed, the (North) Vietnamese did respond to and seem to understand Morrison's act. His suicide, said the North Vietnamese Women's Union, "heralded an even greater and irresistible storm among the American people." Morrison became a national hero in the North. The government issued a stamp in his honor, and named a street after him in Hanoi. Trucks going south along the Ho Chi Minh Trail carried large photographs of him in their front windows. At every "cultural performance" a song about Morrison was sung. A song for his daughter Emily was printed on page 1 of North Vietnam's leading newspaper and "known and sung throughout the country." In factories in Hanoi were posters of Morrison with the legend THE FLAMES OF MORRISON WILL NEVER DIE. A member of the North Vietnamese peace committee said, "We have asked ourselves what it is that makes a man like Morrison burn himself—the holiness, the nobility of his death!" Nearly two years later, in May 1967, two American antiwar activists visiting Hanoi's Revolutionary Museum saw huge photographs of Morrison and of Alice Herz, eighty-two, who had immolated herself on a Detroit street corner in March 1965 after the United States had begun to bomb North Vietnam.

Like Morrison, Alice Herz was a Quaker. She described herself as having been born "part Jewish, part Christian." After Hitler's rise to power she fled her native Germany, traveling first to France and then to the United States. She was an active member both of the Women's International League for Peace and Freedom and of Women Strike for Peace. To the firemen who took her to the hospital where she died ten days later she said, "I did it to protest the arms race all over the world. I wanted to burn myself like the monks in Vietnam did."

Herz had mailed a note to her daughter to explain her action. In it she said, "I do this not out of despair but out of hope. I choose the illuminating death of a Buddhist to protest against a great country trying to wipe out a small country for no reason." Her daughter added to newsmen, "My mother felt that President Johnson's great majority last fall was mainly due to his promise not to escalate the war in Vietnam. She had feelings of great frustration when she decided this country actually was escalating the war there."

One week after Norman Morrison's death, at 5 A.M. on November 9, 1965, Roger A. LaPorte, a twenty-one-year-old member of the Catholic Worker movement, stepped onto First Avenue in front of the Dag Hammarskjöld Library at the United Nations in New York, knelt in the cross-legged position of the Buddhist monks who had immolated themselves in Vietnam, doused himself with gasoline, and set himself on fire. He died the next day at Bellevue Hospital with second- and third-degree burns covering 95 percent of his body; despite remaining conscious, he felt little pain because his body's nerve ends had been destroyed. When asked why he had immolated himself, he replied, "I'm a Catholic Worker. I'm against war, all wars. I did this as a religious action."

LaPorte, a former Trappist seminarian who worked in one of the libraries at

3

Columbia University, had attended a draft card burning ceremony at Union Square three days before at which onlookers had called, "Burn yourselves, not your cards!" Friends said that he had been "melancholy" afterward, but not obviously emotionally disturbed. Although he had been moved by watching five young men burn their draft cards, he had been unable to decide whether to burn his own. In the end he did not. His draft card was found in his wallet after his immolation; he was classified as 2-S (reserved for seminarians), but he was subject to reclassification.

The Catholic Worker issued a statement about LaPorte's immolation which said, in part,

> He was trying to say to the American people that we must turn away from violence in Vietnam, and he was trying to say something about the violence that is eroding our own society here in the United States and our city of New York. And so he made this sacrifice, attempting to absorb this violence and hatred personally, deflecting it from others by taking it voluntarily to himself.

"Perhaps there has been a failure on our part," said Arthur Goldberg, chief U.S. delegate to the UN, when he was asked for his reaction to LaPorte's death. "Perhaps we are not sufficiently communicating to the people of the world our dedication, our attachment and complete commitment to the idea that peace is the only way for mankind in the nuclear age."

The Reverend Daniel Berrigan, S.J., who was later to emerge as a significant figure in the antiwar movement and who was at that time cochairman of the newly formed Clergy and Laymen Concerned About Vietnam, saw the deed rather as had LaPorte himself, in a religious light. Speaking at a memorial service soon after LaPorte's death, Father Berrigan did not call it suicide; rather, he declared, LaPorte "gave his life so that others might live." The New York hierarchy had always been outraged by the pacifism of the Catholic Worker. Now, within three days, Daniel Berrigan was exiled to Latin America by a Jesuit order unwilling to confront the wrath of Francis Cardinal Spellman, the warrior prelate of the American Catholic hierarchy, staunch supporter of the war in Vietnam, military vicar of the armed forces, and archbishop of the communications capital of the United States, New York City. It was a "disciplinary measure," said Berrigan, speaking of "the troubles in which I am in because of my involvement with the peace movement."

Berrigan's punishment was protested both by his fellow Jesuits and by Catholics all over the country. Over one thousand of them signed an advertisement supporting him that appeared in the New York *Times* on Sunday, December 12. Because of this and other protests, Berrigan was back in the United States within three months.

During the years 1965–70, eight Americans burned themselves to death in opposition to the war in Vietnam.* Speaking of Morrison and LaPorte (Herz's death

---

* In addition to Herz, Morrison, and LaPorte, they were: Hiroko Hayaski, thirty-six, of San Diego, a Japanese-American Buddhist who died October 12, 1967; Florence Beaumont, fifty-five, of La Puente,

had been less widely publicized), the New York *Times* editorialized: "They have contradicted their own principles of non-violence by turning upon themselves the full fury of the violence they condemn . . . but they may serve some useful purpose if their self-inflicted agony brings home—alongside the mounting casualty lists —the grisly cost of war. The violence of war feeds upon itself and begets demands for ever more intensifying violence. . . ."

Death by fire is a peculiarly horrible death. The suicides of Morrison and La-Porte shocked many Americans into asking—for the first time—why are we in Vietnam? And what about our involvement there is so monstrous that these two young men protest it in this monstrous way?

Meanwhile, in the fall of 1965, an organized protest movement against the American military presence in Vietnam was already well under way.

California, a housewife who died October 15, 1967; Erik Thoen, twenty-seven, of Sunnyvale, California, a student of Zen Buddhism who died December 4, 1967; Ronald W. Brazee, sixteen, of Auburn, New York, a high school student who immolated himself March 19, 1968, and died April 27, 1968; George Winne, twenty-three, a San Diego State University student who died May 12, 1970. Several other young men tried to immolate themselves but failed to do so. Other self-inflicted deaths attributable to the war include a family of five in Tucson, Arizona, whose mother shot and killed her three children, her husband, and herself in September 1969; her suicide note blamed the war in Vietnam.

1963-64:
The Years of Lonely Dissent

DAVID DELLINGER is a husky man of average height, nearly seventy now but looking at least ten years younger. His ruddy face is creased with laugh-lines; in recent years he has worn a short beard which gives him the look of an Amish farmer. He is a friendly, gregarious man, eminently approachable, who could not be more unlike the somewhat austere and remote pacifists who were his mentors, Mahatma Gandhi and the Reverend Abraham Johannes Muste. He has been described as a "cheery elf," but the term fails to convey either his intelligence or his determination.

He was born in Massachusetts; his grandmother was an active member of the Daughters of the American Revolution and his father, an attorney, a graduate of Yale Law School. In 1937 he was graduated Phi Beta Kappa from Yale with a degree in economics. In both high school and college he was an outstanding athlete, a long-distance runner and a tournament-level golfer. He was awarded a fellowship to study at New College, Oxford; when he returned to the United States he enrolled at the Union Theological Seminary in New York. There, in 1940, he chose to become a conscientious objector and refused to register for the draft. He served a year at the Federal Correctional Institution at Danbury, Connecticut. In 1943 he was sentenced to two years at the Federal Penitentiary at Lewisburg, Pennsylvania, for refusing to report for an induction physical examination. While he was in prison he undertook a hunger strike and was force-fed. When he was released he entered upon his life-long career of radical pacifism and became a leading proponent of Gandhian nonviolence. With Muste and others he founded *Liberation* magazine in 1956 and served as its editor; he worked with the Reverend Martin Luther King, Jr., from the earliest days of the civil rights struggle and served as an important link between King and the white pacifist/activist community.

In April 1963 Dellinger attended the Easter Peace Walk in New York held annually by American peace groups in sympathy with the British Aldermaston

("Ban the Bomb") marches. In the late 1950s and early 1960s, peace activists both in the United States and Europe had concentrated their efforts on the signing of a U.S.-U.S.S.R. treaty that would ban nuclear testing; in England, that day, seventy thousand people marched from Aldermaston (a weapons testing center) to London to protest the arms race.* A founding member of Britain's Committee for Nuclear Disarmament was the famed philosopher and mathematician Bertrand Russell. The week before Easter he had published a letter in the New York *Times* accusing the United States of waging a war of annihilation in Vietnam and of "suppressing the truth about the conduct of this war," which, he said, involved the use of "napalm jelly gasoline" and "chemical warfare." The *Times* huffily editorialized that Russell lived in "never-never land" (in fact he lived in Penrhyndeudraeth, Wales), and that his letter showed an "unthinking receptivity to the most transparent Communist propaganda."

Perhaps seven thousand people gathered that Easter Sunday at the UN Plaza. The speeches they heard were mainly in support of both the test ban treaty and the papal encyclical *Pacem in Terris,* which Pope John XXIII had issued three days before on Maundy Thursday. The encyclical called for disputes between nations to be settled by negotiation rather than warfare, and it stated that "if civil authorities legislate for, or allow, anything that is contrary to [the moral] order and therefore contrary to the will of God, neither the laws made nor the authorizations granted can be binding on the consciences of the citizens, since *we must obey God rather than men* [emphasis in original]." Bayard Rustin, the chairman of the demonstration who would organize the massive civil rights March on Washington the following August, urged his listeners to send telegrams to the Pope, to President Kennedy, and to Chairman Nikita Khrushchev of the Soviet Union supporting the encyclical and the treaty. (A partial test ban treaty halting atmospheric nuclear tests was signed in August.)

Despite the announced purpose of the rally, however, some of the marchers that day carried signs denouncing the U.S. presence in Vietnam. Prior to that time, Vietnam had been viewed as too divisive, and possibly too remote, an issue for the American peace movement. On this day the signs caused trouble: the rally's organizers demanded that they be removed. Dellinger and Fred Halstead, a member of the Socialist Workers Party, insisted that the signs be allowed to remain, and both Dellinger and A. J. Muste spoke about Vietnam during their remarks to the crowd. For this breach of discipline, Dellinger was later warned by representatives of SANE, one of the sponsoring groups, that he would never again speak at one of their rallies.

The incident is illuminating. To the uninitiated, both Dellinger and SANE would have seemed to be in favor of "peace," whatever that was. But in early 1963 the American peace movement was small, isolated, and relatively ineffective. Its newest and most promising group, the Committee for a sane Nuclear Policy, had struggled

---

* Prominently displayed there, and in the United States as well, was the peace symbol resembling an encircled claw-print of a four-toed bird. The symbol had been designed in 1958 by the (British) Direct Action Committee Against Nuclear War; it represented the semaphore signals for N and D: nuclear disarmament.

into existence in 1957 in a cold war climate decidedly hostile to any kind of accommodation with the Soviet Union. Now, with the test ban treaty so close to achievement and *Pacem in Terris* providing moral support, some peace leaders did not want to divide an already weak "peace community" with harsh talk about the U.S. adventure in Vietnam: the audience that SANE hoped to reach—John F. Kennedy's liberals—were the same people who were overseeing the Vietnam agenda, and they would not listen—so the reasoning went—to pleas for nuclear disarmament voiced by critics of their Vietnam policy.

And so the years 1963–64 might be described as the years of lonely dissent—the years when a few isolated voices began to cry out against American involvement in Vietnam. They came mostly from organizations on the fringes of American political life, largely unknown to the ordinary citizen. This fragile, embryonic peace movement was comprised of pacifist, religious, civil rights, disarmament, and student groups, as well as elements of the ". . . Old Left. . . ." Many of them had been working since the mid-1950s to achieve nuclear disarmament; others had been newly energized in the civil rights struggle.

PACIFIST GROUPS

The Women's International League for Peace and Freedom (WILPF), founded in 1915 by, among others, Jane Addams, a pioneer in social work. In 1963 its aims were a complete nuclear test ban treaty; economic planning for disarmament; nonviolent action for human rights; and support of the United Nations.

The War Resisters League (WRL), an outgrowth of the Anti-Enlistment League (1915), founded in 1923 as the American branch of the War Resisters International. WRL offered support to pacifists and conscientious objectors who had no religious ties. It was a "radical pacifist" group, meaning that it followed the Gandhian example of nonviolent direct action/civil disobedience. To protest peacetime conscription after the World War II draft law expired in 1947, WRL sponsored the first draft card burning and turn-in; more than four hundred men participated. In 1948, after the passage of the Selective Service Act, WRL joined other peace groups in founding the Central Committee for Conscientious Objectors. In 1956 WRL started *Liberation* magazine as a forum for social issues—disarmament, civil rights —and the protest tactics of nonviolent direct action. In the late 1950s and early 1960s WRL members actively protested the civil defense "bomb shelter" programs of the Eisenhower and Kennedy Administrations. WRL Executive Secretary Bayard Rustin organized the massive, landmark March on Washington for Jobs and Freedom in August 1963.

The Committee for Nonviolent Action (CNVA), founded by WRL members in 1957. Its specific purpose was direct-action protest against nuclear weapons. CNVA members sailed into the Pacific Ocean nuclear testing zone in 1958; they entered a nuclear testing base in Nebraska in 1959; they protested at the Polaris (nuclear) submarine base in New London, Connecticut in 1960; they initiated the San Francisco to Moscow Walk for Peace in 1960–61; and they sailed *Everyman I* and *Everyman II* into the Pacific testing zone in 1962.

The Workshop in Nonviolence (WIN), founded in 1965, a New York–based outgrowth of WRL-CNVA whose magazine, *WIN*, had wide readership among activists during the antiwar years.

RELIGIOUS GROUPS

The Fellowship of Reconciliation (FOR), a British organization founded in 1914 as "a movement of Christian protest" against World War I. Its American branch was founded by the Reverend A. J. Muste in 1915 to oppose U.S. entry into World War I.

The Religious Society of Friends (Quakers), begun c. 1650 in England, whose tenets include strict pacifism; it is the largest and best known of the many small, pacifist Christian sects.

The American Friends Service Committee (AFSC), founded in 1917 by American Quakers to relieve the sufferings of the European victims of World War I.

The Catholic Worker, founded in 1933 by Dorothy Day and Peter Maurin; now a radical pacifist group whose work began with "Houses of Hospitality" to feed the poor; these continue. Its publication, the monthly *Catholic Worker* (still a penny a copy), has wide circulation among religious and peace groups.

CIVIL RIGHTS GROUPS

The Congress of Racial Equality (CORE), founded in 1942. Its director in the early 1960s, James Farmer, was the moving force behind the "freedom rides" (1961) intended to integrate public facilities and interstate transportation in the American South. Farmer had also organized a CORE-sponsored freedom ride in 1947.

The Southern Christian Leadership Conference (SCLC), founded in 1957 by the Reverend Martin Luther King, Jr., and others as a vehicle for the black struggle for civil rights. Its motto was "To save the soul of America."

The Student Nonviolent Coordinating Committee (SNCC), an umbrella organization founded by blacks in April 1960 after the first sit-ins to integrate public facilities. Its membership came mostly from campus groups.

The Northern Student Movement (NSM), founded in support of the Southern integration struggle; its members were, for the most part, white students, many of whom went south in the civil rights actions and the voter registration drives of the early 1960s.

DISARMAMENT GROUPS

Committee for Nonviolent Action (see p. 9).

The National Committee for a Sane Nuclear Policy (SANE), founded in 1957 to work for a nuclear test ban treaty and for disarmament. Its members frowned on the direct-action, nonviolent civil disobedience of groups like CNVA, and it refused to allow Communists or socialists in its membership—an "exclusionary" policy.

Women Strike for Peace (WSP), founded in 1961 to work for "general and complete" disarmament and the passage of a nuclear test ban treaty. A self-described "grass-roots" organization, its policy of nonexclusion (membership open to anyone regardless of political affiliation) made it the target of an investigation by the House Un-American Activities Committee in December 1962. Although many WSP members described themselves as middle-class "housewives," they engaged in direct-action tactics—always neatly groomed and dressed. WSP picketed at the UN, the White House, and elsewhere; it was the first group to march on the Pentagon.

The Old Left

The inheritors of Marxism-Leninism in the United States were of three main tendencies: Stalinists (Communist Party), Trotskyites (Socialist Workers Party), and Social Democrats (Socialist Party). Although the CP had been active in forming and building labor unions in the 1930s, by the 1950s it had fallen on hard times through government repression and its own internal feuding. After the Moscow-Peking split the CP split also; the leading Maoist group in the United States was the Progressive Labor Party. By the Vietnam era none of these groups had any influence whatever on U.S. politics; their continued ineffectiveness was guaranteed by their bitter internecine fighting over rival political and economic philosophies—matters of interest only to themselves, certain to alienate their few potential recruits.

Student/Campus Groups

The Student Peace Union (SPU), a socialist group founded at the University of Chicago in 1959.

Young Socialist Alliance (YSA), the youth group of the Socialist Workers Party.

Students for a Democratic Society (SDS), founded in 1960 as an outgrowth of the Student League for Industrial Democracy (see pp. 27–32).

All of these groups provided people, organizational support, and money for the movement that was to become the Movement. In 1963–64, they looked back on nearly two decades of cold war, anti-Communist rhetoric—the era of the (Senator Joseph) McCarthy witch-hunts for "subversives," "Reds," "pinkos," and "fellow travelers." This repressive climate made nearly impossible the work of any group seeking rapprochement with Communist nations; any voice raised in favor of "peace" or "disarmament" was viewed as a voice inspired by Communist enemies of the United States who wanted to see her weakened and ultimately destroyed. It was this cold war stance that led to American involvement in Vietnam and to the difficulty of ending that involvement; no President, no politician wanted to appear "soft on communism" or to "lose" Vietnam the way China and Eastern Europe had been "lost" in the late 1940s. The shadow of Joseph McCarthy still darkened the political landscape in the early 1960s; dead since 1957, he haunted every attempt at coexistence with the Communist world. The fact that some atomic secrets were indeed given to the Soviet Union by U.S. and British spies, that some Hollywood screenwriters or some university professors were indeed Communists, did nothing to lessen the national paranoia whipped up and exploited by McCarthy and his congressional cohorts.

The "silent fifties," the time of no protest, was also the time of the "organization man" who dutifully climbed the corporate ladder in order to support his wife and children in the burgeoning suburbs. A kind of underground opposition to this work ethic evolved in the emergence of the beatnik culture—an antiestablishment countercultural lifestyle based in New York and San Francisco. The beats were sullenly macho despite the fact that some of them (male) were admittedly homosexual in a time when such preference could not openly be expressed; they were also avowedly antiintellectual and they experimented with drugs and what was known as "free sex." Their female hangers-on signaled their alienation from the dominant culture by eschewing makeup and by wearing plain dark clothing; later, in the sixties, they blossomed out in colorful hippie costumes, as did their men. Even in the fifties they had long hair—later a monumental point of battle between the generations. In the coffee houses of Greenwich Village and the City Lights Book Store of San Francisco the beats read Allen Ginsberg's *Howl* (published and promptly banned in 1956) and Jack Kerouac's *On the Road* (1957) and cultivated their more or less self-conscious, mostly sincere differences with mainstream America.

The first organized demonstrations against American involvement in Vietnam took place in August 1963, during the annual commemorations by American pacifists of the Hiroshima-Nagasaki atomic bombings.

In Philadelphia members of the Student Peace Union marched in front of the Federal Building; their signs protested U.S. foreign policy in South Vietnam.

In New York the action was inspired by the self-immolation of the Buddhist Thich Quang Duc in Hue, South Vietnam, on June 11. He had killed himself to protest the shooting of nine Buddhists by South Vietnamese government troops; those nine, in turn, had been demonstrating to protest the Roman Catholic President Diem's discriminatory treatment of Buddhists, specifically his banning of the Buddhist flag and his raids on Buddhist pagodas.

"It was a Catholic persecution [of Buddhists]," said Thomas Cornell, then and now a member of the Catholic Worker movement. In the early sixties Cornell lived in the organization's shelter near the Bowery in lower Manhattan; today he and his wife, Monica, run a soup kitchen and shelter for the homeless for the Waterbury (Connecticut) Area Council of Churches. "We felt that the first people to protest this outrage should be Catholics." Further, Cornell feared that if the war heated up, there would be not only antiwar sentiment but anti-Catholic sentiment as well.

And so Cornell and Christopher Kearns, another young Catholic Worker, walked up and down in front of the East Sixties residence of Vietnam's permanent observer to the UN. They carried signs that read WE DEMAND AN END TO U.S. MILITARY SUPPORT OF DIEM'S GOVERNMENT. The demonstration was to last for ten days. For the first nine, Kearns and Cornell were alone save for the observer who emerged from the residence, photographed them, and copied their signs; on the tenth, as they had requested, they were joined by about 250 people from the

Catholic Worker and other New York peace groups. More important, ABC filmed them and broadcast the demonstration on the evening news.

But the issue of U.S. involvement in Vietnam was still far from the center of the nation's attention in the summer of 1963. The continuing civil rights struggle in the (U.S.) South—marches led by the Reverend Martin Luther King, Jr., among others, with sit-ins, beatings, jailings, bombings, assassinations—seemed a far greater threat to the country's domestic tranquility than either nuclear war or the U.S. presence in Vietnam. In August 1963, 250,000 people participated in the March on Washington for Jobs and Freedom, where they and their fellow citizens watching and listening across the country and the world heard King's haunting eloquence: "I have a dream . . ." he cried. (King and other leaders had agreed to hold a mass rally rather than to call for civil disobedience—in the opinion of some civil rights activists, an unacceptable compromise with the government.)

Several weeks later Secretary of Defense Robert S. McNamara and General Maxwell Taylor completed a fact-finding mission to South Vietnam which led to their optimistic appraisal of the situation. McNamara predicted that most U.S. troops would be home by December 1965, and the White House said that the United States would continue to "deny this country [South Vietnam] to communism and to suppress the externally stimulated and supported insurgency of the Viet-Cong. . . ." The military program, the White House statement continued, "has made progress and is sound in principle, although improvements are being energetically sought."†

An editorial in the New York *Times* on October 4, 1963, had a more pessimistic tone than the Taylor-McNamara statement, and provided a contrast to its condescending dismissal of Bertrand Russell's criticisms the previous spring: the war in Vietnam is a "long-drawn-out war of attrition," warned the *Times*, and as such it needed the "support of an informed public opinion." This, it did not have: U.S. public relations policies had been "lacking in candor," and "essential facts were withheld, others distorted," leading to "the confusion, cynicism and frustration of the American public." The government must not "lose the support of an informed public opinion," warned the *Times*, "as, indeed, it appears to be doing." It was an editorial that could have been published any time in the next decade.

By 1963 the war in Vietnam had been raging for eighteen years. The United States had been involved from the start. On September 26, 1945, the first American to die in Vietnam, Lieutenant Colonel A. Peter Dewey of the OSS, was shot down by Viet Minh while driving an unmarked jeep near the Saigon airport. The Viet Minh were a revolutionary political party, the Vietnam Doc Lap Dong Minh (Vietnam Independence League), formed in 1941 to fight for a free, independent, and united Vietnam.

On September 2, 1945, the leader of that party, Ho Chi Minh, using words borrowed from the U.S. Declaration of Independence, proclaimed the indepen-

† Six months later, Neil Sheehan in the *Times* gave an assessment of the military prowess of the Viet Cong: in November 1961, at the beginning of the American military buildup, the Viet Cong had made 1,782 attacks—a situation described as "critical." Two years later, in November 1963, after enormous U.S. economic, technical, and military support, the Viet Cong made 3,182 attacks.

dence of Vietnam before a huge crowd in Ba Dinh Square, Hanoi. His tiny country had preserved its national identity through more than a thousand years of domination by China, and more recently through sixty unhappy years as part of the French colony of Indochina. Ho was a fierce nationalist, but—more important to the United States—he was also a Communist.

Within three weeks of Ho's pronouncement France embarked on the reconquest of her former colony. The United States played an increasingly open role in the effort as the cold war intensified and the "domino theory" took hold: if Vietnam fell to the Communists, all of Southeast Asia, most of the Pacific, and even the Middle East would follow. By 1954, when the French were defeated by the Viet Minh at Dien Bien Phu, the United States had expended over $2 billion supporting the French, and American military "advisers" were on the scene.

In July 1954 the major powers, meeting at Geneva, forced the Viet Minh to accept the division of Vietnam by a military demarcation line at the 17th parallel that was declared to be "provisional and . . . not in any way to be interpreted as constituting a political or territorial boundary." Elections to establish a united Vietnam were promised for 1956; Vietnamese were allowed to settle in either of the two zones. The United States, meanwhile, recognized the puppet state established by France with its seat of government in Saigon; Ngo Dinh Diem, a Catholic from a Mandarin family and a protegé of Francis Cardinal Spellman, was installed as Premier.

Diem proved to be a disaster. In a move endorsed by the Eisenhower Administration, he refused to hold the 1956 elections. Later, in a rigged election in the South, he was elected president of the "nonnation" of South Vietnam with 98.8 percent of the vote. Despite massive U.S. aid and nine hundred American military advisers by the end of 1960, Diem steadily lost both territory and influence to the insurgents in the South, now known as the Viet Cong. His disastrous program of land reform and his repression of dissidents increasingly vexed Washington and drew the United States closer to actual combat to keep him in office. The first official American casualties of the war occurred in 1959 when two U.S. military advisers were killed in a Viet Cong raid on the Bien Hoa military base near Saigon. In December 1960, just before President Kennedy took office, the National Liberation Front (NLF) of South Vietnam was formed as the political wing of the Viet Cong; it immediately endorsed the call issued in September by the Communist Party in Hanoi for the overthrow of the Diem regime.

Influenced by advisers like General Maxwell Taylor, Walt Rostow, Secretary of Defense Robert McNamara, Secretary of State Dean Rusk, and Vice President Lyndon B. Johnson, Kennedy embarked on a policy in Vietnam that one veteran correspondent, Homer Bigart, called "Sink or swim with Ngo Dinh Diem." Kennedy violated the terms of the Geneva Accords by the introduction of new American military personnel, more than 16,000 by the end of 1963. Aggressive new tactics of counterinsurgency, open fire zones, and "strategic hamlets" were adopted. Over eight thousand sorties ("training missions") were flown by the U.S. Air Force. In the years 1961–63, 109 Americans died in Vietnam. Despite this massive aid, the client of the United States, Ngo Dinh Diem, was sinking; he

14

ignored persistent American pleas for political, social, and military reforms and became increasingly alienated from his people. His harsh treatment of Buddhist dissidents was the last straw for his backers in Washington, who needed a stable regime to counter the Communist threat.

More small, sporadic protests against America's Vietnam involvement occurred that autumn. They were inspired by the visit of Mme. Nhu—the beautiful, exotic "dragon lady" who was married to Ngo Dinh Nhu, the chief of South Vietnam's secret police and brother of President Diem. Accompanied by her eighteen-year-old daughter, Mme. Nhu had come to the United States for a coast-to-coast tour to explain and defend the South Vietnamese Government.

On October 14, 1963, Mme. Nhu spoke for seven hours in Cambridge, first at Cabot House at Radcliffe College, where she was warmly applauded, and then in the evening at the Harvard Law School forum, where she was booed by a crowd of about one hundred demonstrators (mostly SDSers) in the street and booed again inside upon finishing her plea for support for her brother-in-law's regime with the statement that there was "absolute religious freedom in Vietnam." As she toured college campuses across the country that fall, protests about her presence—and her message—grew increasingly large and vocal. Only at Fordham, a Roman Catholic university (Mme. Nhu, born a Buddhist, was a Catholic convert), was she allowed to speak without interruption; after she finished she was warmly applauded by her audience of five thousand students. Then she and her daughter lunched with Fordham's president and student leaders.

As a goodwill ambassador for her brother-in-law's regime, Mme. Nhu was hardly a success. She alienated many potential supporters when, asked about the Buddhist immolations, she said that she enjoyed the monks' "barbeques." She criticized the students who picketed and booed her, but her command of English was too slight to allow her to entertain comments or questions on the prepared statements that she read aloud.

On November 2, 1963, while Mme. Nhu was still in the United States, her husband and her brother-in-law were assassinated in Saigon by the leaders of a military coup who had been encouraged by signals received from Washington. Mme. Nhu never returned to Vietnam; she and her daughter flew to Rome and then settled in France, where the daughter, by then a law student, was killed in an automobile crash in 1967.

During the winter of 1963–64, as America struggled to recover from the shock of President John F. Kennedy's assassination, the problem of Vietnam nagged at the edges of the nation's consciousness. On November 24, 1963, two days after taking office, President Lyndon Johnson, in a meeting with Ambassador Henry Cabot Lodge, reaffirmed America's commitment to South Vietnam, whose government was now headed by Major General Duong Van Minh ("Big Minh"). Two months later, after a coup in late January, the commitment was to the new regime of Major General Nguyen Khanh. President Johnson announced that he had requested a pledge from these "new and friendly leaders" that South Vietnam forces would step up their efforts against the Communist guerrillas. During 1964, although America's "commitment" remained "firm," the South Vietnamese Government did not: five different juntas seized control that year, and one dark week in August saw three new governments take charge in Saigon between Monday and Saturday.

By mid-February 1964, the U.S. forces in South Vietnam—Army, Navy, Air Force, and Marines—numbered more than fifteen thousand. They were "advisers," not combat troops; Secretary McNamara told the House Armed Services Committee that he hoped to have most of them home again by the end of 1965. That, in turn, depended on the ability of whatever South Vietnamese Government was in charge to inspire its people to fight. "I don't believe that we as a nation should assume the primary responsibility for the war in South Vietnam," said McNamara. In late February 1964, he made the first of three trips to Vietnam that spring to assess the "military effectiveness" of General Khanh. President Johnson, earlier that month, had ruled out any chance of a negotiated peace; he rejected French President de Gaulle's proposal for a neutralized Vietnam and pledged a greater war effort instead.

In January, New York *Times* columnist James Reston had warned the Administration that the French thought that a U.S. military victory in Vietnam was impossible—a fact that Johnson certainly knew but chose to ignore, perhaps because he was stung by President de Gaulle's sudden and unexpected recognition of the (Communist) government of the People's Republic of China only a few weeks after Johnson had assumed office under extraordinarily difficult circumstances. In early March, Reston raised another, far more difficult issue: congressional approval for what looked like an increasing U.S. commitment to South Vietnam, including suggestions for expanding the war into North Vietnam. "It is odd," he commented, "that nobody has even raised the question of seeking the approval of Congress for such a move."

On March 4, 1964, the day that Reston's prescient column appeared, Senator Wayne L. Morse, the maverick Democrat from Oregon, challenged the Senate to go on record as to whether it supported the Johnson-Rusk-McNamara policies in South Vietnam. No vote was taken; instead, President Johnson defused his opposition by inviting congressional leaders, including Morse, to a White House briefing on Vietnam. But Morse was not so easily put off. All that spring, day after day, in the Senate and out of it, he pounded at the issue of U.S. involvement in Vietnam. It was "McNamara's war"—a war that was "illegal." Moreover, he said, unilateral American intervention was "sheer stupidity" that would lead to a larger war. The United States should withdraw her support for Premier Khanh, whom Morse called a "tinhorn tyrant dictator."

Morse was joined in his public denunciation of the U.S. role in Vietnam by only one other senator, Ernest Gruening (D-Alaska). Both men became known for their colorful, often vitriolic language on the subject of Vietnam: "This bloody and wanton stalemate," cried Gruening; "I consider the life of one American youth worth more than this putrid mess." "Disgraceful and disreputable" was Morse's assessment of a speech by Secretary of State Dean Rusk on March 19 in Salt Lake City in which Rusk assailed the country's "quitters." If they had their way, said Rusk, the United States "would be playing into the hands of its adversaries." Morse replied that this equated criticism with treason, as the "late unlamented Senator

[Joseph] McCarthy had done." Said Morse of the U.S. involvement: "We never should have gone in. We never should have stayed in. We should get out."

In mid-March, the New York *Times'* lead editorial in its Sunday edition explored the notion that many of America's friends, as well as her opponents, thought that she had lost touch with a changing world, defending a *"status quo* or concepts of world affairs that are often invalid or outmoded." The initiative for change, intoned the *Times,* "can only come from the people."

The following week McNamara delivered a speech, widely regarded as a government White Paper, in which he "forcefully" rejected withdrawal or "peace at any price" and announced increased military and economic support for Major General Nguyen Khanh. He did not rule out possible direct military action against North Vietnam. Reacting to this threat, President Ho Chi Minh warned of "shameful defeats" should the United States "encroach" on North Vietnam.

Nearly five hundred American men had died in Vietnam by then; and after the casualty figures—the "body count"—had been disclosed for the week ending April 21, the figure was nearer six hundred. The Senate and House Republican floor leaders, Everett McKinley Dirksen (Illinois) and Charles Halleck (Indiana) accused the Administration of hiding the facts from the American people—a cry that would be heard for years to come from Republicans and Democrats alike.

For the moment, however, only Morse and Gruening carried the burden of dissent. They were an unlikely pair. Wayne Lyman Morse, then sixty-three and possessed of "the most frightening pair of eyebrows in the Senate," held law degrees from the University of Minnesota and from Columbia. He taught law at the University of Oregon, and in 1931, at the age of thirty-one, he became dean of its law school. In 1942 President Franklin D. Roosevelt appointed him to represent the public on the War Labor Board; ever a nay-sayer, Morse resigned in 1944 in a dispute over the power of John L. Lewis, the United Mine Workers president. Nevertheless, Oregon's chapter of the Congress of Industrial Organizations, which Lewis had established, backed Morse's Senate bid (as a Republican) in that year, and he won easily. In 1954, having supported Democrat Adlai Stevenson against Republican Dwight Eisenhower in the 1952 presidential election, he formally announced his switch to the Democratic Party.

Morse was a devastating opponent in debate whose talent for invective was exceeded only by his obsession with whatever issue he was debating. In 1964 it was the issue of American involvement in Vietnam. Day after day that spring his fellow senators as well as the country at large heard his rasping, penetrating voice probing, challenging, trying to shame and cajole and bully them—and the Administration—into admitting their mistake before it was too late, before the country became so entangled in the bloody mesh of war in Southeast Asia that it could not extricate itself. At one point, Premier Khanh called Morse a "traitor" for advocating U.S. withdrawal; Morse insisted on hearing from the President personally that Johnson did not agree.

Ernest Gruening, seventy-seven that year, equally opposed to U.S. policy in South Vietnam, drew fewer personal attacks—perhaps because his appearance and demeanor were those of a courtly, gentle man. But he was as angry as Morse, and equally convinced that his patriotic duty lay in decrying what he saw as the Administration's blind folly. Gruening had shepherded Alaska to statehood, serving for fourteen years as its territorial governor, then two years as provisional senator lobbying for statehood in Congress, then, in 1958, as one of the new state's elected senators. He felt that his patriotism was unassailable, and he exhibited the outraged, proprietary concern for his country's actions that patriots often assume. He traveled across the nation during the spring and summer of 1964, speaking at every opportunity, decrying U.S. involvement in Vietnam, warning the Administration to withdraw. Later in the year, he maintained that it was President Johnson who had "betrayed" the American people by asking approval of the "unconstitutional" Gulf of Tonkin Resolution.

The Administration turned a deaf ear. While Morse and Gruening cried their warnings, Secretary Rusk, visiting a fortified hamlet in South Vietnam, was photographed draped in a garland of flowers and quoted as telling his hosts, in an oddly Oriental phrase, "We are comrades in your struggle."

But the issue of American involvement in Vietnam was still not yet, that spring of 1964, at the center of the nation's consciousness; it was hardly even on the periphery. The civil rights bill had just been passed, with a humorous addition tacked on by the folksy, grandfatherly senator from North Carolina, Sam Ervin: if equality of rights were not to be denied because of one's color or religion or national origin, he said, then it should not be denied because of one's sex either.

Little else was humorous about the civil rights struggle. That summer—"Mississippi Summer"—hundreds of Northern youths would go South to help register disenfranchised blacks to vote, and some of them would die for their pains. Blacks, of course, had met violent death for years in the South both within and outside of the civil rights struggle; black civil rights workers assumed (rightly) that such murders at the hands of Southern white racists would not receive national attention until the deaths were those of (Northern) whites. In June two white civil rights workers from New York, Michael Schwerner and Andrew Goodman, and James Chaney, a black from Mississippi, disappeared in that state. Several weeks later the Democrats in their convention refused to seat the Mississippi Freedom Democratic Party delegation, even though the "regular" delegation—all white and mostly male —had been chosen by an electorate from which blacks had been systematically excluded. Senator Hubert H. Humphrey (D-Minnesota), a leading candidate for Johnson's vice presidential nominee, was given the task of settling the issue. He proposed that two MFDP delegates be seated as delegates at large; many strong civil rights advocates, including Allard Lowenstein and the Reverend Martin Luther King, Jr., urged acceptance of this compromise. The MFDP, however, under the leadership of Robert Moses, felt that it was a betrayal and they rejected it. The convention overruled them; the "regular" delegation was seated with a promise not to seat any delegation in 1968 that had been chosen by an electorate that excluded blacks as they were excluded in Mississippi. This incident had a larger significance than the seating of a delegation—any delegation—important as that was; it signaled to the young civil rights activists that no matter how "right," how moral or just their cause, they would not necessarily prevail, not even among their supposed allies. Afterward many of them felt the onset of an extreme alienation from the "system"—more extreme than that which had led them to work in Mississippi in the first place.

There were a few small bleeps of antiwar protest during this time—faint early warning signals. Because it is our purpose to trace the origins of the antiwar movement, which did not spring suddenly to full-blown life in, say, the spring of 1967 or the summer of 1968, it is necessary to note these events as they happened; they are important for what they nurtured rather than for what they accomplished at the time. For instance, in October 1963 the Friends Committee on National Legislation launched the Vietnam Information Center in Washington. In March 1964 the VIC heard historian Bernard Fall analyze the situation in Vietnam and as a result began its "Write to the President Drive," one of the early attempts to reach the Administration with pleas for withdrawal or, at least, no further involvement.

On April 7, 1964, 250 members of the Women's International League for Peace and Freedom went to Washington for a daylong lobbying effort against the U.S. presence in Vietnam. Their seven-point program included a protest against the brutality of the war; a plea for "honorable" withdrawal of U.S. forces; condemnation of napalm and defoliants; a protest of the continuation of a "war that cannot be won"; a protest of continued support for a [South Vietnamese] government that was not elected and did not have the people's support; a call for a negotiated settlement and a reopening of the Geneva Conference; and, finally, a statement that "we will lose moral leadership in the eyes of the world if we continue a senseless war."

On April 25 a leftist weekly, the *National Guardian,* carried an advertisement signed by eighty-seven youths stating that they would refuse to fight in South Vietnam because "we see no justification for our involvement." A number of "liberal" publications had allegedly refused to carry the ad. The young men were enrolled at Harvard, Columbia, Wisconsin, Haverford, and New York University, among other places; like French youths who had opposed their country's suppression of Algeria's fight for independence, these young men accepted their responsibility to "defend" their country, but not to fight in what they saw as an unjust war. They were all self-described leftists, many of them members of the Progressive Labor Movement.

On May 2, four hundred college students calling themselves the May 2 Movement gathered at 110th Street and Amsterdam Avenue in Manhattan at the Cathedral Church of St. John the Divine, which had been left unfinished over the years because its parishioners felt that their funds could be better spent serving their fellow human beings. (In the late 1970s work on the cathedral building resumed.) The young men demanded the withdrawal of U.S. troops from Vietnam and the end of U.S. military aid to the South Vietnamese Government. Then they marched to Times Square and on to the United Nations; along the way thousands of spectators gawked, astonished, ignorant of what the protesters were protesting.

The M2M, an offshoot of the Progressive Labor Movement, had been organized several weeks previously at Yale; among its fellow groups in this, its first action, were the Young Socialist Alliance and the Socialist Workers Party—hardly groups that were likely to gain the M2M a large following among the general population, but helpful initially to fill out its ranks. Among its aims was the collection of medical supplies—or the money to buy medical supplies—for shipment to North Vietnam.

In late May there appeared in the New York *Herald Tribune*—hardly a "leftist" journal like the *National Guardian*—an advertisement signed by 149 men of draft age, stating that they would not fight if called to do so in Vietnam. Like the previous ad in the *Guardian,* it had been organized by Phillip Luce, who at that time was under federal indictment for defying a State Department ban on travel to Cuba.

On July 3, 1964, President Johnson signed the Civil Rights Act. On the same day, David Dellinger called a demonstration against the Vietnam War to be held in Lafayette Square across from the White House. Present were A. J. Muste, folksinger Joan Baez, Rabbi Abraham Feinberg, Rev. Daniel Berrigan, and Rev. Philip Berrigan. The purpose of the demonstration was to publicize the "Declaration of Conscience" written a few weeks previously by Dellinger, Muste, Bayard Rustin, and others at the *Liberation* office.

The "Declaration of Conscience" was one of two statements in support of draft resistance that year, the other being the M2M declaration. It was a classic radical-pacifist document, written in imitation of the French *Manifeste des 121* (1960), a "Declaration Concerning the Right of Insubordination in the Algerian War." The American version proclaimed a "conscientious refusal to cooperate with the United States government in the prosecution of the war in Vietnam." It called on its signers to "refuse to take part in the manufacture or transportation of military equipment or to work in the fields of military research and weapons development," and stated that "we shall encourage the development of other nonviolent acts, including acts which involve civil disobedience, in order to stop the flow of American soldiers and munitions to Vietnam."

Dellinger remembers:

> After the rally in Lafayette Park, we walked to the fence and kneeled down in front of the White House. It was supposed to be an act of civil disobedience but they didn't arrest us. You have to keep moving, you could picket and walk back and forth but we stopped and we all kneeled down and we stayed there. . . . [When I was going to Washington] I went to La Guardia to catch a shuttle and ran into Bayard. He said he wasn't going to the demonstration. He was going down because LBJ was going to sign the Civil Rights Act and he'd been invited to the White House to be part of it. All the way down he explained how there was no way of stopping the Vietnam War and how smart Johnson was and how LBJ was going to completely nullify Gruening and Morse.
>
> My message to Bayard was—he was going to be given a pen—and I said, "Beautiful! When you come out of the White House, come up to us. I will call you to the platform immediately and you can take the pen that Johnson has signed the Civil Rights Act with and you can publicly sign the nonviolent statement." But he didn't. . . .

Thus was lost a symbolic early joining of the civil rights movement and what would become the antiwar movement; that failure foreshadowed many later ones.

On July 10 came a petition with potentially much more clout: an eighty-six-word appeal, calling on the Administration to "work for a neutralized North and South Vietnam protected by international guarantees. . . ." Delivered to the State Department and announced at a news conference by three spokesmen for the signers, Professors Hans J. Morgenthau of the University of Chicago, David B. Arnold of Princeton, and Robert S. Browne of Fairleigh Dickinson, it had been circulated with the help of SANE, signed by five thousand college and university teachers, and "approved" by several thousand more. Among the two dozen who initiated it were several whose names were to become well known to the public for their antiwar activities, including Dr. Benjamin Spock and Gordon Zahn, a sociologist who had been a conscientious objector in World War II.

The response, given by a nameless spokesman for the State Department, was unencouraging: the government would welcome an end to the "terror and suffering" in Vietnam, but it was unsure what the educators meant by "neutralization" or how it was to be achieved in view of the persistent "sabotage" of the 1954 agreements. Further, a published report of contingency plans to bomb North Vietnamese villages was only "one of many" ideas about how to prosecute the war. In short, the educators, moved by their concern to "do something," had done it, and had seen that their action was like the dropping of a stone into a deep pool: a few ripples and all trace vanished. It was an exercise in frustration for those opposing the government's policies in Vietnam that would often be repeated.

On July 14 the Administration announced that it was sending three hundred more Special Forces to South Vietnam to "advise" the regime of Premier Nguyen Khanh, but apparently neither he nor the U.S. Government thought that number sufficient, for two weeks later, on July 27, came the announcement—from Saigon, not from Washington—that five thousand more U.S. troops would be added to the sixteen-thousand-man U.S. military mission in South Vietnam. General Khanh was a fractious and difficult ally; like Chiang Kai-shek, he wanted to "unleash" his forces against the Communists, in this instance by marching to the North, and he repeatedly stated that South Vietnam had "complete freedom of action" in military operations. In mid-July he led a street rally in Saigon with the cry "Bac Tien!" (To the North!)

On August 2 came the report that "three North Vietnamese PT boats" fired on a U.S. destroyer in the Gulf of Tonkin about thirty miles off the North Vietnam coast. They were driven back by return fire from the destroyer and from four U.S. planes.

"The other side got a sting out of this," commented Secretary of State Dean Rusk. "If they do it again, they'll get another sting."

On August 4 they did do it again—or, at least, the Defense Department said that they did. "They"—the North Vietnamese—denied it. Some years afterward, when the Senate Foreign Relations Committee held hearings on the Gulf of Tonkin incident and its resulting Resolution, the point was one of many that remained unclear despite days of testimony.

21

At a hastily called and nationally televised news conference, an event inherently urgent and dramatic and made more so by its late hour—after midnight—Secretary McNamara announced that U.S. planes had struck North Vietnamese bases used by the PT boats that had attacked, allegedly for the second time, the U.S. destroyers *Maddox* and *Turner Joy,* which were patrolling international waters in the Gulf of Tonkin. In addition to the bases, the planes had struck "certain other targets directly supporting the operation of the PT boats," including, inexplicably, a large open-pit coal mine at Hon Gay.

Premier Khanh, it seemed, had had his way at last: the North had been attacked.

The following day, having addressed the nation on the incidents in the Gulf of Tonkin, President Johnson asked Congress to pass a joint resolution giving him support for "all necessary action" that he might have to take to protect U.S. forces in Southeast Asia. Further, he asked that this Southeast Asia Resolution give prior sanction for any necessary steps, including the use of armed force, to assist nations covered by the SEATO pact if they requested help "in defense of their freedom."

That Resolution, generally known as the Tonkin Gulf Resolution, was to have historic and tragically unforeseen consequences for both the United States and Vietnam, North and South. It had been drawn up in the spring by William Bundy, the Assistant Secretary of Defense. Presented to Congress at a time of apparent crisis, accompanied by a request from a seemingly beleaguered President for speedy action, worded in a way that some members of Congress called "unnecessarily broad," the Tonkin Gulf Resolution was assured of quick passage from the moment it appeared. To have voted against it would have been to lay oneself open to charges of not supporting the President in a time of national crisis—a risk few politicians dare to take.

The Senate debated the Resolution for nine hours—a time period which included, at Morse's insistence, an overnight break. The House debated it for forty minutes. The House vote was 416–0 in favor, with Adam Clayton Powell, the Harlem Democrat who described himself as a "pacifist," voting "present." Representative Eugene Siler (R-Kentucky) was paired against it, but his vote was not recorded. He called the Resolution "buck-passing," the President's attempt to silence later criticism. The Senate vote was 88–2; to no one's surprise, Senators Morse and Gruening voted no.

Morse had threatened a filibuster if he were not allowed two hours' speaking time on both days of deliberation. Although Johnson had wanted the Senate's approval rushed through in one day, the bill's floor manager, J. William Fulbright (D-Arkansas), chairman of the Foreign Relations Committee, was forced therefore to give in to Morse's demand. In an unusually bitter attack, Morse called the Resolution tantamount to a "declaration of war"; "war should not be declared by resolution," he said. The United States was a "provocateur" in South Vietnam, said Morse, every bit as much as North Vietnam was; the incident that inspired the attack on the *Maddox* and the *Turner Joy* was as much the doing of the United States as of North Vietnam. The ships had not been on routine patrol at all, he said, but supporting South Vietnamese naval raids on North Vietnam; further, they had violated the twelve-mile limit claimed by North Vietnam.

Morse was well aware that his arguments fell on deaf ears—on no ears, in fact, for the Senate chamber was nearly empty as he spoke. His fellows had heard his arguments against the war; now at this time of apparent crisis, they did not want to hear them again. Morse knew how they would vote on the Resolution; but, he warned, "Senators who vote for it will live to regret it." "I cannot understand what is happening to my country," he said.

Gruening, as always, was Morse's only ally. "All Vietnam is not worth the life of a single American boy," he said. "We have lost altogether too many American lives already."

Later, Morse returned to the constitutional issue. "A constitutional principle is involved," he said. "It is dangerous to give to any President an unchecked power, after the passage of a joint resolution, to make war. Consider the procedural complications that could develop if Congress decided that the President was making serious mistakes in the conduct of a personal war—for it would be a Presidential war at that point. How would the President be stopped? He could not be stopped. . . ."

Most senators did not share Morse's objections, although they did have two principal reservations. The first was the fear that the Resolution would involve a change in what the Senate understood to be the United States' "mission" in South Vietnam—that is, the providing of training and matériel. The second was the fear that Premier Khanh would extend the war into the North as he and other South Vietnamese generals so longed to do, thus depriving the United States of its "freedom of action." One way or another, Senators Aiken, Brewster, Church, Cooper, Gore, Javits, and McGovern expressed their doubts about the Resolution; in the end, however, they voted "aye."

Senator Gaylord Nelson (D-Wisconsin) went so far as to offer an amendment in an attempt to clarify the language of the Resolution: ". . . it is the sense of Congress that, except when provoked to a greater response, we should continue to attempt to avoid a direct military involvement in the Southeast Asian conflict." This was hardly an ironclad prohibition against America's showing her military might, but even so it was too strong for Fulbright. He told Nelson that there was no time to debate the amendment, but he reassured his troubled colleague that the amendment was an "accurate reflection of what I believe is the President's policy." Further, he "did not believe" that South Vietnam "could involve us beyond the point where we ourselves wished to be involved." Nelson declared that he was satisfied that he had made a "legislative record" of administration intent, and he voted for the Resolution. By August 7 it had been passed by both houses; President Johnson signed it on August 10 before the cameras in a nationwide television broadcast.

In his exhaustive and brilliant dissection and analysis of the Tonkin Gulf crisis, *The President's War*, Anthony Austin quotes an anonymous Senate staffer who had a chillingly matter-of-fact explanation for the overwhelmingly favorable vote. It

was sold to the Democrats on the basis that it would help with the election. "The North Vietnamese have shot at us, and we've shown them, but we

23

musn't let Goldwater get a free ride out of this." As to the Republicans, they were stuck with it. The resolution was in line with what Goldwater was demanding. And the Republicans had always been more gung-ho anyway.

Fulbright? He trusted Johnson not to use the resolution that way. He thought it would help deter the Communists from escalating the war. And it would put Johnson in a stronger position to resist Goldwater's campaign demands for escalating *our* role in the war. He really believed it.

The passage of the Tonkin Gulf Resolution aroused little public concern in a summer filled with more immediate, more pressing events, including news of a war of sorts on America's own soil. On the day that President Johnson first spoke to the country about the events in the Gulf of Tonkin, the FBI announced that it had found the bodies of the three slain civil rights workers, Goodman, Schwerner and Chaney, buried in an earthen dam in Philadelphia, Mississippi—a place not so far away as Vietnam, but one for many Americans equally alien, potentially equally deadly. Howard Zinn, now a professor of political science at Boston University, SNCC's historian who worked in the Southern civil rights struggle during those years and who in the late sixties became one of the most important academic figures in the antiwar movement with the publication of *Vietnam: The Logic of Withdrawal,* remembers the death of the three young men and its significance for SNCC:

> The first joining of the civil rights movement and the antiwar movement that I remember was in early August 1964 when we held a memorial service outside Philadelphia, Mississippi, for the three civil rights workers who had been killed that summer. It was a very tense and very moving memorial. Mrs. Chaney was there. Bob Moses held up a copy of the Jackson [Mississippi] newspaper and it said something like LBJ SAYS "SHOOT TO KILL" IN THE GULF OF TONKIN. The Tonkin Gulf incident had just taken place and here were these three fellows who had been murdered and Bob Moses was making the point of the connection with the violence that the Government was tolerating [in Mississippi]—they refused to send Federal marshals to Mississippi to protect the civil rights workers, [and] they were ready to do violence in Asia.

In addition to the civil rights turmoil, the presidential campaign was in full swing; Johnson was favored to win.

In New York City a rally called for August 6 to support peace and disarmament and to mark the nineteenth anniversary of the explosion of the atomic bomb at Hiroshima also concerned itself with U.S. involvement in Vietnam. About one thousand people gathered in Washington Square to hear Norman Thomas and Bayard Rustin denounce the war, and a statement from Wayne Morse was read. One of the demonstrators' signs read UNITED STATES TROOPS BELONG IN MISSISSIPPI, NOT VIETNAM. Two days later, about sixty people assembled in Duffy Square, at Forty-seventh Street and Broadway, in a rally called by the M2M. WORLD'S FAIR VISITORS—HELP US STOP THE WAR IN VIETNAM read one sign carried by the demonstrators. When ordered by the police to disperse, they refused;

the police arrested seventeen and commandeered taxicabs to carry them to the 16th Precinct station house.

Several weeks later Gaylord Nelson sent a letter to the New York *Times*. He had continued to worry about the wording of the Tonkin Gulf Resolution, for which he had reluctantly voted. Now he wanted once again to explain his understanding of its meaning: although it "does not limit the President's authority, neither does it offer Congressional endorsement and support for an expanded new course of action." After reviewing his clarifying amendment, which was not allowed, Nelson concluded with what he believed "most Senators feel, that our basic mission in Vietnam is one of providing material support and advice. *It is not to substitute our armed forces for those of the South Vietnamese government, nor to join with them in a land war, nor to fight the war for them* [emphasis added]."

Nelson's letter had been a response to a column by James Reston in which Reston had reported that some administration officials were "talking casually about how easy it would be to 'provoke an incident' . . . that would justify an attack on North Vietnam." Such officials apparently did not fear, as many people did, the threat of war with the People's Republic of China—a threat made all the more alarming that month when word came that China had detonated its first nuclear device.

On October 3 twelve people staged a vigil in Times Square to end the war; they announced that they would return every Saturday for the rest of the month if the war did not end. Sponsoring groups included Women Strike for Peace, the Student Peace Union, the War Resisters League, the New York Fellowship of Reconciliation, and the Catholic Worker—all groups that would do much important work in the antiwar movement in the years to come. Such a vigil might strike the reader as naive in the extreme: would President Johnson stop the war because twelve people stood in Times Square? It was not naive; these Americans—mostly radical pacifists —knew what they were up against. The odds didn't matter. Almost a year later they were still there. The war, of course, continued.

Otherwise, no antiwar activity occurred. The country focused instead on the Johnson-Goldwater contest—hardly a contest at all, as it turned out—and, for diversion, on the antics of the students at the University of California at Berkeley, who were involved in something called the Free Speech Movement, led by a curly-haired young survivor of the struggle in Mississippi, Mario Savio. At issue was the freedom of students to organize and collect funds for their various political causes (both off campus and on) on a stretch of university property that had always been used for such purposes but that now had been denied to them by the university administration. The significance of the Free Speech Movement, aside from any immediate on-campus effect at Berkeley, was that it set a pattern for student protest in the years that followed. The President's Commission on Campus Unrest (the Scranton Commission), reporting to President Nixon on student upheaval in 1970, called this pattern, or scenario, "the Berkeley invention": a relatively small number of student activists began a protest over one or more issues involving matters beyond the university (civil rights, disarmament, etc.). Using tactics borrowed from the civil rights movement, the students disrupted the university, which, in turn, called out the campus police. More students became involved; protest escalated; off-campus police were called; mass arrests led to a student strike. The most distinctive aspect of the Berkeley invention, reported the commission, was that the "high spirits and defiance of authority that had characterized the traditional school riot were now joined to youthful idealism and to social objectives of the highest importance. This combination moved the participants to intense feeling and vigorous political activism and provoked from state or university officials reactions and overreactions that promised to keep the movement alive."

The Johnson-Goldwater contest gave the American people a chance to vote their feelings on the war in Vietnam, among other issues. "We want no wider war," said Johnson, and people believed him. Even Barry Goldwater's attempt to tar Johnson with the Vietnam brush did not succeed. Wayne Morse had called it "McNamara's war"; in September, Goldwater called it "Johnson's war." But people associated Goldwater with being trigger-happy (he had suggested the possible use of atomic weapons in Vietnam to defoliate the jungle which hid the Viet Cong supply trails), and no amount of denial could erase that public image. A televised commercial for the Democrats that September showed a little girl counting daisy petals: "one, two, three, four . . ." and an ominous voice-over intoning: "four, three, two, one . . ." as her image dissolved into a mushroom cloud. The Democrats showed this commercial only once before Republican protests forced them to cancel it, but once was enough. Johnson, in the public mind, was the candidate who would keep the country not only out of war but out of nuclear Armageddon. In light of later events, it is important to remember that the vote for Johnson in 1964 was to a large extent a peace vote—or, at least, a vote against nuclear war. He won the election with the largest percentage of the vote ever given to a candidate to that time: 61.1 percent, with a plurality of 16.9 million votes. For the moment people breathed easily: the "war" candidate had been defeated.

Shortly after the election three little-noted events took place. In mid-November the War Resisters League called for "immediate withdrawal of all US military forces and military aid [from Vietnam]"—an extreme position at the time. Over the Thanksgiving weekend members of SANE, in Washington for their annual convention, marched in front of the White House, two hundred strong, carrying signs calling for a negotiated peace in Vietnam—not, it will be noted, for immediate withdrawal. Several weeks later, on December 19, one thousand people gathered in Washington Square, New York City, to hear Norman Thomas, A. J. Muste, and A. Philip Randolph call for an end to the war. The rally was organized by David McReynolds of the War Resisters League, and by Muste, the Committee for Nonviolent Action, and the Fellowship of Reconciliation. Its purpose was "to keep the issue of Vietnam before the public, and before the Administration," said Muste. Demonstrations were held also in Boston, Philadelphia, Chicago, San Francisco and Seattle, among other cities. Little attention was paid.

At the close of the year four senators—all Democrats, but with different points of view—questioned the U.S. role in Vietnam. J. William Fulbright, speaking at Southern Methodist University in Dallas, said that he agreed with the late General Douglas MacArthur that the United States should not get into a land war in Asia;

throwing hundreds of thousands of Americans into the war would be a "senseless effort." On the other hand, he did not advocate getting out. "We should never have undertaken" the aid program to South Vietnam in 1954, he said.

Similar hindsight, 20-20 as hindsight so often is, was voiced by Frank Church (D-Idaho). In an interview in *Ramparts* magazine, Church called for neutralization of Southeast Asia under the aegis of the UN; it would be "folly" for the United States to escalate the war into North Vietnam, he said, and it had been a mistake to become involved in Vietnam in the first place after the example of the French defeat. If the government of Saigon continued to fail to gain the support of its people, said Church, and thereby lost the war, "then I would hope that we would recognize that it is not our country and never has been."

Wayne Morse called once again for President Johnson to lay the problem before the United Nations; in his familiar style, he said that "the loss of one more American life in defense of the hopeless chaos in South Vietnam would be inexcusable."

And Richard Russell (D-Georgia), head of the Senate Armed Services Committee, announced at the end of the month that that group would evaluate the U.S. position in South Vietnam "in view of the lack of support [in Vietnam] for the present Saigon regime." Russell was concerned that the United States would become embroiled in Africa as it had in Vietnam; the United States "made a terrible mistake getting involved in Vietnam," he said.

There was as yet little popular support for such doubts, however, despite the "peace" vote for Lyndon Johnson in November. In mid-December a poll conducted by the Survey Research Center of the University of Michigan revealed that 28 percent of the American people did not know that Communists ruled mainland China; 26 percent did not know that there was a war in South Vietnam. Of the 74 percent who did know it, 53 percent opposed U.S. withdrawal. Senator Church's office, in answer to an inquiry, said that he had received little mail on the subject from his constituents.

And then, at the very end of the year, on December 29 in New York City, in humble surroundings, with no media fanfare, with no celebrities attending, a momentous event took place: the antiwar movement was born. Its midwife was the maverick journalist I. F. Stone. The body which brought it forth was not, as might have been supposed, one of the traditional peace groups but a relatively new organization, Students for a Democratic Society.

In years to come SDS and the antiwar movement would be thought of as synonymous, but they were never that. SDS had begun as the student branch of the old-time, respected (and respectable) League for Industrial Democracy, which had its roots in the Intercollegiate Socialist Society, founded in 1905 by, among others, the muckraker-novelist Upton Sinclair, Jack London, Clarence Darrow, John Reed, Norman Thomas, Walter Lippmann, and Edna St. Vincent Millay. The ISS viewed itself as an educational—not a revolutionary—organization; it languished during World War I and resurfaced in 1921 as the League for Industrial Democracy. Its campus group, the Student League for Industrial Democracy, was active for a time in the thirties around the issues of domestic policy and opposition to international entanglements (i.e., war), but it collapsed with the arrival of World War II. In 1945

SLID was revived as the campus arm of LID, which billed itself as a social-democratic group, explicitly anti-Communist.

In early 1960 SLID changed its name to Students for a Democratic Society. Upon receiving a $10,000 grant from the United Automobile Workers SDS was able to name its vice president, Al Haber, a graduate student at the University of Michigan, as its field secretary—that is, paid organizer. By late 1961, SDS had become heavily involved in the burgeoning civil rights movement. Another member, Tom Hayden, like Haber a University of Michigan alumnus, was sent to Atlanta, where he joined the civil rights struggle and provided periodic reports on the activities of the leading Southern civil rights organization, the Student Nonviolent Coordinating Committee. Haber worked from the group's New York office in the LID headquarters; together Hayden and Haber labored to make SDS a reality, and their early efforts, 1960–62, were directed primarily, although not exclusively, at the Southern civil rights movement. Hayden's reports from the South on SNCC's voter-registration drive were circulated on campuses throughout the country and served to drum up support not only for SDS (which had twenty chapters by the fall of 1961) but also for Northern student involvement in the blacks' Southern struggle to register to vote and to integrate public facilities.

In December 1961 SDS held a conference at Ann Arbor, home of the University of Michigan. Its purpose was to invite those who attended to submit ideas for a national program of action. Since many of those attending were already members of other groups—the Student Peace Union, for example—no agreement was reached on the question of what issue in particular should receive the most attention: civil rights? poverty? university reform? disarmament?

Haber proposed, therefore, that a manifesto be hammered out, an ideology that would provide both an analysis of American society and institutions, and ideas about how they could be improved and strengthened—in other words, how social change could be achieved. Tom Hayden was given the task of composing this paper; with help from others, he did so.

In the 1980s, Tom Hayden is a California state assemblyman (representative) from Santa Monica. He is married to actress Jane Fonda, who was herself caught up in the later years of the antiwar movement. He is a pleasant and unassuming man with a politician's easy friendliness who speaks fluently and sometimes movingly about his years in SDS and the antiwar movement; one has the impression that he has said these things many times before, and that time and circumstance have distanced him emotionally from the turbulent years of his youth when he and his fellows clung to their dream of reshaping America more closely to her—and their—ideals. He recalls the problem of forging the SDS manifesto—of, in effect, forging an ideology for the New Left:

> The history of the late sixties is merely the history of people swept away by various theories and ideologies, having lost faith in their own natural instincts which they followed at the beginning of the decade. Because from the thirties to the fifties there was no mainstream politics in America that had any ideological content, one generation after another would grow up with-

out any acquaintance with serious political ideas and no leadership from adults. So when the New Left suddenly emerged it was a group of very intelligent people, very humanistic people, but suddenly we were asked to do things that adults would normally do, like lead an overdue civil rights revolution, stop a war, end poverty—and the average leader of this movement was about twenty years old. So it was easy to see where this dichotomy would occur, where the energy and the courage would come from the young but we would always look for somebody out there, older, who might be able to put it into some kind of theoretical framework. . . . But they all had ideologies. . . . Everywhere we turned there was someone with a point of view that had been set by the politics of the thirties, politics of the Russian Revolution, politics of McCarthyism, anti-McCarthyism, whatever. . . . It's a very serious problem here that the Left never had its own homegrown point of view.

In June 1962 some SDS members convened at the FDR camp of the United Automobile Workers in Port Huron, Michigan. After four days and nights of discussion and sometimes argument, they succeeded in revising their constitution so that its explicit anti-Communist language was a little less explicit. This deviation proved to be upsetting to SDS's parent, LID, but after several tumultuous sessions with LID representatives back in New York, and an attempted lockout by LID, SDS remained, for the time being, under LID's wing. During the dispute SDSers had the foresight to remove SDS mailing lists from its office.

In attempting to explain its new self, SDS's constitution now said that

> It [SDS] maintains a *vision* of a democratic society where at all levels the people have control of the decisions which affect them and the resources on which they are dependent. It seeks a *relevance* through the continual focus on realities and on the programs necessary to effect change at the most basic levels of economic, political and social organization. It feels the *urgency* to put forth a radical, democratic program counterposed to authoritarian movements both of communism and the domestic right. . . .
>
> SDS is an organization of democrats. It is civil libertarian in its treatment of those with whom it disagrees, but clear in its opposition to any totalitarian principle as a basis for government or social organization. Advocates or apologists for such a principle are not eligible for membership.

The convention elected a new president (not surprisingly, Tom Hayden), but it was unable to finish its primary task of completing deliberation on the manifesto that has come to be known as *The Port Huron Statement.* The document was polished after the convention and sent out to members about a month later. From then on it was an underground classic: requests for copies poured into the SDS National Office and these were read to tatters when new ones could not be produced quickly enough.

The Port Huron Statement is what scholars refer to as a "seminal document"; the explicit masculinity of the term is nicely appropriate in view of the unrelieved machismo of SDS and the antiwar movement in general. Read today, it leaves an impression of innocence and hope, a vision for a better world that, in retrospect, could never have been achieved. Its frame of reference, in the mind-set of the day, was entirely masculine: "We regard *men [sic]* as infinitely precious. . . . Men have unrealized potential . . . fraternity . . . human brotherhood . . . personal links between man and man. . . ."

In 1962 it was important for its identification of the nation's problems, which, it said, were omnipresent: on campus and off, in politics, the economy, the military-industrial complex, the arms race, the colonial revolution (the Third World), American Russophobia, discrimination (seen solely in terms of discrimination against "nonwhites"), poverty, education—among others.

Perceived as the two most urgent problems were (1) how to end the Cold War and (2) how to improve and increase democracy in America.

The Port Huron Statement's prescription for dealing with these problems, in addition to explicit suggestions, was something called "participatory democracy." This was a method of operation which denigrated strong leadership (which came to be called "elitism") and meant that deciding on a course of action—any course of action—became a nightmare of discussion through which, it was hoped, a consensus would emerge. Often it did not. The authors of *The Port Huron Statement* looked mainly to the universities and to the "New Left"—a term coined by the sociologist C. Wright Mills, who died in the year the statement was born—as agents of change.

The Port Huron Statement was important above all because it existed. It was something—some written document, a tangible thing with the aura of importance that print, even mimeographed print, always carries; and it gave to those who read it (mostly students) the sense that here at last was a statement that spoke for them, for the new day that seemed to have dawned when John F. Kennedy was elected President. "We were just one shade from Kennedy," recalls one SDSer. "Just one step—in every sense—optimistic, idealistic, loving. There was anger, too, if you want to call it that. Tom Hayden and Paul Potter got hurt in Mississippi. It was scary. . . ."

During the 1962–63 school year SDS limped along. At its June 1963 convention it took up the question of *America and the New Era*—a position paper somewhat more radical and explicit than *The Port Huron Statement;* it was a critique of Kennedy's "New Frontier," and a further examination of the nation's domestic problems. From this convention and this document came what was perhaps SDS's best-known activity: the Economic Research and Action Project (ERAP), in which SDS members went into the nation's poor, urban districts to organize the residents there to fight for their own betterment—more jobs, better housing, schools, community services, and the like.

ERAP began slowly with a $5,000 grant from the United Automobile Workers, and, in the beginning, as the political activity of blacks increased North and South, it was seen as a project to organize poor, urban whites. But there was no program to offer, no organizational structure, and so at the SDS December 1963 national council meeting the idea was proposed for "An Interracial Movement of the Poor"

—a more massive and organized movement into the nation's slums, black and white, to be made by hundreds of SDS members instead of only a dedicated few.

Al Haber called ERAP the "cult of the ghetto," and he and others were not sanguine about SDS's leaving its natural base, the nation's campuses. He was outvoted, however, and so in the summer of 1964 ("Mississippi Summer") SDS initiated ten ghetto projects: Baltimore, Boston, Chester (Pennsylvania), Chicago, Cleveland, Hazard (Kentucky), Louisville, Newark, Philadelphia, and Trenton. Those who worked in the projects were from perhaps a dozen colleges and universities, including Oberlin, Swarthmore, Michigan, Bryn Mawr, Harvard, Haverford, MIT, Williams, and Wisconsin. (Some SDSers, of course, had already graduated.)

Some attention—not much—was paid. Three adults—W. H. Ferry of the Center for the Study of Democratic Institutions, A. J. Muste of the Fellowship of Reconciliation, and journalist I. F. Stone—published a letter praising SDS and its ERAP project: "SDS has succeeded in attracting some of the best and angriest young minds now functioning, and has been able to put these minds to work in socially relevant ways."

Little was accomplished that summer, but some—not all—ERAPs survived into the following year, when more were begun; more than four hundred people were working in ERAP projects in the summer of 1965. Ironically, it was, in part, the publicity that SDS received from what might be called its foreign affairs work—its organization of the spring 1965 anti-Vietnam march on Washington—that attracted new members, many of whom went into the ghetto with ERAP to work out their newly ignited idealism. Added to the difficulties of organizing the poor (how? for what?) were the difficulties of living and working together in a constant grind of poverty and alienation—from each other, from the system. Todd Gitlin, an early SDSer now on the faculty of the University of California at Berkeley, has said that "ERAP was built on guilt. . . . Guilt and its counterpart, shame, are healthy and necessary antidotes to privilege, but the antidote taken in large doses becomes poisonous." By the end of summer 1965 ERAP was essentially dead. One consequence of its failure was the loss to SDS of much talent; when people left ERAP they left SDS. A consequence of ERAP's very existence had been a loss to SDS of some of its best hearts and minds for crucial months that might better have been used to organize new chapters and give focus to the organization.

Kirkpatrick Sale, the historian of SDS, said that the most important effect of ERAP was not the hoped-for radicalizing of the nation's poor, but the radicalizing of the ERAPers themselves:

Testing some of the reformist hypotheses of *The Port Huron Statement* and *America and the New Era* in concrete and specific ways, they found those assumptions in error; working with the instruments of the state, they found those instruments insufficient, or, worse, corrupt and evil; trying in the only way they could see to make the American dream a reality for the lowliest citizens, to keep the promises about equal opportunity and economic betterment they had heard so often from the nation's leaders, they found that goal impossible and the leaders indifferent. They tried the system, and found it wanting. . . . Many who went through that experience sought more than community unions next time out—they were ready not to challenge the institutions of the system but to resist them.

In December 1964, however, ERAP's success or failure was still in question. SDS held its midwinter convention that year in New York City at the Cloakmakers' Hall—a decidedly Old Left location. When the SDSers arrived they found a ten-foot-high portrait of President Lyndon Johnson in the meeting room; before getting down to business they turned it to face the wall. They had invited as their keynote speaker I. F. Stone, whose *Weekly* was to have a profound effect on the country's consciousness of Vietnam; he was asked to speak on the war and on U.S. involvement in Vietnam. "He always gave interesting, provocative, inspirational talks," says Tom Hayden. "He was very influential with the first generation of SDS leadership, from 1960 through '63–'64. . . . He was the voice in the wilderness." On that occasion Stone spoke with such eloquence and power that the young activists voted to add to the SDS agenda the organization of a march on Washington on April 17, the Easter weekend—the traditional time for peace groups to demonstrate. The purpose of the march was to protest the American presence in Vietnam. To the horror of some on the Left, this was to be a "nonexclusionary" march—that is, anyone who wanted to join it could do so: even socialists, even Communists.

SDS hoped that the march would not be a failure, and with the addition of the American Friends Service Committee to the sponsorship and Senator Ernest Gruening signing on to speak, at least a moderately good attendance seemed assured.

But then President Johnson gave some unexpected help; and at last, although for only a little while, SDS and the engine of mass discontent came together with resounding, reverberating success.

1965:
No Turning Back

IN THE EARLY morning hours of February 7, 1965, the American air base at Pleiku, in the Central Highlands of South Vietnam, was attacked by Viet Cong guerrillas firing 81-mm mortar shells. Eight American men were killed, 126 wounded. As it happened, National Security Adviser McGeorge Bundy was in South Vietnam just then with a team of experts to observe the progress of the war. He telephoned President Johnson to urge a retaliatory strike, which the President then ordered. Within twelve hours forty-nine U.S. Navy fighter-bombers attacked a Viet Cong encampment at Dong Hoi (North Vietnam), just north of the demilitarized zone—Operation Flaming Dart I. South Vietnamese planes with Air Marshal Nguyen Cao Ky in the lead were to have joined the American force but were delayed by bad weather; they attacked another Viet Cong stronghold the next day.

On the plane back to Washington that night with his staff, Bundy drew up a memorandum dated February 7 with the heading "A Policy of Sustained Reprisal." The Pentagon Papers (see pp. 367–69) call the memo a "highly personal Bundy assessment and point of view" and a "unique articulation of a rationale for the ROLLING THUNDER policy" which would begin a few weeks later. ROLLING THUNDER was a program of continuous U.S. air strikes against North Vietnam, intended to "punish" the enemy for his "aggression." It had been devised the previous year to await its moment. "Pleikus are streetcars," said McGeorge Bundy —that is, if you miss one, another one will come along.

At the time the first raids were announced in North Vietnam, Soviet Premier Aleksei Kosygin was in Hanoi; he had gone there to try to arrange a negotiated settlement of the war. The raids were, therefore, a public embarrassment to the Soviets, and they skewered any possibility of Kosygin's acting as a peacemaker.

In Washington, government officials—never named—said guardedly that "the U.S. had adopted a policy of greater flexibility in any future retaliatory strike against North Vietnam."

On February 11, as if in perverse response to the U.S. strikes, the Viet Cong attacked the U.S. barracks at Qui Nhon and killed nineteen Americans and wounded thirteen. On February 12, 160 U.S. and South Vietnamese planes attacked North Vietnam in another reprisal: Flaming Dart II.

As in the previous year, there were a few faint signs of domestic protest, both of the bombing and of the instability and obvious unpopularity of the regimes which the United States was supporting in South Vietnam. (From December 20, 1964, through February 20, 1965, six governments were installed in Saigon.) Small ad hoc demonstrations were held across the country, including many on college campuses; some of these were led by SDS chapters, but many took place on campuses where SDS had not yet appeared.

On February 8, the day that U.S. planes had begun to bomb North Vietnam, SDS put out its call for the April 17 march: "We urge the participation of *all those who agree with us* that the war in Vietnam injures both Vietnamese and Americans and should be stopped [emphasis added]." A full-page ad in *Liberation* (and a half page in the *National Guardian),* the call termed the Vietnam war "a civil war . . . a losing war . . . a self-defeating war . . . a dangerous war . . . a war never declared by Congress . . . a hideously immoral war . . ."

Protests against the U.S. presence in Vietnam continued throughout the month as more and more groups signed up for the April 17 march. On February 11 about three hundred members of Women Strike for Peace and the Women's International League for Peace and Freedom picketed the White House in a call for a negotiated peace and a "dignified withdrawal" in Vietnam. MOTHERS IN 33 STATES WANT PEACE IN VIETNAM read one of their placards. On February 16 faculty from eighteen New England colleges and universities signed an ad in the New York *Times* calling for immediate negotiations to settle the conflict; on February 19 SANE published an ad in the *Times* calling for a halt to widening the war (bombing the North), a cease-fire, and a negotiated settlement.*

On the same day, fourteen people were arrested at the U.S. Mission to the UN after having stood or sat in 20° F temperatures all day blocking the entrances. Only about thirty people appeared at this demonstration (including the Reverend A. J. Muste, age eighty), and once again they represented those organizations which had provided almost all the support for anti-Vietnam actions until this time: the Committee for Nonviolent Action, the War Resisters League, the Student Peace Union, and the Catholic Worker.

Meanwhile, at the Overseas Press Club in New York, Clark Kissinger, the national secretary of SDS, was speaking to reporters about the planned April 17 demonstration. "It's quite clear," he said, "that the major foreign intervening

---

* During the course of the Vietnam War, literally hundreds of ads about the war appeared in newspapers across the country. Most of these were appeals for peace; some were calls for stepped-up fighting. Thousands of people—often but not always university and college faculty—signed them and donated the money to pay for them. They were intended to show the depth and breadth of support for the antiwar cause. They had no discernible effect on any Administration's policy. Nevertheless the practice continues: on April 6, 1983, a two-page ad appeared in the *Times* for a group calling itself "the Bipartisan Appeal [on the Budget Crisis]." It expressed the group's alarm over continued high deficits and appealed for "a coherent, more gradual and affordable multi-year buildup in [the nation's] defense capability." Three of the signers of this ad were McGeorge Bundy, Robert McNamara, and Dean Rusk: former government officials who in the 1960s were among the architects of the Vietnam policy which nearly wrecked the American economy.

power in Vietnam is the United States." A Columbia University student, speaking of the mood on campus, put the matter more succinctly when he said, "I don't think anyone is willing to die for Vietnam." The next day four hundred SDSers picketed the White House to protest the bombing of North Vietnam.

Events appeared to be moving inexorably toward what many people saw as a major war. On February 25 the New York *Times* reported that the State Department had abandoned the "advise and assist" role of American troops in Vietnam, and that the Administration had "changed the rules of United States involvement." The announcements coincided with the disclosure that B-57 bombers and F-100 fighter-bombers had been used to strike a "large concentration" of Viet Cong troops in a mountain pass in Binhdinh Province, on the coast north of Saigon. The official description of American-flown bombing raids as "training flights," with a South Vietnamese pilot always in attendance, had been abandoned. "Congressional authority" for the change was cited—the Tonkin Gulf Resolution.

On February 27 the State Department issued its second White Paper on Vietnam. Titled *Aggression from the North—the Record of North Vietnam's Campaign to Conquer South Vietnam,* the sixty-four-page document charged North Vietnam with aggression against the South and warned that the United States might be forced to renounce its policy of "restraint" if that aggression did not cease.

U.S.S.R. Premier Aleksei Kosygin called the White Paper the "black book" of U.S. "evil deeds." In the Senate, Wayne Morse called it a "Swiss cheese." A week after it appeared, I. F. Stone attacked it in his *Weekly.* Far from showing that the Viet Cong were heavily supported by Hanoi and the North, he argued, the White Paper showed just the opposite: that the Viet Cong received very little support—equipment, arms, and ammunition—from the North, far less than South Vietnamese troops received from the United States. Further, he said, the White Paper failed to mention that the United States, as well as North and South Vietnam, had been criticized in 1962 by the International Control Commission for breaking the Geneva Accords. "The true story is a story of lost opportunities," said Stone—failure to hold the 1956 elections called for by the Geneva Accords, failure by Diem to establish a democracy in the South, failure of land reform, and Diem's establishment of concentration camps for his political enemies *before* 1958, before any support came from the North for the burgeoning guerrilla movement which grew on these injustices without any help from Hanoi.

Before these attacks on the White Paper had had a chance to take effect, however, came a report in the New York *Times* on March 1 which made clear the reason for the timing of its release. Datelined Saigon, the report said that for the past year, the U.S. Administration had had a "peace through pressure" plan which only now it was putting into effect—a plan of "continuing limited air war against North Vietnam to bring about a negotiated settlement of the Vietnam problem on honorable terms." The plan had in fact been announced in April 1964 in an article by William Beecher in *The Wall Street Journal.* Stating that the United States was training South Vietnamese pilots to fly new long-range American bombers, the article went on to say that the decision whether to bomb North Vietnam would be made within two months after the return of Secretary McNamara from yet another inspection trip to the battlefield that spring. Upon the publication of the Pentagon Papers seven years later, documentation was given for the 1964 planning for the stepped-up war on the North. The scenario, which is dated May 23, plotted a thirty-day schedule ending in full-scale bombing of North Vietnam and including the submission to the Congress of a joint resolution to approve "whatever is necessary with respect to Vietnam." Assistant Secretary of Defense William Bundy, a coauthor of the scenario, wrote a draft of the congressional resolution on May 25. As early as March 1, 1964, Bundy had incorporated both proposals—bombing the North and the congressional resolution—in a draft memorandum for the President.

All during the long, hot summer of 1964, while the country simmered through the national political conventions, the state of siege in the (U.S.) South, and the presidential campaign, the "peace through pressure" plan had been kept in abeyance. The attack on American ships in the Tonkin Gulf had not triggered it; the response then had been isolated, not part of a prolonged plan. Even the attack on the Bien Hoa airport outside Saigon three days before the election in November had not been used—as it might have been—as a rationale for the start of the bombing of the North: a fleet of forty B-57 bombers had been attacked by Viet Cong mortar fire, with five bombers destroyed, four Americans killed and twenty injured, and $25 million in damage. It was a far more severe strike than the attack in August on U.S. ships in the Tonkin Gulf. But Johnson, the "peace" candidate, wanted no major expansion of the war until the election was safely won. "We are not about to send American boys nine or ten thousand miles away from home to do what Asian boys ought to be doing for themselves," he said while he campaigned, the Tonkin Gulf Resolution safely approved and signed into law; and even in December, elected but not yet inaugurated, he put a revised version of the bombing plan into the bottom drawer of his desk, to be produced at the appropriate moment. The moment came on March 2, when Operation ROLLING THUNDER went into effect—a policy of sustained U.S. bombing of North Vietnam rather than isolated reprisals like Flaming Dart I and II. It was to last until October 1968; after a lull, further U.S. bombing of the North took place until the end of U.S. participation in the war.

On March 8, immediately following the initiation of ROLLING THUNDER, the 9th Marine Expeditionary Brigade landed in Da Nang, South Vietnam. They were welcomed by a contingent of U.S. Army advisers holding a sign which read WELCOME TO THE GALLANT MARINES, and by South Vietnamese girls who draped them in floral garlands. The 9th Marine Expeditionary Brigade included two battalions and artillery and logistical support; it was the first U.S. infantry to arrive in South Vietnam, although by that date there were 23,000 U.S. "advisers" there.†

† In fact, it was the second time that U.S. Marines had landed at Da Nang. One hundred and twenty years earlier, in May 1845, a contingent of U.S. sailors and Marines landed at Da Nang (then Tourane) in an attempt to free a French bishop, Dominique Lefèvre, supposedly being held captive by the Vietnamese. The Americans were attached to the USS *Constitution* ("Old Ironsides") and were on an around-the-world cruise under the command of Captain John "Mad Jack" Percival. On May 26, 1845, after sixteen days in port and some desultory shelling, they left Tourane, their mission a failure. Lieutenant John B. Dale, one of Mad Jack's officers, had this comment: "It seems, I must say, to have shown a

Reaction to the President's decision to bomb North Vietnam was muted: France and India requested talks or a reconvening of the Geneva Conference; Congress publicly supported LBJ, but "many members felt deep concern." Only the old stalwarts, Wayne Morse and Ernest Gruening, were critical: it was, said Morse, a "black page in American history."

Three weeks after "peace through pressure" was announced, on March 24, 1965, the first "teach-in" on Vietnam took place—a hybrid of protest, education, and festivity which was to have a vogue that spring on campuses across the country. The term "teach-in," like the "sit-in" earlier in the decade, carried with it the connotation of protest: classes were to have been canceled in a "work moratorium" and a day-long analysis of the Vietnam War was to have been held instead—hence, a teach-in. The suffix gave the clue: later years were to see (draft card) "turn-ins," or "lie-ins" to stop traffic or busloads of draftees reporting for induction; some antiwar demonstrations featured "die-ins," a miming of death to protest the war's slaughter.

Held at the University of Michigan at Ann Arbor, organized by forty-nine faculty members, the first teach-in was conducted at night after the university administration and some Michigan legislators had objected to canceling classes during the day. Faculty support for the teach-in grew after the university president stated that they should trust "competent" leaders like Defense Secretary McNamara. To the amazement of the organizers, three thousand students came, women students having been given permission to stay out all night; they were intrigued, perhaps, by the announced torchlight parade and concluding hour of folksinging, but they stayed until 8 A.M. to listen to the speeches and seminars and inevitably they went away knowing at least a little more about Vietnam than when they arrived. Twice during the night the hall where the teach-in took place was evacuated because of bomb threats; the audience and lecturer moved outside and continued the session in weather well below freezing until the building had been searched.

In the following weeks, teach-ins were held at institutions as different as Kent State and Berkeley, on campuses large and small, "liberal" and "conservative," urban and rural: Chicago, Columbia, Pennsylvania, New York University, Wisconsin, Harvard, Goucher, Marist, Principia, Flint Junior College—the idea was to educate rather than to enlist recruits for protest against the Administration, but in the process of learning about what the United States was doing in Vietnam, a good many students, willy-nilly, were turned against the Johnson-Rusk-McNamara-Bundy policies.

Once it became apparent that the teach-in was 1965's sober—even grim—alternative to sillier, more traditional collegiate rites of spring, the Administration acted to rebut the generally anti-Administration line adopted by the teach-ins' participants. But it was too little too late. A "truth team" from the State Department, headed by Thomas F. Conlon of the Agency for International Development (AID), set out in May to visit campuses in the Midwest to try to counter the influence of the teach-ins. It had little success in selling the Administration's position, however,

sad want of 'sound discretion' in commencing an affair of this kind without carrying it through to a successful issue."

and met with hostile receptions everywhere. The team attempted to explain to students and teachers why the United States was in Vietnam and how long it expected to be there. Conlon called the hissing and booing which the team received "exhilarating;" some of the students who heard him called the team "idiotic." Many of those who opposed the war were "extremists," said Conlon; the team was peddling "malarky," replied his audience. At the end of its three-week expedition into the heartland, the "truth team" went back to Washington, not to be heard of again.

The first wave of teach-ins crested during the weekend of May 15–16, when 122 college campuses were connected by special radio hookup to hear, from Washington, perhaps the most extensive discussion to date on U.S. policy on Vietnam. Organized by the Inter-University Committee for a Public Hearing on Vietnam, a group which grew out of the spring teach-ins across the country, the debate reached over one hundred thousand college students and an incalculable number of home listeners. Topics such as "Can the War Be Won?" "Political and Moral Effects of U.S. Policy," "The Realities of North Vietnam," and "The 'Civil War' and 'Aggression from the North' "—plus an afternoon-long "Policy Confrontation"—were debated by more than two dozen men (and one woman) from Yale, Columbia, Chicago, Wisconsin, Harvard, and several other institutions as well as the State Department. Among the speakers were Arthur Schlesinger, Jr., Zbigniew Brzezinski, and Walt Rostow (all defending the administration position), and Bernard Fall, Seymour Melman, and Hans Morgenthau (opposed).

The biggest "draw" to the national teach-in, however, never appeared. McGeorge Bundy, who had agreed to speak as the star defender of U.S. policy in South Vietnam, canceled at the last minute and failed to send a replacement—perhaps on the theory that no replacement for him was possible. The White House refused to explain his absence, and senior officials admitted that they were "uncomfortable" at their orders to remain strictly silent. Later it developed that Bundy had flown on a "secret mission" to the Dominican Republic, where, two weeks previously, LBJ had sent twenty-four thousand U.S. troops to Santo Domingo at the outset of a revolt in that Caribbean country.

While the teach-in was taking hold as a novel way to challenge administration policy, the more traditional form of protest was not neglected. On April 10 in New York Dr. Benjamin Spock, cochairman of SANE, led three thousand demonstrators (including many children and babes-in-arms) on a march and rally from Columbus Circle to the United Nations, where he demanded an immediate cease-fire in Vietnam. In addition, he replied to a speech given on April 7 by President Johnson at Johns Hopkins University in which the President offered to negotiate but not with the NLF; nor did he offer to stop the bombing of the North. The President, said Dr. Spock, "leaves us with the disturbing belief that our policy [in Vietnam] is still based on mistaken views of the fundamental realities there. . . ."

The next weekend, during the Easter recess, SDS's April 17 March on Washington took place. It was the first nationwide demonstration against the war in Vietnam, and it was a resounding success. More than twenty thousand people, both students and adults, took part.

But the ghost of Joseph McCarthy almost destroyed the march before it began. At the eleventh hour, a group of older-generation peace people who had been helping to organize it suddenly decided that they could not, after all, go along with SDS's "nonexclusionary" policy. Nonexclusion meant that anyone from any group could join a march or demonstration. In 1965 the country had only just begun to recover from the long nightmare of the 1950s when the brutal, drunken bully from Wisconsin, Joseph McCarthy, had given his name to the witch-hunts that sought to find a Communist in every government office, every schoolhouse or college lecture hall, every broadcasting studio. Lives were wrecked, careers destroyed, as congressional committees investigated rumors, witnesses were pressured to name names, and any person even suspected of being "Left" or "pink"—let alone "Red"—had the potential to destroy any movement with which he or she was connected. In 1965 the hysteria that had poisoned the climate of political opinion and nearly paralyzed the most powerful nation on earth had calmed but it had not completely disappeared: thus the fears of SDS's elders, people who remembered the McCarthy years as SDS did not. For people like themselves who were seriously worried about the course of U.S. action in Vietnam, the new student groups, and especially SDS, offered some hope of opposing the government's policies there. But not if SDS were smeared by the Red brush; then it would shrivel and die, for no one would join the nascent movement save a few radicals, and the great mainstream of public opinion would flow on, allowing the Administration to lead the country into a major war, oblivious to faint cries of warning from a peace movement made impotent because it had been branded a "Communist front."

Two of the stalwarts of the peace movement who well understood the importance of this dispute were Sidney Lens and the Reverend A. J. Muste. Lens, a Chicagoan and a product of the Old Left, had worked as a labor organizer in the 1930s, and had become an editor of *Liberation* and a prolific writer on social issues; he is today an editor of *The Progressive*. Throughout the Vietnam years he was known for his ability to bridge disputes between warring factions of the peace movement—a talent that had, no doubt, been nurtured by his association with Muste.

Abraham Johannes Muste, born in 1885, was in 1965 a near-legendary figure in the peace and civil rights movements. He was a tall, thin man whose threadbare suits usually needed pressing and mending; his enormous influence came not from wordly display but from his "inner light." He was a native of Holland who came to the United States as a child. He was graduated from Union Theological Seminary and ordained in the Dutch Reformed Church in 1913. During World War I he was removed from his (Congregationalist) church in Newtonville, Massachusetts, for espousing pacifism. He became affiliated with the Society of Friends (Quakers) and was a leader in labor struggles for the next two decades, organizing sit-down strikes and training labor activists at the Brookwood Labor College, which he founded. For a time he was a Marxist. In the 1930s he abandoned Marxism to become a Christian pacifist; he spent the World War II years defending those young men who refused on grounds of conscience to serve in the armed forces. Until 1953 he was the executive secretary of FOR; he had been a founding member of CORE. In the late fifties and early sixties he was a leader of CNVA, participating in many of their nonviolent civil disobedience actions including a protest against nuclear testing in Red Square, Moscow. Muste was a major influence not only on the pacifist community but on civil rights leaders like Martin Luther King, Jr., and Bayard Rustin. Young people gravitated to Muste and he enjoyed their company, supported their peace and civil rights efforts, and encouraged them to do more. Often they did. One acquaintance said that Muste was "a devastating reminder to young pacifists of what a real radical is."

Lens remembers Muste's coming back from a meeting with SDS and reporting to the *Liberation* editorial board: " 'They just took up the position of nonexclusion.' [Staughton] Lynd [a Yale historian] was one hundred percent for that position. But all kinds of people had reservations, not because they were red-baiters but because they were worried that if we came out for including Communists and Trotskyites it would alienate the so-called mainstream of America. And we discussed that for some hours and A. J. just listened. . . . He had some minor reservations but then Lynd came out forcefully and then he did and I did. . . ." SDS asserted its control of the march not only by co-opting the traditional Easter date and issuing the call, but by printing signs with SDS-approved slogans and asking participants to use them: STOP WORLD WAR III NOW, NEGOTIATE, END THE WAR IN VIETNAM NOW, ESCALATE FREEDOM IN MISSISSIPPI. (In November, SANE was bitterly criticized for asking marchers to carry SANE-approved slogans at its own Washington demonstration.)

The dispute over nonexclusion continued right down to the wire; on the eve of the march several prominent members of the older-generation peace groups, including H. Stuart Hughes, Norman Thomas, and A. J. Muste, signed a statement that seemed to disavow the participation of far-left groups: "We welcome the cooperation of all those groups and individuals who, like ourselves, believe in the need for an independent peace movement, not committed to any form of totalitarianism or drawing inspiration from the foreign policy of any government." Originally the objectionable groups had been named (M2M, Progressive Labor, Youth Against War and Fascism, and the W. E. B. Du Bois clubs—all of which were more or less Communist-inspired—as well as the Communist Party itself, of course). The final statement was less specific, but its meaning was clear: the older peace people, some of whom were doubtless offended at the brash new group, SDS, for taking over their traditional day to march for peace, wanted the world to know that they, at least, were not "soft on Communism." Nevertheless their statement was seen by some as red-baiting (attempting to discredit an organization by calling it or its members Communists). Some people refused to sign the statement: David Dellinger, Staughton Lynd, and Ralph DiGia and David McReynolds of the War Resisters League. Muste and others later apologized for having signed.

The day of the march was warm and sunny, a beautiful spring day that showed the nation's capital at its best. The demonstrators picketed the White House, and then rallied at the Sylvan Theatre at the Washington Monument. There they heard speeches by Staughton Lynd, who recalled the French intellectuals' opposition to the war in Algeria; by Senator Ernest Gruening, who reviewed the history of U.S.

involvement in Vietnam and called for a halt of U.S. bombing of North Vietnam; by I. F. Stone, who had inspired SDS to call the march; and, perhaps most memorably, by Paul Potter, the twenty-two-year-old president of SDS. To many in the attentive crowd, Potter's speech was the high point of the rally. Members of the Old Left—the socialist left, which had spent its energies fighting the system (i.e., capitalism), heard this young man, a member of what even then had come to be known as the New Left, call for all of them to name, to analyze, to understand and change the system because it was the system which had brought about the war in Vietnam. But he would not call it capitalism; the New Left was fighting more than the Old Left's battles, and Potter refused to limit the aims of the new generation to those of the old. "I refused to call it capitalism because capitalism was for me and my generation an inadequate description of the evils of America—a hollow, dead word tied to the thirties," Potter wrote later.

Perhaps even more significant was the presence among the speakers of Robert Moses, a hero among the nation's civil rights advocates for his work in the brutal Southern voter registration drives of the previous years. He attempted to connect the war to the civil rights movement, and pointed out that the country's leaders who conducted the war for the ostensible freedom of the South Vietnamese were the same leaders who refused to guarantee the freedom of some Americans in the U.S. South. Many in his audience—perhaps as many as 10 percent—were black. Thus at the outset, at the first national demonstration against the war, a sizable black presence made the occasion truly representative of the country's population. The issue of black participation in the antiwar movement was, as we shall see, a tortured one: but at least in the beginning the two movements were tenuously linked and, in fact, many (white) antiwar activists came from the civil rights movement after whites were no longer welcome there.

After the speeches, after hearing Joan Baez and Judy Collins sing, and a SNCC trio, the Freedom Voices, after singing themselves the civil rights hymn "We Shall Overcome," the throng made its way in the late afternoon sun down the Mall toward the Capitol, a huge mass of humanity carrying its banners and placards, singing peace and freedom songs. It was bent on a peculiarly American mission, the right to which was guaranteed by the Constitution: to petition its elected representatives in Congress.

The petition itself evidenced touching faith in the power and willingness of that Congress to act:

> We, the participants in the March on Washington to End the War in Vietnam, petition Congress to act immediately to end the war. You currently have at your disposal many schemes, including reconvening the Geneva Conference, negotiation with the National Liberation Front and North Vietnam, immediate withdrawal, and UN-supervised elections. Although those among us might differ as to which of these is most desirable, we are unanimously of the opinion that the war must be brought to a halt.
>
> This war is inflicting untold harm on the people of Vietnam. It is being fought in behalf of a succession of unpopular regimes, not for the ideals you

41

proclaim. Our military are obviously being defeated; yet we persist in extending the war. The problems of America cry out for attention, and our entanglement in South Vietnam postpones the confrontation of these issues while prolonging the misery of the people of that war-torn land.

You must act now to reverse this sorry state of affairs. We call on you to end, not extend, the war in Vietnam.

As the marchers approached the statue of Ulysses S. Grant at the edge of the Capitol grounds, where they were to have halted, some of them began to chant, "Get Out!" and, "End the War!" A group of several hundred students broke through the line of police at the Capitol steps. "Let's all go!" cried the crowd, but then some SDSers, alerted to trouble, prevented more from following. About three hundred students conducted a brief sit-in at one of the Capitol doors; finally they gave the petition to a police officer when no one else appeared to take it. Every subsequent antiwar demonstration would see the same split between those who wanted peaceful, legal demonstrations (thus, they hoped, broadening the movement's appeal) and those who urged more radical tactics (thus "upping the ante").

In Texas that day, demonstrators who had hoped to present an antiwar petition to President Johnson called off the attempt when the President himself did not appear; they gave it instead to an aide. The dispatch in the press was datelined "Stonewall."

A few weeks later Staughton Lynd, in an assessment of the march in *Liberation,* observed that as the crowd moved toward the Capitol between rows of chartered buses, it seemed that "there was nowhere to go but forward." By that time, June 1965, the statement was true not only as a description of April 17, but as a comment on the emerging movement as well. They could not then have retreated; they had already gone too far.

And then Lynd added:

> Perhaps next time we should keep going, occupying for a time the rooms from which orders issue and sending to the people of Vietnam and the Dominican Republic the profound apologies which are due: or quietly waiting on the Capitol steps until those who make policy for us, and who like ourselves are trapped by fear and pride, consent to enter into dialog with us and mankind.

The Administration hit back at its emerging opposition a week after the march when Secretary of State Dean Rusk, criticizing the teach-ins, decried the "gullibility of educated men and the disregard of plain facts." In reply, Wayne Morse called for the removal of both Rusk and Secretary of Defense Robert McNamara.

On May 4 President Johnson asked Congress for $700 million in extra funds to pay for the increasing American effort in Vietnam. He could have transferred this money within the Defense Department, without any special request or publicity, but he chose instead to challenge Congress once again to give him a vote of support. Within forty-eight hours he got it: 408–7 in the House, 88–3 in the Senate. Each member who voted in favor, said the President, was voting to "persist in our effort to halt Communist aggression." It was "not the money but the message" that mattered, a message that the United States "will do whatever must be done to insure the safety of South Vietnam from aggression."

Some members of Congress who voted aye were uneasy. A vote for the request was not an "endorsement of a 'command decision' to employ U.S. troops in ground combat in Vietnam," said Senator Jacob Javits (R-New York). Several of his colleagues repeatedly asserted that their vote in favor should not be taken as "blank-check authority for any vast enlargement of U.S. ground forces." When the Senate vote came, however, only the stalwarts, Morse and Gruening, voted against, joined this time by Gaylord Nelson, whose doubts about the Tonkin Gulf Resolution the previous summer had begun to be frighteningly realized.

Nevertheless, Lyndon Johnson had had his way, and once again he had bent the Congress to his will. In an editorial, the New York *Times* sharply chastised the President for conducting "government by crisis" and it criticized the "people's elected representatives" who had "abdicated their constitutional responsibilities." This "caricature" of constitutional procedure, said the *Times,* represented an "institutional failure" on Congress's part. Certainly Staughton Lynd's perception of Congress's "fear and pride" was accurate.

During the week before the nationwide teach-in on May 15, nearly one thousand members of the Interreligious Committee on Vietnam assembled in Washington in a witness for peace—a culmination of that spring's intensified lobbying program conducted by, among others, the Friends (Quakers) Committee on National Legislation. Spokesmen for the three major religious groups, Protestant, Catholic, and Jewish, urged negotiations to end the "terror and destruction of the war;" after a three-and-a-half-mile walk from the Mount Vernon Methodist Church in Washington the group assembled at the Pentagon, where they stood quietly facing the building on three sides. Nine members of the delegation met with Secretary of Defense McNamara, who "expressed sympathy with the aims of the group." McNamara ordered that the demonstrators be allowed to enter the Pentagon through doors usually kept locked to use the water fountains, rest rooms, and restaurants; although he had allotted only fifteen minutes to see their delegation, in the end he spoke with them for over an hour. Afterward a dispute developed between Edward Snyder of the FCNL and Assistant Secretary of Defense Arthur Sylvester. Standing in the rain, Sylvester accused Snyder of making public the contents of what supposedly had been a confidential exchange and of giving a "one-sided, slanted report" of the meeting. McNamara, reported Snyder, had denied that the United States was preparing to attack Communist China, and had emphasized the amount of terrorism conducted by the Viet Cong. "Only church people would do what you are doing," said Sylvester.

On May 21–22 upward of ten thousand people and sometimes as many as thirty thousand attended Vietnam Day at the University of California at Berkeley—that spring's final teach-in. It had been organized by a small group of teachers and graduate students; one of the latter was a young man from Cincinnati, Jerry Rubin. At the last moment, like McGeorge Bundy the previous week in Washington, the proadministration spokesmen, Professors Robert Scalapino and Eugene Burdick, withdrew and left the field entirely to antiadministration speakers: Dr. Spock, Norman Thomas, Dick Gregory, Ernest Gruening, and Norman Mailer. In addition to antiadministration exhortations, a call for antiwar nonviolent civil disobedience was issued by David Dellinger, Staughton Lynd, and SNCC's Robert Moses. The weekend was a success in terms of numbers attending, antiadministration points made by speakers, and media attention; it was more important because it established Berkeley's Vietnam Day Committee, which was responsible not only for major actions on the West Coast in the following months, but for building support for a nationwide antiwar coalition.

Back on the East Coast, Dr. Spock and Norman Thomas appeared together again two weeks later at a SANE-sponsored rally against the war at Madison Square Garden on June 8. Other speakers included Wayne Morse, Bayard Rustin, Hans Morgenthau, and—significantly—Coretta Scott King, a member of Women Strike for Peace. Seventeen thousand people attended. They gave perhaps the biggest ovation of the evening to Morse, who called for a UN peace conference to settle the Vietnam conflict and criticized Lyndon Johnson's attempts to govern the country by consensus. The consensus on Vietnam, said Morse, "is not a consensus of our people, nor even the community of nations; it is a consensus among the State Department, Defense Department, Central Intelligence Agency and the White House Staff." After the rally about two thousand people followed Dr. Spock through the nighttime streets to the United Nations.

Publicity, of course, was always an important by-product of any demonstration, but at least in the beginning the organizers had little skill in getting it and little power to control its slant when they did. The Madison Square Garden rally with its cast of thousands received a modest amount of space and time in the media; a few days previously, however, the individual act of one man hardly as famous as Dr. Spock received front-page coverage. The poet Robert Lowell, having accepted an invitation to a forthcoming White House Festival of the Arts, suffered a change of heart (read "conscience") and sent a letter to President Johnson rejecting the invitation. Expressing his "dismay and distrust" of U.S. foreign policy, Lowell explained his decision not to participate by commenting that "every serious artist knows that he cannot enjoy public celebration without making subtle public commitments."

Other writers and artists who had been invited to the festival were torn between agreement with Lowell's position and wanting to attend the festival in order to give the arts in general a much-needed boost. In the end, most went—some after signing a telegram supporting Lowell. John Hersey read from his account of the nuclear attack on Japan, *Hiroshima;* in his prefatory remarks, he warned that we cannot forget the "truly terminal dangers, in these times, of miscalculation, of arrogance. . . . Wars have a way of getting out of hand."

That fear, that the war in Vietnam would somehow get out of hand and catapult the country—and the world—into the final nuclear holocaust, was at the root of much antiwar sentiment. The stakes were simply too high for the prize involved. Not even the "national honor" was worth such risk, not even saving face—that most Oriental obsession which gripped Washington's policymakers as well.

The aborted revolt of the intellectuals at the White House Festival of the Arts had, of course, no effect at all on U.S. policy; it served only to anger LBJ, and further to alienate him from the intellectual community, which was to turn so bitterly against him in the next few years.

On June 8, the day of the White House Festival of the Arts, in the midst of continuing political turmoil in Saigon, a public relations officer of the State Department announced to the press and public that the United States was, in effect, "in a land war on the continent of Asia," as the outraged editorialist of the *Times* phrased it. The announcement, repeated the next day by the White House, informed the public that U.S. ground troops in Vietnam had been authorized to enter combat if requested to do so by the South Vietnamese Army. Despite the apparent seriousness of this development, the American public, in a survey reported on June 14, continued to back the President's actions in Vietnam. In Washington and in foreign capitals the reaction to this latest step toward full-scale commitment was less enthusiastic. Regardless of their repeated votes in support of the President, members of Congress were reported to be privately "restive and unhappy" about his "high-handed" method of decision making; foreign governments watched with apprehension as the President went his own way without consulting them. As before, the overriding fear was that unilateral action by the United States would embroil the world in a nuclear war; Johnson, who had been the candidate of peace, was perceived as being increasingly like Goldwater, who had been the candidate to advocate a harder line on the war.

On June 14, and again on June 21, McGeorge Bundy performed makeups for the classes he had missed at the National Teach-In on May 15. On June 14 he faced a panel of six faculty and students at Harvard and for two hours and fifteen minutes answered questions from it and from the audience on the Administration's Vietnam policy. Described as "good-natured," the event was perhaps most important as a dress rehearsal for Bundy's confrontation a week later with Hans Morgenthau of the University of Chicago in a nationally televised "debate" on CBS moderated by Eric Sevareid.

Like most such affairs the CBS broadcast was a frustrating question-and-answer session rather than a debate; the terms had been arranged with CBS by Bundy before the arrival of the professors from the National Teach-In who had requested the broadcast. Each man had his "seconds" to back him up. Bundy repeated the Johnson line about "commitment" to South Vietnam; he stated that the United States could (1) escalate "with the view that air power will somehow settle this thing"; (2) withdraw; or (3) "move to sustain our part—and it can only be our part —of a contest which is of as great importance to us as it is to the people of Vietnam." He went on to criticize Morgenthau's "congenital pessimism," and pointed out (correctly) that Morgenthau had been wrong in predicting that Laos would be lost to the Communists.

Morgenthau's rebuttal—accurate but weak—was that because he had been wrong about Laos did not mean that he was also wrong about Vietnam. But the true weakness of Morgenthau's position was revealed when he stated that

I think our aim must be to get out of Vietnam, but to get out of it with honor. I have, indeed, always believed that it is impossible for a great power which must take care of its prestige to admit, in so many words, that its policy has been mistaken during the last ten years and leave the theater of operation. But there are all kinds of face-saving devices by which a nation or a government which has made a series of mistakes can rectify the situation, and I think President De Gaulle has shown how to go about this, with regard to Algeria. . . .

In other words, Morgenthau's problem was that of many peace groups: the fights over slogans that preceded every march and demonstration both in 1965 and in all the years to come simply grew out of a realization that the ultimate slogan—"Out Now!"—was too "extreme," that it would alienate too many Americans who did not like America's involvement in Vietnam but who could not accept the humiliation (as they saw it) of admitting that she had made a mistake and that even one more American life was one too many to lose. Had the selection committee of the National Teach-In picked a more "radical" opponent for Bundy—that is, one who would have advocated unconditional withdrawal—he would have alienated potential support for the antiadministration position.

Thus the dilemma: as much as a few people were beginning to turn against U.S. policy in Vietnam, most people—most of these few—could not yet simply say, "Get out." It would not be until 1971—after more than fifty-six thousand more American deaths—that the majority of the American people, polled by Gallup, chose "immediate withdrawal" as an option.

Meanwhile A. J. Muste led about two thousand people, mostly from CNVA but also including some SNCC members, in a Speak-Out at the Pentagon on June 16. They roamed the corridors distributing leaflets and making impromptu speeches against U.S. presence in both Vietnam and the Dominican Republic; later five of them, including Muste, Staughton Lynd, former Vermont Congressman William Meyer, Sidney Lens, and peace activist Mary Christiansen met for exactly thirty minutes with Secretary McNamara. "The Secretary spoke only very briefly," Muste told his fellow demonstrators later; "what he said was to dispute some of the facts given him. A meeting of this kind leaves one with a sense of frustration." Meyer, in particular, must have been frustrated, for Lens reported that he had a "shouting match" with McNamara. The secretary was not swayed by the group's presentation; in response to their points, he said, "We know things that you don't." The police, who had been instructed by McNamara to make no arrests without his specific approval, eventually formed a line and pushed the demonstrators out of the building.

A week later, WSP demonstrated again at the White House. Among the several hundred protesters was a woman from South Dakota whose son had been killed in Vietnam on Easter Sunday. She said that she did not understand why her son had to die: "People in South Dakota don't even know where Vietnam is."

On June 27 the 173rd Airborne Brigade conducted the first major U.S. combat offensive of the war, a foray into War Zone D, an area northwest of Saigon near the

Bien Hoa air base. The results of the raid were "inconclusive." Defense Secretary McNamara and Henry Cabot Lodge, soon to return to Saigon as U.S. ambassador, took a fact-finding trip to South Vietnam and reported back to Washington that General Westmoreland needed more troops. On July 28 the U.S. troop strength in Vietnam was raised to 125,000; by the end of the year it would be nearly 200,000.

Several important meetings were held that summer as the antiwar movement began to take shape.

The first took place from June 9 to 13 when SDS held its convention at Kewadin, Michigan, a resort area on the shores of Lake Michigan. The meeting proved to be crucial for both SDS and the antiwar movement, for now, instead of seizing the initiative it had gained from its successful April 17 march, SDS fumbled and lost—forever, as it turned out—the possibility of leading that movement.

Prominent that weekend were a large number of new people who turned to SDS for leadership but who became, instead, the organization's new leaders—SDS's "second generation," the replacements for the old guard. They were vocally opposed to a strong centralized organization; they wanted action, not theorizing and debate and self-education; they had little patience with organized groups already in existence (political parties, labor unions, reform groups) with whom they might have joined to achieve their aims. They were not even sure what their aims were, and so the convention foundered in endless debate, unable to agree on the SDS position on any issue.

At last SDS decided upon inaction. It was agreed:

—to leave actions and projects entirely up to local chapters, with no direction from the National Office;

—to *not* build a strong, nationwide campus organization;

—to *not* organize a nationwide antidraft campaign.

"[We] realized that we had made a major blunder [in 1965] in not taking charge of the antiwar movement," recalled one SDSer some years later; "It was too late for us to be the antiwar movement, which is what we should have been."

Instead the thrust of SDS activity over the next year or two was no less than to continue to try to change all of American society—a task which many of its members may honestly have thought they could achieve. By accomplishing that, they said, they might not stop the war in Vietnam but they would stop "the seventh war from now," since that new America would no longer wage wars of aggression against small and backward nations like Vietnam.

In fact the two impulses—antiwar organizing versus community/ghetto organizing—worked against each other, for the ghetto projects drained SDS's strength, and antiwar work impeded organizing the urban poor: those SDSers working in the ERAP projects begged their fellow members not to talk so much about the war, as it was a "sensational" issue which cut away their base. Poor as they might be, and removed from the mainstream of middle-class American life, the people whom SDS was trying to organize were intensely patriotic, and they resented any hint of the anti-Americanism which they perceived in antiwar rhetoric.

Tom Hayden remembers:

I felt very torn. Remember I stayed in Newark [with ERAP] till the end of '67. I had to leave because of the changed relationships between blacks and whites as a result of the violence and the black power movement.

I had at least three missions during those years:

1. The domestic organizing—building some kind of poor people's movement, which was my principal wish;

2. Stopping the war, which I initially saw as an obstacle to dealing with this country's internal problems—a point which I think was extremely crucial, looking back. I see it happening again;

3. I continued to keep up with the left—or the SDS left—participating in meetings and following the debates and so on.

The Vietnam war became more intense and I was constantly struggling with these priorities: where was I the most prepared to make a contribution? I think that's why for a while all the issues became one issue in my mind because I couldn't deal with the choice. . . .

Two issues, however, were decided before the convention adjourned:

—to remove from the SDS constitution reference to the exclusion of Communists;

—to elect as President Carl Oglesby, a relative newcomer to the organization whose studies on Vietnam had formed the basis for SDS's position on that issue.

In 1982, in the bright, white formal dining room of the nineteenth-century house that he is painstakingly restoring in Cambridge, Massachusetts, Oglesby—tall, thin, bespectacled, bearing a resemblance to the young D. H. Lawrence—recalls his transformation from a self-described "redneck," a self-made literary man, into a political animal.

In 1964 he was living in Ann Arbor with his wife and children, attending graduate classes at the University of Michigan, and working as a technical writer for the Bendix Corporation. He had written plays that had been produced in Ann Arbor and Dallas and had had readings at the Actors Studio in New York; he was partway through a novel which was

basically about why doesn't anybody do anything about the wretched way things are? The whole premise of such a novel was that nobody was doing anything. And when somebody started doing anything then if I was going to put my money where my mouth was I would have to leave the novel off and go do those things with them. By definition of my position. So I was open. I can remember reading the stories about what was happening at Berkeley when I was still in the defense industry with no thought in my mind of ever becoming an activist. I got involved in it only because there were some political activists in the Democratic Party at the place where I worked who wanted me to work with their candidate and from that I got into writing a position paper on Vietnam and therefore learning about Vietnam for the candidate. He was worried that it would become an issue in the debate. They couldn't see it either. This was '64—nobody could see how important this thing was. And if I could see it a little clearer than some it was because of being at Bendix. We had some contracts that told volumes about what was happening. And since I was in publications I saw everything they were doing. And I just knew what was happening. I knew there was defoliation when people were just daring to suggest that it could be, I knew that it was already happening. I knew about the problems of the village resettlement programs. We had some projects in those areas. Anyway I did some research on the war and I came up with a position paper and gave it to the candidate and the candidate said, "This is radical." . . .

My position was that the real issue in Vietnam [for the U.S. Government] was America's relationship to China: We were fighting in Vietnam as we had fought in Korea to stop Chinese expansion. [But] Chinese expansion was chimerical. China could not possibly afford to expand even if she wanted to. In any case it's possible for the United States to define China as an ally. So we should do that and avoid the Vietnam War. . . .

The candidate said he thought it was radical because there were parts in it that were sympathetic to revolution. And that made me a little irritated. So I wrote an open letter to him which summarized all this stuff and had it printed in the University of Michigan literary magazine, *Generations.* When the issue came out a play of mine was on at the University theater and the text of the play was in that issue along with this letter about Vietnam. And some SDS folks—I didn't know anything about SDS at this point—went to see the play, saw the play in political terms, liked it, bought the magazine, found the statement on Vietnam and called me up. A couple of guys came out on a motorcycle. . . .

I couldn't have told you the difference between Trotsky and Lenin at that time. I had no interest in it. I thought it was pretty boring. I was a literature guy. I liked to sit around and read exegeses of Joyce. That was my idea of hot stuff. To be in politics was to be detained by a trivial, useless set of problems that were better not to be problems at all. So that one could get on with important things—novels. . . . There were a lot of ironies in it. . . . Although I'd got produced I hadn't gotten published . . . and suddenly when I "gave up" writing I couldn't keep 'em satisfied. Every little squiggle found its way into print. My views were courted from all sides and the next thing you know I had a kind of a reputation as a political theorist. People listened to what I was saying, while frantically at night I was trying to tell the difference between Trotsky and Lenin. But you know how you learn when you want to know something. . . .

Later, Oglesby wrote a sixty-page single-spaced monograph, a history and analysis of European and U.S. involvement in Vietnam. By this time, "fascinated," he was exploring the history of the cold war as a means of "freshening up the batteries" for his novel, which had gone stale. Meanwhile in New York, some SDSers had put up a subway poster, a photograph of Vietnamese children burned by napalm with the caption WHY ARE WE BURNING, TORTURING, KILLING THE PEOPLE OF VIETNAM? FOR THE FACTS, WRITE SDS.

"And there I was," says Oglesby with a smile.

His monograph had wide circulation and became the primary source for SDS's position on Vietnam.

Oglesby's recollection of that time gives a vivid picture of SDS's membership, of its confusion about what it should try to do, and of the deep split in the organization which was never bridged and which ultimately led to its destruction:

> You may have figured it out that when I came into the organization it wasn't long before I was the president. It took me a long time to figure that out. I was embarrassed by it for a long time, and then I had to get over that because suddenly there was a lot of work to do. I can remember talking to the guy who was president just before me, Paul Potter, in Cleveland at the Cleveland project. The presidents would all say, we shouldn't have presidents, everybody's the same thing, and when they got through being president they would disappear into a project—the most meaningful and humblest kind of work. It was like going to the war, to Vietnam to do your tour, to put your time in on the battlefront. In those days the battlefront was ghettos in Cleveland and Chicago and Newark and Boston and Oakland, and I was touring those things trying to get a sense of what they were all about. This was just after I had become president. I remember asking Potter to explain *why* I was president, and the guy just turned over on his bed and faced the wall and wouldn't say a thing, and I couldn't understand what the hostility was about. But later I realized how deep was the conflict between— on the one side—the impulse of the old guard in SDS to make it a more than student movement and therefore to get students off being students and on to being ordinary people in the ghetto; and on the other side, the people who sensed that Vietnam was going to become the leading issue, and that students could be mobilized on that a lot better, a lot faster, with much more impact, than you could ever mobilize the urban poor. So it was a question of, what are you going for? Are you going for what Rennie [Davis] and Tom [Hayden] and Potter and a lot of the beginning [i.e., founding] SDS people saw as a necessary long-term growth of small community projects, ink-blot-like coming together on the long haul, finally forming a constituency on the national level and pressuring the left wing of the Democratic Party to do good? That was the whole strategy. . . .
>
> So Potter was saying to me, "You, Oglesby, represent dangers to this organization. In the first place because you are willing to function in the limelight—to handle debates, to make speeches, to make statements to the press, to be on the TV programs"—which I was. Everybody else was up tight about it, coming out of this middle-class modesty thing. They were so ashamed of being bourgeois kids. . . . So maybe that's where it was good that I was ten years older than most of these kids. I was thirty a few days after they elected me president, in the very year that the slogan was "Don't trust anybody over thirty." So in a way my getting elected president of SDS at that time was that the kids were hedging their bets . . . saying, "We need a little more experience in this thing." The main thing that they were saying was that the war was going to be the SDS issue; or that SDS was not going to shrink from addressing the war and doing antiwar organizing. . . . Nobody could take me at all for a community-organizing person. My whole association with the movement was around Vietnam. . . . I thought it was too bad that the two things were pulling apart, and I didn't see any reason why there had to be such a fight over it. I tried to be a peacemaker between

the two groups, but all I did really was around the war. . . . And they finally couldn't hold together, and then the organization was absolutely vulnerable to factionalism and the fight between the Weathermen extremists and the Progressive Labor extremists and there was no way to stop it. . . .

In late June the Berkeley Vietnam Day Committee met to organize the First International Days of Protest, to be held October 15–16 in conjunction with protests around the world. The VDC had grown out of the success of the Berkeley teach-in the previous month; now, unlike SDS, it was moving ahead to build on its strengths. It invited SDS to participate in building the action, but SDS, in disarray, declined.

A few weeks later in New York the Progressive Labor Party (an offshoot of the CP oriented to Peking) held its first convention. It had something over one thousand members. Two crucial decisions were made:

—to become a "party of the working class" (unlike many of the new organizations forming at this time which were almost exclusively middle class); and

—to focus on the war both as a prime issue and as an organizing tool—an issue to attract potential members to the party.

The fourth important meeting that summer took place in July, halfway around the world in Jakarta, Indonesia, when ten members of Women Strike for Peace held a week-long conference with six North Vietnamese women from the Democratic Republic of Vietnam and three women representatives of the National Liberation Front, the political wing of the Viet Cong. This was the first formal contact between an American peace group and either the DRV or the NLF: it established a personal relationship with the people whom American soldiers were fighting; it allowed the American women to return home with news of the Vietnamese and their thoughts on the war—news that was in short supply in the United States; and it led to later contact such as the Committee of Liaison organized by WSP's Cora Weiss, which served as the conduit between American POWs and their families. One of the NLF delegates was Mme. Nguyen Thi Binh, who became the Foreign Minister of the NLF and its delegate to the Paris peace talks.

On July 29 in New York, four hundred people from the Committee for Nonviolent Action and the Workshop in Nonviolence marched from City Hall Park to the army recruiting building at 39 Whitehall Street. They wore black crepe-paper armbands and carried signs reading THE PRESIDENT HAS DECLARED WAR—WE HAVEN'T, and LBJ: WE ARE NOT A NATION OF KILLERS—NEGOTIATE! At the army building, several young men dropped draft cards, their own or others', into the flames in a small tin pot. One of them, Christopher Kearns, was photographed by a photographer for *Life*. "It's just a nuisance," said the director of Selective Service for New York City; "they'll get a duplicate card."

The fifth meeting took place on August 6–9, the twentieth anniversary of the Hiroshima-Nagasaki atomic bombings, when the Assembly of Unrepresented People met in Washington. This group took its name from the unrepresented, disenfranchised blacks in the South, and also from other groups such as women, Puerto Ricans, and American Indians. Among the organizers for the assembly were A. J.

Muste, Staughton Lynd, David Dellinger, Robert Moses, WSP's Donna Allen, and Eric Weinberger of the Committee for Nonviolent Action; sponsoring groups included the Catholic Worker, the WRL, and CNVA. SDS specifically separated itself from the assembly and did not recommend that its members attend, although some did; one participant remembers that they played a "conservative" role in the discussions and seminars.

The assembly had two purposes: (1) a series of workshops on domestic social issues and on Vietnam, and (2) a march/demonstration to Congress to present a "Declaration of Peace with the people of Vietnam." It had been called in part to respond to what was seen as the enormous turnout for the April demonstration. "The old-line peace people (AFSC, FOR, WRL, Catholic Worker) didn't envision what was going to happen," recalls Tom Cornell. "We were doing our thing as usual when SDS brought down thousands of people for their demonstration. We'd never had more than a few hundred."

On the first day nearly one thousand protesters picketed the White House. After a four-hour rally on the sidewalk outside the gates, where they were addressed by, among others, the Reverend Philip Berrigan, they learned that they had been denied permission to send a delegation to the President to present their "Declaration of Conscience," written in 1964 (see pp. 20–21), which had been signed by six thousand people over the preceding months. The demonstrators then sat down on the sidewalk, but despite the presence of more than three hundred police and Secret Servicemen no arrests were made. "Business as usual" went on in the White House, where President Johnson was discussing the Vietnam problem with Alex Quaison-Sackey, the Foreign Minister of Ghana. The Johnson daughters were reported to be "emotionally upset" by the presence of the demonstrators.

Outside, A. J. Muste was questioned closely about Communist influence in the group. While individual Communists might be taking part in the protest, he stated (although he said he doubted it), he maintained that there was no Communist control of the assembly as a whole—as, indeed, there was not: Muste, the prime mover of the assembly, had explored communism in the thirties and discarded it, and none of the other organizers was affiliated with Communist groups. In 1965, however, the question was still routinely presented to any group that was not mindlessly, loudly xenophobic. The White House guards brought out a chair for Muste, and gave him water in the intense heat. Some of the demonstrators remained all night at the White House gates, and again the following night. On August 8, thirty-six of them were arrested for blocking an entrance.

David Dellinger remembers the assembly as an important early attempt to build a movement that would encompass a broad range of issues:

> It was so much of a multiissue thing. Every workshop met under a tree [along the Mall]. I remember there was a workshop on Puerto Rican independence. There was a workshop on women's rights. There was a workshop on *Indians*. And when everybody today rewrites history—I mean from inside the movement—the whole theory is that it was totally sexist, it was racist up to a point. And what I'm saying is, some of that happened, but

later. Not when it began. We had twenty-eight or thirty-three or twenty-one workshops—all these things that tended later to get put on the back burner or squeezed out. But we didn't start with this narrow one issue, not at the assembly at least.

On the Monday, the last day of the assembly, in a line headed by Dellinger, Staughton Lynd, and Robert Moses, the demonstrators marched down the Mall, eight hundred strong, and attempted to "invade" Congress to urge adoption of their declaration of peace. "We announced that we were going to hold in the halls of Congress an assembly of unrepresented people," says Tom Cornell. "That was rather provocative, I suppose, looking back. They [Congress] thought it was the French Revolution."

More than 350 were arrested that day, including several counterdemonstrators, members of the American Nazi Party, who splashed the marchers with red paint as they approached the foot of the Capitol, where they were halted by police. A photograph of the bespattered trio—Dellinger, Lynd, and Moses—appeared in *Life* in the August 16 issue, adjacent to the photograph of Christopher Kearns burning a draft card in late July.

Dellinger remembers:

> Bob and Staughton and I were leading the march. We got doused with red paint. We got up to the point where the police formed the line and for some inexplicable reason they grabbed Staughton and Bob and pulled them off and arrested them but not me. A.J. was aloof—an observer walking on the sidewalk. Maybe it was just that on that particular day he wasn't ready to be arrested. All of a sudden I was left with a few hundred people. The police formed a barricade and it was a hot sun and I was covered with this stuff. I had burns and scars [from the paint] because I was two hours out in the hot sun. They lasted a long time. And we held a community meeting there because the whole emphasis was participatory democracy, discussing what we were going to do in a nonviolent way. I remember saying we shouldn't turn around just because the police had formed this impenetrable blockade. It went on for a long time. We decided to try nonviolently to proceed, so we crawled between their legs, we dove between their shoulders. . . . To me that was a high point. . . .

Dellinger was subsequently arrested and fined three hundred dollars. He refused to pay, choosing to serve thirty days instead. The Nazis who had thrown the paint on him were fined ten dollars each.

The major result of the weekend was the formation of the National Coordinating Committee to End the War in Vietnam, comprised of thirty-three organizations. This was the first of several umbrella groups that organized nationwide demonstrations and marches against the war in the years to follow; it was succeeded by various "Mobilizations."

Undoubtedly the assembly's activities also fostered Congress's passage of a draft card bill on the day after the attempted "invasion." Angered perhaps by repeated accusations that it was impotent, frustrated by the President's single-handed prosecution of what had in fact become a war, Congress finally took some definite action in the matter of young men and their draft cards. On August 10, at the behest of L. Mendel Rivers (D-South Carolina), the chairman of the House Armed Services Committee, the House passed a bill (392-1) calling for a five-year jail sentence and a $10,000 fine for "willful destruction" of a draft card. Strom Thurmond (D-South Carolina) sponsored the bill in the Senate, where it passed on August 12 by a voice vote. President Johnson signed it into law on August 30.

During the same weekend, protest on the West Coast took the form of an attempt to halt and board troop trains on their way to the Oakland Army Terminal, the embarkation point for Vietnam. This action was organized by the VDC in Berkeley and by the Oakland SDS; about three hundred people participated. They tried again on August 12 and August 23. On the first attempt a few demonstrators slowed the train by sitting on the tracks and jumping out of the way at the last moment as the train slowly proceeded. Three protesters managed to board the train and distribute antiwar leaflets to the troops.

Meanwhile, on July 28, in a classic diversionary bait-and-switch, President Johnson made two announcements: that fifty thousand more American troops would be sent to Vietnam, and—after months of brutal rejections of UN Secretary-General U Thant's proffered aid—that the Administration had asked Thant's help in finding ways to "halt aggression in Vietnam." The increase in troop strength necessitated a rise in draft calls from about 17,000 a month to about 35,000 a month, but to the enormous relief of Congress no reserves were to be called up. The request for UN help was contained in a letter delivered by the new U.S. ambassador to the UN, Arthur Goldberg, named to replace Adlai Stevenson, who had died suddenly in London two weeks before. Stevenson had been viewed in some academic and intellectual circles as a turncoat to the cause of peace in Vietnam because he refused to resign in protest over administration policies there. Now Goldberg, simultaneously with presenting his credentials, was instructed to make a highly publicized plea for help to U Thant. The action smacked of little more than window dressing, however; the President was described as wishing to "seize the opportunity" of Goldberg's arrival at the UN, but at the same time "high government sources" were quoted as having little faith in the ability of the UN to accomplish any move toward peace talks. Thus a sense of unreality pervaded the exercise: all that was certain was that U.S. troop strength in Vietnam would now be 125,000 instead of 75,000, while in the never-never land of conference tables and peace feelers the diplomats would talk about talking.

The last of that summer's meetings which were to have important consequences for the antiwar movement took place on Labor Day weekend in New York City. It had been called by Norma Becker, a teacher in the city's school system who had been active in the civil rights movement, including organizing the Freedom School project in Prince Edward County, Maryland, in the summer of 1963 and in Mississippi in 1964. Later she and another teacher, Sandra Adickes, had organized the UFT Teachers' Committee for Peace in Vietnam (New York City), and had solicited signatures for a newspaper ad opposing U.S. involvement which was put into the *Congressional Record* by Senator Gruening.

Norma Becker is a sturdy woman of average height with brown hair going gray and bright hazel eyes, a New Yorker born and bred whose attitude conveys both the toughness and the good-natured warmth of the big city survivor. She is no-nonsense in her determination to get the job done, whatever it might be, and in those early days she was the catalyst for the New York antiwar coalition, which became one of the strongest in the country.

Having involved her fellow teachers in the Assembly of Unrepresented People, she looked for a way to assist in the upcoming International Days of Protest in October, the first event sponsored by the National Coordinating Committee to End the War in Vietnam. Over Labor Day weekend she called a few people together to discuss how a New York group might contribute to the days:

> I felt we should march down Fifth Avenue the way they do in May for the military parades on Armed Forces Day or Memorial Day. They had just marched this monster missile down Fifth Avenue [in the Armed Forces Day parade on May 15, at which two hundred protesters chanted, "End the War in Vietnam," and twenty were arrested after blocking the parade by sitting down on Fifth Avenue in front of the marching units. Taking part in the protest were members of the New York Workshop in Nonviolence, SDS, the War Resisters League, the Committee for Nonviolent Action, the Student Peace Union, and the Greenwich Village Peace Center]. And I said, "We need to make this a mainstream event, not some kind of peripheral or left-wing event." I didn't know any better so I said, "Let's try." So then I called together the existing peace groups—SANE, WRL, WSP, Women's International League for Peace and Freedom—to discuss having a parade on those days to march down Fifth Avenue.

And so the Fifth Avenue Peace Parade Committee was born. Not, however, without some pain.

> There was such violent disagreement [recalls Becker], such an atmosphere of hostility that it floored me. The contention was over the slogan for the placards—whether to call for withdrawal or for negotiations. There was such passion and such emotional intensity that at one point, when it seemed like the whole thing was going to blow, I said, "Well, look, if the people in this room can't agree on slogans, then I'll find ten other people, or twelve others, and if necessary we'll organize a march down Fifth Avenue without any slogan." Finally Abner Grunauer of New York SANE suggested having one slogan, "Stop the War in Vietnam," and we were in business.

The Fifth Avenue Vietnam Peace Parade Committee was given a "closet" in the offices of the War Resisters League at 5 Beekman Street, where on two floors were housed many radical-pacifist groups including WRL, the Committee for Nonviolent Action, the Catholic Peace Fellowship, *Liberation,* and David Dellinger's and

A. J. Muste's offices. Money and staff for the new committee came from these groups and others.

When Norma Becker predicted that twenty-five thousand might show up for the march, "people shuddered and said, 'That's not realistic.'" Most veterans of the infant peace movement would have settled for five thousand. Meanwhile the city stalled on granting a permit to march, so literature advertising the action had to include the phrase "permit pending." At the last minute, thanks to the intervention of the ACLU legal division, the permit was granted.

The First International Days of Protest took place on October 15–16, 1965. As in the April demonstration the action was divided between the East and West coasts, with smaller demonstrations in between. In Berkeley, a crowd estimated as high as ten thousand set out on a "peace march" to stage a teach-in on a vacant lot across from the Oakland Army Base. On Friday evening and again on Saturday afternoon, the crowd was turned back by police. Hell's Angels interfered—violently —and then Jack Weinberg, one of the leaders of the Vietnam Day Committee, which had organized the march, achieved what the Johnson Administration could not: he negotiated with the enemy in the person of Oakland Police Chief Edward Toothman. Some would have said that Weinberg simply arranged for the demonstrators' defeat, since when he came out of the conference he turned his "troops" back to the University of California campus at Berkeley, where the teach-in was held instead. Unquestionably he prevented considerable bloodshed.‡

In New York, twenty to twenty-five thousand paraded down Fifth Avenue from Ninety-fourth Street on October 16. Along the way they were heckled by as many as a thousand people who threw tomatoes, red paint, and eggs at them and who occasionally rushed into the line of march and attacked them. Signs and banners carried their message, STOP THE WAR IN VIETNAM, as did helium-filled balloons printed with the same slogan; one group wore skeleton masks and carried musical instruments on which they played "The Marines' Hymn." Dozens of the marchers carried enlarged photographs of a Vietnamese mother and her injured child. The most eye-catching devices were larger-than-life-sized dummies contributed by the Bread and Puppet Theater: one of a bloodied Uncle Sam, and two seven-foot ghosts carrying a bandaged child on a stretcher. The marchers had hoped to end their parade with a rally in Central Park, but Newbold Morris, the parks commissioner, forbade them. They rallied instead at Sixty-ninth Street between Lexington and Park avenues, where they were addressed by, among others, I. F. Stone. Protests were held in many other cities that weekend, including London, Stockholm, Brussels, Copenhagen, and Tokyo; estimates were that as many as one hundred thousand people participated in rallies in fifty cities across the United States.

Perhaps the most significant activity that weekend occurred not at the worldwide marches, but at a small demonstration at the Army Induction Center on Whitehall Street, Manhattan, where David J. Miller, a twenty-two-year-old Catholic Worker, burned his draft card—the first person to do so since President Johnson's signing

‡ Around this time Weinberg coined the phrase which captured the spirit of the decade: "Don't trust anyone over thirty."

on August 30 of the bill making such an action a felony. In response to Johnson's action, Tom Cornell had published "Draft Cards Are for Burning" in the September *Catholic Worker*. Cornell saw the new legislation as evidence of the increasing effectiveness of the peace movement; it meant that "we must have a public draft-card burning soon." He recalled previous times when he had burned his draft card (he eventually went through twelve), including an instance in 1962 in Washington Square, New York, during the General Strike for Peace organized by Judith Malina and Julian Beck of the Living Theater. Cornell burned his first draft card in 1960:

> That summer, the first Polaris action summer, I went to New London protesting the [nuclear submarine] *George Washington* [with CNVA]. I was in a rowboat with Robert Stowell and two women on the Thames River approaching the *George Washington*. We had no intention of getting closer to it than the law allowed—something like one hundred feet. A current grabbed the boat and I lost control and it went careening toward the hull. We hadn't intended to get that close. We had intended to get close enough for the workers to see our signs: REFUSE TO WORK ON MILITARY WEAPONS. We were telling them to forego their $3.75 an hour, which they weren't going to do. Go home, don't make these weapons of death. Go live in poverty in West Virginia.
>
> We knew that it was illegal to get any closer than we were and we were not prepared to offer civil disobedience at that point. It was simply a legal demonstration. But there we were crashing into the hull of the submarine. I put my hand out to push the rowboat away from the hull and then I realized here I am in physical contact with this thing that could incinerate all of Europe in a flash and it just became all the more real to me. I'd seen the thing from across the river and of course I'd read everything that Brad Lyttle [of CNVA] could dig up about its destructive capabilities and every piece of scare propaganda that we were trying to generate and it didn't scare me as much as actually touching the thing. So I came back and I went to the Goldenrod Saloon on Main Street and I asked for a beer and the bartender said, "Are you twenty-one?" and I said, "No, I'm twenty-six." And he said, "May I have your draft card?" And I said, "You certainly may." He handed it back to me and I said, "I don't want it." And he said, "I have no use for it," and I said, "Neither do I." So I incinerated it right there.
>
> I had a friend with me and he understood and I understood that this was not as flippant an act as it appeared. But to me it meant that now I have taken the step, I am a noncooperator. It's really not particularly important practically speaking because I'm not going to suffer any consequences, I'm twenty-six years old and they can't even order me to do alternative service. But as far as I'm concerned I have resigned from their system. If it ever comes up then I'll have to follow through on it. I went home and saw that there were several cards in my dresser drawer. A high school deferment, a college deferment, a 1-A-O, a reinstitution of student deferment, a reinstitution of 1-A, I don't know how many cards. So I said, maybe these will be useful at the General Strike. . . .

"No one chose to take notice of that," he recalls; but now in 1965 there was a different climate of opinion, and so

> we knew we had to respond, to demonstrate the punitive repressiveness of this law [wrote Cornell later]. We wanted to expose it for what it is, an attempt to stifle protest and the expression of dissent in the United States. More than that, it made the draft card what it had never been before, something for which there had never been a place in American tradition, an internal passport, a license to breathe for every male between the ages of eighteen and thirty-five. The draft card became the symbol *par excellence* of involuntary servitude for the works of death, and the symbol of moral and intellectual suffocation. It deserved to be burned.

Unrecorded, David Miller's act on October 15 would have had no significance beyond the personal; but television cameras photographed it and broadcast it, and this time people did take notice. And so Miller achieved far more than an individual act of protest: like the later apocryphal "bra-burners" of the women's liberation movement (no bra was burned at Atlantic City, the site of a 1968 protest against the Miss America pageant and the place where the event supposedly took place; nor was one ever burned elsewhere), those young men who burned draft cards in 1965, when the nation was demonstrably at war, aroused people's fears, their outrage and horror. It was a simple act, but committed at a time when American boys were dying in battle, it resonated with defiance.

> We knew we'd touched a nerve [says Tom Cornell]. But still we didn't appreciate the dimensions of the impact we could make. Even with men as experienced as A. J. Muste and as seasoned as Brad Lyttle, who conceived of and/or executed two thirds of the projects of CNVA, we still didn't understand the dimensions of the thing that we'd gotten our hands on.
>
> In psychological terms it's a kind of castration symbol and an Oedipal thing. Your kid is flying in the face of authority. It cuts off something. Burns or cuts or destroys. It has to do with the whole masculine thing. But I thought of it more in terms of religious symbolism. There is a kind of civil or state religion which has subsumed large elements of Christianity, Judaism, whatever else there is, and it has its symbols, obviously secular symbols like the flag, George Washington, Abraham Lincoln. It's subsumed a good part of our traditional real religion. And the draft card then becomes a sacrament. And there's nothing worse that you can do in sacramental terms than defile a species of the sacrament. And this was a defilement, a real blasphemy against the state. And that's where I thought the psychological energy was coming from. Probably it was both. My wife always shunned state rituals, seeing them in competition with the one God who must be adored and He only. So when you're doing these things you're really breaking the First Commandment.
>
> So we called a draft card burning to be held on the steps of the federal courthouse in Foley Square.

Two weeks later in New York, two hundred people gathered at the United States Court House in Foley Square to protest the war and to watch (as announced) another draft card burning, this time by Tom Cornell (who had requested and received a new card for the occasion) and Marc Paul Edelman. Marchers supporting their action carried signs reading BURN DRAFT CARDS NOT CHILDREN and WOULD CHRIST CARRY A DRAFT CARD? while across the street, held back by federal marshals, a hostile crowd jeered, "Burn him, not his draft card," and "Commie scum!" Referring to A. J. Muste, they called, "Who's that old man?" Police would not allow the demonstration to go on, however, until the group obtained and displayed an American flag not less than thirty-six by forty-eight inches, in accordance with the city administrative code regarding street meetings. While some members of the group went to get a flag, Cornell and Edelman tried to burn their draft cards; the crush of newsmen was so great, however, that they were prevented from doing so. Even after the flag was obtained the newsmen refused to back off; finally A. J. Muste canceled the demonstration.

"It is clear," he said, "that we are not going to have a draft card burning under these circumstances." But "this action would have been of great and important significance. These two young men would have made a great contribution to ending the war in Vietnam." The police then put Muste and other protesters into a taxi, not to cart them off to the station for booking, but to protect them from the angry crowd that had begun to attack some of the demonstrators.

Cornell remembers:

> Some guys from the New York *Times* came back with us to 5 Beekman and said, "You know, for demonstrators you really ought to know your business better. Get something that's photographable—a space—time it for the Sunday edition."
>
> So we determined that we would raise the money, about twenty-five hundred dollars, to erect a portable platform at the north end of Union Square, to have a sound system that was respectable, to put out a good-sized mailing, and gather about twenty-five hundred people, which fills the north end of Union Square very nicely. . . .

Meanwhile SDS, which had finally voted in September to support the October 15–16 action, continued to grapple with the issue of the draft and what position SDS should adopt toward it. In October the National Office proposed a mild (and legal) three-point program: urging young men to file for CO status; working to prevent colleges from revealing students' class rank; and demonstrating against local draft boards. The cumbersome process of having the membership vote on the proposal was set in motion.

While the members were voting, however, the proposal caught the fickle attention of the media, both print and broadcast, and for a few weeks SDS's collective ears rang with criticism. Nor was Congress silent: the noted Communist-hunter Senator Thomas Dodd (D-Connecticut), vice chairman of the Senate Internal Security Subcommittee, accused the "anti-Vietnam *[sic]* movement" of having fallen under Communist control, and Attorney General Nicholas deB. Katzenbach warned that there were Communists in SDS. Senator John Stennis (D-Mississippi) demanded that the Administration "pull the anti-draft movement up by the roots and grind it to bits."

Finally, conscious that the "draft-dodging" image was becoming extremely hurtful to SDS, National Secretary Paul Booth and President Carl Oglesby flew to Washington to hold a press conference in which they issued a statement stressing "alternative service" in lieu of the draft, filing for conscientious objector status, and a philosophy of "build not burn" (a reference not only to the destruction of Vietnam but also to the extensive damage of that summer's ghetto riots in Los Angeles' black Watts district).

At last, anticlimactically, SDS's membership vote came in on the proposal that had caused it so much trouble. Only one sixth of the 3,139 people polled had returned their ballots; of those, 243 were in favor, 279 opposed, and 35 abstained. The result was not widely publicized, and the public perception of SDS continued to be wrong on two counts: that it was advocating a "draft-dodging" program, and that it was the leading antiwar organization.

The media had become friendly again, however, and by the end of the year SDS found that it had both growing fame at home and abroad, and a record high number of campus chapters: 124. To the casual observer, or to the naive or badly informed student who wanted to "do something," SDS looked to be in good shape. To those who were more familiar with the organization, however, it was obvious that SDS was floundering: at this relatively late date, it still had no official policies "on Vietnam, on the draft, on university reform, or on domestic priorities." Moreover, it had no strategy either. Older SDSers were already talking of moving on to start a kind of alumni club, the Movement for a Democratic Society.

At Christmas break, an SDS conference was held at the Champaign-Urbana campus of the University of Illinois. It was an attempt to clear the air and to formulate something in the way of SDS policy. The meeting was a failure; participants floundered in endless debate, and in the end they voted down an opportunity to devote the organization to antiwar work. Minimal antidraft actions were adopted: a CO pamphlet was to be distributed, and "Freedom Draft Cards" were to be given out for young men to sign and return to SDS for tabulation (this was never done).

For those who enjoy looking back to see prophetic signs not recognized along the way, the December 1965 SDS conference had two: nasty racial fights erupted, and the first workshop in the New Left was held on "Women in the Movement." This session had been precipitated by a memorandum written in November by Casey Hayden and Mary King—white, female veterans of the Southern civil rights movement. Titled "Sex and Caste: A Kind of Memo . . . to a number of other women in the peace and freedom movements," it recapitulated and expanded what the authors had written anonymously the previous year for a SNCC staff conference: "SNCC Position Paper (Women in the Movement)."

The 1964 paper detailed eleven specific examples of discrimination against women in SNCC and pointed out that, like the paternal white, the average SNCC worker finds it difficult to discuss the woman problem because of the assumption of male superiority. Assumptions of male superiority are as widespread and deep rooted and every much as crippling to the woman as the assumptions of white supremacy are to the Negro. Consider why it is in SNCC that women who are competent, qualified, and experienced, are automatically assigned to the "female" kinds of jobs such as typing, desk work, telephone work, filing, library work, cooking, and the assistant kind of administrative work but rarely the "executive" kind . . . this is no more a man's world than it is a white world.

When Stokely Carmichael heard that such a position paper had been written, he uttered words that served as a clarion recruiting call for the embryonic women's movement: "The only position for women in SNCC is prone."*

In 1965 the "Kind of Memo" led to separate women's discussion groups at the SDS conference, and an acknowledgement by the National Council that, despite SDS's principles of participatory democracy, "many women are neither able to nor encouraged to become participatory democrats in the organization." In the discussion groups that December, "for the first time at an SDS conference women came together to talk about problems of women in the movement or women as an oppressed class."

On November 6 the Committee for Nonviolent Action sponsored an antiwar rally in Union Square, New York. Five young men, all self-described pacifists, burned their draft cards with a Zippo lighter. Only one was 1-A; the others, including David McReynolds of the War Resisters League and Thomas Cornell of the Catholic Workers, were either 4-F, over-age, or, like Cornell, listed as a conscientious objector.

Hecklers booed and jeered the little group, and doused them with water from a pump hidden in a laundry bag (they had feared gasoline; the water did not hinder their efforts). At times the shouting and harassment grew so loud that the speakers could not be heard; "Moscow Mary!" chanted the hecklers when Dorothy Day, a founder of the Catholic Worker, tried to speak. Some of the hecklers' signs read THANKS, PINKOS, QUEERS, COWARDS, DRAFT DODGERS—MAO TSE-TUNG. During the card burning they shouted, "Burn yourselves, not your cards!" They referred to Norman Morrison, who had immolated himself four days before.

The Reverend A. J. Muste, CNVA's chairman, led the crowd, silent now, in a prayer for Morrison and for "the combatants on both sides in Vietnam who are perishing." Morrison's act, said Muste, had "an element of history, an element of terror, an element of courage, and an element of mystery. . . . Do not weep for Norman Morrison or his family. Let us instead weep for the lethargy of this nation and for the future if we do not commit ourselves." After the ceremony, David McReynolds, hustled into a car with some of his fellow protesters, thought that they were being arrested; he was surprised when their police escort delivered them

---

* "Prone": "having the front or ventral surface downward." Either Carmichael needed a dictionary or he was publicly stating his preference for kinky sex. Probably he meant "supine."

to 5 Beekman Street, the office of the War Resisters League. He saw the protective action as evidence that the demonstrators had once again been in physical danger, as they had on October 28, and that the police thought so too.

Three days later, on November 9, Roger LaPorte burned himself to death at the Dag Hammarskjöld Plaza at the United Nations.

Several years after the event McReynolds reflected on LaPorte's action:

> I had been quite disturbed by the [draft card] burning because of the general tension involved—a great deal more tension certainly than on the occasion some years ago when I refused induction and that whole event was a very private confrontation—and I could not help thinking once I realized that the lights had gone out throughout the entire area of the familiar "and darkness fell over the whole land." [The great Northeast blackout of November 1965, which occurred just twelve hours after LaPorte's immolation.] Both Tom Cornell and I feel that LaPorte burned himself in an effort to absorb part of the violence that he had felt at the demonstration on November 6th. He . . . was absolutely appalled at the chants from the right wing that we burn ourselves rather than draft cards. Perhaps we are wrong and perhaps Roger LaPorte would have burned himself to death in any event but I have never since that date been very enthusiastic about burning things because I know that in a society as tense as this one the flame in my hand can very quickly engulf someone else altogether.

LaPorte's and Morrison's deaths, and the burnings of draft cards, were shocking at the time; in retrospect they can be seen as portents, foreshadowings, not only of the napalm and the fire raining from the sky that were to devastate Vietnam and her people, but also of the fire that in the next seven years was to sweep across America: like the prairie fires so dreaded by the pioneers, like the conflagrations that periodically destroyed the nation's nineteenth-century cities, that fire in the minds of men, in the minds of women, would come close to destroying America as well as Vietnam.

As if in grim response to the International Days of Protest, to the draft card burnings and the immolations, a battle took place in mid-November in the Ia Drang Valley between North Vietnamese and American (not South Vietnamese) troops. In one week, 240 U.S. soldiers were killed—triple the highest weekly number to that time.

Families whose sons had died there might have been further distressed, the following week, to read in *Look* magazine an interview with Adlai Stevenson by Eric Sevareid—Stevenson's last interview, as it turned out, conducted on July 12, 1965, and published in the November 30 issue. U Thant, said Stevenson, had obtained in the fall of 1964, before the U.S. presidential elections, an offer from North Vietnam to talk in Rangoon, Burma, with U.S. representatives about "terms" for ending the fighting in Vietnam. The offer was refused: "Someone in Washington insisted that this attempt be postponed until after the Presidential election [wrote Sevareid]. When the election was over, U Thant again pursued the matter; Hanoi was still willing to send its man. But Defense Secretary Robert McNamara, Adlai went on, flatly opposed the attempt." Later attempts by Thant to halt the fighting, including an offer to the United States to write the terms of a cease-fire exactly as it saw fit, were also rebuffed. Thant was reported to have been furious, but he said nothing publicly. Queried by reporters, McNamara called the Sevareid report "totally false"; at the UN, Thant refused comment. A State Department spokesman, replying to reports that Dean Rusk refused even to acknowledge Thant's efforts during the previous year, said, "We saw nothing to indicate that Hanoi was prepared for peace talks and the Secretary of State said he would recognize it when it came. His antenna is sensitive."

The last major antiwar protest action of 1965 was a SANE-sponsored march on Washington scheduled for Thanksgiving weekend. The National Coordinating Committee to End the War in Vietnam, which had been formed out of the Assembly of Unrepresented People in August and had sponsored the October International Days of Protest, had scheduled its convention for Washington at the same time so that its delegates—about fifteen hundred—could join the SANE march.

The NCC meeting was marred by factional fighting over whether to continue as an umbrella organization (which could not, for instance, issue a unified call for "immediate withdrawal") or whether to form a new national organization opposed to the war which would speak with a single voice. The two opposing camps were offshoots of the Old Left, the Du Bois clubs and the Young Socialist Alliance. The New Left, represented by SDS, repeated its plea to restructure American society (ERAP) so that the "seventh war from now" would not occur: the antiwar movement, such as it was, could not influence or halt this particular war, said SDS.

Sanford Gottlieb, Washington political action director of SANE and coordinator for the march, had announced that only SANE-sanctioned placards bearing seventeen different approved slogans would be welcomed at the march, but that SANE would take no action to prevent members of other groups, such as M2M, from carrying their own signs with unauthorized slogans. "We'll just ignore them," said Gottlieb, "and they will just get lost in the crowd." Neither Gottlieb nor his organization wanted any part of "kooks, Communists and draft dodgers." The agony of deciding just which slogans were acceptable and which were not was, of course, another example of the national hangover from the binge of McCarthyism: any sign that was too "radical"—such as those calling for an immediate pullout—would arouse the old cries of "Communist!" and would obscure any good that might come from, say, a big turnout. SANE, having been through a severe bloodletting of its own several years previously, had no wish now to engage again in defending itself against charges of being soft on communism. Younger members of more radical groups, including some from SDS, had no memory of the McCarthy years; they were impatient with their elders' caution, and many of them did, in fact, carry unauthorized signs with messages such as those carried by Youth Against War and Fascism: BRING THE G.I.'S HOME NOW. In the light of later activities of antiwar groups, such slogans seem mild indeed, but at the time they were viewed as much too extreme. One of SANE's approved signs, for example, read NEW ACTION TO SPEED NEGOTIATIONS. A worse nightmare for Gottlieb and other members of SANE was what were seen as little adolescent gestures of rebellion like carrying the

Viet Cong flag. For ten dollars a demonstrator could buy one—a yellow star on a panel half blue, half red. Some demonstrators did; and they carried them, and were photographed and televised doing so. Their presence created a problem of conscience for many older, "straight" demonstrators and those who did not march but who might have liked to: antiwar politics, like every other kind, sometimes produced strange bedfellows.

Perhaps twenty-five thousand people marched that day, Saturday, November 27, 1965; perhaps fifty thousand. As usual, estimates varied. Some would-be demonstrators never arrived because the drivers hired for the buses to take them to Washington refused to make the trip when it was revealed who the passengers were. Coretta Scott King spoke, and Norman Thomas ("I'd rather see America save her soul than her face"), and Dr. Spock, who decried the lack of congressional debate over U.S. policy. Members of the Bread and Puppet Theater, wearing black robes and death masks, performed "A Pageant of Death Based on President Johnson's [April 7] Speech at Johns Hopkins" accompanied by the beating of a bass drum. The sponsors of the march comprised a star-studded list which included playwright Arthur Miller, actors Tony Randall, Ossie Davis, and Ruby Dee, novelists John Hersey and Saul Bellow, cartoonist Jules Feiffer, CORE Director James Farmer, and Dr. Albert Sabin, the developer of the oral polio vaccine; thus in another way was legitimacy achieved. In line with its stance on the far Right of the peace movement, SANE had refused to allow as sponsors of the march SNCC's Robert Moses, Yale's Staughton Lynd, and Nobel Laureate Linus Pauling, a leading figure in the disarmament movement of the early 1960s, to which SANE had contributed so heavily.

During the day a delegation of march leaders conferred at the Executive Office Building next door to the White House with three administration officials including Chester Cooper, a specialist on Vietnam on the staff of McGeorge Bundy and some years later the author of *The Lost Crusade,* one of the most perspicacious of the "insider" books on Vietnam. Although each side praised the other's "sincerity" and "courtesy," some acrimony developed over a suggestion that Dean Rusk had made that the group address itself to the Communists rather than to the U.S. Administration. The delegation, announcing that it had already appealed to Ho Chi Minh, expressed "annoyance" with Cooper's attempt to suggest its phrasing. "We don't speak for this government," said Gottlieb, "we speak to it." Nevertheless, the cable had been sent (on October 28), thereby reinforcing the impression that SANE and the march's sponsors wished to create: that of a moderate, responsible, patriotic demonstration. They had asked Ho to "respond favorably to immediate peace talks"; they warned him that "demonstrations [like this] will continue but will not lead to a U.S. pullout." SANE's, they said, was in support not of immediate U.S. withdrawal but of a "cease-fire and negotiated settlement based on 1954 Geneva accords." Always the antiwar movement was vulnerable to the charge of aiding the enemy: side by side with its front page report of the march, the New York *Times* ran a story with the subhead ASIAN COMMUNISTS SURE PUBLIC OPINION IN U.S. WILL FORCE WAR'S END. The President of the NLF sent his best wishes for the "brilliant success" of the march; to respond to those Americans who turned out to demonstrate against the war, the Viet Cong released two American prisoners, army sergeants, who had been held since November 24, 1963.

The marchers that day were an organizer's dream: thoroughly middle class, largely middle-aged, the crowd "would not have been out of place at the Army-Navy game." Thus readers of the *Times* were reassured: despite a few "fired-up youths," the crowd was like themselves, decent and respectable. The organizers and sponsors of the march had achieved their aim: to hold a demonstration that would strike a responsive chord with the public, a demonstration that would not seem threatening, would not seem "subversive."

But something happened that afternoon, largely unreported, that would have seemed extremely threatening, had the public been aware of it; as it was, it submerged for a time only to surface again as one of the most brilliant and devastating analyses of the men—and their system of "corporate liberalism"—who set the American people on the jungle path that led to the bloody confrontation of the Ia Drang Valley. The analyst—the speaker—was the president of SDS, Carl Oglesby, who had been tacked on, as it were, to the end of the afternoon's array of famous and distinguished speakers as a sop to the youngsters (Oglesby at that time was thirty-one). He said, in part:

> We are here to protest against a growing war. Since it is a very bad war, we acquire the habit of thinking that it must be caused by very bad men. But . . . the original commitment in Vietnam was made by President Truman, a mainstream liberal. It was seconded by President Eisenhower, a moderate liberal. It was intensified by President Kennedy, a flaming liberal. Think of the men who now engineer that war—those who study the maps, give the commands, push the buttons, and tally the dead: Bundy, McNamara, Rusk, Lodge, Goldberg, the President himself.
>
> They are not moral monsters.
>
> They are all honorable men.
>
> They are all liberals.
>
> But so, I'm sure, are many of us who are here today in protest. To understand the war, then, it seems necessary to take a closer look at this American liberalism. Maybe we are in for some surprises. Maybe we have here two quite different liberalisms: one authentically humanist; the other not so human at all. . . .
>
> What the National Liberation Front is fighting in Vietnam is a complex and vicious war. This war is also a revolution, as honest a revolution as you can find anywhere in history. And this is a fact which all our intricate official denials will never change.
>
> But it doesn't make any difference to our leaders anyway. Their aim in Vietnam is really much simpler than this implies. It is to safeguard what they take to be American interests around the world against revolution or revolutionary change, which they always call Communism. . . . There is simply no such thing, now, for us, as a just revolution. . . . We have lost that mysterious social desire for human equity that from time to time has given us genuine moral drive. We have become a nation of young, bright-

65

eyed, hard-hearted, slim-waisted, bullet-headed make-out artists. A nation
—may I say it?—of beardless liberals. . . .

Some will [say] that I overdraw the matter . . . and some will [say] that
I sound mighty anti-American. To these, I say: Don't blame *me* for *that!*
Blame those who mouthed my liberal values and broke my American
heart. . . .

There are people in this country today . . . who aim at nothing less than
a humanist reformation. And the humanist liberals must understand that it
is this movement with which their own best hopes are most in tune. We
radicals know the same history that you liberals know, and we can understand your occasional cynicism, exasperation, and even distrust. But we ask
you to put these aside and help us risk a leap. Help us find enough time for
the enormous work that needs doing here. Help us build. Help us shake the
future in the name of plain human hope.

As the year ended, two groups of Americans journeyed to Vietnam, one (unoffi-
cial) to the North and one (official) to the South. In Hanoi were Staughton Lynd,
Tom Hayden, and Herbert Aptheker, a historian and a leading American Communist, at that time director of the American Institute for Marxist Studies. Aptheker
arranged the trip at the invitation of the government of North Vietnam; he invited
Lynd and a third person, a leader of the New Left, who withdrew at the last
moment for fear of embarrassing his organization. Lynd then invited Hayden, who
said that he was making the trip as an individual and not as a representative of
SDS. Lynd stated that he was on a fact-finding mission for the magazine *Viet
Report,* which had asked him to clarify the peace terms of the NLF and the North
Vietnamese Government. Many Americans had tried to visit Hanoi but had been
denied permission (by Hanoi as well as by the U.S. Government); the opportunity
seemed too good to pass up, and so the three men went. In their book about the
trip, *The Other Side,* Lynd and Hayden recorded at length their conversations with
the Vietnamese; they were deeply impressed by the sincerity and determination that
they found, and they tried to show their American readers the similarities between
the Vietnamese struggle for control of their country and America's revolutionary
struggle against Great Britain two centuries before.

In Saigon that December Senator Mike Mansfield and four fellow senators were
concluding a thirty-five-day tour (in an air force jet) of sixteen European and Asian
capitals. We should pursue negotiations, said Mansfield; his companions agreed.

On Christmas Day the Administration announced a thirty-hour truce including
a pause in the bombing of North Vietnam. At the end of this period, ground
fighting resumed but the bombing did not. Instead the President launched an elaborate "peace offensive" in which he sent emissaries around the world to sound out
North Vietnam's reactions to the pause. He had spent Christmas at his Texas
ranch, and he telephoned his decision on the "peace offensive" to Washington late
at night on December 27. The Bundy brothers, who were attending a debutante
ball, were caught by surprise.

There is evidence that the bombing pause at this time was intended to prepare for an intensification of the U.S. war effort, including increased bombing. Lynd, Hayden, and Aptheker reported that the North Vietnamese had been suspicious of President Johnson's pronouncements of a "peace offensive" because the U.S. arms buildup on the ground was intensifying, the air war over South Vietnam continued, chemical warfare (toxic spraying) had increased, and a parade of high U.S. military officials, including the chairman of the Joint Chiefs and the army chief of staff, had visited Saigon—in the past always a sign of new escalation to come.

In the words of Secretary McNamara, included in a memorandum to President Johnson on November 30:

> It is my belief that there should be a three- or four-week pause in the program of bombing the North before we either greatly increase our troop deployments to Vietnam or intensify our strikes against the North. The reasons for this belief are, first, that *we must lay a foundation in the mind of the American public and in world opinion for such an enlarged phase of the war* [emphasis added] and, second, we should give North Vietnam a face-saving chance to stop the aggression. I am not seriously concerned about the risk of alienating the South Vietnamese, misleading Hanoi, or being "trapped" in a pause; if we take reasonable precautions, we can avoid these pitfalls.

Or, in the words of Secretary Rusk in a December 28 "EYES ONLY" message to Ambassador Lodge:

> The prospect of large-scale reinforcement in men and defense budget increases of some twenty billions for the next eighteen month period *requires solid preparation of the American public* [emphasis added]. A crucial element will be clear demonstration that we have explored fully every alternative but that aggressor left us no choice.

Nineteen sixty-five was a watershed year for the United States because in those twelve months the country's course both in Vietnam and at home was irrevocably set. The events of that year contained all the elements for the drama that would be played again and again in the next seven years: a war conducted by presidential fiat; managed news and outright deceit on the part of the Administration; congressional impotence; and, in the antiwar movement, a struggle to coalesce and to agree on issues and tactics. Virtually every method of protest was tried in 1965: individual acts of witness including suicide; campus speaking and protest; mass marches and rallies; demonstrations and confrontations with the authorities; attempts to appeal directly to the President, the Cabinet, and Congress. By the end of the year the two sides were arrayed: the U.S. Administration was committed to the war in Vietnam; the opponents of that war were committed to ending it.

1966:
Becalmed in a Sea of Uncertainty

ON JANUARY 3, 1966, a black SNCC worker, Samuel Younge, was shot and killed in Tuskegee, Alabama, because he tried to use a whites-only rest room at a gas station.

Three days later SNCC issued a statement linking Younge's murder to America's war in Vietnam, which black men were being asked to fight:

> We believe the U.S. government has been deceptive in claims of concern for the freedom of the Vietnamese people, just as the government has been deceptive in claiming concern for the freedom of the colored people in such other countries as the Dominican Republic, the Congo, South Africa, Rhodesia and the United States itself. . . .
>
> Our work, particularly in the South, taught us that the United States government has never guaranteed the freedom of oppressed citizens, and is not yet truly determined to end the rule of terror and oppression within its own borders. . . .
>
> The murder of Samuel Younge in Tuskegee, Alabama, is no different from the murder of people in Vietnam, for both Younge and the Vietnamese sought and are seeking to secure the rights guaranteed them by law. In each case, the U.S. government bears a great part of the responsibility for these deaths.
>
> Samuel Younge was murdered because U.S. law is not being enforced. . . .
>
> We take note of the fact that 16 percent of the draftees from this country are Negro, called on to stifle the liberation of Vietnam, to preserve a "democracy" which does not exist for them at home.
>
> We ask: Where is the draft for the freedom fight in the United States?
>
> We therefore encourage those Americans who prefer to use their energy in building democratic forms within the country. We believe that work in the civil-rights movement and other human relations organizations is a valid

alternative to the draft. We urge all Americans to seek this alternative, knowing full well that it may cost them their lives, as painfully as in Vietnam.

This statement was one of the first public expressions of a bitterness among many blacks which, by summer, would result in calls for Black Power and the effective expulsion of whites from civil rights activism. Many of them would gravitate to the antiwar movement.

As Howard Zinn comments: "SNCC was psychologically prepared—without the people in SNCC knowing anything about foreign policy—to be hostile to the war effort because they were so furious at the government, they had so little faith in the government of the United States, they so distrusted the leadership in the White House and its promises. . . ."

Meanwhile, in Washington, J. William Fulbright prepared to enlighten the nation further on the subject of Vietnam by holding public hearings before the Senate Foreign Relations Committee. In his introduction to the published version of the hearings Senator Fulbright gave a name to the year 1966: "In China this is the Year of the Horse; in America it appears to be the Year of the Hawk." It was a prescient appraisal, although the report from South Vietnam that 14 percent—ninety-six thousand—of its troops were deserters in 1965 suggested that 1966 might be the Year of the Chicken.

The year began with talk of peace—much talk. The bombing pause was extended indefinitely and emissaries of the President were sent scurrying around the globe carrying, with much fanfare, the peace initiative of the White House. Averell Harriman visited a dozen countries, including Poland, Russia, Japan, and the Philippines, in a matter of days. Vice President Humphrey, McGeorge Bundy, and UN Ambassador Goldberg were part of the traveling show. Even G. Mennen "Soapy" Williams, former governor of Michigan, was dispatched to Africa to carry the message of administrative goodwill. It was an exercise in yo-yo diplomacy, and as such it must have dismayed Senator Fulbright, who, along with his star witness, George F. Kennan, was to plead in the committee hearings for old-fashioned, patient, private, plodding diplomatic consultation as a proper method. Reports coming out of South Vietnam in mid-January made it obvious that the government there had been little consulted on the peace initiative and might well have rejected the stance toward negotiations taken by the United States.

A summary of the U.S. position was prepared by the State Department for the hastily mobilized ambassadors. It came to be known as the Fourteen Points. Taken at face value, the Fourteen Points put the United States perilously close to the NLF-Hanoi position earlier expressed and constantly maintained in four, nonnegotiable points. Both sides seemed to renounce imperialistic interests in South Vietnam and to look for solutions arrived at by the Vietnamese acting alone. The cutting question of the participation of the National Liberation Front—Hanoi asserted that the South Vietnamese settlement must be in accordance with the NLF program—was still open, but point thirteen of the U.S. declaration at least admitted to the possibility of the Viet Cong's being represented at negotiating sessions.

The difficulty lay in the public utterances on either side and rhetoric which exposed the hardened opposing stands. In his January State of the Union message LBJ pledged to stay in Vietnam until aggression stopped and announced a $5.8 billion rise in expenditures on the war. Ho Chi Minh, for his part, made public a letter to foreign governments in which he called President Johnson's words an "impudent threat," expressed equal resolve to stay the course, and labeled the "peace offensive" as "sham" and "tricks." The Chinese, predictably, took up the same cry of deceit as they publicly belittled a Moscow mission to Hanoi that some observers thought was at least partly designed to prod North Vietnam to consider the possibility of negotiations. In the same period both the Vatican and the government of Japan sought independently to open the way to negotiations under cover of the bombing pause.

As the pause continued past the middle of January, pressure to maintain it mounted at home and abroad. The President grew restive. A letter from seventy-six members of Congress urging him to halt escalation and another from fifteen Democratic members of the Senate asking a continuation of the bombing pause perhaps suggested to him that he might indeed become "trapped" in the pause. His response to the congressional letter writers was testy; he said that "he continued to be guided in these matters by the resolution of the Congress approved on August 10, 1964 [the Tonkin Gulf Resolution]." Thereupon Wayne Morse offered a motion to rescind the Resolution, but to pass such a motion, said Russell Long (D-Louisiana), would "fly in the face of tradition, which is to unite behind the President in time of war." Even, apparently, undeclared war.* On January 25, as was his custom before announcing a decision, the President and his top advisers briefed congressional leaders. The President was said to rely heavily on the Tonkin Gulf Resolution at such meetings. "He pulls it out of his pocket and shakes it at you," reported one senator. Said another: "It was so damned frayed and dog-eared the last time I talked to him that I wanted to give him a fresh copy." On January 31 Johnson took to television to announce to the nation that U.S. bombing of North Vietnam had resumed.

The most nettlesome senator for the President was J. William Fulbright of Arkansas, chairman of the Senate Foreign Relations Committee. When Johnson was Senate majority leader in the 1950s he called Fulbright, whom he admired and liked, "my Secretary of State." Fulbright was still respected by his colleagues in the Senate and was always accorded a generous hearing by the press, who tended to "turn off" Wayne Morse, a recognized Senate opponent of the Administration's Vietnam policies. Fulbright was clearly upset by the events of January 1966. Around the time of Johnson's decision to resume the bombing of North Vietnam the senator announced that he regretted his vote on the Tonkin Gulf Resolution;

---

* The story on Morse's initiative ran on page 1 of the New York *Times*. Five paragraphs down in the story, and still on the front page, came a curious aside: "Meanwhile, President Johnson's senior advisers are said to have told him that it would take six or seven years of military action in South Vietnam to bring about a satisfactory solution there." As was to happen more than once during the Vietnam years, such "bad news," even when it was prominently displayed, caused little public reaction—perhaps because it seemed so unbelievable. As it turned out, seven was the correct number of years.

urged that the Viet Cong be invited to peace talks and that the Geneva Conference be reconvened; and let James Reston of the New York *Times* know that Johnson indulged in "briefings" rather than "consultations" with congressional leaders. Finally, in his capacity as chairman, Fulbright announced that the Senate Foreign Relations Committee would hold broad and searching hearings on the matter of U.S. involvement in Vietnam. Lyndon Johnson never forgave his old friend. Accounts of his presidency are scattered with bitter, almost scurrilous references to Fulbright. "Senator Halfbright" was just one of Johnson's epithets for his new foe. Fulbright, on the other hand, had deep instincts of loyalty to both the office and the man to overcome before he moved to challenge his President's Vietnam policies in public. He did not bring to the role Wayne Morse's relish for attack.

The hearings, with four principal witnesses testifying over a three-week period beginning on January 28, were heralded as a kind of national teach-in. However, they scarcely fitted the pattern set by the hundreds of campus teach-ins spawned by the University of Michigan original less than twelve months earlier. The academic version, true to its derivation from the civil rights sit-in, was a (more or less) orderly demonstration against the Administration's Vietnam policy accompanied by (usually) one-sided argument. The argument, as time progressed and those in attendance proved to be the already persuaded, tended to lapse into simple harangue: the United States was woefully, sinfully wrong and should get out of Vietnam *now*. McGeorge Bundy treated with unveiled disdain a distinguished senior research professor at the University of Michigan who had undertaken to explain the point of view of the first teach-in: "it [your letter] does not fill me with admiration for the academic quality of your thinking." The Fulbright hearings, by contrast, were predicated on the assumption that the United States could not "cut and run," that a solution somewhere between "Out Now!" and continued escalation toward inevitable conflict with China should be sought.

There were no hecklers at the Fulbright hearings. The usual courtly decorum of any Senate hearing prevailed. The one exception occurred in an interchange between Senator Wayne Morse and General Maxwell Taylor:

> MORSE: You know we are engaged in historic debate in this country, where there are honest differences of opinion. I happen to hold to the point of view that it isn't going to be too long before the American people as a people will repudiate our war in Southeast Asia.
>
> TAYLOR: That, of course, is good news to Hanoi, Senator.
>
> MORSE: I know that that is the smear that you militarists give to those of us who have honest differences of opinion with you, but I don't intend to get down in the gutter with you and engage in that kind of debate, General. . . . If the people decide that this war should be stopped in Southeast Asia, are you going to take the position that is weakness on the home front in a democracy?
>
> TAYLOR: I would feel that our people were badly misguided and did not understand the consequences of such a disaster.

Morse had touched an administration nerve on the raw. Taylor's responses, which imputed to the opposition both a lack of patriotism and great naiveté, reflected what was more and more to become the embattled stance of the White House.

What made the hearings eligible for the appellation "national teach-in" was the fact that millions watched the proceedings on the ABC and NBC television networks. CBS chose not to preempt reruns (for the fifth or eighth time) of the sitcoms "I Love Lucy" and "The Real McCoys" on the day Ambassador Kennan testified. The resulting uproar over this decision led John A. Schneider, number three man at CBS, to explain: "The opinion makers" (i.e., men) were not at home during the day; mere "housewives" were not interested. Mere housewives, of course, and women from every occupation and of every political persuasion were to provide the sinew of the antiwar movement in the years to come, from its radical fringes to its most sedate expression at the ballot boxes. Fred W. Friendly, a widely respected newsman whose judgment as chief of news for CBS had been overruled by Schneider, quit in protest. Senator Fulbright reported, without giving figures pro and con —or male and female—that twenty thousand letters and telegrams were received in response to the committee's hearings.

On the whole, however, the two principal administration witnesses, Secretary of State Dean Rusk and General Maxwell Taylor, emerged relatively unscathed. Taken as a pair, Rusk and Taylor were both symbol of and agent for America's hard-line policy in Vietnam from the time of its groping beginnings under Kennedy through Johnson's unhappy term of office. The fateful decision by President Kennedy to escalate the carefully capped number of U.S. military in South Vietnam stemmed directly from Taylor's 1961 mission to Vietnam. Since that time he had served the two administrations in several capacities, including that of ambassador. He appeared before the Fulbright group as special consultant to President Johnson. Through the same period Rusk had served the two presidents in one role, Secretary of State, and emerged as a rock of certitude. Schooled in the 1950s era of unswerving devotion to containment of communism that made the department ever the servant and articulator of military policy, never a civilian constraint upon the single-minded enthusiasm of the generals and White House "pragmatists," he was never a doubter or skeptic, never a formulator of new directions. As a lay figure of administration policy through endless years of Vietnam, Rusk, like one of Homer's warriors in the siege of Troy, won his own enduring epithet: "unflappable." His performance before the Senate committee enhanced his claim upon that title.

Rusk and Taylor presented a simplistic, bare-bones argument and stuck to it. The case was not, they said, that of a single Vietnam people engaged in civil conflict among themselves, but rather of two Vietnam nations, one (the North) an outright aggressor against the other. Ours was a war of *limited* objectives and *limited* means: we would persuade the North, by our ever-increasing military presence and pressure in the South and our gradually intensifying bombing of the North, to halt aggression. There was a single, simple solution available, one entirely in the hands of the government of North Vietnam: capitulate either on the field or at the conference table. As Rusk put it, "This is Ho Chi Minh's war."

In his two appearances Rusk also made an elaborate claim that the legal basis for U.S. involvement lay in the SEATO pact. Television viewers must have been mystified to learn that this little-known treaty, rushed into existence in 1954 by John Foster Dulles in order to paper over the failures of the Geneva Conference, and utterly disregarded to this point by all its signatories, the United States included, was now to be viewed as the primary justification for the U.S. presence in Vietnam. It was an argument that the senators, with the exception of Morse and Fulbright himself, did not wish to pursue. That way, after all, led to the admission that the United States had neither right nor reason to be in Vietnam in the first place. None of them—with, again, the exception of the irascible Senator Morse—was ready to use the Ozarks phrase introduced by Fulbright: "Calf rope, I give up."

The dilemma was acknowledged by the two remaining witnesses, Lieutenant General James M. Gavin and George F. Kennan. The two matched in their respective fields the credentials of Rusk and Taylor and were popularly perceived as members of the establishment elite. They saw no justification for America's original involvement, especially when weighed against other worldwide interests and commitments. Kennan saw no benefit in what he called "a precipitate and disorderly withdrawal . . . in present circumstances." Gavin agreed. He proposed, as an alternative, reliance on military "enclaves": a policy that called for standing fast, without escalation, in stronghold positions. Gavin's views were ferociously attacked by administration spokesmen, in some cases by generals brought out of mothballs for the purpose. When his turn came to comment on the Gavin plan, General Taylor used his favorite term of reprobation. It would, he said, be "good news to Hanoi."

Both Kennan and Gavin feared that escalation of the bombing would at some point bring in China, and it was this that the senators pressed hardest on. What were the so-called limits to manpower, to bombing? Taylor would not say; yet within weeks he was to advocate the mining of Haiphong harbor. Rusk, the "unflappable," seemed not to care. Asked by Senator Stuart Symington (D-Missouri) if fear of Red China's reacting "should be decisive with respect to decisions we make on foreign policy," he answered, "No, sir, because if we do not meet those responsibilities, we shall find a Red China much more voracious and much more dangerous, if they should discover that this technique of aggression is successful." "The instrument of aggression," he had earlier told the committee, ". . . is Hanoi. The doctrine which is used to support this aggression is from Peking."

Finally, Kennan, who testified with diffidence despite his thirty-eight years of experience with Communist affairs, made a point that could not fail to tell with his wider audience. Victory in the South against the Viet Cong, said Kennan, "could be achieved . . . only at the cost of a degree of damage to civilian life and of civilian suffering, generally, for which I would not like to see this country responsible." It was a point emotionally echoed later by Senator Fulbright in an exchange with General Taylor.

FULBRIGHT: General, can you imagine, in your wildest dreams, of [sic] a Secretary of Air agreeing to napalm a great city, perhaps a city like Tokyo, with millions of little children, sweet little children, innocent pure babies who love their mothers, and mothers who love their children, just like you love your son, thousands of little children who never did us any harm, being slowly burned to death? . . .

TAYLOR: I am not sure of the situation; I can't visualize the situation you are asking me about.

FULBRIGHT: Isn't it a fact we did just that in Tokyo?

TAYLOR: The fire raid?

FULBRIGHT: Didn't we?

TAYLOR: I am not familiar with the details. . . .

FULBRIGHT: You are not familiar?

TAYLOR: —but we certainly dropped fire bombs on Tokyo.

FULBRIGHT: You hadn't heard about the bombs?

TAYLOR: I had heard about it.

Fulbright apparently had in mind the increasing tendency of administration spokesmen to equate the carnage wrought by American bombers carrying payloads far in excess of World War II with the brutal acts of Viet Cong guerrillas. Dean Rusk had once asked rhetorically what was the difference between a boy carrying a bomb on his bike and what American bombers were doing. Fulbright pressed on and got a chillingly wooden reply from Taylor:

FULBRIGHT: What difference, really morally or any other way, do you see between burning innocent little children and disemboweling innocent citizens? . . .

TAYLOR: I would say that there is no doubt as to the objective in the latter case. In the former case, I would imagine the answer would be that it was an unhappy concomitant of the attack of the targets that happened in the bombing.

The importance of the 1966 Fulbright hearings cannot be overstated, for it was while watching them that millions of Americans learned for the first time that there was a "respectable" basis for opposing the policies of their own government, that sons and daughters caught up passionately in campus movements were not indulging in a newer, more pernicious form of collegiate high jinks. Viewers learned that George Kennan, a distinguished senior statesman and author of the "containment" doctrine that was the theoretical basis for the hard-rock anti-Communist thrust of American foreign policy over the previous twenty years, believed that it had no proper application in Vietnam. They heard and saw that citizens like Morse of near-biblical intensity in their opposition or, like Fulbright, deeply anguished by what their country was doing in Vietnam, were not the "new appeasers" (Chicago

Tribune), or out "to destroy the American will" (Portland *Oregonian),* or agents helping "America to disgrace itself these days, not in Vietnam, but on the home front" (Omaha *World Herald).*

Although there was no immediate response from the antiwar movement, a corner had been turned. If General Taylor had misled the Senate hearing and the citizenry watching when he suggested that the South Vietnamese government controlled 60 percent of the population (Secretary McNamara had just reported privately to the President that the Ky government, by its own estimate, controlled only 25 percent), he was certainly correct in his own appraisal that success in Vietnam depended, in part, on "the picture of a determined United States back home that is not going to be forced off course." But his own testimony, and the hearings as a whole, had suggested to a wide audience of Americans that it was neither illegitimate nor unpatriotic to question the wisdom of that course.

For the antiwar movement itself, its putative leaders and its activists, 1966 was an outwardly quiet year. The leaders only dimly perceived that the ground on which they stood rumbled with the muted, sporadic outbursts that denote seismic activity building. What had appeared to be a vehicle for national leadership, the National Coordinating Committee to End the War in Vietnam, fell apart at a January meeting in Milwaukee. The standing committee split down the middle and narrowly defeated a proposal to make immediate withdrawal from Vietnam the basic demand of the NCC program. The uneasy coalition of Old and New Left, of Stalinists and Trotskyites, and of radical and more establishment-minded pacifists did not survive the division. Before disbanding, the meeting did, however, call for a renewal of the International Days of Protest on March 25–26.

In the sputtering beat of the Movement's progress in early 1966 there faintly echoed the footfall of the Administration: *limited* objectives through *limited* means. For the Movement limited objectives meant a "peaceful solution" or a negotiated settlement; limited means proved to be vigils, newspaper ads, fasts, teach-ins, "read-ins," and an occasional orderly march of protest. Students at Bryn Mawr, Haverford, and Swarthmore colleges began symbolic fasts; others at CCNY, Wesleyan, Amherst, and elsewhere followed suit. In Washington four hundred Quakers conducted a two-hour vigil at the White House and Women Strike for Peace began a continuous lobbying of Congress for "a peaceful solution." In New York City members of Clergy and Laymen Concerned About Vietnam tolled the bell of St. Mark's in-the-Bouwerie church. A national campaign under the auspices of SANE for the election of congressional candidates who favored scaling down the war in Vietnam was announced.

For Lyndon Johnson the antics of students, clergy, and housewives were one thing, the flutter in the Fulbright heartbeat, another. The President reacted like a physician who catches a suspicious fibrillation in a very important cardiac patient. All the resources at his disposal were brought to bear on the problem. Within hours of Senator Fulbright's announcement that his committee would open broad hearings on Vietnam, Johnson held a news conference and unveiled his Honolulu Conference. Once again there was a star-studded cast designed to put the low-budget

Fulbright production in shadow. From the Orient, across the Pacific, would come Nguyen Cao Ky, Premier of South Vietnam, and Nguyen Van Thieu, its chief of state; Ambassador Lodge would attend also, and General Westmoreland. Winging westward with LBJ were Rusk, McNamara, Harriman, Generals Taylor and Wheeler, McGeorge Bundy, and sundry others of star quality. Editorial writers were aghast at so many "indispensables" traveling together. It was a hastily assembled act: only at the last minute did someone remember to inform and to invite the South Vietnamese ambassador in Washington.

So much brass managed only to produce at conference's end a portentously titled Declaration of Honolulu that had all the tinkle of tin. It seemed designed to block avenues that the Fulbright hearings might fruitfully pursue, but in fact did not. The failures of land reform and other social and economic programs in South Vietnam —the very failures on which the Viet Cong and NLF had fed for ten years—were once again papered over with promises. The validity and stability of the Ky government were to be authenticated, it was declared, by real elections in the South. It was, all in all, a routine so familiar to the participants on either side that it could have been done in dumb show. The South Vietnamese had long since learned that the behemoth of the West lacked the political leverage to enforce results from any promise extracted. General Ky felt confident enough in the circumstance to hold his own separate news conference at which he declared, much to the subsequent embarrassment of his Honolulu hosts, that South Vietnam would never negotiate with nor recognize the Viet Cong.

Portents stronger than any promises in the boiler-plate language of the Declaration of Honolulu surrounded the President's trip to Hawaii. Antiwar pickets clashed with administration supporters at the airport on Oahu, and the reception given by the populace at large to their arriving leader was restrained at best. Pickets were on hand again when Johnson returned to the mainland at Los Angeles; they were to become part of an expected ritual for spokesmen carrying the Administration's message abroad in the land. Increasingly, as time went on, the White House messengers sought protected havens in which to set their platforms. Rusk, for instance, would choose his own Atlanta, or Las Vegas, hardly hotbeds of radicalism, for speeches outside of Washington.

More ominous, although not yet known to the President, was the fact that one of his companions on the trip would soon no longer travel with or for LBJ. Even as the Administration was busy assaulting the Gavin notion, McGeorge Bundy was about to find his own "enclave" in the fastness of the Ford Foundation. As president of that bastion of the Eastern establishment, Bundy would at last no longer be another man's servant.

If nothing else—and there was much else—Bundy was the living embodiment of the continuity of policy that Johnson proclaimed at each step of the escalation of the war. Bundy was a "cowhand," in LBJ's terminology, held over from the Kennedy Administration—a link, therefore, in the chain of policy extending, in Johnson's mind, back through Kennedy to Eisenhower and beyond. Moreover, it was Bundy's influential memorandum of February 7, 1965, arguing for a "policy of sustained reprisal" that opened the way to Operation ROLLING THUNDER, the penultimate step in Johnson's irrevocable escalation of the war.

Ironically, the man who had boarded the "streetcar" named Pleiku, dragging the President on after him, was now hopping off. The Bundy memo of February 1965 contained this magisterial reproof:

> There is one grave weakness in our posture in Vietnam which is within our power to fix—and that is a widespread belief that we do not have the will and force and patience and determination to take the necessary action and stay the course.

But it was Bundy who did not stay the course. Much to his dismay, James Reston broke the story of his departure a month after the Honolulu Conference. No defector from the LBJ ranks wished to have the President get the news that way.

On February 23 President Johnson went to New York City to attend a Freedom House dinner at the Waldorf-Astoria Hotel, where he received the National Freedom Award. Four thousand pickets protested outside, including the indefatigable A. J. Muste, who had declined an invitation to attend the dinner itself. As the President began his speech in defense of his Vietnam policies, one member of the audience, James Peck of the War Resisters League, jumped to his feet and shouted, "Mr. President, peace in Vietnam!" and pulled off his jacket to reveal the same slogan across his shirt. Peck was quickly removed. The President's citation read "Freedom at home was never more widely shared nor aggression abroad more wisely resisted. . . ." Meanwhile, in the streets outside, A. J. Muste was presenting the picketing throng's own "Freedom Award" to Elizabeth Sutherland of SNCC, who accepted on behalf of Julian Bond, a black recently elected to the Georgia House of Representatives who had been denied his seat by that body when he refused to disavow his opposition to the war and the draft, or his support of SNCC.

In the President's audience inside the hotel, grimly chewing his cigar, sat the junior senator from New York, Robert Kennedy. Perhaps he was recalling that in 1960, the year before his brother took office, another less savory "freedom" group, the Freedom Foundation, had awarded medals to the three "Democratic Leaders of Asia," Chiang Kai-shek, Syngman Rhee, and Ngo Dinh Diem. Or perhaps his musing carried him back to January when he had sent Johnson a marked copy of Bruce Catton's *Never Call Retreat* in the hope that it would stiffen the President's faltering resolve on the bombing pause. Johnson solemnly read from it to congressional leaders summoned to the White House a passage in which another President, laden with responsibilities, refers to himself as "that unhappy wretch called Abraham Lincoln." It was Johnson's way of indicating that he had resolved to resume the bombing. Kennedy had flown from Washington to New York City with Johnson on *Air Force One* in what must have been an uncomfortable trip for both after the furor created by Kennedy's suggestion in a statement issued on February 19 that the NLF be admitted to a share of power and responsibility in any negotiated settlement. Kennedy was forced by the backlash to refine and water down what seemed in retrospect a mild enough proposal. For nearly twelve months afterward he refused to participate in the public controversy over Vietnam.

The demonstration in the streets outside, kept well away from the President's arrival and departure, was marked by high spirits; it had the aspect and characteristics of many antiwar gatherings for years to come. Older, well-dressed citizens mingled with the young, among whom scruffy clothes and long hair were beginning to show as badges of political position. Numbers were important. No longer were the participants lonely pickets, martyrs in the face of cold and hostile onlookers. From numbers flowed an electric current of pleasurable excitement, anticipation, and existentially created fellowship: *E pluribus unum*. Perhaps. The signs, many carefully printed beforehand, certainly expressed the plurality. They ran from SUPPORT THE VOICES OF REASON IN CONGRESS to THE GREAT SOCIETY— NAPALM, TORTURE, BOMBINGS. Over and over, the chant resounded: "Hey, hey, LBJ, how many kids did you kill today?" echoing with the promise of ugliness to come. And surely not all the elders in the crowd were at one with a bearded, longhaired youth carrying an IMPEACH LBJ sign. He wore a Batman cape with a plastic Christ mask attached to it. Other demonstrators irreverently played upon an old American theme of unity, the flag—but with a difference: some were the red and blue flags of the NLF: another, a Revolutionary American flag of thirteen stars on a blue field. The police detail of two hundred made no arrests outside. James Peck, however, whose peace cry inside had disturbed the President's speech, was arrested and sentenced to sixty days in jail.

The Second International Days of Protest on March 25–26, a last project of the now moribund NCC, showed that the antiwar movement itself was active and growing, with or without effective leadership. Rallies, parades, and demonstrations took place throughout Europe, in Australia and New Zealand, in Tokyo and Manila. In Rome, where Carl Oglesby of SDS was one of the speakers before a rain-drenched throng, the police had prepared for crowds approaching one hundred thousand to descend on the Piazza del Popolo. Unconnected with the Second International Days of Protest, students in Saigon and Nha Trang, the fourth largest city in South Vietnam, took to the streets against the shaky regime of Premier Ky.

In the United States, where nothing equaled Italy's Communist-dominated organization that brought out the crowds in Rome, the turnouts were much smaller. In many cities the local leaders were disappointed by the numbers. Only seven hundred marched in Boston, where the day before eleven persons were arrested in a demonstration outside an induction center at the Boston Army Base in South Boston. Onlookers tried to attack the eleven, and longshoremen spat on them and offered them gasoline "so you can burn yourself." Two days later an even uglier melee broke out on the steps of the South Boston courthouse as several of the eleven tried to burn their draft cards. A mob of South Boston high school students set upon them and beat them bloody ("Kill them! Shoot them! Commie!") while the police looked on.† In San Francisco thirty-five hundred people marched up Market

† In September 1981 the people of South Boston dedicated the first Vietnam Veterans Memorial in the United States. The names of twenty-five South Boston men were carved into its polished black granite surface—the highest number of men killed in Vietnam from any Massachusetts community.

Street in an orderly procession behind flag-draped cardboard coffins; more had been expected. In Washington a small group of two hundred paraded back and forth in front of the White House. The activity of protest against the war in one form or another was repeated in cities across the country. The protests were, perhaps, no more nuisance to officialdom than the brushfires that plague empty city lots and fields in the warm, quickening breezes of spring. Yet they clearly showed that there was dry tinder scattered throughout the breadth of the country.

What was merely felt potential elsewhere burst into full-blown reality on Fifth Avenue in New York City. On March 26 over twenty thousand—a "cross section of Americans," according to the New York *Herald Tribune*—demonstrated against the war. The march proceeded down Fifth Avenue from Ninety-first to Seventy-second Street. Leading the parade, between the ranks of onlookers six or seven deep that lined the sidewalks, were several hundred veterans of the Korean War and the two world wars. The bystanders were, for the most part, friendly. Those who were not, among them a group of younger men, some with VFW and American Legion insignia, gathered near Eighty-sixth Street to hurl abuse, eggs, and, finally, fists, when the NLF flag appeared among the marchers. At Seventy-second Street the paraders spilled over to the Central Park Mall, where ten thousand of the more hardy stood, squatted, or sat on the cold ground through three hours of speeches.

Every shade in the radical/liberal spectrum was present in the march, or so it seemed on that day of almost pristine innocence for the inchoate movement. Again it was young and old together. Mothers pushing their infants in strollers before them walked with the bearded young. There was a black contingent present, Afro-Americans Against the War in Vietnam. The Greenwich Village Bread and Puppet Theater in huge papier-mâché headdresses marched in representation of imprisoned Vietnamese women. The W. E. B. Du Bois Club, the reputedly militant SDS, and the more moderate Women Strike for Peace, SANE,‡ and 150 other groups marched as one. And there were, as well, ordinary citizens by the thousands, brought to the pitch of protest by individual concern rather than group affiliation. Many took the symbolic step from sidewalk to street this day.

In Central Park, the venerable A. J. Muste gave voice to the enthusiasm, hope, and confidence of the occasion. The parade and the response to it, he said, was "evidence of the power of unity. I hope that all of us . . . will take the lesson of what happens when there is unity among the forces opposed to this war, whatever their differences." Using words chosen from the new American lexicon of war, Muste went on to say that "by escalating our activity and protests we can deescalate the war." Not all agreed, however. Carl Oglesby was already on record about the kinds of activity Muste had in mind: "A wilderness of warmed-over speeches and increasingly irrelevant demonstrations."

In his own person Muste represented what the movement most needed and the quality on which a tenuous unity depended: leadership. It was Muste who had reactivated the Fifth Avenue Peace Parade Committee in January and guided it to

‡ In Chicago, SANE and the AFSC had withdrawn from the Days of Protest activities on the grounds that they had a "Hanoi flavor."

the day's success in March. It was the leadership and experience of Muste—along with another veteran of the pacifist struggle, David Dellinger—that kept the Fifth Avenue Peace Parade Committee from splitting as the NCC had in Milwaukee. In New York that leadership persuaded a reluctant SANE and Women Strike for Peace to march behind an "official" slogan (one of seven approved), BRING THEM HOME NOW, and thus kept the organizers a step ahead of their own restless troops. Patience, persistence, unflagging zeal, a decent constraint were all embodied in the patriarchal figure of Muste. He could cool the ardor of restive police, as he did when Dellinger and others snarled the evening traffic of Times Square in early February. In his presence warring factions within the Movement time and again put aside their antagonisms to take up practical solutions. He was a respecter of person, and all in turn respected him. In 1966 A. J. Muste was eighty-one years old.

In April Muste and five other pacifists quietly departed for Saigon as ordinary tourists without special visas. Muste's companions were Bradford Lyttle, a long-time associate and CNVA activist; Barbara Deming, like Muste an editor of *Liberation* and a lifelong pacifist; Karl Meyer of the Catholic Worker; William Davidon, a professor at Haverford College; and Sherri Thurber of Greenwich, Connecticut. It was Lyttle who had proposed the trip to Muste. South Vietnam, where Premier Ky had recently decreed the death penalty for public advocacy of peace, was again in turmoil. Buddhist uprisings in Hue and Da Nang and sympathetic response among Saigon students were bringing paralysis to the junta and jitters to their United States mentors, among them Secretary McNamara, who was forced finally to admit that the war effort was being hurt by the civil disorders there. The nervous reaction in Saigon had included the summary and public execution of a businessman found guilty of corruption and venality. The U.S. partnership, in turn, as if to distract attention from the mess in the South, had used B-52 bombers for the first time against North Vietnam and turned U.S. jets loose to battle MiG-21s within sight of the Chinese border. To add to McNamara's woes, he had to satisfy congressional indignation over the published account that the Saigon PX had imported 142,000 cans of hair spray. The manager of the post exchange, McNamara reported, had been removed. Premier Ky, however, stayed in place. *His* Saigon PX (Senator Fulbright called Saigon an American brothel) would not be asked for an accounting. Again Ky promised national elections for a constituent assembly.

Muste's departure from South Vietnam, somewhat more turbulent than his arrival, served to focus American attention both on the internal problems of South Vietnam and, at home, on our own Internal Revenue Service and the cost of the war. A band of Vietnamese Roman Catholic students frustrated Muste's efforts to hold a press conference called at the Saigon city hall on April 20. The students pelted the Muste group with eggs and tomatoes. Early the next day as the visitors walked from their hotel toward the American Embassy they were arrested, held incommunicado for six hours, denied their request to seek Embassy aid, and expelled from the country. In the melee at the airport American cameramen had film seized, and one newsman was beaten. The American Embassy managed somehow to execute rather poorly, or not to perform at all, the usual ambassadorial function of safeguarding the interests and persons of Americans abroad.

Then, coincident with the wider coverage of the Muste departure, it was announced in the press that Muste and three hundred others, including the popular folksinger Joan Baez, had publicly proclaimed their refusal to pay federal income tax in protest against the war. For the pacifist Muste, it was the nineteenth consecutive year of such refusal. More vigilant in the performance of duty than the embassy in Saigon, the IRS promised to prosecute.

In the spring of 1966 resistance to the draft took a new turn. Barry Bondhus, a young draft-eligible Minnesotan from the town of Big Lake, broke into his local draft board and mutilated hundreds of 1-A draft records. His action was remarkable for more than the fact that it was the first of the draft board raids that would reach to near-epidemic numbers by 1969. Bondhus defiled, so to speak, the records by pouring over them two large buckets of human feces produced and collected at home by Bondhus, his eleven brothers, and a father adamantly opposed to his sons' participation in the draft. Big Lake One, as the Bondhus action came to be known, was celebrated as "the movement that started the Movement."

President Johnson had reason to be on edge. Even as the B-52s, dispatched on bombing runs personally approved by the President himself, carried their mighty loads of fire to the North, fires in the South had greater impact. In Hue the U.S. cultural center and library was sacked and burned. Fire fighters, like laggard volunteers when the alarm is struck for the barn of a hated villager, took an hour to respond, then watched the fire burn. Again in Hue there was self-inflicted death by fire when a Buddhist nun, Thanh Quang, burned herself to death in a pagoda courtyard, leaving behind a letter to President Johnson begging him to abandon the Ky regime. Four other young women in Hue and Saigon soon followed Thanh Quang's example of self-immolation.

The number of American dead in Vietnam for the first three months of 1966 was put at 1,361, half the number killed in the previous five years. Senator Russell of Georgia demanded that "we go in and win or get out"; and Senator Fulbright would not be quiet. By now lost forever to the Administration, Fulbright made news each time he spoke. In a series of speeches at Johns Hopkins University Fulbright coined the phrase "the arrogance of power" to describe the role of the United States in Vietnam, the same arrogance, he said, that led Athens, almost twenty-five hundred years before, to undertake the disastrous and distant Sicilian expedition when no real menace threatened from that far corner of the Mediterranean world. Johnson was sufficiently sensitive, if perhaps not quite historian enough, to infer that he was the unmentioned Alcibiades in this implicit Fulbright parable. Vice President Humphrey, Rusk, and McNamara were kept busy refuting either directly or indirectly the frequent Fulbright charges that the United States had no business being in Vietnam. Finally, the President himself entered the public debate.

With the usual last-minute flurry and with secrecy up to the moment of departure from the White House, the President appeared at a Princeton University ceremony for the dedication of the new Woodrow Wilson School of Public and International Affairs, where John W. Gardner of Johnson's Cabinet had been scheduled to give the principal address. The President faced a sedate and togaed audience of academics. The "exercise of power," he said, ". . . has meant for all of us in the United States not arrogance but agony," and he urged that the task of the "responsible intellectual" was "in the language of the current generation 'to cool it,' to bring . . . 'not heat but light' to public affairs." The small reflecting lagoon between the speaker and his audience seemed to put him oceans away. No applause interrupted his twenty-eight-minute address.

Six days later, on May 17, Johnson took a more strident tone. "There will be some Nervous Nellies," he told a Cook County Democratic dinner group in Chicago, "and some . . . who turn on their own leaders, their own country, and their own fighting men." It was name-calling without names. A prescience not unfamiliar to politicians, whether based on instinct or inside tip, led Senator Fulbright to decline in advance the Nervous Nelly Award and its threefold categorical charge of deserting country, soldiers, and leader. Speaking from Washington earlier the same day, Fulbright denied that the "arrogance of power" phrase—which nevertheless remained as title for the later published version of his Hopkins talks—was aimed at "any American official." Nor did he intend to denigrate or malign either the nation or "the brave young Americans in Vietnam" by his other public remarks.

Lost among the "Nervous Nellies" headlines was a prophetic warning from the President, one that would be borne out only years after his own death: ". . . if we fail in frustrating this aggression [in Vietnam], the war that would surely come in Asia would produce casualties not in the seventeen hundreds [1,705 Americans had died in Vietnam in the first four months of 1966] but in the hundreds of thousands and perhaps millions."

Johnson's Chicago speech was meant to be the kickoff for the 1966 congressional campaign: "I ask you to read carefully the statements of . . . every candidate for every office, then judge for yourselves. . . . Is he trying to draw us together and unite our land, or is he trying to pull us apart to promote himself?" The President was to become obsessed with the notion that the elections would be a referendum on the war and his conduct of it. Once again the Administration evoked antiphonal response in the Movement. On the day before President Johnson spoke to the Democrats in Chicago, SANE, Women Strike for Peace, and other moderate elements in the peace movement gathered, eight thousand strong, in Washington to march and announce that they had seventy-three thousand "voter pledges" to support congressional candidates who "agree to work vigorously . . . to scale down the fighting and achieve a cease fire; for United States initiatives to encourage negotiations with all concerned parties, including the Viet Cong. . . ."

The pledge was too mild a broth by far to tempt many in the Movement. They saw the moderates as seduced by the system and the system itself as morally and intellectually corrupt, nurturing a power structure beholden only to its own berserk bent toward ruination at home and abroad. The *National Guardian* correctly advised that "neither . . . many of the pacifist radical left nor independent antiwar committees actively support the [electoral] drive." The rift between moderates and radicals, heretofore bridged by common concerns, began to take on geological proportions in 1966.

Nevertheless, it was frenzied radical participation in the system that brought the peace movement close to one startling success in the electoral process. In California's Seventh Congressional District, which took in Berkeley and part of Oakland, Robert Scheer, an editor of the crusading lay Catholic publication *Ramparts* magazine, opposed Jeffrey Cohelan in the Democratic primary in June. Cohelan was a four-term, run-of-the-mill "liberal" supporter of LBJ, both of his Great Society and his war. Scheer's credentials, on the other hand, would suggest to the ordinary voter that he was a bona fide radical, despite the fact that his very willingness to participate in the process would disqualify him in the eyes of Trotskyites and others, such as Staughton Lynd, in the antiwar movement. Scheer's attack on Cardinal Spellman in his pamphlet *How the United States Got Involved in Vietnam* was well known. And two months before the primary, *Ramparts* published its devastating exposé of the CIA role in the federally funded Michigan State University program in South Vietnam in the 1950s. To take on two such pillars of conservative belief, Spellman and the CIA, and to campaign bluntly against the war ("The United States should never have gone into Vietnam, should not have stayed there and should now get out") was sufficient to establish a radical position in the eyes of the mid-1960s voter. To take on the exotic and zany Jerry Rubin as campaign manager and Rubin's friends from the Vietnam Day Committee as key supporters may have been a last straw for some voters.

Rubin in fact did not last long as campaign manager. Neither his language (he called Cohelan a "liberal fink") nor his strategy (he suggested a "Marx-Jefferson Day" fund-raising dinner) proved finely attuned to the customary rules of primary politicking. Rubin did bring in student workers by the hundreds, dedicated door-to-door campaigners, predecessors of the "snow children" of 1968 who trudged the chilly streets of New Hampshire for Eugene McCarthy. Scheer himself came to have doubts about his radical support: "Professional non-students," he is quoted as calling them, "who are either drugged on LSD or on Marxist theory."

One watchful politician, however, saw enough to be concerned about California's Seventh Congressional District. President Johnson sent in his big guns to assist. The Postmaster General, Larry O'Brien, was dispatched to advise the Cohelan campaign, which did not lack for funds or outside endorsements, including those of Senator Fulbright and Senator Robert Kennedy. Simon Casady, whose California Democratic Council had endorsed Scheer, was dumped as leader of that group through the efforts of Governor Edmund "Pat" Brown, a loyal Democrat.

Scheer lost the primary, but only narrowly; he won 45 percent of the vote. The message was there, but President Johnson pretended not to receive it: "Even those antiwar people in California couldn't win. I don't think any President in any wartime situation has generally had as clear sailing as I have had."

Some who were not the President's friends took a similar reading. Scheer himself abandoned the electoral route and refused to take on the independent campaign for the November elections that some of his supporters urged. The ineffable Jerry Rubin subsided into the psychedelic street culture for months, emerging only periodically, as when he appeared in 1776 Revolutionary costume before a HUAC hearing in August. For most of the students in the Scheer campaign this first endeavor was also the last. Simon Casady, on the other hand, took his lickings and joined the National Conference for New Politics, which announced in early June a "Committee on 1968" to seek an opponent for Johnson.

By November the two dozen or more single-issue peace candidates who had surfaced in answer to the SANE electoral drive were, like Scheer, gone from the scene. They had been washed away in the detergent tide of off-year American primary politics, where national issues are bleached away by personalities and local concerns. Furthermore, the practiced politicians, unable to read the voters' minds, avoided wherever possible the question of Vietnam, leaving the citizen in the polling booth with no more than his or her own undifferentiated feelings of political malaise as guide: vague concerns about the war; real concerns about an economy faltering under the burdens of war. This alone sufficed to produce a stunning rebuff to the Johnson Administration. The Democratic Party suffered a net loss of forty-seven seats in the House of Representatives—exactly the number gained in the 1964 landslide—and a loss of three Senate seats and eight governorships. The impact of the election on foreign affairs was nil. If anything, more rather than fewer potential hawks were sent to Washington.

There were, however, signs of something more than generalized discontent, and at least one politician was there to read them. In Illinois, for instance, Democratic Senator Paul Douglas's firm stand behind Johnson and the war cost him the needed support of liberals and he lost his seat to Republican Charles Percy. In Oregon, a Republican, Mark Hatfield, made his opposition to the war a major issue; with the help of Oregon's maverick Democrat, Senator Wayne Morse, Hatfield won election to the Senate. And in the Michigan city of Dearborn 40 percent of the voters, 14,124, voted yes on a referendum question, "Are you in favor of an immediate cease-fire and withdrawal of U.S. troops from Vietnam so the Vietnamese people can settle their own affairs?" Richard Nixon, whose voice for years had supplied an off-stage obbligato of support for a hard line in Vietnam and who emerged in 1966 as a constant platform presence in Republican contests, declared, when the results were in, that if the war continued into 1968, "No power on earth [can keep the Republican party] from trying to outbid the Democrats for the peace vote."

In June of 1966 the antiwar movement in the United States was a flotilla of tiny craft becalmed in a sea of uncertainty. The motley fleet included literally hundreds of organizations, local and national, that had shaped themselves to oppose the nation's policies in Vietnam. A minority in their midst saw Vietnam as but symbol of total societal decay. Occasionally an antic breeze, stirred by egregious Washington pronouncement, ruffled sails and gave the appearance of motion, if not direction, to one part or another of this curious, drifting assemblage.

One such flutter had occurred in May when the Selective Service System held qualification tests, first announced in February, for high school seniors, college undergraduates, and graduate students. The test grades, along with class standing, were to be used in determining future student deferments if monthly draft calls, then standing at twenty-five thousand, exceeded thirty thousand per month. Reaction was predictable and loud. Harlem's Representative Adam Clayton Powell, Jr., saw the move as a racist ploy to send blacks to the "slaughterhouse" of Vietnam.

Four hundred students at the University of Chicago took and held the administration building for three days. At City College in New York City, demonstrators neither clean nor quiet sat-in outside the office of President Buell Gallagher. On May 14, 768,000 male college students took the Selective Service Examination. Five hundred thousand of them also received copies (at the door) of the SDS "counter-draft" exam, twenty-five Q & A ("How many South Vietnamese deserted [the Army] in 1965?"), which, it was hoped, would at least stimulate some thinking about, if not opposition to, the U.S. presence in Vietnam. The Selective Service System quickly abandoned its testing program, but opposition to the draft continued to grow. A few weeks later Carl Oglesby of SDS and Stokely Carmichael of SNCC issued a joint call for the end of the draft, and by August SNCC was demonstrating in front of the Atlanta Selective Service Office chanting, "Hell, no, we won't go!" Six of those arrested received prison terms of three and a half years.

In June there came two almost simultaneous decisions at opposite ends of the U.S. military command structure that would give impetus, if not shape, to the flagging antiwar movement. The Commander in Chief, Johnson, decided to bomb petroleum, oil, and lubricant (POL) storage depots in the densely populated Haiphong-Hanoi area. At the same time three privates in his Army stationed at Fort Hood, Texas, decided they would refuse to serve in Vietnam. The decision to bomb the depots would, in its enormity, shock the world at large and enrage American opponents of the war. On June 30, the day that Washington announced the first of the POL bombing strikes (executed, it was emphasized, with "surgical precision"), the Fifth Avenue Peace Parade Committee introduced the Fort Hood 3 at a press conference where they made public their refusal. Although immediate coverage of this latter event was scant, the three soldiers and their supportive families became the focal point for protests against the war that summer.

The two decisions, disparate as they were and distant one from the other in the command scale, nevertheless had much in common. Both were highly personal and highly emotional; each depended in its own way upon agonizing appraisal of what the United States was doing in Vietnam. On June 29, the night the first bombing run took off, a worried LBJ told his daughter, Luci, "Your daddy may go down in history as having started World War III." For two years the Joint Chiefs of Staff had wanted to attack the storage depots, but risk of enlarging the war—i.e., bringing in the Chinese—had deflected this proposal. Finally, in a memorandum to the President delivered on March 28, Secretary McNamara fell in line with the desires of the Joint Chiefs. It was, according to the authors of the Pentagon Papers, the last major escalation of the air war recommended by McNamara. But the authors express some doubt: ". . . despite the comparatively vigorous language of the memoranda, one cannot be sure that McNamara expected or wanted the President to approve his recommendation." Prime Minister Wilson was horrified when he learned of the impending decision and its threat to civilian life in North Vietnam. He dissociated Great Britain from the action and wrote to the President in the strongest diplomatic language possible:

> I am bound to say that . . . the possible military benefits . . . do not appear to outweigh the political disadvantages that would seem the inevitable consequence. If you and the South Vietnamese Government were conducting a declared war on the conventional pattern . . . this operation would clearly be necessary and right. . . . I remain convinced that the bombing of these targets . . . may only increase the difficulty of reaching an eventual settlement. . . . I know that the effect on public opinion in this country . . . is likely to be such as to reinforce the existing disquiet and criticism that we have to deal with.

LBJ chose to ignore this plea. Instead, he followed the advice of his self-confident and highly pragmatic assistants, who, so far as the Pentagon Papers reveal, showed little concern for the issues Wilson raised of public reaction at home, abroad, or for that matter in North Vietnam, where the raids had the not unpredictable consequence of stiffening national morale and determination.

The Fort Hood 3, ordinary soldiers though they were, worlds removed from the elite professional ambience of the Bundys, the Rusks, the McNamaras, and other advisers to the President, did confront these larger questions. Among the issues the Fort Hood 3 addressed was one identified in his memoirs by William O. Douglas of the Supreme Court as the single "most important issue of the sixties to reach the Court," the constitutionality of the war.

Private Dennis Mora, one of the three and a Puerto Rican—the other two were Private First Class James Johnson, a black, and Private David Samas, of Italian and Lithuanian background—read their statement before television cameras on June 30. It said in part:

> We have decided to take a stand against this war, which we consider immoral, illegal, and unjust. We are initiating today . . . an action in the courts to enjoin the Secretary of Defense and the Secretary of the Army from sending us to Vietnam. . . .
>
> No one uses the word "winning" anymore because in Vietnam it has no meaning. . . . We have been told that many times we may face a Vietnamese woman or child and that we will have to kill them. We will never go there—to do that—for Ky!
>
> We have made our decision. We will not be a part of this unjust, immoral, and illegal war. We want no part of a war of extermination. We oppose this criminal waste of American lives and resources. We refuse to go to Vietnam!

A week later the Fort Hood 3, still technically on leave, were picked up by federal agents and brought to the Fort Dix stockade. Their injunction request was denied, and although carried by appeal to the Supreme Court *(Mora v. McNamara)*, Douglas could not muster the votes needed for the case to be heard. To call the treatment of this and other such cases "political" and hence "non justiciable," said Douglas, was "an abdication of duty and a self-inflicted wound on the Court." A court-martial convicted the Fort Hood 3 and they spent two years in prison. The original sentence of the one black in the group, Private First Class Johnson, twenty years old, was especially harsh: five years at hard labor.

The results of the two decisions were disappointing to partisans on either side. Some in the antiwar movement, including David Dellinger, who invoked the "spirit of Nuremberg" in reviewing the actions of the Fort Hood 3, expected that these three men would prove to be forerunners of large-scale disaffection, not to say defection, in the military and that Americans, like the soldiers of Alexander the Great in the distant Punjab of India, would refuse to follow further. This, in 1966, was not to be. Several years and many lives later, however, enlisted men in Vietnam began not only to mutiny but also to murder their officers. Nevertheless, the publicity accorded the Fort Hood 3—thanks to the diligence of leaders in the Fifth Avenue Peace Parade Committee—caused the government to act as if it shared this expectation.

In the Administration, hopes for turning the war around with bombs were equally dashed, at least for insiders in the military and the government. As usual, the American people would be the last to know. The deception with regard to the POL strikes began when Under Secretary of State George W. Ball declared on "Meet the Press" three days before the first attack, "There is no decision on the part of the United States Government to bomb Haiphong or to bomb the fuel installations in Haiphong-Hanoi." The deception continued after the fact in a burst of overly optimistic reports, which led one sardonic Washington observer to comment that the United States seemed to have destroyed 320 percent of Hanoi's oil storage capacity. Inside the Pentagon, however, the facts were known within a month. As the Pentagon Papers put it, there was an "undiminished flow of men and supplies down the Ho Chi Minh trail . . . no significant economic dislocation and no weakening of popular morale." It was months before McNamara began guardedly to report, first privately and then publicly, that bombing had not stemmed the flow of arms southward. He did not report that a team of distinguished outside experts, four scientists from Harvard and MIT who had led in the field of advanced technical weapons systems since World War II, had advised him in a document kept secret even within the upper reaches of the government that ROLLING THUNDER, in its entirety, was of "marginal value." In 1966 over $1 billion was spent on the operational costs of ROLLING THUNDER—$9.60 spent for every $1.00 of damage inflicted. Ho Chi Minh had no difficulty in recouping the losses in materiel by turning to Russia and China. As to physical damage, what one correspondent noted of the Viet Cong was also true in the North: a shovel in the hands of a Vietnamese was an effective countertool to vast American firepower. Pentagon accounting also showed that in 1966 seventeen thousand civilians were killed by bombs.

The fact that an ignorant and deceived American public reacted as always after an LBJ escalation by showing approval in the polls did not deter A. J. Muste. Muste worked at a relentless and even pace to broaden the antiwar movement and give it a firm organizational base. He, Dellinger, and Norma Becker kept the Fifth Avenue Peace Parade Committee alive through the first half of 1966 as one of the few viable groups with a capacity both for quick, effective reaction to the kaleidoscopic shifts on the Washington/Vietnam front and for long-term planning. It was not by accident that the Fort Hood 3 were directed to Muste's group. What was unexpected was the presence of Stokely Carmichael, militant black leader of SNCC, at their television press conference at which they announced their decision. Carmichael had just broken with Martin Luther King, Jr., on the issues of violence/nonviolence, slogans (King shunned Carmichael's "Black Power!"), and cooperation with whites. Yet A. J. Muste was the white man's King, if ever there was a parallel among whites to King in the movement of the early sixties for social justice. By this time Muste was convinced that the antiwar movement should be nonexclusionary. As usual some people did not agree. During 1966 some old-time pacifists pulled away from the nascent antiwar movement because they felt that blacks were being given too much prominence. Carmichael probably frightened them. Moreover, they said, being linked to the civil rights movement would hurt the infant antiwar movement: the American people might accept peace in Vietnam but they would never accept racial equality. Similarly, many black leaders shunned the antiwar movement. What one commentator called the "fateful merging of antiwar and racial dissension" never happened.

Muste also wanted to include labor unions in the antiwar movement. He tried hard to persuade Sidney Lens, a longtime labor organizer and, with his wife Shirley, an early, diligent opponent of the war, to come from his base in Chicago to New York City. Lens was sorely tempted, so great was his admiration for Muste, but chose to stay where he had put down his roots thirty years before and where, in 1965, he had founded the Chicago Peace Council. Whether Muste sought the skills of Lens as an organizer and conciliator or for his ties to labor, the fact remains that the involvement of labor in the antiwar movement was sporadic at best until the Movement split in 1970 on the question of becoming a multiissue force in American society.

Even as Muste was turned down by Lens, however, he met someone who would be even more crucial to the survival and growth of the infant movement that he had nurtured from its beginning. That summer Muste received an invitation to attend a conference sponsored by the Cleveland Area Peace Action Council (CAPAC). The purpose of the conference was to plan a national antiwar mobilization for the fall.

One of the founding members of CAPAC was Professor Sidney Peck (no relation to James), then at Case Western Reserve University in Cleveland, Ohio, and later on the faculty of Clark University in Worcester, Massachusetts. Peck is in his late fifties, stocky and powerfully built, with dark hair and cool, observant eyes and a deceptively quiet manner. He has almost total recall of the events in which he took part during the Vietnam era, and as he speaks the listener discerns, beneath his calm, almost gentle exterior, an iron determination. Sidney Peck is, without doubt, a very serious man.

He was the sixth and youngest child of a poor immigrant family which moved from Annapolis, Maryland, to St. Paul, Minnesota, during the Great Depression. They lived in a neighborhood of Jews and Irish Catholics on the edge of a sizable black community, ensuring that the schools that Peck attended enjoyed *de facto* integration. Peck's early ambition, built on considerable athletic abilities, was to be a football coach. He went to the University of Minnesota on the GI Bill after World War II and soon abandoned football and boxing for new interests in social work, community organizing, and politics. He met his wife while organizing Students for (Henry) Wallace in 1948. Louise Peck, who became an activist in her own right, trained as a psychotherapist and works at that profession today. Peck himself eventually entered upon an academic career as a sociologist. Their consistent desire for an urban setting, combined with left-wing politics that caused uneasiness in college administrators, made for a more than normally peripatetic career. When they went to Case Western Reserve in 1964, Peck resolved to devote himself single-mindedly to the academic life: teaching, research, writing, and service to his department.

And then one night in March 1965 he received a telephone call from a colleague who had word of the planned teach-in at Michigan and wanted Peck to join him in forming a committee to do the same on their campus. "It was a Saturday night and we were in the kitchen. I asked Louise, 'What do you think?' She looked at me . . . 'You know what you're going to do.' It was not like a rational decision and you weigh advantages and disadvantages. . . . So I said, OK, and I went to the meeting."

Thus the University Circle Teach-In Committee was born, a group that soon had as its most prominent member "America's Baby Doctor," Benjamin Spock, M.D. "Of all the people who influenced me [says Spock], Sid Peck influenced me the most. He taught me how to organize, how to raise money, how you have to have courage. He would commit the group to spend money and then we would go out and raise it. This gave you a lot more conviction when you went to ask for money. . . ."

The committee's first teach-in, shortly after the similar event at Michigan, was a success. Nearly three thousand students and faculty attended the night-long affair and eight hundred were still present for an evaluation session at 7 A.M. the next morning. Peck and his group soon came to a decision that had far-reaching implications for the antiwar movement in the United States. The teach-ins led to a national debate aired from Washington in which Hans Morgenthau and other equally prominent professors took on spokespersons from the Administration. That debate, says Peck, "turned us off and made it clear our movement was not going to go anywhere unless we got off the campuses. So we decided to build a movement in Cleveland"—the Cleveland Area Peace Action Council. Its first action was an all-night vigil in October 1965 at the Soldiers and Sailors Monument in downtown Cleveland.

The activists in Cleveland were dissatisfied and concerned about the state of affairs in the antiwar movement. At a time when they perceived a growing opposition to the war, they saw the Movement as "fragmented and fractionated" over tactics, style, demands (on the government), and demeanor. Peck and others in the Cleveland area met for a weekend retreat in May 1966 to discuss the problem. Peck formulated the position that the Movement needed to bring together a single powerful demonstration. The idea came to invite other peace and civil rights groups to Cleveland to discuss the proposition.

The invitation suggested to Muste a new source of energy for the nascent movement: academia. Although his office was astir with planning for local demonstrations nationwide around the annual August remembrance of Hiroshima, A.J. traveled to Cleveland to meet with representatives of thirteen other organizations.* This first Cleveland Conference (there were three in all), like the Movement at large in those summer months, was tenuous and groping; Muste's presence undoubtedly served to save the struggling project from collapsing upon itself.

Little was accomplished at the first conference (July 22) beyond an agreement to adopt Muste's nonexclusionary policy (an indication that the professorial groups were ready to move from words to actions) and an agreement to meet again. Muste added his weight to the call that went out for the second meeting which convened, after one postponement, in September.

A few weeks before the next conference, giving evidence that the spirit of protest was alive in the United States, thousands marched or engaged in other symbolic acts of concern throughout the country on August 6, the twenty-first anniversary of the Hiroshima bombing. As usual, New York City provided the biggest turnout, a crowd large enough (from five to twenty thousand) to prolong the demonstration through many streets and most of a long, hot summer's afternoon, as marchers converged on Times Square from as far away as Greenwich Village and Harlem. On the way, some groups paused to picket at 45 Rockefeller Plaza before the offices of The Dow Chemical Company, manufacturers of napalm. One speaker at the rally, Lincoln Lynch of the CORE national office, declared, "We have become a nation where to work for peace is a traitorous act, where an expression of humanity is considered treason." Some of the onlookers gave substance to this complaint by shouting, "Burn the Reds!" and "Follow the Judas Goat!" at the marchers. Also on the platform were family members of the Fort Hood 3 and a young Marine lance corporal, John M. Martin, who told the crowd, "I will not serve even one more day as a Marine—in conscience I cannot."

A relatively small protest demonstration on the same day in Washington claimed national media mention. An uncharacteristic lapse on the part of the politically canny White House had allowed the wedding of the President's daughter, Luci, to coincide with the Hiroshima date. Protesters appeared before the Shrine of the Immaculate Conception, where the ceremony took place, carrying two small coffins draped with the flags of Japan and North Vietnam. Another group of protesters stood across Pennsylvania Avenue from the White House as the huge wedding reception wound on. The ominous chant of "Hey, hey, LBJ, how many kids did you kill today?" did not penetrate the gaiety of the seven hundred guests on the South Lawn, but Lyndon Johnson was well known for his compulsive tracking of

* Muste represented two: Fifth Avenue Peace Parade Committee and the Committee for Nonviolent Action. Others were: Inter-University Committee for Debate on Foreign Policy (of which University Circle Teach-In Committee was an affiliate), AFSC, NCC, SANE, SDS, SNCC, CORE, National Emergency Committee of Clergy Concerned About Vietnam, MassPax, WSP, University Committee on the Problems of War and Peace, Fellowship of Reconciliation, and Women's International League for Peace and Freedom. A motion from the floor added two more representatives, from YSA and from the W. E. B. Du Bois Club.

press and television coverage of the White House; undoubtedly he was aware of the demonstration.†

The ugly shouts that marred the wedding festivities were still echoing in the retentive mind of LBJ when later in 1966 Hiroshima again impinged on White House discussions. With the POL attacks now demonstrably a failure, the military response was to press for escalation. The military chiefs were urging what amounted to a bombing-into-dust of Hanoi/Haiphong. Three quarters of a million lives had been spared, they said, by using the atomic bomb against Japan. By implication, a fierce and unrestrained conventional bombing campaign against the North Vietnamese capital area would do the same. The young computer experts who had derived these remarkable figures were led before Johnson to explain. Johnson heard them out with apparent interest, only to interject finally, "I have one more problem for your computer—how long will it take five hundred thousand angry Americans to climb that White House wall out there and lynch their President if he does something like that?"

The presidential outburst was understandable. Nothing had gone well of late. Fulbright was at it again, this time resurrecting the follies of the Tonkin Gulf Resolution and the SEATO Pact in new hearings before the Senate Foreign Relations Committee in August. Fulbright and members of the committee insisted that Rusk and Johnson had far exceeded the legislative intent, whatever the wording of these two documents. And de Gaulle was, again, gratuitously pontificating on a Vietnam solution. The two leaders of the West communicated through international headlines: Johnson's response to de Gaulle was addressed "to all whom it may concern." The press, in the meantime, was making household words of the phrase "credibility gap," coined by Murray Marder of the Washington *Post*. Almost daily, discrepancies were revealed in the press around Pentagon estimates of Viet Cong killed, infiltration numbers, and projections ("indefinite," "only eight years") of how long the North Vietnamese could continue to resupply. When the Administration looked outside its own ranks for supporters of stature to participate in the annual patriotic rituals of the veterans' conventions, the best it could do was Cardinal Spellman. A stalwart like Rusk, the shepherd of New York City Catholics was also "in for a dime, in for a dollar." The cardinal continued throughout the year to play the role of Peter the Hermit in the Johnson/Rusk crusade; he declared the war to be "a war for civilization" as he asked, on a Christmas visit to South Vietnam, for total victory. But there were a few strays in the cardinal's flock. The Roman Catholic weekly *The Commonweal* at the same time called the war "a crime and a sin."

Worst of all that autumn for Johnson, who loved the hurly-burly of the campaign trail, congressional candidates of his own party were chary of his overt support. Polls showed that the war in Vietnam was the voters' primary concern, but how that concern would be expressed was a mystery. At any rate, the members of Congress had a taste in late August of what Vietnam could mean when injected

† The next White House wedding, in the Nixon Administration, would be similarly star-crossed and share front-page coverage with the publication of the Pentagon Papers.

into a political scene less controlled than the stately Fulbright hearings. An abortive set of hearings by the House Un-American Activities Committee (HUAC) was turned into theater of the absurd by the antics of the witnesses summoned and their legislative interrogators. The law in question was to make it a federal crime with a fine of twenty thousand dollars *and* twenty years in prison to give material assistance to any "hostile opposition" to the United States. Jerry Rubin arrived, hoping to testify, in the costume of a Revolutionary War soldier. Shouting, hissing, cheering, and jeering greeted every word spoken. At one point Chairman Joe Pool (D-Texas) ("Keep Cool with Pool" was his campaign slogan) ordered the diminutive radical-Left lawyer Arthur Kinoy ejected. As one beefy federal marshal put a stranglehold on Kinoy and a second lifted him by the seat of his pants, another attorney shouted, "Let the record show that Mr. Kinoy is five feet, two inches tall!"

And so, for fear that his presence would cause similar disturbances—or worse—the old campaigner was left to pace the Oval Office in restless constraint. He was as effectively quarantined as if the White House door were placarded, as by local health authorities in the days of his youth, to announce to all in scarlet letters a communicable disease within: VD. In truth, Vietnam Disease had touched the whole body politic, not just the White House.

Denied his homeland, Johnson went abroad. The Manila Conference with the United States' Asian allies was almost as hastily contrived as the Honolulu Conference earlier in the year. The conference convened on October 24. Present were the heads of state of South Vietnam, the United States, and the four governments giving support to Saigon: Australia, New Zealand, Thailand, and South Korea.

Desperate for headlines back home, the presidential entourage produced a promise to withdraw troops from Vietnam within six months, once North Vietnam abandoned its "aggression." No mention was made of the bombing. The President continued on to Vietnam, where he told American officers at Camranh Bay, ". . . may the Good Lord look over you and keep you until you come home with the coonskin on the wall"—hardly a negotiating posture. Before mingling with ecstatic crowds in Manila and homesick troops in Vietnam, Johnson toured in New Zealand and Australia. His visits were marred by embarrassing protests, notably in Sydney, where demonstrators hurled paint-filled bags at his limousine.

The second Cleveland Conference convened on September 10 under A. J. Muste's chairmanship. The National Leadership Conference, as it was called, inched forward in answer to Sidney Peck's call for "the development of a united effort" based on Muste's policy of nonexclusion, embracing all (as Peck put it) "who are in any way, for whatever reasons, opposed to this war." Perhaps it was this policy that kept SANE away from the meeting, as well as SDS, which was increasingly fostering (on the national level) a program without focus on the war. As it was, "nonexclusion" meant few conclusions. The delegates could agree on little in the way of particulars beyond yet one more call for a spate of local actions around the November election under the banner of "noncompliance with the war." (Apparently there was not a single phrasemaker among the 140 delegates present.) The representatives in attendance yielded turf begrudgingly. An *ad hoc* executive structure, once again under Muste's leadership, was adopted. Its writ was to run only through the summons of yet another, postelection, conference. Only Muste, in the view of SWP's Fred Halstead, could have accomplished even this much. Indeed, the absence of both SANE and SDS meant the loss of the two organizations with potential to reach large numbers of citizens unaffiliated with the sectarian Left; but Muste was never one to be daunted by lack of numbers in support of his often almost solitary struggle for peace. And the undercurrent of tension at the conference between SWP and CP was old hat to him; he knew how to knock those heads together.

It was at the September Cleveland conference that Sidney Peck made his proposal for a major mass mobilization on a scale beyond any action ever previously mounted by the peace movement. He describes what he envisioned:

> The proposal was not written down; I just spoke it out. Basically, there's artistry to it. It's important that you have a picture in your head. You have to see the event, you have to have a prevision. Here it's September of 1966 and in my mind I saw the event taking place. I saw it happening. I imagine it's the way an artist deals with a canvas, [he] sees it up there before. . . . So I saw it happening.
>
> Then, when the event takes place and there are pictures of it, it's what you saw. So there is the actual material realization of the event that you're building. You are putting the strokes on the canvas, and little by little the reality of the vision begins to emerge. The exciting thing is when you begin moving on to this. . . .

Sidney Peck's vision took on the shape and substance of reality the following year, 1967, in New York City's Central Park.

The local election protest activities called by the Cleveland Conference for November 5–8 took place with little impact. The combination of deliberately desultory, low-key planning by the coordinating group and generally bad weather in the eastern half of the country left much to depend upon the strength of local units. In Cleveland, despite the rain, more than one thousand marched behind Dr. Benjamin Spock, Sidney Peck, and Darwin Johnson, brother of one of the Fort Hood 3. The New York City march and rally, organized, as usual, by the Fifth Avenue Peace Parade Committee, drew ten to twenty thousand. The New York *Times* account was buried on page 42 and chose to highlight the reactions of fear and distaste on the part of onlookers, and the acting-out of the poet Allen Ginsberg, who wore what he called "white Gandhi pyjamas" as he chanted a Hari Krishna mantra to his own accompaniment.

A very small protest in Cambridge, Massachusetts, however, did receive national attention. There, on the campus of Harvard University the day before the elections, a group of students organized by SDS confronted the Secretary of Defense, Robert S. McNamara. McNamara had come to Harvard as the first "honorary associate" of the John F. Kennedy School of Government. The SDS assembly was no surprise. Michael Ansara, a senior and leader of the Harvard SDS chapter, had earlier sought official permission to demonstrate that day in the courtyard of Quincy

House, where McNamara was to meet with an invitation-only group of fifty students in the common room. Permission was denied. As McNamara tried to slip away alone with his driver to another appointment, however, his car was surrounded by the SDSers in a nearby street and forced to halt by students sitting in the roadway before and behind.

The scene had its ludicrous, mock-heroic touches. The Secretary of Defense, in command of the most awesome armament ever assembled, had been tracked down by a boy on a bike. "I was the 'hunter,'" says Jared Israel, a quondam Harvard student who later led the Harvard delegation to the final SDS convention in 1969. "I was on a bike and my job was—when we found McNamara—I yelled, 'Maac-Naa . . . m . . . a . . . a . . . ra!' He came out a side entrance. They tried to sneak him out through the steam tunnels. He was *mad.* He was like a cornered bull."

Emerging from the car, his face (according to the *Harvard Crimson)* "tightened and grim," the Secretary of Defense of the United States was hoisted onto the hood of a parked convertible and handed a bullhorn. He agreed to give the crowd five minutes and shouted into the bullhorn, "I spent four . . . years at the Berkeley campus doing some of the same things you're doing here. But there was one important difference. I was tougher and more courteous. . . . I was tougher then and I'm tougher now."

McNamara answered only two questions from the unruly crowd, which included as many supporters as opponents, before a flying wedge of police came to his rescue and spirited him away through Harvard's labyrinthine underground tunnels. The second of the two questions was how many civilians had been killed in Vietnam and why was this not reported. The secretary's answer was "We don't know."

Jared Israel, the boy on the bike, was not quite as unsophisticated as the story suggests. A graduate of New York's High School of Music and Art, Israel grew up in Brooklyn, where as a youngster he indulged a kind of "Robin Hood fantasy" of confronting the oppression he saw about him in the streets of the city. After a year at Harvard, he dropped out and worked peddling a radical periodical, M. S. Arnoni's *Minority of One,* at left-wing gatherings. This brought him in touch with a splinter Communist group, the Progressive Labor Movement (PLM). Soon he was an organizer for PLM, first at Columbia University, and then back at Harvard. By the time of the McNamara protest PLM had become the Progressive Labor Party (PL), had disbanded its youth wing, M2M, and had set deliberately about the task of becoming a major, if not the major, force in SDS. The vehicle for doing this was the Worker Student Alliance, a caucus within SDS chapters at many campuses and, eventually, particularly strong at Harvard. "We were sane Communists," says Israel, "and they [the Ansara group of SDS] were sane social democrats, and sane people can always work together." It was a judgment SDS would come to doubt.

The incident had a lasting effect on the Secretary of Defense. Never again, except for congressional testimony, did he offer himself for public questioning on the subject of Vietnam and the involvement of the United States there. In October 1979, thirteen years after the Harvard episode, McNamara appeared at a high school assembly in Belmont, Massachusetts, a town not far from Cambridge. He was there to talk to students about the Kennedy years in connection with the dedication of the John F. Kennedy Library in nearby Dorchester. Companions from the Kennedy era were also speaking that day in other high schools around Boston. McNamara had agreed to an interview with the editors of the student newspaper, but the teenage journalists were told beforehand—much to their indignation—that he would accept no questions on Vietnam.

The Harvard occurrence was, in genteel microcosm, a foreshadowing of what was soon to come. Protest would jostle propriety. Indeed, one Harvardian has declared that the master of Quincy House denied the original request for fear that the tulip-tromping SDS would harm the courtyard flower beds (in November!). Twenty-seven hundred undergraduates signed a letter to McNamara apologizing for the "unruly behavior." A *Crimson* editorial—on the day the lead story announced a change in parietal rules to allow gentlemen to entertain ladies in their dormitory rooms until midnight on Fridays—found the reception accorded McNamara "distasteful." There was no editorial comment on the unanswered question about civilian deaths or on the banners hung to welcome the secretary: KILL FOR PEACE; KILL THE CONG; NAPALM SDS.

On his Cambridge visit McNamara also met privately with Harvard faculty members at the Kennedy School. There, in a more polite context, the other of the two questions bellowed out in the street by angry students arose again. The students had demanded to know if Vietnam was not a civil war with its beginnings as far back as 1958 or 1957. The secretary's response had been cut off by a cascade of shouted epithets. Now the professors gently suggested that these and other questions should be addressed, perhaps by a study along the lines set by Professor Richard E. Neustadt, who had reviewed in detail for President Kennedy the mismanaged Skybolt missile crisis of 1961–62. The implication was clear. Mistakes of judgment, tactics, and strategy had surely been made with respect to Vietnam. A full and true record of U.S. involvement would expose past errors for the enlightenment of future leaders.

It is known that by this time McNamara had his own doubts, misgivings, and questions. In January 1966 he told friends he did not regard a military solution as possible. In July, on the heels of the POL attacks, he set his aide, General Robert Pursley, to seeking intelligence documentation to justify the raids. And in October in the course of a dismal assessment for the President and against the judgment of the Joint Chiefs of Staff, who were always eager for new targets, McNamara suggested "considering the possibility of cessation of bombing" to "split the Viet Cong off from Hanoi." Whatever the reason (some suggest that his son's defection to the antiwar movement played a part), McNamara was slipping from the Johnson fold. The seed of doubt, whether planted by angry students or deferential faculty, would bear fruit a few years later in the massive documentation of the history of the war ordered by McNamara that became known as the Pentagon Papers.

The third and last Cleveland Conference took place on November 26. At last there were concrete results. Sidney Peck's visionary plan for a huge national mobilization to take place in the two metropolitan centers of New York City and San Francisco was adopted. A name was chosen and a date set: the Spring Mobilization

(Committee) to End the War in Vietnam; April 15, 1967. The leadership was infused with new blood. A. J. Muste, doyen and patriarch of the antiwar movement, was the inevitable choice for chairman; his longtime lieutenant, David Dellinger, was elected one of four vice-chairmen. The others were Sidney Peck, Edward Keating, a founder of *Ramparts,* and Robert Greenblatt of Cornell University and the Inter-University Committee for Debate on Foreign Policy. Thoughtful provision, as events in the spring of 1967 would prove, was made for adding to their numbers.

Although most of the 180 delegates to the third Cleveland Conference were young, two vigorous elders exercised a benign and pervasive influence.‡ Dr. Benjamin Spock, then sixty-three years old, addressed the conference in general and encouraging terms, speaking as an individual and not in his role as national cochairman of SANE. Even then, in 1966, Spock was well out in front of his organization, urged on to some degree by his Western Reserve colleague, Sidney Peck, who recalls: "SANE was very reluctant on the nonexclusionary issue. He [Spock] felt as though I pushed him too hard on that." Nevertheless, after resisting Peck's attempts throughout the summer and fall to gain his sponsorship of the Cleveland Conferences, Dr. Spock did finally consent to appear. For the academic wing, still uneasy with the leftish company it was keeping, Spock's presence spelled self-respect. For the movement at large, it meant respectability for the Peck and Muste position of nonexclusion, an opening to the right.

The delegates were inspired by Spock and cheered by their own remarkable accomplishment—the creation of a new national movement without the usual acrimony and petty political maneuvers. They ended the conference with a salute to A. J. Muste. It was this frail, gentle, Christian man who made the new movement happen. Spock's senior by eighteen years, Muste brought something beyond his experience and consummate political skills to the often rancorous gatherings of the Left. He brought an integrity and an openness (not to be mistaken for naiveté) that either disarmed or ambushed the mean in spirit. "He was," says Sidney Peck, "the father." Muste's presence at a meeting meant that the point of agreement, wherever it lay, would be found. This time around had been easier than most. Dr. Otto Nathan, the executor of Albert Einstein's estate, rose to pay tribute to Muste on behalf of all present. Muste was pleased. He had put together a working coalition that could, perhaps, survive without him.

A month later another national organization that would prove a powerful ally to the Spring Mobilization Committee was born. More than two hundred students from all over the country met in late December at the University of Chicago to consider a proposal for a national student strike. The idea for the strike and the meeting's call came from Bettina Aptheker, who had been a student at Berkeley during the Free Speech crisis. Like her father, Herbert, she was a member of the Communist Party; at Berkeley she was also a leader in the Du Bois Club and, in

‡ The proceedings were, in fact, packed by members of the Young Socialist Alliance, the student arm of the Socialist Workers Party. They came to do close-order combat against SDS, their rivals for the allegiance of activist youth. The expected issue, SDS's push for community-level organizing as opposed to the YSA position, a national mobilization against the war, never seriously emerged, perhaps because SDS declined to send even one representative to the Cleveland Conference.

1965, elected to the student government. The Chicago meeting sounded the death knell of SDS as leader of the student antiwar movement nationwide. While it was in progress word came that the SDS National Office would not endorse the Spring Mobilization. The Chicago conference, however, now firmly in the hands of the cooperating but mutually wary CP and YSA groups, elected to do just that, and they voted to form the Student Mobilization Committee to End the War in Vietnam (SMC). An office was set up in New York under Linda Dannenberg, acting executive secretary, and instructed to cooperate, consult, and support the April 15 Mobilization. Dannenberg was a member of the founding group of the Fifth Avenue Peace Parade Committee and a key Muste associate since that time. Her selection as link between the two SMC's would mean much for the success of April 15, 1967.

On December 15, 1966, A. J. Muste was jailed for the last time. He was familiar with the process. Forty-seven years before, in 1919, he went to jail in Lawrence, Massachusetts. On that occasion Muste, still a relatively young Protestant minister, found himself leading mill workers on strike to better their working conditions (eleven dollars for a fifty-four-hour week). Cut off from a march he was heading, Muste was beaten by police until he could no longer stand, then hauled away. Now, in 1966, with sixty others, he was arrested for a civil disobedience protest blocking the entrance to the Whitehall Street army induction center in Manhattan. The protesters were carrying out a "contingency action plan" of the Fifth Avenue Peace Parade Committee, to be set in motion in immediate response to any escalation of the war. On December 14 it had come: after five months of restraint, the United States had renewed bombing in the Hanoi area. With the Parade Committee that day was SWP's Fred Halstead, whose Trotskyite principles ordinarily prevented him from committing civil disobedience. He had joined the demonstration, against his better judgment, out of his devotion to Muste. Predictably, he was arrested. The police took him to the Tombs for deposit in a cell where Muste was already quietly ensconsed on a rear bench. Halstead's joking reproach—"Look what you got me into"—left unsaid but understood his well-known reservations about the utility of this form of protest. Muste, whose long life of protest, much of it through acts of civil disobedience, would end a few weeks later, answered with a shorthand of his own: "It's every man for himself."

The bombs that fell on Hanoi that December had other reverberations. On the morning of the fifteenth Harrison E. Salisbury, an assistant managing editor of the New York *Times* and Pulitzer Prize–winning correspondent, received a cable informing him that his request, entered fifteen months earlier, for a visa to visit North Vietnam would be granted. Salisbury's first dispatch from Hanoi was printed on Christmas Day. What followed from his on-the-spot reports proved that the official Washington communiqués on the December bombings had been deliberately obfuscating, not to say deceitful. American bombs, despite all claims for "surgical precision," had killed civilians and destroyed churches, schools, homes, and factories in Hanoi and other North Vietnamese cities. Also destroyed, for many Americans, was a lingering faith in their government's honesty.

The last casualty of the December air strikes may have been peace. By the end of 1966 there were 389,000 American troops in Vietnam. Combat dead totaled 6,644.

Now a carefully nourished initiative, code name MARIGOLD, was at the point of fruition. The American ambassador to Warsaw, John A. Gronouski, was primed for face-to-face talks there with the North Vietnamese, the culmination of six months of talks and negotiations in Saigon, Hanoi, Rome, and elsewhere. Then, by inadvertence or unconcern—the State Department would not say which—the strikes, on the books since mid-November, were allowed to proceed even as Gronouski waited for the phone call that never came. The North Vietnamese withdrew completely. The State Department was busy for months stonewalling reporters and discounting rumors on the diplomatic circuit of a lost opportunity. The full story is graphically told in David Kraslow and Stuart H. Loory's book, *The Secret Search for Peace in Vietnam.* MARIGOLD was the last flower at the meadow's edge, cut down in December 1966 by the cold plowshare of war.

1967:
"To Break the Betrayal
of My Own Silences"

THE YEAR 1967 began badly, with Harrison Salisbury sending back reports, published in the New York *Times*, of the bombing of civilian areas of Hanoi and other North Vietnamese cities in the face of administration denials; and Francis Cardinal Spellman, the military vicar of the armed forces for the Roman Catholic Church of the United States, extolling the prosecution of "Christ's War" against the Viet Cong: "The war in Vietnam is a war for civilization," he said.

Salisbury's articles drew outraged denials from the State Department and simply outrage from people worldwide who opposed the bombing. Three weeks later the Associated Press reported that aerial reconnaissance photographs of North Vietnam confirmed the extensive civilian damage that Salisbury had described. The *Times* nominated Salisbury for a Pulitzer Prize in 1967 (his second), and the Pulitzer jury (editors) voted to give it to him, but in a highly unusual move the Pulitzer advisory board (publishers), in a close vote, reversed the jury's decision.

Cardinal Spellman's words prompted a protest at St. Patrick's Cathedral in New York during the ten o'clock high mass on January 22 in which demonstrators unfurled posters showing a wounded Vietnamese child framed by the Sixth Commandment, THOU SHALT NOT KILL, and the single word VIETNAM. Twenty-three people were arrested.

Other Americans besides Salisbury visited Hanoi during those early weeks of January 1967 and saw the results of the bombing; their reports, however, did not have as wide an audience as his. Two groups met with Ho Chi Minh: a delegation of Women Strike for Peace and a trio of elderly pacifist clergymen including A. J. Muste. Ho, speaking in English, told Muste:

> Mr. Johnson has stated that he would talk to anyone, anytime, anywhere about peace.
> I invite Mr. Johnson to be our guest, sitting just as you are here, in the palace of the former French Governor General of Indochina.

Let Mr. Johnson come with his wife and daughters, his secretary, his doctor, his cook, but let him not come with a gun at his hip. Let him not bring his admirals and generals.

As an old revolutionary, I pledge my honor that Mr. Johnson will have complete security.

In a statement later, the three clergymen said that "we have every reason to think that the Government and the people of North Vietnam have an iron determination to fight for their independence and the eventual reunification of their country. . . . The people of Vietnam might be exterminated, were any nation capable of such a crime, . . . but we do not believe that they can be beaten into a surrender of submission by any foreign power."

On January 31, two thousand members of Clergy and Laymen Concerned About Vietnam demonstrated in front of the White House. They presented a statement to an assistant to one of the President's special assistants; in it they requested that the bombing of North Vietnam be stopped and the ground war in South Vietnam be scaled down. At the end of their three-day gathering in Washington they announced a nationwide Fast for Peace in February which was joined by over a million people.

On February 11 the antiwar movement suffered a heavy blow: on that date, at the age of eighty-two, the Reverend A. J. Muste died. He had spent his life as a radical —that creature feared above all else by middle America. He has been called "the Gandhi of the American [antiwar] movement"; his mostly young followers affectionately called him "A.J." He had been arguably the single most important person to oppose the war in the early days, the mid-sixties, when the great mass of the American public had yet to awaken to the nightmare that was Vietnam; by the time he died the antiwar movement was just beginning to penetrate the public's consciousness.

Norma Becker remembers the last time she saw A.J.:

It was on February 7. We had all had to appear in court that day. We had been arrested at the Whitehall Street induction center in December of '66 in a contingency action in response to the bombing escalation. The night before we were to appear in court, there was a monumental blizzard, three feet deep. Schools and businesses, everything was closed. We somehow got to court. A.J. wasn't there. We spoke to the D.A. and said A.J. was at home and had tried to get a cab and couldn't and wasn't going to battle the snow. So we told the D.A. And that son of a bitch, I'll never forget, he said, "Well, anyone who can make his way to Saigon can make his way to court." So we got Tom Cornell of the Catholic Peace Fellowship, who was arrested with us. He had a car and he went and picked up A.J. and brought him back. A.J. was his usual self. He came in smiling, not the least bit worried about the fact that he wasn't able to make it. And that was the last time I saw him.

A number of memorial services were held for Muste, and tributes came from around the world, from figures as diverse as Erich Fromm, Robert Kennedy, and

Ho Chi Minh. Representative James Scheuer entered a tribute to Muste into the *Congressional Record.* New York radio station WBAI aired a documentary on Muste, as did CBS-TV. Perhaps the Mobilization newsletter best reflected Muste's life and spirit: "In lieu of flowers, friends are requested to get out and work—for peace, for human rights, for a better world."

A few days later, twenty-five hundred members of Women Strike for Peace "stormed" the Pentagon (according to the UPI dispatch) demanding to see "the generals who send our sons to Vietnam." They carried huge photos of napalmed Vietnamese children. Pentagon guards had locked the doors to the main entrance, possibly to protect the generals, and so the women took off their shoes and banged on the doors with the heels. On the orders of Secretary McNamara the women were finally allowed inside; the Pentagon had always had "an open door policy," he said. McNamara refused to see them, but they were allowed to present their demands to an aide. Senator Jacob Javits met with several hundred of them; he was applauded when he demanded an end to the bombing of North Vietnam, but booed and heckled when he denied that the United States was using toxic gas in Vietnam. Despite such unladylike behavior, unheard of in 1967 when women were supposed to be seen but not heard, Women Strike for Peace always dressed neatly and had the appearance of what, in fact, they said they were: middle-class housewives. "America was not a feminist nation," recalls Cora Weiss, one of the early members of WSP:

> And the antiwar movement was as American as America. Culturally we [WSP] brought to the Movement what our culture provided us in society. [On the other hand] the Movement by definition was a movement that questioned authority—that was the bottom line of the antiwar movement. . . . We couldn't accept the [government] handouts without some question. . . . Women Strike for Peace was very important to the antiwar movement. More women did things first. Women Strike for Peace was born in protest against atmospheric [nuclear] testing and the whole institutionalization of the atomic age. It [WSP] struggled after the first three years as to whether it should concern itself with the Vietnam War because there were many who felt that it should have a single goal—to prevent the development of nuclear weapons. That struggle proceeded for almost a full year before Women Strike emerged [in 1964] fully and solidly as an organization opposed to the war in Vietnam. They [WSP] couldn't support a war carried out in their names which in fact was neither legitimate nor moral nor legal nor justified.

As the meeting with Senator Javits showed, there was, at this time, mounting concern over U.S. use of chemical and biological weapons to prosecute the war. On February 13 four prominent scientists presented a petition to the White House bearing the signature of five thousand of their fellows. The petition asked President Johnson to initiate a study of government policy on chemical and biological warfare, and to stop the use of antipersonnel and chemical and anticrop weapons—cluster, or pellet, bombs and what has come to be known as Agent Orange.

But even more alarming than the growing concern over the nature of the war was a report that Prime Minister Harold Wilson had announced on British television that peace was "almost within our grasp" the previous weekend, and that "one single, simple act of trust could have achieved it." Wilson had spent the week before hosting the Soviet Premier, Aleksei Kosygin; together they had arrived at the brink, so to speak, of an agreement. However, Wilson had apparently been inadequately briefed by the U.S. State Department and had not, therefore, been able to present the up-to-the-minute U.S. position and so the negotiations came to nothing. On February 14 the United States resumed bombing North Vietnam after a week's suspension for Tet, the Vietnamese New Year. The resumption was particularly disheartening for antiwar groups because North Vietnam had indicated that it was willing to negotiate if the bombing was permanently halted.

The following week students at the University of Wisconsin sat-in at the office used by recruiters for The Dow Chemical Company. As evidenced by the scientists' petition to President Johnson, there had been mounting awareness of the horrors of, among other weapons, napalm B, a petroleum jelly which burns at 1000° F and sticks to whatever it splatters on, including human flesh. Dow was the only company that manufactured and supplied napalm to the Defense Department; it also manufactured the plastic body bags in which corpses of Americans killed in Vietnam were shipped home. "Igniting with a roar and a pillar of red flame and oily black smoke," napalm was dropped in thin aluminum 120-gallon containers weighing eight hundred pounds, often onto Viet Cong trenches and the entrances to their protective tunnels, where it sucked out all the oxygen, leaving the occupants to suffocate if they were not burned to death. But death was thought by some to be preferable to surviving a napalm attack, since the victims, often children, were hideously scarred and crippled.

"It's a terror weapon," said one air force pilot who often dropped canisters of napalm from altitudes as low as fifty feet. "People have this thing about being burned to death."

People also had "this thing" about viewing pictures and reading accounts of grotesquely disfigured Vietnamese children. Like so many other forms of protest against the war, the protests against napalm, the public's awareness of its horrors, and the actions against The Dow Chemical Company, which manufactured it, began with Women Strike for Peace. In 1966 four San Jose WSP "housewife terrorists," "napalm ladies," were arrested and found guilty of trying to block shipments of napalm. In January 1967 *Ramparts* ran a lengthy article, complete with color plates, on the children in Vietnam wounded by the war. In the same month a magazine with a far larger circulation, the *Ladies' Home Journal,* printed an article by veteran journalist Martha Gellhorn titled "Suffer the Little Children . . ." "I have witnessed modern war in nine countries," she wrote, "but I have never seen a war like the one in South Vietnam." Gellhorn quoted a New Jersey woman who had adopted three Vietnamese children; she described her trip to South Vietnam:

> Before I went to Saigon, I had heard and read that napalm melts the flesh, and I thought that's nonsense, because I can put a roast in the oven and the

fat will melt but the meat stays there. Well, I went and saw these children burned by napalm and it is absolutely true. The chemical reaction of this napalm does melt the flesh, and the flesh runs right down their faces onto their chests and it sits there and grows there. . . . These children can't turn their heads, they were so thick with flesh. . . . And when gangrene sets in, they cut off their hands or fingers or their feet; the only thing they cannot cut off is their head. . . .

Gellhorn's article was not just a report on civilian casualties; it was an impassioned treatise against the nature of the war that America was waging against the Vietnamese—all Vietnamese. Some American doctors, she wrote, had formed a physician's group, the Committee of Responsibility for Treatment in the U.S. of War-Burned Vietnamese Children. They had received promises of free hospital beds and places in American homes during convalescence of the wounded children whom they proposed to bring to the United States for medical care. The State Department, however, refused to allow the Vietnamese children into the country.

Finally, in October 1967 when five hundred physicians and twenty hospitals across the country had volunteered their services, three Vietnamese children were brought to San Francisco for treatment. More followed—slowly—but no effort was adequate to assuage the wounds of war for thousands upon thousands of Vietnamese children; only a few hundred ever came to the United States.

Shortly afterward campus protests began against recruiters for The Dow Chemical Company, along with so many other campus protests that erupted that year against recruiters for the armed forces, the CIA, ROTC units, the draft and the use of class ranking to establish deferments, and university research for the military and defense industries. Eventually, some students who protested found that university administrators were giving information on their activities to the FBI.

The draft was a particularly sensitive issue for college students, who by their deferments were able to avoid military service, at least for a while, as they watched their less fortunate fellows being drafted or submitting to the "club of induction." The draft was seen as part of the larger, increasingly corrupt "system." In January 1967 New Left Notes published a Selective Service document, originally issued in July 1965, entitled "Channeling." For the first time, students could see how the "club of induction" was used to control their lives: certain occupations, deemed important by the government, were to be allowed deferments. Thus without directly ordering young men to become, say, engineers, the government was able to assure that an adequate supply of engineers would be available by granting deferments to students enrolled in that discipline. The same issue of New Left Notes carried an "Anti-draft Resolution" which called on local SDS chapters to organize groups on campuses to pledge not to serve in the armed forces "as long as the United States is involved in this war."

In early March, the National Advisory Commission on Selective Service proposed a thorough reorganization of the draft. Titled In Pursuit of Equity: Who Serves When Not All Serve? the report's chief recommendations were to eliminate most deferments and to draft the youngest men in the draft pool first; these nineteen-year-olds, the panel said, should be drafted by lot. Headed by Burke Marshall, the former assistant attorney general for civil rights in the Kennedy Administration, the panel had been appointed by President Johnson to study what it later termed the "diffuse, inefficient, often arbitrary and indifferent" Selective Service System.

When Congress passed a new extension of the draft that June, however, it did not incorporate the Marshall commission's recommendations. It left intact the system of deferment for undergraduates and indeed conferred a blanket deferment upon them; the only issue that the President "won" was that of eliminating graduate student deferments. Medical and dental students were automatically deferred, but all others, after a one-year moratorium in putting the law into effect, would be eligible for the draft. The bill was generally seen as a victory for Representative L. Mendel Rivers, chairman of the House Armed Services Committee; Burke Marshall said that "the new bill makes the system worse than it was before."

The most widely publicized protest against Dow Chemical that winter and spring occurred at Madison on February 21, when one hundred students sat-in at the office used by Dow recruiters; nineteen students were arrested. The next day, two hundred angry students blockaded the university chancellor in his office to protest the arrests. The chancellor provided bail money and the protest quieted.

In the fall, however, campus protests began again over the same issues; Dow Chemical seemed to many people to embody the evils of war. At Wisconsin again, at Illinois, Michigan, Boston College, Minnesota, Harvard, Columbia, Brandeis, Boston University, several branches of the University of California, Chicago, City College of New York, Indiana, New York University, and the University of Pennsylvania, among other places, sixty large demonstrations were held, twenty of which were against Dow. Students barricaded Dow recruiters and refused to allow job applicants to see them. Most of these protests were led by SDS, and now, as contrasted to the spring, the protests were deliberately obstructionist rather than actions of moral witness. SDS had itself moved away from the position of nonviolent protests—"from protest to resistance"—and that October, at the University of Wisconsin, its action was met by violence from the Madison (not the university) police. Dressed in riot gear, the police charged the perhaps three hundred students barricading the recruiters' door. In a matter of minutes the building was cleared, but several thousand students, watching and waiting outside, were horrified to see their battered, bloodied fellows who emerged. To disperse this larger crowd, the police used tear gas—the first time it had been used on a college campus. The crowd became angry; people began to throw rocks and bricks. The police sprayed Mace (a nerve gas) but the crowd did not move. Dogs and a riot squad were brought in. At last the crowd melted away. Three policemen and sixty-five students were treated for injuries.

The response of the outraged students was to strike. After two days of a near-total compliance, a student-faculty committee was set up. Dow was temporarily banned from the campus; thirteen students were suspended and three faculty were fired for joining the strike. Later, Wisconsin Attorney General Bronson La Follette deplored the "out-and-out brutality" on the campus.

Dow reacted to the protests by saying that it would continue to recruit employees on campuses and also to manufacture napalm and sell it to the government. Twenty-four thousand students had been interviewed the previous year (1966), while 54,620 tons of napalm B had been produced—an average of 4550 tons a month. In the Korean War (1950–53), the total napalm produced had been 32,215 tons; it had also been used in World War II, when it was developed at Harvard.

In December, H. D. Doan, the president of Dow and grandson of "Crazy Dow," the chemist who founded the company, voiced his concern that the protests—five hundred to date—and the ensuing bad publicity would harm the company by frightening away potential recruits, particularly "creative" people who, like Crazy Dow, might be regarded as eccentrics but who might "invent the great thing for Dow in the future." All the same, he said, Dow did not plan to discontinue its manufacture of napalm B, which amounted to only one half of 1 percent of the company's annual sales of $1.3 billion. He said that he was pleased to receive a letter from Secretary of Defense McNamara in which McNamara praised the company and its employees "for the contributions they are making to our commitment in Vietnam."

The Dow protests sputtered and were finally subsumed in the larger social and political upheavals of 1968, but the horrors of its use were not forgotten. The Russell Tribunal and the Winter Soldier hearings (see chapter "1971: The Winter Soldiers") both gave prominent mention to the use of napalm against the civilian population—women and children—and classified its use as "inhumane" in the sense of "inhumane acts committed against any civilian population" documented at the Nuremberg trials of German war criminals.

Perhaps the most famous act of protest against Dow and napalm occurred two years after the initial protests. It was committed not by students on campus but by nine radical Catholics, mostly priests. On Saturday afternoon, March 22, 1969, they broke into the Washington, D.C., office of The Dow Chemical Company. They wrecked office equipment, poured blood, put up photos of napalmed children, and threw documents out to the street, where one of their number waited for them. After their arrest they fasted for a week before they were released.

Despite the protests the use of napalm continued; none of the actions against it were effective, although arguably they raised the public's awareness of the nature of the war. In June 1972, three years after the action of the D.C. 9, and five years after the initial protests against Dow and napalm, perhaps the most famous photograph of the war appeared in U.S. publications. It was of a naked little girl screaming in agony, her flesh dripping with napalm, running down a road toward the camera.

At the end of February 1967 *Ramparts* reported that since the inception of the National Student Association in 1950, the CIA had been secretly funding its international programs in order to "receive reports on [foreign] student leaders"—the potential leaders of their countries with whom the U.S. Government someday would have to deal. The story was important mainly because it widened the so-called credibility gap: the lesson that was being pounded home, as in Harrison Salisbury's dispatches from North Vietnam, was that the U.S. Government could not be trusted, that in the name of national security it would even stoop to manipulating its own young people. Many other groups had received CIA money, which was "laundered," or channeled through foundations: other student organizations, labor groups, academic and research groups, the National Education Association, the Pan American Fund, the Foreign Policy Research Institute at the University of Pennsylvania. Even the YWCA had received CIA money.

In late February, the Reverend Martin Luther King, Jr., who in 1964 had been awarded the Nobel Peace Prize for his civil rights work, began to attack the war in earnest. He had for some time been wrestling with the fact of the war both as an absolute wrong and as a death threat to the hopes of black Americans. In 1965 he had put the question "Do we love the war on poverty or do we love the war in Vietnam?" Since then it had been increasingly obvious, as the draft quotas were stepped up, that the war in Vietnam was becoming a war in which black men were drafted to fight the white man's war against yellow men.

On February 25, 1967, King addressed a conference on Vietnam organized by *The Nation* magazine and held at the Hilton Hotel in Beverly Hills. "The promises of the Great Society have been shot down on the battlefield of Vietnam," he said, giving his three reasons for opposing the war: violation of the UN charter, crippling the war on poverty, and danger in the United States to the right of dissent. King's fellow participants that day were four dove senators: McGovern, (Eugene) McCarthy, Gruening, and Hatfield. In such company King would not have needed to say a word about his opinions on Vietnam; merely appearing on the same platform with them was statement enough.

One month later King led five thousand people in an Easter peace march in Chicago; addressing the rally that followed, he termed the war in Vietnam a "blasphemy against all that America stands for." Five days later, at a convention of the SCLC in Louisville, he warned that civil disobedience might be called for to "arouse the conscience of the nation" and bring an end to the war: "We are merely marking time in the civil rights movement if we do not take a stand against the war."

But these activities, and the interviews that he gave during this time, were merely warm-ups for the main event, a speech at Riverside Church in New York City on April 4, 1967, sponsored by the Clergy and Laymen Concerned About Vietnam— of which King was to become cochairman the following week.

The audience gave him a standing ovation. Speaking directly to an overflow crowd of three thousand and indirectly to the nation, King spoke words that the nation did not want to hear, words that came from his own torment. He was moved, he said, "to break the betrayal of my own silences and to speak from the burnings of my own heart. . . ." King's concern was for both Americans and Vietnamese; for young black Americans who, with whites, "kill and die together for a nation that has been unable to seat them together in the same schools"; and for Vietnamese peasants who "watch as we poison their water, as we kill a million acres of their crops. They must weep as the bulldozers destroy their precious trees. They wander into the hospitals, with at least twenty casualties from American firepower for each Viet Cong-inflicted injury. . . . They must see Americans as strange liberators," said King; to him, America was the "greatest purveyor of violence in the world today." To young men, both black and white, who considered American policy "dishonorable and unjust," King recommended a "boycott" of the war through conscientious objection.

King suggested a five-point disengagement plan, including a bombing halt and a unilateral cease-fire. More importantly, he spoke to the point made by Carl Oglesby and others outside the mainstream of American politics when he described the war not as an aberration of U.S. foreign policy but as "a symptom of a far deeper malady within the American spirit." If we "ignore that sobering reality we will find ourselves organizing clergy-and-laymen concerned committees for the next generation."

It is difficult even at this remove to assess the results of King's antiwar stand. Certainly, in 1967, the antiwar movement needed all the help it could get, especially from "respectable" sources like Martin Luther King, Jr., with his high standing among the (white) Left liberals and intellectuals—many of whom were leading the fight against the war and who, not incidentally, had given King enormous help in his own civil rights struggle. King's presence in the peace camp did not, of course, mean that blacks would necessarily follow him; but, as David Dellinger has said, many blacks were already there on their own.

On the other hand, many blacks, understanding that the war was more directly harmful to blacks than to whites (proportionately more blacks were drafted and therefore wounded and killed; and the cost of the war eventually drained money from poverty programs), nevertheless feared to alienate administration supporters by declaring against the war. Therefore many black civil rights leaders, who had the most to lose if King alienated the white majority, opposed his Riverside speech. Jackie Robinson criticized King publicly while Roy Wilkins criticized him privately at a board meeting of the NAACP on April 11; on April 12, the sixty members of the NAACP board voted unanimously not to unite the civil rights and antiwar movements. Dr. Ralph Bunche, the UN under secretary for special political affairs and a black who had achieved acceptance in the white man's world far beyond that of most blacks, had strengthened the original language of the NAACP resolution by calling such a merger a "serious tactical mistake." He did not, however, publicly criticize King's antiwar sentiments. A. Philip Randolph, the president of the Brotherhood of Sleeping Car Porters, declined comment. Whitney Young, Jr., the executive director of the National Urban League, said that "civil rights programs and the question of the war in Vietnam should remain separate." By the end of that long, hot summer, when riots had once again ravaged the nation's black ghettos, Young had begun to speak with more militance. The country did not "deserve" order, he said, until there was justice for all: "The greatest freedom that exists for Negroes in this country is freedom to die in Vietnam," he said.

Some black leaders, of course, were fully opposed to the war and they praised King. As one commented, "White Americans are not going to deal in the problems of colored people when they're exterminating a whole nation of colored people." King's own SCLC stood firmly with him on the issue, and Floyd McKissick of CORE said that "Dr. King has come around and I'm glad to have him with us."

Bayard Rustin criticized King's critics: "America really does not believe that Negroes, as citizens, have yet come of age. Like children, we should be seen but not heard."

Reaction to King's Riverside Church address from the white press was not only negative but condescending. He was being "simplistic," they said; he had "diminished his usefulness." The New York *Times* lectured on "Dr. King's error."

Martin Luther King, Jr., having made his commitment to the antiwar cause, did not care who criticized his public condemnation of the war. Such people apparently never understood him, he said. Receiving the Nobel Peace Prize was receiving a "mission to work harder for peace"—and certainly that included Vietnam. "It is more important that I should be concerned with the survival of the world [than with integration]," he said.

On April 15, 1967, the Spring Mobilization to End the War in Vietnam held marches in New York and San Francisco. They were a tremendous success. As usual, estimates of attendance varied according to the source: anywhere from one hundred thousand (police estimate) to four hundred thousand (Mobilization estimate) turned out in New York and probably about fifty thousand in San Francisco.

Much of the day-to-day work of coordinating the marches had been assumed by the Reverend James Bevel of SCLC. David Dellinger remembers approaching Bevel as early as the spring of 1966:

> I wanted Bevel for two reasons: to bring in the black movement and because of his creativity [Bevel's ability to engineer demonstrations]. And because he was the most likely to get King. By June of that year King had said he thought he would take part in our next major demonstration. Little by little the negotiations went on [with him]. But every time he said it he made conditions. His first demand was that the Communists be taken off the letterhead. Now, we had a policy of nonexclusion. And King demanded that Arnold Johnson, who was the public relations director of the CP, be taken off the letterhead. Fred Halstead [of SWP] and I led the debate to say that we would not take Arnold Johnson off the letterhead. Even if we lost Martin Luther King. A.J. was more equivocal but in the end he came to that position. All the traditional antiwar organizations thought that we ought to compromise.
>
> Then toward the end [the time of the April 1967 march] King said he wouldn't speak unless we dropped Stokely Carmichael. Right up to the end we were afraid we were going to lose him. One time he came up to New York and said everything was OK and then there was a fund-raiser and a bunch of his financiers said that if he took part in the demonstration they were going to withdraw their money. That same night Jim Bevel, Andy Young, Ivanhoe Donaldson, Bob Greenblatt and I just had a down-to-earth no-holds-barred discussion and I believe that I convinced Andy Young that we were going to have the biggest antiwar march that ever took place on April 15, 1967, with or without Martin Luther King and that Martin Luther King was going to be left behind in history if he didn't come. And after that I never had moment's doubt that King was going to come. But the blacks were coming anyway, without King, without the NAACP.

A veteran of the civil rights struggle in the South, Bevel was a brilliant and moving speaker with the born preacher's trenchant command of language. Once, responding to the question of whether the Spring Mobilization was more or less "Left," he said, "We're going to get left of Karl Marx and left of Lenin. We're going to get way out there, up on that cross with Jesus."

That, of course, was exactly the fear of some peace organizations that ordinarily would have lent their support to the march. SANE refused to sponsor the march because it objected to the presence of certain groups—for example, YAWF, or members of the Communist Party marching under their banner for the first time since the 1940s, or those who threatened to carry the Viet Cong flag (and did). Dr. Benjamin Spock, cochairman of SANE, failed to persuade the SANE leadership to endorse the march; later in the year he resigned from SANE to join the National Conference for New Politics. In any event, local SANE chapters were given the option to join the march if they wished, and many of them did. Inevitably the Red smear smeared them. The day after the demonstrations, Secretary of State Dean Rusk, interviewed on NBC's "Meet the Press," announced that the "Communist apparatus" was "working very hard" to support the antiwar demonstrations in the United States and elsewhere; asked to elaborate or produce supporting evidence, he refused.

Nevertheless the march was endorsed by a broad enough spectrum to ensure both participation and legitimacy: church and religious groups, political groups, *ad hoc* antiwar groups, pacifists, SCLC, SNCC, AFSC, WSP, and Clergy and Laymen Concerned. Individual sponsors included entertainer Harry Belafonte, Daniel Berrigan, S.J., Dorothy Day of the Catholic Worker, James Farmer of CORE, John Lewis of SNCC, Carl Oglesby of SDS, the Reverend Fred Shuttlesworth of SCLC, historian Staughton Lynd, Norman Mailer, and scientists Linus Pauling, Harlow Shapley, and Albert Szent-Gyorgyi—as before, a representative selection of the best of American activism.

The marchers began to assemble in Central Park on Saturday morning. The parade route lay east along Fifty-ninth Street to Madison, then south to Forty-seventh Street and east again to First Avenue and the Dag Hammarskjöld Plaza at the UN. By two o'clock the plaza was full with people who spilled into the adjacent streets, but some people never arrived, so huge were the crowds in Central Park waiting to step off. Many of them carried signs and banners: STOP THE BOMBING, BRING THE TROOPS HOME, CHILDREN ARE NOT BORN TO BURN, and—from blacks—NO VIETNAMESE EVER CALLED ME NIGGER. Many of the younger marchers chanted "Hell, No, We Won't Go!" and "Hey, Hey, LBJ, How Many Kids Did You Kill Today?" People came from all walks of life: priests and nuns, middle-class "straights," housewives pushing baby carriages, youths who had painted themselves with poster paint, other youths who carried daffodils and chanted, "Flower Power." There were several floats, including one carrying a model of the Statue of Liberty and one carrying the folksinger Pete Seeger and a number of children. And at the head of the march, in memory of the man whose spirit still led them, marchers carried a huge photograph of Abraham Johannes Muste.

At the UN, Martin Luther King urged a halt to the bombing of North Vietnam. Dr. Spock, echoing his argument with SANE, told the crowd that *"all* Americans who are opposed to the war" were welcome, "people of all ages, people of all shades of political opinion." James Bevel spoke, and Floyd McKissick of CORE, and, despite King's objections, Stokely Carmichael of SNCC; Carmichael's speech was interrupted by shouts of "Black Power!" People were still straggling up when, late in the afternoon, heavy rain began to fall, scattering the crowd.

Dellinger remembers his feelings of elation at the success of the march—his feeling that, at last, they had a movement: "Martin Luther King turned to me on the platform and said, 'It's more [people] than the August '63 civil rights march.' Then I somehow felt like 'we're in'—even though that didn't mean that it was the majority of the country."

One of the most significant events of the day occurred in Central Park before the march began: about seventy young men, mostly from Cornell University, stood on an outcropping of rock in Sheep Meadow and burned their draft cards. They were surrounded by a protective barricade of fellow demonstrators and members of Support in Action, an adult support group. A few women burned half of their husbands' or boyfriends' cards while the men burned the other half.

The action had been proposed several weeks earlier by the We Won't Go group at Cornell, which had been organized by SDSer Tom Bell after his attendance at an antidraft conference in Des Moines in August 1966. At an antidraft action at Cornell in December 1966, Bruce Dancis, whose father had been a conscientious objector in World War II, had torn up his card; now, in the spring, the Cornell group sent out "A Call to Burn Draft Cards":

Ithaca, New York
March 2, 1967

The armies of the United States have, through conscription, already oppressed or destroyed the lives and consciences of millions of Americans and Vietnamese. We have argued and demonstrated to stop this destruction. We have not succeeded. Murderers do not respond to reason. Powerful resistance is now demanded: radical, illegal, unpleasant, sustained.

In Vietnam the war machine is directed against young and old, soldiers and civilians, without distinction. In our own country, the war machine is directed specifically against the young, against blacks more than against whites, but ultimately against all.

Body and soul, we are oppressed in common. Body and soul, we must resist in common. The undersigned believe that we should *begin* this mass resistance by publicly destroying our draft cards at the Spring Mobilization. WE URGE ALL PEOPLE WHO HAVE CONTEMPLATED THE ACT OF DESTROYING THEIR DRAFT CARDS TO CARRY OUT THIS ACT ON APRIL 15, WITH THE UNDERSTANDING THAT THIS PLEDGE BECOMES BINDING WHEN 500 PEOPLE HAVE MADE IT.

The climate of anti-war opinion is changing. In the last few months student governments, church groups, and other organizations have publicly expressed understanding and sympathy with the position of individuals who refuse to fight in Vietnam, who resist the draft. We are ready to put ourselves on the line for this position, and we expect that these people will come through with their support.

We are fully aware that our action makes us liable to penalties of up to five years in prison and $10,000 in fines. We believe, however, that the more people who take part in this action the more difficult it will be for the government to prosecute.

The Mobilization had opposed the card-burning action because, like SANE in similar situations, it feared alienating and frightening away potential new support. The night before the march, the Cornell people and others held a meeting to decide what to do. It was agreed that if fifty people would burn their cards the action would be worth doing—that it would be politically meaningful instead of isolated craziness. When the vote was taken, fifty-seven people agreed to burn their cards and the group decided to proceed with the action. As Norma Becker recalls:

> The Mobilization would not let them burn their cards from the podium, where all the media were. [And so] they felt abandoned by the Movement. Some of the more moderate forces—SANE, WSP, Clergy and Laymen, religious groups, Reform [N.Y.] Democrats—went bazongo [at the proposal to burn draft cards]. But it was a positive thing, it enhanced the militance and the commitment, and it served as a model of commitment and risk. It helped give rise to the [draft] resistance movement. But it was sad. The mothers—there was such angst, the young men and their families. And when they came from families that were not supporting them, there was such conflict. The parents were going through agony and anguish, and the young men were going through turmoil. They were arrested later. Bruce Dancis served a year and a half. . . .

On Saturday morning as the group assembled on the rocky slopes of Sheep Meadow they were surrounded not only by Support in Action but by the press (so much for the Mobilization's fears of media coverage), by FBI agents, and by hordes of curious onlookers pushing and shoving to get a look. No orchestrated procedure was possible, so someone simply produced an empty Maxwell House coffee tin with some lighted paraffin in it; some cards were thrown in while others were ignited with matches or cigarette lighters. When the young men had finished they sat down in a group. Then, to their surprise, some of the onlookers began to come forward, men not part of the original group, and they, too, burned their cards. In all, sponsors of the demonstration claimed that about 175 draft cards were burned that day.

Martin Jezer, at the time an editor of *WIN* magazine, wrote about his feelings the night before he took part in the Sheep Meadow action:

That night I hardly slept. I recalled how it was the night before my graduation from college. . . . That was a celebration of my ability to get good grades and to conform, intellectually, to the current catechism of uncritical Americanism. Although I was something of the campus radical, by contemporary standards I was just a good, harmless white liberal, impressed with and convinced of my own powerlessness, prepared to allow politicians, generals, and corporate managers to make decisions over my life. . . . Burning a draft card, I thought, would be a more meaningful graduation. I had finally begun to be educated, to see through the myths of the American propaganda machine.

And afterward, reflecting on the meaning of what he had done:

. . . For me, the burning of my draft card was, symbolically, my graduation or entrance into this world.

To destroy one's draft card, to place one's conscience before the dictates of one's government is in the highest tradition of human conduct. This country was not created by men subservient to law and government. It was created and made great by civil disobedients like Quakers who refused to compromise their religion to suit the Puritan theocracy; by Puritans who openly defied British authority; by provo-type Sons of Liberty who burned stamps to protest the Stamp Act and who dumped tea in Boston Harbor; by abolitionists who ignored the Fugitive Slave law; by slaves who refused to act like slaves; by workingmen who insisted, despite the law, on their right to organize; by black Americans who refused to ride in the back of the bus; and by the more than one hundred young Americans already in prison for refusing to acquiesce in the misguided actions of their government.

So when people tell me that I have no respect for law and order and that I do not love my country, I reply: "Jefferson, Tom Paine, Garrison, Thoreau, A. J. Muste, the Freedom Riders, these are my countrymen whom I love; with them I take my stand."

In San Francisco's Kezar Stadium that day, the crowd heard of a new group formed to resist the Selective Service System and its unfair deferments. Called the Resistance, it had been organized by a former president of the Stanford student body, David Harris, and three others: Dennis Sweeney, Lennie Heller, and Steve Hamilton. Their plan was to hold a national draft card turn-in on October 16 of that year. Other speakers included Coretta Scott King, Julian Bond, Paul Schrade of the UAW, and Edward Keating and Robert Scheer of *Ramparts*.

The Johnson Administration's reaction to the Mobilization's demonstration was swift and predictable. On the day of the demonstrations, the White House announced that the President had received reports from J. Edgar Hoover, whose FBI was "keeping an eye" on antiwar activity. On April 24 General William Westmoreland was produced, fresh from the battlefield, to speak at the annual luncheon of the Associated Press. He spoke frankly. He and his men, he said, had been "dismayed by recent unpatriotic acts here at home." "The enemy," on the other hand, had gained hope that "he can win politically what he cannot accomplish militarily." As to stopping the fighting, "I do not see any end of the war in sight," said the general.

A few days later Westmoreland addressed a joint session of Congress—the first commander ever to do so while battlefield hostilities continued. This time he did not mention protests; he pledged that American forces would "prevail in Vietnam over the Communist aggressor." Later, at a White House luncheon briefing attended by governors, members of Congress, the Cabinet, and the Joint Chiefs of Staff, he elaborated on an analysis of the war by North Vietnam's Defense Minister, Vo Nguyen Giap, the hero of Dien Bien Phu. Giap had predicted that:

—the United States would be able neither to send enough troops "to meet its objective" nor to supply them;

—South Vietnam's morale would collapse;

—the American forces would alienate the Vietnamese population;

—neither American nor South Vietnamese troops would understand why they were fighting the war, and thus would become demoralized;

—opposition to the U.S. role from other countries and—even more—dissent within the United States would impede the U.S. war effort.

The last consideration, said Westmoreland, was the "central" one.

The general's speech to Congress was widely seen as an attempt to gain political support for the war. It was also perceived as an opening wedge to paving the way for even more escalation and more troops—the request for which finally came, with politically disastrous results, ten months later.* But a trial balloon went up (with a Saigon dateline) as soon as Westmoreland returned to Vietnam in early May: he was reported to have asked the President for an increase in U.S. troop strength to between 550,000 and 600,000 men. The previous fall, in fact (1966), he had requested a total troop strength of about 550,000 men by mid-1968. The Administration was reported to have a ceiling of about 480,000 troops by that date. By February 1968, however, there were nearly 500,000 U.S. troops in Vietnam, and again at that time—to cries of outrage—the question of a 200,000-man troop increase was raised.

At the close of Westmoreland's remarks the members of Congress roared their approval—always excepting the President's critics; some added the rebel yell and some, like Senator Russell Long, jumped up and down. L. Mendel Rivers said that the general's speech "separates the men from the boys. . . . The immortal words of Stephen Decatur, 'my country right or wrong,' could never be truer," said Rivers. "It's too late to question whether it's right or wrong."

Despite Senator Thruston Morton's (R-Maryland) complaint of "an epidemic of verbal overkill," the President continued to criticize his critics. At a Medal of Honor ceremony in May, as he had done twice before, he used the occasion to denounce them: the country would pay a price for their dissent, he said.

To drive home the point, in late May the Air Force dropped 1.75 million leaflets on North Vietnam warning the North Vietnamese not to be misled by protests in the United States into thinking that America had lost its will to fight.

* American troop strength in Vietnam at the end of April 1967 was 438,000.

Many Americans might have been surprised to learn that there was a peace movement in South Vietnam also. In mid-March, fifty-nine teachers and students in Saigon circulated an appeal for peace and sent it to peace groups worldwide. One teacher, a thirty-three-year-old woman, Pham Thi Mai, immolated herself in May. She left behind several letters for Ambassador Ellsworth Bunker. In them she pleaded for immediate withdrawal of American troops: "Most of us Vietnamese hate, from the bottom of our hearts, the Americans who have brought the sufferings of this war," she wrote. Another young woman, a disciple of the Buddhist leader Thich Tri Quang, stated that "if the war continues, we will lose not only thousands of lives but all of the cultural and human values of our beloved country."

But a majority of Americans did not agree. In a Louis Harris poll of May 15, 45 percent of those polled said that they favored "total military victory," while 41 percent favored supervised withdrawal of troops of both sides. This was the first poll that showed more people favoring military victory than supervised withdrawal. Despite the number who would have chosen to win the war on the battlefield, 81 percent said that they thought that the war would be a long one.

Following its success with the April demonstration, the Spring Mobilization was faced with the question that always arose after even the most triumphant showing of the antiwar forces: what now? Success in the short term meant pulling hundreds of thousands of people into the streets; in the long term it meant stopping the war. But the war had escalated in the days immediately following April 15, and by the end of the month U.S. planes were bombing industrial targets, power plants and air bases in the Hanoi-Haiphong area—the first time since the previous December that strikes had been made so close to Hanoi, and the first time that Hanoi's only rail link to China had been hit.

In the Senate, Fulbright, Church, and Robert Kennedy attacked the step-up in the fighting; George McGovern, acknowledging the risk to his career, called it a "policy of madness" which "brought us one step closer to World War III," and which "sooner or later will envelop my son and American youth by the millions for years to come."

James Bevel, speaking at the April 15 Mobilization, had threatened massive civil disobedience in Washington, D.C., the following month if the war had not ended—an action which he had not discussed with other Mobilization leaders and which was obviously impossible in any case. Instead, members of the Spring Mobilization went to Washington to present a "demand" to President Johnson to end the war, to stop the "genocide and mass butchery." Martin Luther King, Coretta Scott King, the Reverend James Bevel, Dr. Spock, and Monsignor Charles Rice of Pittsburgh, among others, went to the White House gates for three days in succession, but Johnson refused their invitation to speak with them.

On May 19, as Spock and King stood waiting outside, Secretary McNamara's office delivered a secret Draft Presidential Memorandum to Lyndon Johnson. Titled "Future Actions in Vietnam," it appraised the intensified bombing of North Vietnam:

There continues to be no sign that the bombing has reduced Hanoi's will to resist or her ability to ship the necessary supplies south. Hanoi shows no signs of ending the large war and advising the VC to melt into the jungles. The North Vietnamese believe they are right; they consider the Ky regime to be puppets; they believe the world is with them and that the American public will not have staying power against them. Thus . . . they believe that, in the long run, they are stronger than we are for the purpose. They probably do not want to make significant concessions, and could not do so without serious loss of face.

The authors of the memorandum concluded that "no combination of actions against the North short of destruction of the regime or occupation of North Vietnamese territory" would halt the flow of men and supplies South. In fact, they said, quoting Sir Robert Thompson, the British expert in guerrilla warfare, the bombing "is unifying North Vietnam."

The memorandum then asked the question that had haunted America's Vietnam adventure from the start: "Why not escalate the bombing and mine the harbors (and perhaps occupy southern North Vietnam)?"

The cost, it concluded, would be too high: "the likely Soviet, Chinese and North Vietnamese reaction" was called the most important, but considerably more space was given to the

hard to measure cost [of] domestic and world opinion: there may be a limit beyond which many Americans and much of the world will not permit the United States to go. The picture of the world's greatest superpower killing or seriously injuring 1,000 non-combatants a week, while trying to pound a tiny backward nation into submission on an issue whose merits are hotly disputed, is not a pretty one. It could conceivably produce a costly distortion in the American national consciousness and in the world image of the United States—especially if the damage to North Vietnam is complete enough to be "successful."

The day after representatives of the Spring Mobilization completed their vigil at the White House gates, the "Mobe" (as it came to be known) held a conference in Washington on May 20–21 to assess the results of the April 15 march and to determine future actions. Seven hundred people attended, representing the entire spectrum of antiwar activity. The question of political activity—of supporting a third-party presidential ticket or forming a party around a number of issues—was deferred; it was agreed, however, to support antiwar referenda wherever possible. The major decision arrived at was to issue a call for a civil disobedience action—a "confrontation"—on October 21 in Washington. The "Spring" was dropped from the group's name, which now became simply the National Mobilization Committee to End the War in Vietnam.

While the National Mobilization looked to the fall, two new groups sprang up to begin projects in the weeks just ahead. Negotiations Now! was a coalition of prominent liberals (many from Americans for Democratic Action [ADA]) such as Arthur Schlesinger, Jr., Joseph L. Rauh of the ADA, John Kenneth Galbraith, Victor Reuther of the UAW, and Norman Cousins of SANE. Their goal was to collect one million signatures on a petition calling on the United States to stop the bombing of North Vietnam and calling on Hanoi to join in a cease-fire. Their four-point program also called for a billion-dollar economic assistance program to Vietnam and for the holding of "free elections" in South Vietnam. Eventually endorsed by a number of Protestant, Catholic, and Jewish leaders, as well as other prominent figures, Negotiations Now! was an action of the "right wing" of the peace movement. The demand of the Mobilization for immediate withdrawal of U.S. troops was far too extreme a position for the mainstream types that the new group represented, as was the Mobe's "nonexclusionary" policy. By October, Negotiations Now! backed by ADA, was offering support to candidates either Republican or Democrat who would take a "more flexible attitude toward negotiations" than had the Johnson Administration, but at the same time the group continued to reject both a "dump Johnson" movement mounted by dissident Democrats and Allard Lowenstein's avowed search for a candidate to oppose LBJ (see pp. 124–27).

The other organization was Vietnam Summer, and like Negotiations Now! it was endorsed by Martin Luther King, Jr. Dr. Spock endorsed it also. Patterned on Mississippi Summer of 1964, it was initiated by Chester Hartman, a Harvard professor. Its goal was to recruit ten thousand volunteers for a public outreach program nationwide to build a solid base of antiwar support.

Meanwhile, some members of the New Left continued to show symptoms of the foot-in-mouth disease that hampered the Movement from beginning to end: while many "mainstream" Americans might have found the work of Vietnam Summer and Negotiations Now! unobjectionable, they could hardly have been expected to approve the statements of SDS National Secretary Greg Calvert. Unfortunately, Calvert's remarks, published in May in an overview of the New Left in the New York *Times,* received wide attention; however accurately or not they reflected the organization's position, they were a public relations fiasco, serving only to make more difficult the Mobilization's task of rallying widespread public support to end the war.†

"We are working to build a guerrilla force in an urban environment," said Calvert; "we are actively organizing sedition." Thus throwing a pall of doubt over SDS's cherished community organizing efforts, two of which (Newark and Chicago) survived, he went on to praise the Argentinian revolutionary Ernesto "Che" Guevara: "Che's message is applicable to urban America as far as the psychology of guerrilla action goes. . . . Che sure lives in our hearts." Che, formerly Fidel Castro's right-hand man, at this time had been out of the public eye for more than two years; he was said to be organizing a revolution in the Andes Mountains.

Calvert had nothing but contempt for groups such as the National Conference for New Politics, which had been organized the previous year to field candidates opposed to the war. By trying to work within the political framework, the NCNP

† Again it must be emphasized that SDS was not the antiwar movement or even a major part of it; in the public's mind, however, all factions blurred into one, and that one, unfortunately, often turned out to be SDS.

earned the epithet "left liberals" from SDS, which had by this time, according to Calvert, moved "from protest to resistance."

Some observers attributed SDS's increasing verbal militance to the group's frustration that its announced aims had not been quickly achieved. Others held that in order to match the rising tide of black militance, SDS needed to spout an increasingly hard line. And if SDS was looking for the revolution, it seemed to many people in the spring of 1967 that the revolution would come in the nation's black ghettos.

"Some of the black nationalists are stacking Molotov cocktails and studying how they can hold a few city blocks in an uprising, how to keep off the fire brigade and the police so that the National Guard must be called out," a white Ohio student said. "And they're right. We ought to help them where we can, but we oughtn't be hung up with leading or liberating the Negroes."

Calvert agreed: "Black power is absolutely necessary," he said, acknowledging the split that had occurred between black and white activists since the heyday of the civil rights movement.

Some more moderate voices tried to soften such statements. Staughton Lynd, for instance, said that the talk of guerrilla action was "not descriptive" of the Movement; community-based action to "lead draft resisters or defend the interests of the poor in housing and welfare" were more properly the aim of the New Left. Nevertheless, the fire-eating rhetoric of Calvert and others echoed in the public mind, making more difficult the task of all the many groups working to end the war in Vietnam.

At the SDS convention that summer in Ann Arbor, Calvert claimed that he had been misquoted, that the interview had been a "trap," a distortion by the "capitalistic media." What he had really meant, he said, was that "young Americans who worked for the radical transformation of this society were similar in many respects to guerrilla organizers in the Third World." His disavowal did not repair the damage, however; nor did it allay the fears of those SDS members who were not prepared to follow their leaders into armed conflict in the nation's cities.

On June 23 an unpleasant foretaste of violence to come occurred in Los Angeles. In response to an announced appearance by President Johnson at a Democratic Party dinner at the Century Plaza Hotel, the SMC and the Los Angeles Peace Action Council announced an antiwar demonstration. The police had forbidden the use of sound trucks but some Progressive Labor people brought one anyway. The police smashed the windows and beat the drivers and passengers. In protest, some of the demonstrators sat down in the street in front of the hotel, possibly unaware of a last-minute injunction obtained by the police that required, among other things, that the demonstrators keep moving. The police refused to allow the main body of the march to pass by those sitting down; instead they termed the march an "unlawful assembly" and moved in with motorcycles and billy clubs. Hundreds of demonstrators were injured, sixty hospitalized, more than fifty arrested. It was, according to Fred Halstead, "the first antiwar demonstration in the country to be broken up by police."

War came to the nation's black ghetto streets that summer, and to many observers it was a far more crucial war than the one being waged halfway around the globe. In the first months of the year, 164 "disorders" were reported; many of these doubtless would not have been noted except for the heightened consciousness of the press and public because of the urban riots of the three previous years, most notably Harlem in 1964 and Watts (Los Angeles) in August 1965. In the summer of 1967, however, came the worst "disorder" in the history of the country; in just two months, June and July, eighty-three people were killed, thousands wounded, thousands more arrested, and tens of millions of dollars of property damage done. On July 27, after four days of rioting in Detroit during which the National Guard needed to be called out (with the reluctant agreement of Martin Luther King, Jr.), President Johnson announced a commission chaired by Governor Otto Kerner of Illinois. The commission's job—to find out how and why the riots occurred—was amplified by LBJ in the address that he gave that night: "The only genuine, long-range solution for what has happened lies in an attack—mounted at every level—upon the conditions that breed despair and violence. . . ." But when the Kerner Commission returned its report the following March, its recommendations were rejected on the grounds of cost.

Congress proved to be as obtuse about the nation's ghettos and their attendant problems as it was about the mess in Vietnam. A proposed bill, offered in the midst of the worst unrest in July, would have appropriated the relatively small sum of $4 million to eradicate the rats that so often chewed on black flesh in the slums. The bill was literally laughed out of court; the nation's citizens were treated to accounts of chortling congressmen voting nay, signifying their unconcern for poor black slum dwellers.

Bills were passed, however, to curb riots, to prevent aiding the enemy (the Viet Cong), and to make desecrating the flag a federal crime (all fifty states had laws against desecrating the flag). Emotions ran particularly high during the debate on the flag bill. "Let's deal with these buzzards," said L. Mendel Rivers. One Florida Democrat suggested that flag burners be taken two hundred miles out to sea and dumped overboard with a stone tied around their necks. Despite the opinion of Representative William Ryan (D-New York) that it was equally a desecration to wrap oneself in the flag, the bill passed 385 to 16 and sailed on to passage in the Senate. In all the heat of the debate, no one noticed that the word "burning" had somehow been dropped from the final bill. A year later it was added. In October 1982 the Supreme Court refused to hear a challenge to the law.

On August 3 President Johnson made two announcements: he planned to ask Congress for a 10 percent surcharge on personal and corporate taxes; and he planned to send between 45,000 and 50,000 more American troops to Vietnam. The tax surcharge was necessary, the President said, to prevent an "unsafe and unmanageable" federal deficit, which in turn would bring inflation, high interest rates, and a drop in the balance of payments. Despite the Administration's protestations that America could have both guns and butter, by that time the annual spending ($30 billion) for the war was already two and one half times that for the Great Society programs ($12.5 billion). As for the troop increase, it would bring the American strength in Vietnam to 486,000 by December of that year. Congress refused to enact the surcharge.

1967:
The Pentagon:
Gandhi and Guerrilla

As THE SUMMER drew to a close, and as people looked out across an American landscape still smudged by smoke rising from burned-out ghettos, a landscape still and increasingly shadowed by the clouds of war, the question of the presidential elections a year hence began to assume increasing importance. Was the Democratic Party to have as its standard-bearer the man who had become so identified with the war that he could not even make a public appearance for fear of violent demonstrations?

Richard Nixon was the man for the Democrats to beat. He had little competition for the top spot on the Republican ticket. Of his three possible opponents for the nomination, two—Ronald Reagan and Nelson Rockefeller—failed to muster enough support, and the third, Governor George Romney of Michigan, widely though inaccurately perceived as a dove, did himself out of the race on Labor Day weekend in 1967. While being interviewed on a televised talk show in Detroit, Romney claimed that he had undergone "brainwashing" by American generals and diplomats when he visited Vietnam in 1965. Since his return, he said, he had studied up on the Vietnam problem and had reached the conclusion that "I no longer believe that it was necessary for us to get involved in Vietnam to stop Communist aggression." Romney declared his candidacy in mid-November, but he had damaged himself beyond repair. He was perceived as being either (1) stupid for having allowed the brainwashing to happen; or (2) the bearer of bad news which the American people did not want to hear, for if Romney had been brainwashed, then so had the Congress and the American people. His blunt acknowledgment of the credibility gap made him unacceptable as a presidential candidate; he dropped out of the race in February, two weeks before the New Hampshire primary.

Nixon was preparing himself rather better to deal with Vietnam, one of the two great issues confronting the country. In April, while the Spring Mobilization was taking place, Nixon was in Vietnam conferring with American and Vietnamese officials. Communist defeat, he said, was "inevitable"; the only question was when. It was his fifth visit to Saigon since 1963. One year later, Nixon would refuse to debate the Vietnam issue during the presidential election campaign; he would say only that he had a plan for peace but he would not elaborate.

His democratic opponent would be the incumbent, Lyndon Johnson. Despite the enmity of those Democrats and Independents who hated his war policy, the nomination was the President's. It was inconceivable that some other Democrat would challenge him for it and—worse—win. On the other hand, his candidacy was daily becoming more of a threat to a Democratic victory: if some upstart candidate challenging Johnson in the primaries split the party—as he would—Johnson at the head of the ticket would very likely be so great a liability as to throw the election to the Republicans.

And besides—so the common wisdom went—no one in his right mind would challenge any President, and this one in particular.

But Allard Lowenstein thought that he ought to try.

A former president of the National Student Association, Lowenstein had maintained close contact with students throughout the country in his adult life as lawyer, teacher, congressional aide, Adlai Stevenson campaign worker, special UN delegate, and peripatetic gadfly. In December 1966, at Lowenstein's behest, student leaders from one hundred colleges and universities signed an open letter to Lyndon Johnson stating that "unless this conflict [Vietnam] can be eased, the United States will find some of her most loyal and courageous young people choosing to go to jail rather than to bear their country's arms, while countless others condone or even utilize techniques for evading their legal obligations. Contributing to this situation is the almost universal conviction that the present Selective Service law operates unfairly." These young men were elected student body presidents and the like; they were not "radicals" or members of the New Left. They described themselves as in the "mainstream" of student opinion, and they pointed out that "there are many who are deeply troubled for every one who has been outspoken in dissent."

They received a *pro forma* response from Secretary of State Dean Rusk, repeating the Administration's position that the prosecution of the war was necessary to "protect the vital interests of the U.S." Rusk offered to meet with them, but before the meeting occurred the fighting escalated and the students wrote again, voicing increased doubts about U.S. policy: "We cannot state too forcefully our conviction that *any long-range widening of the war risks domestic responses that could embarrass the government* [emphasis added]."

On February 1, 1967, thirty-eight of the students had an off-the-record meeting with Rusk that was the subject of a column by James Wechsler in the New York *Post* on February 2. Rusk "failed to convince any of the thirty-eight that their anxieties were unwarranted," wrote Wechsler, and in fact "many who had been mildly skeptical emerged as vigorous dissenters." Their mood afterward was one of "apprehension and alienation" caused by what they sensed on Rusk's part as "an almost fatalistic acceptance of an interminable, possibly widened dead-end war." "I don't think Mr. Rusk had a sense of how miserably he had failed," said Gregory Craig, student government chairman at Harvard; "It seemed a little appalling that a diplomat could be so insensitive to the feeling of our group. . . . I think nearly everyone came out more militant than we were when we went in."

On January 26 a group of Rhodes scholars had written to the President with questions and comments on U.S. policy in Vietnam. On February 20 they received from a special assistant to the Secretary of State, like Rusk a former Rhodes scholar, a reply which was condescending and arrogant. On March 6 a group of eight hundred Peace Corps returnees wrote to President Johnson about U.S. Vietnam policy but they received no reply. On April 26 one thousand divinity students wrote to Secretary of Defense McNamara to request that the Selective Service law be amended to recognize conscientious objection to particular wars. The reply was a speech made by Cyrus Vance, then deputy secretary of defense, to the ninetieth annual convocation of the Episcopal Diocese of West Virginia on May 6; in it he presented a standard defense of U.S. policy in Vietnam.

All of this activity, and more, had been inspired by a group of students from the Union Theological Seminary in New York who at Lowenstein's urging had set up a WATS line and had begun to call campuses nationwide to organize the letter-writing effort. In addition, a petition was drawn up requesting that drafted students be allowed to choose some form of alternative service; ten thousand students signed it. It was during this period, too, and at Lowenstein's instigation, that the public began to see statements of protest signed by college faculty and published as newspaper ads, usually in the New York *Times;* one of these took up four pages in a Sunday "News of the Week" section.

In August 1967 Lowenstein addressed the annual convention of the National Student Association, calling on them to organize "Nonpartisans Against the President" to oppose Johnson on the issues of the war and the draft. He received an ovation from his audience. He was, according to all who heard him, an exciting and persuasive speaker. Unprepossessing physically, rumpled, bespectacled, he had the ability to make his listeners, whether one person or a thousand, forget his lack of physical charm and be charmed instead by that more devastating asset, personal and intellectual power. "Nobody ever got me to do more things that I swore I wouldn't do and was glad I did than Al," said Congressman Barney Frank (D-Massachusetts) years afterward. Within days of the NSA meeting Lowenstein and Curtis Gans, formerly an ADA staffer, had founded the Conference of Concerned Democrats and had begun in earnest the search for a candidate to oppose Johnson in the upcoming Democratic primaries. Robert Kennedy seemed to be the obvious choice, but Kennedy would not run. George McGovern and Frank Church, two other senators who were known doves and therefore possible candidates, were up for difficult reelection battles, and both declined.

Lowenstein's task was twofold: to find a candidate, and to drum up support in the hinterland while he searched. He was not deterred by this double difficulty. The key to Allard Lowenstein's behavior was that he had unbounded faith in the American political system: once people were given a choice, he felt, they could be persuaded in the normal political channels—i.e., presidential primaries—to make the wise decision. This adherence to conventional politics (if finding a candidate to oppose a sitting President can be said to be conventional) earned Lowenstein the

125

undying hatred of many in the New Left who preferred to make their opposition known outside the two-party system through mass marches and rallies and civil disobedience. Lowenstein undoubtedly understood this, but he followed his own drummer. He was in his way as committed as any member of the Mobilization: "When a President is both wrong and unpopular," he said, "to refuse to oppose him is both a moral abdication and a political stupidity." Lowenstein's greatest strength—aside from his own superhuman energy—was his network of student contacts built up across the country in the years since his presidency of the NSA. And when he found his candidate at last, the students turned out for him—for Lowenstein as well as for the candidate—as they would have for perhaps no one else.

In late October, Eugene McCarthy, the senior senator from Minnesota, told Lowenstein that he would enter the race. McCarthy was a tall, handsome man who *looked* like a President; reputed to be fearsomely intelligent, he was a poet of some ability, a friend of the poet Robert Lowell, and he had also written thoughtfully on America's foreign policy.

At one point in mid-August, as Lowenstein was addressing the NSA, McCarthy had seemed to reach a kind of personal crisis about the war. As a member of J. William Fulbright's Senate Foreign Relations Committee, McCarthy had heard the testimony of Under Secretary of State Nicholas Katzenbach: with the passage of the Tonkin Gulf Resolution in 1964, Katzenbach said, Congress had given the President the authority "to use the armed forces of the United States in whatever way was necessary," including sending ground troops to South Vietnam and bombing (as had been recently done) near the border of Communist China.

When Fulbright said that the Administration had not asked for, and did not have, a declaration of war, Katzenbach heatedly replied, "Didn't that resolution authorize the President to use the armed forces of the United States in whatever way was necessary? Didn't it? What could a declaration of war have done that would have given the President more authority and a clearer voice of the Congress than that did?"

The Senate Foreign Relations Committee was unhappy with Katzenbach's testimony, and McCarthy was particularly outraged. Leaving the hearing, he commented to a reporter, "This is the wildest testimony I ever heard. There is no limit to what he says the President could do. There is only one thing to do—take it to the country."

Around this time, at the behest of two Massachusetts activists, McCarthy met in Washington with *The New Republic* publisher Martin Peretz and his wife Anne. One of the activists was Chester Hartman; the other was Jerome Grossman, a Boston businessman, president of the Massachusetts Envelope Company. A tall, good-looking, balding man then in his early fifties, Grossman had been, like many in the antiwar movement, an avid sports participant in his youth: tennis, baseball, track, and football. Since the 1950s he had taken part in the peace movement, its demonstrations and its picket lines. Unlike A. J. Muste, whom he first met in 1958, and many other peace activists, Grossman has always maintained a belief in the process of American politics. In 1962 he was a founder of MassPax, one of the earliest citizen-action peace groups. He is today the president of the Council for a Livable World, a lobbying group emphasizing nuclear arms control. He remembers the meeting with McCarthy: "None of us were particularly impressed [with him] . . . he didn't know very much about the Vietnam War. . . . We thought [him] quite bland." Hartman dropped out immediately. "Marty and Anne Peretz were unimpressed also, but I was happy that we had somebody." Grossman returned to Boston to report to a packed meeting of MassPax, where word was out that they had a presidential candidate. "He has gray hair," Grossman told the meeting, "wears a gray suit, he has a gray personality, he has a gray mind, but he's all ours and he's willing to take the Administration on." Grossman became the national director for administration in the McCarthy for President campaign, never believing at the start that it would be anything more than another way of "educating" the electorate on the issues.

In his announcement speech on November 30, McCarthy linked the issue of the war to the other pressing issues of the day: the aborted war on poverty, the reduction of foreign aid, war-related inflation, and, perhaps most important, a desire to bring back a "belief in the processes of American politics and of American government" among the growing numbers of alienated Americans on college campuses and elsewhere; he was concerned that these people would "become cynical and make threats for third parties or other irregular political movements"—as, indeed, many of them were doing in the antiwar movement.

It was hardly a revolutionary challenge, but then McCarthy was not a revolutionary man; he toppled Lyndon Johnson, but he could not have done so without the army of students and adult volunteers that Lowenstein, Grossman, and others had recruited for him.

Neither the New Left nor the Old had a part in that achievement, and many on the Left saw in it bitter confirmation of their deep distrust of electoral politics: you could mount an insurgent movement, you could topple a sitting President, you could even deny the presidency to the offending political party. What you could not do—what no one seemed to be able to do—was stop the war.

Allard Lowenstein was shot and killed in his law office in Manhattan on March 14, 1980. His assassin was Dennis Sweeney, one of the founders of the Resistance and a casualty of the war—the war at home. Sweeney was described afterward as being like "a lot of young people who took part in the civil rights movement, then became radicalized . . . permanently alienated and lost to us just as surely as those who were killed in Vietnam." He was more than alienated, however; he was, in the end, insane. He believed that the CIA had implanted radio transmitters in his teeth (all of which he had pulled), and he was convinced that Lowenstein had conspired to cheat Sweeney's stepfather in a lawsuit.

For Lowenstein it was a grievous end. He was a man who had been above all an optimist, who had believed in the system, who had believed that he could make it work. On the night that he died, he had been scheduled to meet a man who planned to run for Congress from Manhattan's Upper East Side; Lowenstein would have told him that he was running again too.

"He travels fastest who travels alone" would seem to be an unlikely motto for a political organizer like Allard Lowenstein, since politics is, after all, quite literally people; but the dismaying spectacle presented by the National Conference for New Politics in Chicago over Labor Day weekend that year demonstrated that it would have been impossible for the Movement to accomplish what he did—that is, to produce a candidate to oppose Lyndon Johnson within the Democratic Party. Or, for that matter, outside it.

The National Conference was the biggest gathering ever of activist, left-wing, civil rights, and peace groups. More than two hundred organizations represented by over three thousand people gathered at the Palmer House; it was hoped that out of their meeting would come at least a coherent strategy to influence the 1968 presidential and congressional elections toward antiwar candidates, and some delegates even hoped to create a new political party.

What happened instead was a disaster.

Held only a few weeks after the worst riots in the black ghettos in the nation's history, the NCNP conference was conducted in an atmosphere of white liberal guilt. No black demand was too great, no white expression of atonement enough to make up for centuries of white oppression of blacks. Although only about three hundred blacks were present, the black caucus demanded—and got—two "tests of [white] sincerity": 50 percent voting power on every vote, and the acceptance of a thirteen-point program that included such items as calling for "white civilizing committees" to be established in white communities to "humanize the savage and beast-like character that runs rampant through America . . ." and condemning the "imperialist Zionist war" fought the previous June when Israel staged a pre-emptive strike against her Arab neighbors.*

In an orgy of self-abnegation that amounted to self-hate—what the Weathermen would later call ridding themselves of "white skin privilege"—the white majority at the convention thus soured most potential support for the NCNP from the much-maligned (white) liberals throughout the country. In the heat of the moment, however, they were overwhelmed by the blacks' demands; these, together with the endless argument that always accompanied any Left-activist convention, combined to make the NCNP Chicago meeting a "travesty of radical politics at work," a "vulgar joke," and a painful wake for any hope of concerted action from the Left in the 1968 presidential race.

"We are just a little tail," said one white, "on the end of a very powerful black panther. And I want to be on that tail—if they'll let me."

Other whites were not so sure. "One thousand liberals are trying to become good radicals and they think they can do it by castrating themselves," said Arthur Waskow of the NCNP steering committee.

"The black caucus came in and gave us a set of demands which they intended to act as a social barometer of where whites stand," said a member of the executive board. "And we answered, 'We haven't got the imagination to figure it out—we

---

* Only two weeks previously, at the National Student Association conference that had given Allard Lowenstein an ovation, the NSA black caucus had demanded—and received—an endorsement of a Black Power resolution that called for the "liberation of blacks by any means necessary"—an ominous phrase in light of the summer's savage riots.

128

stand wherever you say.' That's not a relationship out of which anything healthy can come."

After the convention passed, by a two-to-one margin, the black caucus's demand for 50 percent of the voting power, one woman stood up and burned her delegate card and went home, saying, "This is the old politics, not the new politics."

The Reverend Martin Luther King, Jr., gave the convention's keynote address. On the platform with him at the Chicago Coliseum were, among others, Dick Gregory and the (white) executive director of the NCNP, William Pepper, who said that the delegates "were taking part in the most significant gathering of Americans since the Declaration of Independence." King asked the delegates to "make the 1968 elections a referendum on the war," but he made no specific proposals for action. King and Dr. Spock had been mentioned as a possible presidential ticket for 1968, but King steadfastly denied that he would run. His speech was interrupted by threats and insults from black teenagers; outside the Coliseum a bongo group chanted, "Kill Whitey . . . Kill Whitey . . ." King quickly left the convention, as did two other well-known blacks, the Reverend Andrew Young of the SCLC, a member of the convention's board, and Julian Bond, the convention's cochairman.

In the end, the conference voted not to support a third-party movement; not to support a third-party candidate; but instead to concentrate on "local organizing" and to permit electoral campaigns in 1968 by groups such as California's Peace and Freedom Party who chose to make them.

Some of its organizers claimed that the tumultuous weekend had been a success. The convention " 'gives us entrée into the ghetto,' said one. He was less sanguine about his entrée into the middle class where the money is, unless 'the false taint of anti-Semitism is overcome.' "

"This whole thing has been a nightmare to me," said one black member of the California Democratic Council. "No revolution has ever succeeded without the middle class and the professionals." His advice to the black caucus to moderate its demands was ignored, however; and so, a victim of good intentions and bad timing, the NCNP faded away, not to be heard of again. Some weeks later Sidney Lens identified two "spies" from the Chicago police who had infiltrated the convention and acted as provocateurs to foment dissension, urging the blacks "not to give in to Whitey." In any case, all the delegates to the NCNP seemed prepared to self-destruct no matter who pressed the button.

Thus the Movement had shown that it was incapable of pulling together to make a political effort; it was a huge and amorphous thing, it had the potential to reach millions of people, but it could do little more than organize street protest. And so it turned its collective attention to its next big event, October's Stop the Draft Week and the March on the Pentagon.

In early October a group of 158 professors, authors, clergy, and others signed and published "A Call to Resist Illegitimate Authority," a statement written by Arthur Waskow and Marcus Raskin of the Institute for Policy Studies in Washington. The "Call" drew on hundreds of versions of a resistance statement that had been circulating for months; it presented legal and moral arguments against the war and supported resistance to it, especially draft refusal:

129

. . . Many of us believe that open resistance to the war and the draft is the course of action most likely to strengthen the moral resolve with which all of us can oppose the war and most likely to bring an end to the war.

We will continue to lend our support to those who undertake resistance to this war. We will raise funds to organize draft resistance unions, to supply legal defense and bail, to support families and otherwise aid resistance to the war in whatever ways may seem appropriate.

We firmly believe that our statement is the sort of speech that under the First Amendment must be free. . . .

At a press conference to introduce the "Call" spokesmen for the group promised sanctuary in churches and synagogues for those who wished it. They pledged civil disobedience during the week of October 16—the Stop the Draft Week of the Resistance—and promised an attempt to return as many as one thousand draft cards to the Justice Department on October 20.

Meanwhile, in a place almost as exotic as Vietnam itself—Bratislava, Czechoslovakia—a meeting occurred between about forty American leftists (not, however, members of either the CP or the PLP) and twenty Vietnamese revolutionaries from both North (DRV) and South (NLF).

The meeting was important because (1) it gave the American Left a chance to meet with representatives of the Third World; and (2) it gave the Vietnamese a chance to say again to a sympathetic audience what they had been saying all along: that they had the support of the people of Vietnam and that a negotiated agreement to be acceptable must exclude the American presence and allow the Vietnamese to determine their own destiny. It was this "revolutionary, passionate nationalism" which so impressed Christopher Jencks, the correspondent for *The New Republic*. That publication carried two articles about the Bratislava meeting, but elsewhere coverage was slight. That was unfortunate, for the American public had had almost no opportunity to learn about the people whom American soldiers were fighting. Most Americans had no idea of the determination of the Vietnamese to force out foreign intruders; the Chinese, after all, had ruled Vietnam for one thousand years and were vanquished in the end, hated all the while, never assimilated.

Jencks included an anecdote about a more recent conqueror, the French, whose representative was warned not to try to regain the country: "You can kill ten Vietnamese for every Frenchman we kill," Ho Chi Minh is reported to have said, "but we are willing to pay that price and you are not."

Rennie Davis was one of the American delegation to Bratislava. A graduate of Oberlin College, he was one of the "old guard" SDSers, a prime mover of ERAP. Now in his forties, Davis still conveys the image that he had in the Movement in the sixties, that of an all-American boy, a "sweet-faced kid." He speaks gently, smiles quickly, and radiates a sense of inner tranquility. He lives high in the mountains of Colorado, a place of magnificent natural beauty far removed from the gritty slums where he and other SDSers tried to keep ERAP alive.

He remembers Bratislava:

We were trying to hold on with the [ERAP] projects, but there were difficulties. It was exhausting, but we were very committed. The trip really made us feel how critical Vietnam was [as an issue for the United States]. It was to be a cross section of antiwar sentiment at that point. We exchanged views with the North Vietnamese, but really it was to present the North Vietnamese case. They sent the highest level delegation to convene outside North Vietnam since Geneva [1954]. The South Vietnamese delegates had traveled for more than a month to get there. After the conference they invited seven of us to go to Hanoi for a two-week trip.

Like many young activists Davis experienced some apprehension about his family's reaction to his activities:

Now, I was always very close to my family. We had a farm sixty-five miles west of Washington [D.C.]. Five minutes away there was an old mine with possibly the hardest rock in the United States. They [the government] moved the shadow government [in event of nuclear attack] out to this underground base. My father [formerly a member of President Truman's Council of Economic Advisors] wound up working there and eventually found himself the Secretary of Labor in the shadow government. It had the most advanced communications system in the world. When I was in Bratislava the trip to go to Hanoi came very quickly. We lived outside a small, rural town. To call the farm you had to go through an operator and if it was a long-distance call the operator would listen in. I thought long and hard about calling, because I was very close to my family. I wanted to tell them about the opportunity to visit Vietnam, but I decided, all things considered, my family would prefer not to have this all over town. So—I just went. I'd tell them when I got back. My father was sitting in his office when I was in Phnom Penh about to go into Vientiane, Laos, and take the ICC [International Control Commission] plane to Hanoi. His colleagues brought a memo to him saying, "There's a Rennard Cordon Davis preparing to make entry into Hanoi. Could this be your son?" Well, that's an unusual name, and he was absolutely adamant there was no way that could be. It was impossible. . . .

Davis had been impressed by the North Vietnamese delegation at Bratislava, but even they had not prepared him for what he saw when he arrived in that country:

North Vietnam had an impact on me. I saw that these people were about something that I could not even comprehend. It was an extraordinary quality that was everywhere. You'd drive down a road and ahead, the road would be hit by a five-hundred-pound bomb. You could see it from a distance. You'd think you were stranded for at least a week. There's no heavy equipment around. Suddenly ten thousand people carrying shovels and baskets would appear out of nowhere. You'd have an hour wait. Even a fifty-foot crater was no problem. . . .

In Hanoi we saw things that *no one* in this country was aware of. It was a combination of factors: the magnitude of the war and the incredible human struggle and the widespread Vietnamese attitude toward the American people. In a crowd I'd be announced as an American. Immediately there was spontaneous applause. It could *not* have been programed. I'd stand up and say through the interpreter, "I'm from Chicago." If every day [Vietnam] bombed Chicago, and a Vietnamese walked the streets, there would be anger and bitterness toward that individual. It took me a long time to understand that the sentiment toward Americans was a deep-seated culture attitude. I would go into fourth-grade classes and every schoolchild had written a poem about Norman Morrison. He was almost on a level with Ho Chi Minh in name recognition. . . .

I found there was something that the Vietnamese nation had that made me consider our own American Revolution in a new light and what it must have been like then. The American Revolution pitted against the greatest power in the world was also a ragtag guerrilla force with an indomitable spirit, fighting for their homeland. [The trip] made the American Revolution something I could understand for the first time. The Vietnamese really did identify with and believe in the American Revolution. Because of our own origins, they seemed to genuinely believe that the American people understood the meaning of "freedom and independence." It was for them not a slogan; it was deep-felt. This belief not only in themselves but in us as well was disorienting and nearly always touched any American going into Hanoi. The result was that Americans would return more patriotic rather than less. For me, personally, it made me more patient and more hopeful for the American people, and more *patriotic*. . . .

Howard Zinn, who traveled to Hanoi with Daniel Berrigan in early 1968 to receive three prisoners of war whom the North Vietnamese had released, reflects on the admiration of many visitors for the North Vietnamese:

It's hard now to accept the truth of that [enthusiastic reports about North Vietnam] because now the North Vietnamese have won the war and they have a different look about them. I suppose it's like the difference between John Reed's describing the Bolshevik revolution—those first exultant days when everything felt wonderful, people were comradely—and then someone describing the Soviet Union later. . . .

We were seeing them at their best moment. They were the embattled defenders, the underdog. It's true that as human beings they were wonderful, touching, sensitive, loving people. They were defending themselves against great odds, fighting back against planes with rifles. When we were there their kids were going into air raid shelters six times a day. We were tremendously impressed. True, sometimes we were bored by their political lectures. The typical thing that happens in newly revolutionary countries is that they feel they have to impress the foreign visitors with all of this. . . .

The population was armed. The rifles were stacked against the walls of the schoolrooms. If they had had any resentment at all against their leadership they could have overthrown it in a day. Everybody was at work, everybody had something to do. They were united in the way that people are united who are desperate. . . . There were no beggars, no prostitutes—

132

. everybody was living down to the bone but the spirit was very high. Norman Morrison! People would say to me, "Did you know Norman Morrison?"

Rennie Davis returned to the United States the day before the Pentagon demonstration. He spoke there, and then returned to Chicago, where he and others, including Tom Hayden, began to think seriously about the Democratic Convention to be held in that city the following summer. There was no question that a demonstration should be mounted; the only question was What kind? Deeply impressed by what they had seen in North Vietnam, convinced that America was betraying all that was best in the nation by fighting the war, the young activists were more determined than ever to force the Administration to end that war: "Chicago was really conceived coming out of [North] Vietnam."

Shortly after this American contact with the Third World, the very symbol of Third World revolution was killed. On October 7, Ernesto "Che" Guevara, who had helped Fidel Castro to victory in Cuba and had gone on to try to export his brand of revolution to all of Latin America, was wounded by government troops in his stronghold in the canyon of Quebrada del Yuro in the mountains of Bolivia. He was taken to a schoolhouse in the nearby village of La Higuera; there he was "executed" (by gunfire) by Bolivian troops. His body was displayed later to newsmen in the laundry room of the Hospital del Señor de Malta in the provincial capital of Valle Grande. His hands were cut off, supposedly to provide identification by fingerprints but possibly to prevent it, and soon his body was hurriedly cremated by a nervous Bolivian Government. The site of his grave is unknown—"a Bolivian state secret."

Hardly unknown before he died, Che now became a kind of secular saint in the Western world. Posters bearing his bearded visage, beret pulled over his dark hair, blossomed like marijuana weed in student rooms and assembly halls all over Europe and the United States—countries where young people were far less oppressed than in Che's native Argentina or other South and Central American countries. In that strange celebrity that death sometimes brings, Che's passing elevated him to a symbolic importance that he had not had in life.

Che Guevara was the second hero of the Left to die that year, A. J. Muste being the first. The two could not have been more different; even the manner of their deaths bespoke their lives and illuminated their opposite (and antipathetic) philosophies. Che appealed to the young who lusted after Third World revolution in the streets of America; Muste, a lifelong pacifist, was loved by a very different group, people in for the long haul rather than a quick fix of violence. Together, they embodied the two extremes of the still nascent antiwar movement.

During Stop the Draft Week, on the designated day, Monday, October 16, hundreds of draft cards were collected at turn-ins all over the country. One of the largest and most dramatic turn-ins occurred in Boston at the (Unitarian) Arlington Street Church. From its pulpit more than a century before William Ellery Channing had joined the abolitionists' pleas to free the slaves; now the church had offered itself for equally radical action.

The Boston action was organized by the New England Resistance under the direction of William Dowling and Michael Ferber, graduate students at Harvard, and Alex Jack, son of Homer Jack (the national secretary of SANE) and a student at the Boston University School of Theology where Martin Luther King, Jr., had also studied. Alex Jack had tried unsuccessfully to organize an antidraft movement in 1966, while he was a student at Oberlin College, and earlier he had taken active part in the Southern civil rights movement. He and Ferber were joined by several others, including James Harvey, then studying for the priesthood and later one of the Milwaukee 14. A morning rally on Boston Common attracted more than four thousand people; some local colleges had canceled classes so that students could take part. The crowd heard, among others, Howard Zinn: "The 13,000 Americans who died in Vietnam died because they were sent there under the orders of politicians and generals who sacrificed them on behalf of their own ambitions. . . . We owe it to our conscience, to the people of this country, to the principles of American democracy, to declare our independence of this war, to resist it in every way we can, until it comes to an end, until there is peace in Vietnam."

After the rally, one hundred clergymen and two hundred members of the Resistance, under banners that read FACULTY FOR THE RESISTANCE, led the crowd the several blocks to the church, whose carillon welcomed them with "We Shall Overcome." Police lined the front of the church not to arrest the demonstrators or to prevent their entering but to protect them from a threatening mob of counterdemonstrators.

Inside, at a "mass burn-in, turn-in" ceremony, the audience heard a message from Dr. Dana McLean Greeley, president of the Unitarian-Universalist Association: "I don't know what justifies a nation in forcing young men to fight and die for a cause in which they do not believe. That is not democracy but totalitarianism, and it is not freedom but tyranny, if the nation is wrong." Father Robert Cunnane (later also one of the Milwaukee 14) represented the Catholics, and at his suggestion Harvard Professor of Philosophy Hilary Putnam was chosen to represent the atheists. Ferber spoke for the Resistance; Alex Jack read a Vietnamese prayer. James Harvey's speech recalled two German Catholics, one a priest and one a peasant, who died protesting Naziism. The Reverend William Sloane Coffin, referring to the justification of civil disobedience, spoke of "hundreds of history's most revered heroes, Socrates, St. Peter, Milton, Gandhi—men who were not disrespectful of the law but who broke it as a last resort."

Then Dr. George H. Williams of the Harvard Divinity School gave the signal and "co-eds" opened the pew doors along the center aisle; the young men proceeded to the altar, where they either turned over their draft cards for collection and presentation to the Justice Department later in the week, or burned them at William Ellery Channing's candlestick. Sixty-seven cards were burned, 214 turned in.

With several hundred draft cards in a battered leather briefcase, Reverend Coffin, Dr. Spock, Mitchell Goodman, Marcus Raskin, and several others visited the Justice Department on Friday, October 20, to deliver the incriminating pieces of paper to Attorney General Ramsey Clark. They were met by a deputy assistant attorney general, John McDonough, who gave them coffee and asked what he could do for them. Each made a brief antiwar statement. When they prepared to leave, Coffin left the briefcase behind. Dr. Spock's biographer quotes his memory of the day:

> McDonough had to ask, "Am I being tendered something?" Coffin offered him the briefcase full of draft cards, which McDonough had to refuse, primly saying that he was not authorized to accept anything. The cards should, he advised, be submitted to the registrants' local draft boards. Coffin tried again, "You are herewith tenderly being tendered some hundreds of draft cards and supporting statements." Again McDonough refused. In a formal and obviously strained manner he read us the draft law and emphasized the penalties for violations, but we left the case there anyway and departed after shaking hands with him.

In California, Stop the Draft Week provided, for a few days, an unpleasant vision of Che Guevara's guerrilla tactics transferred to urban America. After a peaceful protest by the Resistance, the War Resisters League, and other pacifists at the Northern California Draft Induction Center at Oakland on that Monday, in which 125 people were arrested for nonviolent civil disobedience (sit-downs), 3,000 people gathered there before dawn on the next day. They had rallied the previous night, in defiance of a court order, at the Berkeley campus of the University of California. When they arrived at the draft induction center on Tuesday morning—Bloody Tuesday, as it came to be known—the police were waiting; they attacked the demonstrators with clubs and mace and dispersed them before midmorning. Twenty-five people were arrested; more than 20 were injured. Despite the announced purpose of the demonstration—not only to protest the draft but to stop the induction center from functioning—onlookers expressed shock at the degree of police violence, especially toward newsmen. On Wednesday and Thursday, peaceful sit-ins and picketing took place; 97 were arrested. On Friday, however, urban guerrilla warfare returned with a vengeance. Ten thousand people appeared at the induction center; many wore helmets and carried shields. For three hours they succeeded in blocking entrance to the center, occasionally stopping some busloads of inductees, carrying on a running street battle with police, throwing up barricades, grouping and surfacing to attack again in a constant flow. They left behind a twenty-block area spray-painted with antiwar slogans.

In the end, of course, they had to disband; their triumph was intoxicating but short-lived. Some of them may have hoped actually to stop the war in this way; others, more attuned to the reality of American life in the mid-sixties, understood that armed revolution, domestic violence, the mobile tactics of guerrilla street warfare were simply unacceptable to the vast majority of the American people—far more unacceptable than the war in Vietnam. And more, that a great deal of police action would be tolerated by the American public in order to preserve their domestic tranquility, war or no war.

David Dellinger had asked Jerry Rubin to assist with the Washington march and to act as liaison between the East and West coast groups. Rubin, who had directed, among other events, the Berkeley Vietnam Day in 1965, had argued for a march on the Pentagon rather than a rally at the Capitol: the Pentagon was both symbol and substance of America's military power, and to march on it as the climax of a week of antidraft activity seemed nicely appropriate—"confronting the warmakers," as the demonstration's call put it.

In the weeks immediately preceding the October march, the national board of SANE, still haunted by the ghost of Joseph McCarthy, had begun to come apart on the question of nonexclusion—of associating with ragtag and bobtail leftists of all shades of opinion. It was the familiar quandary of what strange bedfellows politics made, but it was complicated in this instance because the fight threatened to destroy SANE and any other organization that even considered the question. In fact, the entire northern California chapter, under the leadership of Robert Pickus, fled national SANE over the issue. Finally SANE decided that local chapters could join the march if they wished; many did. One result of the SANE battle was that Dr. Spock resigned as codirector after suffering harsh words about his "ecumenical promiscuity"; his successor was a more cautious type, history professor H. Stuart Hughes.

SDS wrestled with another question: was the march tactically correct? To be seen with avowed Trotskyites did not worry SDS, but its national officers frowned on the idea of having a march at all. Further, despite the slow progress of SDS projects like ERAP, many of its members still clung to the idea of reforming the whole of American society rather than concentrating on the single issue of the war.

At its annual convention the previous summer, SDS had given only a lukewarm endorsement to October 21: "SDS regrets the decision of the National Mobilization Committee to call for a march on Washington in October." In SDS's opinion, such demonstrations tended to "delude" people into thinking that they were having an effect on policy. If individual SDS chapters did support and join the march, they were urged to call for immediate U.S. withdrawal, an extreme position at the time. In the end, SDS reversed itself as October 21 drew near and the government stalled on granting permits for the demonstration; its leadership urged SDSers to participate, and many hundreds did.

There were other, more critical tensions within the Mobilization itself, primarily over the question of tactics and the location of the proposed action. The Socialist Workers Party, as always, pushed hard for a legal mass march and rally without any civil disobedience or confrontation with the authorities. Others, including many radical pacifists, wanted nonviolent direct action—civil disobedience.

Matters were not helped by Rubin's attempt to recruit the counterculture, which put out a come-to-Washington appeal with an invitation to (in Sidney Peck's words) "come and piss on the White House lawn" or similar suggestions calculated to alarm the middle-class types so necessary to give credibility to any antiwar action. Abbie Hoffman, beginning to emerge as the Pied Piper of the nation's alienated young, announced that he and others would try to "levitate" the Pentagon ten feet off the ground and then drive out its "evil spirits," thereby stopping the war. The first issue of the *Mobilizer,* distributed at the NCNP convention at Chicago, did nothing to enlist anyone's support for what promised to be a freak-show fiasco, and so Peck suppressed it and put out a new issue, calmly stating the theme of the demonstration—"from dissent to resistance"—and its multitactical approach:

1. a rally at the Lincoln Memorial;
2. a mass march to the Pentagon;
3. a second rally at the Pentagon which would include nonviolent direct action (civil disobedience) for those who wished it.

There was also considerable disagreement about the route to be taken from the Lincoln Memorial to the Pentagon. The government had insisted that the marchers take a back-road, circuitous way which was torn up with construction. Many of the Mobe's people wanted to ignore that edict and go directly via the highway; they feared not only that the longer route would delay and dissipate the demonstration, but also that the authorities would cut them off.

On the night before the demonstration and into the small hours a meeting took place in Arthur Kinoy's hotel room. Kinoy, the lawyer who had achieved momentary fame by being forcibly ejected from a hearing of the House Un-American Activities Committee the previous year, argued eloquently for staying with the route assigned by the government. "He laid out his case as if he were before a jury," recalls Peck. "He said that the important thing is to get to the Pentagon, because what you want is for the whole world to see that the American people are no longer afraid to confront their own military, and so the symbol that has to be communicated all around the world is the people wanting this war to end, and the military protecting their household and wanting to continue the war. And anything that is not in line with having that kind of confrontation take place is not in accord with the political goals of this action, which is to continue to surface the dissent, but also to build a sense of resistance to the military."

So they stayed with the assigned route.

The following afternoon, Saturday, October 21, a cool, sunny day, approximately fifty thousand people (some estimates run as high as one hundred thousand) assembled at the Lincoln Memorial to hear speeches and singing. David Dellinger announced that this march marked the end of peaceful protest; from now on, there would be civil disobedience and "confrontation. . . . This is the beginning of a new stage in the American peace movement in which the cutting edge becomes active resistance." "No more parades," commented one young man. Official Washington, indeed, had expected worse: the White House was under "extraordinary" security, with a post-and-cable-fence barricade and police guards posted at intervals of fifty to one hundred yards all around the inside of the main fence. Dr. Spock ("the enemy is Lyndon Johnson . . . who betrayed us"), Dagmar Wilson of WSP, the Reverend William Sloane Coffin, and SNCC's John Lewis spoke, among others. Lewis led the crowd in the chant, "Hell, no, we won't go!" and then asked a moment's silence for Che Guevara. Later in the day, when many demonstrators chose to march on the Pentagon, the relatively few blacks in attendance decided instead to attend a rally at Banneker Park, near Howard University. As Lewis put it to Dellinger, "We don't want to play Indian outside the white man's fort."

The crowd was largely students, many with banners indentifying their schools and colleges, but there were also church groups, old-line peace and leftist groups, unions, a contingent from the Progressive Labor Party—over 150 organizations in all, and a handful of celebrities including Norman Mailer, who commemorated the event by writing *The Armies of the Night*. Many people carried American flags; a few carried Viet Cong flags; the usual plethora of signs included LBJ THE BUTCHER and WESTMORELAND: SUPREME GENERAL OF GENOCIDE.

As the rally drew to a close, people assembled for the march across the river to the Pentagon. Again the dispute broke out: why not go the direct route? People sat down until the issue was resolved. Peck argued strongly—Kinoy's argument—for keeping to the original circuitous way: "If we take the highway, they will block us," he remembers saying, "and you're not going to have a political confrontation with the Pentagon, you're going to have a political confrontation with a highway."

Finally the marchers moved—the long way around—and began to stream into the space reserved for them, the north parking lot of the Pentagon. Suddenly a large group broke away and tried to "storm" the building; they were SDSers and some New York radicals, dubbed the Revolutionary Contingent. Perhaps twenty-five of them managed to enter the Pentagon itself. They were quickly caught, beaten, and arrested. The others, now joined by perhaps five thousand more, remained on the plaza before the building facing the lines of federal marshals carrying nightsticks and soldiers carrying bayonet-tipped M-14 rifles. Some of the demonstrators shouted obscenities, hurling eggs and bottles; some carried the Viet Cong flag. "There was no leadership, that was what was so beautiful," said one participant. Those who were arrested, who had been clubbed until they were broken and bloody, might not have agreed.

Kinoy had tried to negotiate a permit for demonstrators to go legally up onto the steps of the building, but as that attempt failed, wire cutters were produced, the fence was breached, and an eager vanguard pushed forward as Defense Secretary McNamara peered from his office window. These were primarily (1) the "levitators" (counterculturals) and a few radical pacifists, and (2) the "prestigious" delegation—the celebrities. They were all promptly arrested; Bradford Lyttle remembers the eerie sensation he had when the marshals who collared him called him by his first name. And so Sidney Peck was left, so to speak, holding the fort.

As Peck tried to conduct a second rally in the parking lot in the fading light of the autumn afternoon, the air already growing chill, he felt sudden resentment toward his fellow organizers for abandoning him. At precisely the appointed time the sound company came to collect its equipment, leaving him with only a bullhorn for communication. More and more people began to stream through the opening in the fence, dissipating the rally. The Socialist Workers, always critical of civil disobedience, began to urge everyone to go home. People who did not want to approach the Pentagon wanted instead to find their buses, which were parked all around the Pentagon area. Children were lost; people became separated from their groups. The parking lot became an information area, a sea of chaos as people milled about. "There was literally no other leadership," says Peck, "and I felt angry that I hadn't been informed that people were going up to be arrested and angry that all this was being dumped on me. We had never even gotten to the speakers, and the idea of giving people a choice about going up to the Pentagon had not had a chance to present itself."

Darkness fell. They began to smell tear gas drifting down from the Pentagon, and then came requests for blankets and food and wet handkerchiefs through which to breathe. Several thousand people, mostly students, had settled down on the plaza in front of the main entrance to the Pentagon; there, as the night drew on, they tried to have a teach-in with some of the eighteen hundred National Guardsmen and three thousand troops from Fort Bragg, North Carolina. Many of the students were there as members of student religious groups, or were divinity school students, and had come to make moral witness. "Join us!" they cried to the soldiers. "Our fight is not with you!" Some of them, in a sweet and gentle gesture, put flowers into the barrels of the soldiers' rifles.

"Christ, it's getting cold," said someone.

"Burn a draft card! Keep warm!" came the reply—and then and throughout the night, several hundred draft cards were burned, making the Pentagon demonstration of October 1967 the "largest mass draft card burning in the history of protest against the Vietnam War." One SDSer recalled a man wearing a Veterans for Peace hat who burned his discharge papers.

Back in the parking lot the evening wore on, the chaos continuing. In the midst of all the worry and fear and darkness, the badly harassed Peck, on the makeshift stage with his bullhorn frantically trying to keep order, felt sudden pain—physical pain, not psychological. "I just couldn't believe it. Someone had bitten me on my arm. I looked down and saw Norma Becker. 'Norma,' I said, 'what the hell are you doing?' 'Trying to get your attention,' she said. 'I've had it,' " he said, and, dropping his bullhorn (not on Becker), he went up to the Pentagon steps.

It was then around 10 P.M. The young people had settled in for the night, making small bonfires with their placards and posters, sharing food and blankets which had begun to arrive, sent in mostly by the Women Strike for Peace Washington branch and by many local church groups.

Some of the arrests that had been made earlier—not those of the "celebrities"—had been violent, people being clubbed bloody. Young women had been beaten bloodier than young men, possibly to goad the men to fight to "protect" them. David Dellinger, whose pacifism precluded violent action, had hoped for something that he called "Gandhi and Guerrilla"—a "creative synthesis" of "nonviolent militancy" which involved both active resistance (blocking the Pentagon) and a teach-in for the troops who guarded it. He remembers:

> We had upped the ante from protest to resistance. Women Strike, the Socialist Workers had said we would cut down the numbers. This was one of the most uphill fights I ever had to make—all the traditional people, the people who had been in it the longest, were saying we shouldn't do it and I went the other way with a lot of the younger, newer people. And to get there and find all those people were there confirmed my feeling that the older people were wrong in their prediction.

The other thing was that that was the first time they brought out federal troops and that was the big debate, about how to respond to them. Some of us were saying we should approach them as future allies and as victims of the war; others were saying they're nothing but fascists. In my contingent were Monsignor Charles Rice [from Pittsburgh] and Ben Spock. The three of us were up front with a megaphone. All of a sudden the troops came marching out as if a door opened. The three of us addressed them on the agreed-upon theme: "You are not our enemies, you are people like us. Join us. . . ." Then another door opened and I said [to our people], "Get on your knees," or "Sit down . . ." And they were coming in military formation and the sergeant said something like "Bloody up the motherfuckers." I was down like this [he bends over and puts his arms over his head], like [in the civil rights demonstrations] in the South waiting to be hit and they came up and a lot of them just went [gestures a tap] on me, they were like love taps even with batons. Now who knows? At the time the interpretation I made was that they had responded to our thing and they technically fulfilled what they had been asked to do but they were trying not to hurt us.

Now there was some disagreement among the demonstrators: some wanted an all-out confrontation with the troops, while others wanted simply to bear witness. All during the night, in an action reminiscent of the start of the Russian Revolution in 1917, demonstrators had kept up a direct appeal to the troops. Gary Rader, a former Green Beret who had burned his draft card in Central Park in April and had been one of the organizers of Chicago Area Draft Resisters (CADRE), used a bullhorn to address the troops, and at one point his voice and that of the officer giving orders overlapped in a surreal way:

My name is Gary Rader, I'm twenty-three years Company B hold your line. Nobody comes, nobody goes. I was in the Special Forces Reserve Company B hold your line and I quit and I want nobody comes nobody goes I want to tell you what led me up to that Company hold your line what led me up to that decision nobody comes nobody goes we will be heard . . .

As *Liberation* described it:

Rader was heard, for the officer realized that he was shaming his men by plugging their ears in public. He must have guessed, too, what detestation they felt for him. He fell silent and Rader continued, speaking, carrying the teach-in to the troops themselves. It was a beautiful occasion and a rare one, for the troops had no choice but to listen—and some at least had long been softened by the youthful voices, the beards, the lack of beards, the long hair, the short hair, the silky legs, the courage and the communal generosity of the Traitors, the Reds and Drug Addicts assembled before them. Rader spoke in a forthright way, without condescension or moral superiority, telling of his own enlightenment, the history of Vietnam and the lies our government had addressed to its people. He described the experiences of Sergeant Donald Duncan and told how he himself, at Ft. Bragg, had talked

140

with returning Special Forces on leave from Vietnam. Those were not men who needed to believe in the war. They described our blunders, our destruction of civil life, the corruption of Saigon, the hatred the Vietnamese feel for us. It made no difference; they were going back. It had made a difference to Rader, however. He had become hungry to know, and now he described his efforts to find out. For many of the troops who heard him, this was the first real news of the war.

Eventually Rader, like many others around him, was arrested; he served thirty days in jail.

Cathy Wilkerson of SDS tried to reassure those who wanted no part of further bloodshed: leave if you want to, she said, don't feel you have to stay. (Eventually, as we will see, the test of one's commitment to the Movement would be the degree of confrontation one was willing to risk and the amount of punishment one was willing to take. At this time, however, SDS's position was that going to jail or being beaten by the authorities was politically unwise: "the function of a radical was to organize resistance," which was difficult to do from prison, as the experience of the Catholic Left was to show.)

As midnight approached, the media people began to leave. The marshals lined up again to resume their arrests; they began to assault people in the front lines. Peck borrowed a bullhorn. He broadcast an appeal to the marshals, reminding them that the demonstrators had a valid permit until midnight the following night. He called upon the authority of the General Services Administration official with whom he had negotiated. He warned the marshals that any arrests now would be illegal.

His tactic worked: the arrests stopped, and the demonstrators were allowed to resume their action. Around midnight things quieted down. It was a crisp, clear fall night; the sky was filled with stars. People huddled under blankets in their little affinity groups. There was, Peck recalls, a "sense of quietness." Then someone began to sing. The song that she chose was not a rousing antiwar chant, or a mournful folk paean to brotherhood and peace, but the old Christmas hymn "Silent Night." It was, says Peck, "a moment I will never forget. Before you knew it, it was picked up by everyone. It was truly a moment of religious awe. We had a tremendous feeling that what we were doing was a good thing, it was the right thing to do, and it was a profound expression of ending the killing and restoring peace. . . ."

In the hours before dawn the SDS people, who had assumed leadership, announced that the demonstrators would withdraw. This was done in an orderly fashion, a dignified exit from the sit-in, and, it was felt, a statement that the demonstrators were in charge of their own people. It was a conscious use of "guerrilla" tactics: having struck, withdraw to strike again. Some observers and participants felt that Gandhian tactics would have been more appropriate at this time: arrest and jail would have kept leaders and followers together.

On Sunday morning, while attending services at the National City Christian Church, President Johnson heard the pastor excoriate the "bearded oafs who listen to the strumming of lugubrious guitars"; like the "bums" of Richard Nixon's term of office, the protesters' lifestyle and appearance seemed almost more offensive than their politics.

Only a few hundred demonstrators remained at the Pentagon on Sunday. They listened to several hours of speeches. At midnight, when the forty-eight-hour permit had expired and the demonstrators still refused to leave, the arrests began again. In all, 683 persons were arrested—by far the greatest number arrested at any antiwar demonstration until that time.

Was the Pentagon action of October 1967 a success?

"Yes," says Peck unequivocally. "When I arrived at the Pentagon I saw Arthur Kinoy's vision—the people confronting the military establishment. Our fight was not with the GIs, and we told them so."

And did the Mobilization now, at last, have a movement?

"No question. I felt that now there was a resistance movement underway as well —a mass draft resistance movement—a resistance movement in and among GIs, and certainly a resistance to research and development on campuses. I felt that the dissent had surfaced, but that we had also surfaced a movement of resistance: people on a mass basis who would refuse to be complicit, who would refuse to pay taxes, to do the research, to accept the draft, who would refuse to fight, to produce and transport the weaponry—much like the French resistance to the Algerian war. . . . Not that we had it, but that we *could* have it."

To no one's surprise, the Administration did not approve of the Pentagon march any more than it had approved of any of the previous antiwar demonstrations. The protesters were not helping to bring peace closer, said LBJ; peace would come sooner "if the American people were united rather than divided." In late November, two weeks after a particularly nasty demonstration against Dean Rusk, three Republican congressmen, including the House Republican leader, Gerald Ford of Michigan, announced that they had been persuaded that Hanoi had not only applauded but had actually organized the Pentagon march. They had had a long report read to them by the President himself on October 24, they said, detailing meetings between David Dellinger and several other antiwar activists (whom LBJ refused to name) and Vietnamese Communist officials.† The President refused to release the report, despite appeals to do so from the three; nevertheless, they said, they were convinced that the activities of Stop the Draft Week had been "cranked up" in Hanoi. Even more alarming to the unwary was a statement by Senator Frank Lausche (D-Ohio) that "superior forces" were behind demonstrations on college campuses protesting appearances by Dean Rusk. "There are manipulators," said Lausche, "architects behind closed doors watching innocent youth bring shame upon our nation."

The authorities in New York had been alerted to a new force, if not a superior one, when a group calling itself the Revolutionary Solidarity Committee claimed responsibility for burning Lyndon Johnson in effigy after he appeared at a dinner for George Meany of the AFL-CIO at the Hotel Americana on November 9. Police had been warned that Rusk's effigy, too, would be burned when he appeared at a

† Presumably this was a CIA report on the Bratislava meeting; see pp. 130–31.

dinner of the Foreign Policy Association on November 14. Two busloads of riot-trained tactical patrol police were called out; one thousand police guarded the New York Hilton, where Rusk was to speak.

The demonstration against Rusk was the first of two attempts on the East Coast to imitate the "mobile tactics" of the Berkeley Stop the Draft Week actions at the Oakland induction center in October. About three thousand demonstrators turned out, but they were prevented from getting any nearer the hotel than across the street—Sixth Avenue, a broad expanse. Here and there a few demonstrators tried to break through the barricades but they were quickly driven back by mounted police or by police on foot swinging clubs. Eventually things got nastier: one policeman was hit on the head with a bottle, and plastic bags of red liquid—cow's blood, someone claimed—were thrown at the police. Soon a minority split off and roamed through midtown, blocking traffic, filling the sidewalks, trapping pedestrians in stores and shoving them out of the way on the pavements, taunting police, eluding arrest. Some of them sang and chanted and danced; others jeered and screamed obscenities. They ignored the pleas of one of their group, who identified himself as a member of SDS, to return to the vicinity of the Hilton; instead they surged toward Bryant Park, behind the New York Public Library, where they heard another SDSer speaking through a bullhorn: "We're demonstrating against the American establishment, against the liberal fascists." The *Times* described the demonstrators that night as "riotous"; the demonstration "had its own dynamic," said one of the SDS organizers, which the *Times* interpreted to mean that SDS "could not be held responsible for individual pranks." Despite several attempts by the demonstrators who remained at the Hilton to charge police lines, the barricades held and Rusk was not disturbed as he told the dinner guests of the failure of the "other side" to respond to administration attempts to deescalate the war. At ten forty-five he was escorted to the Hilton garage by one hundred policemen; he drove away without seeing any pickets. The demonstrators, frustrated, had been reduced to a rowdy band of several hundred who marched yelling and cursing through the nighttime streets to the United Nations, and then back to the Hilton, where the sight of a long line of police still guarding the sidewalk discouraged them and they left.

Nevertheless, they had begun to have their effect: in a column the next day, Tom Wicker of the *Times* noted that both Rusk and the President were becoming more and more isolated within their inner circles of friends and advisers, reluctant to make public appearances, where they would almost certainly be subjected to pickets at best and screaming, cursing, egg-throwing mobs at worst. The President had begun to limit his appearances to military bases; the week before, Rusk had canceled a visit to Boston to a State Department foreign policy conference.

Johnson was not content to allow his critics to speak and act unopposed, however: they might criticize him in the halls of Congress and jeer him—and worse—at public appearances, but he would fight them as he fought the Viet Cong. One method was to try to link the antiwar movement to Moscow, Peking, and Hanoi. Some weeks before, the CIA had begun surveillance of the antiwar movement; its conclusion, presented to the President around this time, was that "on the basis of what we now know, we see no significant evidence that would prove Communist control or direction of the U.S. peace movement or its leaders." Subsequent CIA studies had the same result, as did those of the FBI and Army intelligence, also begun in mid-1967.

One of Johnson's most dramatic public acts, in mid-November, was to replace his Secretary of Defense. Robert McNamara, of "McNamara's war," would leave at the end of February, it was announced, to become the president of the World Bank; he would be replaced by a well-known LBJ supporter, Washington lawyer Clark Clifford.

McNamara, one of the principal architects of the Vietnam War, had long been troubled by the failure of the policies he had helped to set in motion. In June of that year he had ordered the secret, massive study of the war which four years later would become known as the Pentagon Papers. In August he had testified before the Senate Preparedness Investigations Subcommittee; the session was closed, but in his censored opening statement McNamara criticized the bombing policy then in effect and said that there was "no reason to believe that North Vietnam can be bombed to the negotiating table. The fate of the war," he argued, "will be decided by the fighting in South Vietnam."

In its subsequent publication of the hearing, the committee revealed that McNamara had delivered "the most devastating testimony about the value of aerial bombardment ever heard from a ranking Defense official in wartime." He said that

> *173,000* U.S. bombing sorties had destroyed *$320 million* in facilities—at a cost of *$911 million* in American aircraft [emphasis added]. . . .
>
> Despite heavy concentration on infiltration routes near the demilitarized zone, only 2 percent of the North Vietnamese soldiers going South were reported killed by air strikes. . . .
>
> Despite intensive bombardment, traffic over the roads South had increased; the whole road network had grown.

The senators' reaction was unanimous: they urged Johnson "to widen the air war against North Vietnam and abandon his policy of 'carefully controlled' bombing."

Johnson's response was the "San Antonio formula," a speech in that city on September 29 in which he offered to halt the bombing of North Vietnam if doing so would lead to "prompt, productive" talks, and on the assumption that Hanoi "would not take advantage of the cessation." The speech was a defense of U.S. policy, including the argument that by fighting in Vietnam the United States was staving off World War III (instead of risking it, as critics charged). Senator J. William Fulbright called the speech "nothing new," and indeed it led to nothing.

On November 1 McNamara submitted a memorandum to the President in which he recommended that the United States should:

> Halt the bombing of North Vietnam;
> Announce that the U.S. would send no additional troops to South Vietnam;
> Review American military operations with an eye to reducing casualties,

curtailing the destruction of Vietnam and turning over more of the war to South Vietnamese forces.

This was McNamara's last attempt to reverse the Administration's Vietnam policy, and by the middle of the month his departure had been announced.

Johnson had another plan to win the propaganda war at home: a "Success Offensive" designed to sway public opinion. "Nothing is more important than that the public get the facts," said Walt W. Rostow, one of Johnson's most trusted advisers. On Veterans Day Johnson made a flying tour of eight military installations to exhort the troops. In Vietnam, reporters were given a lengthy briefing to show that Communist strength had declined. Vice President Hubert Humphrey, visiting the war, went on "The Today Show" to announce that "we are beginning to win this struggle." (During Humphrey's stay in Vietnam, Saigon's Independence Palace had been shelled while he was in it attending a reception.) Newspapers were bombarded with favorable information "leaked" by Rostow's Psychological Strategy Committee, the Administration's propaganda unit. Many of them printed the stories.

Most important, Johnson had General Westmoreland speak again, as he had done after the April demonstrations. At the National Press Club on November 21, Westmoreland exuded optimism: "We have reached an important point when the end begins to come into view," he said, predicting that within two years the South Vietnamese would be fighting their own war and U.S. troops would be gone— Nixon's future Vietnamization plan, McNamara's light at the end of the tunnel.

All of this activity had a predictable effect on a public that wanted very much to believe what its government told it. Even before the full effect of the "Success Offensive" could be felt, voters in San Francisco voted on a referendum question about the war: "Should the United States declare an immediate cease-fire and withdraw its troops from Vietnam?" By 63.34 percent to 36.66 percent, San Franciscans voted no. The heaviest no came from the middle- and upper-middle-class precincts; voters in heavily black districts, poor districts which had seen rioting the previous summer, voted yes. Some critics said that the word "immediate" defeated the proposal.

A Stop the Draft Week Committee had been formed in New York shortly after the Pentagon demonstrations; it was composed of antiwar and pacifist groups from moderate to radical—about forty in all. On November 30 it announced that during the week of December 4–8 it would attempt to halt activity at the armed forces induction center at 39 Whitehall Street in lower Manhattan—the second use of the Berkeley "mobile tactics" strategy in the East. Despite warnings that the West Coast demonstrations had not, in retrospect, been markedly successful, the group was determined to go ahead.

On the Monday, a draft card turn-in took place at the Church of St. John the Evangelist in Brooklyn. On Tuesday came the first action at the Whitehall center: a sit-in by older and more moderate factions including the War Resisters League, Women Strike for Peace, and the Women's International League for Peace and Freedom. The demonstrators gathered at 5 A.M. to find twenty-five hundred police awaiting them. The center was barricaded with wooden sawhorses. Those who wanted to commit civil disobedience (and be arrested) were unable to approach the steps of the building to sit-in before being taken away. Dr. Spock tried to crawl under the barricades, then to climb over; finally a sympathetic police officer showed him an opening down the way and he was allowed his few moments of symbolic protest on the steps before he was arrested. Also arrested that day were Allen Ginsberg, the Irish diplomat Dr. Conor Cruise O'Brien, his wife Maire, and 260 others; despite some police who kicked and punched those they were arresting, it was a generally peaceful day.

On Wednesday about twenty-five hundred younger demonstrators had their turn; using the highly touted "mobile tactics," they approached the Whitehall center from Battery Park in three columns. They were badly outnumbered by the police, however, who turned them back at every opportunity; one group, known as the "Lost Battalion," was never able even to get near the center, marching back and forth through lower Manhattan's narrow streets until finally its members gave up in despair. Some forty people were arrested that day.

By Thursday, December 7, the demonstrators had given up the idea of "paralyzing" the induction center; not until they met in Battery Park did their leaders reveal to them where they were headed. Longshoremen attacked some of them before they began to move uptown, only to find that the police, once again, would not let them pass. Fred Halstead, whose SWP was so firmly opposed to confrontational demonstrations which led to arrest, nevertheless found himself on the scene that day as he had been the year before when he attended Stop the Draft Week in solidarity with A. J. Muste and wound up in jail. This time, however, Halstead was determined not to be arrested. He had worn a shirt and tie and a nice-looking overcoat. When he saw that police were beginning to make arrests he picked a *Wall Street Journal* out of the trash can to use as a prop and politely inquired of an officer how he could avoid the fracas and get to the stock exchange. It was a nice maneuver for a dedicated opponent of the capitalist system. Finally a number of the demonstrators reached the UN, where they were all arrested, dragged to police vans, taken to the 7th Precinct station, photographed, interrogated—and then told that they were free to go. Out of some 300 arrested that day, only 137 were charged —an "honest mistake," explained a police spokesman, since police communications were disrupted by the added burden of security for the dignitaries, including President Johnson, who were attending the funeral of Francis Cardinal Spellman.

The last day of Stop the Draft Week began with another breakdown in communications, this time on the part of the protesters, who mistakenly gathered at a government military building at Sixteenth Street and Irving Place. When they tried to march uptown to Forty-second Street the police charged them in what was described as a "massacre." Meanwhile, 25 demonstrators who showed up at 6 A.M. at 39 Whitehall Street were met by 1,000 policemen. The Irving Place protesters finally got to midtown, to the offices of The Dow Chemical Company at Rockefeller Plaza, where their efforts came to an end. One hundred forty people were arrested that day; in all, that week, 585 people were arrested out of thousands taking part in demonstrations.

The business of the Whitehall Street induction center, like the Oakland center, had not been stopped; the draftees were still being inducted, the war went on.

In mid-December, the Louis Harris Poll produced some further bad news for the antiwar groups. The results showed that

—more than three quarters of the population believed that the recent antiwar demonstrations "encouraged the Communists to fight all the harder";

—seven tenths believed that antiwar demonstrations were "acts of disloyalty" to the soldiers fighting the war;

—more than 50 percent believed that General Lewis Hershey was right when he said that youths who obstructed recruiting for the armed forces or defense-related industries should lose their deferments.

And, in a poll at Christmas:

—58 percent favored seeing the war through and stepping up military pressure against the Communists;

—63 percent opposed halting the bombing of North Vietnam to see if the Communists would agree to negotiate.

At the end of December about three hundred members of the SDS National Council met in Bloomington, Indiana. They were faced with three problems:

1. the growing unwieldiness of the organization;
2. the increasing distance between local chapters and the National Office; and
3. the challenge by Progressive Labor for control.

The first problem had arisen out of SDS's rapid growth and its devotion to participatory democracy. But times were changing; SDS needed to be able to act and respond more quickly as events occurred. In an article in the December 18 issue of *New Left Notes,* Greg Calvert suggested a "steering committee" that would organize "strategies and programs" to enable SDS to become a "revolutionary organization."

Such a proposal illuminated SDS's second problem, the distance between membership and leadership. Many members in local college chapters were hardly ready to call themselves revolutionaries; for them, distributing a call to a rally was a radical act, and they were not yet ready to commit themselves to, say, a resistance movement directed against the corporate hierarchy.

The National Office, however, saw itself increasingly as the vanguard of a revolution. And that vision led directly to the way it tried to handle its third problem, the PL challenge.

"It's not my fault that reality is Marxist," Che Guevara had said—and now SDS, in the face of PL's unceasing challenge, had perhaps concluded that revolution is of necessity Marxist as well. Trying to counter PL's arguments, which were always couched in Marxist language, SDS found itself groping for an equally effective ideology.

"There was—and is—no other coherent, integrative, and explicit philosophy of revolution [than Marxism]," wrote Carl Oglesby some months later. And so in order to make its revolution, to fight off PL, SDS began to look to Marx. Increasingly, Marxist terms began to appear in SDS literature: "bourgeois civil liberties," "class analysis," "imperialism." Increasing contacts were being made with Marxists in Europe and in the Third World: Vietnamese, Cubans, etc.

Marxist terminology appeared, too, as the National Council grappled with the question of a proposed student strike in April of the following year. Carl Davidson and Greg Calvert, in an article in *New Left Notes,* "Ten Days to Shake the Empire,"‡ proposed something more than just a strike: they called upon "the radical student movement . . . to develop a political strategy of anti-imperialism," focusing on the war in Vietnam and aimed particularly at "financial and corporate industrial targets."

PL's suggestion for an April action was to concentrate on "base-building" on the campuses—organizing students with the idea of reaching out to the working-class community, to forge eventually PL's worker-student alliance.

This was voted down, and the convention agreed on a compromise: that ten days of resistance would take place in April, but also that local chapters would be free to take such action as they saw fit. The "ten days" would include "education programs, joint actions and demonstrations aimed at a variety of institutions." Nothing more specific was mentioned.

Thus, faced with PL's challenge on the one hand, and the widening distance between the National Office and the local chapters on the other, SDS attempted to hold itself together and make ready for the new year. The war in Vietnam had not been forgotten—far from it—but other issues pressed hard. The idealism of the early years was being sorely tested in the harsh realities of human nature and the nature of the political process. PL aimed to fill the vacuum where SDS's power should have been; the organization was falling apart of its own weight, unevenly distributed between the National Office and the local chapters.

On the last day of the year came New Year's greetings from Ho Chi Minh. Just as the polls had said, he was grateful for the help of Americans who were opposed to the war: "Friends, in struggling hard to make the United States Government stop its aggression in Vietnam you are defending justice and, at the same time, you are giving us support. . . ." He reminded the American people of the eight hundred thousand tons of bombs dropped on North Vietnam, of the destruction that tonnage had caused to homes, schools, hospitals, dikes. He mentioned the damage that the cost of supporting the war had already done to the American economy; further, the "United States aggressors," said Ho, had "stained the honor" of their country. But eventually he and his countrymen would win and would live in "peace and friendship" with the rest of the world: "We enjoy the support of brothers and friends on the five continents. We shall win, and so will you."

"Thank you for your support for the Vietnamese people."

‡ In 1967 few Americans had heard of John Reed's classic work on the Russian Revolution, *Ten Days That Shook the World* (1919). In 1981 Warren Beatty's film *Reds* popularized Reed as a romantic hero; in 1967 the "corporate hierarchy" would never have financed the making of a film that idealized an American leftist such as Reed. Davidson and Calvert's title, of course, was deliberately chosen to recall Reed's account of the greatest Marxist-Leninist triumph of all.

1968:
The Fulcrum Year

NINETEEN SIXTY-EIGHT was the fulcrum year, the year the balance scales tipped against the American effort in Vietnam. It was a year in which events happened so quickly, hammer blow after hammer blow, that in retrospect it seems astonishing that the national psyche survived intact. Perhaps it did not.

It began with an indictment handed down against five men including America's best-known baby doctor. On January 5 a federal grand jury in Boston indicted Dr. Benjamin Spock, the Reverend William Sloane Coffin, Mitchell Goodman, Michael Ferber, and Marcus Raskin on a single count of conspiracy to "counsel, aid and abet young men to violate the draft laws." Four acts were held to make up the conspiracy: circulating the "Call to Resist Illegitimate Authority"; holding a press conference in New York City on October 2, 1967, to promote the call and to announce the events of Stop the Draft Week scheduled for later in the month; accepting draft cards from young men; and presenting those cards to the Justice Department. "The Government is not likely to prosecute us," Spock had said at a news conference announcing the December Stop the Draft Week. "Its bankruptcy in the moral sense is proved by its refusal to move against those of us who have placed ourselves between the young people and the draft." He and the other defendants pleaded not guilty at their arraignment on January 29; they were released on $1,000 bond each without surety.

Meanwhile, the men who had allowed the war to happen were convening in Washington. As the second session of the Ninetieth Congress began, eighty-seven-year-old Jeanette Rankin led a group of more than five thousand women in a protest march at the foot of Capitol Hill. Rankin, from Montana, was the first woman member of Congress. She served two terms, one in 1917–19, when she voted against U.S. entry into World War I, and one in 1941–43, when she voted against U.S. entry into World War II. The women wanted to present Congress with their petition, which demanded the withdrawal of all American troops from Vietnam and the solving of domestic problems in the United States, but they were barred from doing so. Citing long-established precedent, Vice President Humphrey

149

refused to allow any Senate business to be transacted until after President Johnson had delivered his State of the Union message. An indignant Wayne Morse, denouncing the refusal to allow the women their "precious Constitutional right" of petition, forced the Senate to a roll-call vote on adjournment until after the President's speech; it passed 53–3, with Morse, Ernest Gruening, and Gaylord Nelson voting against. The women waited in the snow, singing "We Shall Overcome" with folk singer Judy Collins, until finally a small delegation led by Rankin and including Coretta Scott King was allowed inside the Capitol to present the petition to House Speaker John W. McCormack of Massachusetts (who emphasized his disagreement with them) and Senate Majority Leader Mike Mansfield, Rankin's fellow Montanan.

On January 23 occurred an event that was uncomfortably reminiscent of the Tonkin Gulf incident: the intelligence ship *Pueblo* was captured off North Korea and its commander, Lloyd M. Bucher, and his eighty-two men were taken prisoner by the North Koreans. The incident was clouded in uncertainty, just as the incident in the Tonkin Gulf three and one half years previously had been: North Korea claimed that the *Pueblo* had violated the twelve-mile limit off the North Korean coast, while Washington called North Korea's statement "cynical" and a "distortion of the facts."

Two days later, on the twenty-fifth, President Johnson called up 14,787 air force and navy reservists—the politically sensitive call-up that Congress had long feared. Congress was not notified in advance: newsmen told congressional leaders about the call-up twenty minutes after the White House announcement.

On January 27, the Student Mobilization Committee held a planning conference in Chicago attended by more than nine hundred students from 110 colleges in twenty-five states. Of perhaps even greater significance than those numbers was the attendance of students from some forty high schools: the average age of those attending the conference was twenty, and fewer than a dozen participants were over thirty. SMC during these months was performing what many people thought was the work of SDS—and, in fact, SDS always got much credit for antiwar work done by other groups, such being the power of media identification. In early 1967, shortly after SMC was formed, Bettina Aptheker had called for a protest strike by one million students—a highly unlikely number, so it seemed at the time. Now, in January of the presidential election year, the SMC delegates voted to support the Ten Days of Resistance in April announced by SDS; in the end it was SMC that brought about Aptheker's vision of one million, while SDS once more abdicated.

And then came Tet.

On the night of January 30–31 the United States Embassy in Saigon was overrun by Viet Cong guerrillas; it was not reclaimed until the next day. Part of the attack was filmed for television. When the resulting footage—raw, unedited—was shown to the nation the following evening, Americans had their most terrifying glimpse to date of how far from reality were the official reports on the progress of the war.

The Tet Offensive of January–February 1968 was the turning point in the war. Tet—the Vietnamese New Year—had been a time for truce in previous years. This year, however, the New Year's firecrackers in Saigon and other South Vietnamese cities masked the sound of exploding ammunition as the Viet Cong attacked. In all, they stormed thirty-six South Vietnamese cities; casualties were in the thousands, and thousands more became refugees. It was an assault the length and breadth of South Vietnam. The ancient university city of Hue, on the northeastern coast, was virtually destroyed; while in the Northwest, six miles from the Laotian border and fourteen miles south of the DMZ, six thousand Marines found themselves under attack at an isolated mountain stronghold, the Khe Sanh combat base. From January 21 until April 14 they withstood repeated attacks from North Vietnamese troops whose strength ranged from a few thousand to fifteen thousand to as high as fifty thousand for short periods. One of the North Vietnamese units was the 304th Division, which had helped to defeat the French at Dien Bien Phu. The savagery of the battle for the beleaguered garrison, including hand-to-hand combat with knives, became a microcosm of the entire war, and Khe Sanh became "the symbol of U.S. determination to carry on the war." When the accounts were being drawn up, it was estimated that Khe Sanh had been the most heavily bombed target in the history of warfare: in an attempt to prevent the enemy attack, U.S. and South Vietnamese planes dropped 220 million tons of bombs in the area during the seventy-seven-day siege. President Johnson followed the fighting closely: in the White House situation room he had both a large aerial photograph and a terrain model of the Khe Sanh combat base. The lads at Khe Sanh were photographed by Douglas Duncan for *Life* and were thus seen by millions; the sight of the haunted eyes, the haggard faces, the blood and filth and agony of the war added to the other shocking photographs and television news film of the battles of Tet magnified the nagging doubt about Vietnam that was beginning to grow ever larger in the mind of the American people. In June, the enemy attack never having materialized, Khe Sanh was abandoned by the allied forces. Three hundred U.S. troops had been killed, twenty-two hundred wounded. Estimates of enemy casualties ranged from twenty-five hundred to fifteen thousand. If Khe Sanh had been a symbol of U.S. "determination" and "prestige" in February and March, by June it was for many a symbol of the pointlessness of the U.S. position in Vietnam.

In the end the Tet Offensive was termed a military victory for the U.S. forces in the field, but it was a shocking political defeat at home. For months the American people had been given optimistic forecasts about the prospects of victory. Now those forecasts were shown to be dubious, at best: if the enemy was so close to defeat, how could he mount such a strong attack? Further, some of what came out of Vietnam during those turbulent days cast new doubts on America's rationale for being there at all: the photograph of South Vietnam's police chief, Nguyen Ngoc Loan, summarily executing a Viet Cong suspect on a Saigon sidewalk; the comment (February 7) about the fighting at Ben Tre, a city of thirty-five thousand in the Mekong Delta: "It became necessary to destroy the town to save it," a U.S. major told AP correspondent Peter Arnett. Those words encapsulated the American dilemma in Vietnam, and they struck a raw nerve in the body politic at home, watching and reading with increasing unease as the days of Tet continued.

Walter Cronkite of CBS was perhaps the foremost television newsman in the country. In a time when the public's reliance for news was shifting from newspapers to television, Cronkite's was the most popular news program. People trusted Cronkite; he looked honest, he sounded honest, and he displayed a wide grasp of national and international affairs gained from his long career as a journalist. On his first half-hour evening newscast on September 2, 1963, he had as his guest President John F. Kennedy, who spoke with some unhappiness about the South Vietnamese and President Diem and warned:

> In the final analysis, it is their war, they are the ones who have to win it or lose it. We can help them, we can give them equipment, we can send our men out there as advisors, but they have to win it—the people of Vietnam—against the Communists.

Now, in the midst of the Tet assault, Cronkite went to Vietnam to see for himself how things were. When he returned to New York he made one of the most memorable broadcasts in the history of television: a half-hour CBS News special, *Report from Vietnam by Walter Cronkite*. He concluded the program with his personal summing-up:

> Who won and who lost in the great Tet Offensive against the cities? I'm not sure. The Viet Cong did not win by a knockout, but neither did we. . . .
>
> It seems now more certain than ever that the bloody experience of Vietnam is to end in a stalemate. This summer's almost certain standoff will either end in real give-and-take negotiations or terrible escalation; and for every means we have to escalate, the enemy can match us, and that applies to invasion of the North, the use of nuclear weapons, or the mere commitment of one hundred or two hundred or three hundred thousand more American troops to the battle. And with each escalation, the world comes close to the brink of cosmic disaster. . . .
>
> On the off chance that military and political analysts are right, in the next months we must test the enemy's intentions in case this is indeed his last big gasp before negotiations. But it is increasingly clear to this reporter that the only rational way out then will be to negotiate, not as victors but as an honorable people who lived up to their pledge to defend democracy, and did the best they could.

"*. . . not as victors*": Cronkite had not, after all, joined the antiwar protesters who called for "Out Now!" but he had given voice to the thought that perhaps, finally, this was a war that the United States could not win. Perhaps, finally, the way out would have to be negotiated. Perhaps all the guns and bombs and napalm and poison sprays and the big husky American boys, black and white together, perhaps all of these were not enough to defeat the little yellow folk, the gooks, the slant-eyes, Charlie, Vee Cee.

Earlier that same day, Robert S. McNamara took leave of some of his Washington colleagues at a State Department luncheon. He spoke a few words; his voice was choked with tears, and it seemed to one observer that he was "obviously on edge." McNamara condemned the bombing campaign: "It's not just that it isn't preventing the supplies from getting down the trail. It's destroying the countryside in the South. It's making lasting enemies. And still the damned Air Force wants more." The next day President Johnson awarded the Medal of Freedom to McNamara. After the ceremony, which was held at the Pentagon, McNamara wept as dozens of employees—civil servants, secretaries—cheered him.

Meanwhile, a group that had formed the previous September was announcing plans to step up pressure on the Administration to deescalate and finally to withdraw from the conflict in Vietnam. Calling itself Business Executives Move for Vietnam Peace and claiming sixteen hundred members, the group's spokesman explained that BEM was opposed to American involvement in Vietnam not because it was wrong (the stance of many antiwar activists) but because it wasn't working: "As businessmen we feel that when a policy hasn't proved productive after a reasonable trial it's sheer nonsense not to change it." Like the Administration, the businessmen wanted a negotiated settlement; they felt that the government was keeping to a policy that would not achieve that goal: "We feel it's become mainly a matter of passionate self-righteousness and personal pride to a little handful of men in Washington." The group planned to step up its "educational" campaign throughout the country, and, like many antiwar leaders, it hoped for an "intensive confidential discussion" with President Johnson.

Editorial opinion, as well, had begun to shift, most notably at *The Wall Street Journal*, the bible of the financial establishment, including, of course, many members of BEM. In an editorial on February 23 that was widely reprinted, the *Journal* stated that "everyone had better be prepared for the bitter taste of a defeat beyond America's power to prevent."

There was little organized antiwar protest during the winter, although on February 5 and 6 some members of Clergy and Laymen Concerned About Vietnam, by this time about sixteen thousand strong (out of an estimated four hundred thousand U.S. clergy), convened in Washington in a two-day mobilization against the war. The group tried to get permission to hold a memorial service in Arlington National Cemetery's amphitheater for U.S. servicemen killed in Vietnam, but they were denied; instead, they held a prayer vigil at the steps of the Tomb of the Unknown Soldier. There, under a blue winter sky, twenty-five hundred CLCV members heard the Reverend Martin Luther King, Jr.: "In this period of absolute silence, let us pray." And so, to the accompaniment of the orders of the tomb's army guard, they did. Six minutes later, Rabbi Abraham Heschel of the Jewish Theological Seminary of America broke the silence: *"Eloi, Eloi, lama sabachthani?"* (My God, my God, why has thou forsaken me?)—the last words cried by the crucified Jesus.

Rabbi Heschel's utterance seemed especially appropriate to CLCV's other order of business that weekend in Washington: the release of a 420-page study of American conduct of the war in Vietnam, *In the Name of America.* Begun in November 1966, the book contrasted published news accounts of the war to the Hague and Geneva conventions. CLCV's documentation charged the U.S. military with "consistent violation of almost every international agreement relating to the rules of warfare." The State Department conceded that "moral" conclusions might be made from the study, but the accusation of U.S. war crimes was rejected. Like the 1967 testimony gathered at the Russell tribunal and the 1971 testimony of the Vietnam Veterans' Winter Soldier hearings (see chapter "1971: The Winter Soldiers"), *In the Name of America* had little immediate or discernible effect on public opinion.

A little more than two weeks later, on February 24, the Fifth Avenue Peace Parade Committee rallied at the UN plaza in New York. The protesters were demonstrating against escalation of the war, but some of the two thousand participants also carried signs that read NO NUCLEAR WEAPONS IN VIETNAM and NO MORE HIROSHIMAS. Once again the ultimate horror, the secret terror of everyone save a few unreconstructed hawks, had surfaced: was the United States about to use tactical nuclear weapons in Vietnam, specifically to rescue the besieged fortress of Khe Sanh? The Administration waffled: "As far as I am aware," said President Johnson, "they [the Joint Chiefs] have at no time ever considered or made a recommendation in any respect to the employment of nuclear weapons."

And still the larger question nagged: how had the United States got into this mess—this quagmire, this nightmare, this seemingly endless tunnel whose light at the end receded with every American boy's death?

In late January, as Tet and the *Pueblo* affair were about to erupt, the staff of Senator William Fulbright's Foreign Affairs Committee was completing a study of the Tonkin Gulf incidents. Fulbright's doubts about them had grown in the three and one half years since the Senate, at his behest, had passed the Tonkin Gulf Resolution. In July 1967, before Nicholas Katzenbach's defense of the scope of the Resolution, Fulbright had read an AP account of the incidents in the Tonkin Gulf on the nights of August 2 and August 4, 1964. One of his staff members, in the fall of 1967, had begun to ferret out the precise details of the attacks on the *Maddox* and the *Turner Joy.* By December the New York *Times* had begun to publish John Finney's stories of the renewed interest of Fulbright's committee in the incidents.

Finally the committee voted to hold hearings. Negotiations were conducted to determine when Secretary of Defense McNamara could appear: he was on his way out of the Johnson Administration, on his way to the presidency of the World Bank, and he was reluctant, to say the least, to make this irritating detour back over ground that had been covered, so he thought, in earlier hearings. Eventually, on February 20, he came. In a statement to the committee which the Pentagon released to the press that day, he disclosed that "highly classified and unimpeachable intelligence information" had confirmed attacks on American destroyers on both August 2, 1964 (an incident generally accepted) and on August 4, 1964 (an incident in dispute). Further, as opposed to his testimony of August 6, 1964, in which he stated that the *Maddox* and the *Turner Joy* were on "routine patrol," he now said that they were on "an intelligence gathering mission."

McNamara's testimony was released to the press four days later, simultaneously with the opinion of at least nine of the committee's nineteen members that the United States had overreacted to the attack on the *Maddox* and the *Turner Joy.* What was more, said Fulbright, he (Fulbright) was angered at having been asked to vote on the basis of information which, it now appeared, was so "uncertain." The

154

next day Fulbright called for a full congressional investigation of the Administration's policy in Vietnam. He was particularly concerned at the "process" by which the Johnson Administration had made its decisions. The initial unease at being asked to vote for the Tonkin Gulf Resolution three and a half years previously had never disappeared, not for Fulbright or for many other senators, although at the time only Morse and Gruening had voted no; now the unease had grown, and they wanted back their power to "consent" as well as to offer advice which, often as not, went unheeded.

Less than two weeks later, Fulbright renounced the Tonkin Gulf Resolution as "null and void"; it had been obtained on the basis of "misrepresentations" by the Administration, he said, because the intelligence-gathering role of the two ships had not been disclosed. Nevertheless, neither the House nor the Senate voted to repeal the Resolution.

On March 18, 139 members of the House called for a congressional review of U.S. policy in Vietnam; a resolution to that effect had been languishing (at the behest of the Administration) in the House Rules Committee since the previous fall. Now the members wanted it to be released for debate; failing that, they threatened to recruit a majority of House members to sign a discharge petition. Their motives, they said, were (1) to "unify" the nation's Vietnam effort by a congressional debate and (2) to "reassert the role of Congress" in foreign affairs. Ninety-eight Republicans and forty-one Democrats supported the resolution; one of its sponsors, Morris Udall (D-Arizona), explained that other Democrats who would "welcome" a debate on the Administration's Vietnam policy did not, "for party reasons," want to sign it.

On March 27 twenty-one members of the House urged repeal of the Tonkin Gulf Resolution. They did not propose any specific change in policy, they said; rather, they wanted a "national debate" on future policy, and they wanted Congress to "play a major role in the determination of the policy." No action was taken on either of these proposals.

Events had outrun Congress, and Congress knew it: having allowed itself to be hustled into signing Lyndon Johnson's blank check to make war, it was now faced with the dilemma of how to stop payment. In fact, no Congress ever turned down a request for funds to prosecute the war until 1973, after the peace treaty was signed; the Tonkin Gulf Resolution was not repealed until the last day of 1970. The repeal had no effect on the conduct of the war.

Despite increased sentiment against the war in certain quarters, the antiwar movement in those weeks could take little comfort from the polls. On February 13, two weeks after the Tet strike and before the American command could claim victory, 61 percent of the American people declared themselves hawks—that is, in the words of the question put to them, they wanted to "step up" U.S. military effort in Vietnam. (The figure in December had been 52 percent.) On the question of continuing the bombing of North Vietnam, 70 percent were in favor, as opposed to 63 percent in October. The Gallup people then asked a question that was wildly premature—no one in the Administration, the antiwar movement, or elsewhere dreamed how much so. Would the war end, they asked, as victory, as defeat, or as a compromise settlement? The notion of compromise won handily: 61 percent thought that that would be the final result of the conflict. Twenty percent thought that we would win a decisive victory. Only 5 percent thought that the Americans and their South Vietnamese allies would suffer defeat.

The Louis Harris organization found similar results: support for the war in the weeks immediately after Tet arose from 61 percent to 74 percent. In six weeks, at the end of March, it had slipped to 54 percent.

A poll taken by Gallup in early March, however, showed the public's increasing awareness of the dilemma in which the nation found itself: 49 percent believed that it had been an error to become involved in Vietnam; in August 1965 that number was only 24 percent.

On February 29 the New York *Times* ran a story by William Beecher: U.S. REAPPRAISING ITS USE OF TROOPS IN VIETNAM WAR. Buried in the text were figures that ten days later would set the country on its collective ear: indications were, wrote Beecher, that General Westmoreland would request one hundred to two hundred thousand more troops. Such an increase would have raised the total American manpower in Vietnam to nearly three quarters of a million men. Militarily such a request would perhaps not have been unreasonable; politically it would have been disastrous.

No official word came. *Times* reporters Hedrick Smith and Neil Sheehan began to dig out the story. They discovered not only a precise figure—206,000 men—but also evidence of considerable dissent within the Administration over whether to grant the request. On Sunday, March 10, the *Times* published the report under a four-column headline on page one. Many newspapers around the country picked it up either from the *Times'* news service or from Associated Press reports of the *Times* story. The *Times'* editorialist spoke for many of his fellows, as well as for millions of ordinary citizens, when he wrote of the Administration's "suicidal escalation": "The tunnel has proved to be a bottomless pit. . . . The American people have been pushed beyond the limits of gullibility. . . ."

That night, on an NBC-TV special on the war, correspondent Frank McGee showed an hour of Tet battle footage preceded by clips of optimistic statements by Johnson, McNamara, and Westmoreland. McGee concluded: "The war is being lost by the Administration's definition. All that remains is a mutual capacity for further destruction. . . ." The next week, NBC began a weekly half-hour series dealing exclusively with the war.

On Monday and Tuesday, March 11 and 12, Secretary of State Dean Rusk appeared before Senator Fulbright's Foreign Relations Committee for the first time in two years. In honor of the occasion Fulbright wore a blue tie decorated with white doves and olive branches. When Fulbright demanded that Congress be more fully consulted about administration plans, Rusk replied that if additional troops were to be sent to Vietnam, "appropriate members of Congress" would be consulted—the main concern of the senators. The hearings were nationally televised. Each senator had his turn to voice his opinion. Senator Church worried about the Asian "crocodile" being fed with American lives; Senator Symington worried about the nation's "fiscal security" in the attempts to meet the Vietnam commitment.

Rusk remained unflappable, as was his wont. Only when Senator Claiborne Pell (D-Rhode Island) raised the "moral" question about whether the suffering in Vietnam was worth the effort did Rusk show anger; he himself was worried about "moral myopia," he said. In Vietnam the United States was involved in "the eternal struggle for freedom."

The hearing ended unsatisfactorily. Afterward Senator Fulbright commented to reporters that the secretary had refused to commit himself on the issue of consultation: "He never did answer us. . . . He did not say positively he would and he did not say positively he wouldn't."

The people of New Hampshire, that same day, took part in the ultimate poll: they voted. The New Hampshire presidential primary, first in the nation always, is not necessarily a valid reading of the national temper, but it draws first blood in that brutal quadrennial fight and occasionally it produces a stunning upset. Nineteen sixty-eight was one of those years. When the votes were tallied, Eugene McCarthy had received more than 40 percent of the Democratic vote—not enough to win, but far more than enough to appall the incumbent President against whom he had run. Further, because McCarthy's supporters had been shrewd enough to run only as many delegates as there were places available—twenty-four—McCarthy emerged with twenty of the available number.

In its initial stages the McCarthy campaign in New Hampshire had been dismissed by professional politicians as a "children's crusade"—an army of youthful volunteers, many of whom had "come clean for Gene," who blanketed the state with literature and spent up to sixteen hours a day making telephone calls and personal visits to the Democrats and Independents whose initial skepticism they needed to overcome.* In the end more than ten thousand students from over one hundred colleges and universities worked for Eugene McCarthy in New Hampshire; they were under the direction of a twenty-four-year-old native of Council Bluffs, Iowa, one Sam Brown, erstwhile activist in the National Student Association, erstwhile Harvard Divinity School student, who controlled them as a general controls an army. A young AP reporter, Seymour Hersh, was the campaign's first press secretary. These young people were not, for the most part, antiwar activists; rather, like their mentor Allard Lowenstein, they were believers in the system and were giving it another chance.

Despite McCarthy's strong showing the results of the New Hampshire primary were not evidence that the Granite State Yankees had suddenly sprouted dovish feathers: it was not an antiwar vote. A poll taken two days after the election showed that

—more than half the Democrats voting did not know McCarthy's position on the war;

—the more they knew that McCarthy was a dove, the less likely they were to vote for him;

—the vote showed "dissatisfaction" with the progress of the war—not neces-

---

* Three weeks before he announced his candidacy, McCarthy had said at the short-lived Labor Leadership Assembly for Peace that "this [the war] is not the kind of political controversy which should be left to a children's crusade to save the country."

sarily a wish to deescalate, negotiate, or withdraw, but more likely a wish to intensify the war effort.

It was, more than anything, an anti-Johnson vote. Public approval of the President's performance was dropping (36 percent by late March); and after Senator Fulbright's new, public doubts about the Tonkin Gulf affair, and after the Tet Offensive and the sudden and alarming new figure for troops requested, it was perhaps surprising that Johnson received as many votes as he did. He tried to dismiss the significance of the results, but no one was deceived, least of all himself: his narrow "victory" had in fact been a defeat in the public's mind just as had been the Tet "victory"—and a harbinger of worse to come as the nation's other primaries took place inexorably through the spring.

Four days later, on March 16, Robert F. Kennedy, the junior senator from New York, announced his candidacy for the office of President of the United States. Some people felt that Kennedy had waited until he saw that the challenge was a "safe" one. But Kennedy, while certainly no milquetoast when it came to political maneuvering, was not so cynical as all that. He had hesitated, had anguished, because he had genuinely feared a split in the party.

In his announcement he said that he was seeking the nomination because of the nation's "disastrous, divisive policies" in Vietnam and at home. Senator McCarthy's New Hampshire campaign had shown "how deep are the present divisions within our party and within our country." Kennedy not only feared escalation of the war; he also deplored, he said, the Administration's refusal to enthusiastically endorse the Kerner Commission's report on the previous summer's racial rioting.

Many Democrats welcomed Kennedy's announcement, of course, but many did not. The following day, as he marched in New York's St. Patrick's Day parade, he was greeted not only by cheers but by catcalls of "coward" and "opportunist." Many McCarthy followers felt the same way and never forgave him for his delay in entering the race until McCarthy had shown that anti-Administration sentiment formed a sizable vote.

"There was a real possibility that Kennedy could strike out behind Eugene McCarthy and become an authentic antiwar candidate," recalls Carl Oglesby. Despite their antipathy to electoral politics, "A lot of SDS people would have gone over to a Kennedy campaign, and I would have been pushing and pulling them." Thus Oglesby, the advocate of bridge-building to the moderate center. Tom Hayden, too, would have welcomed a Kennedy candidacy: "In 1968 I believed in an antiwar movement as primary, but I was very much inclined to see an RFK candidacy. I had more faith in him than in McCarthy. I thought Kennedy could reach the hard hats as well as the students. I met with Kennedy in 1967 when Kennedy was just back from Paris.† I went to Hickory Hill [Kennedy's home] a few months

† And after a much-publicized flap in which Kennedy was erroneously reported to have brought back a "peace feeler" from North Vietnam's Paris Mission, supposedly transmitted to Kennedy during his meeting with a French diplomat. Lyndon Johnson was not amused: "I'll destroy you and every one of your dove friends in six months," he is reported to have said. Later Kennedy stated that he had neither received a "peace feeler" nor leaked the story, which, it turned out, had been supplied to the press by a State Department official. A few weeks later, on March 2, Kennedy in a speech in the Senate offered a proposal for the United States to stop bombing North Vietnam and offer negotiations to test the North's

later. I could not become a Kennedy campaigner as opposed to leading the Chicago protests, but I was certainly at the pro-Kennedy end of the antiwar spectrum. I have a feeling that he would have disengaged us from Vietnam. He was moving that way, and his strongest constituency lay in that direction. As a politician he would not have abandoned his constituency." But by the time of the Democratic Convention both Kennedy and Martin Luther King were dead and the possibility for nonviolent change—for the country under either man's leadership to turn itself around from its self-destructive course of war and racial conflict—seemed lost.

Meanwhile the war went on. On March 15 the week's casualty figures for U.S. losses (509 killed, 2,766 wounded) brought the total number of American casualties in Vietnam since January 1, 1961, to 139,801 (19,670 killed, 120,131 wounded). The figure surpassed the number of casualties in Korea (1950–53: 33,061 killed, 103,853 wounded) and made Vietnam to that date America's fourth-bloodiest war.

The next day, the day that Kennedy made his announcement, a company of U.S. soldiers was searching for Viet Cong in the Mekong Delta. They came upon a hamlet called My Lai. In the subsequent report to General Westmoreland's headquarters, it was stated that 128 Viet Cong were killed and three weapons captured.

On March 17, as Robert Kennedy was being booed in the St. Patrick's Day parade in New York, thirty thousand more troops were sent to Vietnam.

In Washington, Senator Fulbright continued his Foreign Relations Committee's "educational" hearings on Vietnam policy. On March 20 General David M. Shoup, the former marine commandant who had called the President's views on the war "unadulterated poppycock," testified that in his opinion up to eight hundred thousand U.S. troops would be needed in South Vietnam simply to protect its cities against Communist attack; in order to win, he said, North Vietnam would have to be invaded.

The new Secretary of Defense, Clark Clifford, had at the President's direction been making his own study of the request for 206,000 more troops. He began to ask questions about the course of the war. The answers that he received unnerved him. Previously he had been known as a hawk. As he told Bill Moyers, "I accepted it [the war] mistakenly, until I got to the Pentagon and after a month in the Pentagon, I knew that we were wrong and I knew that it wasn't really Communist aggression. What we were dealing with was a civil war in Vietnam. And I knew we had an absolute loser on our hands. We weren't ever going to win that war. . . ."

The Pentagon's "hidden doves" (known in some circles as "professional pessimists") challenged Clifford on both the request for 206,000 troops and the Administration's bombing policy. Clifford pressed his investigation: "I sat in a tank with the Joint Chiefs for three days while we tried to talk this thing out. There's where I finally learned they had no plan to win the war."

On March 15, independently of Clifford's efforts, Arthur Goldberg, who at President Johnson's request had given up his seat on the Supreme Court in 1965 to serve as U.S. Ambassador to the UN, presented an eight-page memorandum to the President asking him to stop the bombing of North Vietnam so that peace talks could

"sincerity." The Johnson Administration promptly rejected Kennedy's plan, saying that similar proposals had been tried with no success.

begin. A bombing halt would also, of course, dampen the rising voices opposed to administration policy. "Something had to be done to extend the lease on public support for the war," commented one official.

During the week of March 25 occurred two meetings, hundreds of miles apart, one in Washington, one in Lexington, Kentucky. Neither group knew the other. Both meetings were to have momentous results for the country, although perhaps in ways unanticipated.

In Washington met the "Wise Men"—a group of trusted friends and associates of Lyndon Johnson, most of whom were not currently in government service, who had first gathered six months before at the President's request to assess the progress and prospects of the war. At that time they had said to him that the war could be won in accordance with the Administration's policy. They were a distinguished group: Dean Acheson, George Ball, General Omar Bradley, McGeorge Bundy, Arthur Dean, Douglas Dillon, Abe Fortas, Arthur Goldberg, Henry Cabot Lodge, John J. McCloy, Robert Murphy, General Matthew Ridgway, General Maxwell Taylor, and Cyrus Vance. They were given briefings by Deputy Assistant Secretary of State Philip Habib, Major General William DePuy, and CIA's George Carver. The briefings covered all aspects of the war: political, military, pacification, and the problem of the Viet Cong. The Wise Men conferred also with Rusk, Clifford, and other government officials. The President's friends were struck by the change in the information they were being given; their briefing had been very different the previous autumn. Now, when Dillon asked how long before the war was won, the answer was *from five to ten years.*

On the following day the Wise Men delivered their verdict to the President. Bundy spoke for the group. Although his advice in February 1965 had been to begin the bombing, and although twice the previous November he had urged its continuation, now he had concluded that the bombing was so harmful to American public support for the war that it should be stopped. Acheson agreed: the problem was just that, he said. The American public did not support the war. A few of the advisers present that day spoke in favor of the Administration's policy, but most of them were convinced that it must be changed. They were succinct; they were candid. We could never win, they said; we must find some way to extricate ourselves. Johnson was startled by their bleak, blunt advice; unlike his domestic critics who demanded that the United States get out because the war was morally wrong, these men—trusted friends and counselors all—said that the United States must get out because the war was unwinnable. Further, public support for it, badly shaken by the Tet Offensive, was weakening. Negotiations, not more bombing, were the solution.

The President was stunned. He had not heard the briefings; now he asked that they be given to him. When they were, he understood perhaps for the first time that the information which he had been receiving all the previous months and years had not been correct—or not, at least, complete. In his memoirs, Johnson claimed that all the Wise Men "expressed deep concern about the divisions in our country. Some of them felt that those divisions were growing rapidly and might soon force our withdrawal from Vietnam."

On March 27 SDS held a National Council meeting in Lexington, Kentucky. One hundred and two delegates attended; 19 new chapters were admitted, making a total of about 280 SDS chapters nationwide. (At that time, the Student Mobilization Committee claimed 700 chapters.) Disagreement continued at the center of the organization about what direction to take. Previously, conscientiously, the national leadership had tried to decide such major questions in a democratic way, by having each chapter vote on them; but now, with so many new chapters, that method had become impossible. At Lexington, therefore, the delegates were to decide for the entire membership: should SDS participate in the proposed "Ten Days" of antiwar actions in April being organized by the Student Mobilization Committee—actions that SDS itself had endorsed only three months before? Dissension was bitter: the Progressive Labor faction, which in December had pushed hard for grass-roots organizing rather than participation in the April demonstrations, now again at Lexington argued against what it called pressure tactics by the SDS National Office attempting to force local chapters into an action that many of them did not want.

What did they want? Many of them were not sure. Nothing was decided; the local chapters of SDS were given the option—which they would have taken anyway —to join the April demonstrations if they wished. Like the dog that did not bark in the nighttime in the Sherlock Holmes story, what SDS did not do at Lexington was more significant than what it did: in the face of Tet, in the face of antiwar sentiment that was growing across the land and, perhaps more important, growing in the boardrooms of the Eastern establishment, SDS once again turned away from seizing the issue of the war.

Carl Oglesby tried to put some of the concerns of the moment into perspective for the delegates. Mindful of the National Advisory Commission on Civil Disorders (the Kerner Commission), whose report had been presented to Lyndon Johnson three weeks before, Oglesby attempted in his eloquent way to speak to that issue as well as to the issue of the war. The Kerner Report, it will be remembered, had as its "basic conclusion" a sentence that quickly entered the country's consciousness: "Our nation is moving toward two societies, one black, one white—separate and unequal." The commission determined that the ghetto riots of the past few years had occurred because of ghetto conditions rather than at the instigation of outsiders, and it recommended massive government spending to improve those conditions —a course of action that the Congress and the President, allocating increasing millions to the war, were unable and unwilling to follow.

Oglesby's analysis of the Kerner Report was that it was "outwardly sympathetic to the blacks, but the meaning of it—since the government had no possible welfare program on the shelf to meet the problems that were making the black people rebel —was that there was going to be greater rebellion and police repression." It was important for the delegates to understand that "once they [the government] had officially confronted the fact that the situation was endemic, then their only option was increased repression." Whites needed to understand that "it's a war there" and they must do what they could to protect blacks from what Oglesby saw as inevitable repression.

At the same time, he urged the delegates not to give up on coalition building to the right—the way to broaden the base of the movement. The other way—the way to violence—he specifically denounced: "moderate politics," however pedestrian that might sound, was the way to succeed.

And what of Tet, of the whole Vietnam mess? The "Yankees"—the Eastern establishment—had lost faith in the military, said Oglesby, and thus in America's ability to win in Vietnam, and so they were pulling out. Tet had shown that "people were just not any longer going to believe that the military had the foggiest idea of what they were up to—or up against."

Oglesby's speech was not a plea to stop antiwar activity, but some of the delegates may have thought that it was. In any case, the convention adjourned without taking any antiwar action other than granting local chapters the freedom to do what they would in April—a freedom that was of course hardly the National Office's to deny. In addition the delegates, who were almost 100 percent white, voted nearly unanimously to devote their efforts to the struggle for black liberation —whether the blacks wanted them to do so or not.

Staughton Lynd later dismissed such action as the "politics of guilt"—as indeed it was, a classic American white response to the question of American blacks, the other side of the racist coin. One commentator, Kirkpatrick Sale, attributes the SDS action at Lexington to the fact that the struggle for black liberation was where the revolution was—at least in the opinion of certain of the SDS leadership.

As if in reply to the SDS action at Lexington, two shocking events happened within the week.

The first occurred on Sunday evening, March 31, when Lyndon Johnson addressed the nation on Vietnam. He announced two major changes in policy: (1) the cessation of bombing in North Vietnam except in an undefined area north of the DMZ where the "enemy build-up directly threatens allied forward positions" and (2) a repeated invitation to North Vietnam to participate in negotiations.

At the last moment, Johnson dropped a bombshell of his own; never had the faithful, who listen to presidential addresses in full as a patriotic duty, been so richly rewarded, for Johnson had appended a stunning coda to the main text: citing the need to devote himself both to domestic problems and to the conduct of the war, he said that "I shall not seek, and I will not accept, the nomination of my party for another term as your President."

Some in the antiwar movement were cautiously optimistic at this totally unforeseen development. The Reverend Dr. John C. Bennett, president of Union Theological Seminary and a founder of Clergy and Laymen Concerned, said that Johnson's decision opened "the real possibility that we can move to a different policy. . . . I think he has seen that he himself has become a divisive factor. . . ." Rabbi Abraham Heschel, cochairman of Clergy and Laymen Concerned, said, "It represents a victory for America. Period." Donna Allen, a founder of Women Strike for Peace, was perhaps overoptimistic when she said that "we [the nation] now have to face the real question of whether the war is right or wrong . . ." (a question that had yet to be addressed).

Others were more skeptical. Norman Thomas, the widely respected octogenarian

Socialist leader, offered the thought that Johnson's policies would prove more popular without him—that much of the dislike of the President was directed toward the man and his style rather than to his policies. As for the bombing halt, "I don't think Johnson should be rewarded for any great virtue. He's only doing what he has to do." The Reverend William Sloane Coffin and Dr. Benjamin Spock, two of the Boston 5, cautioned that the bombing halt might lead to more escalation. David Dellinger warned that "it's important to keep up the kind of pressure that brought the Administration to the point of making gestures, whether sincere or not."

Antidraft rallies were held on Wednesday, April 3, in New Haven, Boston, and New York City; more than three hundred young men turned in their cards. At Yale, Staughton Lynd hailed the "growth and increasing legitimization of the antidraft movement."

On that day Hanoi agreed to begin negotiations toward a peace settlement. At the same time, the North Vietnamese issued bitter protests, echoed in the U.S. Congress, that the Administration had misspoken the limits of the bombing halt, and they questioned the "sincerity" of Johnson's peace proposal. "Savage bombings" of North Vietnam had occurred since the President's speech, they said, and the war in the South had been stepped up.

In Congress, news of the continued bombing after the announcement of a halt led to new charges that the President had "misled" the country. The Administration was reported to be "deeply chagrined" at these accusations. Johnson had not, in fact, specifically named a cut-off point; the Pentagon explained on April 2 that bombing would be halted only north of the 20th parallel (225 miles north of the DMZ) and on that day more than 105 missions were flown against North Vietnamese targets—roughly the usual number.

Nevertheless, the bombing "halt" and the new offer to negotiate marked another turning point in the war. At the same time, the President's surprise announcement that he would not run again deprived the antiwar movement of a favorite target. More, it further complicated the question of what, if anything, to do at the Democratic Convention in Chicago. The candidacies of Eugene McCarthy and Robert Kennedy were already beginning to drain talent, energy, and money from the antiwar effort (a quadrennial problem); in a perverse way Lyndon Johnson had given strength to the Movement, had given it some cohesiveness because its members were united in their hatred for him. Now he was gone—or would be soon enough.

On April 4, when the country was still recovering from the shock of the President's announcements, a vastly greater shock occurred when word came that the Reverend Martin Luther King, Jr., had been assassinated.

For twelve years King had been the heart and soul of the civil rights movement. He had gone to Memphis in early April to aid black sanitation workers in their strike for recognition of their union. From there he had planned to go to Washington to lead a Poor People's March—a last attempt to shame the national government into paying attention to the black plight, which new legislation had failed to ameliorate. Housing was still segregated, and schools as well; jobs were hard to come by; black hopes, roused in the preceding decade of struggle, seemed once again to have been dashed on the rock of some more pressing priority—this time, the war in Vietnam, which was killing black youths at a disproportionate rate and diverting money from the war on poverty, now moribund, lost in the escalating expense of funding that other war.

And so at the news of King's murder, the black ghettos once again exploded in rage and grief. On that night, and in the days and nights that followed, it seemed that of the two terrible problems facing the country, the problem of the blacks' condition was more urgent even than the problem of the war. During the week that followed King's death, riots broke out in 125 cities nationwide; Washington, D.C., was the worst, although Chicago and Detroit and Philadelphia were also hard-hit. On April 6, page 1 of the New York *Times* carried a photo of an armored tank in front of the Capitol; the nightly news once again showed scenes of violence and destruction equal to anything in the Kerner Report. Forty-six people died; more than twenty thousand were arrested, and fifty-five thousand federal troops and National Guardsmen were called out to deal with the emergency. Thus was borne out Oglesby's bleak vision.

The Poor People's March the following month became instead Resurrection City —a rain-drenched, muddy encampment adjacent to the Lincoln Memorial. Periodic marches, poorly attended, were made on various government departments; officials paid little attention to the demands that were made, and with each passing day morale sagged, discontent rose, and Resurrection City became a bigger fiasco. It lasted from May 13 to June 24; the Poor People's Campaign made a brief and ineffective appearance at the Democratic Convention in August and then, lacking King's powerful leadership, faded from sight.

On April 10 an edgy Congress passed the so-called Rap Brown amendment to the pending civil rights bill. It was an antiriot provision which would be used in subsequent years against antiwar demonstrators; its genesis, however, was the current ghetto riots. And on April 11, while troops still ringed the Capitol, the new civil rights bill was passed. It provided for

—broader access by nonwhites to housing, including single family homes;

—an antiriot provision making it a federal crime to travel interstate with intent to start a "riot" (defined as three or more people);

—broader rights for American Indians in dealing with tribal governments, the courts, and all levels of nontribal government.

On the same date, President Johnson authorized a call-up of 24,500 reserves—as in February, a politically sensitive and unpopular decision, one that Congress had dreaded. At the same time, Defense Secretary Clifford announced a ceiling of 549,000 American troops in Vietnam, and said that the Administration had decided to shift the burden of the war onto the South Vietnamese. This was the beginning of the policy of "Vietnamization" that Richard Nixon adopted in the following year: a policy which removed the war from the front of the nation's consciousness by lowering the (American) body count—the number of ground troops killed—while continuing the military struggle for "peace with honor" by dropping more tons of bombs onto North and South Vietnam than were dropped by the Allies during all of World War II. Vietnamization, as the saying went, simply "changed the color of the corpses."

And so the country struggled to come to terms with Martin Luther King's death; and the war went on; and April passed; and the time came for the spring demonstrations.

As we have seen, SDS had since its inception tried to foster autonomous local chapters. This went hand in hand, at least in the early years, with a strong sense of the need for a participatory democracy: sometimes SDS even failed to take action on a given issue because the vote had not yet come in from all its membership. In 1967 and 1968, as SDS grew, local chapters lagged behind the national leadership; nevertheless, the feeling was that they were still to be given as much freedom as possible to act in accordance with the temper of the community in which they existed.

What might be called the ultimate in autonomous local action by an SDS chapter took place at Columbia University beginning on April 23, 1968. For some months the university had undergone criticism by students, faculty, and outsiders on three issues which were to come to a festering head on that day:

—student discipline, specifically university punishment of students involved in political protests;

—construction of a gymnasium by Columbia in Morningside Park, adjacent to Harlem—a symbol, many felt, of the university's arrogance in dealing with its neighbors;

—the connection of the university to the Institute for Defense Analysis (IDA), a Pentagon-sponsored group to which a number of universities belonged, and which advised the government on defense strategy in return for funding for the member universities.

On April 23 the Columbia chapter of SDS, under the leadership of its new president, Mark Rudd, had called a rally at "the sundial"—a prime gathering place for Columbia students in the center of what passed for a campus in the concrete jungle of New York City. The rally was to protest a disciplinary meeting to which Rudd and five other students had been summoned after they participated in a protest action against the university's involvement with the IDA. Having refused the previous day to attend the meeting, they had been placed on disciplinary probation. Several hundred students showed up at the sundial, including a delegation from the Student Afro-American Society (SAS).‡

That afternoon, according to the account of the Columbia action written by the editors of the student newspaper, the *Columbia Spectator*, Mark Rudd was given a bit of on-the-job training in demonstration leadership; while he led the crowd in a fruitless attempt to gain entry to Low Library, where the university's administrative offices were, much of his following began to drift away from him. Ted Kaptchuk, whom Rudd had displaced as president of the Columbia SDS chapter the previous month, told Rudd what was happening: "Your demonstration's at the gym!"

Within the hour, a student had been arrested after a scuffle at the gym site and

‡ Despite the fact that one of the issues in dispute was the gym and its availability to Harlem's blacks, there had been little contact or cooperation between black and white students at Columbia, including white SDS members.

the crowd had reassembled at the sundial. Since Low Library was inaccessible, Rudd led the students to a smaller building, Hamilton Hall. There they took a hostage: Henry Coleman, the acting dean of Columbia College. At some time during the night, the members of SAS (blacks) asked the whites, including Rudd and SDS, to leave. Confused, nonplussed, ever guilty about their whiteness, they did.

During the next two days, students succeeded in entering Low Library, where they occupied the offices of Grayson Kirk, Columbia's president; they also occupied Fayerweather, Avery, and Mathematics halls.

The Columbia administration has been criticized for its rigid stance during the 1968 disturbance, but in the context of the times it is not hard to understand its reaction to the dissidents: it feared not only campus chaos but also a full-scale invasion from the black ghetto next door, and in fact on the night of April 25 a group of perhaps forty Harlem community activists, plus the inevitable hangers-on, held a rally at the Broadway gate at 116th Street and then proceeded to march across the campus to the gym site. A thousand Columbia students were with them, cheering a rousing speech by Charles 3X Kenyatta.

In the end, the Columbia occupation was resolved by police action one week after it had begun; earlier police action had been impossible because of the large numbers of police needed at that weekend's scheduled antiwar demonstration. And like the events at the Chicago convention later in the year, what happened at Columbia can only be termed a "police riot."

Kirkpatrick Sale has said that "these months [the spring of 1968] mark the emergence of political violence on a significant scale across the country." But the violence for the previous several years in both civil rights and antiwar actions was *police* violence; demonstrators did not initiate it. Like the police at the Dow protest at the University of Wisconsin and the police and troops at the Pentagon the previous autumn, the police at Columbia vastly overreacted to the event.

The student journalists described the scene at 2:30 A.M., April 30, moments before the bust: Japanese music blaring from a loudspeaker, floodlights set low around the Business School casting huge deformed shadows, a light show of magenta, turquoise, and yellow inside Fayerweather Hall to amuse its occupiers until the attack came. It had, they said, "the appearance of a special corner of hell reserved for left-wing political activists."

Then the police charged. They cleared students at the entrances to occupied buildings and then went in to clear the buildings. They were not gentle; they were armed with nightsticks, which they used freely. Students who would not leave on order were clubbed and dragged away.

One thousand police took part: until that time, the largest police action in the history of American universities. Seven hundred and eleven people were arrested. Of 148 injuries sustained, 120 charges of police brutality were brought—the largest number of complaints received until that time by the New York City Police Civilian Complaint Review Board. Students were clubbed, beaten to the ground, kicked, and dragged away to waiting paddy wagons. As at the Pentagon, girls were beaten as well as boys. In the words of the interim police report, quoting a Columbia administrator, "police pummelled the students as they passed down the stairwell." A New York *Times* reporter, recognized and identified as such, "was seized and struck about the head and body by plainclothes and uniformed officers." His head required twelve stitches. After all the buildings had been cleared the police swept the college grounds, stampeding students who had been watching the drama unfold, charging the crowd repeatedly, clubbing every civilian in sight, kicking them when they fell. Only Hamilton Hall escaped: there, the occupying blacks filed out in orderly fashion, wanting no trouble, disdaining the countercultural whites.

Classes were suspended for three days; when they resumed thousands of students went on strike. Protest action continued with the seizure by community activists and students of a university-owned tenement building on 114th Street; several days later, after the disciplining of four SDS leaders, Hamilton Hall was reoccupied. In both actions police were called in and scores of arrests made.

The Columbia demonstration was an expansion on what the Scranton Commission called the "Berkeley invention." Now in 1968, and in the upheavals that followed in the next few years, the pattern of campus protest changed: the object of the striking students was not just to protest certain university policies, but to force the university to become an institution that would reflect their views—to become a "revolutionary political weapon with which they could attack the system." At Columbia and other universities the students destroyed considerable property including research work; police were extremely violent; threats of bodily harm to university officials and acts of terrorism took place; increased disciplinary measures were taken against troublesome students; and the counterculture (including its use of drugs) played an ever-larger part in students' lives, attracting "street people" who in turn contributed to student unrest.

Tom Hayden, by this time no longer formally connected with SDS, attended the Columbia uprising and later wrote about it for *Ramparts*. He said, in part:

> The goal written on the university walls was "Create two, three, many Columbias"; it meant expand the strike so that the U.S. must either change or send its troops to occupy American campuses.
>
> At this point the goal seems realistic; an explosive mix is present on dozens of campuses where demands for attention to student views are being disregarded by university administrators. . . .
>
> Columbia opened a new tactical stage in the resistance movement which began last fall: from the overnight occupation of buildings to permanent occupation; from mill-ins to the creation of revolutionary committees; from symbolic civil disobedience to barricaded resistance. . . .
>
> In the buildings occupied at Columbia, the students created what they called a "new society" or "liberated area" or "commune," a society in which decent values would be lived out even though university officials might cut short the communes through use of police. . . . Debating and then determining what leaders should do were alternatives to the remote and authoritarian decision-making of Columbia's trustees. . . .
>
> . . . We are moving toward power—the power to stop the machine if it cannot be made to serve humane ends. . . . The students at Columbia dis-

covered that barricades are only the beginning of what they call "bringing the war home."

The bitterness and violence at Columbia were in accord with the year itself. Everything had gone sour—the war, the campuses, the civil rights struggle, the war on poverty. On Broadway a new musical, *Hair,* opened during the week of the Columbia confrontations. It was a fantasy of the new youth culture smartly packaged to entice their parents, the bourgeoisie. No bitterness, no hate here: just the dawn of the Age of Aquarius—some months late, it seemed, since the flowering of the hippie youth culture in San Francisco's Haight-Ashbury and the East Village in New York had already withered into an ugly drug-and-violence scene.

The Columbia uprising overshadowed a far more widespread (and overwhelmingly peaceful) student protest which occurred during the same week. On April 26, one million college and high school students across the country stayed away from classes in a one-day boycott to register their protest against the war. It was the largest student protest in the history of the country. It had been organized mainly by Bettina Aptheker's Student Mobilization Committee; more than a year before she had seen that vision, and now it had happened. In New York City alone, more than two hundred thousand students stayed out. Overseas, students in Mexico City, in Prague, in Tokyo, in Paris joined students in the United States as they marched and rallied in yet another international day of protest against the American presence in Vietnam.

SDS, whose Columbia chapter had tied that university in knots, had little to do with the April 26 strike—part of the Ten Days of Resistance which SDS had endorsed the previous December. Members of the National Office had urged approval of the Ten Days, with emphasis on attacking "financial and corporate industrial targets." But Oglesby's speech on March 26 had shifted their direction, and so now in April SDS presence depended upon the zeal of local chapters—some of whom, of course, did take part.

On the following day, the National Mobilization Committee pulled more than one hundred thousand people to march down Fifth Avenue and Central Park West to a meeting place at Central Park's Sheep Meadow, scene of draft card burnings the year before. On the West Side, the group was led off by six members of a Newark motorcycle club, the Magnificent Riders; the first marchers, including David Dellinger and the Reverend William Sloane Coffin, walked inside a cordon of bodyguards who formed a hand-lock square around them. The peace marchers were carefully routed out of the way of the Loyalty Day parade organized by the Veterans of Foreign Wars; originally called to counter the world-wide leftist celebration of May Day, Loyalty Day had for the past two years been billed as a show of support for the troops in Vietnam and as a response to antiwar rallies. In 1968, the Loyalty Day parade in Manhattan, with Archbishop Cooke and Grand Marshal Frank Gigante at its head, drew 2,669 marchers.

At Sheep Meadow, the Mobilization crowd heard speeches from Dellinger, Coffin, Mayor John Lindsay, comedian/activist Dick Gregory, and actress Viveca Lindfors; they heard songs from Pete Seeger and Arlo Guthrie. Although both "peace candidates," Kennedy and McCarthy, had been invited to speak, neither attended. The most moving moment of the day occurred when Coretta Scott King, three weeks widowed, read to the crowd a decalogue on Vietnam—"Ten Commandments on Vietnam" which, she said, had been found as notes in her husband's pockets after his murder. King had been scheduled to be the keynote speaker at the rally, and these words, Mrs. King suggested, may have been prepared for the event:

> Thou shalt not believe in a military victory.
> Thou shalt not believe in a political victory.
> Thou shalt not believe that they—the Vietnamese—love us.
> Thou shalt not believe that the Saigon government has the support of the people.
> Thou shalt not believe that the majority of the South Vietnamese look upon the Viet Cong as terrorists.
> Thou shalt not believe the figures of killed enemies or killed Americans.
> Thou shalt not believe that the generals know best.
> Thou shalt not believe that the enemy's victory means communism.
> Thou shalt not believe that the world supports the United States.
> Thou shalt not kill.

The crowd applauded after each precept, loudest after the tenth.

On the same day in Chicago, violence came again from the police—an ugly foreshadowing of events later in the year. After more than twelve thousand people marched without incident from Grant Park, the demonstrators were set upon at the Civic Center by police wielding clubs and spraying mace. Many bystanders were injured. The police charged the crowd repeatedly, and at least one police official was injured (he was hit on the head by a demonstrator's sign). A citizens' report on the April 27 demonstration in Chicago, issued three weeks before the Democratic Convention in August, accused the police of "brutalizing demonstrators without provocation." But the investigators did not blame the police entirely: Mayor Richard Daley and his officials had made it plain to the police that "these people have no right to demonstrate or express their views."

Elsewhere that April 27, marchers were fewer but spirits were high: the euphoria of Johnson's retreat and the McCarthy/Kennedy alternatives to a Humphrey candidacy still held. In San Francisco, the march of perhaps ten thousand (or thirty thousand) was led by about forty servicemen (out of uniform); several hundred veterans marched wearing paper hats emblazoned with the slogan VETERANS FOR PEACE. In Philadelphia, one of fifteen other cities where demonstrations were held that day, a black-robed, exiled South Vietnamese Buddhist leader, Thich Naht Hanh, told an orderly crowd that "we are not being saved; we are being destroyed."

On the day of the demonstrations Hubert Horatio Humphrey announced that he was a candidate for the office of President of the United States. In his prepared remarks he called for the "politics of happiness, the politics of purpose, and the politics of joy." The phrases haunted him all year: people felt that he did not understand the deep divisions that were tearing the country apart, that in 1968 neither "happiness" nor "joy" were appropriate political terms.

The presidential primaries continued. The next major primary after New Hampshire was in Wisconsin on April 2, two days after Lyndon Johnson's withdrawal from the race. To the elation of the antiwar forces, already ecstatic over their "defeat" of a sitting President, the Wisconsin results brought euphoria: Eugene McCarthy polled over 400,000 votes to Johnson's 250,000. Several weeks before the election, McCarthy staffers would happily have settled for 150,000, but now, however briefly, the tide seemed running in their favor. Three weeks later, in Pennsylvania (a nonbinding primary), McCarthy polled 428,000 votes to 73,000 write-ins for Johnson (or Humphrey) and 65,000 for Kennedy. Even in conservative Indiana, with Kennedy running a hard race, McCarthy pulled 27 percent to RFK's 42 percent—a vote that anti-Johnson forces could interpret, if they wished, as 69 percent opposed to the President over 30 percent for Governor Roger D. Branigin, a "favorite son."

Kennedy won Nebraska by 51 percent to McCarthy's 31 percent. The next three primaries, Oregon, California, and New York, would be decisive. On May 28 McCarthy won in Oregon, 46 percent to 36 percent. Kennedy had refused to debate McCarthy in Oregon, but the reasons for Kennedy's defeat—the first ever for a Kennedy—went deeper than that; the debate, in fact, might have helped him. McCarthy had had a strong organization in Oregon for months, while Kennedy's campaign, a last-minute affair, of course, was ineptly managed—or so Kennedy people felt in retrospect. Also, Kennedy, a fearsome campaigner, was exhausted. And finally, McCarthy, at last, had developed a fighting speech that he gave in both California and Oregon just before the Oregon primary. In it he attacked Kennedy and the entire Dulles cold-war rationale that RFK continued, said McCarthy, when in his announcement for the presidency he spoke of America's assuming "the moral leadership of the planet." In other words, according to McCarthy, Kennedy still did not understand the reasons for the tragedy of America's involvement in Vietnam.

Kennedy partisans have never forgiven McCarthy for many things, that speech among them. Kennedy himself was more pragmatic. The morning after the election he sent a congratulatory telegram to McCarthy and moved on to California.

It was a frenzied week, that last week: a week in which the crowds, much in evidence all spring thanks to Kennedy's skilled advance men, grew ever larger and more emotional. Kennedy refused protection other than from personal friends like football players Rafer Johnson and Roosevelt Grier; constantly he was mobbed, his clothing pulled awry, his tie pulled off, his cuff links ripped away—even, once, his shoes. The Kennedy crowds were dubbed by the press "the shouters and jumpers and touchers," but they were more than that. They seemed in their frenzy to feed off him, to want to lay hands on him in a kind of primitive ritual, and they frightened Kennedy's staff.

On Saturday, June 1, the long-delayed debate took place between Kennedy and McCarthy. Each side, predictably, claimed that its man "won." The two candidates were more in conflict over how to resolve the problems of the ghetto than over how to resolve the Vietnam issue.

Kennedy won in California by 46 percent to McCarthy's 41 percent. He had planned a meeting with some of McCarthy's people for the morning after the election, seeking to heal some of the deep wounds inflicted by both sides in the weeks just past.

But shortly after midnight on primary night, after a gracious victory speech, Robert F. Kennedy was shot by twenty-four year old Sirhan B. Sirhan, a disgruntled Palestinian immigrant. He lingered, unconscious, until the early hours of June 6. His death killed any hope of uniting the Democratic Party behind an antiwar, antiadministration candidate: McCarthy's showing had been strong but not strong enough. Moreover, Kennedy might have united the country. With his passing went any hope for a healing of the nation's wounds; continued bitter division seemed almost certain.

On the night before Kennedy's funeral mass at St. Patrick's Cathedral, New York, a young man appeared to keep vigil with the Kennedy family and friends; later, during the mass, he sat alone in a back pew, weeping. His name was Tom Hayden.

On June 9, the day after Kennedy's funeral, SDS delegates began to gather at the campus of Michigan State University in East Lansing, Michigan, for their annual convention. Eight hundred people came, more or less: five hundred delegates and three hundred "observers," including some from the FBI. One of the workshops, on sabotage, was designed specifically to draw off all undercover agents, Red Squad agents, FBI, and the like. According to the later testimony of one agent present, it was a successful ploy.

The student union meeting room was decorated with pictures of Lenin and Trotsky and with the hammer and sickle; the stage was adorned with the red flag of communism and the black flag of anarchism; many of the delegates wore red armbands and carried Chairman Mao's *Little Red Book* of thoughts. Were these truly young Communists dedicated to the overthrow of the United States Government? Or were they simply idealists thrown into agony, as idealists often are, by the gap between America's promise and her reality? Bernardine Dohrn said in answer to a question that "I consider myself a revolutionary Communist," but since she was trying to get elected to one of the three top SDS positions her words may have been campaign rhetoric.

It was Progressive Labor, however, which attempted the putsch. Although PL had sent no more than sixty delegates, some of these were authorized to cast five votes apiece; in caucuses, PL members presented a united front, their position agreed upon beforehand, their arguments well rehearsed. Notwithstanding the portraits of Marx and Lenin, many "regular" SDSers were still formulating their ideology; they were no match for PL's ideological juggernaut.

Matters came to a head when the convention was called upon to vote on a proposal written by three non-PL members: Bernardine Dohrn, Tom Bell, and Steve Halliwell. Its intent was to set guidelines for transforming SDS into a revolutionary organization—truly revolutionary now, and not just a group of college youths taking over buildings. (Mark Rudd, fresh from his exploits at Columbia, attended this SDS convention but was not by all accounts taken seriously by the membership; he had become too big a celebrity too quickly, without earning his stripes, as it were.) At the core of the proposal was big-city organizing among workers, welfare groups, high school students, and others. The PL delegates immediately seized upon its weaknesses: lack of ideas, vague language, a general insubstantiality. Although members of the National Office defended the proposal, PL succeeded in swaying enough votes to defeat it, 485–355.

Now the regulars were in trouble, for they had no other proposals, no other weapons with which to fight PL; they themselves had argued for years to keep to a "nonexclusionary" policy, so they could not throw PL out, but at the same time they needed to resist the attempted takeover from this disciplined, purposeful group which never seemed in doubt, as so many SDSers were, about what to do, which way to go.

Finally it was decided to present a proposal for reorganization of the national structure of SDS, with seventeen national officers to be elected. After interminable debate it was defeated—again at the hands of PL.

And so the National Office went to the convention with an outright attack on PL —an unprecedented step in the history of SDS, and one that alienated delegates who were in neither camp. Tom Bell, who was a "first-generation" SDSer organizing in Springfield, Massachusetts, waited his turn to speak; when he did, he excoriated PL in the strongest language for impeding the work of the convention and of SDS, imposing their own hard line on everyone else, threatening to destroy SDS. From the floor came the accusation: Bell was Red-baiting. Infuriated, he shouted back, "PL Out! PL Out!" The response came from the crowd: "PL Out! PL Out," delegates stamping their feet, clapping, shouting. Many were appalled: was this what SDS had become, a group that would not allow PL free speech?

The ruckus faded; the meeting went on; PL was not put out. But neither did the convention accomplish anything: the only event of significance, aside from the attack on PL, was the election of national officers: Mike Klonsky (a "red diaper" baby whose father had been an officer in the American Communist Party); Bernardine Dohrn (not a student; a recent graduate of the University of Chicago Law School who had done Movement legal work); and Fred Gordon, who had no known affiliation. What they had in common was that they were not PL; and they were committed, despite the absence of a supporting vote, to carrying out the Halliwell-Dohrn-Bell proposal to make a revolution. An eight-member National Interim Committee was also selected, among them Carl Oglesby; this group was more or less sympathetic to the new leadership trio, and thus unlikely to yield control to PL.

And so once again, only partly because of PL interference, SDS turned away from the issue of the war.

On June 14, after a three-week trial and a seven-hour jury deliberation, four of the Boston 5 were found guilty of conspiring to "aid and abet draft registrants to refuse service in the armed forces" and to "interfere with the administration of the draft." Marcus Raskin was acquitted.

The defendants' case had been argued on the narrow grounds of conspiracy rather than on the larger issue of Vietnam as an illegal, unconstitutional war—the

Nuremberg defense. The crimes for which Nazis had been tried at Nuremberg after World War II were (in the words of one observer, himself a judge) "crimes against peace, that is, waging wars of aggression; second, war crimes, that is, violation of the laws and customs of war; third, crimes against humanity, including torture, killings of civilians, deportations and forced labor. . . . These are recognized in our own military law. It is in the military orders given to every soldier, sailor and marine corps man: he is told that he does not have to obey his officer if he makes him do one of these things. So, Nuremberg is part of the law of the land. How can you say it isn't? There is no question about it. It's part of the law of the land." At the trial of the Boston 5, however, Judge Francis Ford had ruled that the defense's Nuremberg claims were not relevant.

Many people in the peace movement were disappointed that the trial had not provided a major test of the legality of the war; and even one of the defendants, the Reverend William Sloane Coffin, pronounced the trial to have been "dismal, dreary and above all demeaning to all concerned." Given the ground rules set down by Judge Ford, it could hardly have been anything else.

Dr. Spock comments:

> The purpose of the trial was not so much to punish us as to intimidate other people. . . .
> It was too bad that we didn't make our political point more emphatically, and since we had been denied every single day in court any opportunity to say why we were in it or why we thought we were right, we should have had a press conference every day at the end of court to explain our point of view. We got messages from the Movement: "We're very disappointed in your behavior—you're not fighting at all." It was better reported in *Pravda* than it was in any of the American papers.

A year later the U.S. Court of Appeals acquitted Spock and Ferber and ordered a new trial for Coffin and Goodman. The Justice Department dropped charges and the case was never retried.

1968:
Chicago:
"The Whole World Is Watching!"

IN NOVEMBER 1967 the Fellowship of Reconciliation held a weekend retreat. The purpose of the gathering was to evaluate the Pentagon demonstration of the month before. Those attending included representatives of the Fifth Avenue Peace Parade Committee; radical pacifist groups; SDS; SNCC; CORE; and regional representatives like Sidney Peck of CAPAC. The Socialist Workers Party did not attend; its members had disapproved of the civil disobedience at the Pentagon and wanted no part of any actions in the future which would involve a repeat.

In Peck's words, there was that weekend "an exchange of views with no real clarity." In an effort to sort out his thoughts and to help others clarify theirs, Peck subsequently wrote a paper, whose thesis was that revolutionary tactics were not appropriate for the Movement, but that dissent and resistance tactics were. The Movement's goal, he said, was not to take power but to change public policy.

In other words: where should resistance go next, after the events at the Pentagon? Should the Movement continue simply to bear witness, to make its presence felt in massive demonstrations? Should it move further toward civil disobedience? Or, as some would argue, should it move toward revolution?

"What the Pentagon action did," says Peck,

> was to raise within elements of SDS and sections of the pacifist movement [the idea] that the traditional style of civil disobedience is passé—that just to go there and sit until the cops came and got you or beat you up is not the way to do it. You have to have greater flexibility.
>
> Out of this the idea of affinity groups developed—small groups that had tactical mobility . . . [the idea being that] if you're going to do civil disobedience and engage in resistance-type activity that disrupts the normal course of events, then you've got to be able to move in and move out. You're not there for, quote, moral witness. You're there to resist and disrupt. Some people felt that this would open the door for provocateurs. . . .

No decision was made at the November meeting about what to do, if anything, at the Democratic Convention, but it was agreed to meet again in December to discuss the question further.

And so the following month, members of the Administrative Committee of the National Mobilization met in New York to discuss what action should be taken at the Democratic Convention in August of 1968. Among the sixty or so present were David Dellinger, Rennie Davis, Tom Hayden, Carl Oglesby, Sidney Peck, Robert Greenblatt, and Ron Young of the Fellowship of Reconciliation. Again the Socialist Workers Party did not attend; aside from its policy against civil disobedience, it planned to run its own presidential campaign and did not, therefore, want any involvement, adversarial or otherwise, with the major political parties. Oglesby, too, was beginning to have doubts: "I didn't think there should be a demonstration in Chicago at all. I thought we should declare it 'death city' and get out." No decision was made at the New York meeting about what to do at the Democratic Convention.

In February, Dellinger arranged to have two veterans of SDS, Rennie Davis and Tom Hayden, open an office at 407 South Dearborn Street in Chicago to begin preparations for the convention demonstrations. (As noted above, Davis had returned from North Vietnam the previous fall convinced that some kind of demonstration at the Democratic Convention was necessary. By 1968 neither he nor Hayden was formally connected to SDS.) There they were joined by other "older" SDSers who had given over to the new generation, a generation being about three years in New Left circles; among them were Kathy Boudin, Jeff Shero, and, later, John Froines.

Hayden and Davis put out a position paper outlining possible strategies to be used: "Movement Campaign 1968—an Election Year Offensive." It was a reasoned appeal both for local actions and for "sustained, organized protests" at the convention. It specifically renounced violence: "The campaign should not plan violence and disruption against the Democratic National Convention. It should be nonviolent and legal." Its use of language, however, may have contributed to Mayor Richard Daley's elaborate preparations to secure the city against no one knew how many thousands of intruders: it warned of a "massive confrontation with our government," an "attack on the Democratic convention," "clogging the streets of Chicago," "pinning the delegates in the International Amphitheatre," and "final days of militancy." Later, testifying before HUAC, Hayden denied that he had intended violence (see p. 204), but in March, when the paper appeared, it seemed in the context of both black and student rebellions to be at least ambiguous on the issue.

That same month, the Mobilization held a meeting in Chicago with representatives from black organizations including SNCC, CORE, and the black caucus of the remnants of the ill-fated NCNP. It was an attempt to forge a combination of black and antiwar groups, but no agreement was reached.

The possibility of a black-white alliance was raised again in late March at an invitation-only conference held at a YMCA camp at Lake Villa, north of Chicago, to decide what action should be taken at the Democratic Convention. About two hundred people attended. At that time the target of any action was still Lyndon Johnson. The McCarthy campaign had begun—thereby offering something to be for rather than against—but it was not yet perceived as a viable enterprise, much less as a vehicle for all of the antiwar sentiment which smoldered just under the surface of the nation's affairs, waiting to erupt. McCarthy had specifically offered his candidacy for those who otherwise would go outside the system, but there were many in the Mobilization—not to mention SDS—who scorned electoral politics altogether, McCarthy or no McCarthy. As Carl Oglesby wrote in "An Open Letter to McCarthy Supporters":

> Is McCarthy the pay-off of those years of protest? Does he represent the partial fruition of our efforts to build a movement for changing America?
> Or is he only another attempt to emasculate that protest?
> Is he what the Movement has been working for? Or against?
> How in fact are we to define McCarthy so that we can at least be sure that we're talking about the same thing?
> Perhaps by his record? Surely you're tired by now of listening to the dreary list of his illiberal votes [including "the tardiness of his opposition to the War"]. . . .

Tom Hayden remembers:

> SDS at this point was well on its way to ideological oblivion. They opposed the demonstration [for two reasons]:
> 1. if it was successful it would be co-opted by Kennedy;
> 2. if it was a failure, if it was repressed, it would destroy the leadership of the Left, which was them. So they didn't want to send their experienced cadres into the danger of co-optation on the one hand and repression on the other. . . .

No decision was made at Lake Villa about what to do in August.

One week after the Lake Villa meeting, when President Johnson announced his decision not to run, leaders of the antiwar movement experienced a brief elation followed by an enormous letdown: their infamous target, the man they so loved to hate, had removed himself. The target had become instead the (Vietnam) plank of the Democrats' platform; and as Robert Kennedy had said the previous autumn, "I never saw anyone rallying behind a plank." Further diffusing their energies was the idea of support for the Poor People's March on Washington scheduled for May: now that they had in effect defeated LBJ, should they not at last turn their full attention to the country's racial crisis? The issue seemed all the more urgent in the wake of the riots following the assassination of Martin Luther King, Jr.

Nevertheless the question nagged: what effort should be made at Chicago?

In Washington, in May, as Resurrection City festered on the Mall and McCarthy and Kennedy in the hinterlands battled their way through the primaries and the delegate hunt, the Mobilization's Administrative Committee held a meeting to decide what to do at the Chicago convention. No decision was made. The Chicago office continued to plan for a demonstration of some sort, joined now by Abbie Hoffman and Jerry Rubin of the "Youth International Party," or "Yippies."

In June, after the assassination of Robert Kennedy, Allard Lowenstein attempted to bring together the anti-Humphrey (antiadministration) forces under an umbrella called the Coalition for an Open Convention (COC). At least one major demonstration was planned for Chicago, but as the summer passed and threats of violence and disaster grew, Lowenstein asked those who had volunteered to appear not to come after all. Some heeded his warning; some did not.

Finally, in late July, the Cleveland Area Peace Action Council, which Sidney Peck had chaired, hosted yet another conference of the Mobilization's Administrative Committee to plan for action at the Chicago convention. Peck's feelings of apprehension about the scenario for potential disaster finally surfaced at a meeting arranged between himself, Dellinger, and Hayden: amid talk of violence—were they planning a demonstration or a confrontation?—Peck, exasperated, said, " 'How many people are we willing to risk being killed? . . . I don't think we should risk anyone's life.' But Hayden genuinely believed that we were in a prerevolutionary situation. . . ."

In the end the July Cleveland Conference agreed to organize a mass demonstration the following month, but "to go slow on confrontational challenge. The message was not to disrupt the convention."

In fact, the message was garbled at best. As late as July 31, there was still no date set for a specific action; no agreement could be reached on what to do, how to do it, and who should be in charge of whatever it was that was to be done. At the last major Mobilization planning session for the Chicago demonstrations, held on August 4, Rennie Davis finally gave the proposed schedule:

—"a loose counterconvention"; decentralized and diversified "movement centers" which would help people to "exchange information" and organize small demonstrations;

—picketing the Hilton Hotel (a major delegate site) on Sunday, August 25;

—no official Mobe presence at the COC rally on August 26; Mobilization marshals to be provided if COC requested them;

—an "Un-birthday" party for President Johnson on August 27;

—the major action: the march to the Amphitheatre on August 28;

—"decentralized actions" on August 29.

Fifty thousand flyers containing the schedule were issued within a few days of the August 4 meeting.

David Dellinger has written the postmortem on those weeks:

> Our plan began to founder in the last frantic month before the convention, as we were forced to wrestle with the multiple problems created by external attack and internal uncertainty. It remained the intended framework but suffered from inadequate preparation and attention as energy was drained

into uphill efforts to get permits, housing, facilities for movement centers—and recruits.

Tom Hayden:

The fear of SDS leaders was quite exact—that if we were successful, then we would lose control to moderates, if we were repressed, the leadership would be all wiped out. The crucial thing was the permits, because without the permits you couldn't get the musicians, without the musicians you couldn't get the youth base, and you couldn't draw people who required a promise of personal safety. With permits, you would have clogged the streets with a lot of people. It might have been difficult to get from the convention to the hotels, but you would not have had the running street battles. Some people came hoping for a real savage confrontation that would finally expose the true nature of the beast, as the saying went. . . . My position was, hope for the best, make it a big event, if that's not to be then we have to stay because we're not going to let them take our right to protest away by force and intimidation. So it'll become a battle. That was not my preference but I wasn't going to back away. . . . One way or another we were going to have [either] a massive turnout that would repudiate the President and give the Democratic Party big trouble and indirectly support the Kennedy or McCarthy wing of the party, or, it was going to turn into some kind of awful battle that would expose the bankruptcy of the party and show that only a change in their Vietnam policy would allow them to win in November. So either way we were going to have a major impact on political events. . . .

Their task was complicated by the Yippies' provocative statements flatly predicting violence. The Yippies had been unable to secure permits for their "Festival of Life," and as the convention date drew near, a "festival of blood" was envisioned instead—confrontation with intransigent police, and no clear plan of action. "We had to prepare for war," said Abbie Hoffman afterward.

Rennie Davis remembers:

Initially we saw it as a mass mobilization. . . . We did not see it as a civil disobedience or a militant protest. We were actually concerned about the image promoted by Jerry [Rubin] and Abbie [Hoffman] and that tendency in the beginning. Broad-based constituencies were opposed to [U.S.] Vietnam policies and we conceived of three to four hundred thousand people participating in the protest. Our idea of Chicago was a rank-and-file walkout of ordinary Democrats, spearheaded by the campus, but much, much broader than that. This plan only shifted as the permit issue changed the possibilities. We set out with great sincerity to negotiate a permit. In the beginning, when we had the support of Ramsey Clark [the U.S. attorney general], I didn't anticipate any problem. . . . Daley was making statements, but I assumed we had Johnson's support with Ramsey Clark. . . .
    That assumption shifted quickly. It didn't take too long. And as soon as Daley's unprecedented opposition to permits became clear, we shifted our position to the First Amendment ["Congress shall make no law . . .

abridging the freedom of speech . . . or the right of the people peaceably
to assemble. . . ."]. While the war was the overriding issue, the First
Amendment right loomed large in our minds. . . . I recognized the possibility of people being hurt if plans continued without permits. There was
even the fear of people losing life. . . . We didn't proceed without thought.
◄ . . . There was even deliberation of calling it off.

The week before the delegates and demonstrators arrived, Tom Hayden offered
his opinion of the Mobilization's aims: "Our goal is not to influence the delegates in
the convention, but to re-assert the presence and vitality of the antiwar movement
which had been confused and relaxed by the Paris peace talks and the McCarthy
campaign. . . . The convention is a convenient symbol around which to rally the
movement again. We are not concerned about who gets nominated."
Less than two weeks later, in the midst of the debacle that the convention became for everyone involved, delegates and demonstrators alike, Hayden exhorted
the crowd in Grant Park: "If they want blood to flow from our heads the blood will
flow from a lot of other heads around this city and around the country. . . . It
may well be that the era of organized, peaceful, and orderly demonstrations is
coming to an end and that other methods will be needed."

On August 22, 1968, four days before the Democratic Convention, Jerome Johnson, a seventeen-year-old American Indian from Sioux Falls, South Dakota, was
shot and killed by the Chicago police. The incident happened a few blocks southwest of Lincoln Park, the informal headquarters of both the hippie/Yippie delegation and the Mobilization. Police claimed that they fired only after Johnson, allegedly a Yippie, fired a .32 caliber revolver at them.
The Chicago police were having a difficult year. During the riots that followed
Martin Luther King's assassination they had behaved with admirable restraint,
only to be criticized by Mayor Daley. Police should shoot to maim looters and
shoot to kill arsonists, he said. A few days later, during the April 27 march held by
the Chicago Peace Council, police brutally cleared demonstrators from the downtown Civic Center Plaza. They were criticized for that effort by a citizens' commission called to investigate the incident. Now in late summer they were being put to
the biggest test yet: could they keep order during the Democrats' convention in the
face of increasing threats of disorder, disruption, and worse? How were they—for
instance—to deal with the Yippies' threat to slip LSD into the city's water system?
or to dynamite natural gas lines? or to flood the sewers with gas from service
stations and burn the city to the ground? or to bombard with mortars the
Amphitheatre where the convention was to be held?
The Mobilization had announced plans for massive demonstrations both at the
delegates' hotels and at the convention center several miles away. The Yippies'
plans for a Festival of Life, as ridiculous as they seem now—as ridiculous as they
might have seemed then—were quite deliberately something else: hundreds forni-
cating in the city's parks and on Lake Michigan's beaches; releasing greased pigs all
over the city; slashing tires along the freeways; floating ten thousand nude bodies

on the lake; using Yippie girls as hookers to seduce and drug delegates (in 1968 we are still in the era of the predominantly male delegate); using Yippie men to seduce delegates' wives and daughters (ditto); having one hundred thousand people burn their draft cards with the fires spelling BEAT ARMY.

"Fuck nuns," exhorted the Yippies; "laugh at professors; disobey your parents; burn your money; you know life is a dream. . . . Break down the family, church, nation, city, economy; turn life into an art form. . . . The revolutionary is the only artist. . . . The white youth of America have more in common with Indians plundered, than they do with their own parents. Burn their houses down, and you will be free."

"We wanted to fuck up their image on TV," said Abbie Hoffman; and in that, at least, he succeeded.

From other sources came other threats, real or perceived:

—from *Liberation*, November 1967:

> If there are 100,000 people in the streets, prepared to do civil disobedience, what should their demands be?

—from Dick Gregory, the comedian-turned-activist:

> [Unless racial conditions were improved in Chicago, he would lead demonstrations] which would make it possible for the Democratic Party to hold its convention here only over my dead body.

—from the Mobilization's Chicago organizers, who wanted to

> . . . release the real power of our many forces in a new and significant way at the time that Johnson is nominated, turning delegates back into the Amphitheatre as they attempt to leave. . . .

—from the *Guardian*, February 3, 1968 (a discussion of tactics):

> . . . massive demonstrations probably involving disruption tactics. . . . there are those who say that Chicago should be completely disrupted and the Convention not even allowed to take place . . . a massive confrontation . . . a chaotic confrontation. . . .

—from *New Left Notes*, March 4, 1968:

> It should be clear to anyone who has been following developments in Chicago that a non-violent demonstration would be impossible.

—from a UPI press release, August 13, 1968:

> Their [National Mobe's] battle plan is to raise cain outside the convention hall. As their Chicago coordinator, Rennie Davis, warns, a storming of the convention hall itself is "obviously not out of the question."

David Dellinger and Sidney Peck realized that such confrontation politics were alienating what Peck calls the "mainstream presence"—Middle America: "It became clear that we were going to be isolated in Chicago," says Peck; "and Daley's reaction was a military response."

Indeed it was: the mayor reacted with an array of plans and preparations that were designed to deal with almost any calamity except the one that happened.

As early as January of that year, the Chicago Police Department had set up a Convention Planning Committee made up of representatives from various city, state, and federal agencies, including the police and fire departments, the Secret Service, and military intelligence. Until June, the committee met every two weeks; then until mid-August, when its findings were turned over to the police, it met every week.

To determine what security arrangements were needed the committee used reports fed to it by informers, including police undercover agents and members of the Chicago Red Squad. Davis remembers:

> I arrived at the office one day and there were two plainclothes guys, standing in the hallway, pretty heavy-duty. They just announced their mission in a very stern and direct way. They said they would be with me wherever I went and, "If you try to shake us—don't." The spokesman put his face about this far from me [three inches] and he said, "You understand what I'm saying?"—the implied threat being, "I may blow your head off if you don't play by the rules."

Police coverage included:

—placing the twelve-thousand-man Chicago police force on twelve-hour shifts during convention week, thus increasing capacity by 50 percent;

—deploying three hundred members of the CPD Task Force to specially targeted areas (the Loop, the Amphitheatre, and Lincoln Park); these policemen, who patrolled in cars, usually carried helmets, service revolvers, batons (nightsticks), mace, and one shotgun per car; during the convention week they also had tear gas and gas masks, five hundred of which had been delivered to the CPD one week before the convention began.

—with the help of the Secret Service, securing the Amphitheatre (the convention site):

> —exterior security, including blocking off access streets to all but authorized personnel; erecting a cyclone fence topped with barbed wire around the parking lot (this was done at the request of the Democratic National Committee); letters to be delivered checked by the Secret Service; manhole covers in the vicinity sealed or routinely checked by police; lookouts equipped with walkie-talkies on the rooftop of the Amphitheatre and nearby buildings.
>
> —interior security of 472 men and a reserve force of 50, and a plainclothes policewoman in each ladies' room. Sixty plainclothes detectives worked the convention floor under the command of the Secret Service.

—assigning undercover agents to Lincoln Park, the informal headquarters of the demonstration. In addition, the uniformed police assigned to Lincoln Park were warned that they might be subject to much "taunting and baiting," and they were warned to behave professionally.

—six thousand army troops stationed at Glenview Naval Air Station; trained in riot control, they were equipped with rifles, flamethrowers, and bazookas;

—five thousand national guard troops;

—other government agencies on alert, including the Cook County Sheriff's Office, state police, state fire marshal, Chicago Fire Department, and the Chicago Hospital Council, which implemented a citywide emergency plan; reorganization of the city's arrest and judicial procedures, which were found to be inadequate after the April riots following Martin Luther King's assassination.

In addition, to complete the arrangements, a private security force was hired by the Democratic National Committee.

In an attempt to forestall disaster—i.e., low attendance—Peck and Dellinger spent two frantic days on the telephone in mid-August contacting groups who had never been contacted by the Hayden-Davis leadership or who had refused to join what seemed an increasingly suicidal action. No real call had ever been issued; no real preparation for a mass demonstration had been made. Peace groups and the traditional liberal groups were reluctant to come, and the SWP—the "Trots," the workhorses of so many demonstrations—flatly refused to participate in any action that seemed to recognize the legitimacy of the Democratic Party. They were running their own candidate for President—Fred Halstead—and they wanted to maintain their separate status; to have gone to Chicago, perhaps to bargain with Democrats over a "peace plank," perhaps only to bear witness, would have been to deny the existence and validity of their own party.

Despite Peck's and Dellinger's last-minute efforts, few people came to Chicago: perhaps five thousand at most, matched by another five thousand Chicagoans. As an umbrella group, the National Mobilization Committee had access to every organization in the country that shared its goals, but now these groups were represented sparsely, if at all. SDS sent about five hundred people, a tiny fraction of its membership; other people came from Clergy and Laymen Concerned, the Chicago Peace Council, the Fifth Avenue Peace Parade Committee, the Communist Party, a few from SWP (but not Fred Halstead, who was in South Vietnam), the Progressive Labor Party, American Friends Service Committee, and the Cleveland Area Peace Action Council.

Or, in the words of *Rights in Conflict* (the Walker Report on the convention) submitted to the National Commission on the Causes and Prevention of Violence:

> Communists, anarchists, peace advocates, revolutionaries, New Leftists, bizarre flower folk, draft resisters, radical militants, professional agitators, moderate but discontented liberals, disaffected straights, housewives opposed to the war, black power militants—all with their own motivations and objectives.

As all of these folks began to arrive, the Daley administration was putting an end to the summer-long wrangle over permits to parade and permits to sleep in the city's parks which had been requested by the Mobilization, the Yippies, and Lowenstein's COC, and which had been denied by the Daley administration. All three groups sued in U.S. District Court, and all three lost. On August 23, the Friday before the convention, Judge William J. Lynch ruled in favor of the city: there would be no permits. Finally, on Tuesday night, the twenty-seventh, one permit was granted to the Mobilization for a rally at the Grant Park band shell on Wednesday afternoon, August 28. The permit required that the Mobilization take out a $100,000–$300,000 public liability insurance policy, but this was never done.

Although Hoffman and Rubin had joined forces to produce their Festival of Life, they had felt the strain of their clashing egos and they were not on good terms by the time of the convention. One of their arguments was about Pigasus, the Yippie candidate for President. Hoffman wanted a "cute little pig"; Rubin wanted an "obnoxious, horrible" pig. Rubin won. Obnoxious, horrible Pigasus was released at the Civic Center Plaza on Friday, August 23. His platform, said the Yippies, was garbage. He was promptly seized ("arrested," said the Yippies delightedly) by the police and given to the Chicago Humane Society. Rubin and five other Yippies were arrested too.

With Pigasus, the Yippies showed very clearly their contempt for the system. Now that same system, via the police, began to react in kind. At Lincoln Park, three miles north of the Loop and delegates' hotels, the demonstrators had gathered to prepare for the week ahead. The Mobilization was training marshals in Dellinger's practice of nonviolence: the marshals were to protect demonstrators, to keep them in order, and to prevent physical confrontations with the police. Other groups were practicing karate, judo, and *washoi*—an Oriental protective maneuver, a kind of serpentine dance. Police helicopters monitored this activity even as uniformed patrols, some on motorcycles, watched it from below.

On Saturday afternoon, August 24, an anticipatory crowd including a number of police undercover agents began to gather in Lincoln Park, despite the fact that the much-heralded Festival of Life was not scheduled to begin until Sunday. Late in the day Rubin, Hoffman, Paul Krassner of the *Realist,* and other Yippie leaders issued a statement asking their people to observe the city's 11 P.M. curfew: a mass arrest at this point was seen—correctly—as self-defeating. A crowd had gathered around a bonfire, joining poet Allen Ginsberg in chanting, "Om . . . om . . . om . . . om." Ginsberg claimed that "om" dissipated tension, and that in crowds the sound can work wonders: "A thousand bodies vibrating om can immobilize an entire downtown Chicago street full of scared humans, uniformed or naked." However, no police were immobilized in Lincoln Park on that night or any other; Ginsberg and his thrumming flock moved out, and near 11 P.M. the police moved in, motorcycles in the front rank, and cleared the remaining two hundred or so demonstrators from the grounds. Eleven people were arrested outside the park for refusing to disperse.

Thus ended the first major confrontation between police and demonstrators in Chicago, August 1968.

Early Sunday afternoon an impromptu, ragtag, and bobtail parade of Yippies marched from Lincoln Park to the Loop. Although they shouted slogans as they went, they were a peaceful group and they obeyed police instructions to keep moving. After being blocked at the corner of Jackson and Wabash, they regrouped in Grant Park and then left, all without incident.

Meanwhile, back at Lincoln Park, the Festival of Life was beginning. A lone rock band played. As many "straights" as Yippies watched it—with difficulty, since there was no stage. The park's sound system had been denied to the Festival of Life, so the band had plugged in to the outlet of a nearby concession stand. Late in the afternoon a flatbed truck arrived, driven in to be used as a stage for the band. The police refused to allow it to stay. In the resulting fracas, the crowd turned nasty. "Fascist pig!" and "Pigs eat shit!" and "Kill the pigs! Fuck the pigs!" they cried. The police responded, knocking heads, making a couple of arrests. After a while things subsided.

It was during that afternoon that Jerry Rubin acquired his "bodyguard," a purported member of a Chicago motorcycle gang that had appeared in Lincoln Park, seventy or so strong, more out of curiosity than antiwar sentiment. He was a blond, muscular young man who wore a black T-shirt, dark glasses, and a helmet. His name was Robert Pierson. He was in fact an undercover policeman. He testified for the prosecution during Rubin's trial on a charge of incitement to riot.

As darkness fell, the scene was described by a witness for the Walker Commission:

> It was just before nightfall, and they didn't have any plan. It was supposed to have been a festival of life, but I didn't see any happy people. Everybody I walked past looked depressed and aimless. There was no action, and it was starting to get quite cold. Although there were a lot of police in the park, too, it was a very dead scene. But when it got dark, then things started to speed up.

At 10:30, after an evening of scattered confrontation and name-calling, the police moved through Lincoln Park in a car announcing the 11 P.M. curfew over a loudspeaker. As Mobilization marshals urged compliance, the Yippie crowd cursed them. Eventually most people left the park in time; many of these set off on another impromptu march downtown. They returned later, however, to join those who had stayed; and now came the ugly scene that both sides had anticipated.

Perhaps 1,000 people were in the park versus 458 police, half of whom carried shotguns and tear gas. As the police began their sweep, the crowd threw rocks and bottles at them and taunted them: "Motherfuckers!" "Pig fuckers!" "Fascists!" "Shitheads!" As the police charged and scattered the crowd, it regrouped as if seeking confrontation. Tear gas forced the crowd out of the park and into the streets. Drivers began honking horns, either in sympathy or frustration. The police were as angry as the crowd now: "Kill the commies!" "Get the bastards!" they shouted.

And the crowd replied, "Kill the pigs!" "Your wife sucks cock!"

Police began to clear the sidewalk; people moved. Suddenly some police broke ranks and began clubbing the crowd. Photographers and reporters, who had been busy enough all day and night, now began snapping and scribbling furiously, as they would all week. The police singled out the press for special punishment; on this night they attacked at least half a dozen reporters and photographers, including two from *Newsweek* and one from the Philadelphia *Bulletin.* At last the crowd faded away.

The following day, Monday, August 26, a group of clergy in the Lincoln Park area agreed that because the police had used excessive force on the previous evening, they would offer themselves as buffers on Monday night both to protect people from injury and to observe police operations.

On Monday afternoon at a Lincoln Park baseball field Tom Hayden was arrested. He was charged with resisting arrest, obstructing police, and disorderly conduct. Soon after, Rennie Davis led five hundred or so people on a march to police headquarters to protest Hayden's arrest. Carrying Viet Cong flags and the red flag of communism, they moved downtown toward the Loop and Grant Park. There they joined with other demonstrators at the statue of Major General John Alexander Logan, a Civil War hero. They quickly clambered onto the general, who sat astride his horse, and draped the statue with their alien flags. Police pulled them down, including one boy whose arm was broken and who, like many other protesters, was hit in the groin with billy clubs. Many other people thronged the park, some listening to speeches, some taunting police by throwing rocks and bottles and chanting curses.

By Monday evening, Hayden was released on $1,000 bond. He promptly went underground. For the next two days he moved freely through the city disguised variously in a long-haired wig, false mustache and beard, red helmet, and dark glasses.

By 9 P.M. the crowd in Lincoln Park had begun a march south on Clark Street. Police blocked their way, and after what had by now become routine attacks they arrested more than forty people. Those who had remained in the park were joined by others, including between forty-five and seventy clergymen exercising their "collar power." Toward 11 P.M. several young men began setting up a barricade of picnic tables to block police on motorcycles or in cars. The barricade grew to perhaps thirty-five yards long, curved, with Viet Cong and red and black flags flying. Amid the threats and curses of the demonstrators, in the light of fires set in trash baskets, Allen Ginsberg chanted, "Om." Few people vibrated, however—certainly not the police.

At 11:15 P.M. the announcement came: the park was closed for the night. *"Sieg Heil, Schwein!"* "Hell No, We Won't Go!" cried the demonstrators. By midnight, from two thousand to three thousand people were in Lincoln Park. Many of them were behind the barricade, taunting the police, inviting attack. A police squad car, lights off, became trapped by the crowd as it approached the barricade; the crowd pelted it, breaking its windshield. With great difficulty commanders kept their men in line.

Shortly before 12:30 A.M., Task Force police threw smoke bombs and tear gas canisters at the barricade; then they moved in. Several witnesses claimed that as the police charged, they chanted, "Kill, kill, kill!"

After considerable violence lasting ten minutes or so, Lincoln Park was clear but the adjacent streets were mobbed. With tear gas and nightsticks the police attacked again; bystanders and media persons were clubbed as often as identifiable demonstrators. In return the police were continuously pelted with rocks, bricks, bottles, and any other usable missile. Many police had removed their identification.

By 2 A.M. the crowd had finally dispersed. The city and its visitors, invited and uninvited, rested against the coming day and its promise of renewed violence.

Many demonstrators had planned to arrive in Chicago on Tuesday, August 27, in time for LBJ's "Un-birthday" party. Louise Peck was among them. As Sidney Peck's wife—an identity with which she sometimes needed to struggle—she had heard privately of all of the difficulties and apprehensions about the upcoming events. Publicly she said what she thought she was expected to say: that it would be a good demonstration; that, yes, she was taking her two children ages thirteen and fifteen; that of course she would urge everyone to come.

In truth she felt differently. Although she realized it fully only some weeks after it was all over, "She was in fact pretty angry that I was urging people to come and bring their families," her husband recalls.

> I had to be interviewed [she continues]. And they would say, "Are you going?" and I would say, "Oh yes, I think it's going to be a picnic," and I would say how positive and safe my husband assured me it would be, but I felt very conflicted. When you so want the demonstration to be successful and safe, you begin to deny the doubts, I guess. As we began to enter Chicago my worst fears began to be realized because everywhere you looked you saw tanks and armored cars and National Guard in masks and I began to get more and more frightened. And when we finally got to where we were going and unloaded I was so nervous I tripped over my suitcase and fell down and scraped my nose—really banged it—and blackened one eye, so by the time I saw Sid I looked like I had been beaten up already. . . . I had been at the Pentagon [in October] and I was frightened. . . .

Tuesday night in Lincoln Park, Bobby Seale of the Black Panthers and Jerry Rubin of the Festival of Life harangued the crowd. The Black Panther candidate for President, Eldridge Cleaver, was running on the "Peace and Power" ticket, and the Black Panther message was "developing revolution." Cleaver, who in recent years has discovered Jesus and claims to have been "born again," was at that time a convicted rapist who in his bestselling memoir had claimed that he raped white women as retribution for centuries of black suffering. In any revolution developing out of the Chicago gathering, cried Seale that hot, tense night, blacks would lead and blacks would carry the guns. Whites would be their supporters. It was the scenario of the 1967 Labor Day convention of the NCNP all over again. Jerry Rubin enthusiastically seconded Seale's speech: "We'll take the same risks as blacks take." Several hours of skirmishes between police and demonstrators followed. As many as one thousand people left Lincoln Park at about ten-thirty to walk to Grant Park; it was an orderly march with no arrests.

The clergymen who had expressed alarm at Monday night's violence had gathered meanwhile at the Church of the Three Crosses; they planned to stage a vigil in Lincoln Park to forestall further bloodshed. They began the walk to the park; they carried a twelve-foot-high wooden cross. When they reached the park they were quickly joined by perhaps fifteen hundred people, and as the 11 P.M. curfew approached they began to sing the "Battle Hymn of the Republic."

At eleven-thirty the police announced that the park was closed for the night. A sanitation truck was moved in; it carried a device for spraying tear gas.

Shortly after midnight the clergymen advised the demonstrators to "sit or split." They advised those who didn't want to be "hit, jailed, or gassed" to leave the park. Those who intended to stay were told to sit down, lock arms, and remain calm. Many readied handkerchiefs and surgical masks, dampened with baking soda or vaseline as a protection against tear gas. The demonstrators, perhaps five hundred strong, sang "Onward, Christian Soldiers" and "America the Beautiful."

The police announced curfew several times more; then tear gas began to billow from the sanitation truck. Police lines began to move against the crowd, forcing them out of the park and into the surrounding streets. The truck was hit by rocks and bottles from the crowd, and as people poured out of the park they kept on throwing missiles at the police. Two squad cars were stoned, their windows shattered; in return, five or six parked cars carrying McCarthy stickers were attacked by police, who smashed their windows and released their hand brakes in order to move them out of the way. The sanitation truck continued to spray tear gas. Random violence continued as the police followed the crowd, trying to break it up. Police stopped, questioned, and sometimes clubbed and maced passersby; youths threw rocks, bottles, and bricks at police and their cars.

When the night was over, ninety-three arrests had been made, nine police vehicles damaged, and seven policemen injured. No count of the injured civilians, both demonstrators and passersby, was possible.

During this time Lyndon Johnson's "Un-birthday" party was being held at the Coliseum. Perhaps three thousand people attended and gave an enthusiastic reception to Dick Gregory, David Dellinger, folksinger Phil Ochs, Allen Ginsberg, and others.

Shortly before midnight about three thousand people left the Coliseum to march to Grant Park across from the Hilton, where a confrontation was building. Simultaneously, people were arriving from the confrontation in Lincoln Park; they were in an ugly mood and they joined the chant: "Pig! Pig! Pig! Pig!" "Hell, No, We Won't Go!" "Fascist pigs!"

A line of demonstrators' marshals faced two lines of police who stood with their batons at the ready. When three police officials went to the crowd to speak to Rennie Davis and other leaders, they were greeted (according to their account) by "hippie types" who kept yelling obscenities at them.

Both the crowd and the police were tense; some policemen had worked as long as seventeen hours without a break. The demonstrators, too, were exhausted and angry. They began a sit-down in the park, all the while continuing both verbal and physical abuse of the police, swearing, throwing things, kicking officers who came too close. At about 1:30 A.M. the deputy superintendent of police announced over a bullhorn that if the crowd were peaceful they could stay in the park overnight. He was answered with a loud cheer.

Peter and Mary of the Peter, Paul and Mary trio began to sing and the audience joined in the old favorites, "Blowin' in the Wind," "This Land Is Your Land," "If I Had a Hammer." While they sang, the police, exhausted, summoned replacements. About 3 A.M. the first troops of the National Guard to be used that week—about six hundred—arrived at the Hilton. They were in full battle dress, with M-1 rifles, carbines, shotguns, ammunition, and gas masks. A new crowd control device also appeared: a jeep covered with mesh wire to protect against flying objects and carrying on its front a large square frame of barbed wire.

The crowd was furious. No one had warned them that the troops had been called out, and now they screamed obscenities at the guardsmen. Peter and Mary tried to calm them. One squad leader arrived to hear "Pigs, pigs, fascist pigs!" against a background of "If I Had a Hammer." As Brigadier General Dunn tried to speak to the crowd through a bullhorn they turned up their sound system and drowned him out with "This Land Is Your Land." Speakers mounted the platform; one asked the convention delegates, now returned to the Hilton for the night, to flick their room lights if they agreed with his denunciation of the war. Between ten and twenty did.

Some demonstrators tried to reason with the guardsmen, but many more subjected the soldiers to what was described as an "unbelievable" level of abuse. Nevertheless the guardsmen stood quietly without response.

Very late, about four-thirty in the morning, a figure appeared out of the mist like the ghost of Hamlet's father. It was Tom Hayden, surfacing for only a moment from wherever he had gone "to get the pig off my back." Prophetically, he announced that "now that the pig is on the collective back of all of us, we are going to find a way to go underground." Then he disappeared. The few remaining demonstrators huddled in the damp chill waiting for day, for new confrontation.

On Wednesday afternoon a crowd of perhaps eight to ten thousand had begun to gather at the Grant Park band shell for the scheduled Mobilization rally. Moving among them were uniformed policemen who handed out flyers informing the crowd that this rally was legal, but that no march would be permitted outside Grant Park and no march and rally would be permitted near the Amphitheatre— something that many in the Mobilization wanted to do.

The rally proceeded under the hot sun. Viet Cong and red and black flags were much in evidence, as they had been all week. The Stars and Stripes fluttered on a flagpole near the band shell stage. Speakers came and went at the microphone; many of them called for a march on the Amphitheatre. The audience milled about as if waiting for some exciting thing to happen.

Suddenly, while Carl Oglesby was speaking, a young man began to shinny up the flagpole. Some in the crowd shouted at him to put the flag at half-mast; mindful of the police threat, the speakers on the bandstand told him to leave it alone and get down.

No sooner had the warnings been shouted, however, than the police appeared as if on cue. Two by two, helmeted, visored, nightsticks raised, they quick-stepped into the crowd. They reached the flagpole and began to pull the youth down, beating him in the process.

Oglesby remembers: "They marched in a line of two diagonally into the center of the crowd, with nightsticks, clubbing away at people . . . and they stood in the middle for a while, in a circle clubbing away outward and people couldn't decide whether to run away or to fight, and the thing was, there was nowhere to run away to. The only way you could get out of that place was back the same way we'd come, which was totally lined with cops."

An undercover agent claimed to have been the one who climbed the flagpole, but Dellinger has stated that the act was performed by a "sweet young kid from rural Wisconsin who had acted with innocent enthusiasm and extremely bad judgment." Oglesby says flatly that it was done by a police provocateur.

The crowd, as tense and angry as the police, needed little encouragement to fight back. People seized whatever was at hand: "asbestos, metal and clay floor tiles; placards and placard sticks; balloons filled with paint and urine; bricks; concrete chunks; tree branches; all types of stones; eggs; tomatoes . . . and pieces of park bench."

Led by those on stage, some of the crowd began to chant, "Sit down, sit down!" Rennie Davis went into the crush around the flagpole and was caught and beaten by the police; his head was hit and he was bleeding badly.

"I was never confronted more overwhelmingly with the awful limits of language," says Oglesby, SDS's orator; "when you are actually beholding and taking part in the event, words just can't function. . . ."

Accounts differ as to what happened next. According to the Walker Report, six "burly young men"—unidentified—surrounded the flagpole and lowered the flag. In its place they raised either a red cloth or a girl's bright red slip. Some reports said that the object was a red flag or a black flag or a Viet Cong flag or long red underwear or a bloodied shirt.

In any case, as the red cloth arouses the bull, so it aroused the Chicago police. Fifteen or twenty rushed in to try to arrest the offending youths. Again the crowd attacked them with every missile at hand: "Sticks, firecrackers, shoes, clods of earth, empty fruit juice cans, bottles, flaming rags . . . cellophane bags of human excrement." An unmarked police car (with police inside) was attacked, its windows smashed.

Tom Hayden, aboveground again, exhorted the crowd:

> This city and the military machine it has aimed at us won't permit us to protest in an organized fashion. Therefore, we must move out of this park in groups throughout the city, and turn this overheated military machine against itself. Let us make sure that if blood flows, it flows all over the city. If they use gas against us, let us make sure they use it against their own citizens.

Several months later, subpoenaed to testify before the House Un-American Activities Committee, Hayden—author of *The Port Huron Statement* with its plea for peace and love—explained what he had meant:

> . . . the thing that I did not want to happen on August 28 was for all of these demonstrators to be trapped down by the band shell, and wiped out by the police.
>
> If they were going to be wiped out, if the convention was going to end with mass arrests or with mass gassing, or with mass bloodshed, my feeling was that it should take place in front of the Conrad Hilton, or in the Loop, and I hoped that if I was going to pass out from the gas, that it would waft its way into the fifteenth floor suite of Hubert Humphrey as well, which it did, and make him get the real sweet smell of democracy in Chicago, himself.

Peck, that tense afternoon in Chicago, was afraid that Hayden's words would cause more bloodshed, and so he seized the microphone and urged people to stay quiet, not to run. "I was ready to physically remove him," recalls Peck.

Dellinger also pleaded for calm, but he was ignored. The Mobilization's marshals tried unsuccessfully to quiet the crowd. Tear gas and smoke bombs were thrown. The police stood in formation, making ready to charge. The Mobilization marshals locked arms to hold back the demonstrators, who in any case were now fairly quiet.

Then the police attacked. They marched smartly in a line toward the massed demonstrators, thrusting their nightsticks up with each step. As the crowd retreated before them they broke out in all directions, all discipline gone. Any one in their path was beaten. The crowd panicked. People were trampled as they tried to escape. Women young and old, children, clergy, newsmen—everyone was attacked. The Walker Commission, which viewed films of the melee, stated that the police charged the crowd, not vice versa.

In less than twenty minutes the police stood alone among the benches in front of the band shell. The only demonstrators present were those who lay bleeding and moaning, waiting for medical help. Thirty police were injured; the number of injured demonstrators is unknown.

As the demonstrators straggled back to resume the rally, Allen Ginsberg's "om . . . om . . . om" floated out from the stage. Mostly young people had stayed. They heard, among others, Dick Gregory. He urged his audience to try to change the American political system by nonviolent means, and he told them, bruised and bleeding as they were, that the Chicago police were the "new niggers," not responsible for their actions but under control of the "crooks downtown." "Mayor Daley is a prick and a snake," said Gregory, "and, worst of all, he ain't got no soul."

At about the same time, the Democrats in their convention were debating rival Vietnam planks to the party platform. The antiwar plank had been hammered out over the preceding weeks by a number of antiadministration men, including Richard Goodwin, Blair Clark from McCarthy's staff, Theodore Sorensen, Kenneth O'Donnell, Frank Mankiewicz, Senator Wayne Morse, Senator Claiborne Pell, and

Fred Dutton. They had been brought together by the Democratic senatorial candidate from Ohio, John Gilligan.

Their proposed plank called for:

—a halt to the bombing of all North Vietnam, not just north of the 20th parallel;

—withdrawal of both U.S. and North Vietnamese troops from South Vietnam;

—a coalition government in South Vietnam which would include the NLF.

The proadministration plank, upon which the putative nominee Hubert Humphrey had to run but which, of course, could not repudiate President Johnson's policy, called for:

—a bombing halt in North Vietnam only when "this action would not endanger the lives of our troops in the field";

—withdrawal of "foreign forces" only upon agreement with Hanoi on an end to hostilities;

—free elections for all "who accept peaceful political processes."

Additionally, the pro-Johnson plank, dictated by a Johnson staffer, contained praise "for the initiative of President Johnson which brought North Vietnam to the peace table."*

When the convention delegates arrived at the Amphitheatre on the Wednesday afternoon for the debate on the two opposing Vietnam planks, they found on every seat a mimeographed "fact sheet" which described the peace plank as "emotional, unreasoning, inflexible, unworkable—and a threat to any rational U.S. policy in Southeast Asia."

The proadministration plank won by a surprisingly small margin, 1567 3/4–1041 1/4. The vote set off a tumultuous, emotional demonstration by antiadministration delegates which lasted nearly half an hour. The convention's orchestra tried to drown out their singing of "We Shall Overcome" with choruses of "I'm Looking Over a Four Leaf Clover" and "Happy Days Are Here Again." "We Want Peace!" responded the delegates, many of whom had donned black armbands and put black crepe paper over their badges. Paul O'Dwyer, William F. Ryan, and Herman Badillo of the New York delegation led an impromptu march around the convention hall; they were joined by delegates from California, Wisconsin, South Dakota, and Oregon, all chanting, "Stop the War!"

It was now late afternoon. To the crowd gathering again before the band shell, Dellinger announced that they would attempt a nonviolent march to the Amphitheatre several miles to the south. Since the Mobilization had been unable to get a permit for the march, Sidney Peck undertook to secure one now; he negotiated with Deputy Superintendent of Police James Rochford and a city legal aide.

The demonstrators sat down to wait. There were perhaps ten thousand; about three thousand had lined up to march. At last the negotiations broke down and Dellinger announced that the march would be held anyway. The demonstrators, he said, were to pass through the police lines, cross Michigan Avenue, and regroup in

---

* The week before the convention, as the platform committee held its first hearings in Washington, news came on the night of August 20 that the Soviet Union had invaded Czechoslovakia; thus ended the brief freedom of the "Prague Spring." It was no time for any politician to appear "soft on communism," and from that moment the antiwar plank was doomed.

front of the Hilton Hotel. But they were virtually trapped in the park; when they tried to escape via the Congress Plaza bridge a little farther to the north they were tear-gassed by the national guard troops stationed there. "We were afraid the police would force us into Lake Michigan," recalls Peck. "It would have been the Dunkirk of the antiwar movement." The tear gas wafted into the city, along Michigan Avenue and into the Hilton, where it entered the air-conditioning system and set Hubert Humphrey to weeping. Verbal abuse, including nonstop obscenity, continued on both sides. Night had fallen, but television lights made the scene as bright as day.

The demonstrators finally found a way out of Grant Park at the Jackson Boulevard bridge, and they passed the word back on their loudspeakers: "Open bridge, no gas." They began to stream out of the park onto Michigan Avenue, where by chance they encountered the Poor People's Campaign and its Mule Train.

At first some of the PPC drivers called to the Mobilization people to "Join us!" It was "a moment of exhilaration and enthusiasm," recalls Peck. "The Mule Train now became the symbol of our concern and people began to follow it." For a brief while, there was "a sense that the streets were ours—we'd gotten out of the trap in Grant Park and we were on our way and we had the Mule Train as the symbol of our concerns—peace and justice." But as the crowd grew, it became obvious that the police would not let the antiwar demonstrators pass and that the Mule Train would be trapped as well in the swelling crowd. Viet Cong flags now adorned the civil rights marchers, and they were lost in the huge throng of whites.

The police began to urge people to leave the scene, which had become "total chaos." "Hell No, We Won't Go!" came the reply. The demonstrators were in fact trapped on three sides—north, east, and south. "Two or three people with bullhorns were having an intense argument about what to do," recalls Peck. David Dellinger was not there, nor were Hayden (underground) or Davis (hospitalized).

The police opened a way for the Mule Train to pass, but they would not allow the antiwar demonstrators to follow. The crowd milled uneasily, illuminated by the merciless glare of the television lights. The argument about what to do continued. "People began quoting Lenin," says Peck, "trying to assert their position by reference to—by quoting scripture, an ideological argument. This was so surreal I couldn't believe it. Finally I asked a kid to climb a lamppost, and it was then I learned that we were blocked all the way around."

As the abuse and shoving escalated, the police sent out a 10-1 signal, an emergency call for an officer in trouble. One block west of the Hilton, at the corner of Balbo and Wabash, a busload of police pulled up. Helmeted, visored, batons up, ready for battle, they marched in quickstep down Balbo toward Michigan.

Simultaneously, Sidney Peck was attempting to lead his people away from the Hilton, out of danger, and to another delegate hotel. Balbo was his route. He and the demonstrators were met by the oncoming police line. They tried to back away —an impossible thing to do because of the enormous crowd behind them blocked by more police at the intersection of Balbo and Michigan Avenue. Peck, equipped with a bullhorn (he never knew the name of the young man who carried the heavy battery for him), shouted to his people to sit down and to chant, "No violence . . .

no violence." Then he directed the bullhorn to the police and shouted: "We are not violent . . . we are sitting down." But "they just kept coming on the double-quick."

The police swept through toward Michigan Avenue. Some witnesses testified that they heard the police shouting, "Kill, kill, kill, kill!" People who could not get out of the way were beaten indiscriminately. At the corner of the Hilton Hotel, at the intersection of Balbo and Michigan, what the Walker Commission termed a "violent street battle" took place under the lights of television crews. It was, in the phrase that reverberated in the public's mind, a "police riot."

"The Whole World Is Watching!" chanted the crowd; "The Whole World Is Watching! The Whole World Is Watching!" Indeed it was: and what it was watching, the chaos in the streets, was ultimately more significant and more crucial to the outcome of the election than what it watched of the Democrats' deliberations in the Amphitheatre, for in the pounding rhythm of that chant lay the coming defeat of the political party that played host to the disastrous scenario now being acted out.

"The police were angry. Their anger was neither disinterested nor instrumental [sic]. It was deep, expressive and personal. 'Get out of here you cock suckers' seemed to be their most common cry," testified one witness. "To my right, four policemen beat a young man as he lay on the ground. They beat him and at the same time told him to 'get up and get the hell out of here. . . .' "

The deputy superintendent was "very upset," the Walker Commission stated, and "he pulled his men off the demonstrators, shouting 'Stop, damn it, stop. For Christ's sake, stop it.' "

The crowd that was trapped on the sidewalk between the Hilton's Haymarket Lounge and the police barriers had grown larger as people tried to escape the billy clubs and Mace. Some were rescued to the safety of the hotel lobby and corridors by Sam Brown and Jerome Grossman, who used their McCarthy credentials to persuade police to allow a few demonstrators to escape the crush. Finally, with a "sickening crack," the plate glass window gave way and terrified men and women spilled into the lounge, many of them bleeding, badly cut by the broken glass. The police were on their heels, beating people indiscriminately "like mad dogs."

Peck, having lost his battery-carrier in the crush, was unable to direct the demonstrators—"I didn't have any sound . . . many people had been beaten . . . and people were just shocked at what had happened. . . ."

At this moment he saw Deputy Superintendent James Rochford, with whom he had negotiated previously. One of their understandings had been that "if he had problems with demonstrators he was to approach me, and if I had problems concerning the safety and health of the demonstrators that he was the person to approach. . . ." Hoping to prevent further violence, Peck moved toward Rochford "to find out what the hell had happened."

"I had my hands out like this" (he gestures, hands outstretched, palms up). Rochford's plainclothes bodyguard "began moving at me, at which point I just turned around and tried to get back to where our people were. And then they sent police after me . . . and I went to ground and dropped into a fetal position. The main thing I was concerned about was protecting my head, because that's how I earn a living, so I put my arms over my head and they gave me a real beating with nightsticks. I had to have twenty-two stitches in my head, surgery on my finger, they pounded all over my kidneys, one of them jammed a nightstick between my legs . . . they dragged me about 150, 200 feet to a police van and threw me in." He was taken to the police station and then to the Chicago City Hospital, treated, and released at eight or nine o'clock the following morning.

Louise Peck is moved to tears as she recalls the events of that day and night: how she had been separated from her children in the afternoon in Grant Park and did not know for hours that they had gone safely to Lake Forest with friends; how she had been tear-gassed on the bridges trying to get out of the park; how afraid she had been that she would be beaten; how, separated from her husband, she had returned to the home of friends to watch the events of the evening unfold on the television screen; how she had no idea what had happened to her husband during the violence that she was watching until, around eleven-thirty, she had a call from a young McCarthy worker who had a message from her husband—by that time in the hospital—and a number to call. When she went to the hospital to pick him up she saw him first from a distance. He was sitting in a wheelchair awaiting treatment. He looked like an old man, she recalls, slumped and broken.

Remembering, her tears give way to anger at her husband—anger still felt many years later. "I realized I was angry [then] at you for putting us all in that kind of jeopardy and yet I couldn't express my anger or be anything other than supportive. . . . I was angry because in the face of indications that there would be trouble you were overly optimistic . . . as much as you confronted Tom [Hayden] you still trusted him and that put us in jeopardy . . . when were you going to wake up and realize that their scenario was playing right into the hands of the police? . . ."

In twenty minutes that night the battle was over, although for many demonstrators the worst was yet to come as they fled pursuing police down the adjacent streets. It was now 8:15 P.M. In the Amphitheatre the first reports of the violence had begun to reach the delegates via telephone. No pictures had come in yet because a strike of telephone workers had prevented the installation of lines for instantaneous transmission.

When the pictures finally did arrive, about an hour later, the nomination of Hubert Humphrey was in progress. On television screens in the convention hall, as on those in homes around the nation, horrified viewers saw the bloodshed of the hour before. In the auditorium, which was decorated with posters reading WE LOVE MAYOR DALEY, Carl Stokes, the black mayor of Cleveland, was in the midst of his seconding speech for Humphrey.

Shortly, as the pictures continued to come in, Senator Abraham Ribicoff of Connecticut rose to nominate Senator George McGovern of South Dakota for President. Directly in front of Ribicoff sat Richard Daley. In the heat of the moment, responding to his own feelings and to the outrage of his fellow delegates, Ribicoff broke off from his prepared speech to address the mayor directly: "With George McGovern, we wouldn't have Gestapo tactics on the streets of Chicago."

The convention erupted; Daley exploded. Viewers could not hear what Daley said; they could only see him shouting, his brutal, heavy-jowled face contorted with rage. In one account of the episode, lip-readers viewing the film reported that Daley bellowed, "Fuck you you Jew son of a bitch you lousy motherfucker go home."

Ribicoff responded quietly: "How hard it is to accept the truth. How hard it is."

A motion was made then to adjourn the convention but Chairman Carl Albert overruled it. The balloting began. At eleven forty-seven, with Pennsylvania's 103 3/4 votes, the nomination became Hubert Humphrey's.

In Grant Park, the restive demonstrators, now regrouped, received that not unexpected news from one of their number listening to the balloting on a transistor radio and announcing the results over a bullhorn. At "Oklahoma" the warning went out to the crowd: "Marshals ready. Don't move. Stay seated."

The marshals locked arms and faced the police. The crowd began to boo more loudly than before. Police reinforcements arrived. From the Hilton came the sound of a cowbell. "Sit down. Sit down," chanted the crowd. Someone raised the American flag—not seen much that week—but raised it upside down in the distress signal. The National Guard moved into position between the demonstrators in the park and the Hilton. They brought with them machine guns mounted on trucks; jeeps covered in mesh with barbed wire over their fronts stood parked on streets where the word PIG was written.

At the convention hall, Humphrey's nomination was declared unanimous while hundreds of delegates yelled, "No!"

Allard Lowenstein (who attended as a member of the New York delegation) and Richard Goodwin announced a march of McCarthy delegates back to the downtown area. They had candles from a synagogue to light their way. Earlier, Lowenstein had told a television interviewer that "this convention elected Richard Nixon President of the United States tonight. . . . I never thought it would happen."

And so at 3 A.M. the McCarthy delegates, carrying their candles in Pepsi-Cola cups, having been ferried by buses to a point a few blocks north of the Hilton, began their march down Michigan Avenue. They were led by Paul O'Dwyer, William Ryan, Richard Goodwin, and George Brown. At Balbo Drive a police commander stopped them. O'Dwyer said that they wanted to walk past the demonstrators. The officer replied, "We welcome you and hope you can keep it peaceful. We are here to protect lives and property. Keep it orderly and keep moving."

They did. In the night air heavy with the smell of stink bombs which had been thrown into the Hilton, the demonstrators cheered the delegates as the newcomers arrived. After a brief interval of speechmaking and singing, the delegates went to their hotels and the demonstrators settled down in the park for what remained of the night.

On Thursday afternoon in Grant Park Mobilization leaders Dellinger, Hayden, and Davis announced a march to the Amphitheatre which would take place later in the day. "If we can survive here, we can survive in any city in the country," said Hayden. "When they smash blood from our heads there will be blood from a lot of other heads."

People were already beginning to leave the city; the crowd in Grant Park was perhaps two thousand. Later in the afternoon, Eugene McCarthy came to speak also. His message was different from Hayden's: "Work within the political system and you can help seize control of the Democratic Party in 1972," he said—something that did indeed happen, but with disastrous results that could not have been predicted in 1968.

Later, at dusk, Dick Gregory took the microphone and invited the crowd—about three thousand now—to join him for a glass of beer at his home on East Fifty-fifth Street near the Amphitheatre. Earlier a group of delegates headed by Donald Peterson of Wisconsin had led about two thousand people from the hotel district in the center of the city on a march south toward the Amphitheatre to test citizens' freedom of movement on the streets of Chicago. They were politely but firmly turned back at Sixteenth Street and State. Now Gregory's march set off, only to be turned back at Michigan Avenue and Eighteenth Street. Tear gas was fired, and once again a violent melee ensued, people throwing every available object at police and troops, and in turn being beaten and chased and gassed by police and troops using, among other devices, armored personnel carriers and the by now famous jeeps with barbed wire barriers. Several hundred people were arrested including nine convention delegates. The demonstrators were swept back to Grant Park, where some of them hanged Mayor Daley in effigy. Tear gas hung so thick that "whenever someone moved too quickly, stirring up the gas, he was shouted down."

In New York, relations with the police were somewhat better. Norma Becker remembers that

> there were only two or three of us [leadership people] left in the city, but when the news [of the violence in Chicago] came through people kept coming up to the office to volunteer. People were manning the telephones—listen to that sexist word—they were *personing* the telephones and calling people for bail money, they needed bail money in Chicago. In a difficult situation, adversity breeds a coming together. . . .
>
> We thought we had to have a response to what happened in Chicago, so we set a demonstration for the following day, a Thursday, and we planned it right outside Hubert Humphrey's headquarters in the Grand Central [midtown] area.
>
> Wednesday evening I got a call from some Democratic Party club that was really not actively involved in the parade committee but they said they had called a vigil in Times Square [that night] and were letting us know so that we could spread the word. We of course put it on WBAI [the New York affiliate of the Pacifica network] and then it occurred to me that, being people who were not experienced with the Movement, those people in the Democratic club might not have contacted the police. And I knew from prior experience that if the police don't know what's going on they panic and overreact.
>
> So I called Barry Gottehrer, who was Lindsay's community relations troubleshooter, because there was no time to call the police and go through all that procedure. And he said, "Oh my God, Sandy's going to have a heart attack [Sanford Garelick, New York City police commissioner] because they're so uptight [because the antipolice sentiment at that time was so strong]." So the following morning, Thursday morning when I spoke to

Garelick, he told me that the night before at the vigil in Times Square he had his men under such control that the demonstrators came up with a medal, drawn on a piece of paper, with an expression of appreciation to the police of New York City. So that was already establishing a different dynamic than the one in Chicago. So then I said, "Look, we're having this demonstration right outside Humphrey headquarters and I don't have time to get a permit but it will be out on the sidewalk," and I said, "I don't have marshals, everyone's in Chicago." I didn't know how many people were going to be there and there were three of us who were experienced [at marshaling demonstrations]. And it turned out that word spread through the Democratic Party clubs and we had a demonstration of five thousand people which was called in less than twenty-four hours.

And as people got out of work they joined in. Garelick was there himself. He was in command, and his men couldn't do enough for us. We wanted the wooden horses moved a little bit this way—whatever—they were tripping over themselves [to help us]. But at least he had the sense to be cooperative. At one point I remember he came over to me and he put his arm around me and he said, "Norma, listen, would you speak to that kid?" A teenaged kid with a khaki jacket on and it said FUCK THE PIGS. And Garelick said, "Would you speak to that kid? My men are getting uptight." And I said, "My own kids don't listen to me, you want me to go and tell some stranger who doesn't care?" The police had no understanding of what the sixties Movement and the youth rebellion were about. He saw me as a leader, so he assumed that all I had to do was tell this kid who never saw me before in his life that he should take off his jacket because it's offending the police, whom he hates anyhow. . . .

The final confrontation of the Chicago debacle, and arguably the one that caused the most lasting bitterness, was the police action against McCarthy workers at 5 A.M. on Friday, August 30. Alerted to the fact that objects were dropping from the windows of the Hilton ("ashtrays, beer cans, a silver cream pitcher, and—mysteriously—a bag of military chemical irritant and a grenade with pin unpulled"), the Hilton staff identified the windows as those of rooms on the fifteenth floor used by McCarthy people as staff and reception areas. McCarthy's people, then and later, denied that any objects had been dropped from the windows, stressing that they were in Chicago as campaign workers, not demonstrators. The police were authorized by the management to clear the allegedly crowded corridors and one room. When they arrived they found a badly littered, crowded room where a party had been going on. As more police arrived the group obeyed their orders to disperse; the police moved on to other rooms, beating the occupants, hustling everyone out and into the elevators. Richard Goodwin, a McCarthy speechwriter, found them in the lobby and tried to calm them; then McCarthy himself, having risen early to visit again the demonstrators in Grant Park, arrived on the scene and sent them back to their rooms.

In his memoir of the 1968 campaign, *The Year of the People*, McCarthy makes the point that no reason or explanation for the police action was ever given and, further, that what happened was "a massive invasion of privacy—action without precedent in the history of American politics."

McCarthy delayed his planned Friday morning departure from Chicago to make sure that all his workers had left the city safely. On Friday evening as his chartered plane took off, the pilot said, "We are leaving Prague."

Exhausted, embittered, the young people who had gone to Chicago went home, or back to their schools and colleges. "The children of affluence and technology and Doomsday," Tom Wicker called them; later in the year, at the HUAC hearing in December, Tom Hayden's bitter comment on the younger generation was that "that's our crime, that we exist." At one point the committee's counsel said to him, "And I would ask you, sir, don't you think that the young people who follow you in these various movements should take a second look at you, before they place their lives and their responsibilities in the hands of you [sic]?"

To which Hayden's reply was "Shit."

Eugene McCarthy, whose appeal to the country's youth had been as strong as Hayden's, went to the South of France to recuperate from the rigors of the campaign. When he returned to the United States, he reported on the World Series for *Life*. His fate may be compared to that of Truong Dinh Dzu, the dove candidate for President of South Vietnam who finished second in the 1967 elections. In August 1968, two weeks before the Democratic Convention, Dzu was tried by the military on charges of "actions which weakened the will of the people and army of South Vietnam to fight against the Communists." His sentence was five years at hard labor.

What, finally, did the events of the Democratic Convention at Chicago in 1968 mean to the antiwar movement?

They meant, for one thing, at least the temporary death of Allard Lowenstein's dream of ending the war by working within the system.

They meant, for another, that those who argued for nonviolent protest needed to deal with the fact of police violence. "The Chicago Convention protests were the test," said Dellinger, "and the Movement failed the test"—i.e., was not able to control its people in the face of police violence either actual or threatened.

As Kirkpatrick Sale stated in his history of SDS, they "proved once and for all, for those still needing proof, that the country could not be educated or reformed out of its pernicious system, even by establishmentarian reformers like McCarthy . . . that even resistance, open and defiant resistance, was not enough to wrest changes, for the institutions of American society, grounded in violence, would use violence in their own defense when the threat was regarded as serious enough."

Sidney Peck says of the events at Chicago:

> The Daley military reaction saved the demonstration [in a political sense].
> . . . If the demonstrators had been allowed to march it would have de-
> stroyed the credibility of the antiwar movement as hippie-Yippie revolution-
> ary radicals. There was no sense of a mass base of opposition [to the war],
> whereas the physical actions of the Chicago police were so horrendous and
> the media presentation got into the convention. . . . The march of the

delegates sent a message that mainstream America was obviously shocked and that the young people who were saying there was a war at home were correct. . . . And therefore that the continued pursuit of the war in Vietnam would eventually necessitate a military response here at home to keep [people] repressed. The antiwar movement won a great deal of sympathy although at the same time the nature and character of the action at Chicago stimulated a great many fears in people about participating in demonstrations and that was going to be a huge political problem that we had to overcome. As a result, the whole coalition had to be reconstituted on the basis that the next action would be legal and peaceful.

In other words, the antiwar movement, or at least that part of it that went to Chicago, had succeeded in creating in the public mind an irrevocable link between antiwar protest activity (in the form of mass demonstrations) and violence. The fact that much of the violence came from the police was irrelevant. The public's perception was that the Movement (in this instance, largely young people) had gone to Chicago to demonstrate at the Democrats' convention, and much unpleasantness had resulted. Therefore, somehow, both the Democrats and the young people in the Movement were responsible.

"Chicago, I think, was the place where all America was radicalized," wrote Tom Wicker a year later. "The miracle of television made it visible to all—pierced, at last, the isolation of one America from the other, exposed to each the power it faced. Everything since Chicago has had a new intensity—that of polarization, of confrontation, of antagonism and fear."

Finally, it may be said that what happened in the streets of "nightstick city" that week in August 1968 was more significant than what happened at the Democratic Convention inside the Amphitheatre, for it was in the streets, in the confrontation between established authority and those challenging it, that the festering malaise of the war in Vietnam came home at last, erupting into the living rooms of a nation of onlookers who could no longer turn away from the fact that the war in Southeast Asia, whether a civil war or a war of outside aggression, was causing a kind of civil war in the United States. While the Democrats debated the planks of their platform and made their speeches of nomination, the real issues—the issue of authority run amok (both police authority and the authority of a President who had taken the nation into an undeclared war) and the issue of how to challenge it—were being literally thrashed out in the streets.

There was a last, little-noted postscript to the Chicago demonstrations: on September 28, ten thousand (or fifteen thousand or twenty-five thousand) people reclaimed the right to march through the streets of the city. The event had been organized by the Chicago Peace Council and Citizens for a Free Chicago; its themes were withdrawal from Vietnam and protest against police repression. This was the biggest antiwar event to date in Chicago, and it went off without incident. No arrests were made; the march received little publicity.

On Labor Day weekend some of the Mobilization's Chicago organizers from SDS gathered at Herb Nadelhoffer's 177-acre farm in Downers Grove, Illinois, about twenty miles from Chicago. They were, in effect, on an R and R tour after having seen the front lines. Despite their wounds, they were not discouraged; if anything, their appetite for conflict had been whetted. During the inevitable arguments that arose, Oglesby recalls that he "needed a specific answer to Mike Klonsky's challenge—an alternative to increased militancy as they called it, which meant trashing in the streets. And I pointed out that there was a split in, quote, the ruling circles, quote (to talk like *Pravda),* about the war." His advice was not well received: "It was at that meeting that Mike Klonsky denounced me as the most dangerous man on the Left. For me, the battle lines started being drawn—a group of people in SDS who didn't like my politics."

Having literally tasted blood, the majority of those at the farm hungered for more, even if it were (again) their own. "There's coming a time when the American movement will become more violent for defensive and survival reasons," said Tom Hayden. Speaking of the presidential campaign immediately ahead, he added, "We're going to create little Chicagos everywhere the candidates appear."

They did not do that, although there were some unpleasant incidents that fall. Wherever Humphrey spoke he was greeted by hecklers and demonstrators against the war. A particularly nasty confrontation occurred in Boston on September 19, when Senator Edward Kennedy of Massachusetts, the state's last, beloved (male) Kennedy, a man whom many Massachusetts voters adored, was subjected to an ugly half hour of boos and catcalls as he introduced candidate Humphrey to a noontime rally on downtown Washington Street. Kennedy had not previously been so treated by his constituents, and the experience was a shocking one for him. It was a "mean and ugly sound," wrote Tom Wicker in his account of the incident; "the booing rose and fell throughout speeches by Mr. Humphrey and by Senator Kennedy in deliberate defiance of all pleas for elementary courtesy and customary fair play, and in reckless disregard of the political consequences." Kennedy and Humphrey shouted themselves hoarse to no avail; the crowd's contempt for Kennedy's endorsement of one of the hated Johnson's staunchest supporters would not be quieted.

Humphrey twisted slowly in the wind that fall, strangling in the noose of Vietnam. He faced what was for him an impossible choice: to break openly with LBJ, perhaps even to resign his office in protest against the Johnson Administration's war policy; or to continue to support the Administration and thereby lose vitally needed votes and preelection support from disaffected Democrats.

The polls gave him little encouragement. On September 24 the Harris Poll of the voters' choice for President placed Richard Nixon in first place with 22 percent; then came Edward Kennedy (not a candidate); George Wallace; and Nelson Rockefeller (not a candidate). Humphrey placed last with 8 percent. On September 26 the Gallup Poll gave Nixon 43 percent, Humphrey 28 percent, and Wallace 21 percent.

Maintaining that Vietnam should not be a campaign issue because of the delicate state of the Paris peace talks, Richard Nixon had not proposed any specific plan to end the war other than to seek an "honorable peace." He was assailed for this position: Lawrence O'Brien, Humphrey's campaign manager, suggested that Nixon, referred to over the years as "Tricky Dick," should now be called "Evasive

Dick." Even fellow Republicans criticized him, most notably doves like Senator Mark Hatfield (R-Oregon), who had seconded Nixon's nomination. Writing in the *Ripon Forum*, a liberal Republican monthly, Hatfield said that vague promises of "an honorable peace" were not enough; citing the 1964 election, in which the American people "thought they were voting for peace only to have their trust betrayed," Hatfield said that "voters should not be forced to go to the polls with their fingers crossed; they should not be forced to rely on blind faith that the man they vote for will share their views on the most important issue of the election."

Meanwhile Hubert Humphrey struggled with his Vietnam albatross. In early September he suggested that some American troops might be brought home in late 1968 or early 1969; he was promptly corrected by President Johnson, who said that no such plan was in progress. Several days later he promised simply "peace" to a crowd in Sioux Falls, South Dakota; he received a standing ovation, one of the few of his campaign.

Still, despite the pleas of Democratic doves and despite his dismal showing in the polls, Humphrey refused to break openly with Johnson. When he visited former President Harry S. Truman in Independence, Missouri, Truman told him to "always tell 'em the truth, even if it hurts." Humphrey tried to follow both Truman's advice and the doves' arguments and on September 30, in a speech taped in Salt Lake City for national viewing, he promised, if elected, to halt the bombing of North Vietnam provided that Hanoi gave "some sign" that it was ready to begin "serious" peace negotiations. (Johnson had continued the partial halt announced on March 31.) Such a move, said the Democratic candidate for President, was an "acceptable risk for peace." He did not, however, address the basic questions of American involvement in Vietnam: Why were we there? Should we be? He had been introduced as the candidate—not as the Vice President—and he spoke without his usual backdrop of vice presidential flag and seal. Slowly, agonizingly, he was squirming away from his mentor, his nemesis, Lyndon Johnson, who because of that same war had been forced to give up running for the office now so tantalizingly near to Humphrey's grasp.

The White House response to this speech was to announce, through Press Secretary George Christian, that there had been no change in administration policy concerning the bombing of North Vietnam.

By early October, Max Frankel of the New York *Times* was writing that Humphrey was being allowed to "stray" a bit from the administration line on Vietnam, as if he were an obedient dog. In the middle of the month, while Humphrey was campaigning in St. Louis, the Vice President was called to the phone in the locker room of a Catholic boys' military school, where he had met with a group of housewives vaguely discontented about the war, and was told by his President that there had been a breakthrough in the Paris peace negotiations. Richard Nixon and George Wallace received the call simultaneously. Humphrey was so wary of what he called the "theologians" of the press that he refused to comment on the call, saying that every nuance of what he said would be studied for variations on what he had already said.

On October 31 the breakthrough was explained when Johnson, in a televised speech, announced that he had ordered a halt of all American bombing of North Vietnam. At the same time, he said, the peace talks in Paris would now take place between four sides: North Vietnam, South Vietnam, the NLF (Viet Cong), and the United States. The bombing of the Ho Chi Minh Trail in Laos would continue. The announcement momentarily cheered those who wished a speedy end to the war, but it came too late to help Humphrey. To the bitter end, his association with Johnson's war tormented him and he could not get free of it.†

While the presidential campaign ground on, the antiwar movement tried to recover from the Chicago experience.

The SMC, which had been splintered by infighting early in the summer and was now firmly controlled by the Socialist Workers Party, met immediately after the Chicago convention and issued a call for a week of antiwar demonstrations during October 21–27, and a mass protest on October 26. It was decided to focus on the growing antiwar mood within the armed forces.

In September the administrative committee of the National Mobilization met to call a "strike" on election day, November 5—an action proposed by Tom Hayden and Rennie Davis. The date was chosen to coincide with SDS's proposed two-day student strike on November 4 and 5.

None of these actions amounted to much. The antiwar movement in any and all of its manifestations was fragmented and, as usual in an election year, sapped of energy. In other parts of the world, however, anti (Vietnam) war actions called for October drew large turnouts: one hundred thousand in London, eight hundred thousand in Japan. The largest antiwar demonstration in the United States that fall occurred on October 12 in San Francisco, when fifteen thousand (including five hundred servicemen) participated in a GI's and Vets March for Peace, an action organized mainly by the SMC and Veterans for Peace.

Comic relief came, as it so often did, from Washington. Like a mastodon from another geological era, the House Un-American Activities Committee had reared its shaggy old head to do battle once again: in late September it began hearings to investigate Communist involvement in the Chicago convention action. Abbie Hoffman came wearing feathers in his long, curly hair; Jerry Rubin went naked above

---

† Substantive peace talks proved to be almost as illusory as the light at the end of the tunnel. Although the Administration claimed that the South Vietnamese Government had agreed to negotiate with the NLF, President Thieu balked. Finally, in December, he relented and sent a delegation to Paris headed by Nguyen Cao Ky. Then began a bizarre and ludicrous farce: the acrimonious debate over the shape of the negotiating table so as to accommodate all four sides. Thieu continued to reject the NLF as an equal participant. The delegates seemed to be performing a script from the theater of the absurd: Should the table be round? Square? Should there be two curved tables? Or four tables arranged in a diamond pattern? Or perhaps the table should be doughnut-shaped, but split? By the end of December, in desperation, a South Vietnamese pacifist suggested an eight-sided table. The issue was resolved on January 16 when a circular table was agreed upon. All four sides would sit at it, but they would not be identified by flags, nameplates, or other insignia. The somewhat murky seating arrangements allowed the United States and Saigon to pretend to ignore the independent presence of the NLF, while North Vietnam and the NLF could persevere in their view that four parties of equal standing were present at the table. On the first day of negotiations, January 18, some time was spent arguing about what to call them: the United States and Saigon opted for "meetings," while North Vietnam and the NLF chose "conferences." Since May, when the first peace talks had been held between the United States and North Vietnam, some eight thousand Americans had died in Vietnam.

the waist, his hairy torso bedecked with a bandolier of live ammunition, and carried a toy M-16 rifle. Among those subpoenaed to testify were Dellinger, Hayden, Davis, and Robert Greenblatt. Nothing came of the hearings—which lasted for several months—save publicity, and not even much of that.

In the introduction to *Rebellion and Repression,* Hayden's account of the HUAC hearing, he discussed violence in America past and present:

> The truth is that we all live under a system which requires violence because it is based on the exploitation of man by man. America was founded in genocidal wars with the Indians and the Mexicans. America created the most brutal system of slavery in the Western Hemisphere, killing 50 million people along the way. America was industrialized through the savage exploitation of the working class. Every democratic reform in American history has been achieved only after bloodshed and disruption—from the Boston Tea Party to the Revolutionary War, the Civil War, the women's suffrage movement, the unionizing of farmers and industrial workers. This system of capitalism and racism causes massive violence not only inside our nation's borders but everywhere in the world where it tries to impose itself. Nobody in the world is safe from the "ugly Americans" who come to take their land, their resources, and their cultural identities. Wars like Vietnam are a logical result of the drive for world domination by the American establishment.
>
> Against this backdrop, the "violence of the Left" is minor. . . .

And in his testimony, Hayden declared that in the planning of the Chicago demonstrations, he had explicity renounced the idea of bringing violence to the Democratic Convention:

> I believe that violence should never be ruled out as a method of change, especially, I believe that a country that is burning up Vietnam has no right to lecture people to be nonviolent. However, I believe also, I always believed, that Chicago was no place for a violent confrontation, because you have a disciplined, armed force of 20,000 men waiting for you there, and you have unarmed demonstrators straggling in, nineteen- and twenty-year-old kids from all around the country, who don't know each other, and they would be wiped out. They almost were wiped out in Chicago, simply for existing.
>
> So I wanted to make a distinction in that meeting between the fact that I believe that at some point there may be increased violence in American society on the one hand and/or on the other hand I didn't believe that violence should be part of the planning or preparation or conception of Chicago.
>
> I thought that what we were doing in Chicago was trying to sort of bring the kind of people who are the rank and file of the Democratic party, decent, middle-class Americans of all ages and classes and races, who believe in peace and social justice, to come and protest the abandoning of those ideals by the government of the United States.
>
> And I know very well that for that kind of purpose, violence or the threat

of violence only scares people away, and that is what I think Mayor Daley and President Johnson were engaged in by their buildup, military buildup; they were trying to scare people away from coming to the convention.

So I make no secret of the fact that I am not nonviolent, but often people who are not nonviolent can be the most nonviolent, because they know what they are doing, and they want to make sure that the means suit the ends, and the means in this case for me was a mass mobilization of a peaceful kind. It became a violent situation because of the Chicago Police Department. . . .

In mid-October came a voice from the past: McGeorge Bundy, one of the Wise Men (who had urged deescalation of the war). He wanted publicly to announce that he had changed his mind about the American presence in Vietnam. The United States should withdraw, he said. His opposition had arisen not because the war was wrong, "not on moral outrage or political hostility to the objective, but rather on the simple and practical ground that escalation will not work and that continuation on our present course is unacceptable." The American people would not tolerate "annual costs of $30 billion and an annual rate of sacrifice of more than 10,000 American lives." Further, there was a "special pain in the growing alienation of a generation which is the best we have had." America's only hope of military victory lay in the use of nuclear weapons, and that, too, would be rejected by the American people. The only solution was to "steadily, systematically and substantially reduce the number of American casualties, the number of Americans in Vietnam and the dollar cost of the war."

Except for the last point, Bundy was predicting Richard Nixon's Vietnamization policy—a policy which, it turned out, was Nixon's plan for peace, the plan that could not be divulged during the election campaign. It was also, of course, the policy which had been set in motion when Clark Clifford announced a troop ceiling the previous April.

Nixon won the election. The vote was 43.4 percent for Nixon to 43 percent for Humphrey. Humphrey had come up quickly in the polls during the final days of the campaign, but even a lukewarm endorsement by Eugene McCarthy and, at the last moment on October 31, Johnson's announcement that all bombing of North Vietnam had ceased and that talks would begin were not enough to save the election for the Democrats.

Two senatorial defeats that fall were a blow to the antiwar movement, although neither candidate had been formally a member of it. In Oregon, Wayne Morse was defeated for a fifth term in the Senate by the Republican candidate, Robert Packwood. Morse, always a maverick, had supported Republican Mark Hatfield in the 1966 Senate race on the basis of Hatfield's antiwar stand. The defeated Democrat in that election, Robert B. Duncan, ran against Morse in the 1968 primary and nearly beat him. The race against Packwood was so close that Morse called for a recount but in the end he lost. In Alaska, Mike Gravel, a real estate developer, defeated Ernest Gruening in the Democratic primary. Gruening proceeded to wage a write-in campaign in the general election, but Gravel won over both Gruening and the Republican candidate.

SDS, that fall, received an extraordinary amount of publicity both "good" and "bad," including a not uncomplimentary article in *Life*. New chapters sprang up all over the country—more than one hundred that fall alone. National membership was estimated at between eighty and one hundred thousand, but that was probably a low figure. As applications for new chapters and requests for help and information poured into the National Office, the SDS staff became hopelessly inundated.

Despite its apparent good health, SDS was in fact suffering its death throes. At a National Council meeting at Boulder, Colorado, in October, the old malaise appeared again, this time more virulent than ever: should SDS gather itself to make the revolution, or should it concentrate on community organizing, broadening its base? Individual chapters, that fall, had fallen apart over the issue, and now the national officers did the same. After a fight with PL delegates over their proposal for something called SLAP—Student Labor Action Project, the old never-to-be worker-student alliance—the delegates voted overwhelmingly to organize a two-day protest on election day in November.

But the protest fizzled; SDS simply could not call a national action. Factionalism ate at the heart of what was popularly supposed to be the biggest, most powerful Left student organization. At Ann Arbor in September competing groups argued so bitterly that they dissolved one SDS chapter—at its birthplace!—into two; by Christmas, neither one had credibility. Students seeking political guidance discovered that they had fallen into a nest of vipers; SDS "leaders" seemed more interested in petty feuds between themselves than in organizing and building strong campus organizations. PL was out to make trouble, as always; every meeting had to contend with its arguments, its power plays, its tight control over its members, who invariably voted in a bloc, thus easily triumphing over the more disorganized SDS rank and file.

As Staughton Lynd wrote:

> In 1966 the Progressive Labor Party dissolved its front group, the May 2nd Movement, and directed its youth to join SDS. The new atmosphere of hairsplitting doctrinal debate frustrated SDS members who were pushing the national organization to involve itself in draft resistance, and led to their going their separate way to form the Resistance. PLP had much to contribute, particularly in its emphasis on the blue-collar working class, but imbedded this contribution in a style of work so dogmatic and aggressive that the existing SDS leadership took on the manner of the PLP caucus in order to combat it. Overnight everyone became a Marxist, not because this conviction had grown organically from experience . . . but because quotations from Marxism-Leninism-Maoism had become counters of value in an internal struggle for power.

Other problems faced SDS at this time, most notably the continuing and increasing distance between its leadership and its thousands of recruits on campuses across the nation—campuses which varied widely in their political sophistication. Doctrinal disputes at the national level had little meaning for new members in the provinces who simply wanted to do something—some small thing—to register discontent with the status quo. Many students—putatively members of SDS—took to heckling candidates that fall, thereby calling down on SDS's collective head the machinery of repression and adding to the organization's difficulties as it scrambled to fight the inevitable arrests, jailings, and expulsions. Infiltration by undercover agents, many of whom were not loath to break the law in SDS's name, was a third problem.

Thus when the National Council meeting took place at Ann Arbor December 26–31, the SDS leadership was both exhausted and deeply divided. Mike Klonsky had written an article for the current issue of *New Left Notes*, "Toward a Revolutionary Youth Movement," which argued the case for the student-worker alliance —thus preempting PL's major article of faith. It was Marxist; it was also base-building in its plea to organize nationwide the young "working class," both student and nonstudent, as opposed to SDS's previous constituency, "privileged" students, many of whom had successfully evaded the draft while the blue collars went off to die in Vietnam.

Three issues were debated fiercely at the National Council that year: racism, the embryonic women's movement, and Klonsky's RYM. The first two were almost irrelevant, given SDS's impotence; RYM, however, was fateful. After heated debate designed to undercut PL, the membership adopted Klonsky's proposal and thereby set upon a course that would, in the next year, destroy it. SDS was now committed to a Marxist mishmash of organizing the "workers"; in a country which despite the alarums of the McCarthy witch-hunts had never given the slightest attention to Karl Marx since the Great Depression, SDS had swallowed Marx whole and had determined to make its revolution on the backs of the proletariat, whatever that was. Many SDSers who would go underground as Weathermen in the following year strongly supported RYM; it put them on a path that would inevitably isolate and alienate them from the very people they were supposedly trying to help.

The meeting ended bitterly, PL and the Klonsky faction chanting and yelling at each other, each trying to drown the other out: "Mao, Mao, Mao Tse-tung!" and "Ho, Ho, Ho Chi Minh!"

Thus the bright idealists, working for a newer world, invoking the names of aged revolutionaries whose struggles had been revolutionary, yes, and Communist as well, but who had been, above all, nationalists, profound patriots, men working for nothing so much as for their own countries. For many in SDS at this time (Carl Oglesby most notably excepted), patriotism—love of their native land—was a forgotten impulse; it had begun to be twisted into hate, with Amerika having become everyone's favorite villain.

The last antiwar demonstration of 1968 took place on December 20 when twenty-seven members of Women Strike for Peace and a dog named Prince walked two miles to the White House to present to President Johnson a wreath and telegrams urging an end to the war. A guard at the gate received their tokens; the President was ill with flu at Bethesda Naval Hospital.

And on the last day of the year came yet another New Year's message from Ho

Chi Minh. He greeted his "American friends," thanking those who opposed the Vietnam War. That (antiwar) struggle, he said, defended the "interest and honor of the American people and safeguards the lives of their boys." Ho termed the October cessation of the bombing a "great victory," but he said that "monstrous crimes" were still being committed in South Vietnam by "ruling circles" in the United States.

1969:
"The Shabbiest Weapon"

ON JANUARY 20, 1969, nearly ten months after his announced decision to do so, Lyndon Johnson, thirty-sixth President of the United States, relinquished his office. As Richard Nixon acceded to the presidency, a cautious optimism about Vietnam reigned. One commentator suggested that the war which had dominated all discussion of the previous Administration was destined to "fade from the national agenda." Most Americans agreed with this judgment. Negotiations with the North Vietnamese were under way; Richard Nixon was said to have "a secret plan" to end the war. And had not Eisenhower, the last Republican to hold the presidency, entered office with the promise to end the Korean conflict, and then proceeded to keep that promise?

Leaders in the antiwar movement had no such illusions about Richard Nixon nor any misapprehensions about his path to peace. There was, however, debate on the question of short-term strategy. In December 1968 the coordinating committee of the National Mobilization Committee to End the War in Vietnam, whose leadership was now effectively in the hands of David Dellinger and Rennie Davis, met to discuss a Dellinger-Davis proposal to stage a set of countercultural events around the January inaugural ceremonies. Sidney Peck and Sidney Lens were strongly opposed to what came to be known as the Counterinaugural. Peck, in particular, felt it was the wrong way to go for a coalition movement that had emerged reeling from the political Dunkirk of Chicago. Peck argued that once again to seek confrontation combined with what he called the "hippie-Yippie approach" could only further damage the Mobe, especially since such an action could never expect the numbers needed to raise it to the level of a national demonstration. In his mind the Mobilization existed as a *coalition* that "had to be responsive to the broadest and widest segments" in American life. He circulated a memorandum to this effect within the Movement and did not himself participate in the Washington action.

Peck's prognosis was correct: the Counterinaugural was a sad affair. What little attention it attracted was negative. The lead sentence of the New York *Times* coverage, buried on page 24, said: "A small, hard core of the country's disaffected youth hurled sticks, stones, bottles, cans, obscenities and a ball of tinfoil at President Nixon . . . during the inaugural parade today." How much of this and of other "trashing" incidents was the work of government provocateurs is not known, but at least one, Irwin Bock, was on hand from Chicago. He had led cries of "Stop the bullshit and take to the streets" while a badly disabled Vietnam veteran was addressing a predemonstration rally. There were eighty-one arrests, including two for mutilating the American flag. The Counterinaugural march, on January 19, from west to east down Pennsylvania Avenue in a symbolic reversal of direction *away* from the White House, drew fewer than ten thousand participants. Their banners ranged from bizarre (FREEDOM FOR GREECE) to bathetic (WE MISS BOBBY) to presumptive (NIXON—THE NO. 1 WAR CRIMINAL). One correspondent discerned among the marchers a mood "dampened by the prospect of Mr. Nixon's presiding over the liquidation of the war." That night counterculture held sway. Under a huge tent by the Tidal Basin in a lake of boot-sucking mud, Washington area teenagers by the hundreds attended a rock concert, the "Counterinaugural Ball." Rennie Davis remembers the difficulties surrounding the attempts to rent a circus tent for the concert. By now, FBI harassment of the Movement was an accepted fact of life: "You'd call a place and the FBI would cancel your order. We had to use pay phones."

The Counterinaugural laid bare the organizational bankruptcy of the antiwar movement as the Nixon Administration took up the reins of power in 1969. Leadership of the Mobe was in the hands of men who themselves had no constituencies. First at Chicago and now in Washington, the elements of the once vibrant coalition had failed to respond to their call. As if in recognition of this fact, Dellinger and Davis drifted away and were quickly caught up in their own problems when the indictments arising out of the Chicago activities came down on March 29. Dellinger set up a group called "the Conspiracy" and quickly became devoted to the notion that the forthcoming trial should be the focal point of coalition activity.

Sidney Peck, in the meantime, had problems of another sort. He was, in his own words, discovering that "intense involvement in a dissident movement does have consequences for one's personal life." Intensity there certainly was. For three years he had been playing leading roles—in some cases *the* leading role—in four levels of the peace movement, local, state, regional, and national. Sidney Lens, the self-styled "unrepentant radical," names Peck as the leading organizer on the national level after the death of A. J. Muste. In 1967, when Dr. Benjamin Spock left Case Western Reserve and the Cleveland area, Peck became the Movement's luminary on the campus there and in the local press. In the reflected glare of this publicity his family perceived that they were in danger of losing a father and husband.

Spock's biographer describes Sidney Peck in the early days as "the radical rabbit running before Dr. Spock's greyhound liberalism." Both maintained a hectic pace and both paid a price. In 1964 Spock was hospitalized after his pulse hit 240 beats a minute. He was able, eventually, to resume a busy schedule of platform appearances, but then in the 1970s the Spocks' marriage of more than forty years dissolved in divorce. Peck's rugged, compact physique and his athletic past allowed his frame to carry enormous amounts of psychic strain as he maintained his full teaching load in the midst of the innumerable, incessantly shifting demands of his several roles in the Movement. But, like Spock, he paid his price at home.

Louise and Sidney Peck had been married for nineteen years in 1968. Their two children were in their teens. Family finances were tight, despite the fact that Louise worked regularly as a psychotherapist. Sidney's salary (even by the unprincely standards of his profession) remained low throughout this period. The device, common to his colleagues in the profession, of augmenting income by teaching an extra semester or moonlighting was not available to him because of his work in the Movement. The very travels that carried him away from his wife and children were often financed from the family savings and Louise's earnings.

The children, for whom their father had been, in Louise's words, "a second mother," now saw less of him than did favored outsiders, young men and women of the Movement. Louise was becoming an appendage, "Sidney Peck's wife," no longer known for her own strong role in Women Speak Out for Peace and Justice. The tinder for marital trouble was in place. The dam of emotion did not burst for several months, however, until in January 1969 "a bizarre set of circumstances" around a speaking trip to the West Coast brought the Pecks, through the generosity of a Cleveland friend, to the Flamingo Hotel in Las Vegas. There in alien circumstances, in a hotel room shuttered against the variations of dark and light, an eye in the clockless hurricane of cast dice in the casinos below and the neon flicker of self-indulgent pleasure swirling in corridors around them, the Pecks had what they call "an encounter." Through three days and three nights, stripped of every external indicator of time and place, eating and resting at random, they faced the problems that lay between them. It was, they both agree, a painful, risky leveling with each other at an emotional depth never previously sounded in their almost twenty years of marriage.

For Sidney, the three Las Vegas days were "one of the most powerful emotional experiences of my life." Louise says of it: "It was an emotional watershed, both wonderful and unbearable. We touched each other deeply and found the trust to work things through." The Pecks left Las Vegas feeling "very, very good" about what happened there and determined to persevere both in the Movement and in their personal lives together. Not every participant in the peace movement was as strong or as lucky. All did not endure; many relationships were shattered, many lives were destroyed.

"Burnout" is the word Carl Oglesby uses to describe his own condition in 1969. The years following his election to the presidency of SDS in 1965 had catapulted Oglesby across the Movement's horizon like a meteor. His speech that same year at the November Washington rally placed him on a world stage. His travels took him to South Vietnam; to Europe, where he spoke before crowds in the hundreds of thousands; and, in 1967, to Scandinavia to sit with Lord Russell's war crimes tribunal. In between these intercontinental trips he crisscrossed the United States, a figure in demand on campus platforms everywhere. Then, in late 1968, he was invited to participate in the tenth-anniversary celebration of Fidel Castro's Cuban revolution. It was his position and status in SDS that brought him the invitation.

Life magazine gave him a reporting assignment for the trip, to which neither the national officers of SDS nor his Cuban hosts objected.

Even before he left for Cuba, Oglesby sensed that he had become a "prophet without honor among his own people," SDS. His consistent advocacy of building coalitions to the right while maintaining a hard-nosed, radical critique and opposition to U.S. foreign and domestic policy failures was no longer palatable to the new crop of SDS leaders. Mike Klonsky's attack on Oglesby as "the most dangerous man on the Left" bespoke the new attitude. Even as she extended the Cuban offer, Bernardine Dohrn, now the driving force in the national offices of SDS, warned Oglesby that (as he remembers) there was "a big argument going on about you here. A lot of people say you're a real bad guy, politically, and haven't got a role to play anymore." Dohrn herself, however, claimed to think otherwise and to believe that, in Oglesby's words, he could go to Cuba, "see the Revolution eyeball-to-eyeball . . . and come back a rededicated, revived revolutionary."

Oglesby did come back, not as a revived, gun-toting revolutionary in the Weatherman style (a potential not to be found in the sane Oglesby makeup), but at least an enthusiastic admirer of what the Cubans and Castro were trying to accomplish and the manner in which they set about the task. And he brought back to the SDS National Office an idea and a proposal. True to its history, SDS embraced the idea with some reluctance, eventually set the project in motion, then left its realization to other hands.

For Oglesby, the "image of what the revolution in Cuba was all about" was the consuming, total national effort that year to bring in a sugar harvest of ten million tons, thus enabling the country to be less reliant on Russia's support. "Every back, be it that of accountant, schoolteacher, or city functionary, was bent to the task of cutting cane; Fidel Castro pledged his honor to the ten-million-ton goal and promised to resign if he failed." Oglesby saw the pathos of this monumental effort and thought, "If we could get PTA-type people, church people, Boy Scouts, Girl Scouts, and—who knows what?—Rotarians—to come to Cuba for a month or so and chop away at some sugar cane and get to know the Cuban people and the Cuban situation . . . we could show the middle classes of America that the Cuban Revolution was actually in their interest." The notion, expressed in this way, harks back to the spirit and near-ingenuous earnestness of *The Port Huron Statement* that the present generation of SDS had left far behind. Oglesby presented the idea in an interview with Carlos Rafael Rodriguez, who is today Castro's number two man, and received a preliminary, favorable response. Castro's OK and go-ahead was delivered to Oglesby on the airport runway by a motorcycle messenger as he enplaned for the trip home by way of Madrid.

Back in the United States in January, Oglesby had trouble getting the National Interim Committee of SDS to review the proposal. The worry in the National Office, he feels, was that the Venceremos Brigade, as it came to be known, was a power play on his part, that he would use this bright, new idea, endorsed by one of the Third World revolutionaries they honored, to outorganize them to the right. An added worry for SDS leaders was the antagonism of PL to a "revisionist," Soviet-sponsored Cuban regime. The outcome was that foreshadowed by Dohrn before

Oglesby left for Cuba; he no longer had a role to play. The project was wrested from his hands by the soon-to-be Weatherpeople and given an ideological bent quite different from his original idealistic, perhaps visionary, intent to bring middle-aged, middle-class Americans to the sugar cane fields of Cuba, where through hands-on experience they would discover America's self-interest in the success of the Cuban experiment. Instead, the Venceremos Brigade, commencing in November 1969, sent hundreds of college students to Castro's Cuba for what proved to be a radicalizing experience for those volunteers who were not already well down the road to rejection of the American system. But by the time the first cadres of the Venceremos Brigade departed for Cuba, SDS had been dismantled from within.

For Oglesby the end came earlier, at the March National Council meeting in Austin. There, Bernardine Dohrn, now in full swing after routing the PL forces for what would be the last time, dropped the other shoe on Oglesby: "I was expelled from that group, the National Interim Committee, by Bernardine Dohrn. Arlene Bergman, from San Francisco, acted as the cudgel. Bernardine presided over a star chamber of seven or eight people in a little room off the main meeting hall at the eleventh hour in order to tell me that my politics were not Marxist-Leninist and were therefore no good and I had to accept the discipline of the SDS National Committee. Which at this time was dominated by the Weathermen. So I decided it was time for burnout. . . ."

Burnout for Oglesby took the form of retreat to a Vermont farm commune, an increasingly attractive option for Movement members in retreat or seeking surcease from the action in the streets for whatever reasons. His own recuperation, which included a try at writing music, was marred by echoes of the urban guerrilla street scene. There came to the farm a filmmaker who had made a movie that purported to show what urban revolution in this country would look like. The filmmaker, in what Oglesby thinks of as an effort to make life imitate art, persuaded the commune members that they needed to know how to handle guns. He brought weapons to the farm and set up a target range on the back property. Oglesby, whose instincts were never for violence, left and settled in Cambridge, Massachusetts. His valedictory statement to the Movement was "Notes on a Decade Ready for the Dust Bin," published in *Liberation,* August-September 1969. It is a withering and amazingly perceptive analysis of the remnants of the once powerful, vibrant SDS organization.

Oglesby looks back without rancor on 1969. He comes closest to it when asked why he did not continue his activities under the other available auspices, the National (by this date renamed the "New") Mobilization Committee to End the War in Vietnam. He answers that he'd "had it":

> I'd had it with mass politics dominated on the one side by would-be terrorists who were acting out a temper-tantrum politics, just as though they were still back in their upper-middle-class nurseries . . . and on the other side by a group of old fogies, some of whom I adored and loved, but who were increasingly concentrated on Vietnam as a single issue.
>
> And with the Mobe I didn't see that I had any particular contribution to make. I was always more interested in working out intellectual problems.

Before [1963–64], the war was an intellectual problem; by 1969–70 it had become only a political one. . . . SDS had been attractive to me because of its attempt to create a holistic critique of foreign and domestic policy. When the Mobe emerged, that radicalism, that philosophical radicalism, disappeared. The Mobe was not an intellectual organization and SDS was.

But then Oglesby tempers his criticism, even of the Bernardine Dohrn who read him out of SDS. He takes on the rueful aspect of a bewildered father as he contemplates the younger SDS generation and its bizarre excesses.

The Weathermen, he says, were not "Marxist-Leninist muttonheads. . . . If they used the terms, it was only for their shock value. They were much closer to Dada than the Communist Party. . . . I doubt that Bernardine ever read more than five pages of Marx or Engels, or any of them. She was not an ideologue. She was an organizer and an activist. . . . She could have been a great help." Perhaps, indeed, he is himself to be faulted, at least in part for what was to happen:

. . . I feel some responsibility for the Weathermen. More than anybody else . . . I was arguing an interpretation of politics that very much corresponded with that of Castro, of Che Guevara, or of Ho Chi Minh . . . or the African revolutionaries. . . . As an image of this, as one of the Chinese theoreticians [Lin Piao] had written, the Third World was the world "countryside" to the "city" of the First World, and as the Chinese revolution had succeeded, emerging as an attack from the country on the city, so, in the global sense, the same process was acting itself out. The Weatherpeople took up from this . . . and drew a conclusion that I had never really imagined . . . that the same figure, the revolutionary of the Third World, should materialize in the belly of the Beast, in America, spelled with three k's. . . . There was enormous appeal for that idea . . . I hadn't carried the argument far enough in my mind to conclude that if you liked Che Guevara for Cuba you would love him for Chicago. . . . I never thought that.

It is just here that Oglesby, at the deepest level, parts company with the Weathermen. He never transferred his allegiance to another culture, as they did. He never felt alienated in America, as they were: "Never. Never have. I'm too much of a hillbilly and a redneck. This is my home. It's those other assholes who are alien; you know—screw them. I belong here. I feel like I absolutely, totally belong here, and nobody can raise the least little question. . . . If I want to go off and fool around with the Cuban revolutionaries for a while, then, by God, I will . . . and with the sense that I'm doing a patriotic thing."

By 1969 the patriotic thing was no longer on the SDS agenda.

On February 7, 1969, leaders of the National Mobilization Committee to End the War in Vietnam met in New York City. Few of those attending recall the occasion, perhaps because they accomplished very little. They had met to survey, in the aftermath of Chicago and the Counterinaugural, the wreckage of the national coalition that their committee represented, and also to plan for the future. Norma

Becker, in whose apartment the meeting occurred, has no recollection of it at all, but describes the whole post-Chicago period as "an ebb, a hiatus, a period of powerlessness . . . a real slump." As A. J. Muste had warned them in December 1966 when the Spring Mobilization to End the War in Vietnam was forming with optimistic confidence:

> To maintain a radical anti-war coalition is a difficult and delicate task. It is not, be it noted, an attempt to merge parties or to build a political coalition but a cooperative effort of individuals covering a wide spread of opinion. It demands a high sense of responsibility on everyone's part. Nor does it require slurring over differences and avoiding genuine dialogue, but rather, in a notable phrase of [Martin] Buber's, "bearing these differences in common."

Several assembled that Sunday in February had been either close associates of Muste over the years or partners in forming the Spring Mobilization: Halstead, Dellinger, Peck, Lens, and Becker. They could be counted among those who, in the words of one of Muste's favorite poems by Stephen Spender, "wore at their hearts the fire's centre." And yet no sparks emerged to be kindled. Even a Muste, with his fabled, gentle talent for sitting out the meeting and finding the common ground for the next plausible, possible step to be together taken, might have been sorely tried on this occasion. There were many reasons why.

The perennial issue of strategy and tactics, always matters for endless debate among the coalition, was now of widespread concern in the ranks of the antiwar movement at large. The tilt toward confrontation given to the Movement over the past year did not please everyone. Even the nonviolent Dellinger, whose sometimes apprehensive support was crucial to the influence that Hayden and Davis wielded in 1968, admits to being continually asked, as he moved about the country prior to Chicago, "Is there any chance . . . of a bloodbath? Are you sure Tom and Rennie don't want one?" People needed to be reassured that future demonstrations would be nonviolent.

Another problem for the Mobe lay slumbering undisturbed that day, personified by the genial, indefatigable Fred Halstead. His suggestion, reasonable in the light of things, that the Mobe tie into the SMC demonstrations called for the Easter weekend, was quickly turned aside. Halstead brought more than his own undeniable talents as an organizer to the Mobilization Committee. "Fred was my mentor. He was a pro," says Norma Becker, herself in 1969 the indispensable mainspring of the Fifth Avenue Peace Parade Committee. Halstead also brought in his person the Socialist Workers Party. Even Sidney Lens, who on more than one occasion had found the formula to keep the Mobilization's fragile unity intact, says of Halstead and his Trotskyite party:

> I must say that practically all of us in the leadership of the Mobilization Committee found it easier to work with the communists, not only because their caucus discipline was more lax and they stopped trying to manipulate

people, but because their caucus leaders . . . were flexible. The Trotskyites were harder to live with because they operated in almost military fashion and . . . were less prone to compromise.

Norma Becker, hard-nosed, fair-minded, and direct in manner, had less trouble with SWP. She understood their tactics very well and met them head-on. The paid cadre of young SWP workers were always able to stay late at meetings, long after others with the usual work and family obligations were gone, leaving SWP to wield a disproportionate influence. Like Muste before her, Becker, despite her own full-time teaching job in the New York City system and two young teenagers at home, could sit it out with the best of them. And she "blew their cover."

> I don't think [says Becker] they saw themselves as playing an opportunistic or self-serving role. They really did believe that their position was . . . best . . . for the antiwar movement. They did put in a lot of time and energy . . . they put out for the antiwar struggle. But they're a democratic central-ist organization, and when they come to a meeting, they already have a position . . . otherwise, if something came up, the position that their leader took—usually it was Fred Halstead—would be the position they would follow.
> . . . the SWP were very angry with me because I called their number when they stacked meetings. . . . They would have these little committees, the Tenth Street Committee to End the War, the Washington Heights Com-mittee, you know, and they'd send representatives, so they would have ten or fifteen SWP people there, under the guise of these other committees. So . . . I blew their cover.

SWP's ability to stack, manipulate, and finally control coalition groupings was, especially for the strong-minded leaders who made up the National Mobilization, ultimately a greater problem than its undeviating insistence on a single "correct" line—mass peaceful demonstrations, and nothing else—in the antiwar movement. The men and women of the Mobe had powerful personalities and egos well devel-oped in years of radical and pacifist struggle. None was a likely candidate to join the youthful, docile cadres operating on cue from Fred Halstead. "You could al-ways tell them," says Norma Becker. "They were the clean-cut neat ones, with short hair. Fred was unique among them; he had a sense of humor and could laugh at himself." But the underlying problem of SWP's role in the national coalition was left to smolder untouched for several months more. For the time, they would bear their differences in silence.

If the internal political differences of the coalition were too painful to grapple with in February of 1969, a deeper even less tractable problem enshrouded the entire antiwar movement. A master, protean politician was newly resident in the White House. A "new" Richard Nixon, risen phoenixlike from the ashes of na-tional (1960) and state (1962) defeats, had at last achieved the Oval Office, where his daughter's grandfather-in-law had never made him welcome in the lonely years of his vice presidency. The nation desperately wanted to believe what the venerable columnist Walter Lippmann had promised—that "there really is a 'new' Nixon, . . . bright enough to know that a second term will be impossible if he remains sunk in the Vietnam quagmire." The nation desperately wanted to believe Nixon himself when he declared that he wished the office of the presidency "to be a force for pulling our people back together once again," and to believe the veiled promise of his inaugural address: "The greatest honor history can bestow is the title of peacemaker." Richard Nixon did not, however, seek peace with the anti–Vietnam War movement.

William Beecher, who covered the Pentagon for the New York *Times,* was able to report on March 8, 1969, that "Public pressure over the war has almost disappeared," leaving the Nixon Administration "in something of a quandary." State Department officials visiting college campuses were amazed by the apparent lack of interest in the war. In fact, by providing no targets of opportunity, nothing to react to, Nixon had muffled one of the Movement's strongest weapons. He was himself reacting cautiously to the renewed offensive of the North Vietnamese, designed, some thought, as a test of the new President; he had sent the stately Henry Cabot Lodge to join the diplomatic dance around the Paris peace tables. And Nixon had a "secret plan" to end the war. "I'm the one man in this country who can do it, Bob," he told his chief lieutenant, H. R. Haldeman, during the campaign. "I call it the Madman Theory, Bob. I want the North Vietnamese to believe I've reached the point where I might do *anything* to stop the war. We'll just slip the word to them that, 'for God's sake, you know Nixon is obsessed about Communism . . . and he has his hand on the nuclear button'—and Ho Chi Minh himself will be in Paris in two days begging for peace." With neither this nor any other "secret plan" as yet revealed, Nixon was enjoying the honeymoon period traditionally accorded a new President by the American people. They did not know that Nixon was flirting with an even more dangerous form of brinkmanship than he had observed from the sidelines in the days of John Foster Dulles in the 1950s; they expected peace, and they expected it soon. Nixon himself had assured them that "the long, dark night for America was almost over."

If a madman is to terrify others, he must first have demonstrated a capacity for irrational behavior. Curiously enough, the basic theory had been sketched out ten years earlier by Daniel Ellsberg, who would later figure prominently in the Nixon and the antiwar story with the publication of the Pentagon Papers. In March 1959 Ellsberg, still in his twenties, included in a series of Lowell Institute lectures he gave at the Boston Public Library one entitled "The Political Uses of Madness." In it Ellsberg suggested that Hitler's successful blackmail and bargaining power depended upon the conviction of his opponents that he was "erratic, unpredictable, totally unbound by convention, honor, morality." If Nixon was not familiar with Ellsberg's working hypothesis, his National Security Adviser, Henry Kissinger, was. Ellsberg had, by invitation, spoken on the topic to Kissinger's Harvard graduate school seminar. Now, in March 1969, Nixon took the initial, fatal step down the path of irrationality when he ordered the secret bombings of Cambodia to destroy Viet Cong strongholds. (Fatal it was, for the bombings led by a circuitous route to his own downfall.) When on May 9 the New York *Times* published William Beecher's accurate account of the bombings, the White House reacted frantically. Wiretaps were ordered on several members of Kissinger's staff, the military aide to Secretary of Defense Melvin Laird, and, eventually, four newspapermen. As Nixon states in his memoirs, he had previously (after the publication of several disconcerting leaks in the New York *Times)* "authorized Hoover to take the necessary steps—including wiretapping—to investigate the leaks and find the leakers." On the day that Beecher's story appeared, Kissinger and Nixon were together in Key Biscayne. "Kissinger was enraged, and I was as well," Nixon wrote. Kissinger spoke with Hoover four times on the telephone that day. A Hoover memorandum quotes Kissinger as promising that "they [the White House] will destroy whoever did this if we [FBI] can find him, no matter where he is." None of the taps uncovered any damaging material, but they did put the White House in the business. Illegal wiretapping was but one tool of the White House "Plumbers" two years later in their pursuit of a case against Daniel Ellsberg and his monumental leak of the Pentagon Papers. Then came Watergate, cover-up, impeachment hearings, and the ignominious resignation of Richard Nixon.

Nixon advances as a reason for the secrecy of the bombings the need to keep the antiwar movement off guard: ". . . the problem of the antiwar demonstrators. My administration was only two months old, and I wanted to provide as little public outcry as possible at the outset." Not just his enemies in the Movement were kept in the dark. The computer printouts of the Pentagon were laundered by a system of dual reporting that kept the Office of Strategic Research and Analysis, the chief of staff of the Air Force, and the (civilian) secretary of the Air Force unaware. Nor was the Congress of the United States, except for a few "friends" of the Administration, informed, and thus in the initial weeks of his Administration Nixon struck a mighty first blow at the constitutional structure he was sworn to uphold. Cambodia was a neutral country; the U.S. Congress had not exercised the right reserved to it by the Constitution to declare war on Cambodia. The first operation against a Cambodian area supposedly harboring the headquarters of the Viet Cong was labeled "Breakfast," an Orwellian label in this exercise of *Macht politik.* The carpet bombings of the Breakfast area took place on March 18. Breakfast was followed in search of the ever-elusive target by "Lunch," "Snack," "Dinner," "Supper," and "Dessert"—as if increase of appetite did grow by what it fed upon. The Joint Chiefs of Staff estimated that there were 4,247 Cambodians living in the first six areas struck, but took pains to note that most of them were "peasants." The collective term used for this operation was "Menu."*

Used successfully to escalate and extend the war in Indochina, stealth and secrecy quickly became favorite tools of the Nixon Administration and were soon applied in prosecuting the President's war at home against domestic opposition to the continuing Vietnam adventure. Surveillance of the antiwar movement was a going business in Washington when Nixon took office; what followed were boom times. Nowhere, with the possible exception of the Pentagon, was Parkinson's Law

* For the complete story of the Cambodian tragedy, see William Shawcross's *Sideshow: Kissinger, Nixon and the Destruction of Cambodia.*

better exemplified than in the mushrooming activity of spying on peace activists. Literally thousands of agents were sent into the field to keep an eye on protesters. More ominous for the civil rights of Americans than the oppressive watchfulness of the FBI and, in larger cities, the Red Squads of local police, was the infusion of U.S. Army agents and even the CIA into this intelligence mix. So numerous were the operatives at work that targets for their snooping fell into short supply. To the known, proven, and usually peaceable protesters were added the putative, possible, and in some instances implausible candidates. One brigadier general of the U.S. Army who was on the subscription list of a GI "underground" newspaper showed up in the massive files of Continental U.S. Intelligence (CONUS) at Fort Holabird, Maryland. Church groups of all denominations and purposes, including one meeting of Roman Catholic priests gathered to protest their bishops' stand on birth control, became likely surveillance subjects. The Chicago convention of the Democratic Party was overrun with agents of every stripe.† Army surveillance alone covered eighteen thousand civilians in a two-year period ending in the fall of 1969, according to information developed by Senator Ervin's Subcommittee on Constitutional Rights.

Surveillance, however, as opposed to harassment, was never perceived as a serious problem for the antiwar movement in any of its aspects, at least until Weatherman emerged out of SDS later in 1969, took a revolutionary tack, and went underground. For years J. Edgar Hoover's FBI had two stocks-in-trade: the hidden Communist connection revealed and the secret sexual indiscretion, deviation, or excess exposed. With these two threats in hand, Hoover for decades had cowed congressmen, lofty bureaucrats, and even presidents, not to mention the common citizenry. But time passed Hoover by. The New Left and, in particular, the youth attracted to the banners of SDS simply did not dance to those old tunes. The puritanical, Victorian fears and fantasies that bedeviled the Director and drove him to bursts of moral outrage were beyond their ken, dim and quirky remnants of an age gone by. The Yippies celebrated love, sex, and drugs not in secret trysting places, but *en plein air,* in public parks, all the while performing and proclaiming to the multidecibel accompaniment of their music things Hoover would but whisper of. As for communism, SDS from the start, before the war in Vietnam became an issue, rejected all efforts to bar the far Left from participation in its councils. Marxists, Leninists, Trotskyites—all were welcome to join the melee of SDS debate and decision. If the child is destined to flout the parent's most deeply held convictions, J. Edgar Hoover was father to the children of the sixties.

The governmental response to supposed Communist influence in the Movement was twofold. First, surveillance escalated wildly, driven in part by its own internal dynamics and in part by the fact that, as one agent put it, "We created addicts for this stuff all over the government." On the night before the Nixon inaugural one agent even slept beside Pigasus, the absurd icon-beast of the Yippies, no doubt to spy—like the aged, half-crazed Pentheus in Euripides' *Bacchae*—on the suspected

† These and many other examples of the absurdity and extent of surveillance by the military are found in Frank J. Donner: *The Age of Surveillance.*

219

orgiastic rites of these latter-day devotees of Dionysus. Second, and more important, surveillance was escalated to include the use of provocateurs and "dirty tricks."‡ Nixon's own political hatchet men made a euphemism of the term by destroying Senator Edmund Muskie's 1972 presidential candidacy, and by the infusion of felony and common criminality into the mix (Watergate was a "dirty trick"). Only with the added Nixon nuance did "dirty tricks" become adequately descriptive of the tool in use by governmental agents against the antiwar movement.

The egregious example of FBI activity in this vein was the treatment of Martin Luther King, Jr., even before King spoke out on Vietnam. The FBI put taps and bugs in King's hotel rooms as he traveled around the country, and sent Mrs. King tapes to which she listened in her husband's company. The tapes purported to reveal King as a philanderer. An enclosed anonymous note suggested to King in thinly veiled, morally abusive language that suicide was his only recourse. Hoover's animosity toward King was only exacerbated later, when the civil rights leader began to take a stand against the Vietnam War.

On one level surveillance was police-state harassment of innocent and patriotic citizenry. On another level it was theater of the absurd, revealing the frightening possibilities of the officious, bureaucratic mind at work, unchecked by reason. Henry Kissinger in his tale of the botched 1970 commando raid on the Son Tay prison camp twenty miles from Hanoi illustrates the military version of bureaucratic mind-lock. When the briefing officer reported that the prison camp proved to be empty of American prisoners—in fact a secret, coded message from a prisoner of war had given word four months earlier that the camp was closed—Kissinger essayed a bit of Teutonic "humor." Doubtless, he commented, at least a baby water buffalo had been brought back, and this would endlessly perplex the North Vietnamese. Kissinger's remark was stolidly relayed to the Pentagon and made its way up the command ladder. A frantic search for the water buffalo began, not to end until cabled instructions from the generals in Washington ordered an inspection of the helicopter for traces of buffalo dung. The same mindless will-o'-the-wisp pursuits characterized the basset hounds of intelligence in the war-brought-home. When the Poor People's March set out from the Atlanta burial ground where lay the body of Martin Luther King, Jr., a horde of agents covered the event. The instant communication net available was a technology that often (as in Vietnam) outdistanced the capacity to make effective use of it. It did allow one agent to report from the spot that King's widow, Coretta Scott King, had declared to the assembled Poor People's March that they would see her fallen husband's "dream" fulfilled. Instructions came back immediately: the agent was to stay in place and discover "what dream she is referring to." That the Poor People's March, led by a Mule Train, had its symbolic origin more than 1900 years earlier in the triumphant

‡ "Dirty tricks" was a phrase borrowed from the field of politics, where it more or less accurately described the shenanigans of the campaign trail. Richard Tuck was a Democratic master of the art. He is reputed on one campaign occasion, disguised as a railroad engineer, to have climbed into the cab and moved Nixon's whistle-stop train down the track and out of town as the candidate was in full oratorical flight on the rear platform.

entry into Jerusalem of a malcontent Jew astride an ass, fortunately escaped Hoover's notice.

Provocateurs found easy cover in a movement that had its share of committed militants. It was difficult at times to sort out the insidious suggestion of a provocateur from the escalating rhetoric of spokesmen whose reputations within the Movement occasionally seemed to depend on purely oratorical daring. In this milieu the provocateur moved comfortably. Of the thousands of such informers in the ranks only a handful were exposed or, more frequently, surfaced at later trials. One such was Irwin Bock from the Chicago police, who testified at the Chicago 8 trial. So deeply did Bock penetrate the Movement as both an informer and *agent provocateur* that in October 1969 his name was carried on the letterhead of the New Mobilization as a member of the Steering Committee at the very moment he was appearing as a government witness/informer in the Conspiracy trial in Chicago. At the trial of the Camden 28 (a group of the Catholic Left who planned and executed a raid in 1971 on the post office building where draft boards, FBI, and army intelligence all had offices), an FBI informer, Robert Hardy, gave testimony for the defense. Forty FBI agents, tipped off by the unwitting Hardy, had waited in ambush until the Camden raiders were ready to emerge. In his written testimony Hardy said:

> I am making the affidavit on my role in the Camden 28 case because it is important that the truth come out at the trial. . . . I told the FBI I didn't want my friends to go to jail. They [the FBI] just told me to keep them posted on developments. . . . From then on I was an integral part of the group and one of its leaders. . . . I told the FBI many times that it wouldn't have happened if I wasn't there. Throughout I actually wanted just to stop the action, but I think I became, unknowingly, a *provocateur.* . . . As far as mechanical skills and abilities, they [the Camden 28] were totally inept. . . . It definitely wouldn't have happened without me. . . .
>
> It is important to emphasize that I was promised by the FBI many times that they would stop our activities before they actually happened. . . . I was specifically told that the arrest would come when we did a dry run. . . . The dry run proceeded . . . but nothing happened. . . . I contacted the FBI, and I was told that, against the wishes of some local FBI people, the higher-ups, "someone at the little White House in California," they said, . . . "wanted it to actually happen."

The CIA was a comparatively late entrant in the field of domestic surveillance, and for good reason. The National Security Act of 1947, which brought the agency into being, was intentionally framed to bar the CIA from domestic intelligence operations and any infringement upon the well-guarded territory of Hoover's FBI. Richard Helms who helped organize the Agency in 1947 and became its director in 1966, understood this prohibition well: he regularly appended cautionary notes to his White House reports, beseeching the recipients to accord them the highest security. By 1967 a special unit of the CIA, later known as Operation CHAOS, was at work—unsuccessfully, as it proved—to discover links between domestic protest groups and enemies abroad. The last of several CHAOS reports was delivered to LBJ in late 1968 under the title "Restless Youth." All of them contained the same conclusion: no foreign connections. Richard Helms transmitted the same "Restless Youth" report to Henry Kissinger in February 1969 with the warning "This is an area not within the charter of this Agency, so I need not emphasize how extremely sensitive this makes the paper. Should anyone learn of its existence, it would prove most embarrassing for all concerned." By October Helms had disposed of his qualms and Operation CHAOS was infiltrating the domestic peace movement. By 1973 Operation CHAOS had files on tens of thousands of individual American citizens and included among its targets such threats to the security of the United States as Women Strike for Peace and Clergy and Laymen Concerned About Vietnam.

Like huge icebergs bearing down with chilling effect on the antiwar movement, the work of provocateurs, informers, and perpetrators of "dirty tricks"—government agents all—remained, and to this day remain, largely submerged. Nevertheless, leaders of the Movement were aware of the omnipresent threat in the waters they navigated, and the effect was palpable. The leadership was kept nervous and slightly off-balance, particularly in the planning and execution of major demonstrations, as events later in 1969 show. Under the Nixon Administration, oppressive governmental interference in legitimate protest activity reached a crescendo with the aborted Huston Plan in 1970. The plan carries the name of the young White House assistant, Tom Charles Huston, who was delegated to work on the problem, but the details emerged from a working committee established by the Interagency Committee on Intelligence (Ad Hoc). The CIA representative to the working committee was James J. Angleton, chief of counterintelligence. Its genesis, in turn, lay in a June 5, 1970, Oval Office meeting to which Nixon summoned Hoover, Helms, Lieutenant General Donald V. Bennett, director of the Defense Intelligence Agency, Admiral Noel Gayler, director of the National Security Agency, and, from his own staff, Haldeman, Erlichman, and Huston. The date is significant: less than a month after the Kent State killings had occurred and the nation's campuses had erupted. At that meeting, according to Haldeman, "President Nixon didn't pull any punches in expressing his dissatisfaction with their work of coordination of foreign and domestic intelligence, especially as it related to information regarding the domestic [i.e., antiwar] demonstrations." The resulting recommendations to "authorize" warrantless telephone taps, break-ins, "black bag" jobs, and the opening of U.S. mails were of themselves bad enough. But the proposed linking of the agencies concerned in these activities directly to White House supervision and direction (in the hands, that is, of a President who was to have his own "enemies list") meant nothing less than police-state surveillance, harassment, and interference in the lives of citizens. It was, curiously enough, J. Edgar Hoover, chairman of the task force that produced the report, who saved the country from this fate. Whether he feared that such a wide-ranging program embracing so many illegal activities would sooner or later be exposed, or, more likely, did not care for the new structure that would diminish his stature and elevate that of others with respect to the White House, his objections carried the day. President Nixon shelved the Huston Plan, but not before a copy of it found its way into the hands and White House safe of John Dean. Thanks to Huston and other interested White House parties, the intelligence agencies concerned now included the Internal Revenue Service; at the very least they could continue to engage in the same illegal practices and quasi-legal harassment of the "enemy" with implied sanction at the highest levels of government. The brunt of this oppression fell upon the antiwar movement.

The huge intelligence tapestry, woven of so many individual strands and meant to lie like a suffocating blanket over dissident America, perhaps did lack the controlling hand of a single master weaver that Nixon sought to impose. It began to unravel in 1971. On March 8 of that year a small group of the Catholic Left, perhaps no more than four, broke into an office of the FBI in Media, Pennsylvania, a suburb of Philadelphia, and emerged with documents revealing the agency's deliberate program of harassment. As one of the FBI papers with the heading "New Left Notes," put it, the FBI's counterintelligence program was meant to "enhance the paranoia endemic in these circles—and get the point across that there is an FBI agent behind every mailbox." The leaking of the Media documents to press and selected members of Congress aroused, instead, paranoia in FBI circles. COINTELPRO was ended in April 1971. The investigations of the Subcommittee on Constitutional Rights under Senator Sam Ervin of North Carolina led at about the same time to the piecemeal dismantling of military intelligence operations in the domestic field, beginning with the liquidation of CONUS in December 1970. As for the CIA, by 1973 Helms claimed to have forgotten about his June 5, 1970, meeting with the President of the United States in the Oval Office. Senator Clifford Case (R-New Jersey) raised the question during confirmation hearings on the nomination of Helms as ambassador to Iran: "Do you know anything about any activity on the part of the CIA in that connection [domestic spying on the antiwar movement]?" Helms's response was a model of the blandness and suavity to be expected from an ex-director of the CIA: "I don't recall whether we were asked, but we were not involved because it seemed to me that it was a clear violation of what our charter was." Helms later backed away from this stand and chose to attribute any CIA misdeeds at home to White House pressure from Johnson and, later, from Nixon.

The arsenal Richard Nixon drew upon in bringing the war home had been prepared and stocked by his predecessor. As was the case with the air war in Vietnam, the contribution of the Nixon Administration was to raise the level of intensity and ferocity of the weapons used against domestic enemies. Stealth, secrecy, and deception of the public were not unknown in the Johnson years. Similarly, the misuse of the U.S. intelligence apparatus against the so-called Left and, in particular, the antiwar movement was deeply ingrained in the bureaucratic fabric of government when Nixon took office. Nixon thought his covert approval of the Huston Plan put him in the company of Presidents Franklin Roosevelt and Abraham Lincoln, whose open decisions in times of declared war had infringed upon the constitutional rights of American citizens; he finds irony in the fact that the "investigative techniques" of the Huston Plan—his term for break-ins, mail opening, and illegal bugs and wiretaps—"had not only been carried out long before I approved

the plan but continued to be carried out after I had rescinded my approval of it."
He seems unaware of his own special touch in the matter, which was to take the
illegal invasion of the privacy of Americans away from the loose cannons of the
intelligence bureaucracy and place it under the direct control and the whim of the
President, the elected guardian of the people's interest.*

The last device chosen by Nixon from the armory of LBJ was the pursuit and
harassment of antiwar figures through the courts. Combined with the conspiracy
charge, which Jessica Mitford, chronicler of the trial of the Boston 5 in 1968, calls
"the shabbiest weapon in the prosecutor's arsenal," the 1968 antiriot law gave the
government great leeway as it maneuvered against antiwar figures. Federal prosecutors were able to gain indictments on the flimsiest of grounds, as the vaguely
defined words "conspiracy" and "intent" allowed, and to bring their charges
framed in such a way that the key issue for the defendants, namely, the illegality
and/or immorality of the war, could not be introduced in testimony. (Nevertheless,
harassment through the courts proved at best a double-edged sword.) For the
antiwar activists, the fears that made Fred Halstead and his SWP wary of the civil
disobedience thrust in pacifist and religious segments of the Movement were borne
out in the court cases that inevitably followed: huge amounts of money were
drained off and key personalities were effectively removed from other potential
fields of activity.

Bearing witness, each man for himself, in acts of civil disobedience led inescap-
ably to the courts and often to jail, but now there was a difference. In the past, civil
disobedience ordinarily meant violation of *valid* laws: arrest followed; punishment
was meted out by the court and accepted. Simple trespass, for instance, might be
committed to make a point about the evils of nuclear missiles, as A. J. Muste had
done in 1959 at a Mead, Nebraska, missile base. Conscientiously motivated objectors to the war in Vietnam, however, now wished to declare that the laws they
violated were *not* valid.

The Reverend William Sloane Coffin, a Boston 5 defendant, asserted this version
of civil disobedience in his testimony: "My understanding of . . . civil disobedience . . . is the deliberate testing of a statute or regulation whose constitutionality
is in question. . . ."

And so now a new breed of civil disobedients came to court eager for the fray
and eager to see not themselves but the U.S. Government on trial. Although they
were usually not acquitted, their testimony on the illegality and immorality of the
war, often squelched in the courtroom, received an ever-larger hearing in the world
outside. The examples they offered in their persons of moral courage induced the
already committed to still greater effort and forced many "sideline liberals," intellectually opposed to the war, to reassess their detachment from the active struggle.

* In 1972 a unanimous decision of the Supreme Court declared unconstitutional one of the "investigative techniques" cherished by the President. The 8–0 decision declared that the federal practice of
wiretapping domestic radicals without first obtaining court approval was illegal. The decision does not
merit mention in Nixon's thousand-plus pages of memoirs. Nor does he inform his readers that both
Lincoln's suspension of habeas corpus during the Civil War and Roosevelt's imposition of martial law in
Hawaii during World War II were subsequently declared unconstitutional by the Supreme Court.

"If I am brought to trial, I plan to use my trial as a forum in which to try the United States government before the World." David Henry Mitchell III issued this defy in May of 1964, sixteen months before he was finally brought to trial, charged by a federal grand jury with willful neglect to report for induction. In Mitchell's case the mills of the system ground slow, and exceeding fine. After two trials and two appeals his case reached the Supreme Court, where writ of certiorari (permission to try the case) was denied in 1967, six years after his willfulness began with refusal to fill out the draft board's classification forms. The long interval and the concomitant escalation of the American involvement in Vietnam allowed Mitchell to shift his original rather vaguely stated objection to "military preparation for nuclear war" to a legal defense based on the principles of Nuremberg law. The war in Vietnam, Mitchell asserted, was being conducted in violation of the London Agreement (1945) on which the Nuremberg judgments were based. It was a defense that peace militants who were brought to court on a variety of specific charges ranging from draft refusal to conspiracy attempted to raise time and time again without success. In Mitchell's case, only one of the judges sitting in the five separate court hearings he was granted was willing to permit this line of defense. The lone dissenter was Supreme Court Justice William O. Douglas, who, without expressing an opinion on the merits, believed that Mitchell's petition for writ of certiorari should be granted.

Mitchell was given a long sentence: five years in jail. But if the system dealt harshly with him, he had, in turn, achieved in a certain measure his own avowed goal: "to make sure that they end up with burnt fingers and a kick in the behind." The proximity of the original trial site to Yale University guaranteed the presence of supporting demonstrators in good number, picket lines, and press coverage. The case was followed closely from the start by the peace movement and young people everywhere who were contemplating their own personal response to General Hershey's letters of greeting. Literally thousands of draft-age youths, fortified by his example and the legal basis for objection on what Mitchell himself would call *political* rather than religious, philosophical, or moral grounds, became draft resisters. Judge T. Emmet Clarie, presiding at the retrial in lower court, excoriated Mitchell at sentencing for being an agnostic and flouter of community standards, unfit to claim virtue and morality as motive. He cited particularly the fact that Mitchell lived with a woman in a "common law relationship" for two years. Yet this community outcast, as the judge would have it, and his lawyers did more to spread the basic issues on the legal record—and they carried the test of these questions higher in the courts—than did all the legal talent and pillarlike probity of the defendants assembled for trial in the celebrated Boston case of Dr. Spock et al. in 1968.

The U.S. Army could spot a misfit as quickly as Judge Clarie, and without delving into sexual morality. Captain Howard Levy, M.D., easily matched David Mitchell in his capacity for lonely intransigence. He established his credentials within days of reporting to Fort Jackson, South Carolina, for duty. Levy moved out of the BOQ shortly after his arrival and into private quarters. He then refused to pay his dues at the officers' club. Later, an officer of the military police who clashed with Levy over a parking ticket reported that Levy was insubordinate, smirking, saluted limply, and wore insignia wrongly. "Subject needed a haircut" was the final condemnation. When his commanding officer discovered that Levy was refusing to participate in a five-day training program in dermatology for Green Berets headed for Vietnam, he took action. Levy persisted in his recalcitrance despite a formal order to comply; his commanding officer charged him with willful disobedience, a capital offense in wartime, and with promoting disaffection and disloyalty among enlisted men. The traditional bludgeon for enforcing military discipline was brought into play: a court-martial was called. But Howard Levy was not a traditional soldier.

The trial captured the attention of the press, perhaps because of the list of well-known witnesses called. They included Robin Moore, author of the *Green Berets;* former Green Beret Donald Duncan; Peter Bourne, a U.S. Army psychiatrist, later an adviser on drugs to President Carter; Dr. Benjamin Spock; and Jean Mayer, Harvard University nutrition expert and later president of Tufts University. An abortive attempt to introduce a "Nuremberg defense" was quickly squelched by the presiding officer. The trial reached its foregone conclusion in June 1967, when Levy began three years in Leavenworth at hard labor, only weeks before his required tour of duty was scheduled to end.

Levy's offense, beyond being less than an ideal recruit to the officer ranks of the U.S. Army (although that perhaps is what undid him), was in being equally as stern with others as he was with himself. He had thought through the nature of what the United States was doing in Vietnam, and demanded of others what he asked of himself: noncompliance. He told Dr. Benjamin Spock, his widely revered elder colleague in medicine, that he should and could do more. A young black ophthalmologist who admitted to doubts about training Green Beret aidmen and who testified for him was told by Levy, "You're no better than the rest. You're in sympathy with me, but you want to walk the tightrope." He admonished young protesters against the war who visited him in jail to discard their hippie looks before moving out to proselytize the general public. Levy's story, words, and example traveled far beyond his Leavenworth cell. Protests on his behalf moved from the nearby town of Columbia to the chapel at Fort Jackson in defiance of the colonel who brought the original charges against Levy. The officer assigned as judge at Levy's trial came, in time, to sign published advertisements against the war. Howard Levy did not have a ready-made audience to equal the thousands of potential draft resisters who followed the tribulations of David Mitchell, but if his example bore upon fewer numbers, it struck at a deeper level. He spoke to the solitary conscience, however protective its environment.

"I think we have to follow our consciences and do the work we have set ourselves out to do and to accept it sometimes as small. Yet I have a great confidence that it has affected people's thinking and their interests tremendously." Dorothy Day's explanation of the moral imperative driving individuals to solitary acts of civil disobedience to either law or order well explains the actions of Mitchell and Levy. Her use of the first person plural is equally suitable. A saintly and legendary figure by the time of her death in 1980, she was cofounder in the 1930s of the

Catholic Worker in New York City, a hospitality house for the destitute and broken men of the city streets. Dorothy Day did much more than live and work with the Bowery derelicts served by the Catholic Worker, however. With A. J. Muste, she was a leader of the radical pacifist movement in the United States. *The Long Loneliness,* the title of her autobiography, is in one sense a misnomer. By the power of her own example and the philosophy of social action preached in the pages of the penny monthly *Catholic Worker*—radical, pacifist anarchism based on a Christian view that was only meagerly supported by the theologians of the Catholic Church before the Second Vatican Council in 1962—she drew a steady stream of idealistic youthful followers to her side. The Catholic Worker, its activists and followers, formed a strong support group, not unlike the Quakers, for its own members who engaged in civil disobedience. One of these was David John Miller.

Miller was, in his own words, "an absolute pacifist," a position reached after he had received a student deferment in 1960. He refused to apply for conscientious objector status or to comply with his draft board in any way. On October 15, 1965, he burned his draft card, in lieu of making a speech, at a rally in front of the Whitehall Street induction center. Miller was the first to challenge in this way the recently passed (August 30, 1965) draft card law aimed at anyone who "knowingly destroys, knowingly mutilates . . . any such certificate." The case was argued (unsuccessfully) on First Amendment grounds. The Supreme Court again denied writ of certiorari. But the floodgates were opened by Miller's action and example—perhaps more than by his thoughtfully based and legally acceptable (would he but work within the system) conscientious objection. At his final sentencing the judge gently admonished Miller on the duty to render unto Caesar "what Caesar must have in these circumstances." "I will never," was David Miller's response.

Hundreds were to follow the path set by Miller, Mitchell, and Levy. Robert Luftig was one. Yet Luftig engaged in no civil disobedience nor in disobedience within the military, where he served as an enlisted man in the U.S. Army. Instead, Luftig sought an injunction in the federal courts to prevent his assignment to Vietnam well before receiving any order to duty overseas. The restraining order Luftig requested named some rather big guns: Secretary of Defense Robert McNamara, Secretary of the Army Stanley Resor, and the general in command of Fort Ord, where Luftig was stationed. There was nothing in Luftig's past to suggest that he was a man ready to take on the whole establishment, except perhaps a dangerous propensity to read history. It was reading that led Luftig to the conclusion that the United States was interfering in a civil war in Vietnam. No support group like the Quakers or the Catholic Left or the certifiably secular Mobe that backed the Fort Hood 3 stood behind Luftig. He did, however, come from a family not unacquainted with struggle. His father had fought in the Spanish Civil War, and both parents were labor union members. Perhaps table talk at the Luftigs' was not all box scores. Nevertheless, Luftig decided not to oppose the draft. It was, instead, his basic training experience—being told, among other things, that "if you go to Vietnam you're going to be expected to kill women and children"—that led him to a lawyer's office to seek an order enjoining the most powerful men in the United States from sending him to the jungles of Vietnam.

Robert Luftig's case was joined at the appeals level to that of the Fort Hood 3. In the meantime, the Army, solicitous of its own interests, saw to it that Luftig did not receive an overseas assignment. After being subjected to a tirade from his immediate commanding officer, who declared that Luftig, if not a Communist, was certainly a disgrace to his parents ("No . . . my parents know what I did and they're proud of what I did"), Luftig was offered MP protection against the inevitable reprisals of his fellow recruits. His refusal of this offer was well grounded. What he did get from his fellow draftees, both black and white, was congratulations, admiration, and support: an omen, in 1966, of the widespread disaffection of enlisted men in later years of the war.

Luftig's lawyer, Stanley Faulkner, argued at the appeals level that the case was indeed "justiciable," that is, not a purely "political" question surrounding the right and duty of the executive branch to conduct foreign affairs as well as foreign wars. The Court of Appeals thought not and stated its desire to make clear "to others comparably situated and similarly inclined that resort to the courts is futile. . . ." The Court went on to say:

> It is difficult to think of an area less suited for judicial action than that into which Appellant would have us intrude. The fundamental division of authority and power established by the Constitution precludes judges from overseeing the conduct of foreign policy or the use of military power; these matters are plainly the exclusive province of Congress and the Executive.

It was becoming clear that the antiwar movement would receive no more comfort on the federal level from the judiciary than it had from either the legislative or executive branch.

Stanley Faulkner, nevertheless, carried the issues raised by Luftig and the Fort Hood 3 to the Supreme Court, where he petitioned for a review of the lower court dismissal. This time Justice Douglas gained an impressive ally in Justice Potter Stewart, who was generally viewed as a conservative and middle-of-the-road member of the Court. Stewart, in joining the dissent of Douglas on November 6, 1967, first set forth the basic questions raised: (1) Is the military activity in Vietnam a "war" within the meaning of the Constitution? (2) If so, may the President order citizens to participate when no war has been declared by Congress? (3) What is the relevance of the treaty obligations of the United States? (4) What is the relevance of the Tonkin Gulf Resolution of the Congress of August 10, 1964; that is, does it encompass present military operations and was it a constitutionally permissible delegation of the Congress's power to declare war? Then Stewart went on to say:

> These are large and deeply troubling questions. Whether the Court would ultimately reach them depends, of course, upon the resolution of serious preliminary issues of justiciability. We cannot make these problems go away simply by refusing to hear the case of three obscure Army privates. I intimate not even tentative views upon any of these matters, but I think the Court should squarely face them. . . .

The Army never sent Luftig to Vietnam; he was out of the service by September 1967 and therefore his case was moot before it could reach the high court along with that of the Fort Hood 3. Luftig had no illusions about his situation: "I don't think you can win," he said, ". . . that would change the whole foreign policy of the United States. And that's not going to happen."

By 1970 the number of legal cases arising out of draft resistance reached thousands annually. Many young men took refuge in Canada, Sweden, or other countries.† Few cases, however, received much notice outside their local areas. One which did was that of Muhammad Ali, world heavyweight champion boxer. His petition for CO status was denied by the Department of Justice, which overrode the favorable findings of the original hearing officer. Called for induction in April 1967, Ali refused. He suffered a double penalty. After his sentencing the World Boxing Association stripped him of his title. Ali survived to fight another day and justify his claim, "I'm the Champ!" Ali was also vindicated by the U.S. Supreme Court. In an 8–0 decision in June 1971 the Court found that the Justice Department had misled Selective Service by advising that Ali's conscientious objections were neither sincere nor based on religious tenets.

The pursuit of prominent individual resisters, like Muhammad Ali, or of the egregiously obstinate, like Mitchell and Miller, did not stem the steadily increasing stream of recalcitrants. Instead, each case seemed to produce hundreds of zealous imitators. The government's task, then, involved both a tedious and a counterproductive use of the courts. The trial of the Boston 5 in 1968 was the first conscious effort of the Justice Department to cast a wider net and, at the same time, to substitute for the random targets of opportunity represented by individual resisters targets of careful, premeditated choice. But some groups simply thrust themselves upon the hands of a not necessarily delighted Justice Department. The Catonsville 9, a group of obstreperous and radical Catholics, including six who were or had been members of religious orders, were in this category.

The Spock trial was under way in Boston on May 17, 1968 when the Catholic group entered the office of Local Draft Board 33 in Catonsville, Maryland, and seized 378 files, 1-A classification folders, which they carried to a parking lot across the street. There the files were burned with homemade napalm mixed to a recipe lifted from the Army Special Services Handbook and published in *Ramparts*. A carefully alerted corps of press and cameramen witnessed the deed as the perpetrators, awaiting arrest, joined hands to recite the Lord's Prayer. Their story hit the national news and electrified the tiny pockets of the Catholic Left scattered from coast to coast. Catonsville also set the Catholic Left upon an idiosyncratic path of draft board raids that isolated it from the antiwar movement at large and, of course, from the main body of the Church, whose tenets it thought, not so naively, to proclaim through action.

Nevertheless, from Catonsville two extraordinary figures emerged to leave an ineradicable imprint upon the history of the Movement. "Fifty years from now the

† When in 1981 the veterans of Vietnam were offered the chance to select a highway in Vermont to be named in their honor, they chose the major route to Canada. "It is," they said, "the road we did not take."

Berrigans will be folk heroes," says the Reverend William Sloane Coffin. "I can hear the guitars strumming now." Indeed, in their own lifetime a kind of mythology has already built up around Philip and Daniel Berrigan. The two brothers were bound to each other by a fierce Irish family loyalty and a shared religious vocation. Both were priests; Daniel a Jesuit and his younger brother Philip a Josephite, a religious order devoted to work among the black poor of the United States. Neither was unknown to the Catholic Left at the time of the Catonsville raid, an action conceived in the restless, impatient mind of Philip Berrigan.

James Forest, soon himself to engage in a similar raid on the Milwaukee draft board offices, was a close friend of both Berrigans. "I have the impression that I first met Phil Berrigan on the back of a Wheaties box when I was twelve," he has said. "A human antelope gliding over mountainous line backers . . . he was town marshal in Dodge City . . . a downed American R.A.F. volunteer working with the French resistance. . . ." In her *Divine Disobedience,* largely devoted to the Berrigans, Francine du Plessix Gray cites others who describe Philip Berrigan as "a desperado obsessed by the Gospel" and "the Gary Cooper of the Church." The last is as much a reference to the cinematic good looks and commanding carriage of the tall, blue-eyed, gray-haired priest as to the white-hat persona he projected. Elsewhere Ms. Gray records another admirer as saying, "Meeting Phil was not like meeting a priest, but like meeting—a general or a guerrilla leader. . . . His life is his message, and you feel very small when you're with him." Philip Berrigan, then, had the cowboy image that Henry Kissinger, as he would confess to a later interviewer, cherished for himself. There was about him also the romantic allure of the guerrilla to which the Weathermen would soon succumb. For SDS, however, Che Guevara, not Philip Berrigan, became the model.

Catonsville was not a first for Philip Berrigan. Six months before, on October 27, 1967, he entered a Baltimore draft office in the Customs House with three others and methodically poured a mixture of human and duck blood over records filed there. He and his three companions then had to wait thirty minutes for an embarrassed FBI to arrive for the arrest on federal property. So began what would become J. Edgar Hoover's personal vendetta against the two priests. The Baltimore 4—the press epithet set the nomenclature for all subsequent draft raid groups and conspiracy defendants—came to trial in April 1968 on charges of destroying government records and interfering with the Selective Service System. For those who noticed or cared, including Philip's brother Daniel—"I was at the time very far from their understanding of things"—the reaction to the deed had been one of cautious bewilderment. The trial itself attracted little attention. The nation's concern that April had to do with the murder of Martin Luther King and its consequences. Sentencing was set for May 24, by which time Philip Berrigan had added Catonsville to his felonious record.

Daniel Berrigan, unlike his brother, was not to be mistaken for a general. A poet, he had a poet's ineptitude for (or disinterest in) the minutiae of quasi-guerrilla planning so necessary to successful protest actions. He managed even to forget that he was to lead a protest action by Cornell students at his brother's trial. At this time, Cornell was one of the centers of strength for both SDS and the Movement.

According to Charles A. Meconis, a chronicler of the Catholic Left, the aborted protest, blamed on "those damn Catholics," was the beginning of the Movement's disenchantment with the Catholic Left. Daniel Berrigan's strength was with words and symbols. It lay also in a poet's ability to pluck from the particular, the universal. He was able, to use a phrase he himself borrowed from the French mystic Simone Weil, "to put on the universe for a garment." Dan Berrigan's decision at the last moment to join his brother Phil's second raid ensured that the action of the Catonsville 9 would be woven into the threads of a universal garment for the world to wonder at.

A common element in the careers of the two brothers was difficulty with their religious superiors, difficulty invariably rooted in overzealous or overeffective espousal of social causes, whether civil rights or fair housing or, in the end, Vietnam. For Philip, difficulty at first meant no more than transfer from one parochial assignment to another, as the change from Newburgh, New York, where his local activities and his peace involvements enraged the neighbors of the Josephite seminary there, to Baltimore. Once settled in at Baltimore, Philip, as ever, began to attract followers and stir the pot. By luck, this time his neighbor was the federal government. The results in Daniel's case were different. He became a bird of passage, finally to be netted in 1970 in a howling storm on Block Island, Rhode Island, along the great north/south flyway of migratory fowl, by seventy FBI men disguised as bird-watchers.

Daniel Berrigan's travels after he was ordained a priest in 1952 at the age of thirty-one took him twice to France for year-long stays, to Eastern Europe and into the Soviet Union in 1964, twice to Africa (the east and west coasts), to Latin America, to Hanoi, and to the monastic fastness of Thomas Merton's hermitage in Gethsemane, Kentucky. He taught at Brooklyn Preparatory School and at Le Moyne College (where David Miller was a friend and student); he was the first Catholic chaplain at Cornell University, appointed in 1967, the year of the Cornell-inspired mass draft card burning in Central Park.

He describes his second stay in France as "a watershed in my life." He came that year to know intimately and understand the life of the French worker-priests who lived deeply involved with the daily problems of, and indistinguishable from, the people whose communities they served. He must have recognized it as a priestly mode close to the one his brother Philip had instinctively adopted for himself. (A distressed Vatican would soon call a halt to the European worker-priest movement and its Berrigan-like "excesses.") Even his physical appearance changed to the point that friends who came to visit him that year failed to recognize him when he met them at the Orly airport. He had adopted a manner of dress that would become his trademark: turtleneck sweater, beret, nondescript black pants, and sneakers, a medallion on his chest. To William Kunstler, who met Daniel Berrigan just before he took on the defense of the Catonsville 9, Berrigan looked "more like an East Village freak than a priest of Mother Church." His cherubic, well-scrubbed, young-priest look of earlier years had yielded to the burin of time and experience after just one gray Parisian winter.

It was not only his own uncanny instinct for places of growth, action, and the cutting edge of issues that guided Berrigan. His 1965–66 trip to Latin America was an exile engineered by Cardinal Spellman in retribution for Daniel's founding role in Clergy and Laymen Concerned About Vietnam and for the funeral mass for Roger LaPorte. In Latin America he quickly saw the link between Third World suffering and the American adventure in Vietnam, even as his brother had done for the civil rights struggle at home. Independently the Berrigans were placing Vietnam in the same worldwide context as were SDS leaders like Carl Oglesby. By 1965 Daniel was perhaps the best-known Jesuit in the United States. He was a role model for hundreds of young priests and religious, whose hero worship of the outspoken priest restrained the disciplinary bent of his religious superiors. In 1957 he won the coveted Lamont Prize for poetry, and his poetry as well as his increasingly dramatic public stands on Vietnam helped to make him famous. As noted earlier, public outcry in the winter of 1965–66 forced his recall from Latin America.

For Vietnam, the *Catholic Worker* provided a vital link. In 1961 Thomas Merton, a Trappist monk well known for his contemplative poetry and a bestselling, youthful autobiography written in the 1940s, *The Seven Storey Mountain,* published an article in the *Catholic Worker* entitled "The Root of War." Daniel Berrigan read it and was moved to resume a correspondence with Merton that had lapsed some fifteen years before. Their friendship flourished, built afresh around the issues of war and peace. Merton became a mentor to the Berrigan brothers; the judgment of the contemplative monk made a difference in their activist lives. "Has anyone been arrested? Has Merton written?" Daniel would write to a friend from his exile in Latin America. Merton's accidental death in Bangkok in 1968 cast his brother priest and poet into despair. Dorothy Day, although she became in time a steadfast admirer and imperious supporter of both Berrigans, was not impressed by an early meeting with Daniel in 1961. James Forest recalls her reaction to a long didactic lecture Daniel delivered to what was meant to be a discussion group: " 'Just like a priest!' she snapped. . . . 'He didn't leave room for anyone else to talk.' "

In November 1964 the Berrigans were among a small group who gathered for a retreat at the Trappist monastery in Gethsemane, Kentucky. The topic for this peculiarly Roman Catholic exercise in withdrawal for the purpose of prayer and meditation was "The Spiritual Roots of Protest." Thomas Merton was the retreat master, and the invited guests included A. J. Muste; John Heidbrink, a Presbyterian minister active in both the Fellowship of Reconciliation and the Catholic Peace Fellowship; John Howard Yoder; and several from the *Catholic Worker* milieu who would later be defendants in the draft raid trials of the late sixties. With that meeting, Thomas Merton's monastic cell became the seedbed of the Catholic Left's protest movement.

Merton's notes for the retreat conference lay great stress on the question of justification: "Protest: Against whom or what? *By what right?* . . . *By what right* do we assume that we are called to protest, to judge, and to witness? . . . And are we simply assuming such a 'right' or 'mandate' by virtue of our insertion in a collective program of one sort or another? An institution? A 'movement?' " Thomas Cornell was one of those present. He recalls that an answer to Merton's persistent question was suggested by another in the group, from Jeremiah (20:9): "Then I said, I will not make mention of him, nor speak any more in his name. But his word was in mine heart as a burning fire shut up in my bones, and I was weary with forbearing, and I could not stay." Conscience, then, became the ultimate sanction for the actions of the Catholic Left, and fire the guiding metaphor.

Daniel Berrigan had reason to make the figure of speech his own. Early in 1968 he flew to Hanoi with Howard Zinn, whose testimony on the historical roots of American protest was offered in many protesters' trials, to bring back to the United States three prisoners of war. While there, he saw the charred remains, pickled in jars, of Vietnamese victims of American bombing. Later that same year, at Easter, he visited the bedside of a dying teenage protester who had entered the Catholic cathedral in Syracuse, New York, doused himself with kerosene, and set himself on fire in the street outside. "I smelled, for the first time, and yet again not for the first time, the odor of burning flesh, evidence of what I had seen so often in North Vietnam." A few months later, in his testimony at his trial, Berrigan called Vietnam "the Land of the Burning Children."

A few months after the Spock trial concluded, the Catonsville 9 appeared in federal court before Roszel C. Thomsen, chief judge in the United States District Court for the District of Maryland. The date was October 7, 1968, time enough for their team of lawyers, headed by William M. Kunstler, to have gone to school on the case of the Boston 5. Although the Catonsville 9 succeeded in nearly every instance where the Boston 5 foundered (except verdict rendered), there is no evidence that the prior trial served as a paradigm of errors to be avoided. Rather, a constellation of factors, including the style of the presiding judge, the nature of the crime in question, and, above all, the unanimity of the defendants, combined to give focus, clarity, and impact to the Catonsville trial.

The government helped. A conspiracy charge was dropped, although the Catonsville group was indeed a conspiracy, a "breathing together" (as Judge Ford defined the word for the Boston jurors), of remarkable unanimity. The defendants were thus relieved of the clumsy need imposed upon the Boston 5 to deny the charge while admitting to (most of) the facts. Then, to the astonishment of their lawyer, the Catonsville defendants refused to quibble over selection of the jury and accepted without demur the first twelve jurors presented. Nor were the facts of the case subjected to any dispute by attorney Kunstler. The government was left with the embarrassing task of "proving" what no defendant would deny, that the Nine did remove and burn 378 file folders from the office of the Catonsville Draft Board. The uneasy dispatch with which the technical, prosecutorial aspects of the case were handled served to heighten anticipation in the courtroom for the presentation of the defense.

Judge Thomsen allowed the defense unparalleled leeway, much to the annoyance of the prosecution, in explaining matters of intent. By turn, each defendant was allowed to detail by way of long, autobiographical accounts dealing with experiences among the poor and destitute of three continents how he or she had come to take the action in question. Three of the defendants had been members of the missionary Maryknoll Order in Guatemala and expelled for agitation among the peasants there. Only occasionally did Judge Thomsen remonstrate: "We are not trying the United Fruit Company. . . . We are not trying the bishops of the United States. . . . The United States Marines are not on trial here." Philip Berrigan described in detail frustrating efforts to talk sense to high U.S. officials, including Secretary of State Dean Rusk, which, he declared, led to his acts at Baltimore and Catonsville. Daniel Berrigan was allowed the last word, amounting to sixty-seven pages of court transcript, including excerpts from his own poetry. "I saw suddenly," he said, ". . . that I, too, was threatened with verbalizing my moral substance out of existence. That I, too, was placing upon young shoulders the filthy burden of the original sin of war."

If not a perfect act of contrition, it was for the defendants an act of perfect communication with their supporters inside and outside the courthouse. The word quickly passed through what functioned like an underground Catholic press—the *Catholic Worker, Ramparts, The National Catholic Reporter, The Commonweal,* and others—to tens of thousands of more distant supporters. Charles Knight, an activist from the Boston area, recalls the scene outside the courthouse, where two thousand or more gathered for each day of the trial: "Excitement was high, and the police presence heightened it. There were platoons of uniformed cops watching us as we established an illegal picket. They would wink at me occasionally as I passed by in my suit and tie—the best attire, I thought, for arrest. It soon became known that there were plainclothesmen in our midst, and I had been taken to be one of them."

The trial ended, as was foreordained, in a guilty verdict, but not before Kunstler tried to reveal to the jury what the American system of jurisprudence conceals, that they had the power, in defiance of law and fact, to "decide the case on the principal issues involved."‡ Judge Thomsen, however, quickly intervened before Kunstler could get his point across, and the appeals court upheld his intervention.

An unusual event occurred after the jurors had withdrawn and before they returned to render the verdict. At Judge Thomsen's invitation, a colloquy took place between the judge and the defendants in which both sides spoke from the depths of personal belief. The defendants individually and with quiet passion explained that the imperatives of conscience drove them to act and to appeal through their act to the conscience of America. For his part, Judge Thomsen admitted his own abhorrence of the war, spoke of his grandchildren who would soon be of draft age, and of his admiration for the noble motives on display, but: "The jury are not the representatives of the American people . . . people who are going to violate the law in order to make a point must expect to be convicted. . . ." And again, "people simply cannot take the law into their own hands . . . we either have a rule of law or we do not." Daniel Berrigan's hope that it might be possible, "even though the law has excluded certain very enormous questions of conscience, that we . . . rewrite the tradition for the sake of our people" was not to be. Judge Thomsen

‡ This doctrine of a jury's power of nullification, as it is called, goes back in the history of American courts to the case of John Peter Zenger in 1735. Zenger, a Colonial printer, was on trial for libel, but his lawyer, Andrew Hamilton, persuaded the jury to disregard the law (under which Zenger was clearly guilty) and acquit.

remained, in the end, bound by the law he administered; the Catonsville 9, by their individual and collective conscience.

The remarkable interchange, unique in the history of American jurisprudence, transformed the courtroom into pure theater. The cathartic moment came when Daniel Berrigan asked a startled Judge Thomsen if they could finish by praying together. All in the court rose to their feet and some joined in as the Nine recited together the Lord's Prayer. It echoed through the room like the parting choral ode of a Greek tragedy: ". . . For Thine is the kingdom, and the power, and the glory . . ."

Drama gave way to reality when the jury returned to announce their findings: guilty on all three counts. The crowded courtroom sat in silence, as if stunned by the inevitable, until a strong male voice cried out, "Members of the jury, you have just found Jesus Christ guilty!" Confusion followed. Judge Thomsen ordered the courtroom cleared, and the final word was left to Daniel Berrigan: "We would simply like to thank the Court and the prosecution. We agree that this is the greatest day of our lives."

Philip Berrigan and Thomas Lewis were given sentences of three years, to run concurrently with their six-year sentences for the Baltimore 4 action; the others of the Catonsville 9 received sentences of two or two and a half years each. The appeals process began at once.

Reaction was mixed. Many Americans, then and later, had never heard of the Berrigans. In 1970, two years after the trial, when both brothers were underground and the objects of a massive FBI hunt, *Newsweek* discovered that 62 percent of the American public were unaware of their identity. Of those who did know, many would have endorsed the gravamen of another Catholic priest's complaint: Andrew M. Greeley, who would later add bestselling novels to his credentials as a sociologist, asserted that "the Berrigans and the rest of the protesting rabble may have prolonged the war." Nevertheless, a significant number of Catholics and others were inspired to follow in the footsteps of the Berrigans. A month after Catonsville the Boston 2 poured black paint over draft files in Boston. Then, in September 1968, the Milwaukee 14 napalmed ten thousand draft records in that city. In 1969 the floodgates opened. Nine separate actions, including the first raid conducted entirely by women (the self-named Women Against Daddy Warbucks, in Manhattan) resulted in the destruction of hundreds of thousands of draft board records.

Within the larger antiwar movement reaction was also mixed. For William Kunstler, whose record was already distinguished for his legal participation in a number of "radical" causes, it meant reappraisal:

> Since Catonsville, I have gone considerably beyond this relatively limited concept of the lawyer-client relationship. . . . I will no longer accept the idea that my services can be bought and sold to and by the highest bidder— I must give them away just as the worker-priest donates his own. . . . I have come to understand that it [is] right and decent and sweet to want to make one's life, as Daniel Berrigan put it in his play, *The Trial of the Catonsville Nine,* "a gift to society, a gift to history and to the community."

For Valerie Hendy, it meant a beginning. She was a twenty-one-year-old student at Boston University when a friend showed her the script of *The Trial of the Catonsville Nine*. "Devastated, knocked down, wiped out," by the experience of reading it, she found the money to have it produced and was herself the director of a performance at Boston University before the New York opening of the play. Valerie Hendy dropped out of college, became part of the Catholic Left, and in July 1972, a member of the Great Lakes Conspiracy.

Others in the Movement were more restrained. Douglas Dowd was a founding father in 1966 of the first Mobilization. He was a Cornell professor at the time, active on a campus where SDS members orchestrated the mass burning of draft cards in April 1967 and where black militance erupted in 1969. Dowd, in an essay published in 1971, said that "the initial reaction of most *anti-war* people [to the Berrigans] was one of disbelief and disapproval." When this gave way, as it did, to admiration and approval, "what remained constant was the *distance* between the viewed and the viewer . . . [in] a model of action too heroic to suggest *effective* steps to ordinary people." Staughton Lynd, another of the early leaders of the Movement, echoed this criticism in asking for a "scaling down from actions which are very intense, very self-sacrificial, . . . which the ordinary person (whether he likes them or not) could never seriously consider doing."

Other criticism from within the Movement was less muted. The Berrigans were called "Irish Mafia," "elitist," "arrivistes," and worse. None of this disturbed the serene arrogance of the Berrigans, particularly when they were among friends. James Forest recalls being told by Philip Berrigan after the Baltimore 4 action that he, Berrigan, could no longer take the pacifist Fellowship of Reconciliation seriously, nor—except for his friends who were in it—the Catholic Peace Fellowship, despite the fact that a year or two earlier Berrigan had persuaded Forest to abandon his career plans and sign on with the CPF.

"In the face of what this war has become," Berrigan wrote to Forest, ". . . they are out of it. . . . I will refuse to indict anyone's conscience, but I don't have to cheer their work, which seems to me safe, unimaginative, staffish, and devoid of risk or suffering. . . . To stop this war, I would give my life tomorrow, and I can't be blamed if I have little time for those who want to run ads in the New York *Times*. . . ." Francine du Plessix Gray, in *Divine Disobedience,* describes a similarly airy performance in 1968 by Daniel Berrigan before a devoted group of followers gathered to dedicate a new Catholic Worker home on East First Street, New York City. There, basking in the glow of admiration from a small audience that included the wives of David Miller and Thomas Cornell, both of whom were in jail at the time, Berrigan declared that draft card burning had become "establishment," and explained Catonsville by reference to the acts of the Martyrs and to Christ and the money changers. Despite the Christian allusions the Berrigan stance was more that of the pagan heroes of Greek tradition. Humility was not in the lexicon of an Antigone or an Achilles, to name two uncivil disobedients from the mythology of that land. Nor was it a word for Socrates, whose trial William Kunstler brought to the attention of the Catonsville jurors. "Risk," Socrates told his friends on the day he died, "is beautiful."

The one critic who counted for the Berrigans was Thomas Merton—"My brother," Daniel Berrigan called him in the dedication of his own writings *(No Bars to Manhood)* about the Vietnam conflict. Merton was clearly worried. In a "Note for *Ave Maria,*" written shortly after the Catonsville action and shortly before his death, Merton said, "The Peace Movement may be escalating beyond peaceful protest. In which case it may also be escalating into self-contradiction." While stating that he did not think Catonsville had brought the antiwar movement quite to that point, Merton's words were gloomy nevertheless. "It [Catonsville] bordered on violence and was violent to the extent that it meant pushing some good ladies around and destroying some government property. . . . The evident desperation [of the Catonsville 9] . . . has frightened more than it has edified." Merton went on to plead for what he called "the classic (Gandhian) doctrine of nonviolence" that rises above pragmatism and a self-affirmation of the rightness and conviction of protesters.

The criticism struck home. Daniel Berrigan made it his own and adopted Merton's terminology in his own assessment of others: "The New Left suffers from American pragmatism," he said. "It fights violence with the tools of violence. I fight it with the Gandhian and Christian dimensions of nonviolence. . . . I would like to be more classical and Greek, I am like Socrates . . ."

In fact, Berrigan's rigorous, theoretical abhorrence of random and personal violence—and the deed of Catonsville itself—was more in the tradition of an earlier American resister, Samuel Adams. Adams condemned attacks in Boston on the homes of Loyalists in 1765 as acts of "a truly mobbish nature," yet he sanctioned the carefully controlled destruction of property that was the Boston Tea Party, because all peaceful means of resistance to the East India Company's importation had been exhausted. The Berrigans and their followers were, in this respect, to be distinguished from their rampaging secular counterparts, the Weathermen of SDS. Otherwise the two groups had much in common.

By the end of the decade both the Catholic Left and the Weathermen had worked their way from somewhere close to the center of the larger antiwar movement, their position four or five years earlier, to the radical fringes. Neither group had a strong historical perspective; a few selectively chosen events apart, recorded history seems to have commenced for them with the 1960s, in their own recent, observed past. Their authoritative texts were also documents of that decade: *Pacem in Terris* (1963) and *The Port Huron Statement* (1962). Even with respect to their own holy writ, memory was short. Forgotten were the gentle admonitions in both those texts to work patiently through peaceful means toward goals of peace, love, and justice.

By 1969 *The Port Huron Statement* had about as much currency in SDS circles as a medieval manuscript; it had been, as Kirkpatrick Sale declares, "assigned to the junk-heap of history." So swiftly did the SDS generations succeed one another that it was but an innocent, unwitting kind of atavism that brought the Movement back in 1968 and 1969 to a major thrust of *The Port Huron Statement,* the need to "wrest control of the educational process from the administrative bureaucracy." Certainly no one in 1969 recalled that the authors of *The Port Huron Statement* had explicitly rejected violence as a tool: "We find violence to be abhorrent because it requires generally the transformation of the target, be it a human being or a community of people, into a depersonalized object of hate." What instead rang in the ears of campus radicals in the spring of 1969 was the cry of "Two, three, many Columbias."

"The ruling class," asserted the San Francisco State chapter of SDS, "uses any means necessary to keep people in their place, and we must use any means necessary including people's violence to defeat them." So the shadows cast by the undeniable violence of the war in Vietnam that had flickered across the landscape of 1968 at Columbia and Chicago in the form of police brutality became a darkness that nearly engulfed American campuses in the spring of 1969. Vietnam itself, however, was a neglected or at best peripheral issue, invoked usually as a standard of gruesome horror against which to measure and minimize the violence perpetrated by protesters against college and university administrations.

One survey, based on a study of 232 institutions over the first six months of 1969, discovered 292 protests and demonstrations. Twenty-four percent involved either violence or destruction of property (more than $8 million) or both. There were at least eighty-four bombing or arson incidents on U.S. campuses in these months. In one, at Santa Barbara, a university employee was killed when a bomb he picked up exploded. At least two students were shot to death by police in other, separate incidents. Three thousand, six hundred fifty-two students were arrested; 956 were either suspended or expelled. The major demand in most of these actions (59 percent) had to do with race: instituting of black studies programs; increasing the numbers of black students and faculty; better facilities. The memorable photo of that spring, reproduced by countless media, showed the black students who had seized Willard Straight Hall on the Cornell campus brandishing rifles and (empty) ammunition bandoliers. Student power was the second major issue (42 percent). In only 1 percent of the demonstrations was the draft a factor. Other war-related issues—ROTC, military-industrial on-campus recruitment, university research or investment in tools of war—accounted for 25 percent. As a single issue Vietnam was almost never mentioned.

Had SDS at last found the perfect wave? Like so many beaches in the restless quest of surfers for that elusive goal, one cause after another had been taken up by SDS only to be at once abandoned to others or left deserted. Civil rights; straight-line Vietnam protest; ERAP; draft resistance—each had come and gone, leaving the vague imprint of SDS on the public perception. But now, in the wake of Columbia and Chicago, and in the midst of almost daily press reports of new protests, disorder, and violence, a picture as clear as it was false took shape in the public consciousness: the campuses of the nation were in flames, being torn asunder by a generation of militants lost to its elders, a generation led by a group of radicals symbolized in the popular mind by the letters *SDS*.

The truth lay somewhere else. SDS was riding in a most precarious fashion that huge wave sweeping across the campuses, in control of neither its own fragile conveyance nor the crashing flood beneath. The Urban Research Corporation study on campus disorders found New Left participation in only 28 percent of the demonstrations and takeovers in the spring of 1969. Presumably "New Left" suggests, for the most part, the activity of local chapters of SDS. The events at Harvard University were emblematic of the SDS plight. There as elsewhere SDS lost sight of the essential issues, lost its influence with the student body, lost its fight with an ineptly guided administration, and, finally, lost control of its own organization.

In his annual report to the overseers and alumni in January of 1968, Harvard president Nathan Pusey described the student activists as "Walter Mittys of the Left (or are they left?)—they play at being revolutionaries" and then went on to traduce the rest of the student body by asserting that "the vast majority of Harvard undergraduates went about their essential business seriously and gaily, as students have from the beginning." As even Pusey would discover in time, nothing was on any campus, with the possible exception of General Beadle State College of South Dakota, as it had been from the beginning.

Nevertheless Harvard was not a hotbed of revolutionary activity. Not until President Pusey committed two unnecessary blunders toward the end of March around the long-simmering question of ROTC on campus did SDS have an issue on which to galvanize the students. First, his administration announced reductions in scholarships (financial aid) to student protesters involved in an earlier ROTC incident, and then Pusey himself in an unwonted appearance before students made a gratuitous, hard-nosed, public defense of ROTC and what he called "the military-industrial complex."

Even so, Harvard might have been slow to join campus disruption elsewhere but for the fact that the Harvard chapter of SDS was itself in turmoil. The cause was the Worker Student Alliance (WSA), a caucus organized by Progressive Labor. PL itself had no more than half a dozen members on the Harvard campus. Since 1966 PL had dedicated itself to taking control of SDS on both the national and local levels and converting its nonexclusionary, participatory democracy to sectarian (Communist), monolithic purposes. So Neanderthal was the PL "platform" that years later Carl Oglesby still nurses his suspicions: "If you want to have a group that's always going to be legitimate in any left-wing political scene as a means of penetrating it . . . then let's create an organization ourselves [here Oglesby postulates the New York City Red Squad as an instigator] out of a split-off from, for example, the CP. . . . Operating on dogmatic Marxist terms you could do anything . . . that a Fascist mind could want. . . . And they [PL] did it so consistently that I had to wonder whether or not it was on purpose."

Jared Israel, the PL leader at Harvard, has a different appraisal: "We weren't rigid at all. We were passionate but we weren't rigid. . . . We were trying to conduct a scientific social experiment [to] transform people's thinking. . . . We really weren't Communists, we just thought we were. We really were extreme Left socialists . . . with a little anarchism tossed in. Human beings are best at that. Communism is a distortion of that impulse." But in explaining his later falling-out with PL, Israel acknowledges a certain rigidity as a major flaw in the "democratic centralism" of PL: "We all said the same thing."

In January 1969 the PL positions were formally promulgated. PL was *against:* black nationalism, women's liberation, North Vietnam ("lackeys of Moscow"), the

Viet Cong ("revisionists"), Cuba, drugs, rock music, long hair, and the whole contemporary youth lifestyle, including its pantheon of political heroes, Che, Castro, and Ho Chi Minh. To buttress this list PL invoked a strident antiimperialism aimed at every power center in the world except China, but especially at the United States, and a Marxist-Leninist program of revolution for the working classes.* At Harvard, PL's WSA caucus had reached a standoff by March of 1969 with the "regulars" for control of SDS.

At an evening meeting of SDS on April 8, the PL faction was outvoted three times on the question of immediate occupation of a university building in support of six student demands around the ROTC issue and Harvard expansion in the working-class areas adjacent to the campus. Defeated at the ballot, the PL faction acted on its own. Jared Israel denies that the vote went against the PL/WSA caucus: "I raised the resolution. [It was] that we should not take action tonight, but at *any time* in the future it would be acceptable—and we won. . . . Unlike the right wing of SDS, we were able to meet in the morning because we were not stoned all night." At noon the next day, a handful of PL students, watched by an unsuspecting crowd of several hundred who had come for what they thought would be an SDS rally, mounted the steps of University Hall. University Hall is the administrative seat of Harvard College, housing the office of the dean of students, the dean of the faculty of arts and sciences, and others. Its eastern facade fronts on the main quadrangle of the Harvard Yard. Its western face is guarded by a huge bronze statue of John Harvard, seated, book in hand. The attitude of the seventeenth-century founder is of one disturbed in his reading by some distant sound, years away. On the steps, Norm Daniels, a PL cochairman of SDS, turned to the crowd and, using a bullhorn, read six demands. Shouts of "No, No, Go Home!" arose in the crowd as they began to realize what was happening. Daniels persisted: "There is only one enemy, the Harvard Corporation. It's time for us to tell the Corporation now by action what we've been telling them all fall by words." Whereupon the twenty or thirty students on the steps turned and entered the building.

Inside, those deans and officers who refused to leave quietly were pushed, dragged, or carried out. One, Assistant Dean Archie Epps, went with his fists flailing. According to Israel the charge brought later against the intruders was "touching the elbow of a Dean," and that was the extent of the students' violence. An hour later the occupiers opened the building, which they had renamed Che Guevara Hall, to all comers, and the building filled with student sightseers and curiosity seekers. Soon the carnival atmosphere of a typical Harvard spring "riot" reigned on the lower floor while the radicals gathered in confused discussions in the Faculty Meeting Room on the floor above. The Harvard administration wasted little time on discussion or negotiation. A "bust" was called. Four hundred state and municipal police entered the Yard shortly before 5 A.M. the next morning. The building was cleared with less ceremony, more dispatch, and considerably more violence and brutality than its occupiers had exercised. A chilled and horrified

---

* What brought PL onto the campuses and into SDS via the WSA was the fact that without their recruited students the entire national, truly working-class membership of PL barely outnumbered the Harvard Board of Overseers.

crowd of several hundred witnessed the bloody exit. Among the 196 arrested 145 were Harvard students: 48 required medical attention for injuries that included fractured skulls, legs, and kneecaps. PL and the Harvard administration had at last succeeded in arousing the majority of students.

Archibald Cox, a professor at the Harvard Law School who was later named special prosecutor to investigate the Watergate scandal and then fired by Nixon in the "Saturday Night Massacre," was an adviser to the Harvard administration throughout the spring. Cox had headed a commission to study the Columbia uprising of the previous year. As the Harvard crisis mounted Cox met with the radical students. "They brought in Archibald Cox," says Israel. "He had his glasses down on his nose, and he looked at us and we looked at him. . . . He didn't like it at all. He felt that it was 'quite unreasonable,' the whole thing, 'and probably going to cause a tremendous amount of difficulty for your future—have you considered your future?' We were more influenced by *The Graduate.*"

The infuriated students went on strike. Although there was initially some goodwill toward SDS for revealing the "face of the monster," SDS lost all control over events as the strike developed and, ten days later, petered out. Students were indifferent at this point to an SDS declaration that the strike would continue. SDS became an object of ridicule. A hazy resolution of a few of the strike issues, notably an independent black demand for a reorganized Afro-American studies program, satisfied the general student population. But the only real winners in the demoralized Harvard community were the PL faction of SDS. They were at last in control; almost the entire slate of delegates from the Harvard chapter to the national convention in June were from the WSA/PL caucus.

At the commencement ceremonies that June, a reluctant President Pusey yielded the platform to Bruce Allan of the WSA, one of six seniors suspended for his part in the University Hall takeover. Allan's speech was greeted by hisses, boos, and, when he led fifty seniors in a walkout, angry shouts from the alumni and parents in attendance. The true temper of the audience was shown by the reception given a later student speaker on the program, Meldon Levine of the law school. Levine began with these words:

> The streets of our country are in turmoil. The universities are filled with students rebelling and rioting. Communists are seeking to destroy our country. Russia is threatening us with her might. And the republic is in danger. Yes! danger from within and without. We need law and order! Without law and order our nation cannot survive.

Wild cheering came from the older generation in the audience as Levine spoke these words, but subsided into shocked silence as he went on: "These words were spoken in 1932 by Adolf Hitler." The rest of Levine's speech, a gentle chastisement of the elders and praise of his fellows, won the close attention of his listeners.

At another commencement exercise that June, President Nixon addressed the graduating class at General Beadle State College, where he seemed to take off from the words Meldon Levine had lifted from Adolf Hitler. Nixon's hounds of law and order had been in full cry for months on the trail of scruffy, ragged, disruptive youth. Heading the pack were John Mitchell, who later would become the first U.S. attorney general ever to serve a jail sentence, and Vice President Spiro Agnew, who in 1973 would resign his office in disgrace in the face of multiple charges of conspiracy, extortion, and bribery, and, after the "full equivalent of a plea of guilty," escape jail with a $10,000 fine and three years of probation. Mitchell pinpointed SDS as the villainous catalyst and declared that the "time has come for an end to patience. The time has come to demand that university officials, local law enforcement agencies and local courts apply the law."

At General Beadle State College Richard Nixon himself, the master of the hounds, took up the cry. He stopped at the tiny, little-known college in the flatlands of South Dakota en route to a meeting with President Thieu on Midway Island in the Pacific. The college was, appropriately, dedicating a library to Senator Karl E. Mundt, a virulent anti-Communist who had been one of Joseph McCarthy's staunchest defenders in the 1950s. "This is a small college," Nixon reminded his audience, "not rich and famous like Harvard or Yale"; and then proceeded, from his safe platform two thousand miles away, to rail against those Eastern bastions of "self-righteous moral arrogance."†

Nixon did place himself in agreement with one Harvard figure, Nathan Pusey. The students, he said, were "intoxicated with the romance of revolution"; but then the President widened his field of attack to include "faculty members who should know better" and "in the large community . . . the usual apologists ready to excuse any tactic in the name of 'progress.' " The speech had been six weeks in preparation, and the culminating threat was not an idle one: "We have the power to strike back and to prevail . . . we have a Constitution that sets certain limits on what government can do but that allows wide discretion within those limits. . . ."

"Revolution" blared in the words and music of the Beatles emanating from stereos set up that April by SDS/PL in open windows of a "liberated" University Hall. It was a challenge that Richard Nixon was happy to take on. For the raucous Harvard revolutionaries, like most of their counterparts on other campuses, were "bringing the war home" on terms the President found comfortable. In a stylistically characteristic passage of his memoirs he explains why:

> During the first months of my presidency Vietnam was not the primary issue in campus demonstrations largely because Johnson's bombing halt had suspended the most actively controversial aspect of the war, and my announced plans to establish an all-volunteer Army and our reform of the draft, which made it less threateningly disruptive, also helped in this regard.
> I knew that this situation was bound to change.

Change began long before Nixon realized it, and it began in the bowels of his White House. On April 29, 1969, in an impromptu speech in Washington before

† On the same day, at the commencement ceremonies of Brown University in Providence, Rhode Island, two thirds of the graduating seniors rose to turn their backs upon Henry Kissinger as he received an honorary degree. He was, they said, a symbol of the continuing war.

another safe audience, the U.S. Chamber of Commerce, the President played on a variation of the same theme, the equating of dissent with terror:

> When we find situations . . . where students in the name of dissent and in the name of change terrorize other students and faculty members, when they rifle files, when they engage in violence, when they carry guns and knives in the classrooms, then I say it is time for the faculties, the boards of trustees and school administrators to have the backbone to stand up against this kind of situation.

As Nixon was speaking, two of his aides, Henry Kissinger and John Ehrlichman, were meeting quietly with a small group of student dissenters in the White House situation room. The students were there to display their own version of the kind of "backbone" the President was recommending to the hearts and minds of college administrators.

The group represented 253 campus leaders who had signed a declaration of conscience concerning the war and a petition to the President. Each of the signatories was either editor of his campus paper or a student body president. They were from colleges and universities both large and small across the nation, from thirty-eight states, the District of Columbia, and Puerto Rico. If General Beadle State College was not represented, the President's alma mater, Whittier College in California, was. Representative Allard Lowenstein had introduced the group to the Capitol press corps at a press conference in the House Agriculture Subcommittee room. Reporters were impressed by their demeanor, deference, and determination to use the system—and the fact that one of them was a grandnephew of Elihu Root, Theodore Roosevelt's Secretary of State. The Washington *Post* in a page-one story described them as "clearly middle class in appearance and moderate in their views, . . . from the conventional leadership sector of the universities. They hoped to see the President and 'try to make him understand what [we] are saying.' "

Senator George McGovern introduced their names, their statement, and their petition into the *Congressional Record* for May 1, 1969. The letter to President Nixon was couched in polite and respectful terms. The students reminded him that their predecessors had approached President Johnson in similar fashion in December 1966 and again in 1967, and that he, Nixon, in his inaugural address "stated your confidence and hope in American youth . . . and asked the nation for a resumption of reasonable and rational discussion." They hoped for just that—with the President—even as they "recognized the pressures of your office and the demands upon your schedule." In all, it was the traditional language of petition with roots in the American past. The Stamp Act of 1765 had, after all, addressed "the warmest sentiments of affection and duty for His Majesty's person and Government" in esteeming "it our indispensable duty to make the following declaration of our humble opinion respecting the most essential rights and liberties of the colonists, and of the grievances under which they labour."

The students' declaration that was forwarded with the letter of petition, however, was perhaps too blunt for a George III or Richard Nixon to respond to personally.

The *Statement on the War in Vietnam and the Draft* signed by the 253 closed with these words:

> Along with thousands of our fellow students, we campus leaders cannot participate in a war which we believe to be immoral and unjust. Although this, for each of us, is an intensely personal decision, we publicly and collectively express our intention to refuse induction and to aid and support those who decide to refuse. We will not serve in the military as long as the war in Vietnam continues.

David Hawk had the students in tow. One of Allard Lowenstein's proselytes, he was a graduate of Cornell, where he had been an all-American diver on the swimming team. In 1968, while on leave from Union Theological Seminary, he had been a key figure in the McCarthy campaign through the Wisconsin primary; he left it to work with the National Student Association. He later married Joan Libby, a graduate of Mount Holyoke College and herself an antiwar activist. In recent years he has served as president of Amnesty International, a human rights organization with a particular interest in political prisoners worldwide. He traveled to Cambodia, where he amassed a written and photographic record of the holocaust which occurred there after the Vietnam War; his reports have appeared in *The New Republic* and an exhibition of his photographs was shown (1983–84) throughout the United States.

Hawk remembers that "seminal meeting in the situation room of the White House with Kissinger and Ehrlichman. . . . Kissinger was as if he were back at Harvard with graduate students. He was very professorial. . . . We sat around a very nice conference table with curtains that covered all the maps around us. . . ." Hawk knew how serious the exercise was. Six weeks before the meeting federal agents had arrested him in the chapel of the seminary on the felony charge of refusing induction. Thus he knew the mailed fist of government; now Kissinger showed the velvet glove.

"I don't disagree with you," Hawk recalls Kissinger as saying, "as to the wisdom of our original involvement, but we cannot leave in a way that would cause dishonor, loss of credibility . . ." The students later told reporters that Kissinger said, "If you people come back here next year this time, we could not give you a plea for patience if the state of the war in 1970 is the same as it is now." Kissinger talked with the students in this vein for almost two hours before turning them over to Ehrlichman.

Ehrlichman was as tough as Kissinger had been reasonable and conciliatory. Speaking of the student leaders' assertion that should the war continue, thousands would refuse to fight in a war they considered unjust, Ehrlichman chastised them: " 'If you continue to think that you can break laws just because you don't agree with them, you're going to force us to up the ante to the point where we have to give out death sentences for traffic violations.' " The astonished students stumbled out of the room.

Kissinger's reaction to the meeting is on record in *Look* magazine: "I can understand the anguish of the younger generation. They lack models, they have no heroes, they see no great purposes in the world. But conscientious objection is destructive of society. . . . Conscientious objection must be reserved only for the greatest moral issues, and Vietnam is not of this magnitude." His interviewer, *Look* senior editor Gerald Astor, makes his own comment on Kissinger's statement: "That he [Kissinger] considers several hundred thousand dead and maimed in Vietnam of less than the greatest moral magnitude obviously sets . . . Kissinger and the Nixon Administration apart from the demonstrating generation."

As for the students, they had learned "that the Nixon Administration was as committed to a policy of war as had been the Johnson crowd." The way out of the situation room of the White House was through the press room. The students made a statement, telling the press that "Nixon is not going to end the war . . . and it's clear that we have to resume our efforts to stop the war, because these people aren't going to." Despite the fact that in one form or another the story made the local television evening news, the Washington *Post,* the New York *Times,* and "The Today Show," it plummeted into obscurity, much as would William Beecher's story a few days later on the secret bombings of Cambodia. Nevertheless, the group that emerged on April 29, 1969, from the basement situation room of the White House was to constitute the nucleus for the largest public protest against government policy ever seen in the United States, Vietnam Moratorium Day.

David Hawk describes it as unharnessed energy in search of a sensible strategy to demonstrate the breadth of opposition to continuation of the war. "We had a really good network, these two hundred and fifty student body presidents. It didn't make any difference if they were leaving—their successors would follow through." But the rank and file of students Hawk thought to command had no cause in which to enlist, no banner under which to march. SDS was crumbling, prey to the onslaught of PL. The other national student organization, the Student Mobilization Committee, was already captive of the sectarian Left.‡ The Easter weekend demonstrations of April 5–6 were planned by the SMC/YSA, but generated little recognizable student support. Where there were significant turnouts, local organizations, long-distance runners of the Movement, were the somewhat reluctant partners of the Trotskyites. The Fifth Avenue Vietnam Peace Parade Committee and the Chicago Peace Council, for instance, were by now skilled in turning out goodly numbers of marchers on short notice. Of course they needed the energy and assistance of students in their areas, but they worked without reliance on national organizations. Even the announcement on April 3 that combat deaths in Vietnam (33,641) had surpassed the total for the Korean War lent little impact to the Easter demonstrations, however. The Gallup Poll reported that the number of Americans approving Nixon's handling of the Vietnam problem remained steady: three out of every five

‡ A year earlier, in June of 1968, an SMC meeting of eerie similarity to the confrontation SDS would soon enter broke apart in a cacophony of chanted slogans. It was, as always, the independent students who walked out, unable to resist the relentless, unified pressure of the sectarian element in their midst. They departed to the cadence of meaningless chant, "Up Against the Wall, YSA." YSA was the Young Socialist Alliance, an offshoot of the Trotskyite SWP.

citizens with an opinion supported their President. Thirty-two percent of the American public had no opinion.

On April 20, 1969, one of the most enduring of the regionally based peace groups, MassPax, held an executive committee meeting that was momentous for the antiwar movement in the United States. On that night Jerome Grossman, founder and chairman of MassPax, proposed the idea that would emerge in somewhat modified form some months later as Vietnam Moratorium Day. It was an extraordinary idea, all the more so coming, as it did, from a successful American entrepreneur whose political analyses are dotted with the terminology of business and accounting, whose only agenda is one of fundamental patriotism ("We did not carry the Viet Cong flag, we did not burn the American flag"), and whose personal motto might well be taken from the prayer that opened the First Continental Congress in 1774: ". . . for America, for the Congress, for the Province of Massachusetts Bay, and especially the town of Boston." Grossman's proposal to MassPax called for a nationwide general strike to end the war in Vietnam. His own position paper puts it this way:

> A national call for a deadline strike on Wednesday, October 8. . . . The strike will take effect if American troops are not withdrawn [by that date]. The strike will last one day. If American troops are not withdrawn by November 1, the second strike will last for two days, November 5 and 6. For each additional month an additional striking day will be added. The strike is defined as refraining from reporting for work or to regular occupation. . . .
>
> [The strike] will enable a broad segment of the American people to participate in a legal and traditional protest action which will have a painful effect upon all with power and influence. It . . . will show the Administration and the leaders of American business that those who strike are determined to end the war even if it means shutting down all American institutions by refraining from work.

Big Bill Haywood or Mother Jones could not have asked for more.

In typical business fashion Grossman proposed to his hesitant and only tentatively approving fellow members that "a market survey" be undertaken before the next month's meeting to test support for the idea before going ahead with it. This research bore two results. For one thing, he discovered an unwillingness to participate in something as radical as a general strike. "Like any good businessman," says Grossman, "I backed off."* From one quarter, however, there was a mild expression of interest.

David Hawk had left the White House meeting with Henry Kissinger determined to find new ways to bring Vietnam again to the attention of America's conscience. He turned first to an old friend, Sam Brown, fellow veteran of the McCarthy campaign. Electoral politics were not, however, a possibility in the 1969 off year. At about the same time, Grossman also reached Sam Brown in the course

---

* "*Felix qui cautus*" (Happy the man who is cautious), Samuel Adams had written to Thomas Paine in his last published words, recalling perhaps that he himself had once backed off after making a premature and radical call for rigorous economic sanctions against Britain in 1774.

of his "market survey." He, too, knew Sam Brown from the McCarthy campaign and admired his organizational talents. Hawk and Brown came to the next Mass-Pax meeting. "They thought it [Grossman's general strike proposal] was an interesting idea, but gave no indication that they were willing to do it. . . . I must say, without putting Sam down at all, when he found out we had twenty-five thousand dollars [to put behind the idea] he was a lot more interested. As well he might— there was more where that came from." Brown and Hawk, now deeply interested, suggested a change of name, from "Strike" to "Moratorium." They saw at once that "Strike," in addition to the middle-class aversion Grossman had encountered, would be associated in the public mind with the ugly campus disruptions of the past spring. Grossman went along without observing the irony of abandoning a word from the lexicon of labor in favor of one that had significance only for bankers.

David Hawk and Sam Brown returned to Washington with the idea and the money. The new target date for the first Moratorium action was now October 15. They took an office on the eighth floor of 1029 Vermont Avenue, N.W., an address that would figure in the antiwar movement history for several years to come. A WATS line and telephone bank, indispensable tools of organizing, were set up, and the massive task of tracking down in vacation time some five hundred student leaders—five to ten calls to locate each one, Hawk estimates—began. The campuses had to be ready to move as soon as classes started in September. More imminent was the coming Cleveland national antiwar conference, where Hawk and Brown hoped to win support for the Moratorium from the moribund National Mobilization Committee.

1969:
Vietnam Moratorium Day

"You will be better advised to watch what we do instead of what we say." This amazing piece of advice, with its suggestion that truth in packaging was not a high-priority item for the Nixon Administration, came in 1969 from Attorney General John Mitchell to a disgruntled group of black civil rights workers who had stormed into his inner sanctum at the Justice Department. Mitchell's deputy, Richard Kleindienst, however, did better by the antiwar movement. His small service was to tell the truth of what the Administration and its Department of Justice had in store for protesters: "As soon as we're notified of danger, we'll have the National Guard in the armory and the Army on two-, four-, and six-hour alert. . . . We're going to enforce the law against draft-evaders, against radical students, against deserters, against civil disorders. . . . If we find that any of these radical, revolutionary, anarchistic kids violate the law, we'll prosecute." Prosecute they did, even without the finding. On March 19, a federal grand jury in Chicago indicted eight persons on charges of conspiracy to incite a riot during the Democratic National Convention in that city the previous August. The Chicago 8, as they became known, included David Dellinger, Tom Hayden, Rennie Davis, Abbie Hoffman, Jerry Rubin, Bobby Seale, Lee Weiner, and John Froines. Sidney Peck was one of twelve unindicted coconspirators. The Eight were a representative group: SDS, Yippies, Black Panthers, academics, and the National Mobilization. None of those named had emerged as a suitable target for grand jury action when Johnson's attorney general, Ramsey Clark, called for a study to determine if indictments were in order. He was told that they were not. This same advice from the same source, professionals within the department, was available to Mitchell when he took over Justice; he chose, instead, to prosecute. It was the Chicago case that taught the Nixon Administration how to use the grand jury process, originally designed to protect the rights of citizens, for malicious, contrary purposes. Like the sheriff with his *posse comitatus* in the Western movies so dear to the heart of Henry Kissinger, Mitchell used grand juries to harry and hound dissenters.

Henry Kissinger, however, could not have appreciated Mitchell's advice "to watch what we do, [not] what we say." No magician would. The way in which Kissinger mesmerized the American press—and through it, the American public— is a constant theme of the most revealing book yet written on the Nixon/Kissinger years (including the memoirs of the two principal participants themselves), Seymour Hersh's *The Price of Power.* Hersh says of Kissinger:

> His function in the various interviews and briefings was not merely to garner favorable publicity for Nixon and his policies, but to shield the real goals and strategy of the administration from view. By doing so, Kissinger was also weakening the anti-war movement, and one White House goal . . . was to isolate the anti-war activists who were also against the war but had yet to take to the streets in protest.

While the bombing of Cambodia went on and while plans for an equally savage blow to be directed at Hanoi were being formulated, the President and his National Security Adviser were speaking peace, patience, and Vietnamization. J. William Fulbright was one who succumbed to the "what we say" line. Although Kissinger was loath to follow the democratic tradition that called cabinet-level and other high appointed officers of the government to testify before congressional committees, he did deign to invite Fulbright to a private meeting in March with the President and, of course, himself. The meeting was successful. Fulbright was no less responsive to Kissinger's stroking than the many influential members of the press who received similar treatment. "I left the meeting," Fulbright is reported to have said, "with the belief that the President and Dr. Kissinger were in accord with my views about the war."

How a typical group of American students reacted to this kind of treatment has been described above. A week after that meeting, on May 5, Kissinger, at the prodding of his President, repeated his performance. This time it was for five leaders of a Quaker group, several hundred strong, who had come to picket the White House for peace. The meeting was cordial but unsatisfactory. Kissinger was reported by the New York *Times* to have asked for three months to produce signs of substantial progress. Marvin and Bernard Kalb, however, in their biography written with their subject's assistance, quote Kissinger as asking for six months "and if we haven't ended the war by then, you can come back and tear down the White House fence"—a wildly inappropriate invitation to extend to the American Friends Service Committee. They did return—two months later and after Nixon's June 8 announcement at Midway Island in the Pacific that he would withdraw twenty-five thousand U.S. troops from Vietnam—but found no reason to revise their first review of the prestidigitator's performance: "We believe the United States military and government leaders are fostering illusions in regard to Vietnam."

As the summer went on and Americans continued to die in Vietnam at a rate of more than two hundred per week, the call for patience became a comedy act, fit material for ridicule. In a September column, Russell Baker of the New York *Times* imagined himself coping with a crowd of petulant children ("You'd think they'd invented morality the way they go on about a few deaths") and tells them, "Do I like the war? What a terrible thing to say. . . . I'm doing everything in my power to end this senseless war. . . . What am I doing? I'll tell you what I'm doing, son. I'm doing just what President Nixon asked all of us to do. I'm being patient."

The ninth and last annual convention of SDS began on Wednesday, June 18, 1969. The site was the Chicago Coliseum, six blocks south of Grant Park, where ten months earlier the Chicago police had bloodied up demonstrators and protesters drawn to the city by the Democratic Party's national convention. This time, too, the police were conveniently nearby; police headquarters was just two blocks away. Federal, state, and local undercover agents added to the uniformed presence brought the guardian force in and around the Coliseum close to the total number of delegates in attendance, some fifteen hundred.

Whatever plans the Chicago Red Squad and the FBI may have had to sabotage the convention or SDS itself through the antics of planted provocateurs were entirely unnecessary. The disastrous confrontation that ensued between PL and the SDS National Office contingent under the leadership of Bernardine Dohrn was entirely self-prompted. Together, in one burst of improvisational lunacy, they brought down the whole SDS edifice. And in the dust of that collapse lay the cherished SDS doctrines of participatory democracy and nonexclusion, not to mention the somewhat inflated reputation of SDS as *the* opponent of the war in Vietnam.

Jared Israel, who led the PL/WSA caucus at the convention, estimates that PL controlled about 750 delegates. It was, he says,

> Quite a scene. We had a little more strength than they [the Dohrn faction] did. [But] we didn't want to take over SDS. We didn't want organizational control. . . . Participatory democracy [for them] was for a certain few, but we actually believed in it. We were always arguing, we were a thorn in their sides—"Let's have a discussion." . . . We weren't interested in taking it over. We were interested in having it grow. The split was fomented by them. . . . It was a hysterical action on the part of a politically defeated group. . . . They were on an egomaniacal trip and were so much into drugs that half the time they didn't know *where* they were. . . . We considered it unfortunate that we ended up in control of SDS.

The Dohrn group came armed with a document designed (as in the previous year) to thwart the ideological pressures PL consistently applied against them and to lead SDS in the direction previously designated by the authors as a Revolutionary Youth Movement (RYM). The document was widely distributed, but never brought before the convention for consideration. It took its title, *You Don't Need a Weatherman to Know Which Way the Wind Blows,* from a line in Bob Dylan's 1965 song "Subterranean Homesick Blues." The title was meant to be a chop at a Progressive Labor Party always prepared to tell their troops which way the wind was blowing. Instead, Dohrn and her cohorts used it to name themselves when, a few days later, they marched out of SDS forever. "Weathermen," they were called or, in occasional playful reference to their enemies Left and Right, "Weatherbureau."

Later, some of their followers were to insist upon "Weatherpeople," in stodgy, tardy recognition of yet another movement, feminism, that SDS ignored.

The Weatherman statement displays all the grace and lucidity of what it was, a Marxist-Leninist-Maoist tract composed by a committee of amateurs intent upon dealing death to their doctrinal enemies in PL and promulgating a new dogma for the faithful. Carl Oglesby, who had in three years moved from being an elder statesman active within SDS to a retirement forced upon him by Bernardine Dohrn, provided a thoughtful critique of the document and its call for a revolutionary youth movement subservient to the Black Panther Party in the "mother country":

> But this loss [of all contact with elements in American society to the right of SDS] is primarily compensated by our clarity about the "vanguard." Clarity! Any close reading of the RYM's Weatherman statement will drive you blind. Sometimes the vanguard is the black ghetto community, sometimes only the Panthers, sometimes the Third World as a whole, sometimes only the Vietnamese, and sometimes apparently only the Lao Dong Party. . . . Mostly, though, it's the poor Panthers, whose want of politics was never challenged by the few SDSers who had access to their leaders; this appointment—Vanguard to the People's Revolution—[depends upon a] revolutionary strategy in which the United States is to experience not a social revolution at the hands of its own people, but a military defeat at the hands of twenty, thirty, many Vietnams—plus a few Detroits.

Thus Weatherman—the eleven authors of the document included Bernardine Dohrn and Mark Rudd—embraced the Black Panthers not only as remote leaders of a would-be, mostly white, revolutionary youth movement but as "theoreticians" as well: "In order to get rid of the gun it is necessary to pick up the gun," declared Panther leader Huey Newton.

The Panthers were also intended to be the ultimate weapon in the war against PL inside the convention hall. The Panthers shared with PL a veneration of Mao's *Little Red Book*—and nothing else. On every other issue, including interpretation of Mao's sayings, they were bitterly contemptuous of one another. The five hundred or so SDSers in the Coliseum who were uncommitted, bound neither to Dohrn's National Office/RYM grouping nor to PL, could be expected to be sympathetic to any expression of Panther opinion. SDS was, as Oglesby wrote, "more interested in shining with the borrowed light of Panther charisma than in asking all the hard practical questions." And the Panther "charisma" never had more luster than in June 1969. Within the previous eighteen months the Panthers had drawn national attention on several occasions. They had brandished guns at the San Francisco International Airport and inside the state capitol at Sacramento while the legislature was in session. In October 1967 Huey Newton engaged in a shoot-out with Oakland police after officers following him stopped his car. A policeman was killed. Newton's trial in 1968 became a *cause célèbre,* and when he was sentenced—not for first-degree murder, as the government sought, but for voluntary manslaughter—"Free Huey" became a radical cry. By June 1969 more than one hundred Panthers, nearly one out of every twenty-five, were in jail, twenty-one more were under indictment in New York on charges of conspiring to blow up several public buildings, and eight Panthers were charged in New Haven with the murder of a fellow party member. Bobby Seale, cofounder of the Panthers in 1966 and Huey Newton's chief lieutenant, would soon be arrested on the same New Haven murder charge, just days before his scheduled trial as one of the Chicago 8. Despite or because of all this, the Panthers were being lionized by members of New York's salon society in a short-lived exercise of "radical chic."

Unfortunately for the National Office/Weatherman partisans, the local Panthers introduced to do the hatchet job on PL were not very bright. On the evening of the second day of the convention (a dreary affair to that point, distinguished only by a remarkably low level of debate or just plain name-calling) the Minister of Information of the Illinois Black Panther Party, one Rufus "Chaka" Walls, entered the Coliseum with the customary Panther retinue of bodyguards. Either the Minister of Information was not well informed about the underlying issues or he did not care about them. Whatever the reason, Chaka wandered in his remarks away from the obligatory slashing at PL and on to the topic of women's liberation. The Panthers, he said, believed in "pussy power." Cries of "Fight Male Chauvinism" came from the audience and were picked up at once by the delighted PL faction.* It mattered not that PL opposed women's liberation as a false diversion along the path to armed struggle. They could not resist the chance to mock their enemies. The noise level rose as the well-disciplined PL forces chanted in unison, "Fight Male Chauvinism!" Chaka was bewildered but gave it one more try: "Superman was a punk because he never even tried to fuck Lois Lane." At this point Chaka's colleague, Jewel Cook, took over the mike and tried to restore order by restating in Panther style the doctrinal attack on PL. But then he, too, unaccountably reverted to the taboo topic: he agreed with his brother Chaka, pussy power was good for the revolution . . . and then Jewel launched into a repetition of Stokely Carmichael's opinion about the proper position of women—"prone"—in the movement. Now the only delegates not on their feet screaming "Fight Male Chauvinism" were those RYMers who understood the true significance of what was happening. "We got up," says Israel, "and made a very polite speech about how people should try to curb their chauvinism in the interest of the unity of the Movement." The "vanguard" of Panthers, behind whom the submissive troops of the Revolutionary Youth Movement, discarding their "white skin privilege," were to march, had led them straight into a fatal ambush.

At that moment SDS died. Despite another forty-eight hours of feverish activity on the part of Bernardine Dohrn, the end was inevitable. The Panthers returned to the Coliseum the next night. This time Jewel Cook had a statement approved by Bobby Seale: PL must recant or be counted as traitors to the revolution. More shouted slogans were exchanged by the two sides, both fully prepared for this exercise in revolutionary debate. "Read Mao, Read Mao!" was answered by the

---

* The day before, the convention had already chosen slogans over reasoned debate as a form of argumentation, when the Midwest contingent of RYM parodied the PLers with chants of "Mao, Mao, Mao Tse-tung, Dare to Struggle, Dare to Win" and waved copies of the *Little Red Book* in derision.

Panther rally cry, "Power to the People, Power to the People!" and the echo came back from the PL ranks, "Power to the *Workers!*" The terminology of rebuttal was familiar enough: "Bull-Shit! Bull-l-l-Shit!"†

Not much later that evening Bernardine Dohrn led the penultimate RYM walk-out from the convention hall to caucus on the issue of a split. Dohrn dominated the caucus, which ran on, with pauses, to the early hours of Saturday evening. Finally her speech, which rated as brilliant in the rhetorical context of the convention, moved the rump group to vote to expel PL. "We are *not* a caucus," she bravely asserted. "We *are* SDS." When she and the group returned to the plenary session, led by a phalanx of "bodyguards" in an absurd aping of Panther ritual, Dohrn repeated her bravura performance, ending with the declaration that PL and its WSA stooges were no longer members of SDS. According to Kirkpatrick Sale, the speech provoked a strange response: first silence, then embarrassed titters and giggling, and, finally, the customary clamor of shouted epithets.

To impute laughter of any sort to the PL forces at that moment is, for Jared Israel, "just a slur." Earlier Israel had clashed with Klonsky. "He made a speech quoting Anna Louise Strong [an American long resident in China who died there in early 1974] as saying we were no good and Mao didn't like us anymore. I said it was inappropriate to use the prestige of the Chinese revolution to resolve debates within SDS." But it had come to that. Now, says Israel,

> when they surrounded us to leave and Bernardine Dohrn made this silly speech, the whole group, which filled up most of the room—because we were the majority there—was silent. There was dead silence and absolute horror—we didn't want it [the split]. At that point I . . . ran around the room from person to person, shaking them like this [he gestures] and saying, "Don't you hear what she's saying? She's saying that you are bad, that you are an enemy of the working class." Then people started shouting, "Shame!" I literally went from one person to the other. It was a physical process. Everybody, including the leaders, was frozen. . . . They were in tears. That's what the reaction was . . . stunned horror, because we saw them destroying the organization. We looked around and we saw potheads and crazies and maniacal Panthers—we're talking about sickies. . . .

This time the exit was forever. Several hundred delegates followed a Dohrn bursting with fury from the hall, but soon the Weathermen would number no more than one or two hundred. Most estimates of SDS membership for the preceding year ran between eighty and one hundred thousand. When Dohrn stomped out of the Coliseum to do, as the Weathermen conceived it, revolutionary battle against "pig Amerika," she left behind the corpse of SDS. The stunned PLers remained to gather around the body, declare that it lived, and elect Elgar John Pennington III of Boston as the new national secretary of the defunct organization.

† In 1965 Al Haber, a founder and the first president of SDS, wrote a pamphlet in which he expounded upon the virtues of the New Left. "The power of the left," Haber wrote, "is largely its ability to persuade. . . . Only as we pursue debate do we develop the ability to see and lead others to see beyond the slogans by which truth is obscured. . . ."

The demise of SDS presents an object lesson, to be sure, in the fate of political coalitions too loosely knit, but SDS was also a victim of the times. It caught a mounting wave of youthful revolt in America in the 1960s, rode that wave, and crashed with it. Whenever young America was discontented, disenchanted, angry, or merely disgruntled, SDS turned to proclaim, "We are you!" What began with serious political issues of civil rights in the South, poverty in the Northern ghettos, and the war in Vietnam came to embrace every expression of political and countercultural anomie. The draft; drugs; music; the aridity of getting and spending so assiduously promoted by their generation's baby-sitter, television; the fakery and demagoguery of standard American politics; the culture and lifestyle of their parents; the policies of their government toward its own and other peoples bound in a poverty they, the younger generation, never knew; the patronizing authoritarianism of American universities—all were one to this huge, amorphous organization that scarcely knew, even to number them, its own membership. Vaguely defined notions of participatory democracy and open, endless debate, combined with a disdain for old-fashioned parliamentary procedure, produced within SDS a ruling elite created in the image of its own exotic rhetoric. Style without substance became the SDS hallmark. In the months preceding the denouement at the Chicago Coliseum the rhetoric became increasingly shrill and solipsistic. This, in turn, led rapidly to the alienation of the common folk of SDS, not to mention the Yippies, hippies, anarchists, Spartacists, Wobblies, Communists, and socialists of every stripe represented in the Coliseum. All, equally, were either bored or bewildered, except, of course, PL. PL did not wander aimlessly in through the wide-open door of nonexclusion. Control of SDS, if not outright ownership, was their goal; and if not now, then later. A political party, after all, that was waiting for the armed revolt of the working class in America could afford patience in the matter of SDS. So it was that, in the end, PL joined the others in astonishment at the collapse of SDS, that house of many mansions, and the self-immolation of the Weatherman leadership in the flames of their own rhetoric.

In equally parlous shape as it approached a national conference of its own was the other major coalition of antiwar forces in the United States, the National Mobilization Committee to End the War in Vietnam. The Chicago action at the site of the Democratic National Convention, followed by the lackluster counterinaugural activities in January, left the Mobe, to use Sidney Peck's words, "politically isolated." "It was clear that after the inaugural action there was not much left to the National Mobilization Committee . . . the only remaining faction was the Dellinger-Davis connection—it had moved that far to the left." And Dellinger believed that the focus for any planned national action should be the Conspiracy, a name conjured up from the terms of the indictment of the Chicago 8 to signify both the trial itself and its symbolic trappings. The difficulty here was exactly as Peck suggests: both within the Movement and among the public at large Chicago—the Conspiracy—stood for wild-in-the-streets, radical action. Rightly or wrongly, few would have endorsed Dellinger's recollection that "the will of the people [at Chicago] was so overwhelmingly nonviolent, I couldn't believe it . . . absolutely inspiring." Dellinger's continued faith in his coconspirators caused friction inside the

Mobe. SWP's Fred Halstead, a marshal of the Fifth Avenue Peace Parade Committee's Easter demonstration, was furious when Dellinger not only brought Hoffman and Rubin to the podium, but contravened the agreements of the day and allowed them to speak. Even Dellinger, by Halstead's account, was aghast at their attempts on that peaceful occasion to incite the rabble of Crazies—an exotic offshoot of the Yippies—in the crowd to action against the police presence.

Despite the fact that Sidney Peck knew the coalition had to be rebuilt and that "the time was ripe," he remained cautious when "Fred Halstead and others approached me [in May] to see whether we couldn't initiate an antiwar conference in Cleveland as we did back in 1966." The problem was, as ever, SWP. Peck and other leaders of the National Mobilization had no confidence that SWP, like PL in SDS, would not "stack and pack" a conference with their own party-disciplined representatives. Nevertheless, it was largely SWP—working with Stewart Meacham (national peace secretary of the American Friends Service Committee and himself an ex-socialist), Bradford Lyttle (a long time radical pacifist from Chicago), and others of a loose caucus called National Action Group—that made the actions of the Easter weekend successful. "The Chicago part of that," according to Peck, "—thirty-eight thousand people—showed that there was a mass base ready to come out in the streets when there was a guarantee there would be no physical confrontation." So Peck was ready to proceed—cautiously—with or without, but preferably with, Dellinger.

The conference was held on the campus where Peck taught, Case Western Reserve University, on July 4–5, under the sponsorship of the Cleveland Area Peace Action Council. It was a tense, difficult conference throughout. The issue of whether or not it would be an open conference, susceptible to being packed by the SWP, or an invitational one was resolved by compromise: invitational, but "observers" welcome. Once that decision was made, the Student Mobilization Committee immediately put out a call for its own conference, also in Cleveland, on July 6, and invited its membership units to arrive in Cleveland early as "observers" to the CAPAC national conference, or, better still, to write to CAPAC and demand delegate status. Thus were Sidney Peck's fears confirmed.

Dellinger and Peck, however, were too experienced in matters of this sort to allow the SWP to run away with the conference and, hence, the coalition. Together they established a steering committee for the conference and undertook to keep matters firmly in its hands. The tight control caused some hard feeling among the eight hundred "observers," many of whom followed the SMC lead in demanding delegate status and were disappointed. The roster of the steering committee read, with some notable absences, like a Hall of Fame for antiwar activists.‡ All were

‡ Norma Becker, Fifth Avenue Peace Parade Committee; Barbara Bick, Washington Women Strike for Peace; Rennie Davis, SDS, Chicago Conspiracy; David Dellinger, *Liberation* magazine, Chicago Conspiracy; Douglas Dowd, professor, Cornell University; Al Evanoff, District 65, Retail, Wholesale and Department Store Workers; Rev. Richard Fernandez, Clergy and Laymen Concerned; Jerry Gordon, CAPAC chairperson; Fred Halstead, SWP; Arnold Johnson, CP; Donald Kalish, professor, UCLA; Sidney Lens, Chicago Peace Council; Carol Lipman, SMC; John McAuliff, Committee of Returned Volunteers (Peace Corps); Stewart Meacham, American Friends Service Committee; Sidney Peck, professor, Case Western Reserve; Maxwell Primack, Chicago Peace Council; Carl Rogers, Committee for

scarred and toughened by experience and not about to be steamrollered by the SWP. On crucial votes Halstead could carry only Jerry Gordon and Carol Lipman with him. It was not a youthful group. Davis was in his thirtieth year, and only Lipman, Rogers, and McAuliff were younger than he.

The first test of control came within the steering committee. Dellinger brought Mark Rudd and Kathy Boudin to a meeting where the agenda for the conference was to be set. They reported on the SDS National Office (now virtually synonymous with the Weathermen) plan for major actions around the opening of the Conspiracy trial in September. Dellinger's proposal to support this effort was countered by Jerry Gordon's bid for a fall mass action without civil disobedience in Washington, D.C. Tense and heated debate on the alternative proposals took place; an irreconcilably divided conference became a likely prospect. At this point Sidney Lens moved into action. A congressional investigative committee once labeled Lens "the peacemaker of the peacemakers," a title he embraced and behind which he put his years of labor negotiating experience. Lens's compromise was simple enough: undertake both the Washington and the Chicago actions. Yet the speech Mark Rudd made before the plenary session of the conference the next day was, according to Peck, "so bad and so horrible that it received very little support." But, Peck adds, "at the same time, the conference could not abdicate . . . political support for the Chicago group." Rudd's speech seems to have been a version of the Boudin/Dohrn/Robbins Weatherman manifesto of a month later: "BRING THE WAR HOME! . . . We are coming back to turn pig city [Chicago] into the people's city."

Mark Rudd was not the only representative of the younger generation to address the conference. David Hawk, age twenty-four, also spoke. He came to Cleveland directly from the formal opening of the national Vietnam Moratorium Committee office in Washington, D.C. on June 30. At that opening, Sam Brown made clear that the Moratorium's goal was to galvanize and express a broad, moderate, majority position against the war through a massive student house-to-house campaign on October 15. All normal university activity on that day would be brought to a halt while the young moderates rang doorbells. At the same time, the Moratorium contained the seeds of a radical program in its intention to escalate month by month. That is, the moratorium on "business as usual" would be expanded by one day for each successive month that passed without a satisfactory negotiated peace or a firm American commitment to withdraw from Vietnam. The radical potential of the idea was recognized at once by Peck and others who saw, too, that the Moratorium would provide an opening to the right for their dysfunctional and, since Chicago, politically isolated Mobilization. Unlike Mark Rudd, David Hawk and his Moratorium proposal were well received, although Halstead asserts that many were skeptical.

As Hawk recalls the events, he was added as a member to the steering committee. At any rate, he worked very closely with its members, especially Peck, Weiss, Meacham, and Fernandez. Peck points to Hawk and Lens as the two people who

the Presidio 27; Irving Sarnoff, Los Angeles Peace Action Council; Cora Weiss, New York Women Strike for Peace.

turned a tense, difficult, and potentially disastrous conference into a success. "What David did," says Peck, "was to keep the Moratorium working in sympathy with what was coming out of the conference. . . . He helped bridge things." On the other hand, "the political broker of that conference was Sid Lens. He [was] the communicator between all of the contending groups." Much frantic negotiating lay behind the tripartite "Joint Majority-Minority Resolution" that Lens brought out of the steering committee and saw through to adoption. The new coalition, nameless at this point, would support the October 15 Vietnam Moratorium; the November 15 demonstration in Washington (and, on the same day, in San Francisco); and —Dellinger's original proposal—the Chicago actions around the Conspiracy trial. A proviso was, however, attached to the last of the three items. Because planning for the Chicago actions was initiated by "other groups," i.e., Weatherman, further negotiation on tactics prior to collaboration would be necessary.

Tension surrounding the conference continued throughout. A long, argumentative evening session among the leaders over a name for the reestablished coalition ended only at two or three in the morning with Douglas Dowd's suggestion that they call themselves the *New* Mobilization Committee to End the War in Vietnam. The bickering extended to naming cochairmen and project directors for the contemplated actions. SWP, Peck believes, tried to isolate him—"because they knew I still tried to maintain good political communications with Dellinger"—by placing him on the Chicago task force, a move he frustrated by switching with Sidney Lens and joining Stewart Meacham as cochair for Washington. The last bit of rancor erupted when Jerry Gordon of CAPAC used his position as conference chairperson to take a valedictory shot at the steering committee, lamenting, according to Halstead, the committee's "high-handedness" in manipulating the question of delegate status. The committee was not amused.

Nevertheless, the adult wing of the antiwar movement survived the test that its youthful counterpart, SDS, had failed. SDS abandoned nonexclusion as a principle and collapsed; the zealots in the self-defined elite of the Rudd-Dohrn faction of SDS slammed shut a door at Chicago that left most SDSers outside the pale. At almost the same time in Cleveland the "old fogies" of the Mobe, as Carl Oglesby called them, survived by keeping the basic tenet of nonexclusion which they had borrowed from SDS and found, by inadvertence, an opening to the right. The invitation extended by David Hawk to support the Vietnam Moratorium meant access to moderate America and, more important, to a great body of American youth who were disaffected by the U.S. role in Vietnam and yet still believed in their country's political processes. Followers a year before in Eugene McCarthy's children's crusade, scorned by an SDS they never much cared for, not radicals, not hippies, neither rebels nor revolutionaries, they were nonetheless prepared to take up a cause that both SDS and the McCarthy campaign had let slip away. Peck was justified in counting the Cleveland conference of 1969 a success.

Almost simultaneously with the end of the Cleveland Conference, Richard Nixon came to a major decision about the prosecution of the war in Vietnam: "I decided to 'go for broke' in the sense that I would attempt to end the war one way or the other—either by negotiated agreement or by an increased use of force." Perhaps Nixon was made aware of what went on in Cleveland, although the conference received little publicity. If the President did not know, he is then crediting himself with the same kind of intuition that the antiwar activists claimed for themselves with reference to his intentions. For he says the decision was made because of "my feeling that unless I could build some momentum behind the peace efforts over the next several weeks, they might be doomed to failure by the calendar. Once the summer was over . . . a massive new antiwar tide would sweep the country during the fall and winter"; and he adds that he and Kissinger in several long sessions "developed an elaborate orchestration of diplomatic, military, and public pressures we would bring to bear on Hanoi."

The secret scheme for military pressure, according to Seymour Hersh, carried the code name Duck Hook, a curious label given the well-known fact that Nixon was a notoriously poor golfer.* Duck Hook is gruesome in its details, as reported by Hersh: "massive bombing of Hanoi, Haiphong, and other key areas in North Vietnam; the mining of harbors and rivers; the bombing of the dike system; a ground invasion of North Vietnam; the destruction—possibly with nuclear devices —of the main north-south passes along the Ho Chi Minh trail . . ." Roger Morris, a former Kissinger aide, published a similar description of these plans in the August 1982 *Playboy* magazine. Morris also reports that Kissinger told the planning group, "I can't believe that a fourth-rate power like North Vietnam doesn't have a breaking point." Duck Hook was prepared in great secrecy under Kissinger's direction by the Office of the Chief of Naval Operations and completed on July 20. The Secretary of Defense, Melvin Laird, was not informed.

Equally secret were the diplomatic maneuvers. "I decided to set November 1, 1969 . . . as the deadline for what in effect would be an ultimatum to North Vietnam," says Nixon. On July 15 a message went to Ho Chi Minh, an invitation to peace negotiations. Within days the North Vietnamese responded with a proposal for a secret meeting between Kissinger and Xuan Thuy, their representative in Paris. But the Nixon courier, Jean Sainteny, a French businessman and diplomat who knew Ho personally, was instructed to add a spoken threat: if the deadline passed without a breakthrough, Nixon would be obliged to take "measures of great consequence and force." Through the summer Ho was bombarded with repetitions of the same threatening message, once from Nixon himself through President Ceauşescu of Romania, and again on August 4, when Kissinger held the first of his secret meetings with the North Vietnamese in Paris. The North Vietnamese, said Kissinger after mentioning the November 1 deadline, were attempting in their propaganda to make this Nixon's war. "If it is," Nixon reports Kissinger as saying, "then he cannot afford not to win it." Ho Chi Minh's reply to all of this came in a letter to the President, dated August 25:

> For this [peace] the United States must cease the war of aggression and withdraw their troops from South Vietnam, respect the right of the popula-

---

* A duck hook is a golf shot that veers sharply off course to the left and into the woods or rough shortly after being launched. The basic golfing flaw is one of overanticipation.

tion of the South and of the Vietnamese nation to dispose of themselves, without foreign influence.

Nixon was taken aback; he considered Ho's reply "a cold rebuff."

The American people were kept in the dark. What they heard instead was their President declaring from the South Lawn of the White House upon his return from Midway that "the door to peace [is] wide open. And now we must invite the leaders of North Vietnam to walk with us through that door." From Guam, where Nixon had gone for the July splashdown of the Apollo 11 mission to the moon, the country heard the enunciation of the "Nixon Doctrine." Many took the Nixon Doctrine to be a declaration forswearing future Vietnams, and they were heartened. They would have been less pleased to know that Nixon explained the doctrine in a White House breakfast meeting with Senate Majority Leader Mike Mansfield as "not a formula for getting America out of Asia, but . . . for staying in [emphasis in original]. . . ." Then in mid-September came the White House announcement that an additional thirty-five thousand American troops would be withdrawn from Vietnam by December 1.

Press and public alike were lulled by these developments. The enormous capacity of the White House to manage the news and control the national mood was augmented considerably by external events that summer. The exploits of Neil Armstrong and Edwin E. Aldrin, Jr., the two Americans who dropped onto the moon's surface, captured the attention of a fascinated and proud nation. In August the White House staged an elaborate state dinner to honor the astronauts and their families at the Century Plaza Hotel in Los Angeles. Three thousand antiwar demonstrators organized by SMC appeared in the streets outside, but it was a low-key, scarcely noticed demonstration. The press described the youthful crowd as good-natured and orderly. A few days later a somewhat larger but equally well-mannered crowd of protesters appeared at the Nixon summer residence in San Clemente. They made no attempt to break through police barricades set up one hundred yards from the entrance to the San Clemente enclave, a quarter of a mile from the Nixon home. The highlight of the protest was a "peace picnic" featuring watermelon, soft drinks, and antiwar speeches.

Another and an extraordinary expression of the country's apparently mellow mood was the Woodstock Music and Art Fair and Aquarian Exposition held in Bethel, New York, about seventy miles northwest of the city of New York on the weekend of August 16. Four hundred thousand young rock music fans descended upon the unprepared town before miles of vehicle-clogged roads in every direction blocked further access. The organizers of the music festival had expected no more than one fourth that number. Rain and an ocean of mud compounded the problems caused by the lack of food, shelter, and sanitary facilities. If many in the vast audience could not hear the hours upon hours of music played by celebrated rock groups on stage, few cared. Over 90 percent of those on hand were smoking marijuana or using stronger drugs, including badly manufactured LSD, that were openly peddled in the crowd. From the platform "Wavy Gravy"—real name, Hugh Romney—of the Hog Farm commune in New Mexico, warned against the bad drugs on sale. The Hog Farm group was on hand to minister to those in trouble. There were three deaths, one from a drug overdose, and hundreds of the young were "freaked out" on "bad trips." As amazing as the open use of illegal drugs was the absence of violence. One local policeman described the participants as "the most courteous, considerate, and well-behaved group of kids I have ever been in contact with. . . ." The Age of Aquarius they were celebrating was billed in the rock musical *Hair* as an age of love and peace. Despite the fact that some of the lyrics heard at the "Aquarian Exposition" carried an incendiary, revolutionary message, the audience, or those who could move at all through the haze of marijuana and the seas of mud, wanted only the dancing. Woodstock became an immediate symbol of the countercultural revolt of American youth. The editorial writers of the New York *Times* called Woodstock an "outrageous episode" for which "all the adults who helped create the society against which these young people are so feverishly rebelling must bear a share of responsibility. . . ." A day later the same editorialists had themselves mellowed. Woodstock, they said, was "essentially a phenomenon of innocence."

The SDS/Weatherman appraisal of their contemporaries' activities that summer was less sympathetic: "Fuck hippie capitalism. Build culture in struggle." "Events like the Woodstock gentleness freakout," they declared, "and the demonstration [at San Clemente] indicate that as long as militancy isn't a threat, pig and ruling class approval is forthcoming." These words were part of a Weatherman manifesto issued in August announcing a demonstration for October 8–11 in Chicago. It would come to be known as the "Days of Rage." By this time the New Mobilization had exercised its option on further negotiations before committing itself to participation in and support of Weatherman actions surrounding the trial of the Chicago 8. Both Sidney Peck and Sidney Lens remember the meeting with Weathermen Kathy Boudin, Bill Ayers, and Terry Robbins as cordial and polite. "It was not a shouting match in any way," says Peck. But the differences between a broad antiwar movement and a narrow faction of "antiimperialists" devoted to fighting in the streets were irreconcilable. Boudin and the others were "up front," according to Peck, about what they were going to do, and "they wanted full rein on the politics of the action . . . and us to come up with the money. We just said, 'No way.'" The Weatherman response in print was to call the Mobilization "the twice-yearly Sunday afternoon anti-war movement" and declare that "we declined their offer of support."

"This is an awful small group to start a revolution," said one student from Oregon as he surveyed the small crowd in Lincoln Park on the evening of October 8. The thousands upon thousands of supporters expected by Mark Rudd turned out to be no more than three hundred on any given occasion over the next four days, the approximate number for a street gang rumble in any big city. That evening, Tom Hayden addressed the mob briefly before it set out to rampage: "People have been saying the Conspiracy 8 [whose trial began on September 24] are against this demonstration. That is not true. . . . We are glad to see the militancy of Chicago increased." Bernardine Dohrn also exhorted the crowd before it set off, howling and screaming, pursued by hundreds of Chicago police, to "trash" the streets of

Chicago's plush Gold Coast district. For sixty minutes the berserk mob terrorized that neighborhood, breaking windows, smashing cars, assaulting unprotected civilians and police alike. Only sixty-eight of the nearly three hundred arrests made during the Days of Rage occurred that night. But wherever the Weathermen congregated in the next few days the police moved in to continue the arrests. No one mourned the harsh treatment handed out by the police, who suffered twenty-eight injuries the first night. Least sympathetic of all were the Black Panthers. On the second day, Fred Hampton, an Illinois leader of the Panthers who would himself be shot by Chicago police a few months later, called the action "anarchistic, opportunistic, adventuristic and Custeristic." The "Custer" Hampton had in mind was undoubtedly Mark Rudd, whom he also labeled a "mother-fucking masochist." Rudd, however, was more the Cowardly Lion than a Custer. On the one night of dangerous rampaging he quietly slipped away before the action began.

The Days of Rage were not quite a last stand for Weatherman. The remnants, fast dwindling in number, limped out of Chicago leaving $234,000 in cash behind to cover ten times that amount in bail bonds. A good portion of this money, presumably from parental coffers, was lost when several of the Weatherbureau leadership failed to show up for later trials. Weathermen—along with the Crazies, Youth Against Fascism, Mad Dogs, and others—did take part in the November 15 attack at the Justice Department in Washington that made John Mitchell and Weatherman Bill Ayers think of the Russian Revolution. The last public, aboveground gathering of Weathermen took place toward the end of December at Flint, Michigan. It was there that Bernardine Dohrn, by now a parody of her revolutionary self, made a statement that announced her own alienation even as it glorified the recent Charles Manson gang murders of a young movie actress, Sharon Tate, and her friends: "Dig it, first they killed those pigs, then they ate dinner in the same room with them, then they even shoved a fork in the victim's stomach! Wild!" The Weathermen, now no more than two hundred, went underground a few days later. John Jacobs, a leader in the Dohrn wing of SDS since his days as Mark Rudd's associate in the "action" faction on the Columbia campus, explained to the Flint meeting what would be the underground Weatherman program: "We're against all that's 'good and decent' in honkey America. We will burn and loot and destroy. We are the incubation of your mother's nightmare." The same kind of bullying threat, minus the colorful language, came from the White House underground. Egil Krogh, Jr., the young Nixon attorney who would go to jail for his activities as chief of the undercover White House Plumbers operation, is quoted as boasting, "Anyone who opposes us, we'll destroy. As a matter of fact, anyone who doesn't support us, we'll destroy."

Rennie Davis believes that the Days of Rage were no more than pretext for the Weatherman disappearance underground. From the other side of the SDS spectrum Jared Israel has a somewhat similar view. The Days of Rage were in keeping with what Weatherman was, "hysterical brats." It was a case of, "If I'm going to be dramatic, I'll be hysterically dramatic." The Weatherman walkout in June, moreover, was not a walkout at all: "It was an attempt to destroy SDS. And it was successful. But that was because of us [PL]. We destroyed SDS; they didn't."

More precisely, the destruction of the SDS remnant that now lay in the hands of PL/WSA came about through a decision of the shadowy New York leadership of PL, to whom Israel and other PL campus organizers both reported and submitted. That summer, Israel was summoned before the party chiefs, whose methods owed as much to Stalin as to Mao. Israel and Jeff Gordon, another PL organizer, were told that the war was no longer an issue, that the job now was to organize and win over campus workers and make WSA a reality. "I started crying . . . I said it would destroy SDS. . . . They had never betrayed us before—in their minds, [yes,] but not in practice." Although the two "knew it was wrong," the directive was relayed to the rank and file. Workers on college campuses where WSA retained its influence won some benefits in 1969, but the SDS that Israel and others hoped to keep alive withered away.

Israel was first expelled from the national PL committee for being a male chauvinist, an ironic charge for PL to make, and yet he still remained a subservient member of the party. For him, the "God that failed"—communism—did not fail completely until 1973, when he rebelled against party policy and endured a star-chamber hearing. "It was a secret meeting—no one knew where I was—in a house without any furniture. . . . I had this eerie feeling . . . they began by reading a list of names: so-and-so—dead; so-and-so—dead; so-and-so—out of work. These were all people who had opposed the leadership. I was told, 'This is not a pleasant thing to do, but we have to do it.' " The experience confirmed Israel's suspicion that he was not really a Communist, not really "a slate to be written on." He returned to Boston, lived quietly with his family, started a small business in the classic capitalist-entrepreneurial tradition, and confined his political activity to a parents' association at his children's elementary school.

The antiwar movement in the United States did not fall or rise with the withering away or renascence of national coalitions like the Mobe or SDS. Dependency ran the other way, a fact SDS lost sight of in the end. As with its predecessors, the vitality of the New Mobilization to End the War in Vietnam drew upon the energies of a vast network of independent groups—local, regional, campus—spread across the entire country. Some of these groups, like Women Strike for Peace and the American Friends Service Committee, had their own national offices, but most did not. What they had in common was a determination to work on day by day against the war by their own means, and for their own reasons, whether or not there existed a "twice-yearly Sunday afternoon anti-war movement."

All over the country, not just in Washington, the names of the war dead were read at vigil services; draft board raids continued; the ancient concept of "sanctuary," resurrected in May 1968 at the Arlington Street Church in Boston, spread as far as Honolulu, where twenty servicemen took refuge in a local church; a Taxpayers' Call-in-to-Congress day was announced; small bands of pickets greeted Nixon when he came to address the United Nations in New York City.

On July 8, a historic meeting took place in Canada, not far from the U.S. border. At Rainbow Bridge at Niagara Falls, Ontario, a large delegation of WSP, led by Jane Spock and Helen Boston, a black Gold Star mother from Brooklyn, pushed past vainly protesting U.S. border officials.† Waiting to meet them on the other side were three distinguished women visitors from Vietnam, one from Hanoi, the other two from South Vietnam's National Liberation Front. AMERICAN WOMEN GREET VIETNAMESE WOMEN IN PEACE read the WSP banner. Among the Americans who spoke were Willie Hardy, a mother of five and organizer of the Washington D.C. poor; Helen Boston, who felt her son had "died in vain"; Mary Melville, who had been shaped by her experience as a Maryknoll nun in the barrios of Central America to become a member of the Catonsville 9 and had just recently been arrested for her part in a D.C. raid on The Dow Chemical Company; and Jane Spock, who read a message from her husband, Dr. Benjamin Spock. Cora Weiss, also present that day, remembers that in 1964 WSP plunged in "full steam ahead [against the war] under the banner that all women are our sisters." Thus the meeting at Rainbow Bridge was charged with deep emotion as the common bonds of sisterhood, family, poverty, repression, and wartime suffering were explored. A month later in New York, the Fifth Avenue Peace Parade Committee, still under the firm leadership of Norma Becker, commemorated the twenty-fourth anniversary of Hiroshima in a series of demonstrations. More than twenty-five thousand marchers gathered for the annual parade, this time on Seventh Avenue, to protest the war. Throughout the summer, protesters in swarms of ten, twenty, and thousands—gadflies on the body politic—pestered their government. That so many were women and so many were young was small comfort to the old men in the seats of power.

Unnoticed by Washington, the press, and the general public, the work of the Moratorium continued during those summer weeks. Four skillful organizers, trained and politically matured by their work in the 1968 presidential campaign of Eugene McCarthy, were in charge: in addition to Sam Brown and David Hawk, they were Marge Sklencar, a former student leader at Mundelein College in Chicago, where she had been president of both the student government and SDS; and David Mixner, on leave from Senator McGovern's commission for the reform of the Democratic Party. The Moratorium organizers had the political savvy to avoid the shoals on either hand for those who would sail in New Left waters. "Some elements in the Mobilization," says David Hawk, "were initially suspicious of the Moratorium on the grounds that we were setting up a counter for SDS." Then, adds Hawk, there were problems from a contrary direction. Allard Lowenstein, now a member of the New York congressional delegation, had been political mentor for all four Moratorium leaders in the McCarthy days. It was Lowenstein who engineered the publicity that won Hawk and his student leaders a meeting with Kissinger in April. One Lowenstein project for early in the summer was aborted when his erstwhile lieutenants balked. Sam Brown remembers that "Allard wanted to do a march on July Fourth from Arlington Cemetery to the Washington Monument . . . sort of patriots against the war. We—David [Hawk] and I—thought you'd lose your base, the people who do the work." "There was," says Hawk, "a

† In a masterstroke of irony the guardians of the border had denied the women passage across the Peace Bridge in Buffalo.

short-lived tactical split. Allard was then trying to set up an operation that was very similar in strategy to the Moratorium . . . but that would be explicitly anti-Left. And we said no, that would be divisive. It would get into intra-peace movement fights. And it would give the Administration a handle to attack the peace movement and divert public attention from the war we sought to end. We're going to do our thing."

Doing their thing meant organizing among the current crop of college students. By the time the fall semester was under way, student leaders on three hundred campuses across the country were in full swing and more would join in the weeks to come. There remained, the leaders thought, only the task of getting buttons, flyers, all sorts of printed materials out to the colleges in sufficient amounts, and answering requests for speakers. The Moratorium goal, even as late as mid-September, was to have campus demonstrations on October 15 and then, a month later, to move off the campus into the surrounding communities for two days in November. "Our strategy," admits Hawk, "got blown out of the water, because it caught on like wildfire." Jerome Grossman's original notion of a broad nationwide "strike," obscured as it was by exuberant translation into the language of youthful, campus protest, could not remain submerged. The Moratorium struck a chord deep in the disturbed recesses of the American spirit.

The leaders of the previously isolated Mobilization recognized the opportunity. "It was a very, very mainstream approach," says Sidney Peck. "You didn't have to be out on the barricades. . . . It allowed people to express their opposition to the war in a way that was comfortable. It could be wearing an armband, it could be honking your horn, it could be leaving your lights on. No matter what your politics were, if you were against the war, here was a chance to express it . . . and yet there was a radical potential in the tactic [of escalation month by month]." Stewart Meacham, of the AFSC and a figure in the Mobilization since its beginning in 1966, found a way to capitalize on this opportunity. "The Stewart Meacham Express," as David Hawk called it, consisted of small teams, usually with both the Moratorium and the Mobilization represented, that undertook something like the old whistle-stop campaign treks. Each team trip lasted a week and visited six or seven cities in a network built up over the years by the Mobe. "In many dozens of cities," claims Sidney Lens, "the Mobe *was* the Moratorium." A grass-roots structure was thus put in place over the month of September without the notice of either Washington or the national press.

The sluggishness of the press was an irritation to Jerome Grossman: MassPax turned out a steady stream of press handouts for the local papers on the Moratorium, but to no avail until well into September. He remembers: "The Boston *Globe* —supposed to be so liberal—they wouldn't use any of it. Then the Boston *Herald* called. They heard . . . that here was a businessman telling his employees not to work that day. . . . They ran the story and the *Globe* took it up." In Washington the national press was equally obtuse. On September 27 the New York *Times* finally acknowledged, deep in a story on senatorial reaction, that the Moratorium "shows signs of developing into a national day of protest." On October 5, three months after the Cleveland Conference and long after the Mobe had taken office space one floor above the Moratorium at 1029 Vermont Avenue, the *Times* reported that the Vietnam Moratorium and the erroneously labeled National Mobilization to End the War in Vietnam "joined forces yesterday."

David Mixner was the Moratorium's contact person with Congress. In this capacity he went quietly about the business of securing endorsements for October 15. As the endorsements came in, the Moratorium leaders held them in hand, awaiting the propitious moment to go public. Mixner's task was not easy. Even the closet doves among the Democrats who knew that the President's "honeymoon" period was over and that a Republican administration in office removed the restraints of party loyalty had political costs to calculate. Their constituents at home were as badly divided on the Vietnam issue as Congress itself, if not more so. Senator George Aiken (R-Vermont), who suggested in 1966 that the United States should declare a victory and pull out, endorsed the Moratorium promptly. Morris Udall (D-Arizona) hesitated only briefly. Although Udall had broken with LBJ over the war in 1967, endorsement of the Moratorium was a different question. Sam Brown, spokesman for the Moratorium and its principal money-raiser, tells the story:

> He [Udall] was then running for speaker [of the House of Representatives]. David [Mixner] had been over to see him, and he said, "We've got to go back to see him." It was after the office had closed, and we spent an hour and a half, two hours. He [Udall] had said, "Look, I'd really like to do something. I understand other people are, but it's more important for me to be speaker. I can do more if I'm speaker, and I won't be speaker if I do this."
>
> We went home, and the following morning about seven o'clock the phone rang in the house where we all lived. It was Mo Udall. He said, "Look, I've thought about it overnight and haven't slept very much. What I said to you last night is fundamentally wrong. I ought to do what I think is the right thing to do, not what is . . . politically expedient. Use my name. I'll endorse [the Moratorium]."

Other endorsements came soon after from sources the Mobilization could never hope to tap: dozens of senators and representatives; Averell Harriman, the grand old man of American diplomacy; the United Automobile Workers and Walter Reuther; the United Shoe Workers of America; Arthur J. Goldberg, former U.S. representative to the United Nations and former Supreme Court justice.

Money rolled in, much of it in five and ten-dollar amounts, day after day. Sam Brown estimates the Vietnam Moratorium spent over $700,000 in its nine months of existence. Telephone and postage bills were enormous, and more than thirty-five paid workers, in addition to uncounted numbers of volunteers, were on the Washington staff. Another ten or twelve offices were set up in cities across the country. Three full-page ads were run in the New York *Times* at a cost of $26,328. One of these, according to Brown, was probably the most successful money-raising advertisement ever run in the *Times*. He remembers it as showing a "crew-cut, red-necked father and his long-haired, hippie son standing with their arms around each other. Underneath, it just said, 'October 15, Fathers and Sons Together Against the

War.'" In fact, the father depicted in the ad was a well-groomed, manicured, middle-management type and look-alike for Nixon's Vice President, Spiro Agnew.

By the last week in September, President Nixon realized that something big was afoot. At a press conference on the twenty-sixth at which he was repeatedly questioned about the war and its critics, Nixon stated, "I understand that there has been and continues to be opposition to the war in Vietnam on the campuses and also in the nation. . . . However, under no circumstances will I be affected whatever by it." It was the opening Brown and his Vietnam Moratorium cohorts were looking for. On the day before, Senator Charles Goodell (R-New York) had introduced a resolution calling upon the President to withdraw all troops from Vietnam by December 1970. And even as the President spoke to the press, a group of Democratic senators was meeting in secret caucus for a decision to support the October 15 protest. Senators Muskie, McGovern, and Kennedy were in the group that met at the call of Fred Harris (D-Oklahoma), not a known dove. The next day, a Saturday, Sam Brown, as spokesman for the Vietnam Moratorium Committee, called a press conference.

David Hawk has a vivid recollection of it:

> Suddenly, we were in the extraordinary position of holding a press conference to respond to the President of the United States! Usually you hold a press conference and five or six reporters show up and you can't even get a story out of it. Now there were thirty or forty. And we ended up on the evening news and the front page of the Washington *Post*. What we said was "Surely he [Nixon] didn't mean what he said, for obviously the President of the United States does take into account the feelings and opinions of the American people. Furthermore, it's not only students. We released the list of congressional and other national leaders who were endorsing us. From then on it just mushroomed. CBS news portrayed our logo, the Moratorium symbol. [We became] . . . a major story, and much of the press didn't know who we were. All the Washington press corps were lining up to find out what was going to happen, who was behind this, what was this Moratorium business!

At last discovered by the press and television, and essentially endorsed by centrist Democratic officials who had supported the war under LBJ, a momentary problem for the Moratorium, in Hawk's view, became one of preventing misperception of political partisanship. "We were worried that overembrace by Humphrey Democrats would give Nixon a handle to turn it around." This was a prospect, however, that did not perturb Sam Brown: "I would have regarded that as victory. If the Democratic Party had wanted to make the war the central issue in a campaign against Richard Nixon, . . . amen, brother! Go for it! The intent, as far as I was concerned, was to move the establishment."

The establishment, or that part of it at 1600 Pennsylvania Avenue, did move, and rapidly. On the Tuesday following the Moratorium's press conference, Nixon summoned his congressional leaders to the White House and dispatched the Republican minority leaders, Senator Hugh Scott and Representative Gerald Ford, to the

Front Lawn to lament those who would "bug out," "cut and run," and "capitulate." As for Moratorium Day, Scott declared that the students "ought to demonstrate against Hanoi." Adopting the language of their opponents, Scott and Ford sought a sixty-day "moratorium" on criticism to give the President time to negotiate. Nixon himself went to the Rose Garden, where, in a ceremony honoring the Marine regiment that defended the city of Hue in 1968, he urged Americans not to "buckle under" or "run away." The next day, in a bit of prearranged melodrama, Nixon telephoned Henry Kissinger while Kissinger was in conference with the Russian ambassador, Anatoly Dobrynin, to announce that "as far as Vietnam is concerned, the train has left the station and is now headed down the track." It was the last of the signals on the November 1 deadline. A week later, columnist David Broder wrote that "it is becoming more obvious with every passing day that the men and the movement that broke Lyndon Johnson's authority in 1968 are out to break Richard Nixon in 1969."

But what was going on in Washington hardly bore the marks of a cabal at work. A bipartisan group of nine senators and representatives announced their support of the Moratorium, calling it "positive, constructive, and non-violent." A resolution cosponsored by 108 representatives was introduced in the House in support of the President's "expressed determination to withdraw our forces at the earliest practicable date." A more strongly worded resolution was prepared for the Senate and another, offered by two Republican members of the House, sought repeal of the Tonkin Gulf Resolution. Counting Republican Senator Goodell's S-2000 bill, ten such resolutions were proposed as Moratorium Day drew closer. The intent of the Moratorium leaders to keep the ending of the war from becoming a purely partisan issue on Capitol Hill was realized.

One unhappy example of congressional bipartisanship occurred when the Democratic leadership of the House of Representatives allowed their Republican counterparts to shut off an all-night session on the topic of Vietnam scheduled for the evening and morning hours of October 14–15. Twenty-three members, all but one Democrats, had been granted unanimous consent by the House to speak for one hour each. The idea was to keep the lights of the Capitol ablaze and its flag flying through the night in support of the Vietnam Moratorium activities and protest. The Administration's critics, as usual, were accused of giving "aid and comfort to the enemy"; before the debate began, the White House transmitted a message of support for the Moratorium from North Vietnam's Premier Pham Van Dong. The debate lasted less than four hours, until shortly after 11 P.M., before a motion to adjourn was offered at a point of parliamentary confusion that neither Speaker John W. McCormack nor the Democratic floor leader, Carl Albert of Oklahoma, chose to control. Speaker McCormack, had, in fact, told reporters before the session began that he had no intention of allowing it to run all night. The motion carried by a vote of 112–110 only because of tremendous pressure brought to bear on individual Republicans by the White House that resulted in several members shifting their votes. The House galleries were filled with young people as the disappointing parliamentary maneuvering went on. The debate, such as it was, was the longest ever on the subject of Vietnam in the House of Representatives. Only two of the twenty-three representatives scheduled to speak had done so before the sudden adjournment.

Vietnam Moratorium Day was peaceably observed by millions of Americans in thousands of cities, towns, and villages across the nation. Historians at the Library of Congress told reporters what the young organizers of the event knew well, that it was unique in American history, the largest public protest ever on a national scale. But the special quality of the day went deeper. A Whitmanesque alchemy was at work; a gentle spirit of comradely acceptance pervaded gatherings large and small where every shade of dissent was represented. For some, long kept in silent restraint by radical usurpation of the ground they might have taken, it was, at last, a chance to be safely heard. Only a few minor incidents of violence were reported, and these, as often as not, involved the presence of antidemonstration hecklers. There were no ugly mob scenes; instead, in town after town, there were silent, reproachful vigils, endless reading of the names of the Americans killed in the war, candlelight processions, church services, and, in some cities, larger meetings where politicians spoke in muted terms. The extremes of citizen opposition to the war were come together, and whatever radical impulse strayed about the fringes of these gatherings was submerged in a spirit of civic solidarity and common enterprise. The largest turnout was in Boston, where a crowd of one hundred thousand, most of them students from the many local colleges, assembled under a warm October sun to hear Senator George McGovern speak; the Boston *Globe* headlined the event as a POLITICAL WOODSTOCK ON THE COMMON. But the mellow mood emerged from deeper in the American past. For one twenty-four-hour period the antiwar movement became as American as the Stars and Stripes. The mood of the day was not unlike an old-fashioned, small-town Memorial Day or Fourth of July celebration: solemn, joyous, and, for many, patriotic. Stewart Udall, former Secretary of the Interior, thought the day had the feeling of "a great town meeting." The biggest response for McGovern came when he announced that in the day's World Series game the long-downtrodden New York Mets had defeated the Baltimore Orioles, 2–1. And the crowd saluted with cheers usually reserved for holiday fireworks a skywriting plane that marked out a perfect peace symbol on the cloudless sky blue slate overhead.

What began as a day of student protest spilled out into the adult community. Fifty congressmen and other leaders from the world of politics and diplomacy set out on multiple speaking assignments. Clergy, doctors, and lawyers were caught up in the events. A crowd of twenty thousand gathered on Wall Street to hear Bill Moyers, once an assistant in the Johnson White House. An after-work rally in Bryant Park was jammed with people who left Times Square traffic hopelessly snarled as they marched to the site. Mayor Lindsay decreed the day a day of mourning and ordered the city's flags to be at half-staff. In Washington, as the day's light dwindled, Coretta Scott King addressed a crowd of thirty thousand before leading a candlelight procession past the White House gates. The soft refrain of "Give Peace a Chance" was repeated over and over as the solemn marchers, three or four abreast, reached the Nixon abode. "The whole world is watching. Why aren't you?" one marcher cried out. A presidential spokesman declined comment on Mr. Nixon's mood.

Chilling weather in the northern plains and heavy rains on the West Coast had only slight effect on demonstrations in those areas. In Minneapolis, five thousand nonstudents joined a crowd of equal numbers from the University of Minnesota in a march to the Federal Building. Fifteen hundred gathered in the rain at San Francisco, while further south, in Nixon country, a state college in Orange County held its first antiwar protest, during which the wife of the president of Nixon's alma mater lit a butane "flame of life" on the Whittier College campus as "a constant reminder of those who have died and are dying" in Vietnam. Cleveland had its largest protest demonstration ever. In Chicago, where concern after the Days of Rage led organizers to downplay events, a rally at the Civic Center attracted ten thousand. Over and over, and notably in areas where support for the war was strong, the Moratorium was observed: five thousand in Salt Lake City; crowds of equal size in Atlanta, Little Rock, and Austin; twelve thousand in Pittsburgh, where the city council endorsed the day's purpose. Only where radical protest in previous years had found its strongest expression, at CCNY in New York, for example, or the University of California at Berkeley, were the turnouts small.

Millions of Americans protested on Vietnam Moratorium Day, many for the first time; other millions remained contemptuous and angry at what they considered disloyalty. A Dallas businessman who stood outside the state fairgrounds to read the names of Texans killed in Vietnam was spat upon and his family called "Dirty Commies." In Ithaca, where Senator Goodell was addressing eight thousand Cornell students, a middle-aged man in a business suit rode a horse across the campus carrying a sign that read SUPPORT NIXON, NOT REDS. A New York City councilman, Matthew Troy, Jr., climbed in the wind to the catwalk of the cupola of city hall and raised the American flag to the flagpole's peak.‡ In the sky over Boston Common a plane towed a sign proclaiming WE SUPPORT NIXON. Sharply worded editorials in newspapers across the country reflected people's polarization. An extreme example on the conservative side came from the Manchester, New Hampshire, *Union Leader*. Its publisher, William Loeb, far to the right of most Republicans (President Eisenhower was "A Stinking Hypocrite" and his Vice President, Richard Nixon, "Keyhole Dick"), was fond of displacing the news with his own editorial thoughts. On the day before the Moratorium the *Union Leader* carried this statement across the top of its front page: ATTENTION ALL PEACE MARCHERS: HIPPIES, YIPPIES, BEATNIKS, PEACENIKS, YELLOW BELLIES, TRAITORS, COMMIES AND THEIR AGENTS AND DUPES—HELP KEEP OUR CITY CLEAN! . . . JUST BY STAYING OUT OF IT! Manchester, however, had poignant reason to ponder the wisdom of the war. Two months earlier, five Manchester National Guardsmen were killed by a land mine explosion in Vietnam just a week before they were due to return home.

It was a day of enormous satisfaction for Jerome Grossman. He thinks that as

‡ The battle of the flag was repeated in many cities. In Atlanta the flag was flown at full-staff at the state capitol and at half-staff over city hall.

many as ten million Americans may have participated, although numbers are hard to come by for an observance so scattered and diverse. He could look back to the days of Joseph McCarthy and virulent anticommunism, when Boston's Richard Cardinal Cushing, speaking of Communists, said, "If it walks like a duck, talks like a duck, acts like a duck—then it's a duck"; he could recall the day in 1964 when he was on a picket line outside Fenway Park in Boston, where Barry Goldwater was campaigning as the Tonkin Gulf Resolution was passed, and Grossman turned to another picket on the line to say, "One more thing like Tonkin Gulf and we won't picket Goldwater anymore; we'll picket Johnson." And now a day of protest countrywide that he not only initiated, but had insisted should be open to all: "That was probably my most important contribution, that they should not be aligned—absence of [party] line. . . . You could be against the war for whatever reason you wanted. . . . I think that was as important as any contribution I made—to keep [it] open."

Grossman's Boston was a good example of the unaligned at last aroused. The Boston *Globe* took more than ten pages to cover the day apart from the passive gathering of one hundred thousand on the Boston Common. In the shadows of the Old South Meeting House on Washington Street, white-smocked doctors solicited signatures on petitions against the war from passing businessmen headed for the financial district. Old South was the building in which, in 1773, Samuel Adams gave the signal that began the Boston Tea Party with the words "This meeting can do nothing more to save the country." In Faneuil Hall, Boston's "Cradle of Liberty," four hundred lawyers met to protest the war and listen docilely to a neophyte attorney who chided them for their tardy action. Typically, the stories coming in from the suburbs were of young mothers, middle-aged women, and the elderly giving voice to long-submerged doubt or conviction. The list of towns reads like a Revolutionary War roll call: Sudbury, Concord, Ipswich, Marblehead, Newburyport, Woburn, Wayland, Watertown, Lexington, and many others. On the Green in Lexington, standing near the minuteman statue, Republican Governor Francis Sargent told a crowd that included hecklers, "This war is costing America its soul." In 1775 General Gage, in charge of British troops in the Bay Colony, wrote to Lord Dartmouth: "This province began it. I might say this town, for here the arch-rebels formed their scheme long ago." Richard Nixon and Jerome Grossman each could have his own appreciation of that complaint.

It was Jerome Grossman who had invited George McGovern to Boston for the Moratorium. As the limousine that brought them from the airport and a frosty reception at city hall swung onto Arlington Street, a block from Boston Common, Grossman turned to McGovern and said, "George, I'm not going with you." "What do you mean, you're not going with me?" McGovern asked. "I know where I belong on this day," said Grossman. "I belong in Waban [a tiny enclave in the Boston suburb of Newton], outside the Waban supermarket, handing out leaflets and talking to my neighbors." Whereupon he ducked into the nearby subway that would take him home. Grossman explains his actions:

I was against that demonstration [on the Common], but I was outvoted. . . . So I got him [McGovern]. He came as a favor to me. But . . . what could I do there? I did more at the Waban supermarket. Once [the demonstrations] get too big, they don't need me anymore. . . . My point was there wasn't enough return to the investment. When people go to a demonstration in Washington, it takes one or two or three days. Then I think of the emotional drain. Very important is the recovery, and there is a certain amount of fear. I don't care how cheap you go, it costs a lot of money.

Put all that together—make a package of it—and what else could you do with it? Holy mackerel! If you worked in your own community—ten people —you could convert the whole damn town!

Grossman thought he had done just that on Moratorium night when he spoke without notes to a jam-packed crowd at Roberts Auditorium on the campus of Boston College. His son was in the audience and "got scared, because the audience was responding . . . in such a wave. There was a wave of emotion. . . . At that moment I *knew* that the war had to end that second. . . . It was some day!"

Howard Zinn spoke at Boston College that night also: "I had been invited to B.C. two years before to speak about the war, and at that time I spoke to an absolutely cold group that just tolerated my presence. On October 15, '69, the president and faculty were there and the crowd was enormously enthusiastic. It was a complete turnaround."

Sam Brown, on Moratorium Day, "was in Washington, I was in the office. It was a working day. . . . We had a pretty decent idea of what was going to happen, because we had contact at any given time with four or five hundred communities across the country. We encouraged the media to *see* the events that were most representative of the day. We didn't send them to Bryant Park. . . . When it happens in Kansas, that's a different kind of news. . . . So we spent most of October 15 taking calls."

October 15 was an ordinary working day for President Nixon also, as his press secretary took pains to point out. On his agenda were Latin America, inflation, domestic hunger, and "normal staff discussions." But there are some indications to the contrary. On Tuesday, the day before the Moratorium, Henry Kissinger read to the President a transcript of a Hanoi radio broadcast to the American people by the new Premier, Pham Van Dong. It came not twenty-four hours after the announcement in Washington that President Nixon would make a major speech concerning Vietnam on November 3. The President had hoped the announcement "would give Hanoi second thoughts about fishing in our troubled domestic waters." Pham Van Dong's message, embedded in military phraseology, left no room for hope on that score:

This fall large sections of the American people, encouraged and supported by many peace-and-justice-loving American personages, are launching a broad and powerful offensive throughout the United States to demand that the Nixon Administration put an end to the Vietnam aggressive war and immediately bring all American troops home. . . .

> We are firmly confident that . . . the struggle of the Vietnamese people and U.S. progressive people against U.S. aggression will certainly be crowned with total victory.
>
> May your fall offensive succeed splendidly.

Nixon immediately sent Vice President Agnew before the press to demand that the leaders and sponsors of the Moratorium repudiate the support of a regime that "has on its hands the blood of forty thousand Americans." The press reaction infuriated the President. Their question for Agnew, as reported in the Nixon memoirs, was "Isn't seizing upon this letter a last-minute attempt to dampen down the Moratorium by the administration?" When the press stands up to the White House there is reason to ponder, to worry. The President did, as he himself makes clear. As the night of October 15 came on, "I thought about the irony of this protest for peace. It had, I believed, destroyed whatever small possibility may still have existed of ending the war in 1969. . . . I would have to adjust my plans accordingly. . . . At the top of the page of preliminary notes I was making for my November 3 speech, I wrote: 'Don't get rattled—don't waver—don't react.' "

1969:
Mobilization:
"Give Peace a Chance"

THE SUCCESS of Vietnam Moratorium Day meant that Nixon's decision, taken in July, to bully his way to a negotiated peace on his terms, to "go for broke," was no longer a viable option. The Duck Hook planning pressed so assiduously by Kissinger and his aides suffered the destiny its name implied and was irretrievably lost to the present occasion. Even as the President was coming to this realization in his White House study on the night of October 15, work still went on below in the basement precincts assigned to Kissinger and his staff. One young assistant to Kissinger, William Watts, whose job it was to work on a tough-talking draft of the November 3 speech for the President, recalled for Seymour Hersh how he emerged one October evening for a breath of air and walked over to the gate to observe a demonstration in progress. It was almost certainly the march led by Coretta Scott King from the Washington Monument to the White House on the night of October 15. Watts saw hundreds of people carrying candles. Moving closer, he saw his own wife and children pass by, each with a lighted candle. "I felt like throwing up," Watts said. "There they are demonstrating against me, and here I am inside writing a speech."

The President did not use the draft prepared by the Kissinger team for the November 3 speech. He obliquely and mildly observes only that "Kissinger was advocating a very hard line." Instead he devoted himself wholeheartedly to the task without calling upon the regular staff of White House ghostwriters at his command. He seems to have worked at little else in the interval between October 15 and November 3. The lesson applied came right out of *Six Crises:* as was the case with the 1952 "Checkers" speech, it would be Richard Nixon alone in his own *persona,* speaking directly to the American people over the heads of an unsympathetic, even hostile, press corps. There was, however, some work to be left for other hands.

Testimony in the Chicago Conspiracy trial, which had opened in September and would continue into February, lifted the veil of official secrecy slightly to disclose the government's use of illegal wiretaps, informers, and provocateurs against the Mobe, or at least against its earlier avatar, the National Mobilization Committee to End the War in Vietnam. "Dirty tricks" were also employed against the New Mobilization almost from the day it was formed. The government's aim was to disrupt the planning and logistics for November 15, and it took many forms. One effort took the form of a bogus letter, prepared by the FBI but purporting to come from the Black United Front (BUF) of Washington, D.C. The letter, addressed to Abe Bloom, the Washington coordinator for the Mobilization, demanded an initial payment of twenty-five thousand dollars by the Mobe to BUF as a token of good faith before entering into negotiations around the planned demonstration. Sidney Peck has a copy of the FBI memorandum, dated August 22, 1969, that contemplates the possible results of the forgery: "The resulting bickering, resentment and distrust could be fomented by sources with the hope that the New Left and the Blacks become so ineffective they will be devoting all their time and energy defending themselves. . . . It is conceivable that the resulting situation might force the NMC to cancel its mass rally on [sic] Washington, D.C., 11/15/69." While the Mobilization administrative coordinating committee was in session to discuss a response to the fake demand, Peck was called to the phone. The caller, in the course of threatening physical abuse, used information that made Peck realize that the Mobe had at least one informant in its West Coast ranks.

Peck and others objected vigorously to meeting the demands of the letter—to begin with, the Mobe did not have twenty-five thousand dollars—but it was the principled refusal of a respected member of the Washington black community, Julius Hobson, to dignify that kind of blackmail in any manner, that carried the day. The FBI was not, however, done with the matter. Its next fabrication was a leaflet with the heading GIVE THEM BANANAS, and purporting to come from the hand of Sidney Peck. It was a blatantly racial statement, obscene in every meaning of the word, its message printed on the page around a crude cartoon of an apelike figure. The message conveyed was that the blacks of Washington were a subhuman species, no better than animals, deserving no more than bananas as payment in kind. "Suck on your bananas," it ended, "and someday you might learn how to make fire or build a wheel. Affectionately, Sid." This time the cover letter, dated 10/10/69, proposes anonymous mailings of the leaflet in the New York and Washington areas "prior to the 11/15/69 demonstration," and acknowledges that the "material is racial in tone." Yet another document shows that the FBI readied a spurious press release in which an "unnamed" BUF official is quoted as calling Hobson an "Uncle Tom" and said to doubt his suitability as a candidate for the District of Columbia School Board.*

Nixon depended on his Vice President to savage the antiwar movement. Agnew went on the attack four days after the Moratorium. Speaking of it, Agnew em-

---

* In 1981 the widow of Julius Hobson instituted a successful suit in federal court against national and local FBI executives or agents and against District of Columbia police officials. She was joined in the suit by Abraham Bloom and five other activists. The verdict carried an award of $711,000 for the plaintiffs.

braced not only some of the language used by Fred Hampton about the Weathermen, but also the tactic of using words as a bludgeon: "A spirit of national masochism prevails, encouraged by an effete corps of impudent snobs who characterize themselves as intellectuals." Eleven days later in a speech given in Harrisburg, Pennsylvania, Agnew denounced as "intellectual eunuchs" those politicians who supported the antiwar movement. As November 15 drew closer, Agnew began to call it "a carnival in the streets" on the part of "a strident minority" and equated the word "mob" with "Moratorium" and "Mobilization." John Volpe, a member of the President's Cabinet, declared that the organizers for November 15 were "Communist or Communist-inspired." Whether or not out of fear inspired by Nixon's Vice President, many elected officials backed off from support of the November 15 action.

Not unexpectedly, the government prolonged until the last minute the matter of a permit for the November 15 rally and the marches preceding it. Negotiations for the permit began early in October. Heading the negotiating team for the Nixon Administration was John Dean III, then an associate deputy attorney general. Dean would later become famous for his intimate knowledge of Watergate and the illegal, underground White House unit called the Plumbers, a fact that throws a curious, retrospective light on the early and persistent interest shown by the government team in the question of portable toilets for the demonstration: who would provide this necessity, the government or the Mobilization? It remained, according to Bradford Lyttle, an issue without satisfactory resolution, much to the discomfort of tens of thousands of protesters.

Lyttle, who with Fred Halstead of the SWP was responsible for the logistics of the November event, has written a long, detailed, privately distributed account of the negotiations and other technical problems in mounting November 15. Lyttle is a lifelong pacifist: "full-time in the peace movement all of my life, out of a conviction that the prevention of war is the most important task in the world." He is a Chicagoan who has lived much of his life within three blocks of where he was born on the South Side but has traveled to distant parts of the world in the cause of peace. His mother was a member of the Women's International League for Peace and Freedom. She was active in the pacifist movement, and in his early years her son came to know A. J. Muste. He was with Muste in the "Omaha Action" against the missile base near Mead, Nebraska, in 1959 and through the years after that. He had been deeply involved in the action against the Polaris submarine, the Walk to Moscow, and the Walk from Quebec to Miami in 1964. "I was just exhausted. . . . I needed a rest. . . . I got in the antiwar movement, which, being a mass movement, was less demanding. . . . I became a specialist in practical details of organizing demonstrations of all sizes." Lyttle was among those arrested at the Pentagon in 1967. The demonstrators' attorney on that occasion was Phil Hirschkop, a sharp young man from Alexandria, Virginia, given to a certain flamboyance of manner and dress. He often wore a cowboy hat and a huge silver peace medallion with his business suit. Hirschkop also participated in the negotiations with the government for the Counterinaugural in January 1969. Lyttle gives Hirschkop much of the credit for finally getting the permits to demonstrate in November 1969.

The negotiations dragged on through many meetings in John Dean's office on the fourth floor of the Justice Department. The ultimate question was the march route from the Capitol to the rally point at the Washington Monument. The Mobilization forces wanted permission to use Pennsylvania Avenue, the traditional parade route every four years for the inaugural procession and granted in the past to groups like the Ku Klux Klan. The government insisted upon a route straight down the Mall, a quarter of a mile removed from the White House at its closest point. While the question of a permit remained unsettled, coupled as it was in every news report from Washington with the possibility of violence on November 15, to the dismay and frustration of the organizers the number of marchers expected diminished. Finally, they had had enough of what bore the marks of an orchestrated campaign of insidious suggestion. When Clark Mollenhoff of the Des Moines *Register* rose to ask the question one more time, Sidney Lens lost his temper. "Why the hell don't you ask the man who is really committing violence, Richard Nixon, whether he intends to continue the massacres in Vietnam?"

On November 6, with just a week to go, John Dean announced at a press conference that permission to use Pennsylvania Avenue had been denied. Dean cited reports of possible violence as the reason. Dean and his immediate superior, Richard Kleindienst, declined to name the various groups they asserted were planning disruption, vandalism, and confrontation. Ron Young, Washington project director for the Mobilization, replied by accusing the government of "mounting a fear campaign . . . to scare Americans into staying home." With Hirschkop's insistent encouragement the Mobilization negotiating committee held their ground. Not only did he recommend that they insist on Pennsylvania Avenue until the last possible moment, but he also steadfastly refused to take into the courts what he considered a political issue. The Mobilization began to find influential support. The Washington *Post* backed their stand in its editorial columns. The mayor of the city, Walter Washington, interceded directly with President Nixon. On the afternoon of November 12 the Justice Department negotiating team reversed itself and granted permission for the march to proceed up Pennsylvania Avenue to Fifteenth Street— one block from the White House—and then straight south to the Washington Monument. The permit also allowed the March Against Death to pass by the front of the White House along the sidewalk on the south side of Pennsylvania Avenue.

Another problem for the Mobe was its uneasy alliance with the organizers of the Moratorium. The issue that lay between the two was, in Sidney Lens's view, a simple one: "The Moratorium kids aren't all that conservative. The difference . . . between us is that in their thinking everything goes back to the ballot boxes. In our thinking, everything goes back to the streets." For Sam Brown of the Moratorium, however, it was an intellectual, even philosophical question:

Was in fact the country on the verge of some sort of fundamental and radical change in terms of the way it is going to see itself over the next thirty years, and is the [Vietnam] war going to be the precipitant factor in creating that kind of change? Or is the war aberrational and, therefore, the coalition of people *ad hoc?* And that largely depended on how you saw America. . . .

If [my view] was right, then you needed to appeal to the decent, common, shared instincts of the American people. If we're in a prerevolutionary state, then screw the great middle class . . . put together the coalition that over the next thirty years will change the country.

I always thought that a cynical notion because . . . it took the war as an issue and used it as an organizing tactic to complete some other agenda.

A debate along these lines, says Brown, took place one night in the home of Anne and Martin Peretz, generous backers of the Moratorium. The occasion was a meeting of the board of MassPax. The question was whether or not to endorse the Mobe. "It split husbands and wives and long-time friends . . . twelve or fifteen people were there . . . Marty Peretz was the most articulate opponent." On October 16 Brown announced publicly that support of the Mobe was "an open question." As for the Moratorium itself, it would concentrate on local activities for November 13 and 14. A column by Anthony Lewis in the New York *Times* for October 22 bespoke the underlying hesitation. Some of the Moratorium leaders, Lewis wrote, feared the coming protests would be "a political disaster" and that broad community support was breaking down in "a conflict between radicals and centrist critics of the war." On November 2, one day before the Nixon speech, the Moratorium ran another full-page ad in the *Times* under the banner THE PEOPLE OF AMERICA WILL BE LISTENING, MR. PRESIDENT. The ad, which sought donations, alluded only vaguely to the Moratorium's own plans for November 13 and 14. It carried no mention of November 15 and the mass Washington rally scheduled for that date by the Mobilization.

Whatever qualms, hesitations, and doubts the Moratorium organizers and their moderate followers had about the significance of November 15 and their participation on that date were dispelled by Nixon's speech. The "silent majority" speech, as it came to be known, was surely one of the most divisive ever made by a sitting President of the United States. As Nixon himself admits, "My speech had not proposed any new initiatives; its purpose [was] to gain support for the course we were already following." He did this by identifying the real enemy as a group of citizens within the borders of the United States, "a minority" who were attempting to "impose" their will "by mounting demonstrations in the streets" and threatening the nation's "future as a free society." Apparently now the fighting in Vietnam was no more than the "cruel sideshow" Kissinger would claim it to be. The enemy was at home, for, as the President declared, "North Vietnam cannot defeat or humiliate the United States. Only Americans can do that." Against this internal threat, he made a direct appeal "to you, the great silent majority of my fellow Americans—I ask for your support."

The term "silent majority" caught on at once, much to the apparent surprise of the President. Agnew had used the phrase several times in May, but it was lost in the circumambient flamboyance of his rhetoric. William Safire, a White House speech writer at the time, claims credit for the phrase: "I lifted [it] from a speech by former Senator Paul Douglas: 'That is the silent center, the millions of people in the middle of the American political spectrum, who do not demonstrate, who do not picket or protest loudly. . . . This silent center has . . . transformed from a minority into a majority.' " A more likely inspiration for Nixon, however, was a letter published in the New York *Times* in August. The writer interpreted the nation's pride in landing a man on the moon: "What the American people have been saying . . . is that above all things they love a victory, whether in a ball game or war. There is 'no substitute for victory.' Regardless of loud-mouthed pacifists, the great *silent majority* [emphasis added] wants a victory in Vietnam." The mindless conflation of war, sports, personal courage, and national enterprise might well have attracted the attention of the White House aide assigned to assemble the daily press clips for the President. The "silent majority" speech did sternly promise victory and not defeat. Only the instrumentality had changed, although Nixon's listeners had no way to know that. In place of the savage, punishing blow originally contemplated in the Duck Hook planning there now stood a strategy of withdrawal, a withdrawal "made from strength and not from weakness."

"Very few speeches actually influence the course of history. The November 3 speech was one of them." (The modest judgment is Nixon's own.) In fact, nothing had changed. The claim is based on no more than the President's belief that he now "had the public support I needed to continue a policy of waging war in Vietnam and negotiating peace in Paris until we could bring the war to an honorable and successful conclusion." This assertion, in turn, rested upon a postspeech influx of some eighty thousand letters and telegrams that flooded into the White House as a result of a manipulation campaign largely concocted by the White House public relations team. What the speech did do was to identify public opinion as a moral center of gravity to be won over not by presidential persuasion but to be coerced by the military method of divide and conquer. Richard Nixon was now on all fours with the Weathermen; neither he nor they sought a solution in reasoned debate.

The Movement was quick to respond. Ron Young correctly noted that "the speech gives us just the needed impetus that will carry us into November 15." For Stewart Meacham it meant that one of the two prerequisites for a successful march, good weather and a "bad speech from Nixon," had been met. The Moratorium was left with no option but to intensify their cooperation with the Mobe. "We've just got to work harder," said Sam Brown. Moratorium volunteers poured into Washington and the premises at 1029 Vermont Avenue seethed with activity. The Justice Department negotiating team that had accepted without comment the Mobe's prediction of seventy thousand to a quarter of a million demonstrators began spontaneously to talk of half a million. David Hawk, who had been the Moratorium link to the Mobe ever since the July conference in Cleveland, was by this time joined on the Mobe steering committee by his three colleagues, Brown, Sklencar, and Mixner. "We were never nervous about their [the Mobe's] intentions," said one of them to the press. What the Moratorium forces did realize was that "a great many more people than had been anticipated would be coming to Washington, and that most of those people would be our constituency."

Congressional reaction was something else. A resolution endorsing Nixon's efforts to negotiate a "just peace" was drafted with the assistance of the White House and introduced in the House of Representatives by James Wright (D-Texas) the day after the President's speech. The House Foreign Affairs Committee approved the resolution without hearings. The resolution, with fifty Republican and fifty Democratic sponsors, won the endorsement of three hundred congressmen in a matter of days. Senator William Fulbright, who had introduced and rammed the Tonkin Gulf Resolution through the Senate with only two dissenting votes in 1964, showed some caution on this occasion. He noted that Nixon was now adopting the same assumptions and justifications that had governed the Vietnam policies of the Johnson Administration. Fulbright nevertheless postponed scheduled hearings on Vietnam by his own Senate Foreign Relations Committee for fear they would contribute to the "inflammation of the public mind." Possibly for the same reason, the Arkansas senator announced that he opposed the planned Washington protest. The President paid an extraordinary visit to Capitol Hill to address each house of Congress separately, thank them for their support, and, in a veiled reference to the impending demonstration, seek "constructive criticism" from those who opposed him. The whole scenario was not unlike the unseemly circumstances surrounding the Tonkin Gulf Resolution in 1964. This time the issue was less serious. Yet once again, without hearings, without questioning the meaning of its action, Congress was tumbling all over itself in an effort to escape its responsibilities in matters of war and peace.

Several hours after the President's appearances before the House and Senate, the March Against Death began at 6 P.M. on November 13. Credit for the March Against Death belongs to Stewart Meacham, the community peace education secretary of the American Friends Service Committee. Meacham was fifty-nine years old with a background of long experience in the pacifist and antiwar movements. The son of a Southern Presbyterian minister, he early abandoned plans for a similar career and plunged into the socialist world of the 1930s. After World War II, during which period he supported U.S. participation, Meacham returned to an earlier belief in pacifism and has since remained steadfastly a pacifist. From 1957 his work had been with the Friends and with the peace movement in its many expressions. He was one of those, for instance, who joined with A. J. Muste in an *ad hoc* group to protest the Bay of Pigs fiasco in 1961. In 1968 Meacham campaigned for Eugene McCarthy; in the election, he voted for Dick Gregory.

Sidney Peck thinks of Stewart Meacham as the one person in the antiwar movement who might have taken on the role A. J. Muste played until his death in 1967. "He had," says Peck, "the confidence and the credibility as a person to deserve the respect of a very wide alignment." Presence, integrity, openness, tact, and acceptability are the words Peck uses to describe A. J. Muste before going on to say that Stewart Meacham, among the possible successors, came closest to filling the bill.

Meacham's activities in 1969 exemplified these qualities. Early in the year, when the old Mobe was floundering after the double misfortune of Chicago and the Counterinaugural, he formed, at the prompting of Sidney Lens, the National Action Group (NAG) to organize thirty actions for the Easter season. It was Meacham who talked in a fatherly and firm way to the Weathermen when the

Mobe refused to support the Days of Rage. And it was Meacham, "a grand old fellow," in the words of David Hawk, who was the key to keeping the moderates of the Moratorium in step with the Mobilization for November 15.

On April 4, 1969—Good Friday, a day of solemn observance in the Christian church of the agony and death of Christ on the Cross—Meacham participated in one of the NAG actions in Philadelphia, a sit-in at draft board headquarters in the Federal Building on Cherry Street. The group sat in silence between noon and 3 P.M., at which time Meacham rose and began to read the names of the Americans who had died in Vietnam. He and others read the names from the *Congressional Record,* where they had been entered by Representative Paul Findley of Illinois. The reading lasted for seventeen hours, until eight o'clock the next morning. It was the first occurrence of a ritual that would be repeated elsewhere many times in the next several months.

Out of this experience evolved the idea of the March Against Death. It was first presented by Meacham to the New Mobilization Coordinating committee in August under the name Death March; otherwise its simple elements were in place: a constant file of more than forty thousand citizens passing in front of the White House, each carrying a placard with the name of an American serviceman killed in Vietnam or a Vietnamese village destroyed. The idea had immediate appeal among groups not ordinarily associated with the forces of Mobe. Sidney Peck is unstinting in his praise of Meacham: "He played a very critical role in keeping the Moratorium forces together on the action in November. The major action link—apart from Stewart's negotiating skills—was the March Against Death. . . . [It] was congenial to the style and tone of the Moratorium and allowed a lot of mainstream organizations and groups to come in." Meacham settled in Washington in September and found two able lieutenants in Susan Miller of the Episcopal Peace Fellowship and Trudy Young, then the wife of project codirector Ron Young, to organize the march.

The march began Thursday evening in darkness and near-freezing temperatures, under threatening skies, but on schedule. The assembly area was just across the Potomac River on the Virginia side, not far from the gates of the Arlington National Cemetery. (The Pentagon refused a request that the Tomb of the Unknown Soldier within the cemetery be used as the point of departure.) After crossing the Arlington Memorial Bridge and skirting the west side of the Lincoln Memorial, the marchers proceeded up Seventeenth Street, passed in front of the White House, and then continued down Pennsylvania Avenue to the west front of the Capitol. At the head of the line of march crossing the bridge six drummers rapped out a slow funeral cadence. Behind them was the first marcher: Judy Droz, a twenty-three-year-old widow and the mother of a ten-month-old child. Her husband, Lieutenant Donald G. Droz, had been killed in Vietnam the previous April. Her statement, she said, was that "the United States should get out of Vietnam immediately." Behind Mrs. Droz came other close relatives of men fallen in Vietnam and then the two cochairmen of Saturday's rally, Dr. Benjamin Spock and the Reverend William Sloane Coffin.

Twelve hundred marchers crossed the Arlington Memorial Bridge every hour as they began their nearly four-mile walk, each carrying a name placard and, in the hours of darkness, a lighted candle. From downstream on the Potomac the wavering file of candles on the bridge seemed to mark a rite distant in time and place from secular Washington, a procession of penitents seeking from hidden gods of power surcease in their travail. Hour by hour they silently came, forty-five thousand marchers, through two nights and into Saturday morning, through rain and thunderstorms, wind and biting cold, in what may have been the longest "parade" in American history.

As each marcher paused opposite the main entrance of the White House to say aloud the name of a fallen soldier, it was a moment of highly charged emotion. Bright lights surrounded the building and glared out upon the slowly passing stream of protest. A huge mercury vapor lamp, ten feet long, was mounted on the north facade. It reminded Bradford Lyttle of descriptions he had read "of Special Forces camps deep in VC territory. It was easy to imagine machine gunners stationed in the building's windows." In fact, there were federal troops stationed in the basement corridors running under the White House and the Executive Office Building. But for another young marcher it was a "picture postcard scene." The lawn was still a vivid green, the stark white colonnade of the ceremonial entrance was like a flood-lit Acropolis: light without sound. In the stillness each marcher called out a single name, each in a different way. Mrs. Droz, the first to do so, spoke her husband's name softly. Behind her, in turn, another woman shouted out her brother's name in a loud, firm voice. For Sidney Peck it was "a powerful emotional experience [I] will never forget. For me, it was similar to 'Silent Night' at the Pentagon. I remember it was about one o'clock in the morning when I reached the White House, and when I shouted out the name, it wasn't my voice. It was as though my body was a medium . . . the Yiddish expression for it is *dybbuk*. . . . You just opened your mouth and it wasn't your voice; it was a very haunting sound that came out."

From the White House the marchers passed down Pennsylvania Avenue past Washington's only Peace Monument† to the west front of the Capitol, where they placed their placards in forty waiting caskets. The marchers had hoped to deliver the caskets filled with placards to the White House as a peaceful response to the like number of telegrams the President had received after his "silent majority" speech. Instead the caskets were carried, as if in a funeral cortege, at the head of the mass march to the Washington Monument that began at 10:15 A.M. Saturday morning, two hours after the single file of the March Against Death concluded.

Two events that occurred during the days of the March Against Death attracted varying degrees of attention in the press. Neither event was sponsored or supported by the Mobilization. In one, 186 persons were arrested. Their crime lay in attempting to hold an ecumenical "Mass of Peace" in the Pentagon Mall. Two bishops and many priests, Episcopal and Catholic, were among the culprits. Mrs. Philip Hart, wife of the senator from Michigan, was one of those arrested to the jeering applause

† So called; in fact, it commemorates United States Navy personnel who lost their lives in the Civil War; its two symbolic female figures portray America weeping on the shoulder of History.

of Pentagon workers who mocked the religious ceremony before the police moved in. The story attracted little attention in the national press. The second incident, in which some thirty arrests were made, became front-page news. It smacked of the violence government officials had been predicting, if not inviting, for weeks. On Friday evening some 800 to 1,000 young demonstrators, according to the Washington *Post,* gathered at Du Pont Circle for a rally sanctioned by government permit and began a march toward the South Vietnamese Embassy, only to be met by a cordon of police at Sheridan Circle, one-half block from their destination. Missiles were hurled, the police responded with tear gas, and a melee ensued. Only the Administration and a few Weathermen could have been pleased.‡ Before the evening was over, the Mobilization had issued a disavowal. Sam Brown said that the trouble came from "only an infinitesimal minority . . . who have no relation officially to the Mobilization and obviously not to the Moratorium."

That same night five thousand people, also predominantly young, attended a service at the National Cathedral to hear speeches, prayers, and folk songs in opposition to the war. And, finally, unnoticed by the press, there took place that night in Washington the largest kazoo concert in the history of the nation. Sam Brown explains:

> After the endorsement [of the Mobilization by the Moratorium] our decision was, we had responsibilities to . . . prevent any kind of outbreak. . . . That's why we spent a lot of time, and I don't think it's telling any state secrets to say, with a certain amount of help from the Secret Service . . . in doing the organizational things we thought were important to reduce the threat of violence. . . . The night before actually was more successful, the night of the march on the South Vietnamese Embassy.
>
> That night we had been worried about what would happen, because there were a lot of people just adrift in the city. We went to Wavy Gravy—he runs the Hog Farm commune [in New Mexico] and he's about the smartest person I know in terms of crowd control. "What are we going to do about all these people?" He said, "You create an alternative event." "Well, what?" "Buy me a hundred dozen kazoos, I'll fix the problem." So we had the world's largest participatory kazoo concert the night before. We passed out probably a couple of hundred dozen kazoos, at G[eorge] W[ashington] or someplace and it just sort of sucked up a lot of kids who were very emotional and didn't have any idea what they wanted to do, but wanted to do something, and might very well have gotten themselves involved [in trouble].

Norma Becker did not get to Washington until Saturday, the day of the mass demonstration. Once there, a late arrival, she joined the hordes of people streaming toward the monument, an anonymous figure in the crowd. At least fifty thousand people in that crowd were there directly as a result of arrangements made by her. Many thousands more, come by their own devising, owed the spirit and determina-

‡ "We were the people our parents warned us about," the Weatherbureau proudly proclaimed in the penultimate issue of their national organ, *Fire,* the successor to *New Left Notes.*

tion that brought them there to earlier demonstrations or actions mounted by forces Becker worked with. Since the days when she was a cofounder of the Fifth Avenue Peace Parade Committee and through years of service as a cocoordinator she had chosen a post for herself removed from public view, in the "engine room." She ran the vital machinery that made things go. It was Norma Becker whom the commissioner of police knew and came to count on for reasonable assistance at times of major demonstrations in New York City. The Fifth Avenue Peace Parade Committee maintained a hot line for the Movement that was called Dial-a-Demonstration, the idea of a committee staff member, Eric Weinberger. The New York police came to recognize Dial-a-Demonstration as a reliable source of information for their own purposes. One of Becker's jobs, as she puts it, was "to organize New York City in relation to national actions." So it was for November 15.

At the beginning of October she was busy recruiting for the March Against Death and, in a way reminiscent of small-town activities, raising money for the Fifth Avenue Peace Parade Committee through neighborhood parties—"we didn't have a cent." By November, transportation was the problem. Pressure, not always subtle, was brought by the FBI against bus companies doing business with the organizers. The bank handling the committee's account was turning over to the government copies of checks drawn or deposited to their account. Eventually the ACLU brought suit against the "chilling effect" of this activity. "Thousands of people were stranded that day in New York," says Becker. "Their rental buses never showed." Nevertheless, hundreds of buses did get through, and a hectic, around-the-clock pace was maintained the last few days, selling tickets from an eighth-floor office in a loft building downtown. For Becker this meant late-night hours after her days as a schoolteacher. The Friday night before the demonstration there were so many people crowded into the large loft space seeking tickets that the floor began to sag: "We were really scared; we couldn't sell the tickets fast enough." Late Friday evening, Becker's teenage daughter called: her friend had been mugged outside the Becker apartment. Becker took a taxi home, dealt with the emergency —hospital, police, parents—and returned to the job. It was one-thirty in the morning before she was home at last. At two-thirty her phone rang: another bus coordinator calling in. He had the people to fill another bus, but the company now demanded cash and would not take a check. Becker had a cash reserve hidden away in the piano in the front room. She retrieved it, waited for the pickup, and finally went to bed.

Early the next morning she, her daughter, and friends were on the platform waiting for one of the five trains the committee had rented for the trip to Washington. At Newark the train stopped; a bomb scare had been phoned in. Becker walked through the sixteen-car train to explain the delay and ask passengers to get off while the train was searched. When the train finally reached Union Station it was close to one o'clock in the afternoon of a clear, cold day. The New Yorkers swept down the hill to join the slowly moving carpet of humanity on Pennsylvania Avenue and the Mall. Newspapers already on the street announced its size as 250,000, an "official" figure that never changed, despite the constant influx of demonstrators throughout the afternoon.

Bradford Lyttle visited the assembly area at the west end of the Mall at 6 A.M. The temperature was near freezing and chilly winds were coming in from the northeast under a threatening sky. "This day," he told himself with no pun intended, "will be a bomb." It was not. By noon, the forty-one acres around the Washington Monument were two-thirds covered with people, and wave after wave of massed ranks were entering the area from Fifteenth Street, the Mall, and from beyond the Jefferson Memorial, where some four thousand buses were parked. People were still coming in, headed for the monument, when Norma Becker and her party began the trek back to New York late in the afternoon. Some estimated the crowd as being "two Woodstocks," or eight hundred thousand people. Others were more modest: five hundred to seven hundred thousand. It was by any count the largest political mass march and demonstration in the history of the nation to that time, easily exceeding the numbers present in Washington for the civil rights rally of 1963 or the April 1967 march in New York.

The troubles predicted by the Nixon Administration did not materialize along the line of march or at the Mobe-sponsored rally at the monument. On November 12, the day after reluctantly issuing a permit for the march, the government announced that nine thousand troops were being called in from military installations in Virginia, Maryland, and the Carolinas to be held in a ready-alert status in the environs of the city and to be stationed in federal buildings. It was made known that from this force (considerably more than the number of troops used in the U.S. 1983 invasion of Grenada) troops would be posted in the Capitol, the Justice Department, and the Internal Revenue Service, Commerce, and Treasury buildings. The Secret Service declared that it would "take precautions necessary to protect the White House and the President." The most obvious aspect of these preparations was the solid barrier of buses parked bumper to bumper that encircled the White House. The precautions also included three hundred troops hidden in the White House and the Executive Office Building, which once housed the Departments of State, War, and Navy. Keen-eyed protesters passing up Seventeenth Street during the March Against Death saw soldiers in sharpshooting positions behind balustrades in the upper reaches of that lovely old Second Empire building. All preparations for the war-brought-home were in order.

The need for force did not arise; it was, instead, a day for symbolic statement. The fortress White House with its professedly unconcerned President ostensibly engaged in "normal" routine was silent spokesman for the government. The President, it was reported, watched college football on television that afternoon. Outside, in the streets of the city, three quarters of a million Americans made their statement through sheer presence. And sound: from the river of people packed shoulder to shoulder, coursing up Pennsylvania Avenue and twisting down Fifteenth Street to the delta of the monument grounds, came something like an ocean roar, a steady, mingled din of song, shout, and chanted slogan rising and falling hour after hour, resounding eerily in the deserted precincts around the White House.

Senator Eugene McCarthy spoke at the assembly point below the Capitol before the march began. His theme was echoed on one of the thousands of placards carried that day: TYRANNY HAS ALWAYS DEPENDED ON A SILENT MAJORITY. Cora Weiss of WSP gave the signal to start the march at about 10:20 A.M. She was one of the cochairs of the Mobilization and the person responsible for the remarkable array of musical talent that appeared on the platform later in the day. Behind the Mobilization dignitaries came a grouping meant to continue the theme of the preceding thirty-six hours: three drummers (again, the funeral cadence), then a file of young men carrying the dozen coffins filled with the placards from the March Against Death, and finally four others bearing a large wooden cross. Immediately behind this group, another carried a huge banner saying SILENT MAJORITY FOR PEACE.

But the crush of humanity that edged its way along the avenue was neither silent nor somber. Good cheer, friendship among strangers, and simple civility were the marks of the day. The tens of thousands present who were not white, young, and middle class were not enough to dispel the dominant impression. It was not unlike a homecoming day crowd at a football game: being there was all that counted. Even the most extreme of the slogans chanted—"Ho, Ho, Ho Chi Minh, NLF Gonna Win" and "One, Two, Three, Four, Tricky Dick, Stop the War"—lost whatever edge of ugliness they might have had. At the monument grounds, hundreds of white doves, the peace symbol adopted by the Moratorium, were released to fly in the clear blue November sky above the crowd. The peaceful, orderly demonstration that the New Mobe had promised came to be. Yet it might have been otherwise, for there were in the crowd pockets of angry youths bent on violent confrontation. In the end, they could find no better targets than the Mobilization marshals. Bradford Lyttle and Fred Halstead, "an oddly matched pair," as Lyttle himself admits, had seen to the recruitment and training of four thousand marshals in a prodigious logistical endeavor greatly aided by Quaker groups in several cities and by the New England Committee for Nonviolent Action. The spirit of nonviolence signified by these organizations characterized the work of the marshals along the parade route and at the rally, where they protected the speakers' platform. The marshals formed a nearly continuous phalanx, hand in hand, along either side of the march route. At the turn at Fifteenth Street, the point of the march nearest to the White House, anticipated trouble did arise; three hundred marshals massed to thwart the attempt by militants to break through. Lyttle remembers that later, near the platform, "a contingent of perhaps two hundred people representing themselves as SDS students and New York City radicals" tried to rush the stage while Senator McGovern spoke: Mobilization marshals turned them aside also. The two thousand Washington police on duty were left with little serious work to do.

A curious lethargy gripped the FBI on the day of the rally: given the opportunity to arrest wanted felons, they chose not to. The Boston 8, who had destroyed, defaced, or stolen one hundred thousand draft files in a "hit-'n'-split" (rather than "stand by" for arrest) a week earlier in Boston, chose to "surface" in Washington on November 15 beside the Reflecting Pool in front of the Lincoln Memorial. They telephoned the FBI office of their intention, but the agents were late in arriving, showed little interest as shredded draft records were thrown in the pool, and innocently asked, "Is there a group here called the Boston Patriots [the name at the time of the American Football League entry from Boston]?" No arrests were made. Nor was anyone arrested the following day when the Beaver 55 surfaced, also in Washington. The Beaver 55, the tenth group of the Catholic Left "action community" to strike at draft boards in 1969, were in fact only eight in number; the whimsical name was the choice of Tom Trost, thought to be their leader. The Beaver 55 had destroyed the files of forty-four draft boards in a raid in Indianapolis on October 31; and on November 7 they entered a Dow Chemical data center in Midland, Michigan, where they erased magnetic tapes carrying the records of chemical and biological research.

On the platform at the rally site there were "the usual four or five brigades of speakers," in the breezy estimate of Sidney Lens. The result was a Babel of two dozen voices ranging from Senators McGovern and Goodell, the only establishment figures to approach the microphones, to a shrill melange of representatives of the Left, obscure figures to the huge captive audience they addressed. To the degree the listeners gave any heed, they heard variations on the theme of the New Mobe's manifesto for the day, "A Call to the Fall Offensive to End the War." Sidney Lens was the author of the "explicitly anti-imperialist" document, which excoriated the United States as "the bastion of counter-revolution, the ally of scores of corrupt and reactionary regimes," and took on the individual causes of Eldridge Cleaver, Huey Newton, and Bobby Seale in addition to the Conspiracy, then on trial in Chicago. It was a call not only to stop the war, but also to "Stop the Death Machine" by addressing the problems of "the poor and hungry, the Black and Brown communities, the sick, the cancer victims of air pollution, the accident victims of automobiles—free us all to live, to love, and to run our own lives." The Reverend William Sloane Coffin sums up the oratory: "There were precious few good speeches, and those who tried to make one—like George McGovern—were hooted down by the SDS, many of whom may well have been provocateurs." "We meet today because we cherish our flag," McGovern told the crowd. Immediately in front and below him was a sea of NLF and red revolutionary flags where a purported SDS contingent had clustered in their helmets and leather jackets, constrained by the marshals' presence to no more than vocal abuse. And up the sloping ground a quarter of a mile away from where he spoke, the senator could see the fifty flagstaffs encircling the base of the monument, one for every state in the Union, bleakly mocking his words. No flags were flying that day.

If Coffin was disgusted with the platform party, so (for different reasons) were the Moratorium forces. Sam Brown:

> It's fifteen years later, and I still feel a great deal of anger about the set of decisions that got made and mostly it's anger directed at myself because I was in a position to have stopped it at the time and didn't, out of some crazed sense of solidarity with the Left—no enemies on the Left. . . .
> The Mobe scared the congressmen away. . . . Everyone stayed away in droves. . . . If there had been one hundred members of Congress on the stage on November 15 Agnew was a phenomenon that couldn't have occurred. But the fact is that the speakers' committee of the Mobe—we had to

have a gay-lesbian high school student from southern New Jersey, and we couldn't have politicians because they were corrupt and terrible. . . . In order to appeal to every fringe in the country you throw away the middle. . . .

The congressmen didn't want to have anything to do with it. [They said,] "I'm against the war but I'm not going to hang around with that bunch of clowns [on the platform]." George McGovern wasn't going to be allowed to speak—I guess maybe at the last minute he was allowed . . . there were weeks of debate. . . .

David Hawk, the Moratorium organizer who was closest to the Mobe people throughout, is less angry. He recalls with wry amusement the endless meetings devoted to drawing up a slate of speakers ("At one point there was a resolution that no capitalist could speak") and ruefully admits that the platform performances allowed for no coherent rhetorical response to the "silent majority" speech: "The opposition to the war was not able on that occasion to use its mass to respond to Nixon"; the speeches were "largely rhetoric designed to 'heighten the consciousness' of the marchers. . . ."

It was the music that saved the day. For Tom Hayden November 15 was "the Moratorium and Woodstock." So also David Hawk: a "synthesis of the emerging youth culture, rock and folk music and antiwar politics . . ." The music and the feeling of warm congeniality it engendered gave the day a "Give Peace a Chance" ambience that touched the elders as well as the young in the crowd. Louise Peck had seen a good many demonstrations in her activist career, but none quite like this: "A very beautiful feeling . . . such a sense of community in that crowd . . . even alone, everyone you met was like a friend." For all of this, the music was the catalyst, and it had, very much, a Woodstock flavor.

The sound was pure Woodstock. On the advice of Peter Yarrow (of Peter, Paul and Mary), whom Cora Weiss had enlisted for help in assembling performers for the day, Bradford Lyttle sought out William Hanley to set up the sound system. Hanley was, and is, the best in the business. "Bill was raised a Catholic," says Lyttle, "and I received the impression that reinforcing sound was a religious vocation with him." Hanley grew professionally with the burgeoning music scene through the fifties and sixties, starting with the Newport Jazz Festival. In New York City, at places like Cafe Au Go Go, the Bitter End, and Fillmore East, he met and earned the respect of those he calls "the musicians and poets of the Movement. . . . Mass involvement came from the music, not the political arena. . . . My goal was to make it happen well." Hanley was the inevitable choice to do the staging, sound, and technical facility for Woodstock. Then "Peter [Yarrow] decided Washington was too big for anyone else."

The first of Bill Hanley's two forty-foot semitrailers, loaded with staging and equipment, pulled in to Washington late Tuesday evening. The work of setting up at the spot Hanley had chosen, the southwest corner of the monument grounds near the triangle at Seventeenth Street, began on Wednesday and continued night and day through bad weather until Saturday morning. At one time or another thirty or forty marshals, plus a contingent from the Hog Farm commune, assisted Hanley, his own crew of twelve, and Lyttle's two close associates Eric Small and John Gage. Gradually the facility emerged: stage, scaffolding, towers, protected areas, the five-thousand-watt high fidelity system. On Friday night, when it was time to place the speaker horns and tweeters on the forty-foot towers, the hired crane operator showed up drunk. "That was [the night] when John Gage learned to operate a hydraulic crane." For Hanley, the peace movement people "were great to work with. It was a family-type thing . . . the forerunners were the long-haired, freaky people, and I had been working with them since the fifties and Newport." Hanley was arrested late Saturday afternoon, fifteen minutes before his permit expired, when police cleared the platform area with tear gas. He thinks of it as his merit badge in the Movement.

On Saturday, when the thirty-three-year-old Hanley took his position one hundred feet out into the audience at the end of a catwalk projecting from the platform and sat down before his mixer to control the twenty-five microphones on stage and the huge speakers looming from the crowd's edge, both he and the performers were confident that Woodstock sound had come to Washington. The music was on the mellow side of Woodstock, folk and popular. Mixed in with the likes of John Denver, Pete Seeger, Arlo Guthrie, and Peter, Paul and Mary were four separate touring casts of the hit musical *Hair,* Mitch Miller's big band, the Cleveland String Quartet, and others. Conductor Leonard Bernstein was on the platform, but without baton. The audience, for whose pent-up protest music was the only outlet, reacted with boisterous delight. Time and again they joined the stage, *tutti,* in singing the Movement's favorite songs. The power of the musical message reduced the platform oratory to less than counterpoint, to empty pauses between sets. Typical of the afternoon was a moment when the whole audience joined hands in singing, along with Pete Seeger, "Give Peace a Chance," and the voice of Dr. Benjamin Spock at a speaker's microphone could be heard as an obbligato rising above the chorus: "Are you listening, Nixon, are you listening?" He was not.

David Dellinger was one of those who spoke that afternoon. As nominal leader of the Chicago 8, collectively known as the Conspiracy, he had become the symbol of the federal government's oppression of the Movement, and he was the only unanimous choice of the speakers selection committee. National attention centered on the trial, under way in Chicago since September. Widespread in the peace movement was the perception that the defendants were being railroaded by a head-hunting federal prosecution and a complicit judge. Nevertheless, when members of the Conspiracy announced plans to organize their own demonstration in concert with the larger rally, the reaction within the Mobilization/Moratorium forces ranged from anxiety to consternation. The Mobe had, after all, promised three peaceful days in Washington; a separate Conspiracy action made this prospect unlikely under the best of circumstances. On November 12 the Justice Department, perhaps to guarantee that there would be trouble in some form, had granted a three-hour permit for a march down Constitution Avenue to the Justice Department building at the conclusion of the main rally. To publicize the event one of the Chicago defendants, Jerry Rubin, posed at the site wearing boxing gloves. The

Moratorium organizers, who took it as their responsibility to prevent any kind of outbreak, were horrified. "What a bunch of jerks!" says Sam Brown now. A meeting on the eve of the main rally with Bill Ayers and three other Weathermen did nothing to allay the Moratorium's fears. "They said," David Mixner told reporters, "if we gave them $20,000 for expenses, they would not practice violence . . . as far as I'm concerned, it was nothing less than blackmail." Meanwhile, the New Mobilization decided not to sponsor the action at the Justice Department.

On the platform at the rally Dellinger stood flanked by Jerry Rubin and Abbie Hoffman, both of whom had been explicitly denied access to the microphone. They were well received. Hoffman would soon win new fame by telling his jury, "My name is Abbie. . . . I am an orphan of America. . . . I live in Woodstock Nation. . . . It is a nation of alienated young people." Rubin had already made his comments on the demonstration and the platform dignitaries to a reporter: "I really think Spiro Agnew is right. The leaders of the Mobe are effete snobs. . . . The real test is how many march on the Justice Department." It was left to Dellinger to announce the impending action at Justice and invite those who wished to do so to join it. How many of the thousands who streamed in that direction as the rally wound down were intent on trouble is not known. Most, freezing in the late afternoon chill, were headed, as were Norma Becker and her friends, toward Union Station or other forms of transportation. The Justice Department lay in that direction, a half-mile away from the Monument. Douglas Dowd, a longtime leader in the Mobilization, was at a central command post, in touch with the police. Dowd called in to alert those on the platform of the impending confrontation, and the East Coast cast of *Hair* extended its performance another twenty-five minutes to entice the one hundred thousand still on the monument grounds to remain.

The semblance of a march to the Justice Department was formed among the thousands streaming from the main rally site at about 4:30 P.M. At its head was a line of red and blue NLF flags behind a larger papier-mâché representation of the face of Attorney General John N. Mitchell. The march took one turn around the block formed by the Justice Department building and came to a halt on Constitution Avenue, facing the tall, narrowly proportioned main entrance. Its grayish green, metal-sheathed doors were bolted shut. On the lintel block above them the mandatory Latin inscription reads LEGE ATQVE ORDINE OMNIA FIVNT (All things are accomplished through law and order). From an office window five floors above, the attorney general of the United States looked down on the scene. With him was his deputy, Richard Kleindienst. Both were secure in the knowledge that eight hundred federal troops waited at the ready in the building's inner courtyard.

A few of the marshals trained by the Mobilization for the earlier events were on the scene as volunteers, but they were too few to control the restive crowd and the much lesser number of Crazies, Weathermen, Mad Dogs, and other splinter groups bent on violence. Slogans like "Free Bobby Seale" and "Stop the Trial" were shouted for several minutes; then someone from a militant splinter group ran an NLF flag up a flagstaff at the building's front, a red paint bomb smashed against the facade, and a string of firecrackers and a bottle were thrown at the police lines. The police responded with tear gas. The rout was on. The police largely refrained from using their clubs as they drove the crowd of thousands north into the shopping district and west along Constitution Avenue and past the Ellipse. Tear gas floated down the streets and sidewalks in one large area of the city, entrapping all who happened to be there, innocent and culprit alike. Among the two hundred either arrested (all but three on disorderly conduct charges) or hospitalized for minor injuries, many were law-abiding citizens caught in the wrong place at the wrong time. Police using gas cleared the entire monument area down to the stage. By 8 P.M. Mayor Washington and his chief of police, Jerry Wilson, were able to report that the city was secure. They commended the efforts of the Mobilization marshals to prevent violence and the mayor expressed his sympathy to the Mobilization and Moratorium organizers whose "peaceful demonstration," he said, had been marred by a "small band" of rowdies. John Mitchell held a contrary, Alice-in-Wonderland view of the three days: "The New Mobilization Committee expected violence to occur and that was the result. . . . [It] aided this violence through a combination of inaction and affirmative action." Mitchell told his wife, "Looking out the Justice Department it looked like the Russian revolution going on." For thousands returning home by bus that Saturday night it was a tearful voyage, their clothing saturated with pepper gas.

The gas drifting down on the stage area intensified the crisis atmosphere in an incident of an entirely different nature. Participants refer to it as "the Case of the Lavender Hill Mobe." Money, or the lack of it, was always a problem for the radical/pacifist wing of the peace movement. Just days before the march Peck and Lens were begging small change in the Mobe office and soliciting emergency money on the telephone to satisfy an importunate telephone company. By the day of the rally the Mobe was at least seventy-five thousand dollars in debt. In anticipation of the deficit, Beverly Sterner had been asked to organize the solicitation and collection of money at the rally site.

Sterner entered the peace movement in the early 1960s. Like Tom Cornell, she had a radicalizing experience on the Thames River estuary in Connecticut. The mother of her college roommate in New York City had asked the two young women to baby-sit for friends, Bob and Marjorie Swann, over the weekend of Washington's Birthday, 1961. The Swanns lived in Groton and worked with the New England CNVA. Nearby was the New London Polaris submarine base, a CNVA target over the previous six months. The surprise announcement of the launching of the submarine tender *Proteus* canceled the Swanns' plan for a holiday. Instead of baby-sitting that frigid weekend, Sterner found herself on the river in a canoe, part of a day-and-night floating picket line at the launching site. Like her friend Norma Becker a New Yorker born and bred, she had never before been in a canoe. Nevertheless, she bundled up in foul weather gear several sizes too large and went out on the icy waters, paddle in hand, struggling to keep her craft outside the boundaries marked by buoys while navy launches "tried to swamp us, block us so we couldn't be seen . . . what bothered me was the indiscriminate use of power and authority. I resented it. I was doing a perfectly legal thing." The experience and the enormous impression made on her by the selfless devotion of the Swanns to their cause changed Beverly Sterner. "I went back to New York and I quit school, quit my job, and I took my savings and came up and became a staff member of the New England CNVA."

Eventually she was A. J. Muste's secretary at 5 Beekman Street in New York and learned, among other things, the art of fund-raising. At the Pentagon march in 1967 she raised $35,000. She and a friend stationed themselves at the Arlington Memorial Bridge, used a bullhorn to get their message across to the passing marchers, and collected money in little cloth bags that Sterner's aunt had run up for her on a sewing machine. With proper planning, the potential revealed by the Pentagon experience could be doubled, tripled, or quadrupled on November 15, 1969. Bradford Lyttle thought a take of $250,000 was not impossible.

Sterner worked to the point of exhaustion in the two weeks leading up to the rally. Buttons and posters were designed and produced, as well as six thousand containers for collecting donations. Design of the containers (size, dimension, slot design) was of critical importance. There would be no more than fifteen to twenty minutes for the collectors to work the crowd after actor Ossie Davis made the appeal from the platform. The volunteer collectors needed to be persuaded that a check-off and security system existed, when in fact it did not. The containers were fabricated in two parts and had to be assembled by hand, a process that took several days of donated labor. Sterner recruited and organized a team of one thousand collectors. She arranged to have half a dozen large trailer trucks brought to the site as mobile depots. She negotiated with a downtown Washington bank to deposit the collected money on Saturday evening.

Security fears mounted. Some Mobe organizers thought, especially after the Weatherman-Moratorium confrontation, that a Mafia-type raid by the sectarian Left was possible. The volunteers working inside the truck vans, many of them middle-aged women without previous experience in demonstrations, were given explicit instructions: once all the collection containers for their van were returned, they were to bolt the doors shut from the inside, start sorting the money for deposit, and not open up for any reason before the vans reached the bank. In case of trouble, the plan was to call upon armed union bodyguards who were on hand to protect Coretta Scott King and other platform celebrities.

All went well until the huge trailers lined up near the stage area for the run to the Washington bank. Then the exhaust system of one of the rigs malfunctioned. Like most of the Mobilization working crews, the drivers were amateurs, their services volunteered. They feared that the fumes would penetrate the trailer, and so they rapped for the women within to open up. The women refused; then in turn, they denied Sidney Peck, whose gentle voice they knew, and the rough demands of the union men, who finally and to no avail threatened to shoot the doors off their hinges.

When the curious caravan started out at last it now carried both money and hostages to fate. Peck led the way in a tiny VW "bug." The order of march gave the procession the appearance of a huge Mesozoic reptile, all body and little brain, as it stalled, stuttered, and lumbered through the gas-filled streets to the sounds of breaking glass and police sirens. Their arrival at the bank did not gladden the heart of an assistant manager on hand to receive a large deposit on a Saturday evening.

Peck and his entourage might as well have come for an unscheduled withdrawal. "We're here from the Mobe," Peck told the distracted bank manager. Some of the drivers held handkerchiefs to their faces; Beverly Sterner lay on the backseat of the VW in a sleep of exhaustion; the now somewhat apprehensive women in the trailers tumbled out of their hiding.

And one of the trailers was missing.

"To this day," says Peck, "we don't know what happened to that truck." Bradford Lyttle prefers to think of the lost truck as myth; he believes that the missing trailer never made it to the rally site in the first place. Three days later when all the money had been counted, the Mobe was in the black. Over one hundred thousand dollars had been collected.

The tear gas that flooded the city eventually was blown east as far as Union Station. At that time four thousand people were packed in the waiting room, most of them bound for New York City. In the crowd were Norma Becker and her party, close to the glass-paneled doors giving access to the passenger platforms. The doors had not yet opened when the tear gas drifted into the station waiting room, stirring the immobilized would-be passengers toward panic as they pressed still closer to the platform access. On the outer edges of the station crowd there was more trouble. The Mad Dogs, one of the groups that assaulted the Justice Department, had charged up the hill to hurl bottles at the departing marchers who would not "stay and fight." Becker, to her young daughter's chagrin, had carried plastic bags filled with dampened handkerchiefs through the whole day. Now she passed them out to her immediate neighbors. As the doors slid open, a Fifth Avenue Peace Parade Committee staff member, Marty Green, raised his hand in the protesters' V sign and shouted, "Walk!" The sign and cry were taken up and passed back from person to person in the packed mass. Although the impulse was to run, the New Yorkers moved slowly and safely onto the platforms and aboard the waiting trains.

A calamity had been avoided, and the officers of the Penn Central sought to demonstrate their appreciation. Days later, they delivered to Norma Becker in her capacity as leader of the Fifth Avenue Peace Parade Committee a golden spike in commemoration of the day and event. Becker's recollected emotions of November 15, 1969, are bound up with her memories of the railroaders' presentation. She hoped that the spike, gold-plated though it was, would be a favorable auspice for the Movement.* In the euphoria of November 15 it was possible to believe, as Jerome Grossman had believed on Moratorium day a month before, that the last spike had been driven and now the war must end.

That determination was reinforced during the days of the November demonstrations by newspaper accounts that began to appear on November 13, the day of the March Against Death. They concerned an alleged massacre of an unknown number of Vietnamese civilians—women, children, old men, later revealed to be possibly as many as several hundred—at a hamlet called My Lai on March 16, 1968. A Viet-

---

* Nineteen sixty-nine was a centennial year for railroading. On May 10, 1869, at Promontory Point, Utah, a golden spike was driven to mark the nation's first transcontinental linkup, forged after five years of back-breaking labor, between the Central Pacific Railroad from San Francisco and the Union Pacific from Omaha.

nam veteran, Ronald Ridenhour, had heard of the massacre and after he returned to the United States had begun to write letters about it to government officials, including congressmen. Seymour Hersh undertook to dig out the story; on November 13 his series of reports began to appear in more than thirty newspapers. As the Hersh articles were being published the Army appointed a commission to investigate the My Lai massacre; its report concluded that the Army had attempted a cover-up. For the next two years the nation would be tormented by the issue of war crimes committed by Americans in Vietnam.

The New Mobe mounted another demonstration on November 15 in San Francisco. It was the largest gathering ever on the West Coast in the cause of peace. Estimates of participation on a day marred by rain varied from 100,000 (the press) to 250,000 (the Mobe organizers). Although the Moratorium forces were not a factor at San Francisco, it was, as the reception accorded the various speakers showed, a moderate, well-behaved crowd. There were no untoward incidents on the line of march from downtown San Francisco to Golden Gate Park, seven miles distant. When one of the eight speakers at the rally, Black Panther David Hilliard, spoke of Nixon and said, "We'll kill that ———," the crowd drowned him out with chants of "Peace, Peace, Peace!" and he finally gave up his attempt to finish his speech.

The longest and loudest applause went to Wayne Morse, who had been rejected a year earlier by the voters of Oregon in his bid for reelection to the U.S. Senate. Morse told the crowd what few present were old enough to remember: "It was Eisenhower, Dulles, and Nixon who got us into this war." Morse demanded that American troops "be brought out, and now." Rennie Davis of the Conspiracy spoke in more revolutionary terms: "This generation is committed to taking this country back [from] the new fascism that goes hand in hand with the decision to remain in Vietnam by any means necessary." The crowd, made up of units like the Los Angeles Physicians for Social Responsibility and the Seattle Democratic Council Against [Henry] Jackson seemed willing to interpret the Davis threat in terms of electoral politics.

Television cables rather than railroad ties bind the Union together today. Where and how the moguls of the industry choose to drive their "golden spike" of preemptive live coverage have tremendous bearing on Americans' perception of one another and their nation's priorities. Nixon and his Administration understood this well, and they succeeded in denying the New Mobilization the full, live, and sympathetic coverage on November 15 that the Moratorium enjoyed in October. The football game the President watched on November 15 was not preempted by the largest political demonstration in the history of the country, which was going on very nearly in his own backyard. Nor did either of the other two networks cover the event live.

By contrast, all three networks did cover live a speech given by Vice President Agnew in Des Moines, Iowa, on November 13. On November 4, the day after the "silent majority" speech, Nixon's new appointee to the chairmanship of the Federal Communications Commission, Dean Burch, personally called the three networks to ask for transcripts of the "instant analyses" aired immediately after the speech.

The clear threat to the freedom of the press implicit in this request was spelled out later by the White House, after Agnew's speech. Bias in the press and television, it was announced, meant an invitation to "the government to come in." The networks understood. When the White House sent them the advance text of the Agnew speech, there was, Nixon reports, "pandemonium; all three decided to carry the speech live." What they did not know was that Richard Nixon was editor, if not coauthor, of the speech. According to H. R. Haldeman, "The concept of Agnew's inflammatory speeches against the Eastern 'elite' . . . that controlled communications in this country, came right from the Oval Office." Haldeman and Nixon went over the speech together before the text was released. On November 13 Agnew treated the networks, their owners, commentators, and anchormen to thirty minutes of verbal overkill for their "instant analysis and querulous criticism" of their President. Two days later, the national news portrayed the November 15 demonstration pretty much as John Mitchell saw it. CBS, for one, led off with film clips of the minor incident at the Justice Department.

The leaders of the Moratorium and the New Mobilization had no way to know how great was their success, how real was their achievement. Not until several years later did word leak out that Nixon and Kissinger had been seriously and secretly contemplating at that time a fierce escalation of the war, possibly to include the use of nuclear weapons. The antiwar sentiment generated and aired in the fall of 1969 made it politically impossible for the President to proceed with his plan. As a result, thousands, perhaps hundreds of thousands of North Vietnamese and American lives were spared. Nixon's second plan, to isolate and defuse his opposition in the war at home, was activated and found some success. The Administration did achieve its privately avowed intention of manipulating the press and members of Congress. Only a handful of senators and representatives endorsed the November 15 action. The media, television in particular, treated the event itself with circumspection and trepidation after the White House threats. The "silent majority," on the other hand, was less real than putative. The reality was that millions of Americans, often at considerable personal discomfort and cost, had spoken, marched, and demonstrated in opposition to the war.

An internal White House memo written by Nixon aide Dwight Chapin outlined the steps to be followed by the Administration to undermine the Movement: "the objective is to isolate the leaders of the 'Moratorium' and the leaders of the 'Mobilization' committee. They are one and the same and their true purpose should be exposed." The two groups were not, of course, one and the same, but Nixon's "silent majority" speech did much to bring them together. And neither, as events would soon show, was very clear about its "true purpose." Further efforts to isolate the leaders took the form of Red-baiting. This had little effect on the Mobilization forces. For more than four years the antiwar movement had been nonexclusionary. Communists were welcome, and for years the various Mobilization letterheads had carried the names of such war-horses of the CP as Arnold Johnson, who had once demurred when a proposal was made to invade the Capitol itself in 1967, suggesting instead that "we make it clear we meant the gallery and not the floor of Congress, which could be considered insurrection." The party was a conservative element in the Movement, with a tendency to follow liberal Democratic Party electoral policies. "The CP," says Cora Weiss, "was never the threat [J. Edgar] Hoover made it out to be. It was square. You could count on them to provide bodies but not initiate creative ideas." Nixon's Administration, like Johnson's, was never able to establish a Moscow link with the American peace movement, despite repeated, costly efforts to do so.

Sidney Peck was one of those who fell under scrutiny. Eventually the FBI developed a twenty-thousand-page file on Peck. The most damaging information gleaned in this FBI hunt seems to be that Peck, at the time a college undergraduate, was for seven months a CP member, until he fell afoul of the leadership and was expelled. Peck's assessment of the November 15 action, echoing as it does the language of the Chapin memorandum, does not resonate in the to-the-barricades way of an insurrectionist: "We felt now that we could help bring it to an end and that we had a majority movement. . . . [We were] isolating the Nixon Administration. . . . Now the focus would be on the Congress. The Congress now, at this point, had to put up or shut up. Congress held the purse strings. From here in we were going to have to go to the Congress and force them to act decisively on the war."

In this frame of mind Peck attended a meeting of the coordinating committee of the New Mobilization on December 13–14 in the Hatch Auditorium of Case Western Reserve University in Cleveland, a familiar haunt for the more than fifty persons in attendance. The purpose of the meeting was to evaluate the November 15 action and plan for the future. "It was," says Peck, his voice falling away to a whisper of hurt disbelief thirteen years later,

> a disastrous meeting. Just such a pattern of self-righteous leftism. Here was this great, powerful action [November 15] that a lot of people were really, really hard on. You had people coming from the Left—and they're not bad people, they're decent people—[who] said that we had not accomplished anything . . . and that all we did was give a platform to the phony people in Congress. They just denounced the demonstration as a very liberal thing that had very little impact. . . .

It was a breaking point, and not just for Peck:

> Here was Stewart Meacham, who had broken his back in helping to put this thing together, who had worked hard and kept the Moratorium element together, who had provided the leadership for the March Against Death, and so forth and so on. I think at that point he had had it. He said, "Well, why don't you people take a hand at it. That's it for me." I think he left the meeting. Shortly after—I think, I'm not sure how soon after—he decided to leave his position as peace secretary of the AFSC. And I think that ended his involvement in the antiwar coalition. That was it for him. I know that I just felt I couldn't believe it.

Doug Dowd, like Peck a selfless worker in the Movement since the days of the teach-ins and the Inter-University Committee for Debate on Foreign Policy, was also discouraged. The old-timers drew back, turned over the surplus twenty-five to thirty thousand dollars in the treasury to the radical caucus, and said, "O.K., you folks think you know what you want to do. . . . Take it and move with it." Dowd, Meacham, and Peck, however, were firehorses who could be expected to hear the first clang of the bell and respond. All three were active in the spring of 1970. Meacham, in fact, appeared as a cochairman with Ron Young at the first press conference under the new leadership.

In the politics of the 1969 antiwar coalition the radical caucus meant a loose alliance of radical pacifists with remnants of (SDS) youths loyal to Dellinger, Davis, and the Chicago 8, plus a smattering of radical intellectuals and religious. Measured as troops in the field, they amounted to very little except for the undisciplined adherents of the Chicago 8. The radical caucus gained cohesion and numbers at Cleveland mainly from a shared repugnance for the unswerving stance of the SWP, namely, that the antiwar coalition existed for but one reason, to organize peaceful, legal mass marches and rallies in demand of immediate U.S. withdrawal from Vietnam. An exasperated Fred Halstead spoke to this point—"Haven't you learned anything?"—at the meeting but acknowledges that his "ranting speech was not well received." It was, in Peck's opinion, the rigidity of the SWP position, shared by Jerry Gordon of CAPAC, that gave the radical caucus its slim majority.

The tenuous majority voted to build upon a vague concept of decentralized days of resistance in the spring around tax collection day, April 15, that would "deepen the political message." Says Peck: "Between December and April literature got out, but nothing was building. And in a relatively short time that $30,000 surplus went." Gone too, in every effective sense, was the SWP and its student wing, YSA, which in turn controlled the only viable organization left functioning on the campuses, the Student Mobilization Committee.

Within weeks of its greatest triumph, the huge antiwar coalition thus found itself in disarray. In adversity of the sort encountered in Nixon's Washington, the Movement flourished; its undoing lay in its own success. With no apparent enemy immediately at hand to close ranks against, the coalition discarded old and proven leaders, gave way to all its centrifugal tendencies, and yielded to the quixotic, self-centered politics of its least significant elements. The Moratorium forces—an uneasy ally at best—were, in a different way, likewise the victims of success. "We had essentially peaked in terms of our organizing strategy," says David Hawk. "[The point] where we had hoped to get by December we had reached by October." The Moratorium abandoned its planned escalation of one added day each month— "What could we do for eight days in May?" said Marge Sklencar—and Sam Brown announced that it "was time to go back to the neighborhoods and simple talk." But, in truth, very few of the students who savored the fever-pitch excitement of October 15 and November 15 had ever been in the neighborhoods, and their reception there was problematical. The difficulty was, said Brown, that Nixon had somehow managed "to identify himself with the cause of peace."

A few days before Brown spoke, a minor but ominous incident took place in New York City. It suggested that the country, locked in something like a stalemate position on the war, might be doomed to relive its worst nightmares of domestic violence. What happened was an ugly, small-scale replay of the Grant Park scenario of Chicago 1968. President Nixon was in New York to attend the National Football Foundation's award dinner at the Waldorf-Astoria Hotel. A crowd of some three thousand protesters assembled, just as they had thirty-four months earlier when Lyndon Johnson appeared at the same hotel for a Freedom Foundation dinner event. This time, however, the protesters were younger and their mood angrier. A red flag of revolution was run up a flagpole in the vicinity of the police barricade. The police inspector in charge ordered his men to move in and "get that flag down." They did so, nightsticks at the ready. Rocks were thrown, and one struck the inspector on the mouth. Some of the youths smashed windows in the Saks Fifth Avenue department store. Sixty-five were arrested on charges ranging from misdemeanors to felonious assault. Two of those arrested entered countercharges of police brutality. The incident received little publicity; it was only a possible warning signal.

The fall actions of 1969 were a high point for the antiwar movement, the time of its greatest success. By mounting two huge, peaceful demonstrations it had rescued its public image from the Chicago debacle; furthermore, the revelations of the My Lai massacres had reinforced, for at least some segments of the public and the media, the image of Vietnam as a "bad" war—a war that discredited the United States, a war that should be ended, just as the antiwar movement said that it should.

In the years since its inception, and particularly since the first major antiwar demonstration, in April 1965, the Movement had seen a general expansion. Even the apparent disaster at Chicago produced an explosion of new adherents on the college campuses in the fall and winter of 1968. Now, in December 1969, its leaders might have looked back with justifiable pride on nearly a year of successful organizing which led to the two great demonstrations in the fall. Hundreds of thousands of Americans who had never demonstrated before had taken part in those actions; they provided, for the first time, a truly nationwide base for a mass movement against the war.

But the Movement's success belied its true condition. The Moratorium had not long to live. With only the most nebulous ties to the millions who flocked to its banners in October, it lacked the organic structure to receive, nourish, and retain its new adherents. The Mobilization was deathly ill, its leadership not only divided over how to proceed, without any firm plan for growth, but also taken up by indictments and trials. Further trouble for the Mobilization was the loss, now, of its best conduit to the nation's college youth; SDS had disintegrated and nothing was at hand to replace it. Neither the Moratorium nor the Mobilization offered the Movement firm prospects for growth as 1969 came to a close.

Thus the Movement's time of greatest success was also its moment of greatest peril; for the imperative to grow at that stage held all the force of a biological law for a political movement that had progressed beyond the possibility of dynamic stasis. Opposition to the war was no longer carried on by a small, fluctuating, self-renewing community of "witness," as in the earlier years. In the days when A. J.

Muste and a handful of associates could come forward, make their unavailing point, then retire to return again another day, each martyr lost to the cause for whatever reason was soon replaced, even as molecules and membrane are renewed in living things. In progressing from a state of idealistic witness to the realm of practical politics with a specific, proclaimed political goal, expressed in 1969 as total withdrawal from Vietnam, the Movement exposed itself to the possibility of destruction at each new step. For the countervailing forces of public inertia and denial on the one hand and presidential cunning on the other stood ready to overwhelm a political audacity that could not demonstrate perceptible, steady increase: without mass, no momentum; without growth, decline.

The antiwar movement's root problem was that in 1969 it was engaged (albeit on a larger scale) as it had been for six years in an exercise that since the time of the ancients has been self-defeating: like the Persian messenger in Herodotus, the antiwar movement was bringing, ever more insistently, a message to the American people that the American people did not want to hear. Whether or not it was a correct message was beside the point. Americans in general are proud of their country, and rightly so; they do not like to hear her criticized. They do not like to be told that she is wrong. They do not like to be told that she is engaged in an immoral, illegal, savage, Nazi-like, imperialist war. They do not like to think that America the invincible can be defeated. Presented with such claims, they will exercise all their powers of denial. They will "kill the messenger," even as the ancients did, for bringing such bad news.

Richard Nixon played upon this natural human reaction, this simple and heartfelt patriotism, and never more effectively than in his "silent majority" speech. *His* message—hopeful, inspiring, "patriotic"—gave the American people a rationale for ignoring the unpleasant message of the peace movement, and in that speech (in particular) Nixon laid the groundwork for the crippling of the antiwar movement through the promise of

—Vietnamization,

—troop withdrawal and lowered draft calls,

—lowered (American) body counts, and

—victory through "peace"—"let us unite against defeat."

And so both the "moderate" (Moratorium) and "radical" (Mobilization) elements of the antiwar movement entered 1970 at a moment of triumph, poised to grow and yet fated—almost—to die.

1970:
War on the Home Front

AT 1:30 A.M. on January 1, 1970, a two-engine Cessna 150 took off from an airport outside Madison, Wisconsin, flew thirty-five miles north, and dropped three bombs on the Badger Army Ammunition Plant. An anonymous telephone call to the University of Wisconsin student newspaper, the *Daily Cardinal,* identified the bombers as members of "the Vanguard of the Revolution" and said that members of the group stole the plane from the field where it was used to train University of Wisconsin ROTC flight cadets. "Unfortunately," said the caller, "all the bombs were duds."

The *Daily Cardinal* endorsed the terrorist act in an editorial printed on January 6, and asserted that "the Establishment" had failed to respond to all previous legal and peaceful demands for change in U.S. policy (toward Vietnam). The editorial carried the title "End of the Road." In the same week two campus buildings housing ROTC officers were firebombed and an army reserve building in Madison was broken into with axes and communications equipment destroyed. "If acts such as those committed in the last few days," said the student newspaper, "are needed to strike fear into the bodies of once fearless men . . . then so be it." This was more than youthful frustration; it was the language of insurrection.

The academic year 1969–70 saw a wave of terrorist bombings and arson across the United States both on campus and off. Nearly 250 bombings occurred with at least six deaths and 247 cases of arson, including a $320,000 fire at the library on the Berkeley campus of the University of California. The frustrations of the Movement and perhaps the sense of some radicals that conditions in the country had reached a prerevolutionary stage as 1970 began were also expressed in eloquent if dubious argument by Staughton Lynd. In the March 1970 issue of *Liberation* Lynd wrote an editorial essay entitled "Testimony I Would Have Given at the Chicago Trial." In it he points out the striking surface similarities between the Chicago events of 1968 and two pre-Revolutionary incidents of 1770 in the American colonies, the Boston Massacre and the Battle of Golden Hill in the city of New York: in both 1968 and 1770 there were violent street battles between citizens and armed agents of authority; and just as the epithet "pig" in 1968 echoed the taunt of "lobsterback" that enraged the British soldiers of 1770, so, according to Lynd, did the battle for New York's liberty pole prefigure the skirmish for control of the Grant Park flagstaff.

Lynd then goes on to describe the long and fruitless efforts of the colonists to petition the home government for redress of grievances. Their petition, he says, quoting the Second Continental Congress, "was huddled into both houses [of Parliament] among a bundle of American papers, and there neglected." Coming back to the contemporary event, Lynd argues that "the entire process of assembling and demonstrating in Chicago was an exercise of the right to petition in just that sense . . . intended by the Founding Fathers. The government says the defendants conspired to cause a riot. I, on the contrary, say that they organized a process of petitioning, just as Sam Adams and Tom Jefferson did before them."

The route from this point on, as Lynd charts it, runs from petition to revolution or insurrection. Along this course "are acts of resistance, intermediate between speech and insurrection." The respective examples here are the Boston Tea Party and, again, the events of Chicago. Lynd finally argues not only that the First Amendment right "to petition the government for a redress of grievances" implies the right to alter or abolish that government, but also that the Tenth Amendment may be construed as including among the "powers . . . reserved . . . to the people" the right of revolution.

The Chicago trial to which Lynd alluded in the title of his editorial essay continued through the winter months of 1969–70. It was variously known as the trial of the Chicago 8, then (when Bobby Seale's case was separated) as the Chicago 7, and —more commonly—simply as the Conspiracy, a name the defendants mockingly chose for themselves. The Conspiracy operated in conformity to a dynamic all its own, a segment of the antiwar movement virtually independent of any larger coalition and free of all constraints save those imposed by the U.S. district court in Chicago. All eight defendants were charged with conspiracy to cross state lines with intent to cause a riot (in Chicago at the time of the 1968 Democratic Convention); two of them, John Froines and Lee Weiner, both young, both at the beginning of their professional academic careers, were charged with teaching and demonstrating the use of incendiary devices; the other six were the first to be charged under a provision of the 1968 Civil Rights Act, the so-called Rap Brown law: the act of crossing state lines with the intent to cause a riot. One of the six was a leader of the Black Panther Party, Bobby Seale. Seale had met only one of the other defendants, Rubin, before the trial began. The meeting took place when Seale came to Chicago at the time of the Democratic National Convention as a last-minute replacement for Eldridge Cleaver; he spoke in the usual inflammatory Panther style at two protest gatherings, and departed. The refusal of the presiding justice, Judge Julius Hoffman, either to allow Seale a lawyer of his own choice or to speak for himself led Seale to highly disruptive antics in the courtroom in the first weeks of the trial. The remaining five defendants had indeed planned and organized the protest demonstrations around the Democratic National Convention in August 1968. They were: David Dellinger, Tom Hayden, Rennie Davis, Abbie Hoffman, and Jerry Rubin.

The trial, which lasted for five months from September 1969 to February 1970 and produced a transcript that runs to twenty-two thousand pages, was a travesty of justice and the judicial process from beginning to end. The behavior of Bobby Seale, calculated as it was to affront the dignity of the court in the assertion of what he believed were his rights under the constitutional system, drove Judge Hoffman to distraction. Judge Hoffman was not the only one meeting Seale for the first time. Rennie Davis remembers the impression Seale made on his codefendants as the trial began:

> We were white and he was the black, heavy revolutionary. Yet immediately he was totally one of us, completely one of the team. He completely grasped the mood of what was happening among us: "Wow, isn't this fantastic? Look what we got here! We're running the show, this is our show, our time has come, we are on the stage—and are we ever ready!"
>
> Certainly Bobby was ready—to play this drama to the hilt. No sense of fear; just a delightful sense of humor. He could poke fun at himself as well as the judge.

For all of this, Davis says, "Judge Hoffman was just perfect." After being repeatedly called a racist, a pig, and a fascist, Hoffman had Seale—who was already spending his nights in jail because of a pending trial on murder charges—bound and gagged in the courtroom. When this failed to halt the disruptions, Judge Hoffman declared a mistrial for Seale early in November and sentenced him to four consecutive years in prison on contempt-of-court charges. The spotlight then turned to the seven remaining defendants.

They had several factors working for them. One was that they were not guilty as charged; they had not gone to Chicago for the purpose of fomenting riots. Froines and Weiner were completely exonerated by the original jury, which also rebuffed the government's charge of conspiracy against all seven. The other five, found guilty on the "Rap Brown" charge only because four jurors compromised their beliefs to vote with a majority of the jury panel, eventually won their case on appeal. A major advantage for the defendants was that the trial ran under the full glare of national and international publicity. The defendants thus had the full opportunity they sought to bring to a wide audience what they considered egregious examples of governmental oppression.

Although the government gave Dellinger the prominent role—the case is officially known as *United States of America v. David T. Dellinger et al.*—and he was well known within the antiwar movement as a leader of the Mobilization in all its manifestations, four of his younger codefendants may have been better known to the public at large. Rubin and Hoffman had been in the media spotlight for two years, and all who were aware of SDS knew of Hayden and, to a lesser extent, Davis, despite the fact that their formal ties with SDS had long since been severed. Whatever the case, the trial brought all of them to celebrity status on the college campuses among youth who were opposed to the war and for whom Chicago and Columbia were place-names more honored than Hamburger Hill or Hue.

Hundreds of articles and books were published about the trial, including an edited transcript of the proceedings, *Tales of Hoffman*. Daily press coverage was lavish. It centered, predictably, on the bizarre and unusual: the attempt by the other defendants to introduce into the courtroom a birthday cake for Bobby Seale; Hoffman and Rubin appearing in judicial robes, which they then used to wipe their feet; October 15, when the defense table was draped with the American and NLF flags and Dellinger tried to read the names of the dead from both sides of the conflict. Another occasion for intensive media coverage occurred when Dellinger blurted out, "Bullshit!" when James D. Riordan, a Chicago deputy police chief, was testifying ("an absolute lie," Dellinger called it) about events at Grant Park. The New York *Times* left all but its crossword puzzle aficionados in the dark about this episode when it reported that Dellinger used "an eight letter barnyard epithet."

The defendants, especially the five most responsible for mounting the demonstration in 1968, could not meet the demand for their presence as speakers on college campuses. The one control the judge held over the defendants, the power to revoke bail and put an end to their cross-country speaking trips, was for them a Sword of Damocles. The thread by which it hung was the fraying patience of the seventy-four-year-old Judge Hoffman. It finally snapped with "Bullshit!" Despite Judge Hoffman's protestation that "never in more than half a century of the bar" had he heard a man "using profanity in this court"—to which Abbie Hoffman interjected, "I've never been in an obscene court, either"—Dellinger believes he was punished for talking out of court. At the previous court session Judge Hoffman had referred to a speech given by Dellinger at Marquette University in Milwaukee, one pointedly critical of the judge. The explicit threat was that a repetition would mean loss of bail. Over the intervening weekend Dellinger gave more or less the same speech at Northwestern University, not far from Judge Hoffman's plush home at the Drake Towers. Dellinger's bail was revoked, and his home for the last three weeks of the trial became the Cook County Jail.

At the trial's end and while the jury was deliberating, Judge Hoffman issued over 125 contempt citations and sentenced the seven defendants and their two lawyers, William Kunstler and Leonard Weinglass, to a total of more than twelve years in jail. The judge came down heaviest on the two lawyers, who, wrote Tom Hayden, "had an obligation to be officers in the court of a madman." Their two sentences together fell just short of six years. Press coverage, centering as it did upon the lurid occasion and the flamboyant expression of contempt (one third of the citations, for example, arose out of the binding and gagging of Bobby Seale), shielded from the notice of most Americans a deeper, more pernicious contempt for the whole process of justice on the part of the judge and the prosecution.

In a curious way the trial was a replay of an earlier scenario. This time around, instead of Mayor Daley, the Chicago police, and the street setting, the defendants faced Judge Hoffman and the federal prosecutors in a U.S. district court. Before, they had been refused the necessary permits for a peaceful demonstration; in the court they were denied the right to prove their peaceful intentions. In both instances they suffered from the abuse of legitimate power and authority that so troubled those who saw Vietnam as only the most egregious example of a more pervasive flaw in the American system. The judge and prosecution combined to prevent the defendants from mounting a proper defense on the First Amendment rights at issue: freedom of speech and the right peaceably to assemble. Ramsey Clark (the former attorney general of the United States) and Staughton Lynd, two potentially powerful witnesses on these matters, were not allowed to testify for the defense. Congressman John Conyers and the Reverend Ralph Abernathy were also kept off the stand. Judge Hoffman refused to declare Mayor Daley a "hostile" witness and thereby thwarted attorney Kunstler's desire to cross-examine the mayor, who provided no testimony of value to the defense. The defense was not allowed to enter documents such as the original Yippie application to the city for a permit and the twenty-five-page Hayden/Davis outline of their plans for Chicago, which contained the statement that the demonstration "should be nonviolent and legal." These documents, the prosecution stated, were "self-serving" and therefore inadmissible. The judge agreed. Other documentary evidence, including a memorandum submitted by a Justice Department official to the attorney general of the United States in which Rennie Davis's efforts in the summer of 1968 to obtain a permit and avert violence are set forth, suffered a similar fate. Tom Hayden does not agree that Judge Hoffman was "perfect" for the purposes of the defendants: "If we had had a good judge . . . a straight shooter, we would have won the case."

The defendants had in addition to the First Amendment rights question a second main thrust to their presentation. To this, the federal attorneys offered no objection; they did not see it as threatening the prosecution's case. Tom Hayden, who worked hard in the preparation and planning of this aspect of the defense, says, "We decided to tell the whole history of Chicago in the context of the history of protest in the United States. We had one hundred and fifty witnesses. If you were there and heard it, it was unbelievable—but most of what was said was disallowed. . . . I worked with witnesses and was sort of a third lawyer: bring them into town, go through testimony with them, help them with the kind of questions they would get." Witnesses who were allowed before the jury included Bobby Seale, Norman Mailer, Allen Ginsberg, Arthur Waskow, Mark Lane, Timothy Leary, and Country Joe McDonald—a group that, taken together, was unlikely to set at ease the mind of a typical jury. One defense witness, Linda Morse, was led on cross-examination to admit she practiced shooting an M-1 rifle and had, after Chicago, abandoned her Quaker pacifist upbringing and beliefs in the realization that a nonviolent revolution was impossible. "The theory," says Hayden, "was, we will win in the court of public opinion," but in retrospect it seems a defense more suited to public opinion in the Woodstock Nation or those whom some called "plate glass revolutionaries" than to the twelve citizens of Chicago seated in the jury box.

Fourteen years later, Hayden cautions against this kind of *ex post facto* judgment, because

> it's too difficult to re-create the conditions that could have led an otherwise reasonable person to believe that they were about to be caught up in civil

war. I like to think I was always a reasonable person, looking for whatever was the most practical way to solve a very tough problem, [namely] ending the war. But when I see the coverage of it and hear people talking about the period, I generally pass on even trying to explain. If you were there—it's automatic—everyone felt the same way.

Some felt that between Agnew and Nixon on the one hand and us on the other, and blacks over here, that we were just moving into civil war . . . into those situations where you wind up dead or in prison. A lot of people, myself included, felt that that was quite plausible. . . .

But I place myself in the group [as opposed to those who "dropped out" or went into the armed underground] that took a close look and made a judgment call that it was still a necessity to do political work designed to change the system from within, even if you had to attack it from the outside.

It was in the climate Hayden speaks of that the then governor of California, Ronald Reagan, said, when questioned about militants, "If it takes a bloodbath, let's get it over with. No more appeasement." (Reagan later withdrew the statement.) And Henry Kissinger, speaking of the same period and Nixon's handling of the antiwar movement, reaches a judgment not unlike Hayden's: "He [Nixon] never found the language of respect and compassion which might have created a bridge at least to the more moderate elements of the antiwar movement, so that civil war conditions developed."

Rennie Davis recalls that he and Hayden had at least one serious discussion before the trial began about the likelihood of assassination attempts against themselves or the others. Davis considered Abbie Hoffman, with his reckless, flamboyant, inflammatory speech and manner, to be most in jeopardy. Davis and Hoffman, as it happened, were the only two defendants to take the stand. Hoffman was questioned endlessly on the much publicized 1968 Yippie announcement that there would be nude-ins and public fornication in Chicago's Lincoln Park, but the prosecutors took more satisfaction from one exchange with Davis. Davis was asked, "And you stated, have you not, . . . that 'I have every intention of urging that you revolt, that you join the movement, that you become part of a growing force for insurrection in the United States'? You have said that, haven't you?" Davis replied to the prosecutor, "I was standing right next to Fred Hampton when I said that, and later he was murdered."

Fred Hampton's death had badly shaken Davis and the other members of the Conspiracy. Hampton was shot to death by police in the predawn hours of December 4, 1969, as he lay in his bed. Another Panther, Mark Clark, was also killed when fourteen Chicago police invaded their apartment, guns blazing. The incident was first described as a "shoot-out," but a grand jury investigation found that only one of more than eighty bullets fired could possibly have come from other than a police weapon. The charismatic twenty-one-year-old Hampton had been close to several of the Conspiracy. Davis knew and admired Hampton from his own ERAP days in Chicago and later. The Panthers were running similar community programs in the black neighborhoods and bringing to some Northern blacks the kind of self-esteem engendered in the South by SNCC. Dellinger was present at a postmidnight meeting less than twenty-four hours before the Days of Rage began when Hampton, two other Black Panthers, and William Kunstler tried to dissuade four Weatherman leaders from their intended rampage. "Bobby Seale's life is at stake," Dellinger quotes Hampton as saying. "Revolution is no motherfucking game with us. The black community has too many martyrs already."

The Conspiracy defense became a moveable feast. In his book *Trial*, Tom Hayden estimates that the defendants made at least five hundred campus appearances. He mentioned one thousand dollars as a standard fee and says, ". . . we were a myth in which millions could participate. We were symbols of what millions were going through themselves." Rennie Davis tells what the hectic pace was like:

> It was a real test of endurance. . . . We would get out of the trial and cars would be waiting outside on Dearborn Street. You tried to move as quickly as you could. We'd have staff clear corridors so you could actually move at a fast pace on the elevators, out into the cars, running as fast as possible, to get to the plane on time. Flying into an East Coast city and coming off the plane, you would meet your [police] tail and take a couple of minutes to explain the rules to them—local detectives were usually somewhat new to this form of surveillance and they needed some explanation of how the evening was going to go down. . . .
>
> The last couple of months it seemed like 50 percent of the places I would speak would result in some form of mayhem. Some incidents were extremely unfortunate, like burning down a city block in Tulane. An ROTC center was destroyed in St. Louis. Going into states where the governor had called out the National Guard. You're traveling under extreme time schedules, going into places to face an audience of seven to ten thousand. They've been waiting since seven-thirty [P.M.] and you're entering the hall at nine-fifteen. It's already been a long evening for them and you're about to speak for one and a half hours with a message that will move people to a pitch. . . . And then from that anything may happen. That night, you sleep if you can, and then you're back on a plane at 7 A.M., hoping that the weather's going for you. There were certain rules to this drama, and one of the rules was you must be in that courtroom by 10 A.M. or lose your bail and your right to speak [outside]. There was one tense morning when my plane circled and circled Chicago—was it going to make it? And it came ten o'clock and my seat was empty and Judge Hoffman was ready to revoke bail. The lawyers bought ten minutes through extraneous motions and manipulation. They had no idea if I was coming or not coming. It was just one minute away and it would have been over [for me].

On one late afternoon occasion Jerry Rubin left the courtroom early to make a speaking engagement at Rutgers University in New Jersey. He was halfway to the airport when he heard over the taxicab's radio that Judge Hoffman had issued a bench warrant for his arrest. He returned to the courthouse at once, properly penitent.

The Chicago 8—minus Bobby Seale, whose bail remained revoked—achieved on the campuses a celebrity status equivalent to the leading rock music groups of the day. Even the pictures for which the Seven posed together suggest something of this: hair, costume, youth, and confidence. The balding Dellinger, twenty years senior to the rest, somehow fits in. Under the circumstances it became difficult to distinguish reality from appearance. Could those hundreds of thousands who greeted the Conspiracy defendants on campus with respect, awe, and enthusiasm be an army ready to march? Rennie Davis, at least, seemed to think so. Where Hayden spoke of the court of public opinion, Davis told the judge "my jury will be in the streets all over this country." There was, he recalls,

> a sense that we had now reached a state of truly mass involvement against the war. We had a leadership and a relationship to a giant population. It was short-lived, but there was a sense that what we had been doing since 1960 was in place by 1970.

The happenings that Davis looked forward to then and still remembers as a vindication confirming both the innocence and the power of the Conspiracy were known collectively as The Day After (TDA). TDA took place on February 21, 1970, the day after Judge Hoffman sentenced each of the defendants found guilty to five years in prison, a fine of $5,000, and the "costs of prosecution."* The judge also refused to grant the defendants bail, finding them "dangerous men to be at large." Demonstrations, riots, and vandalism, some of it planned, broke out on TDA in Washington, Boston, Seattle, Santa Barbara (where the Bank of America was burned down), Berkeley, Madison, Chicago, New York, and elsewhere. In *SDS* Kirkpatrick Sale says of TDA that "those protests had no coordination or unified political base . . . they were almost done with and forgotten as fast as the tear gas could clear."

The appeals process took almost three years. Judge Hoffman's verdict was overturned in late 1972, and he was severely criticized by the higher court not only on strictly legal grounds, particularly his refusal to admit certain documents and witnesses for the defense, but also for his antagonistic and sarcastic treatment of the defendants and their two lawyers. The court also rebuked Thomas Foran, the chief prosecutor. A year later, in December 1973, another court disposed of most of the remaining contempt charges. Among those the court let stand were two against Dellinger, one for calling Judge Hoffman a "liar," another for calling Foran a "snake." Judge Hoffman, in the meantime, was scheduled to receive an invitation to visit the White House—until John Mitchell intervened.

The trial of Sidney Peck took place in Chicago in Circuit Court as the Conspiracy trial was drawing to a close, late in January 1970. The case was conducted without a jury but before a packed room of observers each day, many of whom had first tried unsuccessfully to enter the courtroom of the Chicago 7 as spectators. Peck was not named as a defendant in the Conspiracy trial only because state authorities believed they had an open-and-shut case against him on two state

---

* If David Dellinger's estimate of the costs of the defense are correct—close to $500,000, not counting hundreds of thousands more in free legal services from Kunstler, Weinglass, and others—the "costs of prosecution" exceeded $1 million.

charges of felonious assault on police officers. Deputy Superintendent of Police James M. Rochford testified in November in the course of the Conspiracy trial that on August 28, 1969, in front of the Hilton Hotel, he was struck on the head and turned "and found Sidney Peck pummeling me on the head with both his hands." Told he was under arrest, Peck ran off into Grant Park, according to the deputy superintendent, whose testimony strained for the dramatic: "A young Negro officer ran after him. After fifteen feet, he did the bravest thing I ever saw. He reached out and tackled Mr. Peck." With this testimony in hand, the state of Illinois went after Peck. Joseph Ettinger was Peck's attorney, and he passed on to Peck the courthouse gossip: they [the state's attorney's office] were out to get that radical professor from outside and, says Peck, "once they got me, they were going to change my sex."

Peck, however, had his own witnesses. One was a United States senator who had watched the entire scene from the window of his room in the Hilton Hotel, given a written statement to the defense, offered to appear in court, and then, at the urging of his political advisers, backed off. Fortunately, there were others willing to testify. Two of them were photographers who had been on the scene, and one of them, Carolyn Mugar, had a sequence of photos to back up her eyewitness account. The judge hearing the case, a brave man in Sidney Peck's eyes, chose to disregard the testimony of the two police officers. On February 4 Peck was acquitted on the two felony charges and fined five hundred dollars on a misdemeanor. Costs of the trial, which lasted about two weeks, ran close to twenty-five thousand dollars. Peck's friends, under the leadership of the Reverend Ray Miklethun, raised a defense fund in his behalf.

The verdict was considered a victory, but there were disappointments, in particular, the sense Peck had of being an insignificant party, an almost invisible spectator at his own trial. He felt this most keenly on the opening day:

> When I entered a plea of not guilty, I had fantasies of going into court and making some sort of important statement that history will absolve me. . . . I came into the courtroom with Ettinger, and somebody from the state's attorney's office was there and the judge was there . . . for the plea. Ettinger and the fellow from the state's attorney's office were talking, and the judge was waiting for them to finish and finally he said, "Well, what does your client plead?" Ettinger looked up and said, "Not guilty, your honor." And that was it.

But if the bloodless processes of justice denied Peck the sense of his own identity, a chance meeting while the trial was under way miraculously restored it to him:

> We were recessed at one point, and a young man came up to me. He had a little beard, he was white, about my height. He said, "Hi, Sid, how're you doing? How are you holding up?" I said, "Fine, I guess, as well as can be expected." He said, "I'm really glad." Then I said, "I assume that we know each other, but I have to tell you that I can't remember what your name is." "My name is Tom," he said. "You know me, Tom Trost. . . ." The only

Trosts I knew of were people who lived next door to us in St. Paul, Minnesota, where I grew up. Tom Trost was one of about ten kids [in] a Catholic family that lived next door. They owned a grocery store; they had all these kids; they were poor like us. . . . We each had front yards that just had dirt and an occasional blade of grass. . . . They always read Father Coughlin's *Social Justice* [a pro-Nazi, anti-Semitic magazine]. We had fights. We were "kikes" and "dirty Jews," and they were "goyim" and "shanty Irish," and so forth. . . . We used to call them Trost Toasties. . . . But we always had this unity; if anybody else from another neighborhood came around, we'd all be united. Nobody ever fooled around with the Selby-Dale neighborhood crowd.

So here was Tom Trost. I said, "What are you doing here? . . ." Well, he was part of the Beaver 55, part of the Catholic Left. "You're—" I said, "I can't *believe* it!" So, all of the optimism that I have, you know, for our eventually coming together—it was like—I can't express to you the feeling I had. I said, "But *Tom,* do you know that you and I are on the same side?" All the efforts to keep the Irish . . . and Catholic and Jews. . . . We embraced each other. . . . It was a very, very special moment.

I don't know how he got there [to the Catholic Left]. I still have pinned to my lamp at my desk a note that appeared in a WRL newsletter in October 1972 saying, "We are very sorry to report that our friend, Tom Trost, died in a fire in his apartment in Chicago." I never knew if that was for real or not, or whether Tom just went underground. And one time when I went back to St. Paul, I was going to check with his family and I went back to the old neighborhood. That's when I first learned that their house and our house are all paved over by an expressway. Never to this day have I made contact.

As the winter passed and the spring came on, the antiwar movement began to stir with a semblance of life. The plans for action that it announced, however, were tame and almost trite, unlikely to stir wide interest in a public that approved (65 percent) the President's handling of the situation in Vietnam—that is, his announced troop withdrawals.

In January the Moratorium announced its program for the spring. Aimed at "rekindling the fervor" of opposition to the Nixon policies which had surfaced the previous fall, the Moratorium focused on two areas: decentralized actions leading to protests around the country on April 15 (the date when federal income taxes were due), and a long-range program leading into the fall for aiding antiwar congressional candidates in the midterm elections.

In February, the New Mobilization made public its own spring programs: that month to focus on civil rights and "political repression"; in March, on the draft; and in April, like the Moratorium, on tax day and on the issue of the war's impact on the economy.

The most promising spring action was announced by the Student Mobilization Committee at the close of its two-day conference at Case Western Reserve (Cleveland) in mid-February. SMC, firmly controlled by the YSA and SWP, was now, with the demise of SDS, the only student group with a nationwide campus network. Close to thirty-five hundred people attended the conference; SMC claimed about twenty thousand members at this time—nowhere near SDS's membership two or three years before, but enough to organize a more than respectable turnout. The conference was invaded by a contingent of former SDSers, "Revolutionary Youth Movement—II," who, having opposed Weatherman, now had nowhere else to go. They tried to push the conference to support a variety of issues, including women's liberation and the Black Panthers, and they urged that civil disobedience be included in any action. But SMC was tightly controlled, determinedly single-issue (antiwar), and like all Trotskyites, wedded to the tactic of legal mass march and rally. The radicals lost; SMC announced that it would sponsor a week of antiwar demonstrations April 13–18, with a nationwide student strike in high schools and colleges on April 15.

The New Mobilization's draft protests took place as scheduled on March 19, but they were small (no more than a few hundred people) and they received little attention. They occurred in perhaps two dozen cities, including Washington, Philadelphia, Pittsburgh, Kansas City, Boston, and Chicago.

The April demonstrations, sponsored by all three groups, were more successful in numbers but were marred by violent rhetoric and actions. The focus of the protest—the income tax—was recognized by reenactments of the Boston Tea Party in New York, Boston, Chicago, and Des Moines. Many rallies took place at Internal Revenue Service district offices. In line with the plan for decentralization of the antiwar effort, protests were organized in towns and cities across the country; anywhere from a few hundred to a few thousand turned out. In New York twenty-five thousand people came to Bryant Park, some after attending rallies at Columbia and other universities, some after a rally at the New York IRS office in lower Manhattan. But the mood had changed from the previous fall; people seemed to know that those who attended were only the most faithful (or the most angry), and that they were not part of a growing movement that had built its success on the October and November demonstrations. One student who had attended many antiwar rallies but who declined to attend this one said that he felt "cynical and defeated." Pete Seeger, in New York, told the crowd that "most of us are sick and tired of words, words, words." In Bryant Park that day, a band of perhaps one hundred radicals (many of them PL-SDS) refused to allow the rally to proceed. They interrupted the reading of the names of American servicemen killed in Vietnam, prevented scheduled speakers from appearing, and finally took over the podium and shouted, "Revolution Now!" to the rapidly dwindling audience. In Berkeley, police used tear gas and clubs on university students who marched on the ROTC building. Rioting continued into the next day, when the university was closed and declared to be in a state of emergency. A mark of that year's turmoil on the campuses would be the readiness of university administrators, perhaps inspired by President Pusey's example the previous year in Cambridge, instantly to call upon police and other outside forces for assistance. The day's biggest turnout occurred in Boston, where upward of seventy-five thousand people assembled on the Common. Later a small contingent led by John Froines of the Chicago 7 marched across the Charles to Cambridge, where they proceeded to smash windows and set fires in and around Harvard Yard. This self-styled "November Action Coalition," composed of white students and nonstudents, had received a parade permit to protest the trials of Black Panthers Bobby Seale and Huey P. Newton. Harvard administrators claimed that they were not, by and large, Harvard students, and, indeed, the troublemakers chanted outside the dormitories, "How are the nation's elite?" Pitched battles between two to three thousand youths and about two thousand police continued into the night; more than two hundred people were injured and thirty-five arrested.

The postmortems on these less than successful attempts at protest recognized the fact that both the two huge single-issue protests of the fall and the smaller, multi-issue actions just completed failed to achieve an end to the war. In January, Sam Brown had said that the President's plan for Vietnamization was a "policy for continuing the war, not for ending it." He predicted that by the spring it would "become clear that people have been deceived." From a high of 65 percent in January, public approval of the President's handling of the war had dropped to 48 percent (with 41 percent disapproving). But the public's interest in the war seemed to be waning: the environment was rated by many newspaper publishers as the big new story; Earth Day on April 22 that year attracted (or co-opted) many people who had formerly marched for peace.

David Dellinger commented, not for the first time, that protests against the war needed to move beyond dissent to resistance—in Dellinger's lexicon, not armed combat but nonviolent civil disobedience conducted outside the political system. Others, like Rennie Davis, who was now once again an active member of the coalition, wanted to carry matters one degree beyond the level Dellinger advocated. Looking back from 1983, Davis tries to suggest what this meant:

> The defendants [the Chicago 7] were of the view that both things were possible: you continue to build broader- and broader-based support . . . but that a cutting edge of militancy, making it more and more difficult for the government to continue its policy, was necessary.
>
> And we played a kind of one-foot-in, one-foot-out role ourselves. We didn't want to lead the Movement into an SDS stance, *for sure*. But at the same time we didn't see the traditional pacifist groups as being the leadership of the anger. It was a delicate balancing act: mass base was needed, but accelerating the pressure. A little sense in the mind of the government that this thing could really get out of control was not, in our opinion, bad as a political tool against the intransigence of the Vietnam commitment even though it had a cost with image. . . .
>
> There came a certain point—a mood in the Movement—where this war must end. Martin Luther King seemed to possess that mood in Birmingham —a commitment to *whatever it takes*. It was delicate, you know.

And on the other end of the coalition spectrum, the pacifists; Tom Cornell portrays their dilemma:

> The pacifist movement lost control of the overall coalition. It was probably inevitable but we could have exerted more authority and force if we'd fol-

lowed Lens' advice. Lens was a pretty tough fellow. I remember a meeting of the religious and pacifist groups of the Mobilization around 1969 at the AFSC in Philadelphia and Lens stood up and said, "We've got to pull ourselves together and exert more influence in the Mobilization as a group to give greater pacifist cogency in this whole thing or we're going to find things going off in all kinds of directions with all kinds of forces. . . ."

But nonviolent civil disobedience demanded a self-discipline, patience, and dedication which many people did not have—or did not want to have. All spring, while the three antiwar coalitions (the Moratorium, the Mobilization, and SMC) struggled to maintain their semblance of protest, resistance of a very different sort was building—literally—underground. In retrospect it can be seen as—again literally—the dark side of the students' protests, the hellish vision of all that Middle America feared when it thought about its young, its students, its bright hope for a better day: in short, its future.

From the outlaw Weathermen, on March 6, 1970, came a protest message very different from that of the marches and demonstrations: a dynamite blast which destroyed a Greenwich Village town house that had become a Weatherman bomb factory. Three Weathermen were killed: Diana Oughton, Terry Robbins, and Ted Gold. Several others escaped as the house collapsed into ruins around them; only two of these have ever been identified: Cathlyn Wilkerson, whose father owned the house, and Katherine Boudin, daughter of attorney Leonard Boudin, one of Dr. Spock's lawyers in the Boston 5 trial. The explosion occurred when Oughton and Robbins misconnected a wire in an antipersonnel bomb that they were constructing. Later, police found in the ruins enough dynamite to level an entire city block. Oughton's headless torso was studded with roofing nails and was identified only by the fingerprint on the tip of her little finger, which was found as police sifted through the wreckage. Robbins's body was so badly fragmented that police were never able positively to identify him; a Weatherman communiqué in May named him as the third fatality.

The Eleventh Street blast destroyed more than three young lives and an expensive piece of real estate: it destroyed any possibility that the antiwar movement would ever be perceived in the public mind as anything but mindlessly violent. It was the most stunning event in a time of "infernal devices." Bombs were everywhere, it seemed; in the first ten months of 1970 the New York City police had more than 8,700 bombing "cases" (the previous year, 1969, the figure was 3,192 for the entire year). A "case" was described as a telephoned warning (often false), a device, evacuating a building, or any other task performed by the bomb squad. Many of the bombings, police said, were performed by members of organized crime, by the radical Right, by immigrants, and by the mentally ill; undeniably, however, the young, radical Left (or persons claiming to be the young radical Left) had added to the total. Many times, credit for bombings was claimed not by Weathermen but by people who called themselves, say, the Quarter Moon Tribe or the Perfect Park Homegrown Garden Society. They were probably not Weathermen, but no one knew for sure. Weatherman's pattern of three- or four-person cells and its efficient underground machinery made its members almost impossible to find. One policeman, referring to the Ku Klux Klan and the right-wing, heavily armed Minutemen, said, "We know pretty well what they're doing—they're pretty structured." Weatherman was anything but structured, and they continued to plant bombs, usually with a telephoned warning, through January 1975, when the State Department was heavily damaged by a bomb placed in a third-floor men's room.

The fact that there were never more than three hundred Weathermen (probably a high figure); that Weathermen usually gave warning of their attacks; that they claimed to bomb only corporate, military, or government buildings (Socony Oil, the Bank of America, ROTC buildings) as a statement of their hatred for what they viewed as oppressive capitalist/imperialist institutions; and that they killed "only" a few people (many were injured, however) begs the question of the damage that they did. Their turn toward violence came partly out of a sense of rage and deep frustration not only at the continuing war in Vietnam but also at the failure of American society to change to what they thought it should be. (Many Weathermen had worked in the ERAP projects.) They have been compared to the Narodniki, nineteenth-century upper-class Russian youths who went to live with the poor—as uninvited and ultimately unwelcome as the ERAP SDSers had been. The Narodniki were also violent; by assassinating Czar Alexander II they brought down on themselves and others savage reprisals by the Russian police system and destroyed the possibility of democracy in Russia.

Similarly, Weatherman and its imitators (and possibly government provocateurs claiming to be Weathermen) destroyed the true identity of the antiwar movement. The image of its violent rhetoric and its very real war on American society and institutions were indelibly imprinted on the public's mind, and Weatherman and the antiwar movement became irrevocably linked. Thus the actions of a few score insanely angry youths besmirched the historical truth of years of peaceful effort by concerned, responsible, and patriotic citizens, youths and adults alike. Ironically, it had been SDS that in 1965 had insisted on a policy of nonexclusion: when the moderate peace forces had feared destruction if they associated with Communists, SDS had said that no one should be excluded from that year's April march. SDS had won that fight, and the antiwar movement had survived. Now the actions of a few maddened former SDSers—the best and the brightest, some would have said—served to tarnish a peace movement that was far larger than any peace activist could have imagined five years before, and they hurt that movement far more than any member of the Communist Party ever could have done. The antiwar movement in 1970, however, had no way to "exclude" Weatherman, even though Weatherman had excluded itself from the antiwar movement.

The Nixon Administration responded to the (domestic) enemy bombings by announcing, on April 11, an increased program of surveillance on left-wing militants, including wiretapping and the use of informers and undercover agents. By this time, of course, the intelligence apparatus was long since in place; the announcement was only a public acknowledgment of a program of government spying, harassment, and provocation of dissenters that had been going on for nearly thirty years. Through the Freedom of Information Act (1966) many people acquired copies of their files from the FBI; some, like Sidney Peck's, ran to thousands of pages.

Within the system that Weatherman (but not the antiwar movement) was trying to bring down, events moved slowly to respond to public weariness with the war. In Lexington, Massachusetts, lived one John M. Wells, a Unitarian minister; he was also a lawyer, and a onetime legal consultant to the Pentagon. Wells's house faced the Lexington Battle Green, where the American Revolution began; an American flag flies there always to commemorate it. The house had once belonged to Jonathan Harrington, one of the Minutemen who fought that battle; Harrington, the first casualty of that war, died on the front steps of his house on April 19, 1775. The revolution, said John Wells, was fought "for the right of people to participate in the decision-making process, in what the government does. And the process of government that most involves people, their lives, their pocketbooks, is war."

And so Wells drafted a bill which he asked Representative James Shea, Jr., to introduce in the Massachusetts legislature; he had met Shea through Kenneth O'Donnell, former aide to President Kennedy. The bill would have allowed Massachusetts men to refuse combat duty unless Congress, as it is constitutionally obliged to do, had first declared war. One of the bill's provisions empowered the Massachusetts attorney general to bring an action in behalf of any Massachusetts man who refused to serve—in this instance—in Vietnam, thereby enabling the case to go directly to the Supreme Court and, it was hoped, having the Court rule on the issue of whether the Vietnam War was unconstitutional. Lower courts had previously ruled that such dissenters had no case; the Supreme Court had refused all appeals, saying that the war's legality was a political, not a judicial, issue.

The Shea-Wells bill was the most direct challenge until that time to the Supreme Court on the issue of the war's constitutionality; it was passed by large majorities in both houses in early April and promptly signed by Republican Governor Francis W. Sargent. It was not without its critics, who called it everything from treasonous to "nothing more than a symbolic blow." But even symbolically it was viewed as of great importance, since, in the words of Professor Alan Dershowitz of Harvard Law School, "this is the first state to go on record against this atrocious war."

Resolutions similar to the Shea-Wells bill were introduced in at least eight other states that spring, including Connecticut, New York, Ohio, and Illinois; they either died in committee or failed to pass when they came up for a vote. The Massachusetts law reached the Supreme Court in November 1970. The Court refused without explanation to hear the case. In dissenting from that decision, Justice William O. Douglas stated that the question of the constitutionality of the war was "neither academic nor political"—that is, that the Supreme Court was wrong in agreeing that the question was not "justiciable"; the Court could and should rule on the war's legality, he said. Justices Potter Stewart and John M. Harlan, in a separate dissent, stated that at least the Court should have heard arguments on the Massachusetts challenge to the constitutionality of a war not declared by Congress.

Thus failed one more attempt to end the war through the system.

On April 20 the system—in the form of Vietnamization—seemed to be working moderately well as President Nixon announced a further troop withdrawal of 150,000 over the next twelve months. (Like the war itself, Vietnamization was conducted by Presidential fiat.) On the previous day the Moratorium had announced its demise: the "political fad" for mass demonstrations was finished, its coordinators said, as evidenced by what they termed the relatively poor turnout for the tax day protests the previous week. Mass demonstrations were not, of course, what brought the Moratorium into business just six months earlier, almost to the day. The success of October 15—originally intended to be an on-campus day to generate enthusiasm and volunteers for community door-to-door organizing a month later—victimized the youthful organizers. Unable to surpass their own bench mark of October 15, they lacked the endurance of their relatively elderly counterparts in the Mobilization. Jerome Grossman, whose idea the Moratorium was and who instinctively mistrusted the Mobilization forces, comments:

> At that time we were still in the phase of thinking that the world was going to be saved by young people, particularly students on campuses. We don't have that idea anymore. As a matter of fact, the anti-nuclear-weapons movement depends on older people. It depends on community people. And that's the secret of its success. The Moratorium was the first move for me in that direction [toward adults], because the Moratorium, the true Moratorium was not what happened on Boston Common. I was opposed to that rally.

On the evening of April 29 in New York, members of the New Mobilization coordinating committee met at the home of Cora Weiss. They had come together to decide how to keep the coalition alive and moving forward in the light of recent setbacks: the Mobilization's $25,000 to $30,000 surplus was gone; the April 15 actions had had little impact; and the Moratorium was dissolved. Sidney Peck reports that some people present interpreted the disbanding of the Moratorium as a "go-ahead" signal to Nixon; there would be no public outcry on any move the Administration might take to widen the war from the broader focus represented by that wing of the Movement. Suddenly the meeting was interrupted by a telephone call from Washington announcing the invasion of Cambodia by American troops. All dissension evaporated in the face of this new emergency. The group quickly agreed to call a demonstration in Washington on May 9—a seemingly impossible deadline, but one that was unavoidable in the urgency of the moment.

On April 30 President Nixon made the public announcement: American troops, supported by B-52 strikes, had been sent into Cambodia to eradicate enemy strongholds there, specifically North Vietnamese command posts. In addition, air strikes against North Vietnam were being made. The speech stunned a nation unprepared in any way for the sudden presidential decision to widen the war in Vietnam and to invade a neutral country in apparent violation of Article I, Section VIII, of the United States Constitution ("The Congress shall have power . . . To declare war").

The televised speech announcing the decision to the country contained three false statements: (1) that "there has been a great deal of discussion with regard to this decision," when in fact the Congress was not consulted, nor, in any substantial form, were Secretary of Defense Melvin Laird or Secretary of State William Rogers, who were not told of the invasion until the morning of April 27; (2) that "American policy has been to scrupulously respect the neutrality of the Cambodian people," when the Menu bombings had been pounding Cambodia since March 1969 and the so-called Salem House forays across the border by the Special Forces had an even longer history; and (3) that the invasion would "attack the headquarters for the entire Communist military operation in South Vietnam [COSVN]," when Secretary Laird had many times informed the President that no such target existed. Never before had the American people been so greatly deceived or, thanks to television, so thoroughly, as to the facts underlying a presidential decision of such import.

The evident strain of the nervous, sweating, twitching President that night under the television lights—never a friendly medium for Nixon—hinted at a deeper problem than mere prevarication: a psychological state unsuited for decision-making in the Oval Office. Nixon was receiving inspiration from repeated private showings of the movie *Patton* that depicted the career of the unstable, pistol-toting World War II tank commander. In the same vein, he had recently been briefed in Honolulu by Admiral John S. "Red Claws" McCain, Jr., the commander in chief of the U.S. Pacific Fleet (CINCPAC). McCain's epithet came from the Asian maps prepared for him showing vivid, red, prehensile arrows emerging from the belly of China to claw at country upon country in Southeast Asia. McCain was as gung ho as Patton. Nixon's other principal advisers were his drinking companion Bebe Rebozo, John Mitchell, and, of course, Henry Kissinger. Kissinger's admission to this high command was sealed in the days just before the speech by an invitation to join the other three for a cruise down the Potomac on the President's yacht, *Sequoia,* a cruise on which, according to Kissinger, "the tensions of grim military planning were transformed into exaltation by the liquid refreshments." There are other indications of hard drinking in these days: Roger Morris, one of three Kissinger aides who quit in disgust over Cambodia, writes of "the martinis that launched Cambodia." Finally, Nixon, who had been getting little sleep—he worked on the Cambodia speech until four-thirty in the morning of April 30—was infuriated with Congress, more specifically the Senate. On April 8 the Senate had rejected Nixon's second nominee to fill a seat on the Supreme Court that had been empty for nine months. This nominee, as it turned out, had dubious credentials and a segregationist background. Nixon describes his reaction as one of "cold and reasoned anger," but it was much more—or less—than that. He attacked the senators who voted against his nominee as "vicious," "prejudiced," and "hypocritical," and is reported to have told Kissinger that "those Senators think they can push me around, but I'll show them who's tough." Against this background the words of the April 30 speech seem addressed as much to himself as to the American people. "We will not be humiliated. We will not be defeated," he said. "It is not our power but our will and character that is [sic] being tested tonight. . . ." He was unwilling to see the nation "become a second-rate power and . . . accept the first defeat in its proud 190-year history.

. . . If, when the chips are down, the world's most powerful nation . . . acts like a pitiful, helpless giant, the forces of totalitarianism and anarchy will threaten free nations and free institutions throughout the world."

In the Congress, which itself was increasingly perceived to be pitiful and helpless, at least by those who opposed the war, many members supported the President's action. Some, however, did not; the dove faction was gaining adherents. Senator Mike Mansfield, for instance, was reportedly very angry. "It is a difficult situation to reconcile one's mind to," he said, referring to the bombing of North Vietnam; and, in deploring the Cambodian incursion, "there is nothing in past experiences in Indochina to suggest that casualties can be reduced by enlarging the area of military operations. . . . It is not a question of saving face. It is a question of saving lives."

Although the President had briefed about forty congressional leaders (including Mansfield) an hour before his speech, he had not requested their advice and consent. Now the Senate Foreign Relations Committee complained that he was "usurping the war-making powers of Congress"(!). Gearing up for battle, they voted to send the President a letter. They wanted a conference with him. The President agreed, but he invited the House Foreign Affairs Committee to attend also. The senators were annoyed at what they perceived to be a breach of etiquette. The House group was annoyed at what they perceived as the senators' "presumptuousness" in requesting a separate meeting. Meanwhile, the day after the Cambodian invasion, the Senate Foreign Relations Committee approved a repeal of the Tonkin Gulf Resolution; approval by the full Senate came on June 26, and by the full House on December 31. The President said that he would pay no attention to the repeal, and, in fact, he did not.

The meeting requested by the senators was the first time since 1919 that the Senate Foreign Relations Committee had met with a President. At that time the committee, under Chairman Henry Cabot Lodge, grandfather of the ambassador, successfully opposed Woodrow Wilson's wish to ratify the Treaty of Versailles ending World War I and to join the League of Nations. Now, in 1970, the committee had less muscle to work its will upon the executive: the President promised to limit the incursion to thirty-five kilometers; beyond that, he said, he would seek congressional consent. He promised to withdraw American forces from Cambodia by July 1—the announced date.

The reaction of the nation at large, and particularly of its students, to the Cambodian incursion was somewhat more direct and vehement than Congress's. Within hours of the President's speech—that is, on the night of Thursday, April 30— college students across the country had turned out to protest. Early the next morning, after yet another night with very little sleep, Nixon went to the Pentagon for a briefing on Cambodia from the Joint Chiefs. In that setting he responded to the student protest, but not before one more burst of Patton machismo. Pointing to some untouched "strongholds" shown on the Pentagon map of Cambodia, he commanded, "I want to take out all of those sanctuaries. Make whatever plans are necessary, and then just do it. Knock them all out so that they can't be used against us again. Ever." In the lobby of the Pentagon, on his way out, the President paused to talk to an admiring crowd—and to reporters:

> You know, you see these bums, you know, blowin' up the campuses. Listen, the boys that are on the college campuses today are the luckiest people in the world, going to the greatest universities, and here they are, burnin' up the books, I mean, stormin' around about this issue, I mean, you name it— get rid of the war, there'll be another one.

The protests to that point had not been violent, but with the advent of the weekend they became so. Stanford saw the worst riot in its history. At Ohio State the National Guard was called out and one student was shot—at a distance of two hundred feet—by a Guardsman armed with a shotgun. At nearby Kent State, students burned the ROTC building to the ground. In New York student editors from eleven major colleges met on the Sunday to compose an editorial that all of them would print calling for an immediate nationwide student strike; their combined circulation was about fifty thousand. Strikes had already been called on many campuses by that time, including Columbia, Princeton, the University of Pennsylvania, the University of Virginia, Notre Dame, and Brandeis. The National Student Association and the leaders of the defunct Moratorium called for a nationwide university strike starting immediately. A national strike center was established at Brandeis to coordinate information. Within hours of the call more than one hundred colleges and universities had announced their participation; in the next few weeks—the last weeks of the spring term—over 80 percent of the nation's colleges and universities had announced some kind of strike action. In addition to the strike, the NSA called for the President's impeachment. That same night (Sunday), at Kent State, students were herded into their dormitories by police and National Guardsmen; one girl was wounded by a bayonet and sixty-nine students were arrested.

On the Kent State University campus the next day, Monday, May 4, 1970 (almost ten years to the day after the San Francisco police engaged students in that city in the first police-student battle of the decade at a protest over a HUAC hearing), Ohio National Guard troops killed four students and wounded nine. In the words of the President's Commission on Campus Unrest, it was a moment when the nation had been "driven to use the weapons of war upon its youth," a moment when all the violence and all the hatred and generational conflict of the decade just past had been caught in those thirteen long seconds when the frightened, exhausted National Guardsmen, acting perhaps in panic or simple frustration, had turned on their taunters and taken their revenge.

The National Guardsmen who were at Kent State that day had been equipped not only with tear gas canisters but with M-1 rifles, weapons with a range of two miles, which they had been ordered to put into the "lock and load" position—that is, ready to fire. The students had called a demonstration for noon, more to protest the presence of the National Guard on their campus than to protest the President's Cambodia action. The commander ordered his men to disperse the crowd. They fired tear gas canisters at the students; when some of the canisters did not explode the students threw them back. A tear gas "tennis match" ensued. The students were angry with the soldiers; some became not only verbally but physically abusive. They threw rocks and bricks at the troops, but most were too far away to hit their targets. Some Guardsmen, however, were struck. The Guardsmen retreated to the top of a hill. Their heavy helmets and gas masks could not protect them from hearing the jeers and taunts of the students. Suddenly they opened fire. Later their officers denied giving such an order. Sixty-one shots were fired. The battle was quickly done; the dead and wounded lay before them.

And now the nation, and particularly her students, came fully awake to the horror of both her foreign war and her war at home, and higher education—and much secondary and elementary education as well—came to a halt. Faculty and administration joined their students in expressing their outrage, in calling for some action—or reaction—in response to this new cause for anguish. More than five hundred campuses canceled classes and fifty-one of them did not reopen at all that semester. Protest of some kind occurred at more than 50 percent of the nation's campuses; over four million students were involved. A computer printout listing participating schools run off by MIT for the National Student Strike Information Center at Brandeis† was ten feet long. For ease in handling it was taped to the ceiling. One of the schools on strike was General Beadle State College.

In a report on the disruptions for the Carnegie Commission on Higher Education, Chairman Dr. Clark Kerr, who had been president of the University of California at Berkeley at the time of the "free speech" crisis in 1964, stated that the Cambodia protests were without precedent, unparalleled by any previous crisis in the history of American education. Violence flared—arson, bombings, battles with police. Hundreds were arrested. In the week of the Kent State killings thirty ROTC buildings were destroyed by fire or bombs. The National Guard, heavily armed, was called out at twenty-one campuses.

The President was not taken unawares by the uproar. He called an emergency conference with the fifty governors and met with the heads of eight universities; he promised that he would restrain Vice President Agnew's hostile comments about students. On the day before the Cambodia speech Nixon had predicted to his secretary, Rose Mary Woods, "It's possible that the campuses are really going to blow up after this speech," and he summoned home to Washington from their New England colleges his daughter Julie and her husband, David Eisenhower. In the week that followed the speech tens of thousands of other college students also departed for Washington. Many of them believed that they, too, were headed for the White House, the planned target for the New Mobilization's May 9 demonstration.

"Those two weeks [around May 9]," says Norma Becker,

† Run by a twenty-one-year old Brandeis student from Denver, Kathy Power. Since September 1970 she has been sought by police and the FBI in connection with a bank holdup in Boston during which a policeman was killed by another participant.

were *the* high point of activism. I'm talking about the spontaneous upsurge *all over.* The schools closed down, junior highs, highs, colleges—everyone was in the streets protesting—strike center, Alternate University. . . . That's when the kids were beaten up by the longshoremen down by Trinity Church on Wall Street, an ugly, ugly scene.

We put out a mailing of ten thousand on one day's notice—we didn't have computerized mailings then. We had a staff of young people who worked incredible hours. These are the unsung heroes of that period, and their names don't go down in the history books: Linda Morse, Josh Brown, Alan Barnes, Wendy Fisher, Lorri Sandow, Bob Eberwein, and many others. . . . These are the young people who were working for fifty, seventy-five dollars a week, if and when we could pay them—nineteen, twenty, twenty-one years old. . . .

For example, from Pratt Institute the student organization authorized the purchase of half a train, five hundred seats. The students from Pratt Institute were not your revolutionary Communist Party or your Black Panthers, they were just unaffiliated students. I'll never forget this: they came on that train with helmets, with turtlenecks and long sleeves, because they were sure they were going to be maced and beaten by the police. . . . They were not the SDS. They did not go down there to confront or provoke, but they were willing after Kent State . . . to face being beaten and maced. I'll never forget that. I didn't understand. I wasn't wearing a helmet—I was in the Movement all these years—I wasn't going down there prepared to be beaten and maced. I mean, I was afraid, but I wasn't dressed that way. They were. They thought that was what was going to happen to them. They weren't violent. . . . That demonstration was such a sellout.

At least one member of Nixon's Cabinet was sufficiently appalled by the Cambodia speech, the "bums" remark, and the Kent State horror to give expression to his qualms. Secretary of the Interior Walter J. Hickel was a rugged, simple, direct individual whose taste for adventure brought him as a young man to a new home in Alaska. He was governor of Alaska when Nixon called him to Washington to serve as a cabinet officer. After the Kent State killings, unable to get an appointment to meet with either the President or with John Erlichman, the presidential assistant on domestic affairs, Hickel sat down on Tuesday (May 5) to write a letter. In his autobiography *Who Owns America?* Hickel writes that he began to compose the letter in his subconscious six months earlier, when Nixon ignored the hundreds of thousands of young people who came to Washington on November 15 in a vain effort to "reason" with him. Hickel's letter to the President was a single-minded plea to heed what the young people of America were saying; he wrote [in part]:

Today, our young people, or at least a vast segment of them, believe they have no opportunity to communicate with Government, regardless of Administration, other than through violent confrontation. . . .

About 200 years ago there was emerging a great nation in the British Empire, and it found itself with a colony in violent protest by its youth—men such as Patrick Henry, Thomas Jefferson, Madison and Monroe, to name a few. . . . My point is, if we read history, it clearly shows that youth in its protest must be heard. . . .

Faithfully yours,
Wally

Hickel's letter was hand-delivered to the White House on Wednesday morning, just as a leaked version of it was going out over the Associated Press wires. The White House denizens were unamused by the gratuitous history lesson and infuriated by the simultaneous press release. Only the fact that Hickel instantly became a minor hero, much in demand before the television cameras, prolonged his stay in office through the November election period. Then Nixon fired him.

As the young people were pouring into Washington—by Saturday, the day of the demonstration, 130,000 people, mostly students, were on hand—the issue of a permit was still unresolved. The coordinating committee of the New Mobilization was in nearly continuous session through the week. Like the President, they were getting little sleep. The intended site for the demonstration was Lafayette Square, opposite the ceremonial north entrance to the White House. Renovation of the park had been under way for eighteen months in a process stretched out by White House request in order to forestall exactly the use contemplated by the Mobilization. Until the last moment (4 P.M. Friday afternoon) the Administration refused to grant a permit for any site nearer the White House than the Washington Monument grounds—too far away, in the view of the organizers, for the demonstration to make its point of confronting the President in the White House. There was, in fact, no question of a permit at all in the initial stages of discussion, since permits had to be applied for fifteen days in advance. Undeterred, the organizers stated that they would hold their demonstration regardless, since the Administration had not sought a permit (from Congress or the people) for the Cambodian invasion. Anyone who came, therefore, would be engaging in what David Dellinger called the "*de facto* tactic" of nonviolent direct action (civil disobedience). By granting the Ellipse as a site at the last moment, as the government did, the Mobilization was given, as Dellinger put it, a site for yet another day of "sitting on the grass and listening to another round of speeches." It was, he said, "a master stroke of public relations that confused and divided the coalition." In the opinion of many in the Movement, this type of demonstration was an inadequate response to the Cambodian invasion and the nationwide outrage that it had engendered.

On Friday evening, their plans for the next day still chaotic, the leaders of the Mobilization met again. "We had to work out a scenario," says Sidney Peck. "We had a very late meeting. Abbie (Hoffman) and Jerry (Rubin) suggested a delegation to meet with Nixon at the White House—to 'rap' with him. Either a prestigious delegation or—people like Abbie and Jerry." "This," adds Peck with some amusement, "was seriously considered."

In fact, Nixon was in a mood to "rap" that night, although perhaps not with Abbie and Jerry. He describes himself as "agitated and uneasy." He was "dejected when I read that the father of one of the dead girls [at Kent State] had told a reporter, 'My child was not a bum.' " At a press conference that night he sought to associate himself with the goals of the young demonstrators: "They are trying to say they want peace. . . . They are trying to say that we ought to get out of Vietnam. I agree with everything that they are trying to accomplish. I believe, however, . . ." After the press conference Nixon retired to his quarters. William Safire reproduces the presidential telephone log for that night in *Before the Fall.* It shows that the President made or received fifty-one telephone calls between 9:22 P.M. and 4:22 A.M. Twenty-six of them were after midnight. He also received a lengthy visit from Supreme Court Chief Justice Warren Burger. At some point Nixon repaired to the Lincoln Sitting Room, where he played a recording of Rachmaninoff's Second Piano Concerto, a melodramatic piece. His last call at 4:22 A.M. was to Manolo Sanchez, the President's valet. Less than fifteen minutes later, a startled Egil Krogh, Jr., a White House aide on duty at the Secret Service command post in the Peace Corps building, heard the message: "Searchlight is on the lawn. Searchlight has asked for a car." Manolo and Searchlight were headed for the Lincoln Memorial in the company of a solitary Secret Service agent—and without the "Football," the black briefcase containing nuclear retaliatory information that must accompany the President everywhere he goes. A frantic White House staff went into action.

Nixon's "rap" session took place at the Lincoln Memorial, where he found a small group of protesters, perhaps eight in number, growing to twenty-five or thirty as the session went on. Accounts differ as to what was said. Participants later told reporters that the President was tired, dull, and aimless in his rambling remarks about sports and surfing. Nixon later dictated a 2,500-word version of his own. He did ramble. It reads like a dull monologue by a travel agent. There was little give-and-take recorded by any of the parties involved.

The night's escapade was not yet over. Nixon and Manolo were whisked to the Capitol Building and admitted to the House chamber, where the hapless Manolo was asked to mount the speaker's platform and address the House, a most unusual audience of one. William Safire records that worried staff caught up with the President in time to join him for breakfast in the Rib Room of the Mayflower Hotel. Henry Kissinger writes of the whole episode that it was only the tip of the psychological iceberg.

Meanwhile, the coordinating committee of the New Mobilization had adopted the "scenario" put forth by Sidney Peck:

> I said we should send him [Nixon] a delegation that would really express what was happening, and that was that he was causing the death of thousands of human beings by continuing this war. Therefore the delegation should be a delegation of caskets. Let the dead come and deliver this message to him to stop. Just bring several caskets in. We would all go from the Ellipse to the White House and we would be led by the dead—deposit the caskets on the doorstep of the White House. The dead could speak for themselves. As we delivered the dead we would put Nixon under house arrest and post the theses—like Luther—to tell him why we were putting

him under house arrest. Then we would encircle the whole White House area with a sit-in. The reason for this was that Nixon had called a meeting of heads of state National Guards to come in to Washington on Monday morning to deal with the response of the Guard to demonstrations and they would have to come in by helicopter.

Unfortunately, the committee did not leave itself time enough to work out either its practical problems or its tactical difference. Sidney Peck:

Ron Young, John McAuliff, and I were designated to work out how to move the rally to the White House. I think this was Friday night. One casket would be enough. We arranged to have that done. We were getting congress-people to follow the casket. Even somebody like Koch [Edward Koch, D-New York] volunteered. We worked out the scenario whereby people would be prepared to stay through Monday because it was going to be a three-day sit-in. So we worked out the arrangements. We had problems. The casket was slow [a carpenter had been hired to make it]; we had to work out the details with the "notables," work out a statement with them, and that went slowly. Also the Trots were opposed to the sit-in. The White House was already encircled with buses. If we circled it with people, they said, there could be provocateurs who would set the buses on fire and blame it on us. So the marshals [who had been trained by Bradford Lyttle and SWP's Fred Halstead] labeled CD as violent. They violence-baited it.

But Lyttle, Halstead, and the marshals had good reason to be nervous. Until Friday afternoon they had been engaged in a careful review and analysis of the site on the north side of Lafayette Square, the coordinating committee's first choice as a location for Saturday's rally. Out of this analysis came some somber conclusions. Bradford Lyttle states that the Mobilization had been warned that

the government planned to trap the demonstrators between a double horse-shoe of police and troops. The inner shoe, or anvil, would be around the White House. The outer shoe, or hammer, would be west, north and east of the crowd. If trouble broke out, the government's strategy was reported to be to gas or otherwise apply pressure on the crowd from the north, drive a wedge down 16th Street, and force the people down 15th and 17th Streets to what was called a "home free" area at the Washington Monument grounds.

Such a situation posed several serious problems. It was unsuitable for a rally because no sound system could reach everyone. A sit-down demonstration would be difficult because there was no way in the tightly packed throng to separate the civil disobedients from others; only a thin line of people would be able to talk to the police and troops while tens of thousands of others would have nothing to do; multiple sound systems couldn't be used for separate rap sessions because their sound would overlap; and in case of a gas attack, the people couldn't evacuate quickly.

In meetings at the Marshals' Center, a close analysis of this scenario was made and it was calculated that more than an hour would be needed to evacuate a crowd of 100,000 from the H Street area down 15th and 17th

Streets. Clearly, a gas attack from the north could lead to a slaughter, hundreds of people being trampled to death. Many experienced marshals refused to work in such a situation. The marshals finally decided that they would be responsible for no more than 20,000 people in the H Street area. They were about to communicate that decision to the Coordinating Committee when suddenly the government granted the Ellipse.

Again the situation unexpectedly and drastically changed. Winning the Ellipse was a political victory and the Ellipse was highly favorable for a rally. A sit-down at the Ellipse, however, seemed to miss the point. . . .

William Hanley rumbled into town that night with his two semis loaded with sound equipment. He did not know of the change in location and rolled around from one possible site to another until he found that the Ellipse was the spot. Hanley, too, worked through the night and next morning readying the sound equipment. Friday, May 8, may also be the night that Henry Kissinger "slept over" at the White House. Bill Gulley, then director of the Military Office in the White House, describes the situation in his book *Breaking Cover:* "To deal with the real possibility of violence, to organize and run an operation to put it down if it did erupt, we set up a control center in the bomb shelter under the East Wing of the White House. . . . One of the tensest periods was early in May of 1970, after the Kent State killings. Kissinger slept in the President's bedroom in the bomb shelter one night because he literally couldn't get out; demonstrators had the White House surrounded, and it was considered too dangerous for him to try to leave." Kissinger's version of this is that protesters around his apartment building made sleep impossible there.

Saturday, May 9, was a sparkling, beautiful day. The temperature soared into the high eighties; demonstrators splashed about in the fountains. In the center of the Ellipse—the site of the protest—stood a large red sign that said:

WE THE UNDERSIGNED PROTEST THE INVASION OF CAMBODIA AND THE RESUMPTION OF BOMBING IN NORTH VIETNAM, AND ALSO CALL FOR IMMEDIATE WITHDRAWAL OF ALL UNITED STATES TROOPS FROM SOUTHEAST ASIA.

Bradford Lyttle's account of a day that soon was enveloped in sectarian bickering, charge, countercharge, and mutual recrimination is the best we have. Lyttle struggles to tell the story with the dispassion and disinterest proper to his self-described role as "stage manager" for the Mobilization's tortuous demonstration "scenarios." Missing from the account is his later confession to Norma Becker that at one point, seated on the platform, he put his head down, covered his face, and wept:

We knew that a massive civil disobedience demonstration was likely and trained several hundred marshals specifically for that. These civil disobedience marshals were prepared to be gassed, clubbed and arrested along with other demonstrators. They were identified by blue armbands, to contrast them from the rally marshals who wore yellow armbands. . . .

At 1 P.M., Saturday, the stage was set for what might have been a huge civil disobedience demonstration as well as a giant rally. About 120,000 morally outraged people were assembled at the Ellipse, at least 20,000 of whom were prepared for the risks of a determined civil disobedience action. They had 3,000 field officers, marshals, perhaps 500 of whom were ready to direct a massive sit-down and be arrested along with the people. A 4,000 watt sound system was operating with which almost everyone could be quickly informed of the plan of action. Marshals were equipped with sixteen or more powerful bullhorns to organize the action. Many prominent people were on hand, including politicians, entertainers and academic figures to join in the action or give it full moral support. Every major television network was either giving or prepared to give live coverage to what went on. All the other important media were represented.

The stage was set but there was no agreed-on plan of nonviolent battle. The Coordinating Committee announced none when they began the program. Nor, once they were assembled on the speakers' platform, were they able to agree on a plan. Indeed, it can be argued that a serious mistake was for the Committee to try to devise a plan on the platform. Once there, their attention was distracted by a thousand demands. They had to divide their attention between running the rally and trying to come up with an appropriate civil disobedience action. They decided on no action and the program suffered from inattention.

Time passed and no decision was made. . . . At 3:30, the moment of truth had come. It was then or never. The Committee wasn't in agreement. In twenty minutes the decision was made and unmade to have a civil disobedience march. Finally, Stewart Meacham called the civil disobedience marshals to the west side of the Ellipse to prepare for a march up 17th Street to the White House. A few minutes later, Co-Chairman Dave Dellinger directed the march and coffins to go up 15th Street and sent the demonstration off the east side of the Ellipse. No clear instructions were given concerning where or how the march should sit-down. The march had been deprived of the civil disobedience marshals, and, a final mistake, none of the Committee members was leading the march. . . .

What happened after that seems to have been that the rally field officers took over. The rally marshals weren't trained in civil disobedience, indeed, they probably didn't understand the tactic. They were trained in cooling the situation and they did that admirably.

When the march came to H Street the last chance for massive civil disobedience arrived. The chance arrived but there was no united group of New Mobe officers to direct the marshals and lead a sit-down. Instead, the marshals remembered that H Street could be a trap and they discouraged a sit-down; they apparently kept people out of H Street and kept the march moving.

After that, the demonstration disintegrated and the marshals busied themselves discouraging small-scale spontaneous sit-downs that seemed to them actions that would lead only to people being gassed and hurt.

It was all over.

In short, Lyttle concluded, "the New Mobe had an 'uncertain trumpet.' "

The unresolved problems that the Mobilization leaders carried with them up the platform steps were both political and tactical. Sidney Peck, as usual, was in the middle of it all:

> When we finally got down to the demonstration, which had already begun [about one o'clock Saturday afternoon], we found down there the tendency toward the "purist radical" position. We should not have any congressperson speak, they said, because they are part of the establishment. Meanwhile we had congresspeople ready to commit CD, ready to lead the sit-in. And so we had a whole argument on the platform about which congresspeople should speak. Meanwhile we waited for the casket. Dave Dellinger was to announce formation of the line of march. Meanwhile the line began to be formed. Many of the marshals continued to discourage CD as provocative and violent, and eventually they took the line of march to Arlington Cemetery.

The platform was a world apart from the tens of thousands of young people gathered before it on the grass and pathways of the Ellipse. For perhaps 40 percent of the crowd this demonstration was a first. They knew little and cared less about the mysteries of New Mobe politics. The routine, however, was familiar: hours of talk by unknown and near-anonymous Mobilization speakers. The apparent lethargy of the crowd, induced at least in part by the torpid platform oratory, led some reporters to think of Woodstock as they surveyed acre after acre of sprawled young bodies in various stages of undress under the first onslaught of summer sun. It was, in fact, a somber, serious, waiting crowd. Behind the speakers' platform and through the line of buses protecting the frail iron fencing of the White House grounds, some in the crowd could glimpse the South Portico of the White House itself. Many thought they would that day somehow confront the building's occupant. Unlike their counterparts of the previous November, they were prepared for more than collegiate chanting in the streets.

Yet for most of them the uncertain trumpet of the New Mobilization never sounded. Reporters observing the event described the crowd as simply "dispersing" at the rally's end. A few thousand followed the coffins, which had made a tardy appearance on the Ellipse grounds, north on Seventeenth Street and ultimately off in the direction of the Arlington National Cemetery without incident, except for an attempt to push a coffin over the bus barricade. Others followed Dellinger's directions and headed for Fifteenth Street. No call for civil disobedience had come from the platform, but it was in the minds of some, unclear as they were about what or where. These protesters found themselves herded constantly to the north, away from the White House, by marshals not prepared to oversee acts of civil disobedience. A Washington, D.C., police sergeant said of the Mobe marshals, "We could not have kept violence down without them." On H Street, near the corner of Sixteenth Street, some demonstrators tried to crash through or crawl over the barricade of buses. The police fired tear gas to dissuade them. Intermittent attempts to organize sit-downs in the street were discouraged by the marshals. Mobilization leaders were nowhere in evidence as the day sputtered to an end with no more than random, easily controlled skirmishes and acts of trashing. Some three hundred arrests were made, all but a few for misdemeanors.

"Coming back [to New York City]," says Norma Becker, "I remember that it was such a letdown. . . . The demonstration was like a picnic, which did not correspond to the mood or psychology. . . . What happened in Washington on May 9 was not commensurate either to the invasion of Cambodia or to Kent State. . . . There was a deep and pervasive feeling of sellout." Mobilization leaders fell to their typewriters to assess the failings of their colleagues and apportion blame. Articles appeared in *WIN, The Militant,* and *The Village Voice;* these were in turn gathered together and published with his own response appended by Bradford Lyttle under the title *May Ninth.* Alone among the five contributors, Lyttle saw a bright side to May 9:

—It was a giant rally, close to the White House, at which the government's Indo-China policies were denounced and people were called to strike against the war.

—The rally was heavily and objectively covered by the mass media, which mentioned but did not dwell in a critical way on the Woodstockian notes of the day.

—It was an overwhelmingly peaceful, orderly and nonviolent demonstration that silhouetted the violence of the government's war policies abroad and repression of dissent at home. The nonviolent character was established in a political atmosphere of anger and tension so intense that Rennie Davis had predicted martial law in Washington by Thursday, May 7.

—The demonstration was promoted and organized in ten days, six times faster than any previous march on Washington.

—It took place on the Ellipse, an area that had been adamantly denied to the movement Nov. 13–15.

—The New Mobe didn't negotiate for a government permit but simply stated its intention to hold a rally. This affirmed the people's right to demonstrate peacefully where they wished and denied the government's right to issue or deny permits.

These are important accomplishments but they didn't stop the war. . . .

Nor did they honor the maxim of an old revolutionary, Sam Adams, who wrote to his friend Samuel Cooper in 1776: "We cannot make Events. . . . Our Business is wisely to improve them." The "Event" in this case was indisputable. The close proximity in time of Kent State with the Cambodia announcement had drawn a single anguished cry of angry frustration from the American public. May 9 did little to transmute this emotion into effective response. The voiceless army of students who had put themselves under the New Mobe banner for a day returned in sullen silence to their broken campuses. Few among them could have recognized themselves in Bradford Lyttle's listing as he praised the "genius and touch [of the officers of the New Mobe] for holding us all—Panthers, Conspirators, Gandhians,

Pacifists, Liberals, Senators, Congressmen,‡ Quakers, Hippies, Yippies, Women Strikers, Women Liberationists, Trots, C.P.'ers, New Leftists, Old Leftists, Blacks, Pinks, etc.—in the same bag." For a coalition with the announced ambition of ending the war broader support than this was needed.

Remarkably, it was Washington itself, the Administration's town, bastion of its policy-making bureaucracy, that gave evidence of a new, deep, pervasive unease about the war. On Friday morning, May 8, thirteen former members of the Peace Corps entered the Southeast Asia wing of the Peace Corps building at the corner of Connecticut Avenue and H Street, across Lafayette Square from the doorstep of the White House. They declared the building "liberated," flew the NLF flag and a banner proclaiming LIBERATION NOT PACIFICATION. The intruders remained in one room of the building unmolested until they left quietly the next evening. At the Ellipse on Saturday afternoon several hundred federal employees marched into the crowd behind banners that read FEDERAL BUMS AGAINST THE WAR and FEDERAL EMPLOYEES FOR PEACE. Fifty foreign service officers and two hundred other State Department employees signed a letter of petition to Secretary of State William Rogers seeking "reconsideration of the apparent direction of United States policy in Southeast Asia." The Secretary of Health, Education, and Welfare, Robert Finch, was quoted as telling a group of students that "it [Vice President Agnew's rhetoric] contributed to heating up the climate in which the Kent State students were killed," a remark the secretary was quick to disavow in a statement released to the press. "Neither by direct statement or allusion," said Mr. Finch, "have I ever indicated that any statement by the Vice President contributed to the tragedy at Kent State University."

"The very fabric of government was falling apart," says Henry Kissinger in his memoirs. The Administration reversed its policy of the previous November when it had maintained a stance of ostentatious disinterest and disdain for the protesters, and Kissinger and other White House aides held meeting after meeting with student groups. Kissinger also met with a troubled delegation of former colleagues from the Harvard faculty. He tried to explain to the students, who had been reared by "skeptics, relativists, and psychiatrists," that "emotion was not a policy." The professors' problem, on the other hand, was one of "overweening righteousness." Kissinger's answer for both groups was that Cambodia "was *not* a moral issue" but a "tactical choice."

No on-campus activity seemed enough to absorb the tremendous emotional energy unleashed by the combined blows of Cambodia, Kent State, and then Jackson State, a black college in Mississippi, where, on May 14, two students were killed by police during a protest unrelated to the war. The students' course work, which had been put aside for what was thought of as the larger, more immediate concern of the war, was one of that spring's casualties. Many worked out agreements with their teachers to finish the term's work via correspondence, or to take a pass-fail, or to take an incomplete. Some universities canceled graduation ceremonies in fear

‡ Three senators—Charles Goodell and Jacob Javits of New York and Edward Brooke of Massachusetts —mingled with the crowd on the Ellipse, May 9. Nine representatives were on the platform; all but two, Phillip Burton of California and John Conyers, Jr., of Michigan, were from the New York delegation.

that they would turn into antiwar, antiuniversity demonstrations. But something more was needed; the youngsters, as it were, needed to be kept busy, needed to have their energies channeled into some constructive action. The youngsters agreed: they wanted to "do something." Sooner or later such an impulse—in the United States at least—turns to politics.

And so, in concert, students and faculty began a kind of children's crusade to Washington, D.C. By May 5 Congress had been inundated by hordes of students lobbying their demand that Congress end the war in Southeast Asia—students, in short, working within the system. New York *Times* columnist Tom Wicker observed that whatever Congress did, it should do something, for "Congressional impotence" now would mean that "one man alone holds in the world's oldest democracy the absolute power of war and peace, life and death." If "the system" had come to that, said Wicker, "it ought to be changed."

Which of course was what some students—and adults too—had been saying for years.

Such activity within the system came as a relief to worried elders who perhaps envisioned a revolution on the nation's campuses; George McGovern, for one, praised the students' "constructive action." Some of the students, however, were quickly disillusioned. One Bryn Mawr student, visiting House Majority Leader Carl Albert, said of him, "It's really frightening. Here was the leader of the 'good side' and he didn't grasp at all what was going on. I thought he was going to blow a gasket." Many dove members of Congress met with the visitors—a fairly pointless exercise of the students preaching to the converted, and the converted in turn cheering on their supporters—but for the remainder of the month it served to defuse the students' anger and to divert them from what might have been more destructive forms of protest.

By May 13 the hundreds of student lobbyists who had descended on Congress had a name: Project Pursestrings. The group was announced by two nonstudents, Mike Brewer of the Ripon Society (a liberal Republican group) and Sam Brown. The purpose of Project Pursestrings was to lobby for the McGovern-Hatfield amendment, known as the "end-the-war amendment." To be run by an instructor at Princeton, it was a vehicle for young people who wanted to "work through the system"; it claimed membership groups on nearly one hundred campuses. Efforts fell off during the summer, however, and (although certainly not entirely for that reason) the amendment was defeated on September 1.

Meanwhile the Movement for a New Congress (also known as the Princeton Plan, where it originated) was announced on May 9. Its purpose was to provide a "new trend for college students to get back into the electoral process" by working for the victory of antiwar candidates in the fall election; the students would be allowed a two-week sabbatical during the campaign. To be headquartered at Princeton, the group had a wide membership and an elected steering committee of ten students and four faculty.

Other projects to work within—and influence—the system included the National Petition Committee at the University of Rochester, which had a goal of twenty million signatures on an end-the-war petition at fifty cents each; the anticipated ten million dollars would fund a media blitz to convince Congress that nationwide opinion favored ending the war. The Peace Commencement Fund at Yale proposed channeling money that would have been used to rent commencement caps and gowns into a fund for congressional candidates; their goal was $1 million. By commencement season more than 150 campuses had joined this action.

Congress—or, at least, the Senate—moved haltingly to respond. In addition to the repeal of the Tonkin Gulf Resolution, two amendments were offered to curtail the American presence in Southeast Asia:

—the Cooper-Church amendment, which would cut off all funding for American forces in Cambodia after the President's announced withdrawal date of July 1, 1970;

—the McGovern-Hatfield amendment, also sponsored by fifteen other senators. Originally written with a December 31, 1970, deadline, it was changed to read mid-1971 and then to December 31, 1971, in an effort to gain support. It provided that funds for American military operations in Southeast Asia be cut off by that date, and that all American troops be withdrawn unless both houses of Congress declared war.

In addition, Senator Edmund Muskie offered a nonbinding sense-of-the Senate resolution (the congressional equivalent of "writing a letter to your congressman") calling for a cease-fire and withdrawal of American troops by the end of 1971. Muskie described it as a "vehicle for the Senate to express its will."

The Cooper-Church amendment was passed on June 30 by the Senate, but it died in a House-Senate conference. A subsequent version was approved eight months later; like the first, it pertained to ground troops but failed to include any restriction on the air war over Cambodia.

The McGovern-Hatfield amendment was seen initially as the most promising vehicle for Congress to assert its authority over the war-making process; it was the primary focus of that spring's lobbying. On May 12 Senators McGovern and Hatfield bought a half hour of time on NBC television to make a nationwide appeal for support for their amendment. During the program they asked viewers to send contributions to help defray that cost of the air time ($70,000). They received $480,000. After paying the program's expenses and buying radio, TV, and newspaper advertisements they had $110,000 left over, which they gave to charity.

The debate on the McGovern-Hatfield amendment dragged on during the summer. On September 1 it was defeated 55–39. The vote was seen as an endorsement of both the President's policy of Vietnamization and the Paris peace talks. In the same session the Senate defeated, 71–22, a bill to prevent the Army from sending draftees to fight in South Vietnam if they chose not to go.

The vote on the McGovern-Hatfield amendment was termed a "moral victory" by Senator Hatfield; one congressional aide said that the size of the vote showed that "senators are aware of the antiwar sentiment in the country." Senator John Stennis advised his fellows that "this amendment is constitutional. . . . But let's not stampede, let's go on down the road with whatever power our Chief Executive has as a negotiator, as a man of discernment."

As if he doubted the Senate's awareness of the nation's antiwar feeling, George McGovern made an impassioned statement in support of his bill before the vote came:

> Every Senator in this chamber is partly reponsible for sending 50,000 young Americans to an early grave, and in one sense this chamber literally reeks of blood. Every Senator here is partly responsible for that human wreckage at Walter Reed [Hospital] and all across this land—young boys without legs, without arms, or genitals, or faces, or hopes.
>
> If we don't end this damnable war those young men will some day curse us for our pitiful willingness to let the executive carry the burden that the Constitution places on us.

The lobbying drive that Congress chose to ignore was not composed of students alone. The adult establishment responded as well, in greater numbers than ever before. Many college and university faculty members had of course been in public opposition to the war for years. The teach-ins of 1965 that first brought an awareness of the Vietnam problem to the campuses relied heavily, sometimes entirely, on the voluntary services of individual professors. The teach-ins continued in various forms as each new academic year brought a fresh batch of students on campus. But now some administrators began to enter the lists, and a more corporate form of endeavor emerged. Two notable examples were Kingman Brewster, Jr., president of Yale, and Andrew Cordier, president of Columbia. One of the first student-faculty groups to go to Washington that May was from Yale and led by Brewster; about one thousand of them met with the twenty-nine Yale alumni in Congress. At Columbia the lobbying group (all faculty) called itself the Academic and Professional Lobby for a Responsible Congress; it also launched an effort to get similar groups started elsewhere.

Kingman Brewster won greater notoriety, however, for a remark made in the midst of a tense period on his own campus. The atmosphere at Yale and in New Haven was already supercharged before President Nixon announced the invasion of Cambodia. Yale students were on strike to protest the impending New Haven trial of Black Panther Bobby Seale, one of the original Chicago 8. Seale and eight other Panthers faced charges of kidnapping and murder. Radicals of every stripe, notably the violence-prone Youth Against War and Fascism, poured into New Haven for a weekend (May 1–3) of rallies in support of the Panthers. Brewster admitted to "skepticism" about the chances for a fair trial anywhere in America for black revolutionaries. The Conspiracy, living symbols of state oppression for those in attendance, was reunited for the occasion. A bomb was exploded on the Yale campus at the Ingalls Rink following a rock concert; three fires were set at the Yale Law School during the period of the strike. The National Guard was called out for the weekend. Not every Yale alumnus was happy with the Yale President's statement, which received wide publicity and was generally credited with "cooling" an overheated situation. Fear of more than the scattered violence already seen led sponsors to cut the weekend activities short just after Tom Hayden of the Conspiracy issued a call for a national student strike.

Yet another adult delegation to Washington consisted entirely of lawyers, one thousand of whom, some of them senior partners in the most prestigious firms—"the most established of the Establishment"—traveled to the capital from New York carrying legal arguments against the war. "That's when I felt we had a majority movement," says Cora Weiss, "when I heard that Judge [Bernard] Botein went to Washington to lobby Congress." Said Botein: "This is the most exciting thing that's happened to the bar." About fifteen hundred Washington lawyers announced an antiwar lobbying plan of their own; Publishers and Editors Against the War proclaimed itself; jointly and severally, hundreds of scholars, clergy, and other professionals engaged in the lobbying effort.

One group of 350 Asian scholars under the leadership of Professor John K. Fairbank, director of Harvard's East Asian center, brought a damning message to a government that had been embroiled in Asian wars almost constantly for twenty-nine years: in 1970 there was no Vietnam specialist in a tenured position on any faculty in the United States; only six universities offered courses in the Vietnamese language to a total of thirty students; three hundred were studying Chinese; only one university—Yale—offered the Cambodian language (two students). The situation was, said Fairbank, "a scandal."

Organized labor was another adult segment of the population that began to shift against the war that spring. (A few unions and individual labor leaders had been opposed to the war all along, as we have seen.) Under the leadership of George Meany, the AFL-CIO had resolutely backed the Administration's—any administration's—Vietnam policy. (Meany later disavowed his support of the war.) Now, in the wake of nationwide unrest, a few of the major labor unions began to oppose the war. On May 7 one of the largest, the American Federation of State, City and Municipal Employees, endorsed a statement calling for immediate U.S. withdrawal from Vietnam "consistent with the safety of our armed forces." On the same date Walter Reuther, UAW president, had sent a telegram to President Nixon condemning the war; it had been endorsed by officers of the UAW. Expressing his "deep concern and distress," Reuther said that "however this dangerous adventure [the Cambodian invasion] turns out militarily, America has already suffered a moral defeat beyond measure among the people of the world." Two days later Reuther was killed in an air crash. On May 24 Jacob S. Potofsky, president of the Amalgamated Clothing Workers of America, addressing that union's national convention, denounced the war and called on Congress to "exercise its constitutional responsibility of not leaving the war-making decisions to the President alone." Immediate withdrawal was the demand also of 451 labor leaders who took out a full-page ad in the San Francisco *Examiner* on May 18.

In New York, however, many members of other unions clung to their hawk status, and for a few weeks that May the city became a kind of battleground between them and antiwar youth. The workingmen expressed their feelings in a particularly nasty way on Friday, May 8, when several hundred students staged an antiwar protest in the Wall Street area—the financial district, the heart of the system, the heart of corporate America. Their demands were: an immediate pullout of American troops from Indochina; release of all "political prisoners" in the United States (a reference to the Panthers and the Conspiracy); and, once again, that universities halt all defense-related work. Just at noontime, at the steps of the Federal Hall National Memorial, the rally was being addressed not by a student but by a fifty-six-year-old Wall Street lawyer—a member of the establishment who, like so many others in the business and financial community, had come to see the war as a disaster to the American economy. "You brought down one President and you'll bring down another," he told his youthful audience—prophetic words, but in a way that no one could have foreseen in May 1970.

Then the attackers moved in: a band of perhaps two hundred hard hats, construction workers from a nearby site, who marched on the rally, carrying American flags and pushing aside the few police in attendance, and began to beat the students. Some of the workers swarmed up the steps of the memorial and put their flags on its statue of George Washington. Others chased the young people through the noontime crowd, beating them with their orange and yellow hard hats, inevitably attacking bystanders as well as their intended targets. At least seventy people were injured. One lawyer, a candidate for the state Senate, was beaten by several workers shouting, "Kill the Commie bastards." At nearby Trinity Church the hard hats tore a Red Cross banner from the gates and tried to bring down the Episcopal Church flag. "I suppose they thought it was the Vietcong flag," commented the rector. The rampaging men invaded city hall, where the flag on the roof was at half-staff in mourning for the Kent State dead. They demanded that it be raised to full-staff. It was; a mayoral assistant lowered it again; the workers, chanting, "Lindsay's a Red," demanded that it be raised a second time. As it was, they sang "The Star Spangled Banner." The workers proceeded to invade a building of Pace College, where students had hung a peace banner from a window. The hard hats smashed windows, attacked the onlooking, terrified students, and burned the peace flag.

On the following Monday several thousand hard hats—construction workers and longshoremen—staged a Wall Street march of their own in support of the Administration. Carrying signs that read IMPEACH THE RED MAYOR, they were monitored by thirteen hundred police. Occasional scuffles broke out; from time to time the marchers would break ranks to attack an onlooker, like one man who said nothing but simply raised his hand in a peace sign. Many in the crowd cheered them, but some called them "the new Nazis." As the men passed Pace College they called, "Don't worry, they don't draft faggots."

The Lindsay administration had pleaded with a new group of young people not to demonstrate on the following day. But the students—enrolled at graduate schools of business at six Eastern universities—had responded by claiming to be "members of the establishment" and insisting on their right to march and assemble. The police kept them safe from their would-be hard-hat attackers, but only just barely. Occasionally the workers drowned out the rally's speakers (loudspeakers had been forbidden by the police, who in the end lent two bullhorns to the demonstrators). Robert V. Roosa, a partner in the banking firm of Brown Brothers, Harriman & Company and former under secretary of the Treasury, told the crowd that, contrary to a popular theory, the war was not a "conspiracy" of the nation's business interests but rather was opposed by them because war-induced inflation was destroying the nation's economy. At the end of the rally the police held back the workers for twenty minutes to allow the students to disperse without being attacked.

On May 20 more than sixty thousand men turned out under the aegis of the Building and Construction Trades Council of Greater New York for a proadministration rally at city hall. Carrying American flags, wearing their hard hats, they were greeted by admiring crowds and a deluge of ticker tape as they marched through the financial district. Peter J. Brennan, president of the council, told his audience that "history is being made here today because we are supporting the boys in Vietnam and President Nixon." Some time later, Brennan became Secretary of Labor in Nixon's Cabinet.

The next day a group calling itself the Coalition for Peace, a coalition of labor and students, rallied at city hall but their number was far fewer, perhaps twenty thousand. After the rally several thousand tried to march north to Bryant Park at Fortieth Street. They were blocked by police and several violent scuffles broke out. Sixteen complaints of police brutality were filed.

Both sides, proadministration and antiwar, would have claimed to be the true patriots in the marches and countermarches in New York and elsewhere. The country more than ever that May was divided and anguished over the issue of the war. Seventy years before, a few voices had been raised against the U.S. military's brutal suppression of the Philippine insurrection, a conflict similar in many ways to that in Vietnam. At that time Mark Twain, a bitter opponent of U.S. intervention in the Philippines, had commented:

> It would be an entirely different question if the country's life was in danger, its existence at stake; then . . . we would all come forward and stand by the flag, and stop thinking about whether the nation was right or wrong; but when there is no question that the nation is any way in danger, but only some little war away off, then it may be that on the question of politics the nation is divided, half-patriot and half-traitors, and no man can tell which from which.

Meanwhile the antiwar movement proceeded to disintegrate. Sidney Peck's vision for May 9—"a symbolic communication that would have gone instantly around the world . . . a powerful mass action of civil disobedience . . . and, in a political way, putting the Administration 'under arrest' for the crimes it had committed"—vanished in the bickering of the week before and on the platform at the rally. Peck blames the SWP: "There was the rigidity, the absolute rigidity of the Trotskyite position. . . . They fought the idea of multitactics, multiissues. And after that demonstration the SWP and the YSA decided they had enough forces to break with the dominant, multitactic part of the antiwar movement, to go it alone. And so you had a divided movement."

Fred Halstead, speaking for the SWP, had no misgivings. In a retrospective

335

article reprinted in Lyttle's *May Ninth* Halstead gave clear voice to the SWP's position:

> The purpose of these mass demonstrations is not to provide catharsis for frustrated "radicals" who have not yet learned that to stop this war, or to make any fundamental change, much less a revolution, you must involve immense masses. Nor is the purpose of such demonstrations to provide victims for additional examples of ruling-class violence. Their purpose is to provide a visible form in which dissent on the war can manifest itself; and to provide a form whereby new sections of the population can become involved.

In June, SWP formed a new organization, the National Peace Action Coalition (NPAC), with the support of some labor groups and, of course, the SMC, which was now the only group organizing on the campuses from a solid base. The goal of NPAC was that of SWP: single-issue, single-tactic, legal, peaceful mass demonstrations against the war under the slogan "Out Now!" The Mobilization, which had existed under one name or another as *the* national coalition against the war, was dead.

For Norma Becker "that was the worst period in the Movement—after May 1970." She understood the tactical differences that led to the split, but felt that "both styles were legitimate, both styles were valid." The anger of those who said, in Becker's phrasing, "What's running down in Vietnam is an atrocity comparable to the Holocaust. We're not going to *politely* disagree," had to find an outlet in some form of nonviolent civil disobedience. "We were pushed into a corner by 'either . . . or,' " she says.

The split came at a bad moment for the Mobilization, which, under one name or another, had, over the past four years, provided a degree of cohesion, organization, and a (sometimes uncertain) leadership for massive public expression of opposition to the war. In the mutual recrimination and antileadership backlash that followed May 9 most of the Mobilization leaders drew back, emotionally exhausted. "Sidney Peck stepped into the void," says Norma Becker. "He was the only one who did not pull back. He stepped in—and he became the target of the hostility toward the leadership. Anyone who stepped in would have." Out of the ruins rose a shaky edifice with an improbable name, the National Coalition Against War, Racism and Repression (NCAWRR).

NCAWRR was destined for a brief existence. As much to its disadvantage as its name—"the Coalition Against Everything," some derisively called it—was the fact that those who met two or three times in 1970 under its aegis represented very little in the way of organized forces. The Fifth Avenue Peace Parade Committee was perhaps its most substantial element. The student base was gone except insofar as the indefatigable Rennie Davis could claim a campus following. Neither a David Dellinger nor a Tom Hayden was in evidence. The moderate forces that had not been co-opted by NPAC were concerned that summer and fall with electoral politics. And Peck himself had lost control of his original source of strength, the

Cleveland Area Peace Action Council. CAPAC was now in the hands of forces closely aligned with SWP. The radical amalgam—more of tendencies than people —that was NCAWRR did establish a tenuous, mistrustful alliance with some black groups, but at the cost of loss of focus on the war. NCAWRR did mount a small demonstration at the United Nations around the issue of genocide on November 15, the anniversary of the huge Washington, D.C., rally; twenty-six persons (of a gathering of fifteen hundred) were arrested there in a civil disobedience action led by Bradford Lyttle. Thus NCAWRR gave faltering expression to the "multiissue, multitactic" stance around which it mistakenly hoped to form a powerful political alliance.

An added reason for inaction and indecision on the part of NCAWRR was the absence of Peck, who was on sabbatical from his teaching post and based in Cambridge, Massachusetts. William Douthard, a black pacifist who had emerged from the Southern civil rights movement to become a community organizer in New York City, was largely responsible for running the affairs of NCAWRR during these months. Through much of the latter part of 1970 Peck made trips to three foreign countries. In August the Pecks were invited to Japan to participate in a conference on nuclear armaments. Louise Peck went as a representative of Women Speak Out for Peace and Justice, which she helped to organize. As a result of contacts in Japan, Peck was then asked to visit North Vietnam, which he did in October. From Vietnam Peck brought back letters from American POWs and handed them over to the Committee of Liaison With Families of Servicemen Detained in North Vietnam.

The Committee of Liaison developed out of contacts made between a women's delegation from Vietnam and members of Women Strike for Peace in the summer of 1969 (see pp. 263–64). In December of that year Cora Weiss of SWP traveled to Hanoi and established an arrangement under which mail from American prisoners of war would be received by the Committee of Liaison for forwarding to their families. North Vietnam also and for the first time agreed to answer questions on MIAs through the Committee of Liaison—a channel of communication that allowed North Vietnam to snub and bypass the Pentagon and the State Department.* The committee was announced in January 1970; David Dellinger was named as cochairman with Weiss. Washington maintained a wary and uneasy relationship with the Committee of Liaison, receiving and using information supplied by Cora Weiss without acknowledging her committee's existence in any formal way. Nevertheless, by midsummer the Committee of Liaison had established a confirmed list of 335 prisoners detained in North Vietnam and was managing a flow of correspondence between them and their families.

According to Peck, the POW letters he brought back from Vietnam may have been part of the pretext for the commando raid made by U.S. forces against the Son Tay prison camp twenty miles outside of Hanoi, which occurred on November 21. Around that date Peck was out of the country yet again, this time in Sweden for the

* Repeated requests that North Vietnam furnish American delegates to the Paris peace talks with a list of prisoners had been denied.

Stockholm Conference on Vietnam. The Son Tay raid was a failure; the camp had been empty of prisoners from at least the point when planning for the raid was initiated in August.

An enormous tissue of governmental lies built up around the raid and the simultaneous two-day strike by American bombers against targets near Hanoi. The bombings were described by Secretary Laird as "protective reaction" air strikes against missile and antiaircraft sites, a description Henry Kissinger labeled "a patent subterfuge." Similarly, Laird had denied earlier reports of strafing and rocket attacks on the Son Tay area. Before word of the failed prison raid was released, congressmen were reacting angrily to what appeared to be a flagrant violation of the understanding worked out by President Johnson in October 1968 for a halt to bombing in the North. Then, within days, Senator Fulbright bluntly suggested to Secretary Laird, who appeared before the Senate Foreign Relations Committee, that the Defense Department knew there were no prisoners in the camp when the rescue mission was ordered. The implicit corollary to this accusation was that the raid itself was nothing more than a "cover" meant to distract public attention from the resumption of bombing deep inside North Vietnam. For the antiwar movement, the entire episode was a "trial balloon" to test public readiness to accept a new escalation. Sidney Peck and Ron Young returned from Stockholm with a determination to renew the focus of the protest on the war.

On the same day (September 1) that the McGovern-Hatfield amendment was defeated, the military funding bill to which it was to be attached passed the Senate by a vote of 85–5. The administration request for the Pentagon was approved in full. The two votes were a clear signal that Nixon had weathered the Cambodia–Kent State storm. He was able to join enthusiastically in the congressional election campaigns of the fall after returning from a European trip on October 5. In the next twenty-one days he campaigned in twenty-two states. In his memoirs Nixon recalls with some relish the constant attendance of demonstrators at each campaign stand. Bill Gulley, who served under four administrations as director of the White House Military Office, states that there was "speculation at the time of the campaign and after that the anti-Nixon demonstrations, or some of them, were rigged. Even the one at San Jose where they threw rocks."

At San Jose, five days before the election, Nixon emerged from a rally inside the Municipal Auditorium to face a crowd of demonstrators. "I could not resist showing them how little respect I had for their juvenile and mindless ranting," he says. "I stood on the hood of the car and gave them the V-sign. . . . Suddenly rocks, eggs, and vegetables were flying everywhere." While the President was whisked safely away, others in his entourage were less lucky. The fact that police barricades were set up to allow the crowd to push close to the vehicles in the motorcade and that the press had been forewarned of possible trouble lends credence to Gulley's supposition. Nixon's staff seemed pleased with the entire episode, especially the stoning of the press bus.

Two days later the President took up the matter of the San Jose incident in a speech given in Phoenix: "Those who carry a 'peace' sign in one hand and throw a bomb or brick with the other are the super hypocrites of our time. . . . Let's recognize these people for what they are. They are not romantic revolutionaries. They are the same thugs and hoodlums that have always plagued the good people." The President added a typical personal note. "The terrorists, the far left, would like nothing better than to make [me] a prisoner in the White House. Well, let me just set them straight. As long as I am President, no band of violent thugs is going to keep me from going out and speaking with the American people. . . ." The equating of the peace movement with violence, revolution, thugs, and the far Left perfectly expressed the White House view of the issue upon which the 1970 elections should be decided.

So pleased was Nixon with the Phoenix speech that he ordered a taped version of it to be shown on national television on the election eve campaign wrap-up. Speaking for the Democratic Party that night was Senator Edmund Muskie of Maine. He urged the electorate to shun the "politics of fear" and did so in a calm, distinguished, quite "presidential" manner. Nixon by contrast, according to John Mitchell, came across as if he were "running for sheriff." In the eyes of the White House Muskie became a marked man, an obvious target for "dirty tricks."

Nixon's campaign techniques indicated that he had not read, much less heeded, the recommendations of one of the most substantial documents on domestic affairs prepared under his Administration. *The Report of the President's Commission on Campus Unrest* was released on September 26, the day before Nixon's departure for Europe. The commission, under the leadership of William W. Scranton, former governor of Pennsylvania, had prepared its report in ninety days. Apparently the commission was viewed in the White House as a device to quiet the turmoil surrounding the Cambodia invasion and the killings at Kent State and Jackson State. "Just don't let higher education off with a pat on the ass," John Erlichman reports that Nixon warned Scranton in June. The commission noted with somewhat muted approval the essential moderation of the tactics of campus protest in May and the subsequent interest in electoral politics, but warned that radicals had been victorious in politicizing the universities: "In May 1970, students did not strike against their universities; they succeeded in making their universities strike against national policy." And national policy, the commission found, was at the root of the problem of campus unrest: ". . . nothing is more important than an end to the war in Indo-China. Disaffected students see the war as a symbol of moral crisis in the nation which . . . deprives even law of its legitimacy."

The Scranton Commission's ultimate recommendation reads like a commentary on Nixon's behavior on the hustings and no doubt accounts for his failure to mention the commission or its report anywhere in his memoirs. Their most important recommendation, the members of the commission declared, "rests with the President. As the leader of all Americans, only the President can offer the compassionate, reconciling moral leadership that can bring the country together again."

Rennie Davis had much the same reading as the Scranton commission on the mood of the campuses. He saw the war as the root of the problem, and he responded to an adage that he first heard from a Vietnamese on the streets of Hanoi: "A man who has walked four thousand kilometers does not sit down, does not give up, when he has only twenty kilometers to go." Davis, then thirty years old and light-years removed by experience from the current college generation, nevertheless returned to the only power base he knew. With SDS vanished and SMC ill-disposed toward any concept at variance with the Trotskyite line of peaceful, legal, mass demonstrations, Davis turned to the National Student Association (NSA). It was an ironic choice. Sam Brown says of the NSA that it, the WATS line, and Touch-Tone telephones made the antiwar movement possible. Essentially a straight-line, fairly conservative organization of elected college and university student leaders across the nation, NSA was the base from which Lowenstein, Brown, and Hawk drew workers for the McCarthy campaign and, later, the Vietnam Moratorium Committee. Many SDS leaders were at one time involved with NSA, which, unbeknownst to them, had prospered through CIA funding (see pp. 107–8).

In August Davis brought before the annual conference of NSA a proposal to shut Washington down on May 1 in a massive, nonviolent act of civil disobedience that would block roads, bridges, and federal buildings unless the war in Vietnam were ended that date. The proposal was narrowly defeated by a vote of 150–134. The NSA, however, did adopt another notion put forward by Davis. The proposal called for negotiating what came to be known as the "People's Peace Treaty" by sending a student delegation to meet with their counterparts in North and South Vietnam. The NSA action gave Davis, who, since his ERAP days in Chicago, was an adept at organizing "with mirrors," enough to work with. While some were involved in the electoral politics of fall 1970, Davis was busy carrying his two proposals, the People's Peace Treaty and the May Day action in Washington, to the campuses, where he found a receptive audience. He and his supporters were soon known as the "May Day Tribe."

By autumn, student interest in politics had markedly declined. Indeed, many people in the antiwar movement felt, as they always did, that the electoral process was an irrelevant, time-wasting activity. David Dellinger voiced the underlying caution: "Vote for a peace candidate if you wish. But don't leave the decision [on the war] up to him. He probably won't be consulted." Candidates who had taken the Movement for a New Congress and like groups at their word and requested student volunteers for campaign work often found that none were available. Some students worked for hawk candidates.

On October 7 the President proposed a cease-fire in place throughout Indochina and five days later he promised to withdraw forty thousand more troops by Christmas. The two announcements bolstered the public perception that the war was winding down: troops were coming home; Vietnamization seemed to be working. A New York *Times* survey showed that the war would not be the deciding factor in most electoral contests. If the campaign was the apocalyptic exercise Nixon seemed bent on making of it in his frenetic three-week intervention, the Four Horsemen were Apathy, Boredom, Exhaustion, and Despair. The electorate was tired of both the war abroad and the war at home.

The election results proved little. The Republicans lost nine seats in the House and gained two in the Senate. Eight senatorial "peace candidates" (the appellation is questionable) won; six lost. A bitter loss for the peace movement was the defeat of Senator Charles Goodell, who was maneuvered into a three-way race that split the Republican party vote in New York and delighted the White House. ("We got that son of a bitch!" exclaimed Vice President Agnew on election night.) In the House races, twenty-four peace candidates won and five lost. One of the losers was Allard Lowenstein, whose district was gerrymandered in another act of political retribution.

Two first-time winners in the House, both Democrats, would rise to national prominence as opponents of the war. One was Bella Abzug, who represented lower Manhattan and the Upper West Side in New York City. Bella Abzug was a feminist, a founding member of Women Strike for Peace, a longtime, feisty advocate of liberal and radical causes whose flamboyance did not endear her to the House leadership. On the day she was sworn in, she introduced a bill calling for the withdrawal of American troops from Vietnam by July 4, 1971. In Massachusetts' Fourth Congressional District a coalition of antiwar forces led by Jerome Grossman produced a candidate to unseat the conservative, long-established incumbent Democrat, Philip Philbin, in the primaries. Their candidate, who went on to win the election, was Robert F. Drinan, S.J., the dean of Boston College Law School. The election of Father Drinan was an example of how Grossman believed the antiwar movement could be most effective. Drinan's was the second congressional election engineered by the Grossman forces. "We proved we were a moveable feast," says Grossman. Drinan did not disappoint his supporters' expectations in office.

On November 27 there took place a truly moveable feast of the political calendar, J. Edgar Hoover's annual testimony on the FBI budget. The date of this rite changed from year to year but the outcome and surrounding ritual were invariable. The same acolyte, Clyde Tolson, Hoover's lifelong companion and housemate, was always in attendance; the high priest read from a lengthy prepared statement elaborately printed up beforehand so that the faithful could follow along—and the press be informed; responses from the congregation, usually made up of members of the House Appropriations Committee, were muted and properly respectful; the budget request was invariably approved, except for some occasions when it was increased. There were, however, differences this time.

First, Hoover was looking for a dramatic budget increase, something well beyond the usual generous, annual level of gift-giving. He wanted the added funds—more than $14 million—to put one thousand new FBI agents into the field. It was for this reason that on this occasion he was making an extraordinary appearance before the Subcommittee of the Senate Appropriations Committee. Second, Hoover had a sensational announcement to make.

It came toward the end of Hoover's twenty-seven-page prepared statement and after a review of Weatherman terrorist activities in 1970. Bernardine Dohrn, Hoover told the two senators present, was now on the FBI's "Ten Most Wanted" list. Calling their attention to another sector of the antiwar movement, Hoover dropped his bombshell:

Willingness to employ any type of terrorist tactics is becoming increasingly apparent among extremist elements. One example has recently come to light

341

involving an incipient plot on the part of an anarchist group on the east coast, the so-called "East Coast Conspiracy to Save Lives."

This is a militant group, self-described as being composed of Catholic priests and nuns, teachers, students, and former students who have manifested opposition to the war in Vietnam by acts of violence against Government agencies and private corporations engaged in work relating to . . . the Vietnam conflict.

The principal leaders of this group are Philip and Daniel Berrigan, Catholic priests. . . .

This group plans to blow up underground electrical conduits and steam pipes serving the Washington, D.C. area in order to disrupt Federal Government operations. The plotters are also concocting a scheme to kidnap a highly placed Government official. The name of a White House staff member has been mentioned as a possible victim. If successful, the plotters would demand an end to United States bombing operations in Southeast Asia and the release of all political prisoners as ransom.

Hoover's astonishing "revelation" seemed to pass right by the two senators, Byrd and Hruska, receiving the testimony. They clung in a narcoleptic way to the canonical questions about Communist infiltration routinely expected when Hoover testified.

The reaction in every other quarter was one of shock and surprise. At the FBI there was a feeling that the Director had put in jeopardy an ongoing investigation. At the Justice Department there was anger as the realization came that Hoover was forcing the department's hand: they would have to bring down an indictment, whether solidly based or not. For the eleven members of the "East Coast Conspiracy," who counted among their six priests and nuns the only black known to be a part of the Catholic Left (Philip Linden, a priest from Baltimore), there was also bewilderment. The Berrigans were not part of their group and had not participated in their February 1970 draft board raids in Philadelphia. The Berrigans, in turn, were confident that Hoover had outreached himself. Both Berrigans had been in federal jails for several months, hardly, as they saw it, in a position to conspire. They challenged the government either to prosecute or retract the charges.

For the press, the Hoover announcement meant headlines and continuing questions: Who were the "East Coast Conspiracy," the Berrigans, and, for that matter, the Catholic Left? And more intriguing yet, who was the "highly placed Government official" targeted for kidnapping? An answer came on January 12, 1971, when the Justice Department in a news release that pointedly omitted any mention of J. Edgar Hoover or his earlier testimony announced that six persons had been indicted on charges of plotting to blow up the heating systems of federal buildings and to kidnap. The five named in addition to Philip Berrigan included two other Roman Catholic priests, a nun, an ex-priest, and one layman, Eqbal Ahmad, a former professor at Cornell University. The intended kidnap victim was Henry Kissinger.

1971:
The Winter Soldiers

AT THE TURN of the year the antiwar movement faced two threats, one external, one internal.

The threat from without was President Nixon's Vietnamization program, which was intended to shift the burden of the ground fighting to the South Vietnamese Army and allow large withdrawals of American troops while intensifying the air war. Put bluntly, Vietnamization meant that the antiwar movement would be undermined, if not fatally weakened. Most Americans who opposed the war opposed it because their own boys were dying or suffering grievous wounds. When the flag-draped coffins stopped coming home, when the weekly (American) body count dropped, the horrors of the war receded. The stepped-up air war, which inflicted death and destruction on people other than Americans, was a remote war with little immediate impact on American life. The leaders of the antiwar movement, therefore, redoubled their efforts to keep up the pressure for the killing to stop completely. Thus that spring the cry arose, "Stop the air war"—a war which by the end of U.S. participation in it would drop three times as much bomb tonnage on Vietnam, Laos, and Cambodia as was dropped in all theaters in World War II.

The internal strain on the antiwar movement—the strain of carrying on for years its home-front struggle—was beginning to show as well. Tempers were short; patience was thin; lives were disrupted and sometimes destroyed; careers neglected, sleep lost, recreation time lost, friends and families lost—and for what? some people said. For Nixon's secret plan, which may bring some boys home but which in fact extended the war? As David Dellinger wrote in *Liberation*:

> . . . the antiwar movement is paying a price for a period of ideological confusion and tactical mistakes. Even more serious, it has been struggling to overcome the feelings of frustration and despair that have gripped people after they discovered that neither a million people in the streets (November, 1969) nor several hundred schools and colleges on strike (May, 1970) altered Washington's determination to escalate its war of aggression in Indochina.

On January 8 the National Coalition Against War, Racism and Repression met in Chicago. Since "one of the functions of the peace movement was to check further escalations," the delegates knew that they needed to take some action, possibly another mass demonstration. Sidney Peck explains:

> In the fall of 1970, it became apparent that there was going to be another escalation of the war, that the escalation would either be a direct invasion of North Vietnam or an incursion into Laos as another way of moving against the [North] Vietnamese, and that seemed to be apparent from the trial balloon raid on the Son Tay prison camp—would the American public accept it? Well, they would accept it if it was in order to save American lives —that's what they [the government] were testing.

But the Movement was split—had been split for months—and they needed to get themselves together, in the language of the day, before they could decide what to do. For this reason the NCAWRR asked the Trotskyites—the Socialist Workers who formed the base of NPAC—to stay away; they could not find out who they were and what they wanted to do and at the same time handle the Trotskyite argument on every issue.

Peck, recently returned from North Vietnam, remembers the meeting with anguish. "I went through a tremendous personal trashing on elitism and jet-setting," he recalls. Several unidentified women were the worst attackers; two of them later surfaced as government provocateurs. It is at this meeting that we see the ultimate trap of the participatory democracy of the sixties:

> Any leadership element became denounced as elitism, and trashed [says Peck]. The people who made these criticisms were Left people, these were people who would almost genuflect before a strong leader like a Ho Chi Minh or a Mao or a Fidel Castro or a Che Guevara. But there was a current of anarchical pacifism in the movement which fed into a government attack against any recognized leadership formation—which made it easy for the government [informers and provocateurs] to isolate and destroy the credibility of people in a leadership situation. In SDS, for example, the idea of participation got carried to such an extreme that there was a leadership void. The attack against leadership and the equating of leadership with elitism led to the most elitist kinds of leadership. That is a current all the way through the antiwar movement. And it puts such a constraint on people. If you are a leader you are a "heavy" who leans on other people and by sheer weight you crush and overpower people. Therefore people would humble themselves in a false way. . . .

> We are mostly anarchists in our end of the peace movement and we hate authority [says Tom Cornell]. Therefore when authority devolves upon our shoulders we don't want it. And this was a great failure. I think that the pacifists in the Movement could have exerted more authority. Even anarchists have to understand that the authority that is really legitimate is the authority that naturally devolves on your shoulders and you should accept

344

it. I don't think that we did what we should have done. We would never speak to the young folk exerting any kind of discipline. It was, "Do your own thing. . . ." And it was weakening. We could have had something approaching a real nonviolent revolutionary movement in this country.

Some at the January meeting spoke on Peck's behalf; some did not. Like many people trying to appeal to all sides in order to form a coalition, Peck found himself at times under attack from all sides as well. Like the ringmaster of a circus with too many rings, Peck was trying to connect two major issues to the antiwar movement: the war's impact on the economy, and the consequences for the United States of the racist nature of the war.

In order to do this, as he saw it, the NCAWRR needed to keep together the major elements of the coalition:

1. the mainstream of the movement opposed to the war that had a base in traditional peace formations: FOR, AFSC, Clergy and Laymen Concerned, etc.;
2. blacks: SCLC, CORE, National Welfare Rights Organization;
3. the GI movement;
4. Vietnam Veterans Against the War;
5. students;
6. radical pacifists (many of whom wanted a major political confrontation in Washington in the spring, complete with civil disobedience);
7. Rennie Davis's May Day Tribe, which was forming alliances with students who had organized the People's Peace Treaty and with the radical pacifists.

In addition, lines of communication needed to be kept open to the Trotskyites in NPAC who were moving forcefully ahead on their planned April 24 demonstration in Washington—a legal march and rally, the only kind of demonstration that the Trots would sanction.

On January 18, 1971, Senator George McGovern entered the 1972 presidential race. Calling the Vietnam War a "dreadful mistake," he promised to withdraw "every American soldier from Southeast Asia." And so once again those who opposed the war saw some hope that the system might respond to their demands.

In late February the National Coalition Against War, Racism and Repression changed its name to the People's Coalition for Peace and Justice (PCPJ). Its coordinators were David Dellinger, Sidney Peck, Rennie Davis, Bradford Lyttle, Ron Young, William Douthard, and Carol Henderson Evans.

A change of name did not, however, ameliorate the difficulties of holding together a coalition whose members had different, if not altogether conflicting, aims. During the preceding year, fueled by the invasion of Cambodia and the killings at Kent State and Jackson State, the scenario for a spring action (the May Days) had been gestating in Rennie Davis's mind: "Unless the Government of the United States stops the war in Vietnam, we will stop the Government of the United States." Davis envisioned large-scale, nonviolent civil disobedience in Washington which would take the form of sitting-in at selected targets—bridges and traffic circles—thus preventing the capital's normal workaday activity. In PCPJ Davis had finally found a base of support for his May Day action, in which he gave the government until May 1 to sign the People's Peace Treaty or he and his Tribe would try to immobilize the capital. The People's Peace Treaty had been adopted by the National Student Association the previous summer at Davis's behest. It was a symbolic treaty whose ratification by students both in the United States and South Vietnam (and by North Vietnamese professors) was meant to (1) encourage the signing of the real treaty at the negotiations in Paris and (2) serve as a focus for the as yet undecided spring actions. Its provisions included:

—a cease-fire,
—immediate withdrawal of American troops from Vietnam,
—release of prisoners of war,
—free elections in South Vietnam.

Davis remembers:

> After May of 1970 we thought, What more can we do [to stop the war]? It was a summer of solitude for me. I made another study of the war focusing on Agent Orange and the automated weaponry. I decided we needed to do what Martin Luther King had done—take a mass mobilization to the civil disobedience level. The concept of shutting down the government was a more electrifying idea. I thought that mass civil disobedience was needed for its impact on this country and also on North Vietnam. The discouraging thing was the sense of defeat in the coalition [PCPJ]. They rejected the idea as not feasible. The plans had to be developed outside the coalition. Then finally they joined. . . .

And so PCPJ opened its office in Washington and began "to work through the scenario"—that is, to reconcile the "polarities" of the proposed actions in the nation's capital:

—a mass march and rally on April 24,
—nonviolent action intended to "bring everything to a halt" on May 3.

If the groups that wanted a spring action against the war could not agree on goals and tactics, they at least shared a common roof in Washington at 1029 Vermont Avenue. Housed there that spring were PCPJ (in the former offices of the New Mobilization and the NCAWRR), NPAC and SMC (in the former offices of the Moratorium), the Washington Area Peace Action Coalition, the May Day Collective, and the Vietnam Veterans Against the War.

Before the spring actions began to take shape, however, and indeed on the day (February 8) that Dellinger held a press conference to announce plans that still had not been firmly agreed upon, the expansion of the war that he and others had anticipated finally occurred: South Vietnamese troops, backed by heavy American bombing, crossed the border into Laos in yet another effort to cut the Ho Chi Minh Trail. The operation was also a test of Vietnamization—a test which the South Vietnamese failed badly, with a 50 percent casualty rate and a precipitous retreat in the face of heavy North Vietnamese opposition. Within one week of South Vietnam's withdrawal in late March the trail was back in use.

With little time to organize, and in the midst of bitter cold, antiwar groups turned out perhaps fifty thousand people nationwide on February 10 to protest the invasion of Laos. The largest demonstration was in Boston, where upward of four thousand people gathered on Boston Common. Buffeted by freezing winds, the peaceful but "angry and sullen" crowd rallied across from the gold-domed Bulfinch State House. Many of them carried (mock) skeletons or skulls. After a period of speeches, they marched a mile or so to Copley Square, where they burned two American flags. As night fell they proceeded along Huntington Avenue to Northeastern University, growing more unruly, snarling rush-hour traffic, spray-painting antiwar slogans on buildings, smashing windows, and indulging in some violence as police tried to contain them (one officer was beaten with a lead pipe). Fourteen people were arrested.

The Laos invasion indicated to some people that (for instance) Davis's proposal to shut down the government might be the only way, finally, to end the war. Said one young man who had worked for the Moratorium in 1969 and in the fall 1970 elections:

> I'll tell you what this Laos thing means. We've used every straight political tactic there is, and there has been no response from the government, none at all.
>
> Now the time has come to say to the government that either you stop the war or we'll stop you. So I intend to go to Washington in the spring and in an absolutely disciplined, nonviolent way, engage in civil disobedience. . . . The idea for me is to bring the tactics of the civil rights movement ten years ago into today's antiwar movement.

Others fell back on more familiar, less drastic (and, it might be said, less effective) forms of protest. Once again David Hawk and a fellow student at Union Theological Seminary, Dennis Riordan, organized an open letter of protest, this time addressed to President Nixon, signed by more than four hundred college student presidents and editors—the largest number to sign any of the students' open letters since the first in 1966.

In an attack on the President's Vietnamization policy, the students stated that "changing the color of the corpses does not end the war." Calling on Nixon to "reverse futile and immoral policies and use your authority to end the bloodshed in Vietnam," they said that "if not, you will have to take responsibility for an intensification of public divisiveness and disunity which will further weaken the already torn moral and social fabric of American life. The outrage and the purposefulness emerging from beneath the surface despair on our campuses, when it is coupled with the widespread loss of public confidence in your Administration, cannot be deflected or contained. . . ."

By the time the Laotian invasion ended, on March 25, PCPJ had endorsed April 24 as a day for a mass march and rally in Washington on the Capitol steps. The action was announced as a coalition effort by PCPJ and the other major antiwar umbrella organization, NPAC. The aims of the demonstration were:

—to withdraw U.S. forces from Vietnam,

—to end the draft,

—to achieve a guaranteed annual income of sixty-five hundred dollars.

The last point was a concession to civil rights and welfare groups in return for their support; it was also a reflection of PCPJ's attempt to link the war to domestic concerns. Citizens unfamiliar with the agonies of coalition-building would have been astonished to learn how many hours of impassioned debate had been consumed to reach what seemed, on the surface, a fairly simple agreement.

At the suggestion of David McReynolds, in order not to lose momentum, PCPJ decided to use the time between April 24 and May 3 as a time to instruct demonstrators in nonviolent civil disobedience. During that time, also, PCPJ members would conduct the "People's Lobby": a plan to lobby Congress on the war and also to go into government offices and talk to the workers there—the white-collar bureaucracy—so that by the time the May Days arrived with their inevitable disruption and consequent bad feeling toward the demonstrators, the people who worked *for* the government would perhaps understand better why the antiwar forces needed to work *against* the government.

Even before it was approached by the People's Lobby, however, Congress had shown signs of restlessness. Its repeal of the Tonkin Gulf Resolution having failed to have any discernible effect on the war, it now looked around to see what action to take that would end the U.S. presence in Vietnam—preferably in the least painful way.

On April Fools' Day the House, considering a bill to extend the military draft until mid-1973, concluded an intense three-day debate on both the war and the draft—the most searching examination to date that the lower chamber had made of U.S. policy in Vietnam. Some representatives spoke strongly against the war, some against the draft—political daring that would have been unthinkable in the mid-sixties when the United States was sliding into the war. Nevertheless, when the final vote was taken, it was 293–99 in favor of continuing the draft. Members also voted for a huge $1.7 billion increase in military pay: a stratagem which, they hoped, would raise enlistments, thereby making the draft unnecessary.

Despite members' vehement antiwar pronunciamentos, most congressmen were still unwilling to respond in any meaningful way to demands that they act to end the war. At the end of the House debate, when Representative William F. Ryan of New York proposed an amendment to withdraw all U.S. troops from Indochina by December 31, 1971 (an action which a recent Gallup Poll had shown was favored by 73 percent of the American people), he could not muster even the twenty sponsors he needed to achieve a recorded vote.

Things were not much better in the Senate. J. William Fulbright had scheduled public hearings in February on "how to end the war," but he agreed to delay until the Laos incursion had ended. Now, at the end of March, Fulbright announced that the hearings would be held; furthermore he criticized the Administration's statement that the Laos invasion had gone according to plan: "Were I to remain silent, I would be a partner to what is either a massive deception of the American people or what is a massive misjudgment on the part of our political or military leaders. . . .

We are being told that the Laos operation went 'according to plan' when I know it did not go according to plan."

Meanwhile a teach-in—that quaint relic of an earlier, more innocent era of protest—was held at New York University on March 30; its purpose was to drum up support for the April and May actions, but some of its participants also spoke their feelings about themselves and the Movement in this, the ninth year of protest against the war:

> After all the years, all the carnage, I can't help bringing a sense of futility to yet another teach-in. . . . Why do we participate? I guess it's because not to participate is to create greater futility. (New York City Councilman Theodore S. Weiss)

> People are going through a period of tiredness. Yes, it is a protracted struggle. Yes, it is a disappointment. People go to jail, march, refuse to pay taxes. But the truth is we have no choice if we are going to live with ourselves and restore the possibility of building a humane society. (David Dellinger)

> We've got to understand that militant nonviolence is as American as cherry pie. The strike is a traditional and accepted weapon of protest. It is time now to break off relations with the Government. This time we'll stay in Washington. We'll talk to office employees, not the managers, the secretaries. April 24 can't be just an annual spring picnic. Those picnics were good, but they aren't enough. It's no secret that this country is headed for 1984. The alternative to 1984 is 1776, and it's going to begin this spring. (David McReynolds)

On March 29, 1971, at Fort Benning, Georgia, Lieutenant William Laws Calley, Jr., was found guilty of the premeditated murder of twenty-two Vietnamese civilians on March 16, 1968, at the hamlet known as My Lai 4 in the province of Quang Ngai, South Vietnam. He was sentenced to life imprisonment.

Within forty-eight hours his countrymen and countrywomen responded to the news by an unprecedented outpouring of emotion. Hundreds of telegrams were sent to the military judge and jury at Fort Benning, as well as to Calley himself; all but one were against the verdict, and that one read HANG CALLEY. Five thousand telegrams arrived at the White House; they were 100–1 in Calley's favor. Politicians hastened to condemn the verdict; newspaper editorials ran heavily against it. The Veterans of Foreign Wars began a campaign to raise one hundred thousand dollars for Calley.

The Pentagon installed a phone bank to deal with calls; it was staffed by officers above the rank of lieutenant colonel. Most callers protested the Calley verdict, but upon questioning it turned out that most callers did not know why he had been convicted. Those who did know that civilians had been killed at My Lai thought that they had been killed in cross fire with the Viet Cong.

On April 1 President Nixon ordered that Calley be released from the Fort Benning stockade, where he had spent just over twenty-four hours. Calley returned to his apartment, where, according to the Army, he was not allowed to make public statements. However, it was announced that he and a coauthor were to share equally a $100,000 advance on a book. His mail had jumped to twenty thousand letters a day.

In contrast to public reaction to the verdict and sentence, the response to Nixon's order was favorable. The House of Representatives broke into applause upon hearing the news, and politicians like Carter of Georgia and Wallace of Alabama voiced their approval. A few days later Nixon announced that he personally would review the Calley verdict. In August 1971 Calley's sentence was reduced to twenty years; he remained free on appeal. In December 1973 the U.S. Court of Military Appeals upheld his conviction. In April 1974 Calley's sentence was reduced to ten years by Secretary of the Army Howard H. Callaway. In September of that year Calley's conviction was overturned, and in November he was released on bond. In September 1975, six years after he was charged with the murders at My Lai, Lieutenant Calley was released on parole.

Of the fourteen officers charged with offenses at My Lai, only three were tried and they were acquitted. Charges against the others were dropped. No publicity was given to the fact that on the same morning as the My Lai massacre, at a hamlet called My Khe 4 a mile and a half away from My Lai, between forty and one hundred civilians were killed by American servicemen of Bravo Company, like Calley's Charlie Company a part of Task Force Barker.

The issue of war crimes in Vietnam committed by the nation that had conducted the Nuremberg Trials was not a particularly sensitive one; the American people were not capable of seeing themselves as war criminals, and so the initial reaction to the Calley story was one of psychological denial. In *My Lai 4: A Report on the Massacre and Its Aftermath,* Seymour Hersh states that the public's reaction to the first news of the massacre was disbelief—and anger at the press. When the Cleveland *Plain Dealer* published photographs of the victims at My Lai, it was accused of being "anti-American." When Mike Wallace of CBS interviewed one of the American soldiers who participated in the massacre, he was accused by one viewer of "pimping for the [antiwar] protesters." From the beginning of American involvement in Vietnam until December 31, 1970, 117 American servicemen had been charged with murdering Vietnamese civilians; 81 were actually tried, and of these, 38 were convicted of murder, 20 of lesser offenses, and 23 acquitted. None of these had received the attention that Calley had, in part, of course, because of the number of civilian deaths involved, and so the issue of war crimes was a new one to many Americans.

My Lai was one hamlet—one day's massacre. By the time of its occurrence, in March 1968, there had been two extensive inquiries into the subject of American war crimes. Neither one received anything like the publicity given to My Lai from 1969 through 1971.

The first, held in two sessions (May and November 1967), was the International War Crimes Tribunal held under the auspices of the Bertrand Russell Peace Foundation. Lord Russell, it will be recalled, was one of the prime movers of the civil disobedience campaign in England against nuclear weapons (Campaign for Nuclear Disarmament), and it was his mention of Vietnam which prompted A. J. Muste and David Dellinger to refer to the American presence in Vietnam in their speeches at the Easter Peace Walk in 1963.

The Russell tribunal, in the words of one of its participants, accused the U.S. Government of

> aggression, civilian bombardment, the use of experimental weapons, the torture and mutilation of prisoners, and genocide involving forced labor, mass burial, concentration camps and saturation bombing of unparalleled intensity. Our evidence established that eight million people were placed in barbed-wire internment camps by U.S. and South Vietnamese forces. It showed the systematic destruction of hospitals, schools, sanatoria, dams, dikes, churches and pagodas. It demonstrated that the cultural remains of a rich and complex civilization representing the legacy of generations had been smashed in a terror of five million pounds of high explosives daily. Every nine months, this destruction is roughly equivalent to the total bombardment of the Pacific theater in World War II. It is as if the Louvre and the cathedrals of Italy had been doused in napalm and pulverized by 1,000-pound bombs.

In Stockholm in May 1967, where the first session of the tribunal was held after Jean-Paul Sartre, its executive president, had been denied permission by President de Gaulle to hold the hearings in France, the tribunal took testimony from more than thirty experts who had gone to Vietnam to investigate the prosecution of the war—doctors, scientists, engineers, agronomists, journalists, and photographers. Lord Russell himself had begun to gather evidence of atrocities as early as 1961; he did this by culling from published accounts in the European and American press.

The testimony at the two sessions (the second was held in Copenhagen) presented a nightmare of suffering visited upon a primitive peasantry by the greatest power on earth. "Genocide" was the term used by the tribunal, and it substantiated that charge with testimony on six questions:

1. Has the United States and its co-belligerents (Australia, New Zealand and South Korea) committed aggression according to international law?
2. Has the United States bombarded targets of a purely civilian character?
3. Has the United States made use of or experimented with new weapons prohibited by the Laws of War?
4. Have prisoners of war captured by the armed forces of the United States been subjected to treatment prohibited by the Laws of War?
5. Have the armed forces of the United States subjected the civilian population to inhuman treatment prohibited by the Laws of War?
6. Do the combination of crimes imputed to the Government of the United States in its war in Vietnam constitute the crime of Genocide?

Two anticivilian weapons were particularly condemned: napalm and CBUs (cluster bomb units), or pellet bombs. Napalm, arguably one of the most vicious weapons ever to be used in warfare, became the subject of widespread protests across the United States against its manufacturer, The Dow Chemical Company (see pp. 104–5, 106–7). CBUs were first used in Vietnam on February 8, 1965, at Le Thuy in

Quang Binh province. They were called "pineapples" because of their shape; each one contained 300 steel pellets, each 6.3 mm in diameter. A year later the pineapple model was replaced by the "guava," about the size and shape of a hand grenade, containing 260–300 steel balls, each 5.56 mm in diameter. About 640 of the guava bomblets were packed into a hollow "mother" bomb equipped with a timing device which broke the mother bomb and showered the guava bomblets in an area of about one kilometer by five hundred meters. Later there were two "improvements" on the design of the cluster bombs: they were equipped with timing devices which delayed their exploding and scattering their pellets, and they were filled with barbed steel splinters rather than the original pea-sized pellets. Other topics covered by the tribunal were the use of herbicides,* chemicals, poison gas, and phosphorus bombs.

In its verdict of "yes" (in answer to its questions), or "guilty," the Russell tribunal accused the United States of violating numerous international treaties in its conduct of the war, including the Hague Convention of 1907, the Kellogg-Briand Pact of 1928, the Geneva Convention of 1949 (which the United States did sign, in contrast to the 1954 Geneva Agreements, which it did not), and the UN Charter—in addition, of course, to repeating offenses for which Germans and Japanese were tried after World War II at Nuremberg and Tokyo. In the words of Justice Robert Jackson, chief United States prosecutor at Nuremberg (speaking of those trials), "If certain acts in violation of treaties are crimes, they are crimes whether the United States does them or whether Germany does them, and we are not prepared to lay down a rule of criminal conduct against others which we would be unwilling to have invoked against us."

The proceedings of the Russell tribunal were issued in 1969 under the title *Against the Crime of Silence*—a volume of more than 650 pages. The silence continued, however, upon its appearance, with almost no attention paid to the study.

Concurrent with the Russell tribunal, a study of the American conduct of the war was made by Clergy and Laymen Concerned About Vietnam. In January 1968 their report was issued in a four-hundred-page volume, *In the Name of America*.

Taken from newspapers, periodicals, books, and other published sources, the study established that "American conduct in Vietnam has been characterized by consistent violation of almost every international agreement relating to the rules of warfare." In a "Commentary by Religious Leaders on the Erosion of Moral Constraint in Vietnam," which served as the volume's introduction and which was signed by twenty-nine prominent clergy including Robert Drinan, S. J. (later a dove congressman from Massachusetts' Fourth Congressional district), and the Reverend Martin Luther King, Jr., the point was made that

> Any nation that cherishes the religious heritage America claims should set for itself particularly high standards of moral constraint, far beyond the minimum demanded by international law. And yet the awful truth is that on

---

* In the late 1970s, more than twenty thousand Vietnam veterans brought suit against seven manufacturers, including Dow, to recover damages for injuries which they claimed had been caused by the chemical defoliant Agent Orange. In May 1984 a $180 million settlement was reached before trial.

occasion after occasion we have failed in Vietnam to observe even these minimal standards of moral constraint. Our sense of moral shock at the discovery of this fact compels us to present this information to the hearts and consciences of all Americans.

Richard A. Falk, in a prefatory essay, said that the volume "contains the raw data created by the fury of American participation in the Vietnam War." Later he quoted from Hugo Grotius, a Dutch lawyer writing in 1625 at the time of the Thirty Years' War: "It is as if, in accordance with a general decree, frenzy had openly been let loose for the committing of all crimes." What Falk and the Committee of Clergy and Laymen could not have known at that time (January 1968) was that the war in Vietnam—and the American presence there—would also last almost exactly thirty years, from the autumn of 1945 when an American OSS officer was assassinated by the Viet Minh, to the fall of Saigon on April 30, 1975, when the last Americans scrambled into helicopters from the roof of the American Embassy.

Like the Russell tribunal, the study by the Clergy and Laymen dealt with issues such as gas and chemical warfare (including defoliants), the treatment of prisoners, the bombardment of South Vietnam, "mistakes" in the bombing, the use of napalm, phosphorus, and pellet bombs, and the forced transfer of civilians from their homes to refugee centers.

And like the Russell tribunal, the CLCV study failed to arouse public opinion against the war. Neither one received more than cursory notice in the press, and what attention the Russell tribunal received while it was ongoing was extremely negative.

In 1970 several members of Congress convened the Congressional Conference on War and National Responsibility, yet another attempt to come to grips with the issue of war crimes. The proceedings, published as *War Crimes and the American Conscience,* made little impression beyond the relatively small number of citizens already concerned.

On March 28, 1971, the day before the Calley verdict, the Sunday New York *Times Book Review* published a lengthy essay by Neil Sheehan, a former correspondent for the *Times* in Vietnam, dealing with a bibliography of thirty-three books on the U.S. conduct of the war.† It was titled "Should We Have War Crime Trials?"

If you credit as factual only a fraction of the information assembled here about what happened in Vietnam [wrote Sheehan], and if you apply the laws of war to American conduct there, then the leaders of the United States for the past six years at least, including the incumbent President, Richard Milhous Nixon, may well be guilty of war crimes.

† Among them: *Against the Crime of Silence,* ed. John Duffet (the Russell tribunal hearings); *Chemical and Biological Warfare* (Hearings of the U.S. Senate Foreign Relations Committee); *The Destruction of Indochina* by the Stanford Biology Study Group; *In the Name of America,* research director Seymour Melman (the Clergy and Laymen Concerned study); *My Lai 4* by Seymour M. Hersh; and *Nuremberg and Vietnam* by Telford Taylor.

Citing the Geneva Convention, the Nuremberg and Tokyo (war crimes) tribunals held after World War II, and the Army Field Manual, Sheehan recited the litany of unrestricted bombing in the South (not the North, where bombing was more limited), including the bombing of North Vietnamese and Viet Cong army field hospitals, the destruction of peasant villages, the defoliation of the countryside, and the forced relocation of villagers—all of which by 1966 were deliberate U.S. policy rather than accidents of war: "devastation had become a fundamental element in their [American military and civilian leaders] strategy to win the war."

The responsibility for those acts lay not solely with the generals but with the civilians who supposedly commanded them. At the Tokyo tribunal, said Sheehan, "the United States went so far as to establish the legal precedent that any member of a Cabinet who learns of war crimes, and subsequently remains in that Government acquires responsibility for those crimes. Under our own criteria, therefore, Orville Freeman, the Secretary of Agriculture under President Johnson, could acquire responsibility for war crimes in Vietnam."

Sheehan ended his essay with the plea for a "national inquiry into the war crimes question" not for vengeance but so that "if these acts are war crimes, future American leaders will not dare to repeat them."

Later that year came a similar proposal from one of the architects of the war, William Bundy. Speaking at the annual December meeting of the American Association for the Advancement of Science, Bundy suggested an "independent citizens' commission to get at the facts of the war and to re-examine the ground rules of nonnuclear warfare with particular emphasis on how they should be reviewed because of advancing weapons technology." It was important, Bundy stated, to "find a new and much more restrictive set of rules on what is permitted in warfare."

One further attempt to bring to public attention the issue of America's conduct of the war was made by those who knew it best. From January 31 through February 2, 1971, while the nation was receiving reports of the Calley trial, the Winter Soldier hearings under the auspices of the Vietnam Veterans Against the War were conducted in a Howard Johnson's motel in Detroit. The name for the hearings came from Thomas Paine's 1776 pamphlet *Common Sense:* "The summer soldier and the sunshine patriot will, in this crisis, shrink from the service of their country." After the appearance of the pamphlet, in the darkest days of the American Revolution, came the bitter winter at Valley Forge when American soldiers deserted wholesale and General George Washington despaired of having an army to lead. A "winter soldier," therefore, was a true patriot, one who would not desert when the crisis came.

The veterans who testified at the hearings wanted to make clear that the Calley case was not an isolated incident: that the war in Vietnam was a dehumanizing war fought in a dehumanizing way, and that fighting it included atrocities which haunted the men who had committed them. "The purpose of the hearings was not to punish but to preclude the continuance of man's inhumanity to his fellow man," wrote Al Hubbard, the VVAW executive secretary. "The crimes against humanity, the war itself, might not have occurred if we, all of us, had not been brought up in a country permeated with racism, obsessed with communism, and convinced beyond a shadow of a doubt that we are good and most other countries are inherently evil."

More than one hundred veterans testified to acts of brutality that they had committed or witnessed in Vietnam. Senator Mark Hatfield entered the Winter Soldier proceedings into the *Congressional Record* (April 6–7, 1971), but otherwise little attention was paid. In frustration, determined to make themselves heard, the veterans decided to hold a march on Washington—"Operation Dewey Canyon III, a limited incursion into the country of Congress."‡ The week-long rally, lobbying effort, and encampment, attended by several thousand veterans, was timed to take place during the week preceding the April 24 march.

Like the Winter Soldier hearings, Dewey Canyon III reflected the veterans' terrible need to unburden themselves. They were, many of them, haunted by the horror of the war, by the horror of what they had seen and done. Their unprecedented gathering in the nation's capital that spring grew out of their feelings of guilt and their need publicly to confess their private waking nightmares not only in the hope of exorcising their own devils, but also to awaken their fellow countrymen and women to the nature of the war. Jan Barry, a founder of VVAW, wrote in the New York *Times:*

> With the conviction of Lieut. William L. Calley the real dilemma of my generation has finally been brought unmistakably home. To kill on military orders and be a criminal, or to refuse to kill and be a criminal is the moral agony of America's Vietnam war generation. It is what has forced upward of sixty thousand young Americans, draft resisters and deserters, to Canada, and created one hundred thousand military deserters a year in this country and abroad. It is what has created S.D.S. and draft-card burning, the Weathermen and Kent State, the 1967 "siege" of the Pentagon four years ago and much of the impetus for the marches taking place this spring. It is what has caused nearly two and a half million honorably discharged veterans of Vietnam to drop out, to disappear. . . .
>
> One cannot participate in the Vietnam war without being at least in complicity in committing war crimes. . . .
>
> America's Vietnam generation isn't up against the wall: it's bricked in. Going to Vietnam is a war crime, refusing to go is a domestic crime and just sitting still, somewhere or somehow in exile or limbo, is a moral crime. It is a terrible time today to be American and young. In fact, it apparently is a crime.

Intended as an educational experience for the American people conducted by men who knew better than anyone what the Vietnam War was, Dewey Canyon III proved to be educational for the veterans as well. "You feel you're bad off and then you meet someone who's worse—somebody who's lost two legs and an arm, or somebody whose stumps are shorter than yours," commented one. "We're finally bringing the war home," said another. "It's the first time in this country's history

‡ Dewey Canyon I and II had been military operations in Laos.

that the men who fought a war have come to Washington to demand its halt while that war is still going on," added yet another.

To the anger of the veterans (who were, of course, already angry about the war that they had been fighting), word got around Washington that week that the President thought that only 30 percent of them were Vietnam veterans. "Only 30 percent of us believe Richard Nixon is President," retorted one veteran.

Events began on an inauspicious note when on Monday, April 19, eleven hundred veterans made their way across the Lincoln Memorial Bridge to Arlington National Cemetery. The procession was headed by several gold star mothers (women whose sons had been killed in Vietnam) and by veterans in wheelchairs or walking on crutches. By the Tomb of the Unknown Soldier they held a service for those killed on both sides in the war; then several mothers and veterans tried to enter the cemetery itself to lay memorial wreaths. Cemetery personnel refused to allow them to do so. The next day two hundred veterans, determined to be admitted, marched across the bridge again; after some hesitation on the part of the cemetery superintendent they were allowed to enter, lay their wreaths, and hold a brief ceremony.

After the first visit to Arlington Cemetery the veterans went to the Capitol, where they presented a list of demands to Congress and began their lobbying effort. Some of them went to the Mall, where they began to set up camp, despite an injunction against their doing so which had been obtained by the Justice Department. The government's attempts to prevent the veterans from camping on the Mall became a farcical entanglement, with Chief Justice Burger overturning a Court of Appeals order that had overruled the injunction. At last the government began to be aware of the poor public relations involved in arresting peacefully assembled combat veterans and it asked the judge who had issued the injunction to rescind it. The veterans would be allowed to stay on the Mall for the week as long as they did not sleep there. The deadline for their decision was 4:30 Wednesday afternoon: should they defy the authorities by sleeping on the Mall? Sleep won with 480 votes to 400 for staying awake. Later that night park police patrolling the area turned a blind eye to the activities of the young men who had fought and bled for their country in Vietnam. "Camping?" said one officer. "I don't see any camping."

On Tuesday and Wednesday the veterans continued their lobbying of Congress; some of them attended J. William Fulbright's hearings on proposals to end the war, while some staged a guerrilla theater display of "war" on the Capitol steps. Others went to the Pentagon, where they demanded to be arrested for war crimes "along with Lieutenant Calley." A general told them that "we don't take American prisoners." More than one hundred were arrested the following day, however, when they went to the Supreme Court building to ask the Court for a ruling on the war's constitutionality. Washington Police Chief Jerry Wilson refused to arrest either of two double amputees who demanded to be taken with their fellow demonstrators. "I won't do it," said Wilson of one. "I just won't arrest him."

As an effort to draw the public's attention to their cause, the VVAW's April demonstrations were hugely successful; the men conducted themselves well, even planting a tree on the Mall to improve the site before they left, and the nation was moved by the obvious sincerity, the very real pain and anguish that these young men, many of them cruelly wounded, displayed about the war in Vietnam and their part in it. Two events of the VVAW week struck the public particularly hard.

The first was the appearance of Lieutenant (j.g.) John F. Kerry before the Senate Foreign Relations Committee. Kerry was an intelligent, good-looking young man blessed with a way with words, a graduate of St. Paul's School and Yale. He was clean-shaven; his hair was reasonably short; he wore no visible love beads; he did not seem to be high on pot or something stronger; and he did not use hippie-type language or—worse—unprintable expletives. He looked like the son any parent would be proud to have (in 1982 he was elected lieutenant governor of Massachusetts) and his remarks, televised nationwide, were a public relations coup for the veterans. He spoke to the senators with some eloquence:

> In our opinion, and from our experience, there is nothing in South Vietnam which could happen that realistically threatens the United States of America. Any to attempt to justify the loss of one American life in Vietnam, Cambodia, or Laos by linking such loss to the preservation of freedom, . . . is the height of criminal hypocrisy. . . .
>
> . . . we are told that the men who fought there must watch quietly while American lives are lost so that we can exercise the incredible arrogance of Vietnamizing the Vietnamese. Each day to facilitate the process by which the United States washes her hands of Vietnam someone has to give up his life so that the United States doesn't have to admit something that the entire world already knows, so that we can't say that we have made a mistake. Someone has to die so that President Nixon won't be, and these are his words, "the first President to lose a war."
>
> We are asking Americans to think about that because how do you ask a man to be the last man to die in Vietnam? How do you ask a man to be the last man to die for a mistake?
>
> . . . We are also here to ask, and we are here to ask vehemently, where are the leaders of our country? Where is the leadership? We are here to ask where are McNamara, Rostow, Bundy, Johnson, and so many others? Where are they now that we, the men whom they sent off to war, have returned? These are commanders who have deserted their troops, and there is no more serious crime in the law of war. The Army says they never leave their wounded. The Marines say they never leave even their dead. These men have left all the casualties and retreated behind a pious shield of public rectitude. They have left the real stuff of their reputations bleaching behind them in the sun. . . .
>
> We wish that a merciful God could wipe away our own memories of [our] service as easily as this Administration has wiped away their memories of us. But all that they have done and all that they can do by this denial is to make more clear than ever our own determination to undertake one last mission—to search out and destroy the last vestige of this barbaric war, to pacify our own hearts, to conquer the hate and the fear that have driven this country these last ten years and more, so when thirty years from now our brothers go down the street without a leg, without an arm, or a face, and

small boys ask why, we will be able to say "Vietnam" and not mean a desert, not a filthy obscene memory, but mean instead the place where America finally turned and where soldiers like us helped it in the turning.

The final event of Dewey Canyon III took place on Friday, April 23, when nearly one thousand veterans returned their Vietnam combat medals to the government that had issued them. Originally the men had planned to return the medals in body bags, but then the authorities had a fence built around the Capitol steps, where the ceremony was to take place, and the veterans decided to throw the medals over the fence. Their act may be compared to the burning of draft cards: an act overtly defiant but not done lightly, filled with profound significance for those who performed it and also for those who witnessed it. Some of the men, before tossing their medals over the fence, dedicated them to comrades either American or Vietnamese who had died in battle—commendation medals, Purple Hearts, Silver Stars, the Vietnamese Cross of Gallantry, all went into the pile at the feet of the statue of the fourth chief justice of the Supreme Court, John Marshall. Said one veteran: "This was the final act of contempt for the way the executive branch is forcing us to wage war." Said another: "I just want to ask for the war to end, please." And another: "I'm not proud of these medals. I'm not proud of what I did to receive them. I was in Vietnam for a year and our company policy was to take no prisoners. A whole year we never took one prisoner alive. Just wasted them with the door gun, dropped down to check their bodies for maps or valuables, and split. If it was dead and Vietnamese, it was a VC." And another, speaking of his time in the Air Force: "It was a disservice to my country. As far as I'm concerned, I'm now serving my country."

Afterward, some of the veterans experienced the same sense of temporary euphoria that many antiwar demonstrators had felt over the years: now, they thought, now we have taken an action that will end the war. Said one: "We wouldn't have been surprised if somebody said, 'Hey, Nixon just announced that all the troops will be out of Nam and back home by suppertime.' We would have believed it at that instant. . . . We thought we'd finally done it and we'd reached everyone."

The next day, April 24, half a million people came to Washington to protest the war in Vietnam. In their numbers, their peacefulness, and their diversity, they represented one of the greatest triumphs of the antiwar coalitions which for six years had been mounting demonstrations against the war. This year, the tenth year of the American presence in Vietnam (or the eighteenth, or the twenty-seventh), they had come to convince their elected representatives to end it.

The marchers assembled at the Ellipse, just behind the White House (not barricaded now by a ring of buses, as it had been during previous demonstrations), and proceeded down Pennsylvania Avenue to the Capitol steps. Vice President Spiro Agnew, president of the Senate, had given them permission to rally on the Capitol grounds after receiving their assurances that they would assemble peacefully—as, indeed, they did. It was the first time that the site had been granted to an antiwar demonstration.

On the morning of the march, traffic bringing in would-be demonstrators was backed up into Maryland for twenty miles. The procession from the Ellipse to the Capitol continued all day; long after the speeches had begun, Pennsylvania Avenue was filled with marchers from one end to the other. Representatives from all walks of American life were there: students and adult professional groups, religious, trade union, and political groups, local antiwar groups, active duty servicemen, veterans of previous wars, government employees, blacks, and Third World groups, as well as newer special interest groups such as women's and gay liberation.

Like the few hundred who had come to the Assembly of Unrepresented People in August 1965, these hundreds of thousands in April 1971 had come to petition Congress. ENOUGH—OUT NOW! read their blue and white placards. "You have come to the right place," Representative Herman Badillo (D-New York) assured them.

David Livingston, president of District 65 of the Retail, Wholesale and Department Store Workers, explained the demonstrators' mission: "We would like for the whole world to know why we are meeting—to appeal to the members of the House of Representatives and the Senate, and to say to them, 'Under the Constitution you can end the war.'"

Said Representative Bella Abzug: "Your presence here today means that you're going to force the Congress to undeclare the war."

Coretta Scott King spoke, and the Reverend Ralph David Abernathy of SCLC, and former Senator Ernest Gruening. As had often happened at antiwar rallies, the order of speakers was in constant flux, new people constantly being added as different groups jockeyed for a moment's attention, new speakers being pushed onto the program to preempt those already scheduled. One woman, a member of SMC, was upset that after three hours, no one under the age of thirty-five or forty had had a turn at the microphone. She had promised the presidents of the National Student Association and the Association of Student Governments a place on the program, but they had been constantly shunted aside by older speakers. Her dilemma is an ironic and revealing comment on the much-criticized "student" movement that by 1971 had achieved such stature that all the adults, many of whom in former years wanted nothing to do with the antiwar cause and its occasionally scruffy youngsters, now were eager to be counted as part of it. "The peace movement has risen from the ashes of Vietnamization and withdrawal," wrote I. F. Stone of the April 24 demonstration. "But it still has a long, hard way to go."

The rally lasted for five hours. Afterward, mindful of Earth Day, the marchers cleaned up their trash. The day in Washington was everything that NPAC had hoped for: "Totally legal, peaceful and orderly." Ten people—an insignificant number—were arrested on minor charges.

The next morning, however, 150 pacifists—Quakers unconnected with NPAC—were arrested when they tried to transfer their ongoing peace vigil in Lafayette Square to the sidewalk in front of the White House. And that evening, 1,000 homeward-bound demonstrators undid much of the goodwill engendered by the rally by stalling their cars on the New Jersey Turnpike, stopping traffic for nearly four hours. Abandoning their vehicles, they danced in the northbound lanes, chanting antiwar slogans, and started a bonfire in the southbound lanes. State police arrested more than 100 of them.

Upward of 150,000 people attended the April 24 demonstration in San Francisco. Led by active-duty servicemen, they marched peacefully for seven miles to a rally at Golden Gate State Park, but violence erupted there when militant Hispanic and Indian (native American) groups forcibly took control of the microphone on the speakers' platform. The peace movement, said one militant speaker, was "a conspiracy to quench the revolution."

When the April 24 Washington demonstration was over, the Trotskyites (NPAC) left town. They had been concerned for weeks about possible violence on that day, about confrontation or scattered acts of civil disobedience, and they wanted no part of the People's Lobby the following week or the disruption of the city promised by the May Day Tribe.

The People's Lobby visited the Department of Labor, the Selective Service Office (where two hundred were arrested after a sit-in on the steps), and the Department of Health, Education, and Welfare, where they found a thick cardboard wall in the lobby barring entry to any of the offices or to the elevators. The wall was perhaps thirty feet long, painted black, and guarded by black U.S. Park Police. Since the way to the building's auditorium was not blocked, the People's Lobby proceeded to hold their meeting there. Black speakers were on the program, including the Reverend Ralph David Abernathy and the Reverend Hosea Williams of SCLC, and HEW employees were invited. This was, in effect, a teach-in; its purpose was to protest the Nixon Administration's proposed $2,400-a-year family assistance plan. Meanwhile, black women in the People's Lobby who were members of the National Welfare Rights Organization talked to the black police guarding the wall, and half a dozen other members of the People's Lobby went to talk to one of the senior officers of HEW about having the wall removed. When they returned they found that the police had left and that some of their fellow demonstrators had knocked the wall down to the accompanying cheers of HEW employees. But as they stepped through they found the police waiting for them, still not permitting them access to the building. So, carrying pieces of the wall, they began to march to the White House. Two hundred were arrested for parading without a permit.

Other lobbying efforts were more directly connected to the antiwar effort, if no more effective. Dressed in burlap sacks and smeared with "blood," some People's Lobbyists invaded the Senate Foreign Relations Committee to "beg and sob and cry mournfully for peace" instead of demanding it as they had in previous years. Senator John Stennis locked the door of the Senate Armed Services Committee, of which he was chairman, to keep out protesters in army costume staging mock war maneuvers. Some protesters painted a peace symbol on the floor of the Capitol rotunda, and they were arrested when it could not be wiped off.

A later delegation to the Senate Foreign Relations Committee, members of the May Day Tribe, accused the senators of a "lack of initiative" in ending the war; Congress, said the demonstrators, was "the puppet of the madmen who are in power." Such talk did not sit well with the senators. Jacob Javits told several of the demonstrators (who had been invited to testify before the committee) that they would not "intimidate" him. J. William Fulbright was more astute: "I can detect that some of you have lost all confidence that this system can work."

By and large, however, the People's Lobby was neither disruptive nor offensive to those whom it was attempting to persuade. The May Days that followed were a very different matter. They are remembered for, among other things, totting up the largest number of arrests of any demonstration in U.S. history, antiwar or otherwise: more than twelve thousand by the end of the third day.

There were, in fact, arrests even before the demonstrations began: 242 of them made at dawn on Sunday, May 2, at the end of an all-night rock concert in West Potomac Park. Revoking a permit for use of the park, the police based their action on the "numerous and flagrant" violations of the permit's conditions, including the "rampant" use of narcotics. Many of those arrested chose to be, remaining in the park after the police announced the revocation of the permit, debating whether to stay or go while police helicopters hovered overhead, their rotors beating the air—the whirlybirds, the sound and symbol of the war.

During the day, that Sunday, the demonstrators gathered at Washington's two largest campuses, those of George Washington and Georgetown Universities, to make their final preparations for the planned 6 A.M. assembly at the Washington Monument and march across the Potomac to the Pentagon. One leaflet counseled demonstrators "Don't get busted."

About seven thousand were arrested, however, on the Monday, the first "official" May Day. The government had prepared itself by amassing fifty-one hundred metropolitan police, fifteen hundred National Guardsmen, five hundred National Park Police, and (despite the denials of Deputy Attorney General Richard Kleindienst) ten thousand federal troops, some of them paratroopers from the 82nd Airborne Division at Fort Bragg, North Carolina.

In the predawn hours of Monday, May 3, members of the May Day Tribe readied themselves for their planned invasion of downtown Washington. They had bivouacked at the city's college campuses, waiting for the hour to strike, and now they listened to last-minute advice: no contact lenses, no earrings, telephone numbers of lawyers written in pen on their wrists. Just before 6 A.M. they began to move out, chanting, running into the streets, where they planned to stop traffic and shut down the city. The police were waiting for them at their announced targets, however, and the arrests began promptly amid clouds of tear gas and a few pitched battles.

In addition to the march on the Pentagon, the May Day plans had included disrupting traffic at Du Pont, Thomas, and Scott circles and Mount Vernon Square. Again, as so many times before, the demonstrators seized whatever was at hand for weapons: bottles, stones, trash, bricks, tree limbs, and lumber. They did succeed in halting traffic and harassing government employees, but the march to the Pentagon was a failure.

Howard Zinn remembers:

> We had a funny little affinity group, a little academic group with Noam Chomsky [professor of linguistics at MIT], Daniel Ellsberg, and others.

. . . We went out near the Fourteenth Street bridge and sat down in the middle of the street to block traffic and the police were all around us. The march had gone by. There were hundreds of police. They would throw tear gas into our midst and we would scatter and regroup. I remember sitting in the middle of the street and looking at Noam Chomsky and thinking, he is a very smart person and I don't want the police to hit him on the head—his head is very precious. But we weren't arrested at that point. A passerby stopped to discuss the war with us, and as we were standing there talking to him a policeman came up and sprayed mace directly into my eyes. I was blind for ten minutes. The next morning I walked out into Du Pont Circle. There was a helicopter in the middle. The 100th Airborne was occupying Du Pont Circle. Washington looked as if it was under martial law. The police were picking up just anyone. They arrested this fellow and put him up against a car and I walked over and said, "Why are you arresting him?" and the policeman said, "Get over there." And that was my arrest. . . .

The arrested demonstrators and bystanders alike were taken to a practice field for the Redskins, the Washington football team, or to the Washington Coliseum, a hockey arena. Conditions were bad, with no toilets or even drinking water available; those in the open field broiled in the hot sun.

After the first rush of incidents on Monday morning, the leaders of the demonstration held a press conference. Rennie Davis was one of those who participated. He announced that the action had failed.

Sidney Peck disagreed. "I couldn't believe it [what Davis had said]," he recalls. "We were not in a situation of military or physical confrontation with the government. We wanted to politically communicate with the American people that we could not carry on with our usual routine, that we were taking this drastic action to call attention to the fact that the war was still going on, escalating, that it could move into North Vietnam or the use of tactical nuclear weapons, and the war had to come to an end and people were now willing to put themselves in a situation of arrest. It was not a question of 'winning' over [i.e., defeating] the government."

Upon leaving the press conference, Davis was promptly arrested by the FBI and held on $25,000 bond on a charge of "conspiring to violate citizens' rights to travel in interstate commerce and to work for agencies of the U.S. Government." John Froines, another of the Chicago 7, known to the FBI in this instance as "Echo," was arrested the next day on the same conspiracy charge.

By midnight Monday the three judges assigned to handle the May Day arraignments had been able to hear only five hundred cases, and nearly all those who had been arrested were freed either by posting a ten-dollar bond (some had higher bail set) or by the order of Judge Harold Green, who ordered the immediate release of all those for whom arrest forms had not been filled out.*

On Tuesday, May 4, about three thousand demonstrators assembled at Franklin Square in Northwest Washington and marched fourteen blocks to the Justice Department, where they held a two-hour rally. From time to time Attorney General

---

* Some years later a class action suit brought about $10,000 to each improperly arrested person.

John Mitchell, puffing his pipe, would appear on his balcony to gaze down at the throng. During the period from April 24 through the May Days, the Justice Department directed the actions of the Washington police. Afterward, Mitchell compared the May Day Tribe to Hitler's Brownshirts and said that he hoped that police in other cities would copy the "decisive" tactics used by Washington's police in dealing with "mob force."

That night, with most of the leadership arrested, the remaining members of the coalition met at St. Stephen's Church and, very late, decided to hold a rally at the Capitol on the following day. On Wednesday, May 5, therefore, nearly two thousand May Day demonstrators assembled at the east front of the Capitol on the House steps to demand that Congress adopt the People's Peace Treaty, whose original provisions, in recognition of the realities of coalition-building, had now been expanded to include a $6,500 guaranteed annual income for families of four and the release of all "political prisoners" in jail in the United States.

Four congresspeople spoke to the crowd, all representatives of "minorities," a white woman and three black men: Bella Abzug, Ronald Dellums (D-California), Charles Rangel (D-New York), and Parren Mitchell (D-Maryland). In the midst of Abzug's speech came comic relief quickly followed by alarm: a young man off to one side began to strip. Without missing a beat, Abzug glanced at him and told the crowd to pay no attention, that there was nothing of interest to be seen. Humorous in itself, the incident was seen by some as another "red flag": like the flagpole incident at Grant Park in Chicago in 1968, a cue for the police to move in fast.

They did move in, but not at once. Coming from below, at the bottom of the steps, they worked their way up over the protests of Abzug and her fellow representatives. In the end, 1,146 people were arrested, including, finally, Sidney Peck.

Along with the others, he was taken to the Washington Coliseum. Two or three hundred of those arrested allowed themselves to be processed, but the rest refused because, they said, the arrests had been illegal. It was decided to have a demonstration in the Coliseum. The police produced a bullhorn so that their "prisoners" could have sound. People began to coalesce into groups by region; each group elected one man and one woman to meet to decide what to do: should they send word to people outside to go home? to organize further actions? A strong sense of community arose: some people sang, some danced, everyone shared food and blankets sent in largely from Washington's black community.

Word was got out that those arrested wanted those on the outside to stay in Washington, pick another target, and continue the May Day actions. But word came back that Rennie Davis, now released, had called for a march on CIA headquarters in Langley, Virginia—the very kind of action that would dissipate the effect of any demonstration. Word went back out to bring people to Washington from Baltimore and Philadelphia in order to form and keep a political base so that demonstrations could continue until those being held were released. But that did not happen. Instead, on Thursday, about sixty demonstrators tried to reach the South Vietnamese Embassy but were kept at two blocks' distance by police who outnumbered them five to one. That afternoon at a news conference, Rennie Davis warned that "We are coming back again. They are going to have to jail every young person in America before we can be stopped."

When Peck and the others were told that they were to be taken to city jails they went limp and refused to cooperate. In the jails they were packed like sardines into a big bull pen so tightly that one of them, a person with a "computer mentality," organized a head-to-toe sleeping arrangement.

They were held for forty-eight hours. When they were released they learned that all their fellow demonstrators had left the city.

Although the May Days failed in their announced purpose (the government did not stop the war; the protesters did not stop the government; the People's Peace Treaty was not signed or even delivered), Davis remembers positive things about the action: "its impact on Vietnam, the ability to maintain the pressure [on the government], maintaining the focus [of the protest], and using your base to have an impact on key [government] people—asking them in effect, 'Is this the kind of society you want to live in?' I believe it planted the seed in Nixon and his closest advisers to finally pull the plug."

Ten of the leadership were indicted for disturbing the peace of the Congress. The trial took place that summer. Known as the trial of the D.C. 10, it provided two moments of unexpected humor for the defendants. In the first, the government prosecutor showed a film of the demonstrators at the Capitol steps; the jury, largely female, largely black, was treated to the sight of antiwar protesters, led by a contingent of Vietnam Veterans Against the War, chanting (at full volume), "One, Two, Three, Four, We Don't Want Your Fucking War!"

Was this not disturbing the peace of the Congress? demanded the government's lawyer, also black, not female. Further, how could this noisy, obscene crew claim allegiance—as they did—to the goals and the quiet, dignified tactics of the slain leader Martin Luther King, Jr.?

In its turn, the defense showed a film of equal noisiness: a Chinese drum and bugle corps from Los Angeles who entered the Capitol building to serenade their congressmen and whose volume was at least equal to that of the May Day protesters. Why, demanded the defense, were these folks not arrested also for disturbing the peace of the Congress?

The point was decided for the defendants on the basis of a previous case involving the precise level of noise that could be called "disturbing the peace."

The second incident involved the alleged obscenity of the word "fuck." One of the defendants, a woman who taught English literature at the University of Maryland, was questioned by the defense counsel:

Did the witness believe that the word "fuck" was obscene?

Witness certainly did not.

Could the witness explain?

"Fuck," explained the witness, is a juridical term that has been used for many years.

Defense was puzzled: How is it a juridical term?

It is a term used by barristers in England, said the witness in her best professorial manner. It refers to "fornication without carnal knowledge." "FWCK" is the acronym. In Old English a *w* looks like a *v*, which once represented the consonantal value of the Latin *u:* hence, fuck. Nothing obscene about it.

The other defendants were slightly bemused and highly entertained by this display of ersatz erudition; nevertheless, aware that their fate lay in keeping straight faces, they struggled not to laugh. In the end the jury found them not guilty—a happy conclusion, at last, to a government prosecution of the antiwar movement.

While the May Days were still in progress in Washington, nationwide memorials to the students killed at Kent State and Jackson State were taking place. These observances were joint efforts of the major antiwar coalitions (SMC, PCPJ, and NPAC) together with the National Student Association and the Association of Student Governments. On May 4, seven thousand participated in a memorial on the Kent State campus, and on May 5, ten thousand people congregated in New York at Bryant Park to hear, among others, Senator Vance Hartke (D-Indiana), Victor Gotbaum of District 37 of the Municipal Workers, David Livingston of District 65 of the Retail, Wholesale and Department Store Workers, and VVAW's John Kerry. Thousands rallied in other cities.

Howard Zinn remembers Boston that day: "I came back just in time to speak to a rally of about fifty thousand on Boston Common. The next day we had civil disobedience—several thousand people encircling the Kennedy [Federal] Building. I was pulled out of the encirclement by the police and knocked around a little. They knew me. They had singled out a number of people. . . ."

The large-scale participation of VVAW in the April demonstrations, as well as the growing civilian antiwar sentiment and of course the nature of the war itself, contributed to a burgeoning antiwar movement within the armed forces. On May 15, Armed Forces Day (or, as it was known, "Armed Farces Day"), antiwar actions occurred at nineteen bases, including air force and navy bases. The biggest turnouts were at Fort Hood, Fort Bliss, Fort Bragg, and Fort Lewis; there were marches, rallies, festivals, and fairs attended by several hundred active duty personnel. In San Diego, nearly fifteen hundred members of the crew of the carrier USS *Constellation* signed an appeal requesting that the Jane Fonda FTA show be allowed to be presented on the deck. Although Bob Hope's USO show was always allowed on board, Fonda's was not. However, her appearance in San Diego drew four thousand people, a majority of them in the armed forces.

Armed services protests continued through Memorial Day, abroad as well as at home: on May 31, three hundred air force personnel presented an antiwar petition to the U.S. Embassy in London. Just one of them, their legal counsel (who was also a Vietnam veteran), was court martialed. They were members of a larger group, People Emerging Against Corrupt Establishment (P.E.A.C.E.), which had members at all eight U.S. Air Force bases in England.

Antiwar sentiment among servicemen not in combat generally followed the pattern of civilian protest: meetings, marches, rallies, publications, and dozens of GI coffeehouses which served the same purpose as student meeting places. To protest the war while fighting it in Vietnam was a different matter, and a far uglier one. One method was to refuse to fight: mutiny. Between August 1969 and April 1972 ten major incidents of mutiny occurred; it is not possible to know how many "minor" incidents were unrecorded.

"Man, the war stinks," complained a member of Company C, 2nd Battalion, 1st Infantry, 196th Brigade. His company had been ordered to patrol an area around Phubai, about ten miles south of the DMZ; it was April 1972 during the height of that spring's North Vietnamese assault. "It's a damn waste of time. Why the hell are we fighting for something we don't believe in?"

"We're not going!" shouted another. "Why should we fight if nobody back home gives a damn about us?"

Eventually the men did move out, but only because they were told that their fellow soldiers—about twenty-five hundred of them just below the DMZ—would be endangered by their refusal. The battalion commander lambasted reporters who covered the incident: "All you press are bastards, I blame you for this and you can quote me on it."

A new battle technique appeared during these years: "working it out," in which enlisted men would refuse an order (generally to advance), whereupon their superior officer would bargain with them to determine exactly how much they would be willing to do and under what circumstances.

Many times the enlisted men's response to a direct order was that of Bravo Troop, an armored cavalry unit of the Americal Division. In the spring of 1971, when the South Vietnamese Army was reeling from the counterattack to their attempted invasion of Laos, men from Bravo Troop rescued their commander from an ambush attack but failed to retrieve his armored personnel carrier. No one volunteered for the job, nor would anyone do it on the direct order of the lieutenant colonel who was the squadron commander. "You must be out of your f—— mind," said one trooper. "Why should we die for an APC?" said another. "It's just a piece of junk."

Far worse than mutiny was murder, known in Vietnam as "fragging." Overzealous officers who pushed their men too far were often punished with a grenade in their bunk or a Claymore mine thrown into officers' quarters. From 1969 to July 1972 army records showed 551 incidents of assaults with explosive weapons; eighty-six men (mostly officers and NCOs) were killed and more than seven hundred injured.

In his study of antiwar sentiment in the armed services, *Soldiers in Revolt,* David Cortright says that

> for every one of the more than five hundred reported assaults, there were many instances of intimidation and threats of fragging which often produced the same result . . . as internal defiance spread within many units, no order could be issued without first considering the possibility of fragging. The ardent young West Point graduate, eager to succeed in combat and push his men to medal-winning heroics, was a doomed figure. The majority of grunts in Vietnam had but one aim, to return home safely, and few were willing to risk their lives for a hopeless cause. As violent and ruthless as it may have been, fragging was an essential tool of soldier democracy . . . [it

was] the final manifestation of a breakdown in the U.S. mission in Vietnam and signaled an Army at war with itself.

Sabotage was another weapon used by disaffected servicemen. By the end of 1971, the Navy alone reported 488 "investigations on damage or attempted damages" during fiscal year 1971: 191 for sabotage, 135 for arson, and 162 for "wrongful destruction." With increasing navy participation in the war during 1972, incidents of sabotage increased as well. The most devastating was a fire on the carrier USS *Forrestal,* based at Norfolk, Virginia, which damaged its radar center and caused $7 million in damage. Less than two weeks later, $1 million in damage was done to the carrier USS *Ranger* at Alameda, California: a paint scraper and two twelve-inch bolts were put into the ship's number-four-engine reduction gears. Defense lawyers for the serviceman accused of the crime documented more than two dozen acts of destruction on the carrier during the preceding few months, many of which were the occasion for bragging by men who claimed responsibility for them. The sailor accused was acquitted the following year.

On Sunday, June 13, 1971, the New York *Times* began to publish what it called the "Vietnam Archive," since known as the Pentagon Papers. This was an extraordinary collection of documents and a history of U.S. involvement in Vietnam from 1945 to March 1968. Drawn from official records—Department of State, Department of Defense, CIA files, National Security Agency files, some White House files, etc.—it had been secretly prepared at Robert McNamara's direction beginning in June 1967. Originally scheduled to take half a dozen men three months to complete, the history ultimately used thirty-six men for eighteen months. The final version comprised forty-seven volumes: three thousand pages of narrative and four thousand pages of documents.

As Senator Mike Gravel (D-Alaska) wrote in his Introduction to one edition of the Papers, it was

> the most complete study yet performed of the policy-making process that led to our deepening involvement in Vietnam, and the most revealing insight we have had into the functioning of our government's national security apparatus. . . . The Papers prove that, from the beginning, the war has been an American war, serving only to perpetuate American military power in Asia . . . as the leaders of America sought to preserve their reputation for toughness and determination.

In perhaps the truest and most damning comment on the history contained in the Papers, Gravel continued:

> No one who reads this study can fail to conclude that, had the true *[sic]* facts been made known earlier, the war would long ago have ended, and the needless deaths of hundreds of thousands of Americans and Vietnamese would have been averted. This is the great lesson of the Pentagon Papers.

As Max Frankel stated in the New York *Times* edition of the Papers, "the predominant American objective was not victory over the enemy but merely the avoidance of defeat and humiliation." Government leaders, as revealed in the Papers, showed "an arrogant disregard for the Congress, for the public and for the inherent obligation of the responsibilities of leadership in a democratic society."

Attorney General John Mitchell moved to halt the *Times'* publication, but meanwhile other newspapers had begun to publish portions of the Papers. They, too, were enjoined. In an effort to make the full contents of the Papers known, Senator Gravel tried to read them aloud in the Senate. He was prevented from doing so by a parliamentary maneuver. Thereupon he convened his Subcommittee on Public Buildings and Grounds and took testimony on the lack of funds for public buildings because of the high expenses of the war. During this testimony he read into the record parts of the Papers and had the remainder incorporated for release. The next day (June 30, the day that the Twenty-sixth Amendment took effect, giving eighteen-year-olds the right to vote) the Supreme Court ruled 6–3 for the *Times,* and publication resumed.

The *Times* had received the Vietnam study from Daniel Ellsberg, a former Rand Corporation analyst, former Marine, former member of McNamara's staff, and himself one of the authors of the Papers. Believing that the study proved that the war was wrong—that the United States had been wrongly involved from the start, and that each administration was simply repeating the mistakes of previous administrations—Ellsberg had begun to photocopy the archive in 1969. Then, like the Ancient Mariner, he had for many months sought to unburden himself of the documents and the story that they told, but the members of Congress whom he approached, including J. William Fulbright and George McGovern, declined to make them public. Finally, in early 1971, Ellsberg went to *Times* reporter Neil Sheehan.

Ellsberg's leak prompted the White House to put into effect, in July 1971, a version of the discarded Huston Plan: Nixon instructed John Erlichman to form an independent investigating team within the White House ranks. Erlichman put in charge his young aide Egil Krogh, Jr., and, in a move designed to cover his flank from Henry Kissinger, borrowed David Young from Kissinger's office. The group's assigned task—to stop leaks—gave them their name: the Plumbers. In September 1971 the Plumbers staged their first operation when a team of Cubans, under the field direction of former CIA agent E. Howard Hunt and G. Gordon Liddy, a former employee of the Treasury Department, broke into the office of Ellsberg's psychiatrist, Dr. Lewis Fielding, in a fruitless search for Ellsberg's psychiatric records.

In July and again in December of that year Ellsberg and another Rand employee, Anthony J. Russo, were indicted for their role in giving the archive to the *Times* and other newspapers; the second indictment included the government's by now standard "conspiracy" charge and, like the first, charged violation of the Espionage Act (1917). Their 1973 trial ended in a mistrial after the judge announced a series of government illegalities in the case, including unauthorized wiretaps, the burglarizing of the files of Ellsberg's psychiatrist, and the fact that the Nixon Administration had offered to the judge the directorship of the FBI.

Coming as it did after six years of intensifying antiwar activity, the publication of the Pentagon Papers might have been expected to raise a huge public outcry for immediate American withdrawal. The Gallup Poll for August showed just such sentiment: 61 percent favoring a pullout and 28 percent for staying. The Harris Poll showed that a majority thought the war was "immoral." But despite these findings no great public outcry developed. No big antiwar action was mounted, and those that were attempted in the fall were poorly attended. Nixon's Vietnamization plan, a failure in Vietnam, was succeeding in the United States.

What next? was the question that the antiwar movement always needed to ask itself after every major action, and never was the question more appropriate—and more disquieting—than after the spring actions of 1971. Antiwar sentiment across the country was at its height, demonstrations had aroused—if not produced—an unprecedented number of people, and even the Senate seemed finally, reluctantly, ready to go on record against the war. Although five resolutions had been introduced in February and March aimed at extricating the United States from its involvement in Vietnam, none had passed. Now, in June, the Senate was willing to commit itself in what it perceived as the least politically damaging way: it passed, 57–42, the Mansfield "Sense of the Senate" resolution (nonbinding) "to terminate at the earliest possible date" U.S. military involvement in Indochina. The resolution had no force, but undoubtedly it assuaged some senatorial consciences.

Once again, however, instead of capitalizing on this public mood, the antiwar movement fell afoul of its tendencies to self-destruct. Both NPAC and PCPJ held conferences during June and July. Prior to these meeetings, three union leaders (Abe Feinglass, Moe Foner, and David Livingston) acted as mediators between the two groups. Their help was needed because to some observers it seemed that the two coalitions were more interested in fighting each other than in fighting the Administration's pursuance of the war. The disagreements were both tactical and political:

NPAC advocated:
   —legal march and rally,
   —immediate withdrawal from Vietnam,
   —a single-issue coalition focusing on the war,
   —nonpartisan antiwar activity unaligned with electoral politics.
PCPJ advocated:
   —legal march and rally plus opportunities for nonviolent civil disobedience and confrontation,
   —a negotiated date for withdrawal from Vietnam—"set the date",
   —a multiissue coalition with a multiissue focus (i.e., $6,500 guaranteed income),
   —participation in party and electoral politics.

Under the mediators' guidance, however, the two coalitions did agree to cooperate on three actions during the rest of the year: Hiroshima-Nagasaki commemorations on August 6–9, a "national moratorium" on October 13, and regional antiwar demonstrations on November 6.

Some days later, around the middle of August, the May Day Tribe assembled for an acrimonious meeting in Atlanta. This time lines were drawn between women and gay liberationists, on the one hand, and white male heterosexuals on the other; each side saw the continuing struggle very differently, and they divided bitterly over their respective visions.

Meanwhile the war went on. To dramatize the fact that the killing continued in Indochina, Women Strike for Peace, the Fellowship of Reconciliation, and the War Resisters League participated that fall in Project DDT (Daily Death Toll). Every day people from all over the country came to Washington to stage a "die-in" in front of the White House. Each American wore a Vietnamese paper hat and a banner with the name of a dead Vietnamese. Approaching the White House gate, the Americans would "drop dead" on the sidewalk—an experience described by one WSPer as a "new dimension" in her already staunch resistance to the war, "a quality in the commitment of your body to the sidewalk where you are told it should not be, which is a commitment, symbolically, to pit yourself, the individual, against the power of the U.S. government." After being arrested, her group was jailed in Washington's Second Precinct House, a cold, filthy, cockroach-infested "dungeon." There the women found the walls of their cells covered with graffiti, messages written by the May Day protesters who had been jailed there the previous spring; among them: TO SPEAK OF GOD AND REMAIN SILENT ON VIETNAM, IS BLASPHEMY. RESIST! DON'T PAY WAR TAXES. PRAY FOR LIFE, NOT DEATH. —THOREAU.†

On October 13 a number of small demonstrations were held around the country under NPAC's aegis; NPAC's biggest efforts, however, were reserved for November 6. Meanwhile, PCPJ's and the May Day Tribe's "Evict Nixon" campaign took place in Washington on October 25 and 26. It was a resounding failure: no more than eight hundred to one thousand people attended. Prior to the scheduled march and rally intended to "close the White House," a "grand jury investigation of

---

† Not paying war taxes had been a technique dating to Henry Thoreau's one-night jailing for his tax refusal during the Mexican War in 1846. During World War II this form of protest was made more difficult when the government began withholding taxes from employees' paychecks. In 1948 the Peacemaker committee was formed to assist citizens who wished to protest military spending by refusing to pay taxes. Among Peacemaker's founders was A. J. Muste. During World War II Muste had not felt that tax refusal was a practical or viable way for pacifists to protest war, but in 1948 he began to refuse to pay his federal income tax because of the government's production of hydrogen bombs in addition to atomic bombs. Every year Muste wrote a letter to the director of the IRS and made a public statement explaining that he would neither pay his taxes nor even file a return. Citing "Divine Guidance" for his conscientious refusal, Muste one year sent along to the IRS Thoreau's essay "Civil Disobedience" and portions of the Scriptures.

During the Vietnam years the tax refusal movement grew to include thousands of Americans. They refused to pay not only their federal income tax (or that portion of it allotted to the defense budget) but also the surtax instituted in 1966 on private telephones—a tax that was specifically targeted for the war. War Tax Resistance, formed in 1969, aided in publicizing tax refusal; by the end of the war more than two hundred local tax refusal groups were in existence.

citizen grievances and American power" was held at Washington's First Congregational Church. In accordance with PCPJ's philosophy, this three-day teach-in covered a broad spectrum of concerns of which the war was only one. The moderator told the audience that sitting through hour after hour of speeches would make them a " 'community of suffering' drawing them close to society's various victims." Eqbal Ahmad, Tom Hayden, David Dellinger, John Froines, Staughton Lynd, Richard Falk, and Rennie Davis were among the speakers. Strategy for 1972 seemed to be in question; there was general recognition of the fact that the American people were not, after all, prepared for revolution. "We have to get into the arena where most of the people are and most of the people in this country still believe in electoral politics," said Davis.

"We have developed a rhetorical style that speaks to ourselves and to no one else," said Froines. "Now we have to go back to the American people with a new kind of humility, a new kind of seriousness which recognizes that people are not, by and large, bad people, but people who are confused, frightened, manipulated and controlled. . . ."

The "grand jury," as expected, handed down "indictments" of the "organs of the American government" and the "social and economic basis of American society." No one save themselves seemed to care. Davis called for a rally at the Washington Monument, announcing that "it should be the most important gathering of people in twenty-five years." It was postponed for a day because of rain. When it did take place, only about seven hundred people showed up. The FBI, it was said, had deliberately kept away its infiltrators so as to embarrass the rally's sponsors by diminishing the crowd. The day took on a surreal tone: "Prepare to launch rubber duckies!" cried one marshal into his walkie-talkie. "Away duckies! Away duckies!" Said Davis to the dampened crowd: "We intend to affect the outcome of the 1972 presidential election." And then, most unreal of all, came the voice of Nguyen Minh Vy, a member of the Viet Cong delegation to the Paris peace talks, his voice and that of his interpreter coming over loudspeakers hooked up to receive the transatlantic call.

"Is there any great dishonor for the United States to end a war that is prejudicial to American honor?" said Vy.

He was told in reply that "the demonstrators feel nothing but shame."

The sun came out at last, and then it began to set. At dusk the demonstrators, perhaps eight hundred strong, began to make their way to the White House. Police blocked them at Fifteenth Street and Pennsylvania Avenue, however, and so they sat down in the street, snarling the rush-hour traffic. They carried "eviction notices" for the President that read WE THE PEOPLE HEREBY SERVE NOTICE OF OUR DETERMINATION TO EVICT YOU FROM PUBLIC OFFICE. Three hundred were arrested, including Davis, Dellinger, and Father James Groppi of Milwaukee.

On November 6 the regional demonstrations that had been agreed on by NPAC and PCPJ took place in several cities. In San Francisco forty thousand came; in New York thirty thousand, in Denver fifteen thousand, in Boston ten thousand, and thousands elsewhere. As respectable as these numbers were (the antiwar movement's "body count"), they gave no evidence of a growing public sentiment against the war. To many people, in fact, it seemed that the war was indeed ending, at least for American combat troops, just as President Nixon had said it would. In the period October–December 1971, draft calls were ten thousand per month, as opposed to seventeen thousand during the first part of the year. Nixon had also removed, or at least softened, people's fears of a war with China by his trip there, announced in the summer of 1971 but not occurring until February 1972. However, even the promise of the journey gave people hope in the intervening months: while the Administration was talking to the Chinese it would hardly go to war with them.

Finally, and most heartening of all, the American casualty rate had dropped. In May 1970, during the Cambodian incursion, it had stood at two hundred per week. In May 1971 it was down to 35 per week. This drop was partly due to the reduction of American troop strength; by the end of June, 150,000 troops had been brought home.

Thus, in light of a shift in the public's attention from the war, the late-autumn meetings of PCPJ and NPAC assumed a special urgency: how could they return public notice to a war that was no longer being perceived as escalating uncontrollably and, more, was no longer killing Americans at an unacceptably high rate?

The war had become automated to a great degree—an "electronic battlefield." For example, in the perennial and always fruitless effort to stem the flow of supplies down the Ho Chi Minh Trail, the U.S. command had planted "man-sized" sensors along its length. When North Vietnamese trucks rolled by, an electronic signal was sent to an IBM computer in Thailand; its printouts were translated into bombing orders for American pilots. Now, in the late fall and early winter of 1971, the Ho Chi Minh Trail was particularly busy as the North Vietnamese prepared for a spring offensive. What Herbert Mitgang of the *Times* called the "truck count" was escalating, even as the (American) body count dropped.

In Chicago on November 27–28, the national steering committee of PCPJ met and decided to work in the upcoming presidential primaries and to demonstrate at both parties' conventions. But the delegates refused to endorse a date for a spring action in conjunction with NPAC; rather, they chose to continue to try to build a multiissue coalition—in effect, an American Left.

A week later in Cleveland NPAC met December 3–5. The convention was "open to all antiwar activists"; it passed resolutions to continue to build demonstrations against the war and, in line with its Trotskyite principles, to stay independent of party politics. April 22 was chosen as the date for the major spring demonstrations, to be held in New York and Los Angeles.

Meanwhile, in Dallas, a group called the Peoples Party was holding its own miniconvention (no more than 200 to 250 delegates attended). It nominated stand-in candidates for President and Vice President, with the understanding that they would stand aside in the (unlikely) event that a politician of national stature would accept their spots on the ticket. Benjamin Spock and Julius Hobson, a black educator and antiwar activist from Washington, D.C., were the candidates. The Peoples Party had hoped for a defection from the Democrats but none was forthcoming, perhaps because of the party's platform, a laundry list that no politician interested in reelection would have dared to endorse: giving "minority communities" control over police, welfare, courts, and schools; a $6,500 guaranteed income; giving control of industry to "workers and consumers"; making hospitals and drug companies "nonprofit"; eliminating I.Q. or maximum age level or amount of schooling as a condition for employment; providing community "free" schools designed to meet the "needs of real life" . . .

One further sign of disaffection in the antiwar movement occurred at the Remember the War Benefit for PCPJ held on December 6 at the Cathedral Church of St. John the Divine in New York. The brainchild of David McReynolds and Dotson Rader, a former SDSer, it was intended not only to erase PCPJ's sixty-thousand-dollar debt, but also to breach the media blackout which they felt had descended upon the Movement. "New respectability for the antiwar movement" was a third goal. The event was not a success on any of these counts.

The benefit was organized by Rader, David Dellinger, Rennie Davis, William Douthard, and Norma Becker. Typically, its planning was marred by arguments over everything from the advertising copy to the uses to which the presumed profits would be put. To the disgust of feminists in the May Day Collective, Norman Mailer's play *D.J.*, based on his book *Why Are We in Vietnam?* was to be performed at the benefit. Like a lightning rod, Mailer in the late sixties and early seventies invariably attracted feminist ire; trapped in his male image, he never failed to elicit what eventually became almost automatic reactions. According to Dotson Rader, the women working on the benefit hated Mailer more than they hated anyone—and certainly more than they hated the war:

> Every day at the mention of his name—*whammo!* Sexist male chauvinist pig right-wing opportunist objectively contrary to Marxist-Leninist-Maoist liberation counterrevolutionary cake-eater rip-off artist decadent bourgeois culture-vulture running dog . . .

Nevertheless the audience saw *D.J.* that night. It was performed on a sixteen-foot-high stage which Wm. J. Hanley & Sons of Medford, Massachusetts, had erected at a cost of ten thousand dollars.

Speakers included Bishop Paul Moore, rector of the cathedral; David Dellinger; Tennessee Williams; Ossie Davis; and, finally, Mailer himself. The audience was not friendly to him; catcalls and boos came from the vast darkness of the cathedral. Mailer spoke prophetically of the future:

> . . . when that war in Vietnam is over, you have to ask yourself what you will do next, what are your values going to be, what are your desires going to be when there will no longer be a war in Vietnam to boo. . . . The more we go in for self-righteousness and piety beyond this point, the more we are in danger of becoming left-wing totalitarians. That is the danger when we all of us get together.

While Mailer's play was being performed approximately one third of the audience walked out. Meanwhile, backstage, the organizers of the benefit discovered that they would not make a penny from all their months of work. The "security" forces in charge of tickets had not only allowed people to come in without paying, they had also stolen the collection. Creditors appeared, pressing for immediate payment, but there was no money to give to them.

Later, Dellinger and Norma Becker and a few other organizers confronted the "security" people with the theft—more than nine thousand dollars, by Rader's reckoning. The security people denied everything. In the end PCPJ decided not to press charges because the attendant publicity would be more harmful than the loss of the money.

On December 26, 1971, Operation Proud Deep Alpha was launched—the heaviest U.S. bombing of North Vietnam since 1968. According to the Pentagon, the one thousand sorties flown December 26–30 were all below the 20th parallel, about seventy miles south of Hanoi.

PCPJ and NCAP hurriedly put together a few small demonstrations, but the actions that attracted the greatest public notice came from the Vietnam Veterans Against the War, who seized upon national monuments as sites for protest. In Philadelphia on December 27 twenty-five VVAW entered the Betsy Ross House, where, according to tradition, Ms. Ross stitched the first American flag. The protesters flew a modern-day flag upside down in front of the house; after an hour they were removed by police. In Washington the next day a group of 150, including some from the Betsy Ross protest, marched through the city and dropped bags filled with blood ("to bring the bloodbath home") at the White House gates. They proceeded to the Lincoln Memorial, where they placed a coffin in front of Abraham Lincoln's statue and then blocked the entrance to the memorial. Eighty-seven were arrested.

The most spectacular protest, however, took place December 26–28 at Liberty Island in New York harbor, where fifteen VVAW entered the Statue of Liberty with the usual flow of tourists, remained after closing time, and barricaded themselves inside for forty-two hours. Calling themselves Operation Peace on Earth, they flew the American flag upside down first from Liberty's crown and then from her torch, access to which had been barred since 1960 by the National Park Service because it was considered structurally unsound. They issued statements about the purpose of their protest; one said:

> The reason we chose the Statue of Liberty is that since we were children, the statue has been analogous in our minds with freedom and an America we love.
> Then we went to fight a war in the name of freedom. We saw that freedom is a selective expression allowed only to those who are white and who maintain the status quo.
> Until this symbol again takes on the meaning it was intended to have, we must continue our demonstrations all over the nation of our love of freedom and of America.

Feeling that they had made their point, the veterans evacuated Liberty on the order of a federal judge. They left no debris, and they put five dollars in an envelope in the lunchroom to pay for coffee and sugar that they had used.

By the end of 1971 there were 140,000 American troops remaining in Vietnam.

1972:
"Peace Is at Hand"

IN JANUARY 1972 Senators Edmund S. Muskie (D-Maine) and Hubert H. Humphrey (D-Minnesota) announced their candidacies for the presidency. Vietnam was high on their list of issues. Muskie demanded total withdrawal, stating the politically unpalatable opinion that fifty-five thousand American lives and $130 billion had been "wasted" in Vietnam—an assessment that would have been unthinkable (even given the lower numbers) in the previous presidential election, when Muskie had been Humphrey's running mate. Humphrey, opening his campaign a week later, did not offer so specific a denunciation of the war which he had formerly so enthusiastically supported, but, in typically trenchant style, he said that "it has taken Mr. Nixon longer to withdraw our troops than it took us to defeat Hitler."

That same week in January Eugene McCarthy entered the presidential race also, saying that all his competitors "looked like losers." To no one's surprise, he promised to make the war one of his major campaign issues.

But opposition to the war—which had been "McNamara's war" and "Johnson's war" and was now "Nixon's war"—was not an issue upon which a candidate for national or state office (with a few exceptions) could campaign and win, although it was an issue upon which many candidates could and did lose. And in any case, the Nixon Administration was determined to pursue its course of Vietnamization in which the American casualty rate went down while the American government pursued the war by a different strategy—mostly bombing. Having undertaken Project Proud Deep Alpha against North Vietnam in the last days of 1971—"protective-reaction air strikes," they were called—Nixon proceeded apace with massive bombings of both North and South Vietnam, Laos, and Cambodia. He also continued the promised withdrawal of troops. On January 13 it was announced that seventy thousand additional American men would be withdrawn by May 1, leaving only sixty-five thousand.

At the end of January the President spoke to the nation and revealed that his National Security Adviser, Henry Kissinger, had been conducting secret talks with the North Vietnamese while the formal public talks were going on, but that no agreement had been reached secretly, just as none had been reached publicly. Thus the war was largely defused as an issue for the Democrats, since the Nixon Administration had portrayed itself as sincerely trying to achieve a treaty of peace. Even though the carnage continued, and everyone knew that it continued, the troop withdrawals and news of secret efforts to find peace reduced the public's fear that the war was out of control. To add to his public image as a peacemaker and thus to further deprive the Democrats of their issue, Nixon made much-heralded trips to Peking (in February) and Moscow (in May). The danger of precipitating World War III and/or a nuclear war—a danger that those opposed to the war had feared from the start—seemed much less when heads of state toasted each other at banquets that were televised around the world.

In February, a week before President Nixon's trip to the People's Republic of China, members of the American peace movement traveled to Versailles to attend the World Assembly for Peace and Independence of the Peoples of Indochina. The assembly was sponsored by the Stockholm Conference on Vietnam and the World Peace Council, a group dominated by Communists oriented toward Moscow. Over twelve hundred delegates from eighty-four countries attended, including delegates from North and South Vietnam and Laos and Cambodia. Despite the fact that NPAC was a Trotskyite organization, it was invited to this conference because the NLF wanted to meet representatives from the entire American peace movement. Other Americans came from NWRO, VVAW, AFSC, WSP, CLCV, WILPF, political and church groups, and PCPJ. The U.S. representative to the Paris peace talks (which had been broken off) called the U.S. delegates "communist claques": like all meetings between American citizens and their Communist adversaries, the Versailles conference was frowned upon by officialdom. The major outcome of the conference was the delegates' pledge of international support for a series of spring antiwar actions in the United States.

The first of these came on April 1, two days after North Vietnamese troops had invaded South Vietnam and begun a major spring offensive. Ten thousand people marched in front of the state capitol in Harrisburg, Pennsylvania, to protest the war and the conspiracy trial of the Harrisburg 7: the Reverend Philip F. Berrigan, Sister Elizabeth McAlister, the Reverend Neil McLaughlin, Anthony Scoblick, his wife Mary Cain Scoblick, the Reverend Joseph Wenderoth, and Eqbal Ahmad, a Pakistani Moslem and a research fellow at the Adlai E. Stevenson Institute for International Affairs.

The trial of the Harrisburg 7 was perhaps the most bizarre of all the antiwar trials. The defendants were charged with conspiracy to kidnap Henry Kissinger and to ransom him for "certain demands"—the freeing of political prisoners in the United States and ending the bombing in Southeast Asia; to blow up generators in heating tunnels in Washington, D.C.; and to vandalize draft boards. Defense counsel included Ramsey Clark, who had been attorney general under LBJ at the time of the indictment of the Boston 5, and Leonard Boudin, a well-known defender of political activists including Benjamin Spock in the Boston trial.

By April 1 the Harrisburg trial had been in session for two months and now the

378

jury had begun its deliberations. All the preceding week there had been protests by hundreds of people who had come to the small, conservative state capital not only to march but also to take part in Holy Week workshops, rallies, and liturgies. The April 1 demonstration once again reflected the pressures put on the Movement to allow itself to be a vehicle for more than just protest against the war: the theme of the day was "Dr. Martin Luther King's message of a unified nonviolent struggle against war, poverty and repression." (The date was three days shy of the fourth anniversary of King's assassination.) Ten thousand people saw the Bread and Puppet Theater's Mr. Bigman, a giant Uncle Sam who "eats the children of the world." They heard Father Daniel Berrigan (an unindicted coconspirator) bring a message from his brother Philip, one of the defendants: "The real indictment is to be violent in any form; to hate to any degree." Representative Bella Abzug spoke, and Daniel Ellsberg, and the Reverend Ralph David Abernathy; telephoned greetings, broadcast to the crowd, came from Mme. Nguyen Thi Binh in Paris, Foreign Minister of the Provisional Revolutionary Government (PRG), successor to the NLF.

Four days later, on April 5, the jury returned with the announcement that it was hopelessly deadlocked, and a mistrial was declared. Father Philip Berrigan and Sister Elizabeth McAlister were found guilty, however, of smuggling contraband letters in and out of Lewisburg Federal Penitentiary—hardly a "lesser charge," since it carried a possible sentence for them of forty and thirty years, respectively. The charges were later dismissed.

"I thought the whole thing was kind of funny, the idea of a bunch of priests and nuns zipping off with Henry Kissinger," commented one juror after the trial—and, indeed, the government had had so little faith in its original two-count indictment that it had added a third, the conspiracy to vandalize draft boards. Its case had rested on the testimony of a paid FBI informer, Boyd Douglas, and the jury simply had not found him credible.

The Harrisburg trial had served as a rallying point for antiwar activists as had the Conspiracy two years before. The Harrisburg Defense Committee raised half a million dollars for the expenses of the trial; like the Chicago defendants, the Harrisburg defendants undertook heavy speaking schedules. But the HDC was riven by dissent as the Conspiracy had not been; Charles Meconis, the historian of the Catholic Left, recounts the way in which "movement professionals"—i.e., non-Catholic political activists, antiwar and otherwise—moved in and took charge, much to the dismay of some in the admittedly "elitist" Catholic Left. Even more damaging to the Catholic Left was the reading in open court of the letters smuggled into and out of prison between Father Philip Berrigan (imprisoned for the Catonsville action) and Sister Elizabeth McAlister—letters transmitted by the informer Douglas. They included, among other things, expressions of personal feeling each for the other, not "bad" in itself, but deeply shocking to devoutly religious followers of two individuals who had taken vows of chastity in obedience to that religion. Philip Berrigan, in fact, had spoken of the need for activists to remain celibate in order to concentrate fully on their work. Finally, the cost of the Harrisburg trial in both money and energy proved too great; although individuals would go on to organize and take action in later years, for all practical purposes the Catholic Left ended with the Harrisburg verdict.

On April 6, the day after the verdict, the Administration ordered the formal resumption of air strikes against North Vietnam, and on April 15, fighter-bombers and B-52s struck Hanoi and Haiphong—the first acknowledged attacks against those cities since Lyndon Johnson's partial bombing halt at the end of March 1968. The Administration announced that it was ready to extend the attacks to any military target in the North. Angered by what he saw as Soviet support of a sudden movement into the South of North Vietnamese men and equipment, President Nixon was willing to jeopardize his upcoming visit to Moscow in order to deter further North Vietnamese advances. Ruled out, however, was an option that had been considered earlier in the war: the mining of Haiphong harbor.*

Reaction to the renewed bombing was swift and severe. "Only a madman could believe, now, that more bombing will bring peace to Indochina," wrote Anthony Lewis in the New York *Times;* and, with an eye to domestic upheaval: ". . . the most disastrous effects of the bombing escalation must be inside the United States."

Only a few hours after news of the renewed bombing of Hanoi-Haiphong, PCPJ drew eight hundred people to an emergency demonstration in Washington. After hearing speeches by their own leaders and by Senator Mike Gravel at St. Stephen's Church, they marched thirty blocks to Lafayette Square across from the White House. Upon refusal of orders to disperse by U.S. Park Police, more than two hundred were arrested, including Sidney Peck and David Dellinger. Earlier in the day, U.S. Park Police had dispersed (without any arrests) members of a Quaker peace vigil which had been encamped on Pennsylvania Avenue in front of the White House for ten months. Day and night, week in and week out, Quakers and non-Quakers alike had kept their vigil. Begun the previous June 2 by members of the New York Yearly Meeting of the Religious Society of Friends, the protest had initially been in support of some of its number who were going on trial that day for their part in the April 1971 demonstration. Like Topsy, it just grew, attracting a bizarre collection of hangers-on until a permanent encampment was in place.

Until the President's announcement the nation's campuses had been relatively quiet for some months. The students of 1972 were a different generation from those of 1968–69; with the demise of SDS—never a reliable antiwar vehicle in any case—they had not found a new organization to channel their discontent. (The Trotskyite tendencies of SMC were too sectarian for most college youth, even for most antiwar youth.) In early April a study was released showing that as of spring 1971 as many as 30 percent of American college students said that they would prefer to live in some other country. Their mood had shifted from "personal despair and depression" in 1970 to "confused but not despairing" in 1971. Titled *The Changing Values*

---

* The antiwar movement had had advance notice of the bombing of Hanoi-Haiphong: on April 8 the Ad Hoc Military Buildup Committee was formed, and on April 13, two days before American B-52s attacked those cities, the Ad Hoc Committee knew about it. Composed largely of antiwar veterans and civilians in the GI coffeehouse movement, the committee had hit upon the tactic of telephoning contacts at military bases to learn what buildup and alerts, if any, were occurring. Sometimes the committee shared its scoops with the media: on April 13 it informed the wire services that an air force reconnaissance group in Hawaii had been preparing "extra-large targeting charts for Hanoi and Haiphong."

on Campus, the study showed that one in ten students were "left radical," while two in ten were "conservative" and the rest "mainstream." Whatever their characterization of themselves, since the Kent State killings of 1970 during that spring's protest against the invasion of Cambodia, students had more or less withdrawn into themselves and their campus lives.

Now Richard Nixon was giving them a chance to make themselves heard again. On April 17, two days after the bombing of Hanoi-Haiphong, the National Student Association, affiliated with 515 campuses, issued a strike call for Friday, April 21. The campus newspapers of the eight Ivy League schools published a joint editorial endorsing the strike; calling for a one-day Moratorium, the editorial urged students and faculty to attend meetings to plan other protests. Moreover, students were encouraged to join NPAC's April 22 demonstration.

That same day a rock-throwing crowd, three thousand strong, taunted police at the University of Wisconsin during an antiwar rally there; in San Francisco fifteen hundred demonstrators surrounded a federal building and forty-one people were arrested in a protest at the Alameda Naval Air Station. In New York five hundred demonstrators at Columbia University tied up traffic as they marched down Broadway to 107th Street, where they were halted by police.

Protests escalated during the following days. On April 18, during a march of two thousand from Boston Common to Harvard Square, Harvard students attacked Henry Kissinger's former bailiwick, the Center for International Affairs. About two hundred broke in, smashing windows and destroying offices, overturning desks, throwing typewriters out the windows, strewing papers and books, spray-painting obscenities with Nixon's name, and setting a fire which was quickly put out by firemen. Police sealed off Harvard Square and imposed a curfew, whereupon students roamed through Cambridge smashing windows of stores, a post office, and the IBM building. At Columbia and Princeton strike votes were taken for April 21, and a peaceful rally was held at Columbia. At Cornell, at Berkeley, at Wisconsin, Yale, Fordham, NYU, Tufts, and countless other campuses students and faculty met in an atmosphere of crisis to vote to join the nationwide strike.

Their elders watched them anxiously. The goal, said the *Times,* was "not to shut down the universities but to end the war." Students were urged to use their new voting rights to defeat candidates who equivocated on the war or propounded "secret, evasive" plans to win it militarily. That is, the students were being asked once again to work within the system, which until that date had not been notably responsive. Alarmed at the prospect of continuing disruption, the presidents of the eight Ivy League universities plus MIT issued a statement: they "deplored" the renewed bombing of North Vietnam and its civilians; they expressed the hope that all Americans would find "nonviolent, constructive outlets" to show their concern —specifically, in that election year, working for political candidates or "communicating their feelings to appropriate government officials." (In other words, "Write a letter to your congressman.")

Some students were tired of hearing such advice. At a rally at Fordham on strike day, a group of about five hundred listened to Allard Lowenstein, always a supporter of the system, urge them to work against President Nixon in that fall's elections: "Anyone who says we can't defeat him is ridiculous." One student, watching the crowd, offered her opinion: "The trouble with demonstrations is that they give you the feeling that you've accomplished something. You're opposed to the war and you do feel guilty because you don't do anything positive, so you come out here and release your guilt. But you still haven't done anything constructive."

Like stopping the war.

As the waves of B-52 attacks continued against North Vietnam, and the South Vietnamese Army continued to fall back from North Vietnam's offensive, the nationwide student strike took place on Friday, April 21. Most demonstrations were peaceful, but some were not. At Princeton 350 students seized the building of the Woodrow Wilson School for Public and International Affairs, demanding to know the identity of its donor. Sister Elizabeth McAlister spoke to them, urging them to widen their protest by reaching out to the community beyond the university. At Stanford over 100 students were arrested for blocking highways; previously they had attacked an electronics lab which, they said, did war-related research. At the University of Michigan students attacked an ROTC building, vandalizing its offices; later 1,500 of them roamed through Ann Arbor, tying up traffic for four hours. At Boston University 1,500 students attacked the administration building, smashing doors, taking files, ripping out telephones; the next day 40 students took over the office of the dean of students. At the University of Texas at Austin police dispersed demonstrators with tear gas and nightsticks. Twenty-seven students were arrested at Syracuse University while barricading the entrance to an air force recruiting office; 15 were arrested at Idaho's Boise State University. Some protests were more extensive. At Columbia, 500 students rallied and then, chanting and singing (falling silent as they passed hospitals) and carrying Viet Cong and Cuban and black nationalist flags, marched downtown via Broadway to the Veterans Administration building at Seventh Avenue and Twenty-fourth Street. Trying to avoid serious trouble on a campus that had seen more than its share, Columbia president William McGill had ordered the school closed for the day. At the midday campus rally, blacks joined whites for the first time in that spring's demonstrations. Many of the white speakers welcomed them with contrition, criticizing themselves for not fighting in the black "revolution." Later, as the marchers arrived at the VA building, they found that the sixteenth floor had been occupied by eighteen Vietnam veterans who were later arrested.

The most serious trouble erupted at the University of Maryland at College Park, where on the night of April 20 Governor Marvin Mandel called up an eight-hundred-man force of the National Guard to keep order. Two thousand student demonstrators had blocked U.S. Route 1; police, using armored vehicles and tear gas, had scattered them. Battles between police and students had occurred, and "scores" of demonstrators were arrested, many after trying to set fire to an ROTC armory. The following night, after a rock-and-bottle attack on the school's administration building, five more were arrested, including the university chaplain.

In the next week most campuses quieted, but at Columbia the protesters, having seized five buildings in an action reminiscent of 1968's miniwar, kept up their occupation in the face of massive disinterest on the part of their fellow students. On

April 28 a group calling itself the Majority Coalition threatened to sue the university if the buildings were not reopened (two buildings had, in fact, been "liberated" by nonprotesting students). Similar lawsuits, or threats of lawsuits, occurred on other campuses around this time. Classes were held outdoors, or in cafeterias, fraternity houses, professors' apartments, and even in neighborhood barrooms. Eventually, however, pressure to resume normal campus activity became too great, and on April 29 University President McGill used campus police to free Kent Hall, but not others. With the help of a front-end loader and nightsticks, police routed the occupiers, most of whom jumped out the ground-floor windows and ran to an adjacent occupied building, Hamilton Hall. Two were arrested: one a university employee, one a former student. They claimed to have been threatened with beatings by their fellow demonstrators if they spoke to reporters.

Despite these actions and others, the majority of students, even though they disliked the war, wanted to finish their course work and receive their diplomas. Nevertheless, the threat of disruption remained sufficiently strong for the presidents of sixty Midwestern colleges, including the Reverend Theodore Hesburgh of Notre Dame, to issue on May 6 a statement expressing their "grave distress over the war" and calling for "the immediate withdrawal of American military forces from Indochina."

NPAC's long-planned and much-disputed Peace Action Day, which PCPJ had not endorsed until April 11, took place on April 22. Demonstrations were held not only in the United States but around the world: in Belgium, Canada, Denmark, England, France, Ireland, Lebanon, Luxembourg, Scotland, Sweden, Switzerland, and New Zealand. The weather in the eastern United States was cold and rainy, a factor that undoubtedly cut into the size of the crowds. Still, the turnout in the major designated city, New York, was very low even after the weather was taken into account: only about thirty-five thousand. In San Francisco, listening to speeches from Bobby Seale, Jane Fonda, and Richard Hongisto, the city's sheriff, there were about thirty thousand; in Los Angeles, about twelve thousand. The sodden marchers in New York, having made their way from Central Park West and Seventy-sixth Street to Bryant Park, heard speakers as diverse as David Dellinger, Ossie Davis, Daniel Ellsberg, Senator Mike Gravel, David Livingston, the exiled Greek leader Andreas Papandreou, Jeannette Rankin, (age ninety-five) and David Schoenbrun, one of the most perceptive journalists to have covered the war. A group called the Rhinestones sang John Lennon and Yoko Ono's "Give Peace a Chance." The crowd was overwhelmingly young and white, but there was also a sprinkling of older people, blacks, and special-interest groups such as the Vietnam Veterans Against the War, labor unions, the CP, and SWP. PEACE NOW was one of the more popular slogans to be seen (and chanted), but there were others: MY SON AND 45,000 (?) GIS WERE KILLED IN VIETNAM IN VAIN read one carried by a black man; and DROP NIXON IN HAIPHONG. A few Viet Cong flags were to be seen; some marchers carried black balloons.

Even before the April 22 demonstrations a call had gone out from antiwar groups for a nationwide Moratorium on May 4, the second anniversary of the killings at Kent State. Its purpose was (1) to protest the increasing escalation of the air war, and (2) to mark the start of intensive lobbying of Congress (once again) to pass legislation to end the war. Twenty representatives and senators backed the call; fifty antiwar groups and individual leaders joined them. As usual, disagreement arose among those who might have been considered natural allies. NPAC, the prime mover behind April 22, called for local demonstrations on April 29, claiming that they would not interfere with the May 4 Moratorium but would in fact help to build it.

Neither day, however, saw very large turnouts. The May 4 demonstration drew only about one thousand people in New York; smaller groups gathered elsewhere. In Washington, several antiwar activities took place. At noon on May 3, congressmen and their staffers began a thirty-six-hour reading of the names of American and South and North Vietnamese soldiers killed in the war since the beginning of U.S. involvement. On Pennsylvania Avenue in front of the White House, one thousand Quakers held a five-hour silent witness for the Quaker in the White House, calling on him to stop the war. Later, five of them met with John Negroponte, a Kissinger aide. Thirteen demonstrators sat in at the office of Representative Thomas E. Morgan (D-Pennsylvania), chairman of the House Foreign Affairs Committee, to encourage him to support legislation to end the war. On the evening before the Moratorium, on the west steps of the Capitol, a drama and liturgy on the air war took place; participants included William Kunstler, Judy Collins, Sister Elizabeth McAlister, and Daniel Ellsberg.

After the April 22 demonstrations, but before the May 4 Moratorium, and while protests continued at Columbia and other universities, Senator Mike Gravel made public another government study classified as secret. Titled *National Security Study Memorandum No. 1,* it was a 548-page study made early in 1969 for President Nixon by his White House National Security Adviser, Henry Kissinger. It reflected the deep division between the Joint Chiefs of Staff and the American Saigon military and diplomatic command, on the one hand, and the Department of State, Department of Defense (Pentagon), and the CIA on the other. The Joint Chiefs and Saigon urged a resumption of the bombing of North Vietnam, which had been halted by President Johnson, and, further, they urged a naval blockade (mining) of North Vietnam's ports. Like the use of nuclear weapons or the invasion of North Vietnam, a naval blockade had always been perceived as too extreme, too risky and confrontational even in light of the stated American determination to "win" the war; moreover, the *NSSM 1* study concluded that it would not be effective. Both military and civilian opinion in the study reflected pessimism about the success of "Vietnamization" (as it came to be known). Estimates ranged from *eight to thirteen years* before the South Vietnamese Army could regain control of the South, and then only with the help of extensive American bombing. The study was labeled top secret, not surprisingly in view of its grim assessment of what was, in effect, Nixon's secret plan for peace.

NSSM 1 had been prepared with the help of Daniel Ellsberg, brought in from the Rand Corporation in late 1968 and early 1969 to help newly appointed National Security Adviser Henry Kissinger assess the Vietnam problem for President-elect Nixon. And it was Ellsberg, appropriately enough, who leaked the study in April

1972; he did so in response to the bombing attacks that month on Hanoi-Haiphong. It was Ellsberg's contention that Nixon knew that the attacks would do no good. Ellsberg was scheduled to appear at an antiwar demonstration at the Capitol on May 3, 1972, an event planned long before the death of J. Edgar Hoover on May 2. Hoover's body lay in state under the dome of the Capitol Rotunda the day of the demonstration. Acting on orders from the White House, E. Howard Hunt and G. Gordon Liddy brought in Bernard Barker, who had worked with them in the Plumbers operation against Ellsberg's psychiatrist; Barker in turn enlisted the aid of a band of Cuban exiles from Miami to disrupt the demonstration and, if possible, assault Ellsberg, who appeared that day with Jane Fonda, William Kunstler, and others. At least two demonstrators were physically attacked, but Ellsberg was untouched. After the incident Hunt and Liddy drove Barker around Washington in a car and "debriefed" him. As they drove past the condominium and office complex known as Watergate, Liddy turned to Barker and, using Barker's self-selected nickname, said, "That's our next job, Macho."

One American strategy to win—or at least not to lose—was the "pacification" of Vietnamese villages, the policy of grouping peasants into villages protected by government troops. During the week preceding the April 22 demonstrations came a tragic ending to one of the most infamous events of the war: twenty-three villages near My Lai, including two that had been rebuilt in 1971 by survivors of the 1968 My Lai massacre as part of the "return to the village" program of the pacification effort, were burned to the ground by the Viet Cong's 48th Battalion. Twenty-three people (the initial count) were killed, an undetermined number captured, and thirty thousand made homeless. American officials inspecting the area in helicopters saw only charred mounds where the villages had been; they saw no survivors, most of whom were presumed to be hiding in the surrounding fields. It was the Viet Cong's 48th Battalion for whom Lieutenant William Calley and his men were searching on the morning of the massacre four years before.

At the beginning of May, while the withdrawal of American troops continued, the policy of Vietnamization crumbled in the face of the North Vietnamese sweep. The northeastern province of Quang Tri fell on May 1 while panicking South Vietnamese soldiers fled toward Hue "like a rabble out of control," wrote Sidney H. Schanberg of the New York *Times*. "Commandeering civilian vehicles at rifle point, feigning nonexistent injuries, carrying away C-rations but not their ammunition, and hurling rocks at Western news photographers taking pictures of their flight. . . . No one tried to stop them; their officers were running too."

The Administration's response—from "well-placed sources"—was to threaten to increase the bombing of North Vietnam, particularly Hanoi and Haiphong.

What the President actually did, however, was to order on May 8 the mining of all North Vietnamese ports and the bombing of North Vietnamese rail lines leading to China—actions proposed and rejected in the national security memorandum leaked by Daniel Ellsberg two weeks previously.

And now the response was not only swift but outraged—and, from those who had platforms from which to be heard, almost unanimously opposed. Editorial opinion at home and abroad was opposed; congressional Democrats were opposed;

the leading contenders for the Democratic presidential nomination were opposed. Disruption, demonstrations, and sit-ins intensified and expanded on college campuses; thousands of people took part in sporadic, *ad hoc* protests and violence which broke out in cities and towns across the country. One thousand people battled police in Boulder, Colorado; thirty-five hundred did the same in Berkeley. The protest technique of blocking streets and highways was carried out nationwide. The most violent confrontations with police occurred in Minneapolis, Madison, Berkeley, and the unlikely college town of Gainesville, Florida. Forty protesters who invaded the galleries of the House of Representatives were ejected, leading the speaker, Carl Albert, to order that the galleries be closed. At the UN, seventeen people chained themselves to seats in the visitors' gallery and demanded to see the U.S. ambassador, George Bush; outside, ten members of VVAW tried (and failed) to scale the fence surrounding the UN buildings.

Like the war, during the following days the protests escalated in violence and desperation. At Albuquerque, a twenty-two-year-old law student was wounded by police; the next day thirteen University of New Mexico students were hit by no. 17 birdshot from police guns. In Madison, three policemen were shot but not seriously wounded during the third night of student disorder. During the next few days clashes occurred between police and protesters in more than a score of cities including Boston, Burlington (Vermont), Athens (Ohio), Chicago, Honolulu (where Vice President Agnew was visiting), New York, Princeton, Philadelphia, San Francisco, Cambridge, Hartford, New Haven, and Ithaca (Cornell University).

In Washington an unusual demonstration occurred when four senators and fifteen representatives took part in a protest sponsored by the Americans for Democratic Action, whose president was former Congressman Allard Lowenstein. At 6 A.M., the hour when the mines laid in North Vietnamese harbors would be activated, they gathered with one thousand others at the east steps of the Capitol to hear Senators Edward M. Kennedy, John V. Tunney, Alan Cranston, and Harold E. Hughes, and Representatives William F. Ryan, Bella Abzug, Robert F. Drinan, Edward Koch, Robert Kastenmeier, and others. Later they returned to a Capitol building and congressional offices jammed with groups and individuals from all parts of the country, all of whom had descended upon Congress to lobby for end-the-war legislation.

Although Richard Nixon had bitterly divided the nation, he had succeeded in bringing together the fractious peace groups. On May 10 an emergency meeting was held in New York to plan a protest march in answer to the newest escalation of the war. In attendance were both NPAC and PCPJ, the largest of the umbrella groups, as well as Americans for Democratic Action, SANE, SMC, the Fifth Avenue Peace Parade Committee, Women Strike for Peace, and a number of union representatives. May 21 was selected as the date, with May 22 reserved for civil disobedience; the city was Washington.

Meanwhile NPAC and SMC called "emergency demonstrations" across the country on May 13. They were held in a number of cities including Boston, New York, Chicago, Minneapolis, Denver, and San Francisco; they drew several thousand each and were generally peaceful.

Despite the fact that final exam time was upon them, some campus officials still feared at least disruption if not total chaos, and if not in May, then in September when classes resumed. On May 17 the presidents of seven Ivy League colleges visited Henry Kissinger to warn him that they feared losing control of their institutions if escalation of the war increased. Kissinger, in his memoirs, quotes one as saying, "We try to introduce fairness and reason to the debate—but only at risk to our own lives. That is a fact." Kissinger comments, "It was the ultimate expression of the abdication of institutional leaders in our society, of the abasement of the middle-aged before the young, of the dismissal of rational discourse by those with the greatest stake in reason."

Antiwar leaders had, perhaps rashly, predicted an attendance of as many as fifty thousand for the May 21 march. The actual number—always in dispute—was nearer fifteen thousand. One reason for this low turnout may have been the explosion of a bomb in a Pentagon rest room on May 19. Callers to the New York *Times* and Washington newspapers claiming responsibility for the blast said that they were Weathermen, but several aboveground, nonviolent radicals disputed the authenticity of that title. "Weathermen" had long since been replaced by "Weather People" or "Weather Underground" in response to demands for equality by female members of the group.

No matter: the bombing set an unpleasant tone for the day, a rainy, cold day near the end of that spring's long run of presidential primaries. Proceeding from the Mall near the Washington Monument down Constitution Avenue to the west front of the Capitol, the crowd was somewhat older than usual with a large contingent of union members, many of them from a new umbrella group calling itself Labor for Peace; students who might have taken part had chosen to stay on campus and take their final exams.

Although the demonstrators were, by and large, peaceful and well disciplined, the day was marred by small groups of ragged youths, some carrying red banners and Viet Cong flags, who first attempted to block traffic on Constitution Avenue and then broke away from the main crowd to attack the Justice Department, where they broke some windows. Chased by mounted police and foot patrols who threw tear gas grenades at them, they rejoined the larger group only to break away again to attack the HEW building. Again they were dispersed with tear gas, and this time they returned it, along with bottles and bricks.

Despite these diversions the rally proceeded at the Capitol, where the crowd heard Julius Hobson welcome them to Washington "for the one thousandth damn time." Representative Bella Abzug, one of the thirty-one members of Congress who had endorsed the rally, demanded that the President be impeached for "high crimes and misdemeanors"; a number of labor leaders spoke, and representatives of gay and women's groups; Sidney Peck of PCPJ and Jerry Gordon of NPAC; and Gus Hall, the Communist Party's presidential candidate. About two hundred of the troublemakers were arrested; twelve policemen reported minor injuries. On the following day about five hundred people were arrested at a PCPJ-sponsored sit-in at the Pentagon.

The last major antiwar protest of 1972 before the Republican Convention occurred on June 22 when members of WSP, working with Coretta Scott King and Joan Baez, staged their "Ring around Congress" demonstration. The action was plagued first by cries of protest from some members of the capital's black community, who charged that insufficient attention had been given to their needs.† The women agreed to a "summit" meeting at a later date between blacks and the peace movement; but the demonstration had to take place as scheduled, they said, because Congress was near adjournment. The second problem for the "Ring around" demonstration was the weather: heavy rains that month had caused major flooding in the Northeast, and some demonstrators were unable to get to Washington because of washed-out roads, bridges, and railroad tracks. Eventually, however, three thousand women, many with children in tow (the Capitol Rotunda was used as a child-care center), showed up to circle the Capitol in a demand that Congress cut off funds for the war and use the money instead for domestic needs. Later many demonstrators lobbied their congressmen, an exercise in frustration that left most of them "disappointed and discouraged." One group of "militant women from Michigan had to chase Senator Robert Griffin from his office to the Senate floor and back in an attempt to confront him face to face to discuss his reactionary pro-war stand."

Some of the women who traveled to Washington had thought of North Vietnam as they crossed flooded rivers in the United States. The heavy U.S. bombing had posed a severe threat to North Vietnam's system of dikes. It was charged that U.S. planes deliberately bombed the dikes, but the Pentagon denied this. If the dikes went, not only would North Vietnam's rice fields be destroyed (and contaminated for years if seawater entered), but thousands of North Vietnamese would be drowned.‡

Later that summer former Attorney General Ramsey Clark traveled to North Vietnam with an international group headed by Sean MacBride, former Foreign Minister of Ireland, to view the extent of the bombing damage. He reported (in *Life,* among other places) that he had seen destruction in cities as well as villages, that he had visited churches, hospitals, and schools that had been hit—and six dikes and two sluices. Clark also stated that when he visited Haiphong he had been told that 101 raids had been staged on the city since the renewal of the bombing in April, with 2,208 blast bombs having been dropped as well as 250 "mother bombs" holding hundreds of antipersonnel bombs, each of which contained hundreds of steel fragments or pellets. Like the reports of other visitors to North Vietnam, some of Clark's had been broadcast over Hanoi radio. His visit and his report on it was an issue in his 1974 New York Senate race against Jacob Javits, who did not hesitate to attack him for it.

In May, while the demonstrators marched in Washington with little media cover-

† The multiissue/single-issue problem; some observers, however, saw the black protest as a message to Congress that if Congress would grant autonomy to the District of Columbia the black leadership of Washington would clamp down on protest actions.
‡ In Holland during World War II the German High Commissioner, Seyss-Inquart, opened the dikes and flooded half a million acres with seawater. He was warned by Allied commander Dwight D. Eisenhower to close them, which he did; nevertheless, he was convicted of war crimes and condemned to execution by the Nuremberg tribunal.

age, Richard Nixon wined and dined and talked in Moscow with typical media overkill. It was his second foreign extravaganza in four months; he had risked scuttling the conference with the Soviets by his actions of May 8, but he had won the gamble: they had not canceled.

Nixon also won the gamble that he had taken with American public opinion. On May 14 the New York *Times* reported that a survey by the Louis Harris organization found that 59 percent of the American people backed his actions on May 8; 24 percent disapproved and 17 percent were not sure. This statistic, in a year of voter surveys and poll-watching, was perhaps the most significant finding in 1972. Perhaps it should have been more of a warning than it was to the Democratic candidate who, running on an antiwar platform, was to be Richard Nixon's opponent in the general election.

But Nixon's luck was not inexhaustible, and in the early morning hours of June 17—almost exactly one year after the publication of the Pentagon Papers—it came to an end. At about 2 A.M. a guard at the Watergate office and apartment building in Washington saw that a door latch on the door leading from the garage into the office complex had been taped. The tape was affixed not vertically, as a professional burglar would have done, but horizontally, so that it showed on the door's front and back surfaces. The guard removed the tape. When he checked the door a short time later, the latch had been taped again. He called police. When they arrived they discovered five men in the offices of the headquarters of the Democratic National Committee. Presumably they were interested in more than burglary, although that is the charge on which they were booked that night: they carried with them cameras, electronic surveillance equipment, walkie-talkies, tear gas, and a large amount of cash. At the moment of their arrest they were installing a listening device in the office of Lawrence O'Brien, the DNC chairman.

The break-in, it was later learned, was the second successful effort by the same team illegally to enter the DNC. On May 28 the group had photographed documents in the files and placed transmitters (bugs) on the phones of O'Brien and a staff person, Spenser Oliver. Oliver's bug (monitored from a Howard Johnson's motel room across the street) worked; O'Brien's did not. Hence the June 17 break-in to repair it.

Within days it was known that the burglars had impressive connections. One of them, James W. McCord, was a former CIA agent in the employ of the Committee to Re-elect the President, popularly known as CREEP. And papers found on one of the burglars led investigators to E. Howard Hunt, whom they traced to his working address at the White House, and to G. Gordon Liddy. Hunt and Liddy had monitored and supervised the break-in from the Howard Johnson's motel across from the Watergate. One of the five arrested in the DNC offices was Bernard Barker, their accomplice in the Ellsberg affair of May 3 and their chief operative in the Plumbers break-in at the office of Dr. Lewis Fielding, Ellsberg's psychiatrist, in September 1971. The seamy recent past of Hunt and Liddy was, in June 1972, known by only a very few persons, but those few included highly placed individuals in the White House: John Ehrlichman, Charles Colson, and—possibly—Richard Nixon. The White House cover-up began.

At the beginning of the primary season George McGovern had not been the favored Democratic candidate; Edmund Muskie held that place. But Muskie fumbled badly in New Hampshire, winning, but not by enough (46.4 percent to 37.2 percent for McGovern). Later it was disclosed that CREEP's "dirty tricks" had much to do with Muskie's failed campaign in New Hampshire and elsewhere. The most infamous of these was the "Canuck letter," reproduced in the Manchester *Union Leader,* which implied that Muskie had spoken derisively about "Canucks," or Americans of French-Canadian descent, who make up a significant portion of New Hampshire's population. Despite the attempts by more than fifty reporters to unearth the author of the letter, he was not found at the time. The Canuck issue blurred into another: a short piece, reproduced in the *Union Leader* from *Newsweek* (which in turn had run it after it appeared in *Women's Wear Daily),* that seemed to be unflattering to Muskie's wife. When Muskie climbed onto a flatbed truck parked in front of the *Union Leader's* office on a snowy February day to castigate the newspaper, he appeared to be so emotionally upset that he shed tears. Muskie's performance that day was said to have cost him much voter support; from then on, despite a good fight by Hubert Humphrey, McGovern was the front-runner. His lieutenants (among them Gary Hart, later a Democratic senator from Colorado and himself a presidential candidate in 1983–84, and Frank Mankiewicz, a former press secretary to Robert Kennedy) built a campaign "army" that matched Eugene McCarthy's 1968 organization in fervor and outdistanced it in money and numbers. By the time McGovern won California and New York in June, he was nicely poised to go to the convention and take the nomination.

On the day after he became the Democratic candidate, which is to say the Thursday of the convention, George McGovern and/or his strategists made two major errors, one not immediately apparent, one obvious at once.

The first was the selection of his vice presidential candidate, Senator Thomas Eagleton of Missouri, an excellent choice save for the fact (which he did not at first disclose) that he had twice been given electric shock treatment and three times been hospitalized for mental strain or nervous exhaustion. When in the week following the convention this news began to be known, McGovern wavered agonizingly for several days. During that time he made the most memorable statement of his campaign, saying that he would not drop Eagleton from the ticket, that he stood behind him "1,000 per cent." But within another week Eagleton was gone, to be replaced—after several others refused—by Sargent Shriver, Senator Edward Kennedy's brother-in-law.

The second error of the McGovern campaign, immediately obvious, was to allow the assembled Democrats at their convention to bicker about party structure and other vice presidential candidates until well past midnight—until 2:48 A.M. (EDT), when McGovern finally rose to make his acceptance speech, perhaps the best speech of his campaign. It was an eloquent plea to "come home America" from the war, from "secrecy and deception in high places" (a reference to the Watergate break-in), from wasteful military spending, from "special privilege" and "prejudice." "I have no secret plan for peace," said McGovern; "I have a public plan"— to stop the bombing and return both the troops and the POWs within three months of his inauguration. How helpful this speech might have been to McGovern's campaign will never be known, for only 3.6 million people heard it—a fraction of the prime-time audience.

Antiwar protest at the Democratic Convention had been minimal, but in August a number of demonstrators arrived in Miami to confront the Republicans. It was a bad time for the antiwar movement, as election years always were; moreover, the years of protest had taken their toll. Rennie Davis remembers his sense of frustration and very real desperation:

> It was a discouraging period for me personally. Our ability to mount a mass movement was rapidly diminishing. Delegations would come to me and say we should do this or that. . . . I had a sense that even if it comes down to myself alone and there's no one left who cares at all, that still this is something I have to see through if it takes my whole life —until it [the war] was over—and if it never ended, until they just kill me. I'd struggle and struggle about what to do. I went on a hunger strike. I fasted for forty-two days and I was considering fasting to death, if it could break loose and get attention. I was prepared to do that. . . .

What did get some attention was a series of protests as the Republicans convened. Several thousand Yippies, "Zippies," members of PL-SDS, and others, as well as more than a thousand Vietnam Veterans Against the War, converged on Miami to confront the delegates. The VVAW staged a silent, orderly march, fists raised, on the Fontainebleau Hotel (the Republican headquarters); the nonveterans spent several days and nights harassing delegates who occasionally needed to venture outdoors to get from one site to another. Shrieking, "Murderers!" they cursed the Republicans and taunted them as they came and went. Over one thousand demonstrators were arrested during the convention week. Three of the veterans made a more pointed—and painful—protest inside the convention hall on the night of Nixon's acceptance speech. All of them had been gravely wounded in Vietnam and were confined to wheelchairs for life. Having acquired passes, they positioned themselves at the top of the main aisle leading to the podium. When Nixon appeared, and after the ovation which the party faithful gave to him, the three veterans held aloft a sign reading STOP THE WAR. One of them, Ron Kovic, tells in his wrenching account of his injury in Vietnam and his agonizing recovery, *Born on the Fourth of July*, how he felt that night:

> This was the moment I had come three thousand miles for, this was it, all the pain and the rage, all the trials and the death of the war and what had been done to me and a generation of Americans by all the men who had lied to us and tricked us, by the man who stood before us in the convention hall that night, while men who had fought for their country were being gassed and beaten in the street outside the hall. I thought of Bobby [Robert Muller, later executive director of Vietnam Veterans of America], who sat next to me, and the months we had spent in the hospital in the Bronx. It was all hitting me at once, all those years, all that destruction, all that sorrow.

President Nixon began to speak and all three of us took a deep breath and shouted at the top of our lungs, "Stop the bombing, stop the war, stop the bombing, stop the war," as loud and as hard as we could, looking directly at Nixon. The security agents immediately threw up their arms, trying to hide us from the cameras and the President. "Stop the bombing, stop the bombing," I screamed. For an instant [Walter] Cronkite [of CBS] looked down, then turned his head away. They're not going to show it, I thought. They're going to try and hide us like they did in the hospitals. Hundreds of people around us began to clap and shout, "Four more years," trying to drown out our protest. They all seemed very angry and shouted at us to stop. We continued shouting, interrupting Nixon again and again until Secret Service agents grabbed our chairs from behind and began pulling us backward as fast as they could out of the convention hall. "Take it easy," Bobby said to me. "Don't fight back."

I wanted to take a swing and fight right there in the middle of the convention hall in front of the President and the whole country. "So this is how they treat their wounded veterans!" I screamed.

A short guy with a big FOUR MORE YEARS button ran up to me and spat in my face. "Traitor!" he screamed, as he was yanked back by police. Pandemonium was breaking out all around us and the Secret Service men kept pulling us out backward.

"I served two tours of duty in Vietnam!" I screamed to one newsman. "I gave three quarters of my body for America. And what do I get? Spit in the face!" I kept screaming until we hit the side entrance, where the agents pushed us outside and shut the doors, locking them with chains and padlocks so reporters wouldn't be able to follow us out for interviews.

All three of us sat, holding on to each other, shaking. We had done it. It had been the biggest moment of our lives, we had shouted down the President of the United States and disrupted his acceptance speech. What more was there left to do but go home?

I sat in my chair still shaking and began to cry.

The campaign progressed chaotically for the Democrats (partly because of the Republicans' "dirty tricks"), and somewhat more smoothly for the Republicans. The Administration continued to downplay the war. On August 12 the last American ground troops left Vietnam; 43,500 air force personnel and support personnel remained. On August 29 President Nixon was able to announce that by December only 27,000 U.S. troops would be in South Vietnam. McGovern had made a "flat pledge" to bring home every American soldier and POW within ninety days of his inauguration, but Nixon seemed to be working ahead of that deadline while at the same time making peace with both the Chinese and the Russians. Inevitably, control of the Vietnam issue remained with the Administration.

Although conventional political wisdom holds that a single-issue candidate cannot win, George McGovern had at least succeeded so far as to become the Democratic nominee. Naturally he claimed to be more than a single-issue candidate, and he had the Democratic platform of positions on a broad spectrum of issues upon which to run, but generally he was perceived as the "antiwar candidate." As the campaign progressed his chance for victory seemed increasingly slim; and if Nixon were reelected, the antiwar movement would once again have failed to end the war through the (presidential) electoral system. Some people in the Movement, therefore, turned to intensified congressional lobbying. Tom Hayden remembers:

We started to shift gears to the Indochina Peace Campaign [IPC]. It started as a conception late in 1971; it was an organization by spring 1972. My idea was to go to the mainstream based on an analysis that the system had partially opened up, we had a much wider audience now, that now it was possible to pressure Congress. The other assumption was that the Movement had gotten itself isolated at the very moment that large numbers of people were ready to be mobilized and that we had gotten ourselves isolated by being anticountry, antiflag, antieverything, and engaging in the politics of provocation that came from powerlessness. We were no longer powerless, so we should start organizing differently. And this attracted a range of people across the country who had more of a community-organizing background. They didn't feel comfortable being fully in the establishment, nor did they feel comfortable with where the Movement had gone. So it attracted these types, typically early New Left activists. We reacted to whatever situation we were in, not so much guided by theory. If the system was open you flow into it. If it closes down you confront it. Now it was reopening, partly due to our efforts, partly due to the broadening of public opposition [to the war]. . . . Another thing we felt was very important, therefore, was to reeducate the American people. So we started IPC. Twenty or thirty trusted people from around the country met in Washington. We decided we were going to do this; we were not going to be involved with any quarrels with any other organizations. Our program was very simple: to cut off aid to Indochina by convincing Congress to do so, and we could convince Congress by building a public pressure organization in the eight or ten states that had the greatest number of electoral votes and the largest number of antiwar activists—California, New York, Pennsylvania, Massachusetts, Ohio, Michigan, Illinois, Wisconsin, Minnesota, later expanded to Texas and Georgia. We developed an organization in each of these states—speaking tours by myself and Jane [actress Jane Fonda, whom Hayden later married]; educational programs on Saigon's political prisoners; a pledge to cut funding for the war that we would try to get newspapers to endorse and congressional representatives to sign. We opened a Washington office to lobby Congress and through that office all the pressure was coordinated on our behalf. . . .

We picked the period of the McGovern campaign, but we stayed organizationally separate. Jane and I and a former POW, George Smith, and the singer Holly Near campaigned and spoke in ninety cities in September–October 1972. We urged everyone to vote against Nixon. We thought that while McGovern was very important to us in one sense, we preferred to make the issue of the war paramount and we didn't want to get into debates about McGovern and Eagleton, how much stress McGovern was putting on the war versus the economy. . . . We just said, "There's only one issue in this election and that's ending the war." This was the year of the eighteen-year-old vote. It was exciting—like real political barnstorming. We talked to one hundred thousand people. There was a sense of excitement about finally being accepted, fitting into the mainstream that had been falsely appropriated by Spiro Agnew and his famous Middle America concept that left us all out.

The IPC was, in fact, the only visible antiwar activity that took place during the 1972 campaign, so heavily did the McGovern effort drain the Movement.

On October 26 Henry Kissinger announced that, after months of both secret and public negotiations, "Peace is at hand." It was an unbeatable last-minute campaign slogan. A peace agreement, however, had not been signed; details needed to be worked out. In essence the agreement provided for a cease-fire in place (the "leopard spot" arrangement), with North Vietnamese, South Vietnamese, and Viet Cong troops all holding what areas they had; President Thieu controlled about 75 percent of the territory in South Vietnam and 85 percent of the population. Arrangements for a U.S. troop pullout and POW return would be agreed upon, as would a Council of National Reconciliation, comprised of Vietnamese of all sides, which would decide where and when to hold elections. By and large, these were the conditions upon which the North Vietnamese had insisted since 1965.*

McGovern tried to counter the effect of the announcement with a bitter attack on the President's "cruel political deception," calling it "not a path to peace but a detour around Election Day." His words had little effect on the voters.

On November 7 Richard Nixon was elected to his second term as President. He received 60.7 percent of the vote—a landslide second only to LBJ's 61.1 percent in 1964. Nixon carried forty-nine states, all except Massachusetts;† he received 521 electoral votes to McGovern's 17.

Fred Halstead, speaking from a stance not only outside the two-party system but critical of it, wrote of the 1972 election:

> It had certainly been an odd campaign. A man who was already the most isolated American president in modern times ran for reelection while the greatest scandal ever to hit the presidency had begun to unravel, presented himself as a lover of peace while carrying out the heaviest bombing in history in a war the majority of the people had repudiated, and carried the election in an unprecedented sweep while his own party lost ground. I leave it to supporters of the two-party system to explain that anomaly.

* A "Policy Declaration" by Premier Pham Van Dong of North Vietnam, reprinted in the New York Times, April 14, 1965, set forth the four basic points:
1. United States withdrawal from South Vietnam;
2. Observance of the military provisions of the 1954 Geneva Agreements that temporarily divided Vietnam into two zones;
3. Settlement of the internal affairs of South Vietnam by the South Vietnamese people themselves in accordance with the program of the NLF;
4. Peaceful reunification of Vietnam to be settled by the Vietnamese people in both zones, without foreign interference.

† In 1973 and 1974, as Nixon's Watergate troubles expanded, a popular bumper sticker in the Bay State read DON'T BLAME ME, I'M FROM MASSACHUSETTS.

The presidential campaign and the reelection of Richard Nixon further crippled the antiwar movement. On November 18 NPAC held demonstrations in twenty-one cities, but the largest turnout, in New York, did not exceed two thousand. NPAC and PCPJ were feuding once again, this time over whether to demand immediate withdrawal of all U.S. forces (NPAC) or simply to demand that the United States sign the agreement announced by Kissinger (PCPJ). The difference between the two, imperceptible to the general public, was crucial to some (not all) in the Movement. As Tom Cornell explains:

> "Sign the agreement" [a cease-fire in place] would leave the Communist forces not in complete control and that was not acceptable to [some on] the far Left. . . . But who in the world cares out there in the great public? They don't understand "Out Now!" and "Sign the agreement now" as politically opposed. "Cease-fire in place" had its legitimacy. It may have had a greater legitimacy, looking back, because look what's happened.

Although December was often the time when spring marches and demonstrations were announced, in December 1972 no announcement was made. Energy levels were low; the Movement was becalmed, waiting with the rest of the world for the news that what Kissinger said was true, that the details of the agreement were finally to be resolved and that after all the years of war, all the years of bloody pain and death and ruination, that now at last, at Christmastime, peace would come to that tiny, tortured, faraway place called Vietnam, and America could rest easy in her soul again, she could awaken from her nightmare.

They waited. Nixon had promised peace, Kissinger had promised peace. Peace, they had said, was at hand. The American public yearned to believe them.

On December 4 Hanoi began to evacuate all of its children and much of its adult population.

On December 13 the New York *Times* published a story by James Reston, apparently from an interview with Henry Kissinger in Paris, that said that the peace talks were progressing and that a settlement would be reached.

In Washington, however, the *Times'* Pentagon correspondent, William Beecher, was discovering from his sources a very different story: the peace talks were on the verge of collapse, and extreme measures were being considered by the Administration to resuscitate them. The resumption of the bombing of North Vietnam was one of the possibilities. Beecher filed his story on December 14. The *Times'* New York editors were suspicious of Beecher's information and reluctant to print his story, which ran counter to what Kissinger had said. They asked Beecher to get more supportive information, which he did. Still they hesitated; the story did not appear.

On December 16 Henry Kissinger in effect confirmed Beecher's story and contradicted Reston's when he announced that his talks with the North Vietnamese in Paris, privately resumed on November 20, had broken off because, although the agreement was "99 percent completed," Hanoi continued to demand "changes in the text."

The North Vietnamese denied that they had obstructed the talks and said that the United States had changed its position on the nine-point draft agreed upon in October. North Vietnam's party newspaper charged that the United States had challenged the same points in the agreement that had been brought up by President Thieu in a speech to the legislature in Saigon on December 12. Some unnamed (U.S.) administration officials declined an opportunity to deny this interpretation of events. Kissinger's deputy, Major General Alexander M. Haig, Jr., had meanwhile been dispatched to Saigon to "brief" South Vietnam's leaders on the break in the talks; he was to convey to them President Nixon's refusal to sign an agreement that would be "a disguised form of victory" (Kissinger's phrase) for North Vietnam. President Thieu's points of disagreement included the number and mobility of an international team to monitor the cease-fire; Saigon's insistence that it control South Vietnam as a separate state; the removal of North Vietnamese troops; and the recognition of the demilitarized zone between North and South Vietnam (which, like separate sovereignty for the South, effected a divided Vietnam, unsatisfactory to North Vietnam).

On December 18 the *Times* ran Beecher's story, but by then it was no longer news because on the same date Hanoi radio—not the U.S. command and most certainly not the White House—announced the resumption of attacks against North Vietnam, including the dropping of mines in Haiphong Harbor, rocket attacks on Haiphong City, and the bombing of Hanoi; many people, said Hanoi, were killed and wounded and damage was heavy. On December 18 (U.S. time) the Nixon Administration acknowledged that it had resumed the full-scale bombing and mining of North Vietnam: Operation Linebacker Two. Hundreds of planes, fighter-bombers, and B-52 stratofortresses carrying twenty-four tons of bombs each, were conducting the heaviest raids of the war not only on Hanoi-Haiphong but on targets not struck before. The fighter-bombers were used for "pinpoint bombing"; the B-52 raids were carpet bombing in a pattern half a mile wide and a mile and a half long. In the first two days twenty thousand tons of bombs were dropped on North Vietnam—the equal of the atomic bomb dropped on Hiroshima. After five days, one hundred thousand tons had been dropped. The attacks would continue, said the White House, until a settlement was reached.

During the first night of the raids, which lasted from 8 P.M. until 6 A.M., nine waves of planes struck Hanoi; the reporter for Agence France-Presse described the glowing red and white sky northeast of the city, where suburbs had been hit, and the sight of "immense incandescent mushrooms" rising like a display of fireworks. Because the central power plant had been damaged, reporters filed their stories by candlelight. Toward dawn, during the final and most severe raid, the French correspondent descended to an air raid shelter. There he met Joan Baez, who had traveled to Hanoi with three other Americans including retired Brigadier General Telford Taylor, a U.S. prosecutor at the Nuremberg trials and author of *Nuremberg and Vietnam: An American Tragedy.* They brought with them five hundred letters and a duffel bag of Christmas presents for American POWs. As American bombs fell on the city above them, Baez played her guitar and sang antiwar songs to entertain her companions in the shelter.

Administration spokesmen said that President Nixon had ordered the resumption of the bombing so that North Vietnam "would comprehend the extent of his anger" at North Vietnam's failure to sign the peace agreement. (In other words, the "madman" theory [see p. 217] was being tested again.) The raids were described by "senior planners" as part of an effort "to force North Vietnam into a more conciliatory position at the bargaining table." That effort failed: the agreement that was signed in January was essentially the one arrived at in October. The real reason for the raids was to assure Thieu that if he would agree to the peace terms, the United States would continue to back him, peace treaty or no peace treaty, if he still needed help against the Communists. Nixon had secretly pledged such aid, and had already begun a huge increase of arms shipments to South Vietnam.

As the raids continued, increasing numbers of American planes and pilots were lost. After the fourth day, the U.S. command listed four fighter-bombers and eight B-52s downed, and forty-three American airmen either killed or captured. Hanoi's accounting was higher, and in Washington, the Senate Armed Services Committee said that the Pentagon had informed it that thirteen B-52s had been lost. The Pentagon denied that figure. Because the American military command had declined to comment on specific targets, Pentagon spokesmen were unable to deny Hanoi's charges that civilian areas were being bombed. These included the Bach Mai Hospital, the largest in Hanoi, where twenty-five doctors and nurses and an uncounted number of patients were killed and the hospital itself completely destroyed. Also struck was the "Hanoi Hilton," a POW camp, where a number of American prisoners were injured; many urban residential areas and country villages; Hanoi's (civilian) international airport (a "mistake," the U.S. command said later); and several foreign embassies including those of Cuba, India and Egypt. The French mission had been destroyed in previous U.S. bombing on October 11; six people including the delegate-general had been killed.

On December 28, ten days after the bombing had resumed, the U.S. military command in Saigon finally issued a statement. In a ten-page report, it listed military targets that had been bombed; the civilian targets that had been hit were not mentioned. A spokesman refused to answer questions about Bach Mai Hospital or other civilian sites.

Because Hanoi had relatively good antiaircraft defenses by December 1972, the loss of U.S. planes and pilots was particularly high. By December 30 fifteen B-52s and eleven other planes had been downed, sixty-two crew members killed, thirty-one captured—thus adding considerably to the number of POWs to be returned. The men who flew the missions were aware of the dangers; a number of them were rumored to have refused to fly and at least one was court-martialed for his refusal.

The Christmas bombings of 1972 were universally condemned. Voices of protest cried out in the United States and abroad. Olof Palme, the Swedish Premier, likened the bombings of Hanoi-Haiphong to other outrages of the twentieth century whose names reverberate with horror: Guernica, Lidice, Treblinka. The Administration, angered, asked Sweden not to send an ambassador to its U.S. Embassy. In London, Berlin, and other cities citizens took to the streets to protest the bombings. In Rome twenty-five thousand marched; in Amsterdam one hundred thousand. Australian and Italian maritime unions voted to boycott U.S. ships. In an open letter to British Prime Minister Edward Heath, Roy Jenkins, a leader of the Labour Party, condemned the bombings as "one of the most cold-blooded actions in recent history" and urged the government to speak out against them.

One of the most eloquent and passionate condemnations of the Christmas bombings came from New York *Times* columnist Anthony Lewis. "A Christmas of horrors," he called it on December 25; "the Christian peace offered by the United States is the peace of the inquisition: conformity or tormented death." The men who ordered the bombings were "men without humanity. They talk about football while arranging to impose on little countries that thwart them the punishment of mass death.

"In the sentimental myth, Christmas is a time of forgiveness. But only saints can forgive mass murder. . . ."

In a column two days earlier,‡ Lewis had excoriated the men who made U.S. policy in Vietnam:

> Worst of all has been the failure of a single person in the United States Government to break with a policy that many must know history will judge a crime against humanity.
>
> To send B-52s against populous areas such as Haiphong or Hanoi can have only one purpose: terror. It was the response of a man so overwhelmed by his sense of inadequacy and frustration that he had to strike out, punish, destroy. . . .
>
> Whatever the cause, whatever the rights or wrongs of the parties in Vietnam, the means used by the United States in this war have long since passed the point where they could be justified by the end. . . .
>
> Human indifference in the face of cruelty to others is hardly a new phenomenon. . . . Still it does seem remarkable that no one in the United States Government has now made himself a witness against what his country is doing. . . .

There were a few token acts of protest. In York, Pennsylvania, five members of the East Coast Conspiracy to Save Lives were arrested at midnight on December 18 as they poured concrete into a Penn Central Railroad switch near a siding which led to the American Machine and Foundry Corporation, a manufacturer of bombs. In New York City on December 21, one thousand demonstrators called out by the Fifth Avenue Peace Parade Committee blocked traffic for two hours in Times Square. Fifteen were arrested. At the United Nations, twenty-five demonstrators sat in at the U.S. Mission to the UN; twenty-one were arrested. On December 22

‡ Titled "Vietnam Delenda Est": the phrase recalls the oft-repeated injunction of Cato the Censor to the Romans: *Delenda est Carthago* (Carthage must be destroyed). At the time, Carthage represented no greater threat to Rome than Vietnam did to the United States, although fifty years earlier it had nearly destroyed Rome. After the surrender of Carthage (146 B.C.), its population was nearly annihilated, the remnant sold into slavery, its city razed, and its earth cursed and ritually sown with salt—a gesture that forever after symbolized the complete destruction of an enemy and his land. It was Vietnam, Lewis's title suggests, that was being destroyed as Carthage was. Both North and South, vast areas of Vietnam today still resemble a barren moonscape; even where bombing destruction does not exist, toxic chemicals (a twentieth-century "salt") poison the land.

several hundred demonstrators from the Puerto Rican Student Union and the Attica Brigade demonstrated at Herald Square; fifty people handed out antiwar leaflets at Westover Field in Chicopee, Massachusetts; small turnouts occurred in San Francisco and Boston; fifty people attended an antiwar rally in Madison at the University of Wisconsin. On the day before Christmas, three hundred members of Women Strike for Peace demonstrated across from St. Patrick's Cathedral on Fifth Avenue. On Christmas Day, two hundred people took Christmas communion during a service across the street from the White House; guards refused to receive from them a letter of protest to the President. In Hartford, two hundred people demonstrated at the Federal Building, where they heard a speaker exhort them to work harder for peace. On December 28 the largest science organization in the world, the American Association for the Advancement of Science, declared that it condemned America's presence in the war. In Washington two thousand people marched from the National Cathedral to the White House, where they prayed for peace.

One Movement veteran remembers: "By that time it was just one blow after another after another and you just get numb and know you have to keep on working. You don't feel any particular surge of rage because it's spent. It was a kind of quiet dull horror—what are these people capable of? What next?" Norma Becker was visiting her mother in Florida that Christmas; she remembers her feelings of outrage at "the inhumanity and the callousness—the arrogance, the inhuman arrogance—and my powerlessness as this atrocity was going on. That's when I got this gray streak in my hair." Sidney Peck, Tom Cornell, Bradford Lyttle, and others undertook "marathon work at the telephone" to recruit Movement supporters to sign newspaper ads opposing the bombings and to send money to pay for the ads. The response was generous and immediate, and the ads appeared in newspapers throughout the country.

Meanwhile NPAC and PCPJ, never firm allies, struggled with their disagreement over what slogan might be used at any joint protest. NPAC favored "Out Now!"; PCPJ wanted "Sign the Agreement Now." Jerry Gordon of NPAC issued a call for massive protests at Nixon's second inaugural on January 20, and in the end PCPJ joined the call. Both groups began intensive work to prepare for the demonstration.

1973-75:
"The War Is Over!"

"OUR CHILDREN have been taught to be ashamed of their country, ashamed of their parents, ashamed of America's record at home and its role in the world. . . ." Thus spoke President Richard M. Nixon in his second inaugural address; he did not mention Vietnam by name. Unlike President Abraham Lincoln in his second inaugural address, written as the Civil War was drawing to a close, Nixon did not express compassionate understanding or a determination "to bind up the nation's wounds." The desire for atonement, rather than the anger of other years, was, however, the mood of the antiwar forces that gathered in Washington and elsewhere to mark the occasion—a desire comprised of shame, sorrow, guilt, and despair for what America had wrought in Vietnam. In New York City a six-hour vigil of prayer was conducted in the Cathedral Church of St. John the Divine, with the participation of authors, poets, and musicians, in a program that called for healing the wounds of war. At the same time, the Catholic Worker, Pax Christi, and other groups offered a Mass of atonement at St. Paul the Apostle Church on Fifty-ninth Street. In Central Park a group describing itself as "the largest assembly of Jewish organizations ever to protest the Vietnam war" planted a tree as a symbol of dedication to the work of "healing and rebuilding" after "the ravages of an abhorrent war." It was the same in other parts of the country, including cities like Montgomery, Alabama, where whites in black robes, their faces whitened and their hands dyed red, marched in solemn protest for the first time ever against the war.

Two concerts given in Washington on the eve of the inauguration reflected the deep division of feeling in the country at large. More than fifteen thousand people gathered at the Washington Cathedral of St. Peter and St. Paul to hear Haydn's *Mass in Time of War* conducted by Leonard Bernstein. Only three thousand could be accommodated inside; the rest stood in the raw, rainy night and heard the performance over a public address system. Bernstein, the soloists, and orchestra appeared in street dress. The Mass, written at a time when Napoleon was overrunning the armies of Austria, is famous for the mournful kettledrum accompaniment to the words of petition that bring the Agnus Dei, its final section, to a close:

401

"Dona nobis pacem" (Grant us peace). Some in the audience recalled the drumbeat of three years earlier that led off the March Against Death on a similarly chill, damp Washington night. Meanwhile, at the John F. Kennedy Center for the Performing Arts, the inaugural committee was presenting its concert to a formal dress audience, including the presidential party, that did not quite manage to fill the hall, perhaps because tickets started at $250 each. A highlight of the concert was Tchaikovsky's *1812 Overture*, a retrospective set piece, scored for cannon and celebrating the rout of Napoleon's army in Russia. At this concert, however, Eugene Ormandy of the Philadelphia Orchestra,* who conducted, omitted the cannon blasts. Also omitted from the program at the last minute was a work especially commissioned for the occasion. The composer, Vincent Persichetti, had written a piece for narrator, chorus, and orchestra based on Abraham Lincoln's second inaugural address. It was explained to Persichetti by the inaugural committee that the piece would not be heard because the text, the most famous words of which are "With malice toward none; with charity for all," might embarrass the President.

The Counterinaugural demonstration sponsored by PCPJ and NPAC drew a crowd of more than sixty thousand persons to the by now traditional site of the Washington Monument grounds. It was a generally peaceful gathering, its foreboding expressed by the two competing slogans, "Out Now!" (NPAC) and "Sign the Treaty!" (PCPJ). Members of VVAW, some twenty-five hundred of whom were in the demonstration, staged a mock treaty-signing ceremony, and Bella Abzug told the crowd, "We are not going to stop protesting until he takes all forces out of Vietnam." On the inaugural platform the President was asking, "As America's longest and most difficult war comes to an end, let us again learn to debate our differences with civility." From the direction of Union Station, where the Yippies and SDS-PL were gathering for their own demonstration, some reporters could make out the faint cries of "Murderer" as the President took the oath of office at the Capitol. The mood of the major demonstration at the monument, however, was one of witness. Most were there because they were unable not to be; they had come to manifest silent concern for a war in which, as Lincoln's forbidden text had put it, "Neither party expected . . . the magnitude or the duration which it had already attained."

The stale rhetoric from the monument platform on a day when little remained to be spoken that had not already been said many times before could not hold the audience. Most wandered off in the direction of Pennsylvania Avenue to watch, unbelieving, the inaugural parade and its anticipatory bicentennial theme of 1776. Neither they nor Richard Nixon on the reviewing stand suspected that Gerald Ford would be President of the United States in the bicentennial year of 1976.

On the evening of January 22, Lyndon B. Johnson died. Harry S. Truman had died on December 26, 1972. For the first time in sixty-five years, with the exception of the two months preceding the inauguration of Franklin Roosevelt, the country was without a living ex-President. Johnson died only hours before a final agreement

---

* Sixteen members of the orchestra asked to be excused on the grounds that the concert was a *"de facto* political situation." When Ormandy characterized the recalcitrants as "left-wing sons of bitches," Richard Nixon was pleased: "What a man he [Ormandy] is."

was reached in Paris on the peace settlement to end the war that had escalated so dramatically during his term of office. Henry Kissinger had kept him informed of the progress of the negotiations.

President Nixon announced to the nation in a televised statement on the evening of January 23 that Henry Kissinger and Le Duc Tho had initialed on behalf of their respective governments the "Agreement on Ending the War and Restoring Peace in Vietnam." He declared that, at last, "peace with honor" had been achieved. In that same broadcast Nixon began the presentation to the American people of a distorted view of the agreement with the statement that "the United States will continue to recognize the government of the Republic of Vietnam as the sole legitimate government of South Vietnam." While this was indeed the intention of the Nixon Administration, it was a view of the political status quo nowhere endorsed in the agreement Kissinger had initialed.

The agreement was formally signed in Paris on January 27. The joyful reaction of the American public centered on three major and almost immediately visible effects of the signing: a cease-fire in Vietnam that began on January 27; the withdrawal of the remaining American force of 23,700 troops, to be accomplished within sixty days; and, in the same time span, the release of all American POWs. The fact that North Vietnamese troops would not also be withdrawn seemed not to matter; nor did the fact that the dissenting portion of the population of South Vietnam, long represented by the NLF (now by the PRG), was recognized as one of "two parties" upon whom the peace depended. For most Americans at least, the war was over. In Hanoi, the government and the people took a longer view. "Now," said Premier Pham Van Dong, "we must lean on the agreement and *on the texts* [emphasis added] to pursue our struggle to complete the revolutionary work carried out by the Vietnamese people." Few Americans saw, much less read, the text of the Paris Agreement. In Hanoi, however, the text was broadcast over the city's public address systems and Radio Hanoi began forty-eight hours of constant repetition of the full text. The announcers were instructed to read slowly to allow the people to feel the full impact. Millions of copies were printed by Hanoi and distributed to troops in the field and to citizens at home.

The American public, by contrast, received primarily explanation and analysis of the text of the Paris Agreement. Henry Kissinger served as interpreter. For Americans who cared to know more than the simple fact that American troops would no longer fight and die in Vietnam, certain crucial aspects of the agreement emerged only dimly from the Kissinger exegesis: (1) the agreement specifically recognized the existence of "two parties" of equivalent status in the South. The "two parties" had been named in the October version and they were the two signatories to the final Paris Agreement in January: the PRG and the government of South Vietnam; (2) the only "sovereignty" at stake in the South depended upon the guarantee to the people there of self-determination, free from outside interference, and upon the "two parties" reaching agreement on the internal matters of South Vietnam; (3) the military demarcation line at the 17th parallel "dividing" North and South Vietnam was "only provisional and not a political or territorial boundary"; (4) when the "two parties" in the South resolved their differences, reunification of North and

South Vietnam was to be carried out "step by step through peaceful means" (Article 15 of the Paris Agreement); (5) The Paris Agreement was in no significant way an improvement upon the terms of the rejected October 1972 agreements that Hanoi had been ready to sign; in fact, it basically followed what had been the consistent demands of the NLF since 1962.

How bleak a prospect the Paris Agreement presented to the Thieu government was not generally recognized in the United States. No one knew at the time that Thieu was relying on secret commitments made to him by Nixon in November of 1972 and again in a letter of January 5, 1973. Nixon assured Thieu that "far more important than what we say in the agreement on this issue [of the North Vietnamese troops that would remain in the South] is what we do in the event the enemy renews its aggression." He promised "swift and severe retaliatory action" and, again, that "we will respond with full force." The letters constituted an invitation to Thieu to disregard at will the provisions of the Paris Agreement. Equally unknown to the American public—and to Thieu—was another Nixon letter, this to Premier Pham Van Dong, in which he indicated that "United States contribution to postwar reconstruction [of North Vietnam] will fall in the range of $3.25 billion of grant aid over five years." One American understood very well what all this meant for the future of the Thieu government. John Ehrlichman writes in his memoirs, *Witness to Power,* that he asked Kissinger on January 24 how long South Vietnam could survive under the terms of the Paris Agreement. "I think," said Kissinger, "that if they're lucky they can hold out for a year and a half."

Like most Americans, members of the antiwar movement, although less than trustful of Richard Nixon and Henry Kissinger, took the Paris Agreement at face value as a document that would end the war and restore peace in Vietnam. Rennie Davis was more cautious than most. He flew to Paris in late January to meet with Mme. Nguyen Thi Binh, the PRG representative, and Xuan Thuy, who had represented North Vietnam in many of the secret discussions with Kissinger:

> I stepped on a plane and flew to Paris. . . . The question in the antiwar movement at that time was "Is this for real?" I went right to the delegation. I wanted to know their position. And their position was, "This is it."

Davis returned reassured by Mme. Binh of "the great victory we have won." David Dellinger declared that "there can't be any peace with honor until we face up to the fact that the war was without honor. . . . We'll have to go through some dark night of the soul to find what human values made it possible for that war to go on." And, from an anonymous "fallen-away Trotskyite": "The peace movement has won, so they've [also] lost. They'll be the last to realize they changed the course of United States foreign policy. They'll be disorganized and aimless for a number of years. And precisely because they were right about the war, they're going to be hated."

One person prominent in the Movement did attempt to raise warning signals about the Paris Agreement, or rather the Administration's interpretation of the document. Noam Chomsky, a scholar of world renown in the field of linguistics and a professor at Massachusetts Institute of Technology, had been active in the antiwar movement since 1964, a time when none but a very few were receptive to the notion that America's policies represented error, much less that they constituted a moral wrong. In response to a perceived need, Chomsky devoted his enormous intellectual talents to mastering the field of Vietnamese and Indochina studies. His writings on the subject became a major resource and an important part of the intellectual and moral foundation of the antiwar movement. Chomsky could be as scornful of doves who opposed the war on "pragmatic" grounds as he was of the successive Washington administrations that led the nation into Vietnam and kept it there. He reserves his harshest criticism, however, for the press.

"If there were an honest and independent press, the headlines in January [1973] would have read U.S. ANNOUNCES INTENTION TO VIOLATE PARIS AGREEMENTS," wrote Chomsky in an analysis of the Nixon-Kissinger presentation of the diplomatic achievement at Paris. "An informed press would have observed further that the Paris Agreements incorporate the essential principles of the original enemy program, never modified except in detail." Chomsky feared that an elaborate groundwork of misinterpretation was being laid to justify a subsequent reentry of U.S. bombing and air power in the Vietnam theater of war. His letter to the New York *Times,* expressing similar opinions and also signed by Professor Salvatore Luria of MIT, evoked little response. America wanted to forget.

For yet some others in the antiwar movement the task continued. Sidney Peck joined Tom Hayden and Jane Fonda in a Boston press conference to announce plans for action on several fronts: to seek support for the rebuilding of the Bach Mai Hospital destroyed in the Christmas bombings, to establish committees to keep watch on adherence to the terms of the Paris Agreement, to press for the termination of American aid to the Thieu government, and to ask for congressional inquiries on the thousands of prisoners detained in South Vietnam.

Tom Cornell remembers his work in behalf of Saigon's political prisoners:

> We recognized that this would be a tender issue for American political liberals, to lift up the cause of people who are *just like us*—religious people, humanists, artists—liberals. They were being imprisoned for doing the things that we do—for signing petitions, going to rallies, for associating with other people. For having children who do things. And they are held upside down and water is forced up their nostrils, they are held in tiger cages. And so we started gathering evidence. . . . Thich Naht Hanh headed up the Vietnam Buddhist Peace delegation, which was shunted aside by the North Vietnamese and the Viet Cong in Paris. He had just a minor lobbying presence there. One of his people had access to the files in the jail in Saigon, so he took out all the papers, Xeroxed them, and put the papers back.

Cornell traveled to a Pax Christi International Assembly held at the Conseil de Europe in Strasbourg to call attention to the plight of the political prisoners:

> I doubt very seriously whether we alleviated the suffering of any significant number, but we did make their cause known. It had a political effect in

undercutting support [in the United States] for the war effort among people who were sitting on the fence and couldn't be intellectually convinced. After the war the North Vietnamese put the same people back into the tiger cages. What happened to the Viet Cong? Where is Mme. Binh? The far Left didn't want to hear these things. . . . Jim Forest, Pastor Neuhaus, and I wrote the first letter to the North Vietnamese asking about possible human rights violations that may be occurring in the context of our heartfelt support for their gains in Vietnam. And there was never a response. Only from the American peace movement, in the most hostile manner. If you ask any questions about the propriety of what's going on in the new regime you undermine the new regime and give ammunition to the American Right, which would undo all the gains made everywhere under any socialist banner. And that is true. But I don't believe that raising these questions in fact undermines. I think these questions have to be raised. That there really are not two kinds of political morality, one for capitalist countries and one for socialist countries. . . .

Nineteen seventy-three was a troublesome year for Richard Nixon. What little solace he found among the burdens of office and the exercise of power came in the first few months. He might be said to have taken refuge in patriotism. Early in the year, inspired by a scene in the movie *The Man,* he began to wear in his lapel a small replica of the American flag. White House staff were encouraged to follow his example, which, he wistfully confessed in his memoirs, he hoped would be "an impetus for a new rebirth *[sic]* of optimism and decisiveness and national pride."

In March Nixon carried his patriotic show to Nashville's Grand Ole Opry to join in the celebration of a new home for the famous country music radio show. Talk of impeachment was already in the air and the loyal crowd in this Southern bastion told the President in song that they would have none of it. Nixon in turn declared to the audience that "the peace of the world for generations . . . may depend . . . on our character, our love of country, our willingness to stand up for the flag, and country music does that." He played the piano while the crowd sang "God Bless America," but then he took the act a step too far. In imitation of singer Roy Acuff, and before a national television audience, Nixon pulled a yellow yo-yo from his pocket. The President notoriously lacked manual dexterity: the string of the yo-yo unwound to its full extent, and the yellow disk hung motionless, unresponsive to the hand that sought to control it.

As the troops and the POWs began to return from Vietnam on schedule there were less contrived opportunities for patriotic display. In May the President and Mrs. Nixon gave a lavish formal dinner for thirteen hundred people in honor of the POWs† on the South Lawn of the White House. A tiny flag, made out of salvaged odds and ends of cloth in a North Vietnamese prison by air force Lieutenant Colonel John Dramesi, was carried in the presentation of the colors by the military honor guard. Nixon told the gathering that but "for the brave men that took those

† All of whom had been returned by the end of March. There are, however, approximately twenty-five hundred Americans who served in Vietnam and are listed as Missing in Action (MIA).

B-52s in [against Hanoi in December] and did the job . . . you wouldn't be here tonight."

One returned POW who later became a United States senator, navy Captain Jeremiah A. Denton, Jr., in a private session with the President had a particularly pleasing bit of information to relate. Denton said that not only did the North Vietnamese consider Nixon "a very tough fellow," but "[they] really thought that the President was off his rocker—was totally irrational." The President, Denton went on to explain, was like the POWs, whom the North Vietnamese thought—to use Nixon's words—"so irrational that they could not break them and they could not take risks with them." Thus, the madman theory found confirmation in the example provided by Denton and other POWs.

In a speech to the full assembly of returned POWs on May 24, Nixon spoke indirectly of what truly soured the year 1973 for him. He told the group it was "time in this country to quit making national heroes out of those who steal state secrets and publish them in the newspapers." The reference was to Daniel Ellsberg, whose trial had just ended, all charges against him dismissed by a judge angry at the government's duplicity in the case. But the deeper problem—for Nixon—was Watergate.

Most of the nation's travail over the previous ten years was tied in one fashion or another to Vietnam. Watergate was no exception. "Deep Throat," the purported White House leak in the Watergate scandal, persistently urged two young reporters working on the story to "follow the money." A second suggestion, never made and never pursued, might have been in order: "Follow the Vietnam thread." John Dean, who warned Nixon in March that there was "a cancer on the Presidency," described for the Ervin committee the paranoia induced in Nixon and his aides by the antiwar movement:

> The White House was continually seeking intelligence information about demonstration leaders and their supporters that would either discredit them personally or indicate that the demonstration was in fact sponsored by some foreign enemy. We never found a scintilla of viable evidence indicating that these demonstrations were part of a master plan.

It was this mind-set that drove the White House to pursue their quarry by the illegal means of bugging, break-ins, and burglary—what John Mitchell referred to as the "White House horrors." For these purposes the Plumbers unit was formed, with Daniel Ellsberg as a first target in 1971.

Daniel Ellsberg was number two on Nixon's "enemies list," in a place of honor right behind Edward M. Kennedy, the senator from Massachusetts and brother of John F. Kennedy, who defeated Nixon in the presidential race in 1960. The harassment of Ellsberg was therefore relentless, the means more foul than fair.

Nixon's downfall and ultimate resignation in disgrace from the office of the presidency came about through exposure of his role in the Watergate cover-up. But H. R. Haldeman, Nixon's closest White House associate, the person to whom he confided the madman theory, has suggested that it was not Watergate, but the

"Vietnam thread" and the Ellsberg link that Nixon sought to cover up. In his book *The Ends of Power,* Haldeman lists Nixon's three "personal motives for a cover-up." The first, says Haldeman, was to prevent himself from being connected to the Watergate break-in; the second, to prevent disclosure of John Mitchell's involvement, if any. Then:

> *Third*—and perhaps most important—to avoid exposure of the "other things" (as he always called them), the actions ranging from the Ellsberg break-in to Chuck Colson's projects which had brought such a gleam to his eye when they were happening. In other words, to "contain" the investigation to Watergate.

Colson is said by J. Anthony Lukas in *Night-Mare* to have given the orders from the White House (in Nixon's name) that led to the May 3, 1972, attempt on Ellsberg. The Watergate investigations did not pursue the question of what "other things" Colson may have set in motion against leaders of the antiwar movement.

According to Haldeman, Nixon is not solely to blame in the Ellsberg matter; he was goaded into it by Henry Kissinger. "It shows you're a weakling, Mr. President," Haldeman quotes Kissinger as telling Nixon after the release of the Pentagon Papers. "The Pentagon Papers affair," writes Haldeman, "so often regarded by the press as a classic example of Nixon's paranoia, was Kissinger's premier performance. Unfortunately for Henry, it was recorded, and may some day be played to standing room audiences." It was, of course, the existence of the Oval Office tapes, an ironic exercise in bugging, that ultimately sealed Nixon's doom.

In the estimate of Tom Cornell, "the most important thing that happened in the whole protest movement was what Dan Ellsberg did with the Pentagon Papers, because it gave the lie to the whole government line [on Vietnam]." Perhaps there was more. Henry Kissinger writes of a privately envisioned program, distinct from the provisions of the Paris Agreement, for the indefinitely continuing existence of two Vietnams, one in the North, the other (protected by "the implicit threat of our retaliation") in the South. He asserts: "But for the collapse of executive authority as a result of Watergate, I believe we would have succeeded." In other words, Daniel Ellsberg's release of the Pentagon Papers—an action nurtured in the supportive climate of the antiwar movement—not only gave the lie to the government's line on Vietnam, but also destroyed that government's policy and, indirectly, brought down its leadership.

Like the yo-yo demonstrated so ineptly by the President in Nashville, the Vietnam thread had its own spindle weight: the White House obsession with "enemies" in the antiwar movement. Coaxed out to an ultimately unmanageable length by the dead weight of hatred, it is a strand not hard to follow:

> February 1969. Richard Helms delivers to Henry Kissinger the "Restless Youth" report in which the CIA found no proof of foreign (i.e., Communist) direction of the antiwar movement;

408

May 1969. White House orders telephone taps on government officials and newsmen after William Beecher's New York *Times* story on the secret Cambodia bombings;

June 1969. White House requests new investigation by CIA, FBI, and other intelligence agencies of foreign links to antiwar movement and is disappointed in the results;

June 1970. White House proposes abortive Huston Plan to put Administration directly in charge of illegal surveillance activities aimed at domestic protest movement. J. Edgar Hoover's objections force Nixon to withdraw the plan;

December 1970. White House establishes the Intelligence Evaluation Committee under the Justice Department, again with the goal of removing restraints on intelligence-gathering operations against domestic radicals. Hoover is once more obstructive;

July 1971. In response to Daniel Ellsberg's release of the Pentagon Papers, the White House takes direct action. The Plumbers, led by Egil Krogh, Jr., of Ehrlichman's staff and David Young from Kissinger's office, are formed as an independent investigative unit. Through Nixon confidant Charles Colson, E. Howard Hunt is brought in and joins Liddy on the Plumbers team;

September 1971. The Plumbers (Bernard Barker and two Cubans operating under the on-scene direction of Hunt and Liddy) burglarize the office of Daniel Ellsberg's psychiatrist, Dr. Lewis J. Fielding. (John Ehrlichman has called this incident "the seminal Watergate episode");

May 1972. Barker and a team of Cubans, again under the direction of Hunt and Liddy, attempt to assault Daniel Ellsberg at an antiwar demonstration at the steps of the Capitol in Washington;

June 1972. The Barker team, ostensibly working for CREEP and augmented by former CIA operative James McCord and directed by Hunt and Liddy, break into the Watergate headquarters of the Democratic National Committee and are arrested in the act. The White House containment and cover-up begin;

March 1973. As federal prosecution of Watergate burglars proceeds, Nixon orders John Dean to get additional hush money to E. Howard Hunt to forestall Ellsberg case disclosures;

Spring 1973. Testimony of John Dean to federal prosecutors and to the Senate Select Committee on Presidential Campaign Activities (the Ervin committee) reveals information on the Huston Plan, the Plumbers, the break-in at Dr. Fielding's office, wiretapping, bugging, and other White House "horrors";

July 1973. Alexander Butterfield reveals existence of Nixon tapes in testimony before the Ervin committee. Representative Robert F. Drinan of Massachusetts submits resolution to impeach Nixon for Cambodia bombings and for lying to Congress about them;

February 1974. House Judiciary Committee commences formal constitutional process to consider impeachment resolutions;

July 1974. House Judiciary Committee votes three articles of impeachment. Article 1 deals with the Watergate cover-up and Article 3 with the President's refusal to honor the committee's subpoenaing of tapes and papers. Article 2 states that "Richard Nixon, in violation of his constitutional oath . . . has repeatedly engaged in conduct violating the constitutional rights of citizens, impairing the due and proper administration of justice and the conduct of lawful inquiries. . . ." A fourth article on the Cambodia crimes, introduced by Representative Robert F. Drinan the previous summer, is voted down.

August 9, 1974. Richard Nixon resigns the office of President of the United States.

In April 1973, while Nixon was intensively engaged in the Watergate cover-up, Representative Elizabeth Holtzman (D-New York) and four air force officers filed suit in federal court to halt the bombing of Cambodia on the grounds that it had not been approved by Congress. In June, Congress voted to halt funding for the bombing as of August 15. On July 25, in response to Holtzman's suit, Judge Orrin G. Judd issued an injunction to halt the bombing but it was lifted by the Court of Appeals. The ACLU, acting on behalf of Holtzman, appealed to Supreme Court Justice Thurgood Marshall; on August 1 he refused to overturn the Court of Appeals decision. An appeal was then made to Justice William O. Douglas. On August 4 Douglas ordered that the Cambodia bombing be halted. He said that he considered that the case had the urgency of a capital case, since "we know that someone [either Cambodian peasants or American pilots] is about to die." Douglas explained that as in a capital case, there were doubts about due process. For the Cambodia bombing, the "due process" in question was the constitutionality of the war. After the Pentagon Papers decision in 1971, Douglas believed that he could carry four votes in addition to his own to grant certiorari—that is, to have the Court consider the next case that arose involving the constitutionality of the war in Vietnam. But two of those votes, Justices Harlan and Black, were no longer on the Court in 1973. Instead, in an unprecedented action, Marshall overruled Douglas after conferring with each of the other justices not in person but by telephone. On August 9 and again on August 13 Chief Justice Warren Burger rejected an application by the ACLU on behalf of Holtzman and the four air force officers to call a special term of the Court to consider the question of the constitutionality of the U.S. bombing of Cambodia.

On August 15, as mandated by Congress, the bombing ceased. The question of its constitutionality, or, indeed, that of the war itself, was never resolved. Since January 28, the day after the signing of the Paris Agreement, the officially acknowledged bombing of Cambodia—no longer of Viet Cong strongholds along the border but of the capital of Phnom Penh—had involved 27,626 sorties by fighter-bombers and 7,784 B-52 sorties at a cost of $422.8 million. Six pilots were killed and four were reported missing.

On the day that the bombing was halted sixty antiwar demonstrators including the Reverend Daniel Berrigan and his brother Jerome were arrested in a prayer vigil at the White House, part of a five-week campaign by the White House Prayer Group that met daily to kneel and pray at the East Portico during tour hours. Daniel Berrigan had been paroled in January 1972 after having been jailed on his Catonsville conviction; his parole had ended only a week before this latest arrest. Sister Elizabeth McAlister had been among those arrested during the vigil several days before.

While the prayer vigil was taking place on the White House grounds another demonstration was occurring in front of the fence along Pennsylvania Avenue. Organized by WSP, VVAW, and the Fifth Avenue Peace Parade Committee, its spokeswoman, Cora Weiss, said to newsmen that the group had come to begin a "national campaign for the impeachment of President Nixon"—a response to Representative Robert F. Drinan's introduction on July 31 of a resolution to impeach the President for carrying out—and denying—the illegal Cambodian bombings. Drinan's fellow House members did not want an impeachment vote at that time because they feared it would fail, thereby making any later impeachment attempt more difficult. Impeachment hearings were finally begun by the House Judiciary Committee in May 1974.

On October 16, 1973, the Nobel Committee announced that it had awarded the Nobel Peace Prize for 1973 jointly to Henry A. Kissinger and Le Duc Tho for their success in negotiating a peace agreement for Vietnam. It was the most controversial award in the history of the prize. Two members of the committee resigned in protest. One week later Le Duc Tho rejected the prize because "peace has not yet really been established in Vietnam." Kissinger did not decline his prize but accepted it in London rather than Oslo.

Although the United States had for the moment ceased her active military participation in Indochina, the threat that she would reenter the conflict remained. In November 1973, in order to avert future Vietnams in an era of war by Presidential fiat, Congress passed, over the President's veto, the War Powers Resolution. It provided that if the President sent U.S. troops to any foreign area where they might be involved in hostilities, he had only sixty (or, in some cases, ninety) days in which to secure congressional approval or withdraw the troops. The first test of this Resolution came almost exactly ten years later in September 1983, when President Ronald Reagan sent U.S. troops to Lebanon. A compromise agreement somewhat weakening the War Powers Resolution was worked out in which the troops could remain for eighteen months—until after the 1984 elections.

The first anniversary of the signing of the Paris Agreement passed almost unnoticed, save by a few activists. Outside the White House, whose occupant was now engaged in a kind of war for his personal survival, Father Philip Berrigan and about thirty others demonstrated to protest further aid to South Vietnam. Some of them said that they would try to meet with the President. They did not succeed.

Continued military aid to President Thieu was one of the three issues emphasized by those Americans still actively involved in "antiwar" work a year after the war ended for the United States, the other two being a demand that the peace accords be enforced and that the Thieu regime's political prisoners held in the infamous tiger cages be released.

Congress, after ten years, finally acted to wind down U.S. participation in Vietnam. On April 4 the House of Representatives, in what the Washington *Post* called a "staggering blow," voted down an administration request for a $474 million increase in military aid to Saigon.

A new lobbying group had been formed the previous fall to pressure Congress for the cut-off of funds. Calling itself the United Campaign to End the War, it was an outgrowth of the Indochina Peace Campaign. In October 1973 some two hundred representatives from fifteen or twenty peace and religious groups met at Germantown, Ohio, to form a strategy to end the U.S. presence in Indochina, honor the Paris Agreement, and work for the release of South Vietnam's political prisoners. By March 1974 the United Campaign had begun to have some success. Tom Hayden remembers working in Washington:

> Very interesting things happened. Jane and I were here for about six weeks. I taught a class in the House of Representatives for about eighty staff on the history of the war—the same course I was giving on campuses. . . . There was a critical moment when I think our efforts paid off in the sense that occasionally, when a vote is close, you can make the difference between winning and losing. It was the day the Democratic caucus decided by a binding vote to oppose any further aid. . . . There was a meeting that morning at eight o'clock that I attended. . . . The idea was hatched there to take it to the caucus because there was a fear that the leadership would go along with the President and wouldn't have the "wherewithal" to cut off aid and take the consequences. So there was a binding vote and that did it. That ended the war as far as I was concerned. . . . You don't know how drastic this was, to cut it off. If you're part of the system you don't usually do things like this. . . .

Having been rebuffed by the House, the Administration tried to find aid for Saigon through a bookkeeping sleight of hand. The sum of $266 million was discovered to have been previously appropriated but never spent; now the Senate was requested to appropriate the windfall. It refused: by a vote of 43–38 it endorsed an amendment offered by Senator Edward Kennedy which barred additional military aid to Saigon for that fiscal year. Several weeks later, however, an amendment offered by Kennedy and Alan Cranston (D-California) to cut $150 million in aid from a new Pentagon budget was defeated. The vote was close, 46–45, with several proclaimed antiwar senators absent. By August, however, with the Nixon Administration tottering before the onslaught of Watergate revelations from the Oval Office, the House was as ready to forget Vietnam as was the public at large: on August 7 it voted, 233–157, to limit military aid to Saigon to $700 million for the next year (the Administration had requested $1.6 billion).

Meanwhile the war went on, as did protest against it. More than fifty thousand Vietnamese soldiers, North and South, had been killed in 1973. In May 1974 a crowd of ten thousand gathered at Kent State University on the fourth anniversary of the Kent State killings. Singers Holly Near and Judy Collins performed; speakers included Jane Fonda, who had just returned with her husband Tom Hayden from North Vietnam and "liberated" (PRG) areas of South Vietnam. A film of their trip was made showing much devastation from the war and showing also the attempts by the Vietnamese to rebuild. Others who spoke at the rally were Julian Bond, Daniel Ellsberg (with newly released transcripts of White House tapes; such revelations came thick and fast that spring), and two casualties of the war—Ron Kovic, wounded in Vietnam, and Dean Kahler, one of the students injured during the Kent State shooting (like Kovic, Kahler is paralyzed). The audience also heard a message from Cambodia's exiled Prince Norodom Sihanouk protesting continued U.S. intervention in his country.

That summer renewed antiwar protests took place in Washington. From June 24 through August 15 the American Friends Service Committee, the United Campaign to End the War, and seventeen national and international peace organizations maintained a "tiger cage" vigil at the Capitol in which a replica of a tiger cage was set up to symbolize the imprisonment and torture of an estimated two hundred thousand political prisoners by the Thieu regime. A tiger cage was also set up outside the White House; on July 4 Philip Berrigan was arrested as he sat chained with another demonstrator inside the cage. About two thousand Vietnam Veterans Against the War staged a four-day demonstration demanding (1) universal amnesty for draft refusers and deserters, (2) implementation of the Paris Agreement, (3) ending aid to Thieu and Lon Nol, (4) a universal discharge and benefits for all veterans, (5) President Nixon's removal from office. As they had done in April 1971, they requested a permit to camp on the Mall, and like the earlier permit it was granted with the proviso that sleeping was prohibited. This time, however, the authorities did not condone violations, and the veterans were harassed every night through their stay. Undoubtedly their choice of flags to fly—PRG, Pathet Lao, and Cambodian United Front—served to anger the police.

In July 1974 the underground Weatherman issued the little red book *Prairie Fire,* which contained their self-criticism (a Weatherman constant) and their continuing hope that the revolution—whatever that was—would come. Ominously, they stated their ongoing support for the Black Liberation Army; Weatherman's guilt over "white skin privilege," it seemed, never lessened. They lived in hiding throughout the 1970s. The FBI could not find them. From time to time a bomb would be set in some public place and Weatherman would claim credit for it. Eventually some of them began to surface and surrender: Mark Rudd (1977), Bernardine Dohrn, Bill Ayers, and Cathlyn Wilkerson (1981). They were the lucky ones; others were less fortunate—or more foolhardy. In October 1981 the most spectacular, if unintended, "surfacing" occurred when Weatherpeople Kathy Boudin, David Gilbert, and Judith Clark were arrested during a shoot-out in the aftermath of an armed robbery of a Brink's truck. A Brink's guard and two Nyack, New York, police officers were killed. The three whites had been allied with members of the Black Liberation Army, which had as one of its goals the establishment of a "Republic of New Afrika" in the American South—a nightmarish replay of the effort by white students two decades previously to help black students in the Southern civil rights drives.‡

Richard Nixon had strongly opposed any form of amnesty for young men who had opted out of the war. On September 8, 1974, President Gerald Ford announced a full (and highly controversial) pardon for his predecessor, who had so narrowly escaped impeachment. One week later Ford announced an "earned re-entry program" for fugitive draft resisters and military deserters. Unlike the fallen President, these young men would have to pay for their return to society. Charges against resisters would be dropped upon completion of up to twenty-four months' alternative service. Deserters who completed the same alternative service would receive either an undesirable or a clemency discharge, neither of which provided veterans' benefits. A special Clemency Board was set up to handle these cases; it was headed by former Senator Charles Goodell.

About 350,000 men were eligible to apply for the Ford program; only 6 percent of them did so, and fewer than half of those completed their alternative service. Avenues outside the Ford program provided better results: clemency could be granted through other channels without alternative service, and deserters had a chance to apply independently for upgraded discharges providing veterans' benefits. The Ford program ended on March 31, 1975, as the North Vietnamese Army overran South Vietnam. When the board disbanded, Goodell said that he would "never advise anyone to work for two years to earn a Clemency Discharge."

On January 21, 1977, the day after his inauguration, President Jimmy Carter announced a pardon to approximately 10,000 draft evaders, many of whom were in exile in Canada, Sweden, and elsewhere. Deserters, he said, would have their cases considered individually to determine if their less-than-honorable discharges could be upgraded. Those young men who had never registered for the draft—about 250,000—would not be prosecuted.

Carter was criticized by conservatives who considered his program too lenient, and by amnesty groups who protested that the plan excluded those most in need of help—poor and minority young men who did not know that they could have evaded military service, who had had no choice but to submit to the draft, and who had then deserted.

Few men took advantage of the Carter program. By mid-1977, fewer than a hundred had asked for a pardon, and fewer than a hundred exiles returned. For those veterans with undesirable or clemency discharges (about 430,000), the Defense Department undertook a review program. In the first six months of the program only about 37,000 men applied for upgraded discharges; 28,000 cases were processed, and of these, 60 percent received them. The question of upgrading discharges became academic, however, when legislation was enacted which denied

‡ In September 1983, Gilbert and Clark were each found guilty of murder and were sentenced to seventy-five years to life in prison. In April 1984, Kathy Boudin, refusing to cooperate with the prosecution of another member of the group, pleaded "guilty" to charges of robbery and murder. Judge David S. Ritter stated that he would sentence her to twenty years to life in prison. The forty-year-old Boudin will be eligible for parole in 2001, when she is fifty-eight.

benefits to any veteran who had received an upgraded discharge under the Carter plan.

Although deserters, evaders, and refusers aroused considerable hostility during the Vietnam years, particularly from parents whose sons had died in the war, attitudes toward them seemed to change. In late 1983, one father who lost a son to the war commented that "I respect those who went to Canada. They followed their conscience when it became clear that things weren't what they seemed over there [in Vietnam]."

By the fall of 1974 the American public had suffered through more than two years of leaks, testimony, and news reports about the internal workings of the Nixon Administration. The nation's faith in its government, undermined during the Vietnam years, had been, to say the least, further badly shaken. But there was worse to come, as the public discovered on December 22 when the New York *Times* published an investigative report by Seymour M. Hersh on the CIA: "The Central Intelligence Agency, directly violating its charter, conducted a massive, illegal domestic intelligence operation during the Nixon Administration against the antiwar movement and other dissident groups in the United States, according to well-placed Government sources. . . ." Many people in the antiwar movement, of course, had known for years that they were under surveillance by one or another government agency; in addition to the CIA, surveillance and infiltration was carried out by the FBI (Operation COINTELPRO), Army intelligence, and local police Red squads.

President Ford responded to Hersh's revelations by appointing a "blue-ribbon" commission headed by Vice President Nelson Rockefeller to investigate the CIA; within weeks both the Senate and the House of Representatives set up their own intelligence committees for the same purpose. The Rockefeller commission was criticized by some because of its members' close ties not only to Rockefeller but to the CIA. Nevertheless, its 299-page report, delivered the following June, contained a sobering assessment of CIA domestic surveillance including an astonishing figure for the number of entries indexed in the CIA's "Hydra" computer: some three hundred thousand. The commission report also detailed evidence of CIA penetration of dissident groups, particularly antiwar and black groups, and mail openings, wiretaps, buggings, and burglaries. Under the name Operation CHAOS the CIA had, in short, conducted espionage against American citizens since 1967; other, less intense surveillance had been ongoing almost since the CIA's inception in 1947. Operation CHAOS was administratively part of CIA's counterintelligence unit, whose legendary chief, James J. Angleton, had resigned along with three other CIA staffers shortly after Hersh's report appeared. Demoralization within the CIA on other counts may have led to Angleton's resignation. President Ford withheld the Rockefeller commission's findings on the CIA's reported assassinations of foreign leaders, but the Senate Intelligence Committee under the chairmanship of Frank Church did consider that issue in detail.

In January 1976 the report of the House Intelligence Committee under the chairmanship of Otis Pike (D-New York) was suppressed by a vote of the full House

(246–124), over Pike's protest, until President Ford and the CIA had censored it. Portions of the report found their way into *The Village Voice*, however.

Meanwhile the war went on, as did protest against it. In Washington in late January 1975 several thousand people attended an Assembly to Save the Peace Agreement—workshops and a candlelight march to the White House. They listened to familiar voices: Bella Abzug, Joan Baez, Robert Drinan, Daniel Ellsberg, Tom Hayden, George McGovern, and Pete Seeger. Said McGovern, "Incredibly, the Ford Administration has plans to prolong and escalate the fighting in Vietnam. But they forgot one thing. The war-makers did not plan on you . . . on the resistance of the people to a war the people sought to end years ago. . . ."

In the spring of 1975, South Vietnam crumbled under North Vietnam's advance. The northern provinces fell; the cities of Quang Tri, Pleiku, and Hue were taken by late March, and a mass exodus of refugees headed toward Da Nang, there to seek escape by sea. The North Vietnamese pushed on toward Saigon.

On April 17, Cambodia fell to the Communists (Khmer Rouge). On April 21, as North Vietnamese troops began their final push to Saigon, President Thieu resigned. Four days later he fled to Taiwan. The North Vietnamese continued their drive to South Vietnam's capital.

In Congress, a debate arose over the question of whether to use U.S. troops to evacuate the remaining Americans in South Vietnam as well as their Vietnamese dependents and other Vietnamese who, having worked for or with the American forces, might be in danger from a Communist takeover. The House debated the measure for fourteen hours—considerably longer than its consideration of the Tonkin Gulf Resolution—and voted approval by 230–187. The Senate passed a similar bill 75–17.

Meanwhile the nation turned with relief from the traumas of Vietnam and Watergate to the celebration of the bicentennial. On April 19, 1975, President Ford journeyed to Massachusetts to commemorate the two-hundredth anniversary of the battles of Lexington and Concord. He was greeted by a crowd of one hundred sixty thousand, most of whom were friendly; a sizable minority, however, booed him and shouted curses at him as he spoke at Concord's Old North Bridge. They were members of the People's Bicentennial Commission, many of whom were, or had been, antiwar activists. Later that month Ford declared that America should put Vietnam behind her; the war, he said, was done with. He issued a proclamation stating that May 7, 1975, was the last day of the "Vietnam era."

On April 30 Saigon fell; it would be renamed Ho Chi Minh City. Howard Zinn remembers that day:

> I was in what I call "the last teach-in of the war." It was in the last days of April '75—a teach-in at Brandeis to try to get the U.S. and the Ford administration to stop sending arms to Saigon. It was a huge meeting—four or five speakers, including Noam Chomsky and me. In the midst of the meeting a fellow broke into the hall and came down the aisle waving this little piece of paper—he worked for the Brandeis student paper—and he said, "It just

came over the teletype that the Saigon government has surrendered. The war is over!" And everybody stood up and cheered.

In the days after the fall of Saigon the first of the boat people began to flee Vietnam. Many of them came—or wanted to come—to America. It was estimated that something over one hundred thousand could be expected; over half a million arrived in the United States by the end of 1983, out of a total of approximately two million who fled Indochina after the spring of 1975. In a latter-day version of the old Yellow Peril hysteria, many Americans did not want them. A Gallup Poll that spring reported that by 54 to 36 percent, the American public opposed the resettlement of South Vietnamese refugees in the United States. People were afraid that they would take jobs from Americans;* they were afraid that the Vietnamese would bring with them strange Oriental diseases; they were afraid, oddly, that these refugees from communism would bring with them a Communist virus to afflict the American body politic. Mostly, Americans were fed up with things Vietnamese and did not want reminders of the war that the United States lost. The refugees, therefore, met a hostile reception; many of them in 1984 are still unwelcome in communities where they try to settle along with refugees from Cambodia and Laos. Nevertheless many have adapted well: in 1983, at least three valedictorians of high school graduating classes were Vietnamese.

Since the end of the war in Vietnam, thousands of Americans who worked against it have eased back into the mainstream, which many of them, of course, had never fully abandoned. Most of them today are not actively involved in issues of public policy, but a large number are, most visibly in the movement for nuclear arms control. In June 1982 nearly a million Americans marched and rallied in New York City to support a freeze on nuclear weapons—a demonstration organized in large part by former antiwar activists. In January 1984 the eight Democratic presidential candidates, in a nationally televised campaign debate at Dartmouth College, concentrated on the question of a nuclear freeze and disarmament for nearly a third of their time—a question made more urgent for them not only by the possibility of nuclear war but by the activism of thousands of citizens working to challenge the authority of their government on the issue of nuclear weapons proliferation, thus forcing politicians to confront the problem. Like the war in Vietnam, to many citizens the question of nuclear arms control has appeared too important to be left to their political leaders or to "experts." The resulting nationwide citizen movement for weapons control and/or reduction is a direct descendant of the antiwar movement, and many of its key organizers are veterans of that earlier struggle.

A third party encompassing these and other interests did not evolve, however:

> The average leadership in the antiwar movement had no ideology [says Tom Hayden]. They were involved because they wanted to stop the Vietnam War, not because they wanted to build nonviolent resistance, not because they wanted to build a socialist movement, not because they wanted to build a third party or whatever else was grafted on. Others wanted to get involved

* The unemployment rate from the 1974–75 recession was 8.7 percent in April 1975.

because they wanted to get elected to high office. A lot of motives. But the thrust of it, the power of it, was the simple, spontaneous, unorganized repugnance that people had toward the war. So it didn't surprise me afterwards that there came of it no Left, no Catholic Left, no New Left, no third party, because it was a mass outpouring in a country that has no ideological history, no multiparty systems, no Left in its history in the sense of a third party, a labor party, a class-based party. But our country does have a history of morally- or class-driven politics when a group of people feel disenfranchised whether it's women or labor or a single major issue like Vietnam. Then reform follows, the dust settles, people go back to their normal lives. Because normal life in this country is defined as private. Not public, not belonging to political associations. So these little groups played a key role in directing it [the antiwar movement], giving organizational structure to it. But if they hoped as many did that out of it would come a permanent movement based on certain key ideological principles, those hopes vanished.

There was, in fact, a constant pull toward staying "in the system"—toward not splintering into a permanent third-party alignment. Many antiwar activists had worked mightily to keep the peace movement "respectable":

The moderates who helped force Johnson out had political control and dominance of the peace movement until 1965 through SANE [says Sidney Peck]. They wanted a respectable peace movement and a respectable opposition. They were exclusionary. They continued the pattern of McCarthyism [red-baiting] in the peace movement. They excluded the Left. SDS won that fight in the April 1965 demonstration. From 1965 on, the dominant leadership of the antiwar coalition was in the hands of progressive Left people based on a nonexclusionary orientation. . . . We assumed the public leadership of the Movement over the tremendous opposition of these other [moderate] forces. The only way they could come back was to try to pick up the momentum of the April 1967 demonstration and orient it to electoral politics. The success of that demonstration led the business community to decide to act, to do something. This led to the call for Vietnam Summer and the NCNP conference in September 1967—electoral activities [within the system] as opposed to street action. In other words they were saying, "There are other ways to oppose the war than by getting into the streets or burning your draft cards." . . . The [Eugene] McCarthy campaign was a substitute for the debacle of the NCNP. The Moratorium and the McGovern campaign were further expressions of this wing of the peace movement. . . .

But the traditional two-party system could not accommodate the protest against the war. As Fred Halstead wrote: "The American movement against the Vietnam War—the greatest moral resurgence in the U.S. since the struggle to abolish slavery—had to arise and maintain itself apart from and in defiance of both parties."
Tom Hayden:

The question of working in the system is a hard one to analyze because you usually don't have to factor in assassination [of Robert Kennedy and Martin

Luther King]. Assassinations in 1968 reinforced the feeling that you could not work in the system. The leaders were being killed off.

Had Kennedy lived, there was a good chance we would have seen a Kennedy nomination and presidency. I think that would have led to an end of the Vietnam conflict and a greater focus on the domestic issues that Dr. King stood for. Had that occurred, there might not have been the conflict in Chicago and no Conspiracy trial and no Kent State. It's complicated because Martin Luther King represented civil disobedience and mass mobilization. Robert Kennedy was a politician who was moved by these forces. The lesson is: only through a combination of mass mobilization and effective leadership within the system interacting can you get real change without violence. My life and a lot of other people's lives would have been quite different had King and Kennedy lived.

Most of the antiwar movement and pacifist movement had a different view. They felt that Kennedy and King were token rather than real agents of change. The new leadership of SDS in fact thought that we who planned the demonstration in Chicago were "stalking horses" for Kennedy.

[But] Congress ended the war following popular protest. In a ten-year period the whole Congress was transformed. Ten years is not a long time. People who take that view are just venting their frustration. What actually happened?

—military frustration—we couldn't win;
—the economy was destroyed;
—the country was threatened with internal chaos;
—the rise of political opposition within the system starting with the Kennedy and McCarthy campaigns—the political equivalent of Mendès-France back in the French model;
—Watergate.

These things in sequence and together happened. What other country in the world could it happen in? We would have been arrested or shot immediately in most other places. The press would have been clamped down on; Congress would have had its powers eliminated. From the point of view of someone who's still living entirely in those times, they will tell you Congress was catastrophically irresponsible for taking so long to deal with the war. I think Congress did pretty well. I think that it was a miracle that we didn't plunge into civil strife. I give credit to the antiwar movement, but I'm not going to rule out Congress's role.

As we have seen, the system did not welcome the dissenters and, indeed, it tried to stifle them. The reason why it did not succeed is problematical. As Howard Zinn comments:

Maybe one of the reasons [that the government did not suppress the antiwar movement] is that they did not foresee how it would develop. It may be if they could have foreseen that development in an early stage they would have been tougher and rougher. In World War I they moved fast [to suppress antiwar sentiment]. Neither they nor the antiwar movement could predict how fast the antiwar movement would grow, how large and effective it would be. Because this government is capable of repression. . . .

Like the war it opposed, the antiwar movement arose from obscure beginnings, held the nation's attention for a time, and then faded away. Afterward those who took part in it, like those who fought the war, found that the nation did not want to hear about their decade-long struggle to speak truth to power. One of those truths, and one of the most important lessons of the war itself, was that America learned that she could be wrong—a profoundly maturing lesson for either an individual or a nation.

On May 11, 1975, on a sunny afternoon in Central Park's Sheep Meadow, where eight years previously a group of frightened young men had burned their draft cards in opposition to the war, fifty thousand or more people gathered to celebrate the war's end both in Vietnam and Cambodia.† It was not a solemn and angry antiwar rally but a joyful welcome to peace. The demonstration had been organized in just ten days. The crowd heard mostly music: from Odetta, Peter Yarrow, Joan Baez, Phil Ochs, Harry Belafonte, Tom Paxton, Richie Havens, Paul Simon, and the Deadly Nightshade (a women's group). David Dellinger spoke, and Bella Abzug, and Elizabeth Holtzman. Norma Becker attended the rally but she did not speak; she seldom did to an audience and never to such a large crowd. Many people that day sang with the singers, giving voice to their overflowing emotions. On a banner on the platform, and on white balloons and placards, were the words that many in the crowd had worked ten years and more to achieve: THE WAR IS OVER!

And so, for America, it was.

---

† For Cambodia, the horror—the holocaust—had only just begun. After Nixon expanded the war into Cambodia in 1970 the Viet Cong and the North Vietnamese forces had been driven westward deep into the country; the communist Khmer Rouge gathered strength and eventually toppled the weak Lon Nol regime. After the Communist takeover in April 1975 a reign of terror ensued under the leadership of Pol Pot. It is estimated that during Pol Pot's regime from two to four million Cambodians (half the population) perished. In December 1978 the Vietnamese invasion stopped the slaughter. Cambodia now languishes under the harsh rule of Hanoi.

Afterword

In the same winter, the Athenians following their ancestral custom, held a burial, at the public expense, of the first to die in this war. They do this in the following way:

They erect a tent where the bones of those who died lie in state for a three-day period, and each one brings to his own dead whatever offering he chooses. When the funeral procession goes out, wagons carry coffins made of cypress wood, one for each tribe. The bones of each man are in the coffin of his own tribe. One bier is carried empty and covered with a cloth. This is for those who are missing and could not be found for burial. All who wish to do so, whether citizen or foreigner, accompany the funeral procession; and women who are relatives of the dead are at the burial and cry in lamentation.

They put the bodies in the state burial mound, which is at the fairest approach to the city. In it they always bury the dead from their wars. . . . And when they have covered the bones with earth, a man chosen by the people, who in their judgment is wise and has risen to a place of honor in their esteem, speaks at the gravesite a eulogy suitable to the occasion. After this, the people depart.

This is the way they bury their dead, and throughout the entire duration of the war, whenever events demanded, they followed this custom.

Thucydides 2.34.1–7

Thus does Thucydides tell how the people of democratic Athens did on frequent occasion confront the meaning of a war that would last for almost thirty years and carry their young to distant corners of the world to die. Only rarely in America, as when a President loved of his nation dies young, do the emotions of grief combine with the rites of religious and state observance, and the people face the meaning of their loss or muster strength to persevere. Neither public ceremonies of sorrow nor words by one wise in the judgment of the people called Americans to ponder the meaning and moral questions of Vietnam. Those who fell there returned home in an unending stream of anonymous plastic body bags and aluminum caskets; their families mourned alone. Those who survived came home and were not heeded.

Instead, Americans, their deepest democratic instincts denied, allowed the face of war to be obscured by devious public policy and ugly words: military advisers, "guns and butter," an unjust draft law, Vietnamization, and "peace with honor." Congress did not debate, the Supreme Court did not consider, and one President after another refused to reconsider. No Lincoln arose from among our leaders to make eloquent expression of public grief or national resolve. The voice of the people was heard only in the streets.

Once, very nearly, a part of the people performed on their own a national ceremony of solemn reflection and honor to the dead. Forty thousand Americans walked in silence through the streets of Washington for forty hours, past the monuments and majestic buildings of the city, past the home of the President, in a March Against Death. But this was, after all, only protest. It was the peace movement, not the nation whole, that spoke. The peace movement was a conscience only; not all heard, and still fewer heeded.

Then, seven years after the last soldier died in Vietnam and more than thirty years (as some believe) after that war began, the people spoke again. A small group of Vietnam veterans determined that Washington should have a monument to those who died in that conflict. On July 1, 1980, Congress authorized a two-acre site near the Lincoln Memorial. Funding for the monument came from private contributions. It is a remarkable work, and, remarkably, it was designed by a young American woman of Asian descent. Maya Ying Lin, who was at the time a twenty-one-year-old undergraduate at Yale, submitted the winning entry among 1,421 in the largest design competition of its kind ever held in the United States.

The monument lies in the northwest corner of the Constitution Gardens, near the Reflecting Pool, almost in the shadow of a seated, brooding Lincoln, who once, in the midst of war, expressed the hope to "bind up the nation's wounds." No brave general on prancing, caparisoned horse adorns the site; no America weeps there on the shoulder of History; no figure of human form gazes off into space; no flag flies.

The monument consists entirely of two walls of black, polished granite set into a gentle downward slope of land that forms something like a shallow amphitheater. The walls rise gradually, each from its farther end, in the shape of the letter V inverted; at the apex where they meet, the walls reach a height of ten feet. On the highly polished slabs, like the stelai of the Athenians, are carved the names of the 57,939 who died in Vietnam; nothing else.* The monument is a silent, encompassing, mysterious, feminine statement. Thousands of Americans approach it every week, and "each one brings to his own dead whatever offering he chooses": a bunch of flowers, a framed picture, a tiny American flag. They touch the surface of the

---

* The unadorned monument as described accords with Ms. Lin's design and the appearance of the memorial on the dedication date. In March 1982, federal approval was granted for the addition of a flagstaff and a life-sized sculpture to stand near the entry to the memorial. The sculpture shows three servicemen in the uniform and equipment of war.

stone and trace with their fingers the name of a brother, son, or friend lost. Men weep.

It is a monument that speaks for those who died in Vietnam; for those who fought, suffered, and were wounded there, but yet returned; for those who did not return and yet may live. It speaks to the families of the fallen, their wives, parents, sisters, and brothers, and it speaks to those who protested the war. It speaks to the hearts and minds of all—and it speaks to the folly of war.

The Vietnam Veterans Memorial was formally dedicated on November 13, 1982, to honor the "courage, sacrifice, and devotion to duty and country" of all who served in that war. The dedication ceremony was attended by tens of thousands of veterans, their families, and others. Except for Senator John W. Warner (R-Virginia), who supported the memorial project from its beginnings, no political figures spoke at the ceremony. No representatives from the administrations that conducted the war were present on the platform. But in the attending crowd that chill November day were two figures from the past: the Honorable Ellsworth Bunker, then eighty-eight years old, ambassador to South Vietnam from 1967 to 1973; and James J. Angleton, chief of counterintelligence, CIA, from 1954 to 1974. They were both bundled against the cold, and they clutched small American flags as they stood side by side and listened attentively to the speakers and joined in the singing of "God Bless America."

Glossary

ACLU	American Civil Liberties Union
ADA	Americans for Democratic Action
AFSC	American Friends Service Committee
BEM	Business Executives Move for Vietnam Peace
CADRE	Chicago Area Draft Resisters
CAPAC	Cleveland Area Peace Action Council
CIA	Central Intelligence Agency
CLCV	Clergy and Laymen Concerned About Vietnam
CNVA	Committee for Nonviolent Action
COC	Coalition for an Open Convention
CORE	Congress of Racial Equality
CP	Communist Party
CPF	Catholic Peace Fellowship
CREEP	Committee to Re-elect the President
DRV	Democratic Republic of Vietnam
ERAP	Economic Research and Action Project
FBI	Federal Bureau of Investigation
FCNL	Friends Committee on National Legislation
FOR	Fellowship of Reconciliation
HUAC	House Un-American Activities Committee
IDA	Institute for Defense Analysis
IPC	Indochina Peace Campaign
ISS	Intercollegiate Socialist Society
LID	League for Industrial Democracy
M2M	May 2nd Movement
NAACP	National Association for Advancement of Colored People

NAG	National Action Group
NCAWRR	National Coalition Against War, Racism and Repression
NCC	National Coordinating Committee to End the War in Vietnam
NCNP	National Conference for New Politics
NLF	National Liberation Front
NPAC	National Peace Action Coalition
NSA	National Student Association
NWRO	National Welfare Rights Organization
PCPJ	People's Coalition for Peace and Justice
PEACE	People Emerging Against Corrupt Establishment
PL(P)(M)	Progressive Labor (Party) (Movement)
PPC	Poor People's Campaign
PRG	Provisional Revolutionary Government
ROTC	Reserve Officers Training Corps
RYM	Revolutionary Youth Movement
SANE	Committee for a Sane Nuclear Policy
SAS	Student Afro-American Society
SCLC	Southern Christian Leadership Conference
SDS	Students for a Democratic Society
SLAP	Student Labor Action Project
SLID	Student League for Industrial Democracy
SMC	Student Mobilization Committee to End the War in Vietnam
SNCC	Student Nonviolent Coordinating Committee
SPU	Student Peace Union
SWP	Socialist Workers Party
UAW	United Automobile Workers
UFT	United Federation of Teachers
VVAW	Vietnam Veterans Against the War
WILPF	Women's International League for Peace and Freedom
WIN	Workshop in Nonviolence
WRL	War Resisters League
WSA	Worker Student Alliance
WSP	Women Strike for Peace
YAWF	Youth Against War and Fascism
YSA	Young Socialist Alliance

Notes

DEATH BY FIRE

1 "American youth": Baltimore *Sun*, November 5, 1965.

2 "Norman Morrison has given": Baltimore *Sun*, November 3, 1965.

3 Morrison in North Vietnam: Lynd and Hayden, *The Other Side; Liberation*, May–June 1967.

4 Alice Herz: Detroit *News*, March 17, 1965; March 18, 1965.

4 "He was trying": *Catholic Worker*, November 1965.

4 Goldberg statement: New York *Times*, November 10, 1965.

4 "gave his life": Richard Curtin, *The Berrigan Brothers* (New York: Hawthorn Books, 1974), p. 52.

5 "They have contradicted": New York *Times*, November 10, 1965.

1963–64: THE YEARS OF LONELY DISSENT

8 Editorial reply to Russell: New York *Times*, April 8, 1963.

8 "if civil authorities": *Pacem in Terris*, p. 18.

12 Cornell statement: *Catholic Worker*, August 1963.

13 to "deny this country to Communism": Raskin and Fall, *The Viet-Nam Reader*, p. 128.

13 Viet Cong attacks: New York *Times*, April 27, 1964.

16 "I don't believe": New York *Times*, February 19, 1964.

19 WILPF lobbying effort: *National Guardian*, April 11, 1964.

20 "Declaration of Conscience": *Catholic Worker*, February 1965.

21 Morgenthau-Arnold-Browne petition: New York *Times*, July 11, 1964.

22 Tonkin Gulf debate: Powers, *The War at Home;* and Austin, *The President's War*. On senators' fears and Nelson amendment, New York *Times*, August 8, 1964.

23 "was sold to": Austin, *The President's War*, p. 104.

25 Nelson letter: New York *Times*, October 6, 1964.

25 "the Berkeley invention": *The Report of the President's Commission on Campus Unrest*, pp. 22–28.

26 "high spirits": ibid., p. 28.

26 "immediate withdrawal": Powers, *The War at Home*, p. 36.

27 SDS history: Sale, *SDS*.

29 "It maintains a *vision*": ibid., p. 56.

31 "SDS has succeeded": ibid., p. 115.

31 "ERAP was built": ibid., p. 143.

31 "Testing some of the reformist": ibid., p. 145.

1965: NO TURNING BACK

33 "A Policy of Sustained Reprisal": *The Pentagon Papers*, 3:687–691.

34 SDS Call: *Liberation*, March 1965; and Powers, *The War at Home*, p. 73.

35 I. F. Stone reply to White Paper: *I. F. Stone's Weekly*, March 8, 1965.

36 The scenario: *The Pentagon Papers*, Quadrangle ed., pp. 254–57.

36 Bundy draft memorandum: Porter, *Vietnam*, 2:240–46.

36 In fact, it was the second: Tyrone Martin, *A Most Fortunate Ship* (Chester, Conn.: Globe Pequot Press, 1982), pp. 236–39.

37 Teach-ins: Menashe and Radosh, *Teach-ins*.

37 "truth team": New York *Times*, May 5, 1965.

40 "We welcome": Halstead, *Out Now!* p. 38.

41 "I refused": ibid., pp. 42–43.

41 "We, the participants": ibid., pp. 43–44.

42 "Perhaps next time": Staughton Lynd, "Coalition Politics," *Liberation*, June–July 1965

43 FCNL Pentagon demonstration: Wilson, *Uphill for Peace;* and New York *Times*, May 13, 1965.

46 "I think our aim": Menashe and Radosh, *Teach-ins*, pp. 204–5.

46 CNVA Speak-Out: Lens, *Unrepentant Radical*, pp. 299–301.

47 "[We] realized": Sale, *SDS*, p. 221.

47 "the seventh war from now": Ferber and Lynd, *The Resistance*, p. 34.

47 ERAP vs. antiwar organizing: Carl Oglesby, Remarks to the Ethical Society of Boston, February 7, 1982.

58 "we knew we had to respond": Lynd, *We Won't Go*, p. 37.

60 "Sex and Caste: A Kind of Memo": Evans, *Personal Politics*, p. 235.

60 "SNCC Position Paper (Women in the Movement)": ibid., p. 233.

62 "I had been quite disturbed": Ferber and Lynd, *The Resistance*, p. 26.

63 Rusk's "antenna": New York *Times*, November 16, 1965.

63 NCC meeting: Halstead, *Out Now!* pp. 104ff.

64 Telegram to Ho: New York *Times*, October 29, 1965.

65 "We are here to protest": Carl Oglesby, "Trapped in a System," in Teodori, *The New Left*, pp. 182–88.

67 McNamara memorandum: *The Pentagon Papers*, 4:33.

67 Rusk message: *The Pentagon Papers*, 4:40.

1966: BECALMED IN A SEA OF UNCERTAINTY

69 "We believe": SNCC: statement on Vietnam War, January 6, 1966, in Teodori, *The New Left*, pp. 251–52.

70 The Fourteen Points: Cooper, *The Lost Crusade*, pp. 293–94, gives the entire "text."

72 "it does not": the Bundy letter is quoted in full in Menashe and Radosh, *Teach-ins*, p. 147.

72 Exchange between Senator Morse and General Taylor: *The Vietnam Hearings* (New York: Random House [Vintage], 1966), p. 187.

73 "This is Ho Chi Minh's war": ibid., p. 52.

74 Exchange between Senator Fulbright and General Taylor: ibid., pp. 221–22.

76 If General Taylor had misled: ibid., p. 173.

76 Secretary McNamara had just reported: *The Pentagon Papers*, 4:622.

76 "the picture of a determined United States": *The Vietnam Hearings*, p. 211.

77 Bundy's influential memorandum: *The Pentagon Papers*, 3:687–691.

78 "There is one grave weakness": *The Pentagon Papers*, 3:311.

78 James Peck of the War Resisters League: Halstead, *Out Now!* p. 138.

78 a marked copy of Bruce Catton's: Schlesinger, *Robert Kennedy and His Times*, p. 792.

79 "so you can burn yourself": New York *Times*, March 26, 1966.

79 "Kill Them!": *Time*, April 8, 1966.

80 in Chicago, SANE: Lens, *Unrepentant Radical*, p. 308.

80 "A wilderness of warmed-over": *Studies on the Left*, January–February 1966, p. 54; cited in Halstead, *Out Now!* p. 146.

81 It was Lyttle: authors' interview.

82 Barry Bondhus, a young: Francine du Plessix Gray, "The Ultra-Resistance," in *Trials of the Resistance*

(New York: A New York Review Book, 1970), p. 125.

83 Speaking from Washington: New York *Times,* May 18, 1966.

83 On the day before: New York *Times,* May 16, 1966.

84 "The United States should never": cited from Scheer's campaign literature in Powers, *The War at Home,* p. 126.

84 (he called Cohelan a "liberal fink"): *VDC News,* January 28, 1966; cited in Halstead, *Out Now!* p. 157.

84 "Professional non-students": Powers, *The War at Home,* p. 125.

84 "Even those antiwar people": *Newsweek,* September 26, 1966.

86 "Your daddy may go down in history": New York *Times,* May 5, 1967.

86 It was, according to the authors: *The Pentagon Papers,* 4:107.

87 "I am bound to say that": ibid., 4:78.

87 "most important issue of the sixties": Douglas, *The Court Years,* p. 152.

87 "We have decided to take a stand": *The Fort Hood Three* (New York: Fort Hood Three Defense Committee, 1966), pp. 9–11, cited in Halstead, *Out Now!* pp. 177–78.

87 To call the treatment of this: Douglas, *The Court Years,* p. 55.

88 "Spirit of Nuremberg": Dellinger, *Revolutionary Nonviolence,* p. 281.

88 "There is no decision": New York *Times,* June 27, 1966.

88 "undiminished flow": *The Pentagon Papers,* 4:110–11.

88 a team of distinguished outside experts: Leaders of the team were Dr. George Kistiakowsky (Harvard), Dr. Karl Kaysen (Harvard), Dr. Jerome Wiesner (MIT), and Dr. Jerrold Zacharias (MIT). Their project, the Jason Summer Study, and its summary finds are described in *The Pentagon Papers,* 4:114–22.

88 In 1966 over $1 billion: see "1966 Summary," in *The Pentagon Papers,* 4:136.

88 a shovel in the hands: New York *Times,* June 28, 1966.

89 Lens was sorely tempted: Lens, *Unrepentant Radical,* pp. 302–4.

92 "I have one more problem": Halber-stam, *The Best and the Brightest,* p. 641.

93 "may the Good Lord look over you": Sidey, *A Very Personal Presidency,* p. 150.

94 A very small protest: the account here relies on the *Harvard Crimson,* November 8, 1966.

96 the other of the two questions: Salisbury, *Without Fear or Favor,* pp. 57–58.

96 "considering the possibility": *The Pentagon Papers,* 2:597.

96 Some suggest that his son's: Salisbury, *Without Fear or Favor,* p. 58.

98 "Look what you got me into": Halstead, *Out Now!* p. 267.

1967: "To Break the Betrayal of My Own Silences"

101 "Mr. Johnson has stated": Robinson, *Abraham Went Out,* p. 218.

108 "Do we love the war on poverty": Miller, *Martin Luther King, Jr.,* p. 238.

108 "to break the betrayal": *Declaration of Independence from the War in Vietnam,* in A. J. Muste Memorial Institute Essay Series (War Resisters League); see also *Ramparts,* May 1967.

111 "We're going to get left": *WIN Magazine,* April 7, 1967.

112 "A Call to Burn Draft Cards": Lynd, *We Won't Go,* pp. 216–17.

114 "That night I hardly slept": ibid., pp. 220–21.

114 "For me, the burning": ibid., p. 225.

116 South Vietnam peace movement: New York *Times,* May 17, 1967.

116 "Future Actions in Vietnam": *The Pentagon Papers,* Quadrangle ed., pp. 589–92.

118 Gregory Calvert interview: New York *Times,* May 7, 1967.

119 "young Americans who worked": Sale, *SDS,* pp. 359–60.

1967: The Pentagon: Gandhi and Guerrilla

123 "I no longer believe": New York *Times,* September 5, 1967.

126 "When a President": Chester, Hodg-

son, and Page, *An American Melodrama,* pp. 58–59.

126 Katzenbach testimony: New York *Times,* August 18, 1967.

127 McCarthy announcement: Richard Stout, *People* (New York: Harper & Row, 1970), pp. 116–17.

127 "a lot of young people": Boston *Globe,* March 17, 1980.

128 NCNP meeting: *The New Yorker,* September 23, 1967; *The Nation,* September 25, 1967; New York *Times,* September 24, 1967.

129 "A Call to Resist": *The New Republic,* October 7, 1967.

130 Bratislava meeting: ibid.

134 "the 13,000 Americans who died": Boston *Globe,* October 17, 1967.

135 "McDonough had to ask": Bloom, *Dr. Spock,* pp. 287–88.

136 "SDS regrets": Halstead, *Out Now!* p. 311.

139 "largest mass draft card burning": Ferber and Lynd, *The Resistance,* p. 136.

140 "My name is Gary Rader": *Liberation,* November 1967.

142 Lausche's statement: New York *Times,* November 29, 1967.

144 McNamara testimony: Don Oberdorfer, *Tet!* (New York: Avon Books, 1972), pp. 113–14.

144 McNamara memorandum: ibid., p. 115.

145 "Success Offensive": ibid., pp. 101–4.

148 Ho's New Years greetings: New York *Times,* December 31, 1967.

1968: THE FULCRUM YEAR

149 "The Government is not likely": New York *Times,* December 1, 1967.

152 "In the final analysis": New York *Times,* November 27, 1966.

152 "Who won and who lost": Don Oberdorfer, *Tet!* (New York: Avon Books, 1972), pp. 268–69.

156 "suicidal escalation": New York *Times,* March 11, 1968.

157 "this is not the kind": Halstead, *Out Now!* p. 360.

159 "I accepted it": "Bill Moyers' Journal," March 6, 1981.

159 "I sat in a tank": ibid., March 6, 1981.

160 On the Wise Men, see Schandler, *The Unmaking of a President.*

167 "The goal written": *Ramparts,* June 15, 1968.

169 "Thou shalt not": New York *Times,* April 28, 1968.

170 "the shouters and jumpers": New York *Times,* June 9, 1968.

173 "crimes against peace": Bannan and Bannan, *Law, Morality, and Vietnam,* p. 202.

1968: CHICAGO: "THE WHOLE WORLD IS WATCHING!"

177 "Is McCarthy the pay-off": Oglesby, "An Open Letter to McCarthy Supporters." A detailed account of the 1968 Democratic National Convention can be found in Walker, *Rights in Conflict;* Chester, Hodgson, and Page, *An American Melodrama;* White, *The Making of the President, 1968;* and Viorst, *Fire in the Streets.*

178 "Our plan began to founder": Dellinger, *More Power than We Know,* p. 128.

180 "Our goal": New York *Times,* August 18, 1968.

180 "If they want blood": New York *Times,* August 30, 1968.

190 "sweet young kid": Dellinger, *More Power than We Know,* p. 70.

190 "This city and the military machine": Hayden, *Rebellion and Repression,* p. 163.

191 "the thing I did not want": ibid., p. 164.

194 "The police were angry": Walker, *Rights in Conflict,* p. 256.

199 "that's our crime": Hayden, *Rebellion and Repression,* p. 76.

200 "Chicago, I think": New York *Times,* August 24, 1969.

201 "There's coming a time": New York *Times,* August 31, 1968.

201 "mean and ugly sound": New York *Times,* September 22, 1968.

202 Hatfield article: New York *Times,* September 29, 1968.

204 "The truth is": Hayden, *Rebellion and Repression,* p. 13.

204 "I believe that violence": ibid., pp. 72–73.

205 Bundy statement: New York *Times,* October 13, 1968.

206 "In 1966": *Liberation,* January 1971.

1969: "THE SHABBIEST WEAPON"

209 "fade from the national agenda": New York *Times,* January 14, 1969.

209 "A small, hard core of the country's": New York *Times,* January 20, 1969.

210 but at least one: Dellinger, *More Power than We Know,* p. 67.

210 a mood "dampened by the prospect": New York *Times,* January 20, 1969.

210 "the radical rabbit": Bloom, *Dr. Spock,* p. 258.

215 "To maintain a radical antiwar": *Mobilizer* #1, no. 1 (December 1966); cited in Halstead, *Out Now!* p. 225.

215 Several assembled that Sunday: see Halstead, *Out Now!* pp. 450–51.

215 "Is there any chance": Dellinger, *More Power than We Know,* p. 122.

215 "I must say that": Lens, *Unrepentant Radical,* p. 318.

217 "I'm the one man": Haldeman, *The Ends of Power,* pp. 82–83.

217 "The long, dark night": Nixon at the Republican National Convention, 1968.

217 In March 1959, Ellsberg: the story is told in Salisbury, *Without Fear or Favor,* pp. 53–55.

217 When William Beecher: New York *Times,* May 9, 1969.

218 "the problem of the antiwar demonstrators": Nixon, *RN,* p. 382.

219 One brigadier general of the U.S. Army: New York *Times,* January 18, 1971.

220 Henry Kissinger in his tale of: Kissinger, *White House Years,* pp. 982–83.

220 "what dream she is referring to": New York *Times,* January 18, 1971.

221 "I am making the affidavit": Robert Hardy, "Affidavit," in Cowan, Egleson, and Hentoff, *State Secrets,* pp. 222–27.

222 "This is an area not within": *Report to the President by the Commission on C.I.A. Activities,* p. 134.

222 "President Nixon didn't pull any

punches": Haldeman, *The Ends of Power,* p. 108.

223 "enhance the paranoia endemic": Donner, *The Age of Surveillance,* p. 178.

223 "Do you know anything about any activity": ibid., p. 277.

223 "had not only been carried out": Nixon, *RN,* p. 475.

224 "The shabbiest weapon": Mitford, *The Trial of Doctor Spock,* p. 69.

224 "My understanding of": cited from the court transcript by Bannan and Bannan, *Law, Morality, and Vietnam,* p. 99.

225 "If I am brought to trial": David Mitchell, "What Is Criminal," in Lynd, *We Won't Go,* p. 99.

225 "to make sure that they end up": ibid., p. 98.

225 Captain Howard Levy, M.D.: see Andrew Kopkind, "Captain Levy I—Doctor's Plot" and "The Trial of Captain Levy II," in *Trials of the Resistance* (New York: A New York Review Book, 1970), pp. 14–42.

226 "I think we have to follow our consciences" interview with Dorothy Day, in Bannan and Bannan, *Law, Morality, and Vietnam,* p. 169.

227 Miller was the first to challenge: Miller's case is considered by Bannan and Bannan, *Law, Morality, and Vietnam,* pp. 40–62.

227 Robert Luftig was one: see interview with Luftig, "Suing the Army," in Lynd, *We Won't Go,* pp. 168–80.

228 "It is difficult to think of an area": *Luftig v. McNamara,* 373 F 2d 665–66 (1966); cited in Bannan and Bannan, *Law, Morality, and Vietnam,* p. 77.

228 Stewart, in joining the dissent: the questions raised are from the trial transcript, ibid., p. 82.

230 "I have the impression that": James Forest, "Philip Berrigan, Disturber of Sleep," in Casey and Nobile, *The Berrigans,* p. 166.

230 "Meeting Phil was not like meeting a priest": Francine du Plessix Gray, "Phil Berrigan in Hawaii," ibid., p. 155.

230 "I was at the time very far": Daniel Berrigan, *No Bars to Manhood,* p. 23.

231 "those damn Catholics": Charles

Meconis, *With Clumsy Grace* (New York: Continuum, 1979), p. 173 n.

231 "more like an East Village freak": William Kunstler, "Some Thoughts About the Berrigans et al," in Halpert and Murray, *Witness of the Berrigans*, p. 167.

232 "Has anyone been arrested?": Francine du Plessix Gray, *Divine Disobedience* (New York: Random House [Vintage], 1971), p. 104.

232 "Just like a priest!": James Forest, "Daniel Berrigan: The Poet and Prophet as Priest," in Halpert and Murray, *Witness of the Berrigans*, p. 86.

232 "Protest: Against whom or what?" Thomas Merton, *The Nonviolent Alternative*, ed. Gordon C. Zahn (New York: Farrar, Straus, 1980), pp. 259–60.

232 Thomas Cornell was one of those present: Charles Meconis cites from interview with Cornell in *With Clumsy Grace*, p. 9.

233 "I smelled, for the first time": Daniel Berrigan, *No Bars to Manhood*, p. 26.

234 "We are not trying the United Fruit Company": unless otherwise noted, quotes from the trial come from Daniel Berrigan's dramatization of the trial, *The Trial of the Catonsville Nine*. Berrigan's Introduction describes changes from the original words spoken as "minute."

234 "I saw suddenly": cited from the court transcript in Bannan and Bannan, *Law, Morality, and Vietnam*, p. 134.

234 "The jury are not the representatives": cited from the court transcript, ibid., p. 144.

235 "the Berrigans and the rest of the": New York *Times*, February 19, 1971.

235 "Since Catonsville, I have gone": cited in Halpert and Murray, *Witness of the Berrigans*, pp. 170–71.

236 "Devastated, knocked down": quoted in Meconis, *With Clumsy Grace*, p. 98.

236 "the initial reaction of most": Douglas Dowd, "The Strengths and Limits of Resistance," in Halpert

and Murray, *Witness of the Berrigans*, pp. 176–78.

236 "scaling down from actions": "A Conversation With Staughton Lynd," ibid., p. 198.

236 "In the face": quoted by Forest in "Philip Berrigan, Disturber of Sleep," in Casey and Nobile, *The Berrigans*, p. 177.

236 a similarly airy performance: Gray, *Divine Disobedience*, pp. 50–58.

237 "The Peace Movement may be escalating": Merton, *The Nonviolent Alternative*, p. 230.

237 "The New Left suffers from": Gray, *Divine Disobedience*, p. 140.

237 Adams condemned attacks in Boston: see Maier, *The Old Revolutionaries*, pp. 26–32, for Adams's views on violence.

237 "assigned to the junk-heap of history": Sale, *SDS*, p. 496.

238 One survey, based on a study: survey conducted by Urban Research Corporation of Chicago; reported in New York *Times*, January 14, 1970.

239 Nevertheless Harvard was not: for a complete recounting of the events at Harvard in the spring of 1969 see Eichel et al., *The Harvard Strike*.

240 "There is only one enemy": ibid., pp. 85–86.

241 "The streets of our country": ibid., pp. 324–25.

242 "full equivalent of a plea of guilty": This is the assessment of the judge who sentenced Agnew. The actual plea was *nolo contendere*.

242 "time has come for an end to": speech before the Detroit Bar Association, May 1, 1969.

242 The speech had been six weeks: New York *Times*, June 1, 1969.

242 "During the first months of": Nixon, *RN*, p. 399.

242 The Washington *Post*, in a page-one: Washington *Post*, April 22, 1969.

243 The letter to President Nixon: *Congressional Record*, vol. 115, no. 71, May 1, 1969.

244 Kissinger's reaction to the meeting: *Look*, August 8, 1969.

246 "for America, for the Congress": cited in Maier, *The Old Revolutionaries*, p. 19.

246 "A national call for a deadline strike": from copy in authors' file.

246 *"Felix qui cautus":* cited in Maier, *The Old Revolutionaries,* p. 20.

1969: VIETNAM MORATORIUM DAY

249 "You will be better advised": cited in Harris, *Justice,* p. 206.

249 "As soon as we're notified of": ibid., pp. 163–64.

250 "His function in the various": Hersh, *The Price of Power,* pp. 76–77.

250 "I left the meeting": Kalb and Kalb, *Kissinger,* p. 130.

250 Kissinger was reported: New York *Times,* May 6, 1969.

250 "and if we haven't ended the war": Kalb and Kalb, *Kissinger,* p. 120.

250 Russell Baker of the New York *Times:* New York *Times,* September 30, 1969.

251 The ninth and last annual convention of SDS: the account here relies on Sale, *SDS,* pp. 557–79; Andrew Kopkind, "The Real SDS Stands Up," *Hard Times,* June 1969; Viorst, *Fire in the Streets,* pp. 487–91; and interview with Jared Israel, a participant.

252 "But this loss is primarily": Oglesby, "Notes on a Decade Ready for the Dustbin."

254 Al Haber, a founder: the pamphlet, *The New Left Methodology: Nonexclusionism, Participatory Democracy, and Direct Action,* is reprinted in Teodori, *The New Left,* pp. 218–28.

256 SWP's Fred Halstead: Halstead, *Out Now!* pp. 452–53.

256 The roster of the steering committee: listed ibid., p. 467 n. 19.

257 Rudd's speech: *New Left Notes,* August 23, 1969.

257 although Halstead asserts: Halstead, *Out Now!* p. 474.

258 the committee's "high-handedness": ibid., p. 473.

258 "I decided to 'go for broke' ": Nixon, *RN,* p. 393.

259 "my feeling that unless": ibid., p. 393.

259 The secret scheme: Hersh, *The Price of Power,* pp. 120–26.

259 "I decided to set November 1": Nixon, *RN,* p. 393.

259 "measures of great consequence": ibid., p. 394.

259 Ho Chi Minh's reply: ibid., p. 397.

260 "not a formula for": ibid., p. 395.

261 The editorial writers: New York *Times,* August 18, 1969.

261 The SDS/Weatherman appraisal: *New Left Notes,* August 23, 1969; cited in Jacobs, *Weatherman,* p. 176.

261 "the twice-yearly Sunday afternoon": Jacobs, ibid., p. 180.

261 "This is an awful small group": Tom Thomas, "The Second Battle of Chicago," ibid., p. 201.

261 "People have been saying": ibid., p. 201.

262 Only sixty-eight of the nearly: Sale, *SDS,* p. 608.

262 "anarchistic, opportunistic": Tom Thomas, "Second Battle of Chicago," in Jacobs, *Weatherman,* p. 207.

262 "a motherfucking masochist": Sale, *SDS,* p. 602.

262 "Dig it, first they killed": ibid., p. 628.

262 "We're against all that's 'good and decent' ": ibid., p. 628.

262 "Anyone who opposes us": Karnow, *Vietnam,* p. 634.

267 "I understand that there has been": New York *Times,* September 27, 1969.

268 The next day: Nixon, *RN,* p. 399.

268 "it is becoming more obvious": Washington *Post,* October 7, 1969.

270 the wife of the president of Nixon's alma mater: the New York *Times,* October 16, 1969.

271 "This province began it": cited in Howard Mumford Jones and Bessie Zaban Jones, eds. *The Many Voices of Boston* (Boston: Atlantic Monthly Press, 1975), p. 99.

272 "This fall large sections": Nixon, *RN,* p. 401.

273 "has on its hands the blood of": ibid., p. 402.

273 "I thought about the irony": ibid., p. 403.

1969: MOBILIZATION: "GIVE PEACE A CHANCE"

275 "I felt like throwing up": Hersh, *The Price of Power*, p. 131.

277 "A spirit of national masochism": New York *Times*, October 20, 1969.

278 "Why the hell don't you ask": Lens, *Unrepentant Radical*, p. 356.

278 "The Moratorium kids": New York *Times*, November 30, 1969.

279 "I lifted [it]": Safire, *Before the Fall*, p. 50.

280 "What the American people have been saying": New York *Times*, August 21, 1969.

280 "Very few speeches": Nixon, *RN*, p. 409.

280 "public support I needed": ibid., pp. 410–11.

288 "usual four or five": Lens, *Unrepentant Radical*, p. 361.

288 "bastion of counter-revolution": ibid., p. 354.

288 "the poor and hungry": Lens, *Unrepentant Radical*, p. 354.

291 "if we gave them": New York *Times*, November 18, 1969.

292 "Looking out the Justice Department": New York *Times*, November 22, 1969.

1970: WAR ON THE HOME FRONT

301 "Unfortunately": New York *Times*, January 7, 1970.

301 "If acts such as those": ibid.

304 "had an obligation": Hayden, *Trial*, p. 73.

306 "If it takes a bloodbath": Boston *Globe*, April 9, 1970.

306 "He never found the language": Henry Kissinger, *Vietnam* (PBS), December 13, 1983.

306 "And you stated": Clavir and Spitzer, *The Conspiracy Trial*, p. 490.

307 "Bobby Seale's life": Dellinger, *More Power than We Know*, p. 163.

307 "we were a myth": Hayden, *Trial*, p. 84.

308 "my jury will be": New York *Times*, February 21, 1970.

315 "for the right of people": New York *Times*, December 23, 1970.

317 "those Senators think": Morris, *Uncertain Greatness*, p. 174.

318 "It is a difficult": New York *Times*, May 3, 1970.

318 "It is not a question": New York *Times*, May 2, 1970.

318 "I want to take out": Nixon, *RN*, p. 454.

319 "You know, you see these bums": New York *Times*, May 2, 1970.

321 "Today, our young people": Hickel, *Who Owns America?* p. 227.

322 "sitting on the grass": *The Village Voice*, June 14, 1970.

322 He described himself: *RN*, pp. 457, 459.

323 "Searchlight": Safire, *Before the Fall*, p. 202.

324 "the government planned": Lyttle, *May Ninth*, pp. 10–11.

325 "To deal with": Gulley, *Breaking Cover*, pp. 166–67.

325 "WE THE UNDERSIGNED": New York *Times*, May 10, 1970.

325 "We knew that a massive": Lyttle, *May Ninth*, pp. 12–13.

325 "We could not": New York *Times*, May 10, 1970.

328 "It was a giant": Lyttle, *May Ninth*, p. 9.

329 Petition to Secretary of State Rogers: New York *Times*, May 9, 1970.

329 "it contributed to heating up": ibid.

329 "Neither by direct statement": New York *Times*, May 10, 1970.

330 "one man alone holds": New York *Times*, May 5, 1970.

332 "Every Senator": New York *Times*, September 2, 1970.

333 "however this dangerous adventure": Halstead, *Out Now!* p. 546.

335 "It would be": John Elderkin et al., eds., *After Dinner Speeches at the Lotos Club* (New York, 1911), pp. 14–15; quoted in Morison, Merk, and Freidel, *Dissent in Three American Wars*, p. 95.

338 "speculation at the time": Gulley, *Breaking Cover*, p. 198.

338 "I could not resist": Nixon, *RN*, p. 492.

338 "Those who carry": ibid., p. 493.

339 "The terrorists": ibid., p. 493.

339 "In May 1970": *The Report of the President's Commission on Campus Unrest*, p. 46.

339 "nothing is more important": ibid., p. 9.

339 "rests with the President": ibid., p. 231.

340 "Vote for a peace candidate": New York *Times*, May 10, 1970.

341 "We got that": Hickel, *Who Owns America?* p. 251.

341 "willingness to employ": Nelson and Ostrow, *The FBI and the Berrigans*, pp. 17–18.

1971: THE WINTER SOLDIERS

343 "the antiwar movement": *Liberation*, January 1971.

347 "I'll tell you": Boston *Globe*, February 11, 1971.

348 "Were I to remain silent": New York *Times*, March 31, 1971.

349 "After all the years": New York *Times*, March 30, 1971.

351 "aggression, civilian bombardment": Duffet, *Against the Crime of Silence*, p. 8.

351 "Has the United States": ibid., p. 48.

351 "Have prisoners of war": ibid., no page number.

352 "If certain acts": ibid., pp. xxiii–xxiv.

354 "independent citizens commission": New York *Times*, December 31, 1971.

354 "The purpose of the hearings": Vietnam Veterans Against the War, *The Winter Soldier Investigation*, p. xiv.

355 "With the conviction": New York *Times*, April 23, 1971.

355 Dewey Canyon III: Kerry and VVAW, *The New Soldier*.

357 "In our opinion": ibid., pp. 12ff.

359 Platform incident: Halstead, *Out Now!* p. 611.

360 May Day Tribe visit to Senate Foreign Relations Committee: New York *Times*, April 29, 1971.

365 GI antiwar movement: Cortright, *Soldiers in Revolt*.

366 "Man, the war stinks": New York *Times*, April 13, 1972.

366 "You must be out": *Time*, April 5, 1971.

366 "For every one": Cortright, *Soldiers in Revolt*, pp. 46–47.

367 "the most complete study": *The Pentagon Papers*, pp. x–xi.

367 "No one who reads": ibid., p. xi. On the Pentagon Papers and the New York *Times*, see Salisbury, *Without Fear or Favor*.

369 Labor leaders' mediation between NPAC and PCPJ: Halstead, *Out Now!* pp. 646ff.

370 "Evict Nixon" campaign: New York *Times*, November 7, 1971.

372 "electronic battlefield": New York *Times*, December 20, 1971.

373 "Every day at the mention": Rader, *Blood Dues*, p. 89.

373 "When that war": ibid., p. 98.

374 "The reason we chose": New York *Times*, December 29, 1971.

1972: "PEACE IS AT HAND"

378 Harrisburg 7: Charles Meconis, *With Clumsy Grace* (New York: Continuum, 1979); Nelson and Ostrow, *The FBI and the Berrigans*.

382 "The trouble with demonstrations": New York *Times*, April 22, 1972.

384 *National Security Study Memorandum No. 1:* Hersh, *The Price of Power*.

385 Attack on Ellsberg: ibid., pp. 520–21; Lukas, *Night-Mare*, pp. 195–96.

385 "Commandeering civilian vehicles": New York *Times*, May 2, 1972.

388 "Ring around Congress": WSP *Memo* #2, no. 4; Halstead, *Out Now!* pp. 680–84.

388 Ramsey Clark in North Vietnam: *Life*, August 25, 1972.

389 Watergate break-in: Wise, *The American Police State;* Lukas, *Night-Mare*.

394 "It had certainly been": Halstead, *Out Now!* p. 690.

395 Beecher bombing story: Morris, "Kissinger and the Media"; idem, *Uncertain Greatness*.

1973–75: "THE WAR IS OVER!"

403 Paris Agreement on Vietnam peace: New York *Times*, January 25, 1973.

404 "there can't be any peace": New York *Times*, February 7, 1973.

404 "The peace movement has won": ibid.

405 "If there were an honest": Chomsky, *Towards a New Cold War*, p. 124.

405 Chomsky-Luria letter: New York *Times*, February 12, 1973.

407 "The White House was continually": *Vietnam* (PBS), December 6, 1983.

408 *"Third*—and perhaps": Haldeman, *The Ends of Power*, p. 284.

408 "But for the collapse": Kissinger, *White House Years*, p. 1470.

412 Kent State rally: *Indochina Focal Point* #1, no. 19 (May 16–31, 1974).

413 VVAW rally: *Indochina Focal Point* #1, no. 22 (July 15–31, 1974).

414 On clemency and amnesty: Baskir, *Chance and Circumstance*.

415 "I respect those": Boston *Globe*, December 4, 1983.

416 "Incredibly": *Indochina Focal Point* #2, no. 9 (January 29–February 19, 1975).

Bibliographical Note

The single most important resource for the authors in writing this book has been interviews with men and women who helped to make the antiwar movement happen. All, except those who requested anonymity, are listed below. Unless specifically noted as taken from their own writings or from other sources, all quotations attributed in the text to the individuals listed below come from interviews with the authors.

For general information on the events of the years covered, the authors have relied upon dispatches in the daily press, notably the New York *Times* and the Washington *Post*. Fred Halstead's *Out Now!* is a history of the antiwar movement told in great detail by a member of the Socialist Workers Party who was an active member of the Movement. Kirkpatrick Sale's *SDS* is the most comprehensive of the several accounts of Students for a Democratic Society. Charles Meconis's *With Clumsy Grace* is a valuable history of the Catholic Left.

Interviews with: Norma Becker, Sam Brown, Noam Chomsky, the Reverend William Sloane Coffin, Thomas Cornell, Rennie Davis, David Dellinger, Ralph DiGia, Ann Froines, Jerome Grossman, William Hanley, David Hawk, Tom Hayden, Jared Israel, Charles Knight, Katherine Knight, Sidney Lens, Jennifer Littlefield, Lawrence Lowenstein, Bradford Lyttle, David McReynolds, Stewart Meacham, Carl Oglesby, Louise Peck, Sidney Peck, Benjamin Spock, M.D., Beverly Sterner, Cora Weiss, Gordon Zahn, and Howard Zinn.

Selected Bibliography

Arlen, Michael J. *Living-Room War.* New York: Viking Press, 1969.

Ashmore, Harry S., and William C. Baggs. *Mission to Hanoi.* New York: Putnam, 1968.

Astor, Gerald. "Henry Kissinger: Strategist in the White House Basement," *Look,* August 8, 1969.

Austin, Anthony. *The President's War.* New York: Lippincott, 1971.

Avorn, Jerry L., and members of the staff of the *Columbia Daily Spectator. Up Against the Ivy Wall.* New York: Atheneum, 1968.

Ball, George W. *The Past Has Another Pattern.* New York: Norton, 1982.

Bannan, John F., and Rosemary S. Bannan. *Law, Morality, and Vietnam.* Bloomington, Ind.: Indiana University Press, 1974.

Baskir, Lawrence M. *Chance and Circumstance.* New York: Knopf, 1978.

Becker, Theodore L., *Political Trials.* Indianapolis: Bobbs-Merrill, 1971.

Berrigan, Daniel. *No Bars to Manhood.* Garden City, N.Y.: Doubleday, 1970.

————. *The Trial of the Catonsville Nine.* Boston: Beacon Press, 1970.

Berrigan, Philip. *Prison Journals of a Priest Revolutionary.* New York: Ballantine Books, 1970.

Bloom, Lynn Z. *Doctor Spock.* Indianapolis: Bobbs-Merrill, 1972.

Braestrup, Peter. *Big Story* (abridged edition). New Haven, Conn.: Yale University Press, 1983.

Carling, Francis. *Move Over.* New York: Sheed & Ward, 1969.

Casey, William Van Etten, and Philip Nobile, eds. *The Berrigans.* New York: Praeger, 1971.

Caute, David. *The Great Fear.* New York: Simon & Schuster, 1978.

Charlton, Michael, and Anthony Moncrieff. *Many Reasons Why.* New York: Farrar, Straus (Hill & Wang), 1978.

Chester, Lewis, Godfrey Hodgson, and Bruce Page. *An American Melodrama.* New York: Viking, 1969.

Chomsky, Noam. *American Power and the New Mandarins.* New York: Pantheon Books, 1969.

————. *Towards a New Cold War.* New York: Pantheon Books, 1982.

————, Ronald Dworkin, et al. *Trials of the Resistance.* New York: Random House, 1970.

Clavir, Judy, and John Spitzer, eds. *The Conspiracy Trial.* Indianapolis: Bobbs-Merrill, 1970.

Cohen, Mitchell, and Dennis Hale, eds. *The New Student Left.* Boston: Beacon Press, 1967.

Cook, Fred J. *The Nightmare Decade.* New York: Random House, 1971.

Cooney, Robert, and Helen Michalowski. *The Power of the People.* Culver City, Calif.: Peace Press, 1977.

Cooper, Chester L. *The Lost Crusade.* New York: Dodd, Mead, 1970.

Cortright, David. *Soldiers in Revolt.* Garden City, N.Y.: Doubleday (Anchor Press), 1975.

Cowan, Paul, Nick Egleson, and Nat Hentoff with Barbara Herbert and Robert Wall. *State Secrets.* New York: Holt, Rinehart, 1974.

Dellinger, David. *More Power than We Know.* Garden City, N.Y.: Doubleday (Anchor Press), 1975.

———. *Revolutionary Nonviolence.* Indianapolis: Bobbs-Merrill, 1970.

Donner, Frank J. *The Age of Surveillance.* New York: Knopf, 1980.

Douglas, William O. *The Court Years.* New York: Random House (Vintage), 1980.

Drinan, Robert F., S.J. *Vietnam and Armageddon.* New York: Sheed & Ward, 1970.

Duffett, John, ed. *Against the Crime of Silence.* New York: Simon & Schuster (Touchstone-Clarion), 1970.

Duncanson, Dennis J. *Government and Revolution in Vietnam.* New York: Oxford University Press, 1968.

Ehrlichman, John. *Witness to Power.* New York: Simon & Schuster, 1982.

Eichel, Lawrence, Kenneth W. Jost, Robert D. Luskin, and Richard M. Neustadt. *The Harvard Strike.* Boston: Houghton Mifflin, 1970.

Ellsberg, Daniel. *Papers on the War.* New York: Simon & Schuster, 1972.

Emerson, Gloria. *Winners and Losers.* New York: Harcourt Brace (Harvest), 1976.

Epstein, Jason. *The Great Conspiracy Trial.* New York: Random House, 1970.

Evans, Sara. *Personal Politics.* New York: Random House (Vintage), 1979.

Falk, Richard A., chairman, and John H. E. Fried, rapporteur. The Consultative Council of the Lawyers Committee on American Policy Towards Vietnam. *Vietnam and International Law.* Flanders, N.J.: O'Hare, 1967.

Fall, Bernard B. *Last Reflections on a War.* Garden City, N.Y.: Doubleday, 1967.

Ferber, Michael, and Staughton Lynd. *The Resistance.* Boston: Beacon Press, 1971.

Finn, James. *Protest.* New York: Vintage Books, 1967.

Fitzgerald, Frances. *Fire in the Lake.* New York: Random House (Vintage), 1972.

Fortas, Abe. *Concerning Dissent and Civil Disobedience.* New York: New American Library (Signet), 1968.

Garrow, David J. *The FBI and Martin Luther King, Jr.* New York: Norton, 1981.

Gelb, Leslie H., with Richard K. Betts. *The Irony of Vietnam.* Washington, D.C.: Brookings, 1979.

Gitlin, Todd. *The Whole World Is Watching.* Berkeley: University of California Press, 1980.

Goldman, Eric F. *The Tragedy of Lyndon Johnson.* New York: Dell, 1974.

Goodman, Mitchell, ed. *The Movement Toward a New America.* New York: Knopf (Pilgrim Press), 1970.

Guiles, Fred Lawrence. *Jane Fonda.* New York: Pinnacle Books, 1981.

Gulley, Bill, with Mary Ellen Reese. *Breaking Cover.* New York: Simon & Schuster, 1970.

Halberstam, David. *The Best and the Brightest.* New York: Random House, 1972.

Haldeman, H. R., with Joseph DiMona. *The Ends of Power.* Dell, 1978.

Halpert, Stephen, and Tom Murray, eds. *Witness of the Berrigans.* Garden City, N.Y.: Doubleday, 1972.

Halstead, Fred. *Out Now!* New York: Monad Press, 1978.

Harris, Richard. *Justice.* New York: Dutton, 1970.

Hayden, Tom. *Rebellion and Repression.* New York: Meridian Books, 1969.

———. *Trial.* New York: Holt, Rinehart, 1970.

Hentoff, Nat. *Peace Agitator.* New York: Macmillan, 1963.

Hersh, Seymour M. *Cover-Up.* New York: Random House, 1972.

———. *My Lai 4.* New York: Random House, 1970.

———. *The Price of Power.* New York: Summit Books, 1983.

Hickel, Walter J. *Who Owns America?* New York: Paperback Library, 1971.

Hoffman, Abbie. *Revolution for the Hell of It.* New York: Dial Press, 1968.

———. *Soon to Be a Major Motion Picture.* New York: Berkley Books, 1980.

Hoopes, Townsend. *The Limits of Intervention.* New York: McKay, 1969.

Hurwitz, Ken. *Marching Nowhere.* New York: Norton, 1971.

Jacobs, Harold, ed. *Weatherman.* Berkeley, Calif.: Ramparts Press, 1970.

Kalb, Marvin, and Bernard Kalb. *Kissinger.* Boston: Little, Brown, 1974.

Karnow, Stanley. *Vietnam.* New York: Viking, 1983.

Kearns, Doris. *Lyndon Johnson and the American Dream.* New York: New American Library (Signet), 1976.

Kennan, George F. *Democracy and the Student Left.* Boston: Little, Brown (Atlantic Monthly Press), 1968.

Kerry, John, and Vietnam Veterans Against the War. *The New Soldier.* Edited by David Thorne and George Butler. New York: Macmillan, 1971.

Kiernan, Thomas. *Jane Fonda.* New York: Putnam (Delilah), 1982.

Kissinger, Henry. *White House Years.* Boston: Little, Brown, 1979.

Knightley, Philip. *The First Casualty.* New York: Harcourt Brace (Harvest), 1975.

Knoll, Erwin, and Judith Nies McFadden. *War Crimes and the American Conscience.* New York: Holt, Rinehart, 1970.

Kovic, Ron. *Born on the Fourth of July.* New York: Pocket Books, 1976.

Kraslow, David, and Stuart H. Loory. *The Secret Search for Peace in Vietnam.* New York: Random House (Vintage), 1968.

Krause, Patricia A., ed. *Anatomy of an Undeclared War.* New York: International Universities Press, 1972.

Lacouture, Jean. *Vietnam.* New York: Random House (Vintage), 1966.

Lang, Daniel. *Patriotism Without Flags.* New York: Norton, 1974.

Lens, Sidney. *Unrepentant Radical.* Boston: Beacon Press, 1980.

Lewy, Guenter. *America in Vietnam.* New York: Oxford University Press, 1978.

Lukas, J. Anthony. *Don't Shoot—We Are Your Children!* New York: Random House, 1967.

———. *Night-Mare.* New York: Viking, 1976.

Lynd, Alice, comp., *We Won't Go.* Boston: Beacon Press, 1968.

Lynd, Staughton, ed. *Nonviolence in America.* Indianapolis: Bobbs-Merrill, 1966.

———, and Thomas Hayden. *The Other Side.* New York: New American Library, 1966.

Lynn, Naomi B., and Arthur F. McClure. *The Fulbright Premise.* Lewisburg, Pa.: Bucknell University Press, 1973.

McCarthy, Eugene. *The Year of the People.* Garden City, N.Y.: Doubleday, 1969.

Maclear, Michael. *The Ten Thousand Day War.* New York: St. Martin's Press, 1981.

Magruder, Jeb Stuart. *An American Life.* New York: Atheneum, 1976.

Maier, Pauline. *The Old Revolutionaries.* New York: Random House (Vintage), 1980.

Mailer, Norman. *The Armies of the Night.* New York: New American Library (Signet), 1968.

———. *Miami and the Siege of Chicago.* New York: New American Library (Signet), 1968.

May Ninth. Commentaries by David Gelber, Fred Halstead, Bradford Lyttle, and Arthur Waskow. Midwest Pacifist Publishing, n.d.

Meconis, Charles A. *With Clumsy Grace.* New York: Continuum, 1979.

Menashe, Louis, and Ronald Radosh, eds. *Teach-ins: USA.* New York: Praeger, 1967.

Merton, Thomas. *The Nonviolent Alternative.* Introduced by Gordon C. Zahn. New York: Farrar, Straus, 1980.

Michener, James A. *Kent State.* New York: Random House, 1971.

Middleton, Neil, ed. *The I. F. Stone Weekly Reader.* New York: Random House (Vintage), 1973.

Miller, William D. *Dorothy Day.* San Francisco: Harper & Row, 1982.

Miller, William Robert. *Martin Luther King, Jr.* New York: Weybright & Talley, 1968.

Mitford, Jessica. *The Trial of Dr. Spock.* New York: Knopf, 1969.

Morison, Samuel Eliot, Frederick Merk, and Frank Freidel. *Dissent in Three American Wars.* Cambridge: Harvard University Press, 1970.

Morris, Roger. "Kissinger and the Media: A Separate Peace," *Columbia Journalism Review,* May–June 1974.

———. *Uncertain Greatness.* New York: Harper & Row, 1977.

Nelson, Jack, and Ronald J. Ostrow. *The FBI and the Berrigans.* New York: Coward, McCann, 1972.

Newfield, Jack. *A Prophetic Minority.* New York: New American Library, 1966.

Nixon, Richard. *RN*. New York: Grosset & Dunlap, 1978.

Oglesby, Carl. "An Open Letter to McCarthy Supporters," in Teodori, *The New Left*, pp. 445ff.

———. "Notes on a Decade Ready for the Dustbin," *Liberation*, August–September, 1969.

———, and Richard Shaull. *Containment and Change*. New York: Macmillan, 1967.

Patti, Archimedes L. A. *Why Vietnam?* Berkeley: University of California Press, 1980.

The Pentagon Papers as Published by the New York Times. New York: Quadrangle Books, 1971.

The Pentagon Papers. The Senator Gravel Edition. 4 vols. Boston: Beacon Press, 1971.

The Pentagon Papers. The Senator Gravel Edition, vol. 5. Critical essays edited by Noam Chomsky and Howard Zinn, and an index to volumes 1–4. Boston: Beacon Press, 1972.

Podhoretz, Norman. *Why We Were in Vietnam*. New York: Simon & Schuster, 1982.

Porter, Gareth, ed. *Vietnam*. 2 vols. Pine Plains, N.Y.: Coleman Enterprises, 1979.

Powers, Thomas. *Diana. The Making of a Terrorist*. New York: Bantam Books, 1971.

———. *The War at Home*. New York: Grossman, 1973.

Rader, Dotson. *Blood Dues*. New York: Knopf, 1973.

Raskin, Marcus G., and Bernard B. Fall, eds. *The Viet-Nam Reader*. New York: Random House (Vintage), 1965.

Reeves, Thomas, and Karl Hess. *The End of the Draft*. New York: Random House, 1970.

Reischauer, Edwin O. *Beyond Vietnam*. New York: Vintage Books, 1967.

Report of the National Advisory Commission on Civil Disorders. New York: Bantam Books, 1968.

The Report of the President's Commission on Campus Unrest (William W. Scranton, Chairman). New York: Arno Press, 1970.

Report of the Select Committee to Study Governmental Operations with Respect to Intelligence Activities (United States Senate). 6 Vols. Washington, D.C.: U.S. Government Printing Office, 1975.

Report of the U.S. Congress, House Committee on Armed Services. Special Subcommittee on Intelligence Inquiry into the Alleged Involvement of the C.I.A. in Watergate and Ellsberg Matters. Washington, D.C.: U.S. Government Printing Office, 1973.

Report to the President by the Commission on C.I.A. Activities Within the United States. Washington, D.C.: U.S. Government Printing Office, 1975.

Robinson, Jo Ann Ooiman. *Abraham Went Out*. Philadelphia: Temple University Press, 1981.

Rubin, Jerry. *Do It*. New York: Ballantine Books, 1970.

Safire, William. *Before the Fall*. Garden City, N.Y.: Doubleday, 1975.

Sale, Kirkpatrick. *SDS*. New York: Random House, 1973.

Salisbury, Harrison E. *Behind the Lines—Hanoi*. New York: Bantam Books, 1967.

———. *Without Fear or Favor*. New York: Ballantine Books, 1980.

Schandler, Herbert Y. *The Unmaking of a President*. Princeton, N.J.: Princeton University Press, 1977.

Schell, Jonathan. *The Time of Illusion*. New York: Knopf, 1976.

Schlesinger, Arthur M., Jr. *Robert Kennedy and His Times*. New York: Ballantine Books, 1978.

———. *A Thousand Days*. New York: Fawcett, 1965.

Schoenbrun, David. *Vietnam*. New York: Atheneum, 1968.

Shawcross, William. *Sideshow*. New York: Pocket Books, 1979.

Sidey, Hugh. *A Very Personal Presidency*. New York: Atheneum, 1968.

Skolnick, Jerome H. *The Politics of Protest*. New York: Ballantine Books, 1969.

Stevens, Franklin. *If This Be Treason*. New York: Wyden, 1970.

Stone, I. F. *In a Time of Torment*. New York: Random House (Vintage), 1967.

———. *The Killings at Kent State*. New York: Random House (Vintage), 1971.

Taylor, Telford. *Nuremberg and Vietnam*. New York: Quadrangle Books, 1970.

Teodori, Massimo, ed. *The New Left*. New York: Bobbs-Merrill, 1969.

Vietnam Veterans Against the War. *The Winter Soldier Investigation.* Boston: Beacon Press, 1972.

Viorst, Milton. *Fire in the Streets.* New York: Simon & Schuster (Touchstone Books), 1979.

Walker, Daniel. *Rights in Conflict.* New York: Dutton, 1968.

White, Theodore H. *The Making of the President: 1964.* New York: Atheneum, 1965.

————. *The Making of the President: 1968.* New York: Atheneum, 1969.

————. *The Making of the President: 1972.* New York: Atheneum, 1973.

Wilson, E. Raymond. *Uphill for Peace.* Richmond, Ind.: Friends United Press, 1975.

Wise, David. *The American Police State.* New York: Random House, 1976.

————. *The Politics of Lying.* New York: Random House (Vintage), 1973.

Woodward, Bob, and Scott Armstrong. *The Brethren.* New York: Simon & Schuster, 1979.

Zahn, Gordon C. *War, Conscience, and Dissent.* New York: Hawthorn Books, 1967.

Zinn, Howard. *Disobedience and Democracy.* New York: Random House, 1968.

————. *SNCC.* Boston: Beacon Press, 1964.

————. *Vietnam: The Logic of Withdrawal.* Boston: Beacon Press, 1967.

INDEX

See also Catholic Left; John XXIII; Spellman,
  Francis
Catholic Left
  draft-board raids of, 229–30, 233–37, 287–88,
    310
  end of, 380
  FBI office break-in of, 223
  See also Berrigan, Daniel; Berrigan, Philip;
    Catholic Peace Fellowship; Catholic
    Worker
Catholic Peace Fellowship (CPF), 55, 102, 232,
  236
Catholic Worker, 3–4, 10, 56, 227, 236, 401
  in demonstrations, 12–13, 25, 34, 52
Catholic Worker (publication), 4, 10, 57, 227,
  232, 234
Catonsville 9, 229–30, 233–37, 264
Catton, Bruce, 78
CBS (Columbia Broadcasting System), 45–46,
  350
  Cronkite of, 151–52, 392
  Fulbright hearings and, 73
  Muste documentary on, 103
  1969 Washington rally on, 296
CBUs (cluster bomb units), 351–52
CCNY (City College of New York), 76
  demonstrations at, 86, 106, 270
Ceaușescu, Nicolae, 259
Center for the Study of Democratic Institutions,
  31
Central Committee for Conscientious Objectors,
  9
Central Intelligence Agency (CIA), 44, 415–16
  fundings by, 107–8
  investigation of antiwar movement by, xii,
    143–44, 219, 221–23, 408, 409, 415
  protests vs. recruiters for, 105
  Ramparts exposé of, 84
Chaney, James, 18, 24
Chapin, Dwight, 296
Chemical warfare in Vietnam, 103, 352
  See also Defoliants; Napalm
Chester (Pa.), 31
Chiang Kai-shek, 21, 78
Chicago (Ill.), 31, 50, 83, 118, 150
  black riots in, 164, 180, 183
  demonstrations in, 26, 80 n., 108, 169, 200,
    255–56, 270, 311, 386
  1967 NCNP conference in, 128–29
  1969 SDS convention in, 251–55
  police of, 129, 169, 182–98, 221, 238, 262, 306
  See also Conventions—1968 Democratic
Chicago, University of, 11, 21, 37, 38, 106
  1966 occupation of, 86
  SMC founded at, 97–98
Chicago Area Draft Resisters (CADRE), 140
Chicago 8 *(later* Chicago 7; *also* "the
  Conspiracy"), 210, 249, 255, 257, 258,
  261, 275–76, 288, 290, 295, 298, 332, 362
  description of trial of, 302–8
Chicago Peace Council, 89, 180, 183, 200, 256 n.
Chicopee (Mass.), 399
China, People's Republic of, 49, 74, 214
  Nixon's trip to, 372, 378
  threat of war with, 25, 43, 72, 74, 86
Chomsky, Noam, 362, 404–5, 416
Christian, George, 202

Christiansen, Mary, 46
Church, Frank, 23, 27, 116, 125, 156, 331, 415
Citizens for a Free Chicago, 200
City College of New York. *See* CCNY
Civil disobedience (CD), 312–13, 322, 337
  Coffin's definition of, 224
  new laws vs., 224
  1967, 136–42, 146
  1970, 322–28
  1970 proposed, 340
  1971, 345–48, 360–64, 365
  1972, 380, 386
  SWP opposition to, 138, 324, 335–36
  See also Conscientious objection; Nonviolence.
Civil rights acts, 18, 20, 164, 302
Civil rights movement, 10, 18–19, 24
  antiwar movement and, 69–70, 89
  FBI attempt to make trouble, 276
  King's policy, 108–10
  NCAWRR, 345
  1968 Democratic Convention and, 176
  SDS, 28, 30–31, 41, 86
  See also Black Power; Blacks
Clarie, T. Emmet, 225
Clark, Blair, 191
Clark, Judith, 413, 414 n.
Clark, Mark, 306
Clark, Ramsey, 134, 179, 249, 305, 378, 388
Cleaver, Eldridge, 187, 288, 302
Clergy and Laymen Concerned About Vietnam
  (CLCV), 4, 76, 102, 108, 162, 183, 222,
  345, 378
  D. Berrigan and, 232
  draft card burning opposed by, 113
  In the Name of America, 153–54, 352–53,
    353 n.
Cleveland (Ohio), 31, 50, 90, 94, 270
  Mobe conferences in, 91, 93–94, 96–97, 178,
    255–58, 297–98
Cleveland Area Peace Action Council (CAPAC),
  89–90, 178, 183, 256, 298, 337
Cleveland String Quartet, 290
Clifford, Clark, 144, 159, 164, 205
Coalition for an Open Convention (COC), 178,
  184
Coalition for Peace, 335
Coffin, William Sloane, 134–35, 137, 163, 168,
  230, 282, 288
  draft-conspiracy prosecution of, 149, 173, 224
Cohelan, Jeffrey, 84
COINTELPRO, 223, 415
Coleman, Henry, 166
Collins, Judy, 41, 150, 384, 413
Colson, Charles, 389, 408, 409
Columbia University, 19, 37, 39, 95, 106, 311,
  319, 332, 381
  1968 events at, 165–68
  1972 occupations at, 382–83
Committee for a Sane Nuclear Policy. *See*
  SANE
Committee for Nonviolent Action (CNVA), 9–
  10, 55, 58, 91 n., 287, 293
  demonstrations by, 26, 34, 40, 46, 51–53, 55,
    57, 61, 292
Committee for Nuclear Disarmament, 8
Committee of Liaison With Families of